PRAISE FOR THE

Insider's Guide to
Graduate Programs in Clinical and
Counseling Psychology

"A 'must read.' . . . Like many other Directors of Clinical Training, I could continue to pull my hair out over the increased individual inquiries regarding how to get into graduate school, or simply refer each individual to the well-written, fact-based latest edition of the *Insider's Guide*."
—**Sally H. Barlow, Ph.D., Director of Clinical Training, Brigham Young University**

"Your book is simply a godsend! I found it to be instructive, informative, and a great comfort."
—**Emily M. Douglas, psychology undergraduate**

"There is a definite need for this book, which improves with every edition. Prospective graduate students will significantly increase their chances of gaining admission to clinical doctoral programs when they use this outstanding guide."
—**Arnold A. Lazarus, Ph.D.,**
Distinguished Professor Emeritus of Psychology, Rutgers University

"[Helps] students prepare to gain entrance into the two specific subfields of psychology that are popular but extraordinarily competitive. The book is written in a pragmatic, conversational tone that is easy to understand. The advice is realistic, which is important when each year applicants in the triple-digits usually compete for slots in the single-digits. Highly recommended."
—*Choice*

"Your book has helped me immensely. It was fun to read and contained great suggestions and insights that I would have been clueless about. Thank you for providing this resource for students!"
—**Timothy G. Lock, graduate student**

"The essential and practical guide for those who are considering pursuing graduate-level degrees in clinical or counseling psychology. . . . Should be considered mandatory reading for all undergraduates and those considering graduate school. It is objective, informative, and almost like having your own personal advisor to guide you along the way. ★★★★★"
—*Doody's Review Service*

"Imagine for a moment, a growing crowd of people who are all attempting to get through doors that are passageways to the careers they desperately want. If you find yourself in this reality that students face in attempting to gain admission to graduate programs in clinical psychology, the *Insider's Guide* is a 'must read.'"
—**C. R. Snyder, Ph.D.**
Director of Clinical Psychology, University of Kansas

"Your book means so much to me. The *Insider's Guide* was the most helpful piece of literature I came across during my years of research into graduate programs. It was almost like a bible to me."
—**Sharon Lee Hudson, doctoral student**

"I love your book! This book is excellent for focusing upon specific areas of interest as well as going about the process in a systematic, logical manner. Great job!"
—**Helen Rowan, M.A.,**
clinician returning for her doctorate

"The authors have created a valuable guide for applicants. The wealth of practical information and insights gleaned from their research and personal experiences should help applicants make the strongest possible application to the schools of their choice. This well-written, encouraging book will be a great asset for anyo_____ to clinical or counseling psychology programs."
_____ng, Ph.D., Washington University School of Medicine

"The *Insider's Guide* focuses on the complete application process with sample documents, worksheets, and timelines. Advice, warnings, and an easy-to-read format give this book an edge over resources providing program descriptions only, such as the American Psychological Association's *Graduate Study in Psychology* and *Peterson's Graduate Programs in the Humanities, Arts, and Social Sciences*. The text is supplemented with helpful statistics and the worksheets assist readers in defining the most important criteria for choosing schools."

—American Reference Books Annual

"I was lost and confused before I stumbled across this *wonderful* piece of literature! It answered every question I had, narrowed down my choices. The ranking system was great!"

—Lisa Oldfield, clinical psychology applicant

"I bought your book at the suggestion of my undergraduate psychology advisor once I decided to go back to school after spending nearly 10 years in the nonprofit sector. Your book has been extremely helpful and I have used it as my road map in guiding my efforts to set myself up to be successful in applying to schools this year. Thank you for writing this book—I really would not have known how to navigate the process without it."

—George Lewis

"I am writing to thank you for the second time for the remarkable resource the *Insider's Guide* has been. My girlfriend has just successfully utilized your most recent edition and has been accepted into a clinical Ph.D. program. Great stuff!"

—Jason Paris, graduate student

"I cannot express enough gratitude to you for the *Insider's Guide*. Your book was *the* most important resource that I used during my applications to Ph.D. programs in counseling psychology. It is exceptionally written, incredibly applicable, and, most important, it is clear, concise, and pragmatic. Thank you so much for remembering how stressful and chaotic the application process can be, as well as being empathic enough to pull together a resource that I am sure has helped so many graduate students."

—Kimberly Tran, doctoral student

INSIDER'S GUIDE TO
GRADUATE PROGRAMS
IN CLINICAL AND
COUNSELING PSYCHOLOGY

INSIDER'S GUIDE to
Graduate Programs in Clinical and Counseling Psychology

2012/2013 Edition

John C. Norcross
Michael A. Sayette

THE GUILFORD PRESS
New York   London

© 2012 The Guilford Press
A Division of Guilford Publications, Inc.
72 Spring Street, New York, NY 10012
www.guilford.com

Printed in the United States of America

Last digit is print number: 9 8 7 6 5 4 3 2 1

ISBN: 978-1-60918-932-7

ISSN 1086-2099

CONTENTS

CONTENTS ──

TABLES AND FIGURES

Tables

Figures

ABOUT THE AUTHORS

John C. Norcross received his baccalaureate *summa cum laude* from Rutgers University, earned his doctorate in clinical psychology from the University of Rhode Island, and completed his internship at the Brown University School of Medicine. He is Professor of Clinical Psychology and Distinguished University Fellow at the University of Scranton, Adjunct Professor of Psychiatry at SUNY Upstate Medical University, and a clinical psychologist in part-time independent practice. He also edits the *Journal of Clinical Psychology: In Session*. Past-president of the American Psychological Association's (APA's) Division of Clinical Psychology and Division of Psychotherapy, he currently serves on APA's Board of Educational Affairs. Dr. Norcross has published more than 300 articles and has authored or edited 20 books, including *Leaving It at the Office: Psychotherapist Self-Care; Psychotherapy Relationships That Work; History of Psychotherapy;* and *Systems of Psychotherapy: A Transtheoretical Analysis*, now in its eighth edition. Among his awards are the Pennsylvania Professor of the Year from the Carnegie Foundation, Distinguished Practitioner from the National Academies of Practice, and the Distinguished Career Contribution to Education and Training Award from APA. Dr. Norcross has conducted workshops and research on graduate study in psychology for many years.

Michael A. Sayette received his baccalaureate *cum laude* from Dartmouth College. He earned his master's and doctorate in clinical psychology from Rutgers University and completed his internship at the Brown University School of Medicine. He is Professor of Psychology at the University of Pittsburgh, with a secondary appointment as Professor of Psychiatry at the Western Psychiatric Institute and Clinic, University of Pittsburgh School of Medicine. Dr. Sayette has published primarily in the area of substance abuse. His research, supported by the National Institute on Alcohol Abuse and Alcoholism, the National Institute on Drug Abuse, and the National Cancer Institute, concerns the development of psychological theories of alcohol and tobacco use. Dr. Sayette is a Fellow of the APA and of the Association for Psychological Science. He has served on National Institutes of Health grant review study sections and is on the editorial boards of several journals. He is also an associate editor of the *Journal of Abnormal Psychology* and a former associate editor of *Psychology of Addictive Behaviors*. Dr. Sayette has directed graduate admissions for the clinical psychology program at the University of Pittsburgh, and has presented seminars on applying to graduate school at several universities in North America and Europe.

ACKNOWLEDGMENTS

To paraphrase John Donne, no book is an island, entire of itself. This sentiment is particularly true of a collaborative venture such as ours: a coauthored volume in its 12th edition comprising the contributions of hundreds of psychologists and the program reports provided by training directors throughout North America. We are grateful to them all.

We are particularly grateful to Dr. Tracy J. Mayne, who coauthored the previous editions of the *Insider's Guide* and who collaborated on many of our program surveys over the years. We wish him the best of success as he immerses himself in the private sector and in research on cancer-supportive therapies.

We are also indebted to the many friends, colleagues, and workshop participants for their assistance in improving this book over the years. Special thanks to John Dimoff for marvelously collecting and organizing data on individual program reports, and to Kavita Shah for updating the Web addresses of every APA-accredited program in this book. William Burke, Director of Financial Aid at the University of Scranton, updates our sections on financial aid and loan options every 2 years. Seymour Weingarten and his associates at The Guilford Press have continued to provide interpersonal support and technical assistance on all aspects of the project. Special thanks to our families for their unflagging support and patience with late night work!

Finally, our efforts have been aided immeasurably by our students, graduate and undergraduate alike, who courageously shared their experiences with us about the application and admission process.

PREFACE

One of the benefits of applying to clinical and counseling psychology programs is that you earn the right to commiserate about it afterwards. It was a night of anecdotes and complaints (while doing laundry) that led us to review our travails and compare notes on the difficulties we each experienced during the admission process. We emerged from diverse backgrounds but wound up in doctoral programs in clinical psychology.

Although we approached graduate school in different ways, the process was much the same. We each attempted to locate specific information on clinical and counseling psychology admissions, looked to people around us for advice, took what seemed to be sound, and worked with it. Not all the advice was good (one professor went so far as to suggest a career in the theater instead!), and it was difficult to decide what was best when advice conflicted.

All in all, there was too little factual information available and too much unnecessary anxiety involved. No clearly defined or organized system was available to guide us through this process. So we decided to write an *Insider's Guide to Graduate Programs in Clinical and Counseling Psychology*. That was 11 editions, 22 years, and more than 120,000 copies ago.

The last dozen years have seen the entire process of choosing and applying to schools become progressively more complex. Approximately 95,000 bachelor's degrees are awarded every year in psychology (National Center for Education Statistics, 2009), and about 20% of the recipients go on to earn a master's or doctoral degree in psychology. Clinical and counseling psychology programs continue to grow in number and to diversify in mission: 234 APA-accredited doctoral programs in clinical psychology, 66 APA-accredited doctoral programs in counseling psychology, 8 APA-accredited programs in combined psychology, dozens of non-APA-accredited doctoral programs, and hundreds of master's programs.

How can you develop your qualifications for graduate school in psychology? How should you prepare for admission into these competitive graduate programs? To which should you apply? And which type of program is best for you—counseling or clinical, practice-oriented Psy.D. or research-oriented Ph.D.? We'll take you step by step through this confusing morass and help you make informed decisions suited to your needs and goals.

In clear and concise language, we assist *you* through this process, from the initial decision to apply through your final acceptance. In Chapter 1, we describe clinical and counseling psychology and both practice and research alternatives to these disciplines. We explain the importance of program accreditation and warn against many online graduate programs that seek to separate you from your money. In Chapter 2, we feature the Boulder model (Ph.D.) and the Vail model (Psy.D.) of training psychologists and highlight their salient differences so that you can make an informed choice between them. In Chapter 3, we discuss the essential preparation for graduate school—the course work, faculty mentoring, clinical experiences, research skills, entrance examinations, and extracurricular activities.

From there, in Chapter 4, we get you started on the application process and assist you in understanding admission requirements. In Chapter 5, we show you how to systematically select schools on the basis of multiple considerations, especially research interests, clinical opportunities, theoretical orientations, program outcomes, financial assistance, and quality of life. Then, in Chapter 6, we take you through the application procedure itself—forms, curricula vitae, personal statements, letters of recommendation, academic transcripts, and the like. In Chapter 7, we review the perils and promises of the interview, required by three-quarters of clinical and counseling psychology programs. Last, in Chapter 8, we walk you through the complexities of the final decisions. With multiple worksheets and concrete examples, we will help you feel less overwhelmed, better informed, and, in the end, more aware that *you* are the consumer of a graduate program that best suits *your* needs.

In this new edition, we provide:

- Information on the new format and score report of the Graduate Record Examination (GRE)
- Updates on financial assistance and government-sponsored loans
- Discussion of APA's discontinuing its accreditation of Canadian programs
- Coverage of the new PCSAS accreditation system for programs in clinical science
- Advice on acquiring the licensure pass rate for the graduates of any doctoral psychology program
- Direction on conducting a Web self-audit to assess and probably enhance your presence on the Internet

In addition, we describe how you can capitalize on the Internet revolution to ease the graduate school admissions process—locating compatible programs, communicating with potential faculty mentors, submitting application forms, and helping faculty send letters of recommendation electronically. We also provide specific advice for racial/ethnic minority, physically disabled, and lesbian, gay, bisexual, and transgendered (LGBT) applicants. Throughout the book, we provide Web sites to access for additional information and direction.

We have conducted original studies on graduate psychology programs for this book in an effort to inform your decision making. These results provide crucial information on the differences between clinical and counseling psychology (Chapter 1), the distinctions between Ph.D. and Psy.D. programs (Chapter 2), the importance of various graduate school selection criteria (Chapter 3), acceptance rates (Chapter 4), the probability of financial assistance (Chapter 5), and interview policies (Chapter 7). The results of our studies allow you to search for particular research areas (Appendix E), clinical opportunities (Appendix F), and concentrations/specialties (Appendix G) as you consider which graduate programs to apply to. Indeed, we have extensively surveyed all APA-accredited programs in clinical, counseling, and combined psychology for 24 years now and present detailed information on each in the Reports on Individual Programs. A detailed Time Line (Appendix A) and multiple worksheets (Appendices B, C, and D) supply assistance on the heretofore treacherous journey of applying to graduate programs in clinical and counseling psychology.

This volume will assist anyone seeking admission to graduate school in clinical and counseling psychology, both master's and doctoral degrees. However, the primary focus is on Ph.D. and Psy.D. applicants, as the doctorate is the entry-level qualification for professional psychology. Just as a master's degree in biology does not make one a physician, a master's in psychology does not, by state licensure and APA regulation, typically qualify one as a psychologist. Forty-eight states require the doctorate for licensure as a psychologist; almost half the states grant legal recognition of psychological associates, assistants, or examiners with a master's degree (APA Practice Directorate, 2008). But the material presented here is relevant for master's (M.A. or M.S.) applicants as well.

With this practical manual, we wish you an application process less hectic and confusing than ours, but equally rewarding in the end result. Welcome and good luck!

CHAPTER 1
INTRODUCING CLINICAL AND COUNSELING PSYCHOLOGY

If you are reading this book for the first time, we assume you are either considering applying to graduate programs in clinical and counseling psychology or are in the process of doing so. For even the best-prepared applicant, this can precipitate a great deal of stress and confusion. The mythology surrounding this process is foreboding, and you may have heard some "horror" stories similar to these: "It's the hardest graduate program to get into in the country"; "You need a 3.7 grade point average and outrageous GREs or they won't even look at you"; "If you haven't taken time off after your bachelor's degree and worked in a clinic or research lab, you don't have enough experience to apply."

Having endured the application process ourselves, we know how overwhelming the task appears at first glance. However, we find that much of the anxiety is unwarranted. It does not take astronomical test scores or years of practical or research experience to get into clinical and counseling psychology programs. Although these qualifications certainly help, they are not sufficient. Equally important are a knowledge of how the system works and a willingness to put in extra effort during the application process. In other words, in this book, we will help you to work smarter and work harder in getting into graduate school.

Clinical and Counseling Psychology

Before dealing with the question of "how to apply," we would like to address "why" to apply and what clinical and counseling psychology entail. Reading through the next section may be useful by making you aware of other programs of study that may better suit your needs.

Let us begin with clinical psychology, the largest specialty and the fastest growing sector in psychology. Two-thirds of the doctoral-level health service providers in the American Psychological Association (APA) identify with the specialty area of clinical psychology. A census of all psychological personnel residing in the United States likewise revealed that the majority reported clinical psychology as their major field (Stapp, Tucker, & VandenBos, 1985).

A definition of clinical psychology was adopted jointly by the APA Division of Clinical Psychology and the Council of University Directors of Clinical Psychology (Resnick, 1991). That definition states that the field of clinical psychology involves research, teaching, and services relevant to understanding, predicting, and alleviating intellectual, emotional, biological, psychological, social, and behavioral maladjustment, applied to a wide range of client populations. The major skill areas essential to clinical psychology are assessment, intervention, consultation, program development and evaluation, supervision, administration, conduct of research, and application of ethical standards. Perhaps the safest observation about clinical psychology is that both the field and its practitioners continue to outgrow the classic definitions.

Indeed, the discipline has exploded since World War II in numbers, activities, and knowledge. Since 1949, the year of the Boulder Conference (see below),

TABLE 1-1. Popularity and Doctorate Production of Psychology Subfields

Subfield	% of doctoral-level psychologists	Number of Ph.D.s awarded		
		1976	1994	2006
Clinical	44%	883	1,329	1,118
Cognitive	1%	—	76	181
Counseling	11%	267	464	411
Developmental	4%	190	158	202
Educational	6%	124	98	60
Experimental & physiological	3%	357	143	220
Industrial/organizational	6%	73	124	173
Quantitative	2%	27	23	20
School	5%	143	81	123
Social and personality	4%	271	165	202
Other or general	12%	387	560	553
Total	100%	2,883	3,287	3,263[a]

Note. Data from Stapp, Tucker, & VandenBos (1985) and National Research Council (selected years).

[a]Plus 1,400 Psy.D. degrees awarded annually.

there has been a large and significant increase in psychology doctoral graduates. Approximately 2,800 doctoral degrees are now awarded annually in clinical psychology—1,400 Ph.D. degrees and 1,400 Psy.D. degrees. All told, doctoral degrees in clinical psychology account for about half of all psychology doctorates (Norcross et al., 2005). Table 1-1 demonstrates the continuing popularity of clinical psychology and the growing number of clinical doctorates awarded annually.

These trends should continue well into the future. The percentage of psychology majors among college freshmen has increased nationally to almost 5% (CIRP, 2005). A nationwide survey of almost 2 million high school juniors, reported in the *Occupational Outlook Quarterly*, found that psychology was the sixth most frequent career choice. Indeed, according to data from the U.S. Department of Education, interest in psychology as a major has never been higher (Murray, 1996). So, if you are seriously considering clinical or counseling psychology for a career, you belong to a large, vibrant, and growing population.

Counseling psychology is the second largest specialty in psychology and another rapidly growing sector. As also shown in Table 1-1, counseling psychology has experienced sustained growth over the past three decades. We are referring here to counseling *psychology*, the doctoral-level specialization

in psychology, not to the master's-level profession of counseling. This is a critical distinction: our book and research studies pertain specifically and solely to counseling psychology programs, not counseling programs.

The distinctions between clinical psychology and counseling psychology have steadily faded. Graduates of counseling psychology programs are eligible for the same professional benefits as clinical psychology graduates, such as psychology licensure, independent practice, and insurance reimbursement. The APA ceased distinguishing many years ago between clinical and counseling psychology internships: there is one list of accredited internships for both clinical and counseling psychology students. Both types of programs prepare licensed, doctoral-level psychologists who provide health care services.

At the same time, five robust differences between clinical psychology and counseling psychology are still visible (Morgan & Cohen, 2003; Norcross et al., 1998). First, clinical psychology is larger than counseling psychology: in 2011, there were 234 active APA-accredited doctoral programs in clinical psychology and 66 active APA-accredited doctoral programs in counseling psychology (APA, 2010) currently accepting students. About 50% of all doctorates awarded each year in psychology are in clinical psychology; about 8% are in counseling psychology. Second, clinical psychology graduate programs are almost exclusively housed in departments or schools of psychology, whereas counseling psychology graduate programs are located in a variety of departments and divisions. Our research (Turkson & Norcross, 1996) shows that, in rough figures, one-quarter of doctoral programs in counseling psychology are located in psychology departments, one-quarter in departments of counseling psychology, one-quarter in departments or colleges of education, and one-quarter in assorted other departments. The historical placement of counseling psychology programs in education departments explains the occasional awarding of the Ed.D. (doctor of education) by counseling psychology programs.

A third difference is that clinical psychology graduates are more likely trained in projective and intellectual assessment, whereas counseling psychology graduates conduct more career and vocational assessment. Those applicants particularly interested in vocational and career assessment should concentrate on counseling psychology programs. Fourth, counseling psychologists more frequently endorse a client-centered/Rogerian approach to psychotherapy, whereas clinical psychologists are more likely to embrace behavioral or psychodynamic orientations. And fifth, both APA figures (APA Research Office, 1997) and our research (Bechtoldt, Norcross, Wyckoff, Pokrywa, & Campbell, 2001) consistently reveal that 15% more clinical psychologists are employed in full-time private practice than are counseling psychologists, whereas 10% more counseling psychologists are employed in college counseling centers than are clinical psychologists.

Studies on the functions of clinical and counseling psychologists substantiate these differences, but the similarities are far more numerous (Brems & Johnson, 1997; Goodyear et al., 2008; Watkins, Lopez, Campbell, & Himmel, 1986a, 1986b). Thus, as you consider applying to graduate school, be aware of these differences but also remember that the two subdisciplines are similar indeed—which is why we feature both of them in this *Insider's Guide*!

In order to extend the previous research, we conducted a study of APA-accredited doctoral programs in counseling psychology (95% response rate) and clinical psychology (99% response rate) regarding their number of applications, characteristics of incoming students, and research areas of the faculty (Norcross, Sayette, Mayne, Karg, & Turkson, 1998). We found:

- The average acceptance rates of Ph.D. clinical (6%) and Ph.D. counseling (8%) psychology

programs were quite similar despite the higher number of applications to clinical programs (270 vs. 130).
- The average grade point averages (GPAs) and GRE scores for incoming doctoral students were nearly identical in Ph.D. clinical and Ph.D. counseling psychology programs (3.5 for both).
- The counseling psychology programs accepted far more master's students (67% vs. 21%) than the clinical psychology programs.
- The counseling psychology faculty were more interested than clinical psychology faculty in research pertaining to minority/cross-cultural issues (69% vs. 32% of programs) and vocational/career testing (62% vs. 1% of programs).
- The clinical psychology faculty, in turn, were far more interested than the counseling psychology faculty in research pertaining to psychopathological populations (e.g., attention deficit disorders, depression, personality disorders) and activities traditionally associated with medical settings (e.g., neuropsychology, pain management, pediatric psychology).

When interpreting these findings, it is important to realize that Ph.D. clinical programs include an enormously diverse set of schools. Accordingly, comparisons between clinical and counseling Ph.D. programs reflect general trends. For instance, as we describe in more detail in chapter 4, there exist professional schools offering a Ph.D. in clinical psychology that accept more than half of those who applied (see Sayette, Norcross, & Dimoff, 2011). In contrast, the median values among Ph.D. programs that are members of the American Academy of Psychological Clinical Science (APCS; see Table 2-1) are vastly different. Please rely on the reports on individual doctoral programs at the back of the book, rather than on these generalizations alone.

In addition, please bear in mind that these systematic comparisons reflect broad differences in the APA-accredited Ph.D. programs; they say nothing about Psy.D. programs (which we discuss in the next chapter) or nonaccredited programs. Also bear in mind that these data can be used as a rough guide in matching your interests to clinical or counseling psychology programs. The notion of discovering the best match between you and a graduate program is a recurrent theme of this *Insider's Guide*.

As shown in Table 1-2, clinical and counseling psychologists devote similar percentages of their day to the same professional activities. About one-half of their time is dedicated to psychotherapy and assess-

TABLE 1-2. Professional Activities of Clinical and Counseling Psychologists

Activity	Clinical psychologists		Counseling psychologists	
	% involved in	Average % of time	% involved in	Average % of time
Psychotherapy	80	34	74	28
Diagnosis/assessment	64	15	62	12
Teaching	50	10	60	18
Clinical supervision	50	6	54	6
Research/writing	51	14	50	8
Consultation	47	7	61	7
Administration	53	13	56	15

Note. Data from Norcross, Karpiak, & Santoro (2005) and Watkins, Campbell, & Himmell (1986a).

ment and a quarter of their time to research and administration. A stunning finding was that over half of clinical and counseling psychologists were routinely involved in all seven activities—psychotherapy, assessment, teaching, research, supervision, consultation, and administration. Flexible career indeed!

The scope of clinical and counseling psychology is continually widening, as are the employment settings. Many people mistakenly view psychologists solely as practitioners who spend most of their time seeing patients. But in truth, clinical and counseling psychology are wonderfully diverse and pluralistic professions. Consider the employment settings of American clinical psychologists: 39% in private practices, 22% in universities or colleges, 8% in medical schools, 6% in outpatient clinics, 4% in psychiatric hospitals, another 4% in general hospitals, 3% in the Veterans Administration, and 15% in "other" placements (Norcross, Karpiak, & Santoro, 2005). This last category included, just to name a few, child and family services, correctional facilities, rehabilitation centers, school systems, health maintenance organizations, psychoanalytic institutes, and the federal government.

Although many psychologists choose careers in private practice, hospitals, and clinics, a large number also pursue careers in research. For some, this translates into an academic position. Continuing uncertainties in the health care system increase the allure of academic positions, where salaries are less tied to client fees and insurance reimbursements. Academic psychologists teach courses and conduct research, usually with a clinical population. They hope to find a "tenure-track" position, which means they start out as an assistant professor. After a specified amount of time (typically 5 or 6 years), a university committee

reviews their research, teaching, and service, and decides whether they will be hired as a permanent faculty member and promoted to associate professor. Even though the tenure process can be pressured, the atmosphere surrounding assistant professors is conducive to research activity. They are often given "seed" money to set up facilities and attract graduate students eager to share in the publication process. (For additional information on the career paths of psychology faculty, consult *The Psychologist's Guide to an Academic Career*, Rheingold, 1994, or *Career Paths in Psychology*, Sternberg, 2006.)

In addition, research-focused industries (like pharmaceutical and biomedical), as well as community-based organizations, are increasingly employing psychologists to design and conduct outcomes research. The field of outcomes research combines the use of assessment, testing, program design, and cost-effectiveness analyses. Although lacking the job security of tenure, industry can offer greater monetary compensation and is a viable option for research-oriented Ph.D.s.

But even this range of employment settings does not accurately capture the opportunities in the field. Approximately half of all clinical and counseling psychologists hold more than one professional position (Norcross et al., 2005; Goodyear et al., 2008). By and large, psychologists incorporate several pursuits into their work, often simultaneously. They combine activities in ways that can change over time to accommodate their evolving interests. Of those psychologists not in full-time private practice, more than half engage in some part-time independent work. Without question, this flexibility is an asset.

As a university professor, for example, you might supervise a research group studying aspects of alcoholism, treat alcoholics and their families in private practice, and teach a course on alcohol abuse. Or, you could work for a company supervising marketing research, do private testing for a school system, and provide monthly seminars on relaxation. The possibilities are almost limitless.

This flexibility is also evident in clinical and counseling psychologists' "self-views." Approximately 60% respond that they are primarily clinical practitioners, 20% are academicians, 7% administrators, 5% researchers, 5% consultants, and 2% supervisors (Norcross et al., 1997; Watkins et al., 1986a).

Also comforting is the consistent finding of relatively high and stable satisfaction with graduate training and career choice. Over two-thirds of graduate students in clinical and counseling psychology express satisfaction with their post-baccalaureate preparation. Moreover, 87 to 91% are satisfied with their career choice (Norcross et al., 2005; Tibbits-Kleber & Howell, 1987). The conclusion we draw is that clinical and counseling psychologists appreciate the diverse pursuits and revel in their professional flexibility, which figure prominently in their high level of career satisfaction.

According to *Money* magazine and Salary.com, psychologist is one of the 10 best jobs in America. And so, too, is college professor.

Combined Programs

The American Psychological Association (APA) accredits doctoral programs in five areas: clinical psychology, counseling psychology, school psychology, other developed practice areas, and combined psychology. The last category is for those programs that afford doctoral training in two or more of the specialties of clinical, counseling, and school psychology.

The "combined" doctoral programs represent a relatively new development in graduate psychology training, and thus are small in number, about 3% of APA-accredited programs. In emphasizing the core research and practice competencies among the specialties, combined programs try to enlist their respective strengths and to capitalize on their overarching competencies. In doing so, the hope is that a combined program will be "greater than the sum of its parts" (Salzinger, 1998). For students undecided about a particular specialty in professional psychology and seeking broad clinical training, these accredited combined programs warrant a close look.

The chief reasons that students select combined doctoral programs are for greater breadth and flexibility of training and for more opportunity of integrative training across specializations. The emphasis on breadth of psychological knowledge ensures that combined training will address the multiplicity of interests that many students have and that many psychologists will need in practice (Beutler & Fisher, 1994). The chief disadvantages of combined programs are, first, their lack of depth and specialization and, second, the fact that other mental health professionals may not understand the combined degree. Our research on combined training programs (Castle & Norcross, 2002; Cobb, Reeve, Shealy, Norcross, et al., 2004) does, in fact, substantiate the broader training and more varied employment of their graduates. Consult the Reports of Combined Programs at the end of this book for details on these innovative programs. Also consult two special issues of the *Journal of Clinical Psychology* (Shealy, 2004) on the combined-integrative model of doctoral training in professional psychology.

A Word on Accreditation

Accreditation comes in many guises, but the two primary types are institutional accreditation and program accreditation. Institutional applies to an entire institution. Seven regional accreditation bodies, such as the Commission on Higher Education of the Middle States Association of Colleges and Schools, oversee accreditation for the university or college itself. A school receives accreditation when it has been judged to have met minimum standards of quality for postsecondary education.

Beware of any institution that is not accredited by its regional accreditation body. A degree from this institution will probably not be recognized by licensing boards, certifying organizations, or insurance companies (Dattilio, 1992). Be particularly careful about nontraditional or external degree programs that offer the option of obtaining a degree based on independent study, typically away from the institution itself. Some of these are reputable programs, but many are "diploma mills" (Stewart & Spille, 1988). Many diploma mills have names similar to legitimate universities, so you must be vigilant. Here are several diploma mills with potentially misleading titles: Columbia State University (Louisiana), La Salle University (Louisiana), Chadwick University (Alabama), American State University (Hawaii), American International University (Alabama). (For additional information about diploma mills, consult the fact sheets at the Council for Higher Education Accreditation at www.CHEA.org, www.degreefinders.com/distance_

learning/diploma.php and www.web-miner.com/deu-naccredited.htm).

The second type of accreditation pertains to the graduate psychology program itself. Specialized accreditation of the discipline is performed by APA. This accreditation is a voluntary procedure for the doctoral program itself, not the entire institution. Most programs capable of meeting the requirements of APA accreditation will choose to apply for accreditation. Accreditation of a clinical or counseling psychology program by the APA presumes regional accreditation of the entire institution.

As of 2011, APA had accredited 234 active clinical psychology programs (62 of these awarding the Psy.D. degree), 66 active counseling psychology programs (3 of these awarding the Psy.D. degree), and 8 active combined professional–scientific psychology programs (Accredited, 2010). The Reports on Individual Programs in this book provide detailed descriptions of these 300+ clinical psychology, counseling psychology, and combined programs, respectively.

Take note that APA does *not* accredit master's programs. Accordingly, references to "accredited" master's psychology programs are to regional or state, not APA, accreditation.

The program accreditation criteria can be obtained from the APA Office of Program Consultation and Accreditation (www.apa.org/ed/accreditation). The general areas assessed include institutional support, sensitivity to cultural and individual differences, training models and curricula, faculty, students, facilities, and practicum and internship training. These criteria are designed to insure at least a minimal level of quality assurance.

The APA (Accredited, 2010) recognizes three categories of accreditation. "Accredited" means that the programs meet or exceed the criteria in a satisfactory manner. "Accredited, inactive" is the designation for programs that have not accepted students for several years. This indicates that the program is taking a hiatus as part of a restructuring process, or is phasing out the program. "Accredited, on probation" is the designation for programs that were previously accredited but are not currently in compliance with the criteria. We do not feature programs on probation in our Individual Reports at the end of this book.

In the past decade, there has been concern among some clinical psychologists about the proliferation of professional schools unaffiliated with universities offering doctorates in clinical psychology. Some psychologists believe that these professional schools, especially the for-profit chains, have eroded the quality and scientific training of new psychologists. Thus, a new accreditation system—Psychological Clinical Science Accreditation System (PCSAS; pronounced *pee-cee-sass*)—was launched in 2010 to "accredit clinical psychology training programs that offer high quality science-centered education and training, producing graduates who are successful in generating and applying scientific knowledge" (Baker et al., 2008). It is too early to know how this new accreditation system will fare, and only a handful of programs have sought accreditation by PCSAS so far. But it is important for you to know that there is spirited discussion about the quality of for-profit professional schools and the proper role of research training in clinical and counseling psychology doctoral programs.

For more than 30 years, doctoral psychology programs in Canada have enjoyed the option of simultaneous accreditation by the Canadian Psychological Association (CPA) and the American Psychological Association (APA). This dual accreditation enabled United States citizens to travel north to attend APA-accredited Canadian programs and facilitated internship placement and licensure in the United States for both American and Canadian students. Graduates of APA-accredited programs, whether located in Canada or the United States, were eligible for the same privileges.

In 2007, APA decided to phase out accrediting Canadian psychology programs. The phase out will occur gradually over a 7-year period. Mutual recognition agreements will continue, but formal APA accreditation of Canadian programs will not. Most jurisdictions in the United States recognize CPA-accredited or National Register-designated programs for the purposes of licensure. But a few do not. Thus, be aware of this transition and the potential consequences on internship and licensure in selected U.S. states. We do *not* want to discourage anyone from attending excellent Canadian doctoral programs in psychology; we *do* want you to be informed consumers. For this edition we have continued to provide information for APA-accredited Canadian programs if they chose to participate.

Our Reports on Individual Programs provide crucial descriptive and application information on each APA-accredited doctoral program in clinical, counseling, and combined psychology. The APA Education Directorate updates the listing of accredited programs annually in the December issue of the *American Psychologist* and bimonthly on their Web site, www.apa.org/ed.

How important is it to attend an APA-accredited program? The consensus ranges from slightly important to absolutely essential. APA accreditation ensures a modicum of program stability, quality assurance, and professional accountability. Graduates of APA-accredited programs are practically guaranteed to meet the educational requirements for state licensure. Students are in a more advantageous and competitive position coming from an APA-approved program in terms of their internship choices (Anderson, 2009; Drummond, Rodolfa, & Smith, 1981) and their eventual employment prospects (Walfish & Sumprer, 1984). The federal government, the Veterans Administration, and most universities now insist on a doctorate and internship from APA-accredited programs. Graduates of APA programs also score significantly higher, on average, than do students of non-APA-accredited programs on the licensure exam (Templer, Stroup, Mancuso, & Tangen, 2008; Kupfersmid & Fiola, 1991). Licensure and employment as a psychologist are not precluded by attending a non-APA-accredited program, but the situation is tightening. Several states now license only graduates from APA-accredited programs. All other things being equal, an APA-accredited clinical or counseling psychology program gives you a definite advantage over a nonaccredited program.

Online Graduate Programs

Practically every institution of higher education now offers some online courses and distance education. Some institutions have gone further to create graduate programs that are almost entirely online, with all discussions being conducted electronically on bulletin boards and all assignments being submitted by computer. The only on-campus contact might be a couple of weeks or several weekends per year.

Several of these online or distance learning institutions offer doctoral programs in clinical and counseling psychology, including Walden, Capella, and Fielding. Fielding Graduate University requires several weeks of in-person residency per year, making it the only distance program that is APA accredited.

We are frequently approached by students intrigued with these and other distance-learning doctoral programs and asked whether we think they are credible programs. Our answer is that some are credible, but definitely not preferred, for several reasons. First, we recommend that students favor APA-accredited programs, and only one of these programs has met the minimum educational criteria set forth by APA. Second, many psychology licensing boards will not issue licenses to graduates of distance learning programs (Hall, Wexelbaum, & Boucher, 2007).

Third, online programs lack quality control over their clinical supervisors, who are scattered around the country. Fourth, much of the learning in doctoral programs occurs in close, interpersonal relationships with faculty on a daily basis. Frequent computer contact is useful, but in our opinion, not equivalent. And fifth, without sounding too stodgy, we believe online programs are still too new and alternative to have developed a track record of producing quality psychologists. Most internship directors and potential employers feel likewise; graduates of non–APA-accredited distance programs have experienced difficulty in securing employment as psychologists.

Online or distance education increases accessibility for students in many areas of study. However, this benefit does not extend as readily to students in graduate psychology programs because they need, in addition to course work, practical experience, clinical supervision, research mentoring, and residency requirements (Murphy et al., 2007).

Of course, each online program needs to be evaluated on its own merits, and each doctoral student must be considered for his or her individual abilities. In the end, graduate students will get out of a program what they put in—whether through a traditional, bricks-and-mortar institution or an innovative, online program. The early research on distance and online education indicates that it produces comparable outcomes to traditional education, at least in acquiring knowledge and academic skills. Unfortunately, there is insufficient research on the online preparation of professional psychologists to render any conclusions.

Recent research demonstrates that many psychology majors—45% or so—are interested in online graduate programs (Bendersky et al., 2008). Given the aforementioned problems with online graduate education in psychology, we repeat our warning to be wary. Students matriculating into these programs often do so under the false belief that these online, distance programs will offer comparable training, licensing, and professional benefits as traditional, accredited programs. They rarely do.

Should you decide to apply to online doctoral programs in psychology, we would advise you to:

- complete your master's degree in a conventional program to secure one in-person degree and to meet the admission prerequisites of most online doctoral programs.
- obtain information on the program's track record of producing graduates who secure APA-accredited internships and eventually licensure as psychologists.

- determine the residency requirement (how much time per year is expected on campus).
- expect no financial assistance from the online institution itself (but loans are available).
- become very comfortable and savvy with computers, as most of your contact and assignments will be conducted online.
- be an organized, self-motivated individual who can meet deadlines without supervision.
- realize that the vast majority of interaction with fellow students and professors will occur online, not in a conventional classroom.
- be prepared for intensive research and writing on your own.

Practice Alternatives

In addition to doctoral programs in clinical and counseling psychology, we would like to describe several alternative programs of study that should be considered. We have classified these programs along the practice–research continuum. The practice-oriented programs are outlined first. Portions are abstracted from APA's (1986) *Careers in Psychology*, which can be found online at www.apa.org/careers/resources/guides/index.aspx. Additional details on helping professions can also be accessed online at www.teachpsych.org/otrp/resources/resources.php. *A Student Guide to Careers in the Helping Professions* by Melissa Himelein provides information on typical job duties, potential earnings, required degrees, and the like.

You are restricted neither to clinical/counseling psychology nor even to psychology in selecting a career in mental health. School psychology, as discussed below, is a viable alternative. Also note that psychology is only one of six nationally recognized mental health disciplines, the others being psychiatry (medicine), clinical social work, psychiatric nursing, marital and family therapy, and counseling.

We do not wish to dissuade you from considering clinical or counseling psychology, but a mature career choice should be predicated on sound information and contemplation of the alternatives. A primary consideration is what you want to do—your desired activities. Conducting psychotherapy is possible in any of the following fields. Prescribing medication is currently restricted to physicians and some nurse practitioners, although psychologists are steadily securing prescription privileges around the country. Psychological testing and empirical research are conducted by psychologists. As discussed previously, psychologists also enjoy a wide range and pleasurable integration of professional activities. Following is a sampling of alternatives to a doctorate in clinical and counseling psychology.

1. School Psychology. Some undergraduates have a particular interest in working with children, adolescents, and their families. Admission into the Boulder-model programs with a child clinical specialty is particularly competitive. A doctorate in school psychology is much more accessible, with two or three times the acceptance rate of clinical psychology programs. The APA (Accredited, 2010) has accredited 61 of these programs, which provide doctoral-level training in clinical work with children in school settings.

One disadvantage of pursuing a career as a master's-level school psychologist lies in the fact that, unlike the other alternatives, one's professional work may be limited to the school. If this limitation is not a concern, then training as a school psychologist can be an excellent option for those interested in working with children and families (Halgin, 1986).

At the doctoral level, school psychologists are credentialed to function in both school and nonschool settings. Research finds substantial overlap in the coursework of child clinical programs and school psychology programs (Minke & Brown, 1996). Some differences remain, of course—such as more courses in consultation and education in school programs and more courses in psychopathology in child clinical programs—but the core curricula are quite similar. School psychology training at the doctoral level is broadening to include experience outside of the school setting and with adolescents and families as well (Tryon, 2000).

For further information, check out the following Web sites:

- www.indiana.edu/~div16/
  (APA's Division of School Psychology)
- www.naspweb.org
  (National Association of School Psychologists)
- www.ispaweb.org/
  (International School Psychology Association)
- www.schoolpsychology.net
  (comprehensive links to the field and graduate schools)

2. Community Psychology. This field shares with clinical and counseling psychology a concern with individual well-being and healthy psychological development. However, community psychology places considerable emphasis on preventing behavioral problems (as opposed to only treating existing problems), adopting a broader ecological or community perspective, and changing social policies.

Graduate training in community psychology occurs within clinical-community psychology programs or within explicit community psychology programs. The former are clinical psychology programs with an emphasis on or a specialization in community; these doctoral programs are listed in Appendix E (Research Areas) under "community psychology." Ten universities in the United States offer a doctorate in community psychology, and an additional 15 offer a doctorate in clinical-community. If your interests lean toward prevention and community-based interventions, then by all means check out a specialization or a program in community psychology. The Web sites at www.scra27.org/ and www.communitypsychology.net provide further information about the field and training programs.

3. Clinical Social Work. A master's degree in social work (M.S.W.) is a popular practice alternative these days. One big advantage of this option is a much higher rate of admission to M.S.W. programs, with about 65% of applicants being accepted to any given program, on average (O'Neill, 2001). Other advantages are GREs less often required for admission, fewer research requirements, an emphasis on professional training, and completion of the M.S.W. in less than half the time necessary to obtain a psychology Ph.D. With legal regulation in all 50 states and third-party vendor status (insurance reimbursement) in 49 states, clinical social workers are increasingly achieving autonomy and respect, including more opportunities for independent practice.

The major disadvantages lie in the less comprehensive nature of the training, which is reflected in a lower pay scale as compared to psychologists. Not becoming a "doctor" and not being able to conduct psychological testing also prove troublesome for some.

Students interested in clinical social work as a career should peruse an introductory text on the profession, consult career publications (for example, Wittenberg, 2003), and contact the National Association of Social Workers (NASW). This organization provides detailed information on the emerging field, student membership, and accredited programs in clinical social work. NASW resources can be accessed via the Web (www.naswdc.org) or the telephone (1-800-742-4089). Three other Web sites on social work programs also prove handy: www.petersons.com/graduate_home.asp?path=gr.Home; www.socialworksearch.com; and www.gradschools.com.

4. Psychiatry (Medicine). Students often dismiss the possibility of applying to medical schools, believing that medical school admission is so difficult that it is out of the question (Halgin, 1986). However, the student interested in neuroscience and the more severe forms of psychopathology may find this to be an attractive choice. Although the application process necessitates more rigorous training in the "hard" sciences than most psychology programs, the admission rate may also be higher than the most competitive doctoral programs in clinical and counseling psychology. Of the 42,000 people applying to medical school annually, about 43% are admitted, and half of them are women. The average GPA of applicants accepted to medical school is between 3.5 and 3.6 (see aamc.org for details).

Medical school thus remains an attractive option for many students headed toward a career in mental health. For further information and demystification of this subject, refer to the data-driven *Medical School Admission Requirements 2009-2010: The Most Authoritative Guide to U.S. and Canadian Medical Schools* (Association of American Medical Colleges Staff, 2009) and *Medical School Admissions: The Insider's Guide* (Zebala, Jones, & Jones, 1999). Prime Web sites include www.premedonline.com and www.aamc.org, the official Web site of the Association of American Medical Colleges.

The advantages of a medical degree should be recognized. First, an M.D. (allopath) or D.O. (osteopath) allows one to prescribe medication. Second, the average income for psychiatrists is higher than for psychologists. Third, a medical degree permits more work in inpatient (hospital) facilities. Applicants should not dismiss this possibility out of hand, and should explore medicine as a career, especially if their interests lie on a more biological level.

5. Psychiatric Nursing. The employment opportunities for nurses are excellent at this time, especially for psychiatric nurses who have the flexibility of working in hospitals, clinics, health centers, or private practice. Of course, psychiatric nurses are nurses first and are required to obtain a bachelor's degree (B.S.N.) and to become registered (R.N.) prior to obtaining their Master of Science in Nursing (M.S.N.). They do not conduct psychological testing and rarely perform research, but psychiatric nurses practice psychotherapy in both inpatient and outpatient settings. Further, certified nurse practitioners now have the authority to write medication prescriptions in 48 states. Consult a textbook on mental health nursing and visit the Web site of the American Psychiatric Nurses Association at www.apna.org/ to learn more about psychiatric/mental health nursing and its graduate programs.

6. Counseling. A master's degree in counseling, as distinct from a doctorate in counseling psychology, prepares one for state licensure as a professional counselor. The high acceptance rates of counseling programs, their two years of practical training, and eligibility for state licensure in all 50 states represent definite assets. Master's-level clinicians, such as social workers and counselors, have become the front-line providers of most mental health services in community clinics and public agencies. For those students committed to practice and untroubled by the lack of training in conducting research and psychological testing, the profession of counseling deserves consideration. Visit the Web page of the American Counseling Association (www.counseling.org/) for more information on careers and the Web page of accredited counseling programs (www.cacrep.org/directory.html) to locate counseling programs of interest to you.

7. Marital and Family Therapy. Another master's-level mental health profession is devoted to conducting couples and family therapy. The simultaneous strength and weakness of these graduate programs are its specificity—training in couples and family therapy, as opposed to broader and more comprehensive training in multiple professional activities. Securing a master's degree in this field should certainly be considered by students with this definite and specific interest. All 50 states now legally recognize marital and family therapists. Check out the [...] he American Association for Marriage [...] erapy at www.aamft.org.

8. Psychology and the Law. There is a great deal of interest in the burgeoning amalgam of psychology and law, as evidenced by an APA division, two energetic professional societies, and many scholarly journals (Bersoff et al., 1997; Otto & Heilbrun, 2002). Doctoral students must be trained in both fields, of course, increasing the length of graduate training. At least five programs now award law degrees and psychology doctorates together—joint J.D. and Ph.D./Psy.D. programs (Arizona, Drexel, Nebraska, Pacific, and Widener Universities). Graduates pursue both practice and research careers—practicing law in men-

tal health arenas, specializing in forensic psychology, working in public policy, and pursuing scholarship on the interface of law and psychology, for example. This is an exciting career, albeit one requiring extra commitment in terms of effort and knowledge during doctoral studies.

Another two dozen clinical programs offer Ph.D.s or Psy.D.s with specializations in forensic psychology or clinical forensic psychology. (Consult Appendix G and the following Web sites for a list of the programs.) These clinical psychologists specialize in the practice of forensic psychology. It's a growing and exciting specialization in psychology, but one that rarely involves the criminal profiling featured in television shows and *Silence of the Lambs*! Instead, forensic psychologists are far more likely to conduct child custody evaluations, assess a patient's psychological damage, evaluate a person's competence to stand trial, consult with lawyers on jury selection, and conduct disability evaluations. For tips on undergraduate preparation and graduate training in forensic psychology, consult these Web links:

- www.teachpsych.org/otrp/resources/index. php?category=advising
- (Undergraduate Preparation for Graduate Training in Forensic Psychology)
- www.ap-ls.org/ (APA's American Law–Psychology Society)
- www.abfp.com/ (American Board of Forensic Psychology)

9. Other. Student guidance, art therapy, occupational therapy, and a plethora of other human service programs present attractive alternatives to clinical and counseling psychology. They are typically less competitive master's-level programs in which admission rates are quite high and in which the training is quite practical. Relative disadvantages of these programs, in addition to lack of a doctorate, include less prestige, lower salaries, diminished probability of an independent practice, and variable licensure status across the United States.

If one or more of these options seem suited to your needs, discuss it with a psychology advisor, interview a professional in that field, peruse the Web sites, or write to the respective organizations for additional information.

Research Alternatives

Some graduate students enter clinical or counseling psychology to become researchers. They are less interested in working with patients than researching clinical phenomena. If you are most interested in research, here are some nonpractice alternatives that might appeal to you.

1. Social Psychology. Social psychology is concerned with the influence of social and environmental factors on behavior. Personality, attitude change, social neuroscience, group processes, interpersonal attraction, and self-constructs are some of the research interests. Social psychologists are found in a wide variety of academic settings and, increasingly, in many nonacademic settings. These include positions in advertising agencies, personnel offices, corporations, and other business settings. Check out the official Web sites of the Society for Personality and Social Psychology (www.spsp.org) and the Social Psychology Network (www.socialpsychology.org) for additional resources.

2. Industrial/Organizational Psychology. This branch of psychology focuses on the individual in the workplace. Industrial/organizational psychologists frequently select and place employees, design jobs, train people, and help groups of workers to function more effectively. Master's programs generally prepare students for jobs in human resources and personnel departments, whereas doctoral programs are geared to preparing students for academic positions and for management and consulting work on larger-scale projects. Industrial/organizational psychologists earn among the highest median salaries compared to other areas of psychology (Kohout & Wicherski, 1992). Academics find positions in both psychology departments and business schools.

The Society for Industrial and Organizational Psychology (2009) produces a useful list of *Graduate Training Programs in Industrial/Organizational Psychology and Related Fields*, which describes 200 plus graduate programs in "I/O" psychology and how to contact each. It is available free from the society's Web site (www.siop.org). Students interested in pursuing a career in I/O psychology should obtain, beyond psychology classes, courses in management, marketing, and organizational behavior as well as research experience.

3. Behavioral Neuroscience. For the student interested in the workings of the brain and its influence on behavior, programs in neuroscience may be a better match than clinical psychology. By employing animal subjects, researchers can control the conditions of their studies to a rigor often elusive when

using human participants. Research areas include learning, psychopharmacology, memory, and motivation. For example, recent investigations on memory have provided valuable insight into the etiology and course of Alzheimer's disease. Go to the Society of Neuroscience Web site (www.sfn.org/index.aspx?pagename=professionalDevelopment_ndp) for a list of graduate programs in neuroscience.

Research demonstrates that neuroscience graduate programs expect entering students to possess course work and lab work beyond the standard psychology curriculum (Boitano, 1999). Essential courses would include biology, chemistry, calculus, and introduction to neuroscience. And desirable courses would sample from cell biology, biochemistry, and anatomy and physiology. These are all possible, with adequate planning, to incorporate into the psychology major, should you decide on this path relatively early in your undergraduate career. The Web site (www.undergraduateneuroscience.org/) of Faculty for Undergraduate Neuroscience (FUN) provides a bounty of useful information on preparing for a career in neuroscience.

4. Developmental Psychology. The developmental psychologist studies behavior change beginning at the prenatal stages and extending through the lifespan. Areas such as aging, identity, and development of cognitive and social abilities are popular areas within developmental psychology. The characteristics of individuals at different age ranges, such as the work of Piaget on child cognition, are of particular interest to developmental psychologists.

Geropsychology, or the psychology of aging, has become a popular specialty as the elderly population in this country presents special needs that are insufficiently addressed. Employment opportunities in geropsychology are sure to grow over the next several decades. Visit the Web sites of APA's Division of Adult Development and Aging (apadiv20.phhp.ufl.edu/) and the friendly Geropsychology Central (www.premier.net/~gero/geropsyc.html) for more.

5. Cognitive Psychology. Cognitive psychology presents an attractive option for students whose interests lie in the exploration of human thought processes. Major areas include language structure, memory, perception, attention, and problem solving. Research in cognitive psychology has gained insight into what in the past was considered inexplicable behavior. For example, research into how moods affect the interpretation of ambiguous events has implications for the study of depression. Much research on the accuracy of eyewitness testimony has been conducted by cognitive psychologists. Cognitive programs emphasize artificial intelligence, cognitive neuroscience, and affective neuroscience. Indeed, interest in cognitive neuroscience and affective neuroscience has increased of late.

6. Experimental Psychology. Often a student is interested in research but has not yet defined an area of interest. Or a student is fascinated with a certain psychopathology but does not desire to practice. In both cases, a graduate program in experimental psychology might be the ticket. These programs allow a student to explore several research areas, such as learning, measurement, and memory. Other programs focus on experimental psychopathology, which is geared more specifically for the researcher interested in clinical populations.

Experimental programs offer excellent training in research methods, statistical analysis, and hands-on research experience. In fact, some experimental programs now classify themselves as quantitative or measurement programs. If interested in these programs, consult www.apa.org/divisions/div5/docprogs.html for a list of graduate psychology programs with a measurement and quantitative focus.

7. Sport Psychology. This emerging specialization typically entails both research and applied activities. Research focuses on all aspects of sports, whereas application involves psychological assessment, individual skills training, and group consultation. Research and training encompass stress management, self-confidence, mental rehearsal, competitive strategies, and sensory-kinetic awareness. Consult the *Directory of Graduate Programs in Applied Sport Psychology* (Burke, Sachs, Fry, & Schweighardt, 2008) for information on specific psychology programs. Consult, too, the Web site of APA's Division of Exercise and Sport Psychology at www.apa.org/about/division/div47.html for information on career possibilities in this area.

8. Medicine. A medical degree (M.D., D.O.) earned concurrently or sequentially with a psychology doctorate (Ph.D.) may allow the greatest flexibility of all the aforementioned programs of study. This option allows one to practice medicine and psychology while also affording advanced training in research and statistics. For an extremely bright and motivated student, this can be a real possibility, but it is certainly the most challenging of all the alternatives. Earning two doctoral degrees will take longer

than earning either alone. This choice is for someone interested in the biological aspects of behavior in addition to gaining a rigorous education in the scientific study of human behavior.

Once again, if your interest lies in research, there are many options available besides clinical and counseling psychology. Talking to professionals in the relevant discipline and consulting textbooks about the discipline will help you to explore that option more fully. An increasing number of Web sites also offer valuable career advice. Five of our favorites are:

- www.psychwww.com/careers/index.htm
- www.lemoyne.edu/CareerServices/tabid/865/default.aspx
- www.apa.org/students/
- www.socialpsychology.org/career.htm
- www.gradschools.com

Acceptance Rates

As you have quickly learned, there are dozens of options for practice and research careers, inside and outside of psychology. Our intent in this opening chapter is neither to confuse nor to bedazzle you with these multiple choices. Rather, our intent is to acquaint you with the options so that you become an informed consumer and make the choices that best suit your career trajectory.

Toward that end, let us summarize here the average acceptance rates in graduate psychology programs. Table 1-3 does just that for the various subfields in psychology, separately for master's and doctoral programs.

The numbers in Table 1-3 represent the average percentage of students who apply and are accepted into a single, particular program (*not* the percentage of students accepted into any graduate program, which will be higher). Take the example of developmental psychology graduate programs: the typical master's program in developmental psychology will accept 44% of its applicants, and the typical doctoral program will accept about 20% of its applicants. The acceptance rates are surprisingly high for master's degrees in all of psychology; about half of the applicants to any master's program are accepted. These numbers should prove comforting to you and reduce some of those pre-application jitters. And remember: you will be applying to several graduate programs, thereby increasing the probability of acceptance even more.

Doctoral programs are obviously more competi-

TABLE 1-3. Average Acceptance Rates in Graduate Psychology Programs
(% of students who apply and are accepted to a particular program)

Area	Master's	Doctoral
Clinical Psychology	37%	(Table 4-1)
Clinical Neuropsychology	—	26%[a]
Cognitive Psychology	40%	16%
Community Psychology	61%	24%
Counseling Psychology	63%	(Table 4-1)
Developmental Psychology	44%	20%
Educational Psychology	57%[a]	48%
Experimental Psychology	39%	15%
Health Psychology	41%	16%
Industrial/Organizational Psychology	52%	27%
Neuroscience	32%[a]	15%
Quantitative Psychology	78%	36%
School Psychology	34%	31%
Social & Personality Psychology	39%	12%

Source: American Psychological Association. (2010). *Graduate Applications, Acceptances, Enrollments, and Degrees Awarded to Master's- and Doctoral-Level Students in U.S. and Canadian Graduate Departments of Psychology: 2008–2009.*

[a]Data taken from Norcross, Kohout, & Wicherski (2005).

tive than master's programs. The applied areas of psychology—clinical, counseling, health, school, and industrial/organizational (I/O)—tend to be the most selective.

For those interested in doctoral programs in clinical and counseling psychology – approximately one-half of undergrads—the situation is more complex as there is huge variation in acceptance rates. We shall take you step-by-step through the acceptance rates to these programs later in this *Insider's Guide*. For now, we want you to gain a general sense of the odds of getting into graduate school in psychology and to feel confident that there is a place for most serious students in graduate school, even if it is a part-time master's program.

On "Backdoor" Clinicians

The APA ethical code outlines two pathways to becoming a clinical or counseling psychologist. The first is to complete a doctoral program and formal internship in clinical or counseling psychology. The second is to obtain a nonclinical psychology doctorate and then to complete a formal respecialization program in clinical or counseling psychology, which includes the internship. Formal training and supervised experience, not simply the desire to become

a clinical or counseling psychologist, are required according to the APA ethical code.

In the past, some psychologists obtained doctorates in developmental, experimental, social, or educational psychology or in a psychology-related discipline and managed to practice as "clinical psychologists" or "counseling psychologists." This was possible because of the paucity of clinical and counseling psychology doctoral programs and because of generic state licensure laws, which recognize only one broad (generic) type of psychologist. However, this educational and licensure process circumvents the established pathway, increases the prospects of inadequate training, and in some cases results in unethical representation. Hence the term *backdoor*—unable to enter through the front door, they sneak in through the back entrance. Major universities, the federal government, the Veterans Administration, and practically all universities now insist on the doctorate (or respecialization) in clinical or counseling psychology for employment as a clinical or counseling psychologist. Although individuals with nonclinical psychology doctorates may be eligible for state licensure, they will be increasingly unable to identify themselves as clinical or counseling psychologists.

Circuitous routes to becoming a clinical or counseling psychologist may still exist, but they have become far less common and ethical. We emphatically recommend against these "backdoor" practices on both clinical and ethical grounds.

To Reiterate Our Purpose

The purpose of this book is to help you navigate the heretofore unknown and frightening process of applying to clinical and counseling psychology graduate programs. Gaining admission to such competitive programs requires a good deal of time and energy. There are the matters of taking the appropriate undergraduate courses, gaining clinical experience, acquiring research competencies, requesting letters of recommendation, locating compatible schools to which to apply, succeeding on entrance examinations, completing the application, creating personal statements, traveling to interviews, and deciding which program actually to attend. We have known people who have quit jobs or taken months off just to invest all their time to the application process. However, with this book and a fair degree of organization, you can make such extreme measures unnecessary.

Emotional strain is an inherent part of the application process. This is unlike many job interviews, where you are marketing yourself merely as a provider of services. Here you are marketing yourself as a human being. This is a personal process. The application forms and interviews require self-exploration and even a certain amount of justification. Why do you like clinical work? What do you enjoy about spending time with people who are disturbed? Do you really like research? You may end up questioning your answers and may feel compelled to examine the beliefs that have led you to this point in your life.

With the help of our book, you ultimately become the consumer for a program best fitted to you. And 86% of students say that their sense of fit with a program is the single most important factor in choosing a graduate program (Kyle, 2000). By negotiating this process in a systematic manner, you can become an informed consumer of psychology graduate programs. Many interviewers recommend that the final interview should be approached by the applicant in this way. With this approach to the admission process, much of the stress can be allayed.

Although the application process itself can appear intimidating, or the prospect of being rejected upsetting, we urge you *not* to allow fear to cause you to abandon your goal. Do not allow yourself to be one of the students who gets rejected unnecessarily. If you apply to the appropriate programs and present yourself effectively, your chances of getting in are vastly improved. In this book, we will demystify the graduate school application process, help you successfully navigate it, and showcase your credentials.

Our Approach

Having now counseled thousands of clinical and counseling psychology aspirants and conducted scores of workshops on applying to graduate school, the two of us have gravitated toward a particular approach to the topic. It might be called *realistically encouraging*.

It is realistic in that we present the hard facts about the competition for entrance into doctoral psychology programs. We will not resort to the disservice of feeding you illusions ("Anyone can become a clinical/counseling psychologist!"), even though the reality may leave you feeling discouraged at times.

Still, our approach is unabashedly encouraging in that we support people seeking their goals. With knowledge and perseverance, most of our students have made it. Consider the real-life story of Justin, a success story in the quest for a doctorate in clinical psychology.

Justin almost flunked out of college during his first 2 years, before discovering his abiding interest in psychology. He took his GREs late in his senior year without adequate preparation but obtained combined verbal and quantitative scores of 1100. His applications to doctoral programs that year were hastily and poorly prepared. Justin was, to complicate matters, grossly unaware of typical admission requirements, acceptance rates, and application guidelines. He had no clinical experience whatsoever and had never engaged in research beyond course requirements. Not surprisingly, letters of recommendation about him were mildly positive but without detail or conviction (the deadly, two-paragraph "He/she's nice, but we haven't had much contact" letters). He received dismal rejections, not even a hint of a possible interview or finalist pool.

Well, as people are apt to do, Justin was about to give up and throw in the towel. But he then attended one of our workshops and began to understand that he had neglected virtually every guideline for sophisticated application to graduate school. The next year was devoted to preparing himself for the hunt: he took extra courses after receiving his degree in order to increase his GPA and to improve his GRE psychology score; he volunteered 10 hours a week at two supervised placements; he worked 20 hours a week for a small stipend as a research assistant; and he copublished three articles. Not surprisingly, his letters of recommendation were now enthusiastic and detailed. That year, Justin obtained six acceptances into clinical doctoral programs with full financial support at three of them.

There *are* concrete steps you can take to improve your application. Knowledge of the application process can be as important as your actual credentials.

And if you do get rejected once, many steps can enhance the probability of acceptance the next time around, as in Justin's case. Knowledge of the process makes a tremendous difference. Over the past 22 years, this *Insider's Guide* has helped tens of thousands of students reach their goal of a doctorate in clinical or counseling psychology—and we hope you will be among them. In the following chapters, we provide suggestions and strategies that will increase your attractiveness as an applicant. Let's get to it!

CHAPTER 2

CHOOSING THE Ph.D. OR Psy.D.

Clinical psychology now has two distinct training systems by which students earn their doctorates. Without a firm understanding of the differences in these training models, many applicants will waste valuable time and needlessly experience disappointment. In this chapter, we explain and distinguish between the two prevalent training models in clinical psychology—the Boulder model (Ph.D.) and the Vail model (Psy.D.). Counseling psychology has parallel differences in training emphases; however, it offers only a handful of Psy.D. programs. Thus, we spend most of our time on clinical psychology in this chapter.

The Boulder Model (Ph.D.)

The first national training conference on clinical psychology was held during 1949 in Boulder, Colorado (hence, the "Boulder model"). At this conference, equal weight was accorded to the development of research competencies and practice skills. This dual emphasis resulted in the notion of the clinical psychologist as a *scientist–practitioner*. Clinical psychologists were considered first and foremost as scientific psychologists and were to have a rigorous, broad-based education in psychology. Their training would encompass statistics, history and systems, and research, with core courses in development, biopsychology, learning, and the like. The emphasis was on psychology; clinical was the adjective.

The Boulder conference was a milestone for several reasons. First, it established the Ph.D. as the required degree, as in other academic research fields. To this day, all Boulder model, scientist–practitioner programs in clinical psychology award the Ph.D. degree. Second, the conference reinforced the idea that the appropriate location for training was within university departments, not separate schools or institutes as in medicine and law. And third, clinical psychologists were trained for simultaneous existence in two worlds: academic/scientific and clinical/professional.

The important implication for you, as an applicant, is that Boulder-model programs provide rigorous education as a researcher along with training as a practitioner. Consider this dual thrust carefully before applying to Boulder-model programs. Some first-year graduate students undergo undue misery because they dislike research-oriented courses and the research projects that are part of the degree requirements. These, in turn, lead to the formal dissertation required by Boulder-model programs. Many applicants are specifically seeking this sort of training.

Other applicants are seeking training focused on clinical practice. For these applicants, there is an alternative to the Boulder model: the Vail model of training psychologists.

The Vail Model (Psy.D.)

Some dissension with the recommendations of the Boulder training conference emerged at later meetings; however, there was a strong consensus that the scientist–practitioner model, Ph.D. degree, and university training should be retained. But in the late 1960s and early 1970s, change was in the wind. Training alternatives were entertained, and diversification was encouraged. This sentiment culminated in a 1973 national training conference held in Vail, Colorado (hence, the "Vail model").

The Vail conferees endorsed different principles than the Boulder model, leading to a diversity of training programs (Peterson, 1976, 1982). Psychological knowledge, it was argued, had matured enough to warrant creation of explicitly professional programs along the lines of professional training in medicine, dentistry, and law. These "professional programs" were to be added to, not replace, Boulder-model programs. Further, it was proposed that different degrees should be used to designate the scientist role (Ph.D.—Doctor of Philosophy) from the practitioner role (Psy.D.—Doctor of Psychology). Graduates of Vail-model professional programs would be *scholar–professionals*: the focus would be primarily on practice and less on research.

This revolutionary conference led to the emergence of two distinct training models typically housed in different settings. Boulder-model, Ph.D. programs are almost universally located in graduate departments of large universities. Vail-model programs are housed in three organizational settings:

- a psychology department (as Ph.D. programs)
- within a university-affiliated psychology school (for instance, Rutgers and Adelphi universities)
- independent, "freestanding" university (for instance, Alliant University, Argosy University)

These last programs are part of independent institutions, some of which are run as for-profit companies. Although they are titled "universities," they are frequently not comprehensive universities offering degrees in dozens of subjects. Rather, they only offer degrees in a handful of subjects and thus not "universities" in the traditional sense of comprehensive universities.

Table 2-1 lists APA-accredited clinical Psy.D. programs. (For a listing of non-accredited Psy.D. programs, see www.apadiv2.org/otrp/resources/brynolf07psyd.pdf.)

Clinical psychology now has two established and complementary training models graduating an equal number of psychologists each year. Although Boulder-model programs still outnumber Vail-model programs, Vail-model programs enroll, as a rule, three to four times the number of incoming doctoral candidates. This creates numerical parity in terms of psychologists produced.

Salient Differences

The primary disparity between Boulder-model and Vail-model programs lies in the relative emphasis on scientific research: Boulder programs aspire to train producers of research; Vail programs train consumers of research. Even Vail programs require research and statistics courses; you simply cannot avoid research sophistication in any APA-accredited psychology program. The practice opportunities are very similar for students in both types of programs.

Several studies have demonstrated that initial worries about stigmatization, employment difficulties, licensure uncertainty, and second-class citizenship for university-based Psy.D.s have *not* materialized (see Hershey, Kopplin, & Cornell, 1991; Peterson, Eaton, Levine, & Snepp, 1982). There do not appear to be strong disparities in the pre-internship clinical skills of Ph.D. and Psy.D. students as evaluated by internship supervisors (Snepp & Peterson, 1988). Nor are there discernible differences in employment except, of course, that the more research-oriented, Boulder-model graduates are far more likely to be employed in academic positions and medical schools (Gaddy et al., 1995). While Vail-model graduates may be seen as second-class citizens by some Boulder-model traditionalists, this is not the case among health care organizations or individual patients.

Which training model do clinical psychologists themselves prefer? In one of our studies (Norcross, Gallagher, & Prochaska, 1989), we found that 50% favored the Boulder model, 14% the Vail model, and the remaining 36% both models equally. However, preferences varied as a function of the psychologist's own doctoral program: 93% of the psychologists trained in a strong Boulder tradition preferred the Boulder model or both equally. Likewise, 90% of the psychologists trained in a strong Vail tradition preferred the Vail model or both equally. In short, psychologists preferred the training model to which they applied and in which they completed their training.

As we discuss in subsequent chapters, there are important trade-offs between Vail-model and Boulder-model programs. Here are 8 differences to bear in mind as you read through our book and as you become an informed consumer.

1. *Research skills.* Vail-model, Psy.D. programs provide slightly more clinical experience and courses

TABLE 2-1. APA-Accredited Psy.D. Programs in Clinical Psychology

Adler School of Professional Psychology
Alliant International University–Fresno[a]
Alliant International University–Los Angeles[a]
Alliant International University–San Diego[a]
Alliant International University–San Francisco Bay[a]
Antioch University New England
Argosy University, Atlanta
Argosy University, Chicago
Argosy University, Hawaii
Argosy University, Orange County
Argosy University, Phoenix
Argosy University, San Francisco Bay Area
Argosy University, Schaumberg
Argosy University, Tampa
Argosy University, Twin Cities
Argosy University, Washington, DC
Azusa Pacific University
Baylor University
Biola University[a]
California Institute of Integral Studies
Carlos Albizu University–Miami Campus
Carlos Albizu University–San Juan Campus[a]
Chestnut Hill College
Chicago School of Professional Psychology
University of Denver[a]
Florida Institute of Technology
Forest Institute of Professional Psychology
Fuller Theological Seminary[a]
George Fox University
George Washington University[a]
University of Hartford
Immaculata University

Indiana State University
Indiana University of Pennsylvania
University of Indianapolis
John F. Kennedy University
La Salle University
University of La Verne
Loma Linda University[a]
Long Island University, C.W. Post Campus
Loyola University Maryland
Marshall University
Marywood University
Massachusetts School of Professional Psychology
Nova Southeastern University[a]
Pacific Graduate School of Psychology/Stanford University Medical School Consortium
Pacific University
Pepperdine University
Philadelphia College of Osteopathic Medicine
Ponce School of Medicine
Regent University
Roosevelt University
Rutgers, The State University of New Jersey[a]
Spalding University
Virginia Consortium Program in Clinical Psychology
Wheaton College
Widener University
Wisconsin School of Professional Psychology
The Wright Institute
Wright State University
Xavier University
Yeshiva University[a]

[a]These institutions also have APA-accredited Ph.D. programs in clinical psychology.

but less research experience and courses than do Boulder-model programs (Tibbits-Kleber & Howell, 1987). Psy.D. programs typically require a clinical dissertation, substantially less than an original research dissertation required by Ph.D. programs. An important caveat: if you desire to teach full time at a 4-year college or university, we strongly advise you *not* to seek the Psy.D. degree. The Psy.D. is an explicitly professional or practitioner degree; your training

and expertise will be as a practitioner, not as a professor, researcher, or academician.

2. *Length of training.* The additional research training and the large dissertation required in Boulder-model Ph.D. programs translate into an additional year of training, on average. Students in Ph.D. programs take significantly longer, 1 to 1.5 years longer, to complete their degrees than do Psy.D. stu-

dents (Gaddy et al., 1995; Norcross, Castle, Sayette, & Mayne, 2004). Various interpretations are given to his robust difference, from "Psy.D. training is more focused and efficient" on one pole, to "Ph.D. training is more comprehensive and rigorous" on the other.

3. *Class size.* Each year, Boulder-model Ph.D. programs in clinical psychology will take in 7 to 10 new students. The rule of thumb is to accept one new student annually for each full-time clinical faculty in that program. Each year, Vail-model Psy.D. programs in clinical psychology will take in 20 to 60 new students (Norcross et al., 2011). The natural consequence is that the number of students in graduate courses tends to be much larger in Psy.D. programs than in Ph.D. programs. The amount of individual mentoring by full-time faculty will also be less in Psy.D. programs.

4. *Acceptance rates.* Both Vail and Boulder programs have similar admission criteria, which favor grade point average, entrance examination scores, letters of recommendation, and so on. (All these topics are covered in detail in later chapters.) But Vail-model programs afford easier admission than Boulder-model programs. On average, clinical Ph.D. programs accept 6% to 10% of applicants, whereas clinical Psy.D. programs accept 41 to 50% of applicants (Norcross et al., 2010) (see Table 4-1 for details).

5. *Financial assistance.* Admission rates are higher in Psy.D. programs, but financial assistance is lower. These numbers are plainly visible in the Reports on Individual Programs. As a rule, only 1 to 10% of Psy.D. students will receive full financial assistance (tuition waiver plus a paid assistantship), whereas 61 to 98% of clinical Ph.D. students will (Norcross et al., 2010) (see Table 5-3 for details).

6. *Loan debt.* The paucity of financial assistance to Psy.D. students translates into increased personal debt. If the program does not provide funding, then students are forced to rely on personal funds or loans. The median debt for Psy.D. recipients is now $90,000 (Pate & Finno, 2009). In fact, about one-third of recent Psy.D. recipients are saddled with more than $120,000 of graduate school debt. The median debt for clinical Ph.D. recipients is $45,000, half that of Psy.D.s but still substantial. (For comparison, the median debt for psychology Ph.D.s in non-clinical fields is $35,000; Pate & Finno, 2009.)

7. *Accredited internships.* All doctoral students in clinical and counseling psychology will complete the equivalent of a year-long, full-time internship before receiving their degrees. Students desire an internship accredited by APA or APPIC (Association of Psychology Postdoctoral and Internship Centers). The competition for an APA or APPIC-accredited internship can be keen, and in recent years, only 75% of intern applicants matched with an accredited internship. The research consistently demonstrates that students enrolled in large, freestanding Psy.D. programs match at a lower rate than students enrolled in smaller, Ph.D. programs (APPIC, 2006; Norcross et al., 2010; Parent & Williamson, 2010).

8. *Licensure exam scores.* One disconcerting trend is that Vail-model, Psy.D. graduates do not perform as well as Ph.D. graduates on the national licensing examination for psychologists (Templer et al., 2008; Maher, 1999). That is, doctoral students who graduate with the Psy.D. score lower, on average, than doctoral students who graduate from a traditional clinical psychology Ph.D. program on the Examination for Professional Practice in Psychology (EPPP), the national licensing test. Higher EPPP scores have been reliably associated with smaller-sized clinical programs and larger faculty-to-student ratios, in addition to traditional Ph.D. curricula.

From a student's perspective, these 8 differences between the Boulder Ph.D. programs and the Vail Psy.D. programs do not reliably favor one training model over the other. As a potential applicant, you will probably prefer the shorter training and higher admission rates among Psy.D. programs, on the one hand. Easier to get in and quicker to finish. You will probably prefer the greater probability of financial assistance, accredited internships, and higher licensure scores among Ph.D. programs, on the other hand. More money and better internship matching.

In the final analysis, the decision comes down to your personal interests and career trajectory. Certainly if you have primarily academic or research aspirations, then a Boulder model Ph.D. program would be wise. Certainly if you adore clinical practice and dislike much of research, then a Vail model Psy.D. program would be your choice. These truly represent choice points for an informed student.

A Bolder Boulder Model (Ph.D.)

The rise of the Vail model and the Psy.D. degree has always concerned many research-oriented academic psychologists, but their simmering concern has risen to collective action in the past decade. Some psychologists believe that the professional schools, especially the large multi-campus institutions, have seriously compromised the quality of training and the scientific nature of psychology. In a provocative monograph, three prominent clinical psychologists argue that the "evidence shows that many clinical psychology doctoral training programs, especially Psy.D. and for-profit programs, do not uphold high standards for graduate admission, have high student–faculty ratios, deemphasize science in their training, and produce students who fail to apply or generate scientific knowledge" (Baker, McFall, & Shoham, 2009). These authors argue for a return to the Boulder model of training and endorse the new accreditation system—Psychological Clinical Science Accreditation System (PCSAS)—which is supported by the Association for Psychological Science and the Academy of Psychological Clinical Science.

This movement toward a "bolder" Boulder model was crystallized by the 1995 creation of the Academy of Psychological Clinical Science (APCS). APCS is an alliance of scientifically oriented, doctoral and internship training programs. APCS programs are strongly committed to research training and to the integration of such training with clinical practice. They are also committed to raising the standards of graduate education in psychology and upholding a science of psychology, even within professional training. APCS includes 52 clinical psychology Ph.D. programs, which are listed in Table 2-2. (More information on APCS can be found on their Web site: http://acadpsychclinicalscience.org/).

Our research has determined that APCS programs are indeed distinct from other APA-accredited clinical psychology programs in that they are more selective and more research-focused. Based on the data from previous editions of our *Insider's Guide*, we found that APCS Ph.D. programs, compared to nonmember Ph.D. programs, admit a lower percentage of applicants (who had higher GRE scores) and were more likely to provide full financial support. APCS programs also subscribe more frequently to a cognitive-behavioral orientation, report a stronger research emphasis, and engage more frequently in research supported by funding agencies than non-APCS programs (Sayette, Norcross, & Dimoff, 2011). Students interested in a "bolder" Boulder-model clinical Ph.D. program may find these APCS programs to be especially attractive in that they represent empirically based, research-focused training.

A Continuum of Training Opportunities

In truth, the doctoral training opportunities in clinical and counseling psychology are more nuanced than the either/or, Ph.D./Psy.D. dichotomy we have presented above. There is considerable variation within the Ph.D. and Psy.D., not only between them.

Think of a training continuum in psychology programs running from practice oriented on the left side to research oriented on the right. In the middle are programs equally emphasizing science and practice. Such a practice-research continuum is displayed below.

Practice-Oriented Programs	Equal-Emphasis Programs	Research-Oriented Programs
	(Scientist–Practitioners)	(Clinical Scientists)
(Practitioners)		
1 2 3	4 5	6 7
Psy.D. Programs	Ph.D. Programs	

The practice-oriented Psy.D. programs account for roughly one-third of APA-accredited programs. Psy.D. recipients are typically known as *practitioners*. In the middle of the continuum are the equal-emphasis Ph.D. programs that account for another one-third of the APA-accredited programs. Graduates of these programs are typically called *scientist–practitioners*. On the other end of the continuum are the research-oriented Ph.D. programs that account for the final one-third. These Ph.D. recipients are called either *scientist–practitioners* or increasingly *clinical scientists*, especially if they graduate from an APCS program.

As you will soon discover in the Reports on Individual Programs, training directors rated their programs along this continuum. They assigned themselves a number from 1 to 7 corresponding to their training orientation.

Consider the heterogeneity of Psy.D. programs (Norcross, Castle, Sayette, & Mayne, 2004). Yes, all are dedicated to training practitioners (1 to 3), but they do so in different settings and in different ways. Some are small, university-based programs accepting 15 students a year, and others are huge, for-profit campuses enrolling 70 to 80 students per year. It's inaccurate to simply lump them all together. For example, the smaller, university-housed Psy.D. programs are more likely to offer financial assistance than the larger, multi-campus Psy.D. programs.

TABLE 2-2. APA-Accredited Clinical Psychology Programs That Are Members of the Academy of Psychological Clinical Science (APCS)

University of Arizona	University of Minnesota
Arizona State University	University of Missouri
Binghamton University	University of Nevada–Reno
Boston University	Northwestern University
University of Buffalo	University of North Carolina at Chapel Hill
University of California–Berkeley	Ohio State University
University of California–Los Angeles	University of Oregon
University of California–San Diego and San Diego State University	University of Pennsylvania
University of Delaware	Pennsylvania State University
University of Denver (Department of Psychology)	University of Pittsburgh
Duke University	Purdue University
Emory University	Rutgers University
Florida State University	University of Southern California
University of Georgia	University of South Florida
Harvard University	Stony Brook University
University of Hawaii	University of Texas
University of Illinois at Chicago	University of Toronto
University of Illinois–Urbana Champaign	Vanderbilt University
Indiana University	Virginia Commonwealth University
University of Iowa	Virginia Polytechnic State University
Kent State University	University of Virginia (Department of Psychology)
University of Kentucky	University of Washington
University of Maryland	Washington University in St. Louis
McGill University	West Virginia University
University of Memphis	University of Wisconsin
University of Miami	Yale University

Also look at the diversity of Ph.D. programs in clinical psychology. They range from 4 to 7, from equal-emphasis, scientist–practitioner training to the research-oriented, clinical scientist training. It is mythical to treat clinical psychology Ph.D. programs as homogeneous and unified (McFall, 2002). The differentiation among types of clinical programs—beyond the dichotomy of Ph.D. and Psy.D.—is now abundantly clear and consistently replicated.

Our research substantiates a similar continuum among counseling psychology, except that there are only 3 or 4 Psy.D. programs in counseling psychology. Counseling psychology has historically endorsed scientist–practitioner training and, with a few exceptions, actively resisted the practice-oriented Psy.D. (Neimeyer, Saferstein, & Rice, 2005). Hence, the practice-research continuum in counseling psychology begins with equal-emphasis programs (3) and ends with the research-oriented programs (7). As in clinical psychology, the practice-oriented and equal-emphasis Ph.D. programs in counseling psychology accept a higher percentage of applicants but offer less financial assistance than the research-oriented programs (Norcross, Evans, & Ellis, 2009).

In short, you are not simply restricted to the Ph.D. or the Psy.D., but to all the variations and permutations within the practice-research continuum. Most students are, at once, excited and dismayed by this diversity. Excited because they can select doctoral programs that best match their interests and career goals. But also dismayed because the application process becomes more complicated. Do not fret;

we shall take you step-by-step through the process of selecting schools and applying to programs.

Can you apply to both Ph.D. and Psy.D. programs? The answer depends on you. Yes, if your interest lies mostly in practice (a rating of 3) or in equal-emphasis (4). Both Psy.D. and Ph.D. programs would fit your career goals. No, if your interests are almost exclusively practice (1 or 2) or research (5, 6, or 7). In those cases, you would be poorly served by applying to a program that trains students for a career in direct conflict to your career goal.

Your Informed Choice

In order to become an informed applicant, know the crucial differences between the Boulder-model Ph.D. and the Vail-model Psy.D. training models and the diversity within them. But more importantly, know the specific data on programs to which you will apply. The Reports on Individual Programs later in this book present these data—ratings on the practice-research continuum, length of training, acceptance rates, financial assistance, students securing accredited internships, and more—for each APA-accredited program.

The key tasks for you as a potential applicant are, first, to recognize the diversity in training emphases and, second, to understand your best fit. The bottom line for applicants to psychology doctoral programs is one of choice, matching, and parity. You have the choice of two training models (and all the programs in between the two extremes). The choice should be matched to your strengths and interests. Parity has been achieved in that half of all doctorates in clinical psychology are now Psy.D.s. The choices are yours, but make informed decisions. The remainder of the *Insider's Guide* is designed to do just that.

CHAPTER 3

PREPARING FOR GRADUATE SCHOOL

People begin the graduate school application process at different stages in their lives. You may be a junior or a senior in college. Maybe you have a bachelor's degree in psychology and have worked for a year or two. Perhaps you are a master's-level counselor or social worker who has decided to return for a doctorate. Or maybe you were not a psychology major but have decided you want to make a career change. Depending on your situation, your needs will be somewhat different. Therefore, each situation is addressed separately throughout this chapter.

But whatever your current status, recognize this about becoming a clinical or counseling psychologist: *Do not wait until the year of your application to begin the preparation.* Securing admission into competitive doctoral programs necessitates preparation throughout your undergraduate career and any intervening years. Good grades, adequate test scores, clinical work, and research experience cannot be instantaneously acquired simply because you have made a decision to pursue psychology as your career.

Plan ahead of time using the knowledge and strategies presented in this chapter. Preparing for graduate study is *not* for seniors only (Fretz & Stang, 1980). Timeliness is everything, or, in the vernacular, "you snooze you lose" (Mitchell, 1996).

Much of the "advice" bandied about by fellow students and even some faculty is hopelessly general. Their well-intentioned comments are meant to be universal—one size fits all. However, this advice is akin to the bed of the legendary Greek innkeeper, Procrustes, who insisted on one size bed and who stretched or shortened his unfortunate guests to fit that bed! Do not fall prey to these Procrustean maneuvers; different applicants have different needs. Understanding your particular circumstances and needs will produce an individualized plan for applying to graduate school.

Different Situations, Different Needs

Undergraduates

Some of you are undergraduates, not yet in your senior year. By getting a head start, you can take the prerequisite courses and attain the optimal clinical and research training possible at your institution. The more time invested in preparation, the better able you will be to meet the requirements of the application process with confidence, which puts you in a very desirable position. This *Insider's Guide* will provide you with information that can help guide your undergraduate experiences, academic as well as practical. The "Time Line" presented in Appendix A outlines important steps to be taken during your freshman, sophomore, and junior years.

Seniors

Some of you are seniors, deciding whether to go directly to graduate school. This is a difficult time, and you are likely to be given advice ranging from "everyone *must* take time off" to "if you take off a year, you'll lose the momentum and study skills and never go back." Obviously, this decision is based on the needs and experiences of each individual. There are two guidelines, however, that can help you muddle through these decisions.

1. Are you primarily interested in becoming a practitioner and desire only minimal research training? If so, a practice-oriented psychology program will probably best suit your needs. These programs tend to put the emphasis on clinical experience (Piotrowski & Keller, 1996). They favor applicants who have a master's degree or have been involved in a clinical setting and who will come into a program with some practice skills already in their repertoire. The average age of students admitted into these programs is slightly older than that in research-oriented programs, reflecting time spent out of school in a work environment. Consequently, if you are interested in a practice-oriented program, you could take time off to gain relevant experience in clinical work and research.

2. Are you interested in a program that is primarily research oriented? If you have a solid grounding in research as an undergraduate, such a program is less likely to emphasize the need for clinical experience. The necessary and sufficient research experience can certainly be obtained during an undergraduate education without taking time off. Adding research experiences and clinical skills to an application, however, can only improve your chances of acceptance into a research-oriented program.

The decision to postpone graduate school for a year or more can be influenced by the time constraints of the application process. Applications for doctoral programs in clinical and counseling psychology are typically due between mid-December and mid-February of the year before you plan to attend school. First-semester seniors just beginning an honors or research project may not be in a position to showcase their talents by application time. The additional preparation for the Graduate Record Examination (GRE; see Entrance Examinations) may lead a potential applicant to wait a year before applying.

For all these reasons, first-semester seniors may not easily meet the requirements of the recommended Time Line presented in Appendix A. This is a frequent predicament, the solution to which is to wait another year to apply or to do what you can in the remaining time available. In either case, do not

give up! Rather, review the Time Line carefully and check off what you have and have not accomplished before making the momentous decision to go for it this year, or to wait until next year. Some shortcuts may well be necessary to apply this year; the ideal time line will need to be modified to fit your reality (Keith-Spiegel, 1991). Some of the items will have to be sacrificed, some accomplished later or more hastily, and others with great energy.

Should you elect to wait a year after receiving your baccalaureate degree, you will begin the application process almost immediately after graduation. In addition to gaining research and clinical experience, the year away from school is spent applying to graduate school. This is not a year to relax or "goof off"; rather, it should be an intense year of preparation for graduate admission.

Our research on the admission statistics of APA-accredited clinical psychology programs demonstrates that, on average, 79% of incoming doctoral students held bachelor's degrees only and 21% possessed a master's degree (Norcross et al., 2010; Oliver et al., 2005). However, this generalization is limited by significant differences among the types of programs: research-oriented Ph.D. programs enrolled a significantly higher percentage of baccalaureate-level students (87% on average; 13% master's), while Psy.D. programs enrolled more master's-level students (35% on average).

In summary, the advantages of taking time off depend on the type of psychology training you desire and the strength of your current credentials. If you desire to focus exclusively on clinical practice and a Psy.D. degree, it may be advisable to take time off to gain some practical experience and to save some money. If you are more research oriented and already possess skills in this area, you may be in a position to apply at present. If your current credentials—grades, GRE scores, research—are marginal, then another year may also be required.

In using this book, you will be introduced to the admission criteria for graduate school. By using the worksheets, you can determine how well prepared you are to apply to schools at this point. Following the steps in this book will help you assess how prepared you are to apply to graduate school successfully and whether some time out in the "real world" would be advised.

Previous College Graduates

Some of you are college graduates and have already taken time off, or you are a member of the working world contemplating a career change. A solid work record and a mature perspective on psychology are certainly advantageous.

Those of you who have been out of school and in the real world for several years may feel at a disadvantage in terms of taking the GREs, finding academic letters of recommendation, and locating research opportunities. But by faithfully following the strategies in this book, you can master these steps—as have thousands of returning students before you. And by reviewing the admissions criteria for graduate programs and using the worksheets provided, you will evaluate the degree of your preparation in order to decide whether it is prudent to begin the application process immediately or to bolster your credentials before beginning. Pay particular attention to the steps listed under "application year" in the Time Line (Appendix A).

Returning Master's-Level Clinicians

Some of you will be master's-level clinicians interested in obtaining the doctorate in clinical or counseling psychology. Although your wealth of clinical experience gives you an immediate edge over undergraduates in the admissions race to Psy.D. programs, you cannot ignore the importance assigned to entrance examinations and research experience.

Psy.D. programs and practice-oriented Ph.D. programs tend to accept proportionally more incoming students with master's degrees than with baccalaureate degrees only. Interestingly, counseling psychology programs also seem to prefer master's-level students: Two-thirds of incoming students in APA-accredited counseling psychology programs already held their master's (Norcross, Evans, & Ellis, 2009). Of course, these are merely averages that mask the huge differences between, for example, the one-third of counseling psychology programs which *only* accept master's recipients and the one-tenth of programs which primarily accept baccalaureate recipients (Turkson & Norcross, 1996).

Hines (1985) conducted a survey of clinical psychology doctoral programs regarding their policies and experiences in accepting students with master's degrees in psychology. Following are several of the salient findings.

The first question was "What effect (if any) will having a master's degree have on an applicant's chances for admission to your program?" Most responses indicated that having a master's per se made little or no difference, with some respondents suggesting that it was the student's performance in the master's program that was more important. However, 10% answered that having a master's degree had a definite positive effect. Only 3% indicated that having a master's would have a definite negative bias.

The second question requested that respondents rate the importance of seven criteria for admission to their programs. Each criterion was rated on a 5-point, Likert-type scale ranging from least important to most important. The three highest ratings were for GRE scores, letters of recommendation, and research experience. The rest, in descending order of importance, were undergraduate grades, graduate grades, quality of the master's program, and practicum experience.

As you can see, GRE scores and research experience definitely count in admissions decisions for master's-level applicants. The lower ratings given to graduate grades and to undergraduate grades reflect a difference among schools in whether graduate or undergraduate grades are considered more important. The standard deviation for graduate grades was particularly high, indicating wide variability in the importance placed on graduate grades among different programs. Comments suggested that some schools tended to downplay graduate grades "because they are universally high"; another suggested that "high grades don't help, but poor grades hurt."

Thus, a master's degree by itself neither helps nor hinders your chances in most doctoral admission decisions. It is not possessing the master's degree itself that matters, but the quality of performance in academic courses, clinical practica, and research experiences during master's training and thereafter that give an edge in the admission process.

Master's degree recipients with combined Verbal and Quantitative GRE scores below 1,000 can take hope from a study of similar students admitted to Ph.D. programs (Holmes & Beishline, 1996). Ten such applicants were admitted by virtue of "compensatory virtues," such as research presentations or publications that helped mitigate the effect of low GRE scores. If you find yourself in this position, emphasize the other, positive elements of your application and, again, seriously consider Psy.D. clinical and Ph.D. counseling psychology programs that enroll a higher percentage of master's-level students (Norcross et al., 1998). Assuming other parts of your credentials are acceptable, master's recipients should not be discouraged from applying to doctoral programs on the basis of GRE scores alone.

While clinical experience is valued, for most doctoral programs this factor is a secondary consideration to research. The vast majority of clinical and counseling doctoral programs prefer a research thesis or a journal article over a graduate internship or post-master's clinical experience (Keller, Beam, Maier, & Pietrowski, 1995). All programs expect evidence of conducting empirical research: Ph.D. programs favor it over clinical experience and Psy.D. programs weigh it equally with clinical experience.

A Master's Degree First?

A common question during our graduate school workshops is whether students should secure a master's degree before seeking the doctorate. Fortunately, our workshop participants and you realize that no simple answer is possible to such a complex question. Nonetheless, the following are some broad reasons for seeking a master's degree first.

- *Low grade-point average.* The vast majority of doctoral programs will not consider applicants with a GPA below 3.0.
- *Weak GRE scores.* Similarly, most university-based doctoral programs rarely accept bachelor's-level applicants whose combined Verbal and Quantitative scores fall below 1,000.
- *Scarce research or clinical experiences.* Doctoral admission committees understandably desire that you have had some direct experience with those activities you intend to pursue for a lifetime.
- *Uncertain career goal.* Indecision about your subfield in psychology, or outside of psychology, is a strong indicator for a master's program initially.
- *Late application.* Doctoral programs hold to earlier deadlines than do master's programs, so those students waiting too late to apply will be redirected to master's programs.
- *Terse letters of recommendation.* By virtue of late transfer into a university or into the psychology major, some students lack sufficient contact with faculty for them to write positive and detailed letters of recommendation expected by doctoral programs.
- *Inadequate coursework in psychology.* Doctoral programs require a minimum level of education in the discipline prior to acceptance, typically at least 15 to 18 credits of psychology course work.

Completing a rigorous master's program in psychology can correct many of the foregoing impediments to acceptance into a doctoral program. As we describe in Chapter 8, students typically strengthen their grade point average, acquire clinical and research experience, sharpen their career goals, and establish close relationships with faculty during the 2 years of a master's program. For these and other reasons, many students opt for a master's degree at one institution before seeking the doctorate at another.

Doctoral psychology faculty were surveyed in detail regarding the value of a clinical master's degree for gaining admission to their programs (Bonifzi, Crespy, & Rieker, 1997). Assuming a *good* undergraduate GPA and *good* GREs, the effect of having a master's degree on the applicant's chances for admission was negative for 7% of the programs, neutral for 48% of the programs, and positive for 45% of the programs. However, assuming *mediocre* GPA and *mediocre* GREs, the effect of having a master's was more neutral than positive overall. Put another way, it is clearly the applicant's overall credentials—rather than possession of a master's degree per se—that carries the day.

This same study (Bonifzi et al., 1997) and our own research (Mayne et al., 1994; Norcross et al., 2004) consistently demonstrate that Ph.D. clinical programs hold a positive bias toward baccalaureate-level applicants. By contrast, Psy.D. clinical, Ph.D. counseling, and Ph.D. school psychology programs view master's degree recipients more favorably and accept higher proportions of master's-level applicants. Keep these biases in mind as you consider the selection criteria of graduate schools.

Graduate School Selection Criteria

As an applicant, your perceptions of graduate admissions criteria probably differ from those of the admissions committee. Some of the things you may think are important are actually not so important (Collins, 2001). For two examples, your GRE Psychology Subject score is way less important than your GRE Verbal and Quantitative scores, and your extracurricular accomplishments do not count as much as you might like (Cashin & Landrum, 1991). On the other hand, you probably underestimate the importance of other admissions criteria; two examples are letters of recommendation and research experience, which students routinely undervalue compared to admissions committees (Nauta, 2000).

In this section we acquaint you with the evidence-based practices of graduate admissions committees. Learn what they value in graduate applicants and then tailor your application to those criteria in order to maximize your success.

TABLE 3-1. Importance of Various Criteria in Psychology Admissions Decisions

Criteria	Master's programs		Doctoral programs	
	Mean[a]	SD	Mean[a]	SD
Letters of recommendation	2.74	.49	2.82	.42
Personal statement/goals	2.63	.55	2.81	.41
GPA	2.75	.43	2.74	.45
Interview	2.30	.76	2.62	.60
Research experience	2.04	.74	2.54	.65
GRE scores	2.36	.66	2.50	.55
Clinically related public service	1.94	.70	1.91	.69
Work experience	1.91	.65	1.87	.68
Extracurricular activity	1.46	.54	1.41	.55

Note. Data from Norcross, Kohout, & Wicherski (2005).

[a]Means are calculated on ratings where 1 = low importance, 2 = medium importance, 3 = high importance.

A number of studies have been conducted to determine the relative importance of selection criteria in psychology graduate programs. The findings of one of our studies (Norcross, Kohout, & Wicherski, 2005) are summarized in Table 3-1. This table presents the average ratings of various criteria for admission into 410 doctoral programs and 179 master's programs in psychology. A rating of 3 denotes high importance; 2, medium importance; and 1, low importance.

The top-rated variables for doctoral programs were letters of recommendation, personal statements, GPA, interview, research experience, and GRE scores. All received ratings of 2.50 and higher on the 3-point scale, indicative of high importance. Extracurricular activity and work experience were valued substantially less.

The implications for enhancing your application are thus clear and embedded throughout this *Insider's Guide*: secure positive letters of recommendation, write compelling personal statements, maintain your GPA, ace the preadmission interview, obtain research experience, and prepare thoroughly for the GREs. At the same time, being heavily involved in student organizations and campus activities does not carry nearly as much weight as these other criteria. Being a volunteer soccer coach is not a path to graduate school!

Another study (Eddy, Lloyd, & Lubin, 1987) investigated the selection criteria of only APA-accredited doctoral programs in clinical psychology. Program directors rated the importance of each type of under-

graduate preparation on a scale ranging from very low importance, 1, to very high importance, 5. Table 3-2 presents the mean ratings and standard deviations for clinical psychology programs.

Research experience emerged as the top-rated variable. The authors of the study concluded that there is simply no better way to increase one's chances for graduate school acceptance than research. Personal visit to a department on an invited interview, computer proficiency, and paid clinical experience were also highly valued. However, as in the previous study, extracurricular activities, such as Psi Chi membership, were rated relatively unimportant.

Not all research experiences count equally in graduate admissions. The most important are published articles in referred journals and paper/poster presentations at national conferences. Of course, serving as first author counts more than second or third author. Paper/poster presentations at regional conferences follow in importance, then state conferences. Publishing in nonrefereed or undergraduate journals bring less credit in graduate admissions decisions, but still some credit (Kaiser et al., 2007; Keith-Spiegel et al., 1994).

In sum, the results of these and other studies (e.g., Briihl & Wasielski, 2004; Mayne et al., 1994; Munoz-Dunbar & Stanton, 1999; Purdy, Reinehr, & Swartz, 1989) consistently indicate that the ideal applicant has high GRE scores, strong letters of recommendation, research experience, clinical experience, and high GPA. The results also consistently demonstrate that the admission requirements for

TABLE 3-2. Importance Assigned by Clinical Psychology Doctoral Programs to Various Types of Undergraduate Preparation

Preparation	Mean	SD
Research methods	4.28	0.91
Personal visit to department	3.14	1.41
Computer knowledge and skills	3.00	0.85
Paid human service experience	2.90	1.07
Volunteer human service	2.85	1.13
Double major with basic science	2.78	1.10
Master's degree	2.16	0.99
Double major with social science	2.08	0.84
Psi Chi membership	2.00	0.94

Note. From Eddy, Lloyd, & Lubin (1987). © 1987 Lawrence Erlbaum Associates. Reprinted by permission.

doctoral programs are more stringent than for master's programs.

The remainder of this chapter highlights these pivotal criteria used by graduate admissions committees in selecting their students. We consider, in order, course work, faculty mentoring, clinical experience, research skills, entrance examinations, and extracurricular activities.

Course Work

Although graduate programs differ slightly in the courses they prefer you to have taken prior to admission, there are several "core" courses that nearly all require (Smith, 1985). These include Introduction to Psychology, Statistics, Research Methods, Abnormal Psychology, Physiological/Biopsychology, and Learning/Cognition.

Our research on clinical doctoral programs in the United States and Canada reveals that both Vail- and Boulder-model programs hold similar expectations on desirable undergraduate courses (Mayne et al., 1994; Oliver et al., 2005). Approximately 60% of the programs require or recommend specific undergraduate courses, 15% require an undergraduate psychology major, 10% specify a minimum number of psychology credits (but not specific courses), and the remainder have no set policy on the matter.

Table 3-3 presents the percentage of psychology courses required (first column), recommended (second column), and either required or recommended (third column) for entry into APA-accredited clinical programs. Bear in mind that these figures system-

atically *underestimate* the actual percentage of programs requiring these courses as they do not include those graduate programs requiring a psychology major as a prerequisite and thus probably requiring most of the courses listed in Table 3-3. Introduction to Psychology was presumed to be a prerequisite for these advanced psychology courses and was therefore omitted from the table. Courses you should complete, according to these results, are Statistics, Research Methods, Abnormal Psychology, Physiological Psychology, Learning/Cognition, Personality, and Developmental Psychology.

Doctoral programs require more courses on average than do master's programs (Smith, 1985). Accordingly, both to meet admissions criteria and to improve your GRE Psychology Subject score, we heartily recommend that you complete Social Psychology, History and Systems, Psychological Testing, and at least one laboratory course. The safest plan, of course, is to complete a rigorous undergraduate major in psychology to satisfy all these courses, but a well-planned minor in psychology may suffice. The rule of thumb: the more competitive the graduate program, the more stringent the required undergraduate course work.

If you were not a psychology major, it is still important that you take the minimum of six core courses mentioned. In addition, you may have to invest additional time studying for the Psychology Subject Test of the Graduate Record Examination (more about this later).

If you have been out of college for several years and feel deficient in this course work, you might consider taking a course or two as a part-time student at

TABLE 3-3. Undergraduate Courses Required or Recommended by APA-Accredited Clinical Psychology Programs

Psychology course	Percentage of programs		
	Required	Recommended	Either
Statistics	65	29	94
Research methods	48	19	68
Abnormal/psychopathology	29	22	51
Physiological/biopsychology	10	23	33
Learning/cognition	10	19	30
Personality	15	13	28
Child/developmental	11	13	24
Social psychology	7	16	23
History and systems	6	9	16
Psych testing/assessment	6	8	15
Laboratory course	6	5	11
Sensation and perception	3	2	5
Clinical/psychotherapy	1	1	2
Comparative psychology	1	1	2
Motivation and emotion	1	1	2
Neuropsychology	1	0	1

Note. Adapted from Mayne, Norcross, & Sayette (1994).

a local university. This will shore up your record and prepare you more fully for admission and the GRE. Those of you who are not psychology majors but have studied extensively for this test and have done well will often be considered favorably by admissions committees.

Graduate selection committees prefer a broad undergraduate background in a variety of arts and sciences (Fretz & Stang, 1980). Exposure to biological sciences, math competency, and verbal skills are generally valued. If you are anxious or phobic regarding oral presentations, then by all means complete a public speaking course. Composition and writing courses are also vital; you may well face three or four major papers each semester in graduate school.

At this point, you may want to glance at the Reports on Individual Programs following Chapter 8 to get a better idea of which courses particular doctoral programs recommend or require of applicants. You will find the specific courses that each accredited clinical, counseling, and combined psychology program recommends or requires applicants to have taken.

For students who have gotten an early start or who are seniors, we would like to suggest considering advanced course work. To allay any anxieties, we would emphasize that the vast majority of applicants do *not* take these courses as undergraduates. Your application can be very strong without taking the courses we are about to mention. However, those fortunate enough to be in a position to add these to their academic transcripts should seriously consider taking advantage of the opportunity.

Consider an advanced or graduate statistics course. Statistical acumen is highly regarded, especially in research-oriented programs, and advanced knowledge may pave the way for you receiving funding as a graduate assistant or research assistant. Another suggestion would be to take a course specifically focused on one of the data analysis programs. Learning one of the major statistical packages—Statistical Analysis System (SAS), Statistical Package for the Social Sciences (SPSS), or R—is a definite advantage. Such knowledge increases your employability and may catch the eye of a professor in need of a data analyst. Recall that computer proficiency is rated a moderately important admission variable by doctoral programs. Lastly, we suggest an advanced course in biopsychology, genetics, or neuroscience. This is certainly helpful in increasing your understanding of the biological aspects of behavior, an increasingly important focus in psychology today. If you have the time and abilities, these courses can help distinguish a strong application from an outstanding one.

As mentioned earlier, your GPA is a very important criterion for admission. Two types of GPA are usually considered by graduate programs: overall GPA and psychology GPA. Most programs focus only on your overall or cumulative GPA. Determine which GPAs programs evaluate and also how much importance they place on them. For example, if you have an overall GPA of 3.2 (on a 4-point scale where $A = 4$, $B = 3$, $C = 2$, and $D = 1$) and a psychology GPA of 3.6, you might concentrate on schools that emphasize the latter.

Our research has shed light on the average GPAs among incoming doctoral and master's students in psychology (Norcross et al., 2005). For doctoral programs, the mean GPA is 3.54 for all undergraduate courses and 3.66 for psychology courses. For master's programs, the mean GPA is 3.37 for all undergraduate courses and 3.48 for psychology courses. Of course, when interpreting these figures, recognize that roughly half of the incoming students will possess GPAs above these scores, and half of the students will possess GPAs below them.

Although we do not want to discourage anyone, a GPA below 3.0 is considered unsatisfactory by most APA-accredited programs. Regardless of the prestige of the institution, admissions committees view a GPA under 3.0 as below the acceptable limits of course performance. If your GPA is below 3.0, then consider the following steps:

- Take additional courses to bolster your GPA.
- Retake courses to improve it.
- Wait another year to apply in order for all of your senior-year grades to be factored into your GPA.
- Complete a master's program to show doctoral admissions committees you can perform academically at a higher level.

Try to speak with an academic advisor about how best to improve your standing within the workings of your own institution. Academic performance in your junior and senior psychology courses is particularly vital. Your grades in these courses affect your overall and psychology GPAs.

Your "academic" performance is not limited to exam grades in the classroom. Faculty members—several of whom may submit a letter of recommendation on your behalf—also assess your interpersonal skills, verbal ability, and professional commitment in the classroom, outside formal course work, and in everyday interactions. The direct implication is

to avoid undesirable interpersonal behaviors—for instance, silliness, arrogance, and hostility—in any interactions with your professors (Keith-Spiegel, 1991). The wisdom of avoiding such undesirable behaviors should be obvious, but students are frequently unaware of the importance faculty attach to good questions, genuine attentiveness, respectful disagreements, office visits, mature disposition, interpersonal responsibility, and so forth. These are the characteristics a student heading for graduate studies should manifest in and outside of the classroom.

Finally, there is a corpus of general knowledge regarding clinical and counseling psychology that may not have been covered in your courses. This body of information includes at least a cursory understanding of diagnosis, for example, the *Diagnostic and Statistical Manual*, 4th ed. (DSM-IV); various assessment devices, such as the Minnesota Multiphasic Personality Inventory-2 (MMPI-2) and the Wechsler Intelligence Scales (WAIS-IV, WISC-IV); and ordinary therapy practices, such as individual, group, and family therapy. You must have a passing familiarity with theoretical orientations, for example, cognitive-behavioral, psychodynamic, family systems, and integrative/eclectic, in order to understand program materials. If you are not already familiar with these concepts, it would be wise to review an introductory textbook in clinical or counseling psychology.

You should also be gaining knowledge specifically about psychology as a field and about the current issues within this field. Toward this end, we suggest you begin reading the *Monitor on Psychology*, a publication sent to all APA members and student affiliates, or the *APS Observer*, the publication distributed to all members of the Association for Psychological Science (APS). Both publications feature articles dealing with psychology in general and clinical/counseling psychology in particular. You can become an APA or APS affiliate and receive a subscription, peruse your library's copy, or ask to borrow a professor's old issues.

Faculty Mentoring

Learning about psychology and achieving good grades are important components of academic work. But classes are also important in that they provide you with the opportunity to become acquainted and form relationships with faculty. It is natural to feel shy around faculty, especially if you are part of a 300-person lecture class. Substantial courage is required to muster the nerve to ask a question or to stay after class and introduce yourself. Equally anxiety provoking is a visit alone to a professor's office during office hours. In the one case, you expose yourself in front of your peers; in the other, you are individually vulnerable and do not have a crowd of faces to blend into. *But find a way to become comfortable in approaching faculty members.*

The irony of student reticence to approach faculty is that professors generally would like more students to visit them. Many faculty sit alone during office hours wondering why students never come to see them. They love to have students come after class or during office hours with questions. Ideas for questions can include something mentioned in the lecture, something you encountered in the readings, or something that puzzles you about graduate school. You do not have to be a star pupil or ask brilliant questions to begin a conversation with a professor. If you want to develop a relationship, ask professors about their research or other courses they are teaching. Faculty are passionate about their research, and they will be flattered that you investigated their interests online before visiting them during office hours.

What is the importance of meeting faculty? Three compelling reasons spring to mind. First, having a mentor to advise you in your growth as a future psychologist is invaluable. There is no better way to learn about psychology than in a one-on-one, mentoring relationship. When you apply to graduate school, having a professor to guide you through the process is a huge advantage. Second, eventually you will need faculty to write letters of recommendation on your behalf. Whether you are applying to graduate school or for employment, everyone wants a few references regarding your performance and responsibility. Occasionally faculty members are asked to write a letter for a pupil who has taken a lecture course with 100 or more students—the professor may not even know the student until he or she requests a letter! It makes a huge difference if you have spent some office hours or time after class with a faculty member, and he or she knows you more personally.

And third, once you get to know professors, you may have the opportunity with work for them on a research project or as part of their clinical activities. You will be working closely with your major professor in graduate school, and you might as well begin as soon as possible as a colleague-in-training. Though more will be said about this later, we cannot overemphasize the need to cultivate such a relationship and obtain the rewards that can ensue.

To put it bluntly, the single largest contributor to preparedness for graduate school is students' interaction with faculty members at their undergraduate institution. That's what the research concludes and what graduate students report (Huss et al., 2002). Psychology students who had a mentor and who had high-quality interactions with faculty felt more prepared for graduate school. And the second largest contributor to graduate school preparedness is research activity—a point to which we shall return in a few pages.

Odysseus, the hero of Homer's epic poem *The Odyssey*, left for the Trojan War and entrusted his wise friend, Mentor to oversee the education of his son, Telemachus. The eponym "mentor" now refers to a trusted guide, positive role model, and caring teacher (Wang, 2010). Your task is to be Telemachus (or a mentee) and find at least one Mentor to guide you through the graduate admissions process. This *Insider's Guide* also serves that purpose, but another real-time person is highly recommended.

Beyond meeting professors, read your textbooks with an eye toward graduate school. If you come across an interesting study, note the author and check in the back of the text for the reference. When you have time, go to the library or online and read the original article. If it is recent, note the author's university. You will be surprised at how much you can learn about the field just by doing your typical class work.

Clinical Experience

What is clinical experience? In its loosest sense, it involves spending time working in human service or mental health agencies. Graduate programs in clinical and counseling psychology expect that you will have some experience working with emotionally, intellectually, or behaviorally disadvantaged people. Many students volunteer or intern during their undergraduate years, whereas other people get paid as part of a summer job or during their time off. In research-oriented Ph.D. programs, you will be expected to have some clinical experience as a prelude to your clinical training and as an aid to researching clinically relevant problems. Experience of this nature will be considered essential.

What kinds of clinical experience count? Largely two types—paid and volunteer—under individual supervision. Paid part-time work in a clinical setting may be available in your community (but your involvement should not be at the expense of your academic performance). Returning master's-level clinicians will obviously have a multitude of employment possibilities, whereas undergraduates will have to search vigilantly for part-time employment.

For college students, a prime opportunity is to complete an undergraduate practicum or field experience for academic credit. This is a great way to "kill two birds with one stone." More than 80% of colleges and universities provide undergraduate internships in psychology (Stoloff et al., 2010). Further, students consistently rate fieldwork as one of the most rewarding experiences and relevant courses in their college career. Internships "pay" in multiple ways: clinical experience, academic credit, familiarity with behavioral health agencies, professional supervision, potential sources for letters of recommendation, and a shot at a full-time job.

Check with your undergraduate advisor, faculty mentor, and the college catalogue to determine whether such an opportunity exists for you. To learn more about the specific placements, you should consult the Psychology Department or the faculty member responsible for internship placements.

In selecting a place to work or volunteer, please consider several factors. Although it may be difficult to accomplish, it is ideal to gain clinical experience in a setting that complements a research interest. For example, if your research is in the area of alcohol abuse, you might seek experience in a college counseling center or a substance abuse prevention program. Determine exactly what your responsibilities will entail.

The optimal program is one that will train you in clinical skills (such as crisis counseling on a hot line), will allow you to deal directly with clients, and will provide regular supervision by an experienced clinician.

Supervision is probably the most important consideration in choosing a clinical setting. It is important that you be supervised by a professional, one with a master's degree or higher. Determine the qualifications of the person who will be supervising your work. Aside from the valuable insight supervisors can offer, they may also be familiar with faculty at different graduate programs and assist you in selecting schools. In addition, you may eventually decide to request letters of recommendation from them. Letters from a clinical supervisor are particularly important for practice-oriented graduate programs. In a later section we offer suggestions regarding approaching professors for letters of recommendation. The same strategies apply here.

If you are volunteering, you should insist on receiving supervision. Learn not only who will supervise you, but also how often and for what length of time. You will need to be assertive when searching out and interviewing possible agencies. If this seems challenging for you, try to remember that you are a volunteer—giving your time and energy, without financial compensation, to an agency that is in need of people like yourself. You seek only experience and supervision. You are a valuable commodity, so do not sell yourself short!

Numerous settings are available to people seeking clinical experience. Here are several excellent sources of hands-on experience that can be found in most communities:

- *Crisis hot lines.* These typically provide training in counseling skills, suicide prevention, and outreach services. The clientele range from sexual assault victims to suicidal teens to lonely elderly who need to talk with someone. Volunteers usually provide telephone counseling, although opportunities to work with an emergency outreach team may also be available. This can be a great way to gain exposure to a multitude of psychopathologies and to acquire fundamental helping skills. One word of caution: new members of most crisis hot lines are expected to take a large share of the midnight to 8 A.M. shifts. Be prepared to pay your dues.

- *Centers for homeless or runaway adolescents.* Much of what is done in these settings is similar to case management, in that these teenagers are connected with social service agencies. However, in-house counseling may also be provided to these youths, who frequently come from disadvantaged families. Be particularly careful about specifying the supervision arrangement before starting. The facilities are often understaffed and financially strapped, meaning you may have to be assertive to get the training you desire.

- *Schools for emotionally disturbed children and adolescents.* These placements offer exposure to both educational and clinical services. Educational activities might include tutoring, classroom management, and one-on-one homework supervision. Clinical activities typically involve recreational supervision, art therapy, and perhaps individual, group, and family therapy.

- *Supervised homes for the developmentally disabled or chronically mentally ill.* These are unlocked transitional facilities where clients live and work in a therapeutic milieu (an environment consisting of peers). Depending on your prior experience, you might be expected to conduct skills training, recreational counseling, and work/school supervision. The programs are often behavioral, affording you experience with reinforcement schedules, shaping techniques, and token economies. Often the goal is to graduate clients to the outside world.

- *Summer camps for the physically challenged, developmentally disabled, or emotionally disturbed*. These can be either day or overnight camps, where counselors are expected to supervise recreation and train campers in skills and vocational activities. The positions are usually paid, ideal for college students who want to gain field experience while working for the summer. They also tend to be full-time positions, while they last. They offer short-term but intensive training.

- *Community mental health centers*. These provide experience with patients suffering from serious mental disorders, such as schizophrenia, bipolar disorders, substance abuse, and anxiety disorders. The programs vary but are likely to include an outpatient department, partial (day) hospitalization, and an education/outreach wing. Duties may include helping out during recreational activities or assisting with individual and group therapy. Though supervising recreational activities allows contact with patients, you might not be observing any clinical methods. Do not be shy about asking for greater responsibilities!

- *College peer programs*. These provide students with peer education and assistance on specific disorders, such as bulimia or substance abuse. Less common but still available is peer counseling on more general concerns, for example, "Need to Talk? Call Us." Both peer education and peer counseling programs are typically flexible in the number of hours you must work and usually provide training in listening and counseling skills. They may also provide an opportunity to begin learning about a specific clinical problem.

- *Women's resource centers*. These multiservice centers offer or coordinate a plethora of human services for women—rape crisis counseling, domestic violence education, victim advocacy, "safe homes" for victims of abuse, and so on. Possible activities likewise vary, but the training and *esprit de corps* are highly regarded. Students with abiding interest in women's issues and feminist therapy will find these placements particularly satisfying.

- *Drug and alcohol treatment facilities*. These offer a variety of detoxification and rehabilitation interventions designed to help patients cope with the physical and psychological components of addiction. Although not all "D & A" programs will afford undergraduate placements, sub-

stance abuse is one of the most popular research areas in clinical and counseling psychology (see Appendix E). Students can gain exposure to several models of addiction, interact with a multidisciplinary treatment team, and observe clinical services with substance abusers across gender, racial, and socioeconomic lines.

- *Psychiatric hospitals*. These offer comprehensive behavioral care in an inpatient setting and typically feature individual psychotherapy, group treatment, psychoactive medication, psychological assessment, occupational therapy, and recreational therapy. Students are likely to observe patients with severe disorders receiving many treatments provided by multidisciplinary staff. In addition, large state hospitals depend upon the kindness of volunteers to staff social events, community outings, and recreational opportunities for patients.

- *Legal and probation offices*. These offer ideal experiences for students interested in forensic applications. Students frequently volunteer or intern with District Attorney's offices, probation officers, criminal lawyers, state police, and other criminal justice professionals. In these settings, ask to be exposed to the psychological or psychiatric side of criminal justice.

A word of caution about initial clinical encounters. Be careful not to generalize from one experience. One of the authors worked with runaways at a crisis center for adolescents in the Times Square area of New York City. The rate of employee turnover at this facility was exceptionally high. The "success" rate for clients was low, and the population was difficult indeed. Although it was a rich experience, some of the volunteers became disillusioned with psychology as a result of working there. Settings vary considerably, depending on the populations they serve and the resources available. An unpleasant experience may only mean that the particularpopulation or setting was not ideally suited to you. Try something else, and you may feel quite differently.

Though clinical work is important (and often rewarding), remember it is only one of several experiences you must acquire for admission to graduate school. Some Ph.D. applicants make the mistake of accumulating a wealth of clinical experiences at the expense of gaining research training. By doing so, you may be inadvertently presenting yourself as being uninterested in research or perhaps better suited to a Psy.D. than a Ph.D. program. Clinical experience must be balanced with research competencies. This balance will be weighted toward clinical work or research depending on your desire to gain either a Psy.D. or Ph.D. or whether the Ph.D. program is practice or research oriented.

Research Skills

Research experience, as discussed earlier in this chapter, consistently emerges as a top admission criteria to nearly all Ph.D. programs in clinical and counseling psychology. To a lesser but still significant degree, Psy.D. programs also value your research experience for what it communicates about your intellectual ability and professional commitment. Recall the conclusion of one study on graduate school admission: there is simply no single better way to enhance an application than by obtaining research experience (Eddy et al., 1987). The desired skills—to reason critically, to review the research literature in pursuit of what works, to write in scientific language, among others—are essential. Even though all psychologists need not produce original research, all must intelligently consume and apply research.

The benefits of student research, according to research (Landrum & Nelsen, 2002), boil down to two dimensions. The first might be labeled specific skills and abilities. These skills include developing clear research ideas, conducting literature searches, choosing appropriate measures, analyzing data, using statistical procedures, preparing conference presentations, and improving writing ability. The second dimension might be called interpersonal goals. These tend to be overshadowed by the technical skills listed above, but they are critical benefits in preparing and mentoring psychologists-in-training. These entail influencing decisions about graduate school, meeting other students involved in research, getting to know faculty members better, improving teamwork, forming relationships for the basis of letters of recommendation, developing leadership, and improving interpersonal communication. You seek *both* types of benefits in securing a research experience or assistantship.

Gaining research experience is largely dependent on your own initiative. It can be an intimidating process, and a knowledge of the potential opportunities can help you to maximize your gains during the course of your research.

Common Paths

Let us begin by outlining six common avenues for students engaging in scholarly research. The first is probably the most frequent—volunteering to work with a faculty member on one of his or her research projects. A second avenue is to complete a student research program for a notation on your transcript but not academic credit. Students identify potential professors to work with from a faculty directory of research interests, jointly complete a learning contract, and then devote a minimum number of hours (say, 75) throughout a semester working directly with the faculty sponsor. A third option is to enroll in independent psychology research for academic credit. This entails individual study and research under the supervision of a faculty member and is ordinarily limited to junior and senior psychology majors.

A fourth and increasingly common approach is to work or volunteer for a researcher outside of your university—in a hospital, medical center, research institute, industry, or community-based organization, for example. Especially in large cities, researchers with major grants depend upon individuals (both pre- and post-baccalaureate) for many elements of study management, data collection, and statistical analyses. Many industries, especially biomedical and pharmaceutical research, offer summer research internships. These positions can provide valuable experience in randomized controlled trial research. Conversely, community-based organizations commonly conduct outcomes research around clinical or community interventions and accept interns throughout the year. If you have taken a statistics or research methods course that included SPSS or SAS, you may have sufficient skills for an entry-level position on an active research team outside of a university.

A fifth alternative, restricted to matriculated undergraduates, is to complete an honors thesis in either a departmental or a university-wide honors program. As with additional courses and post college work, an honors thesis is a "feather in your cap." For students desiring to move straight into a Ph.D. program, it is one means of presenting evidence to graduate admissions committees that you are capable of performing graduate-level work. Many schools allow motivated students to complete an honors thesis, an original study that the student conceptualizes, conducts, analyzes, and has some hope of presenting at a regional conference or even publishing. An honors thesis shows a genuine commitment to psychology and is a palpable sign of ability in the applicant.

A sixth and final avenue toward acquiring research competencies is restricted to master's students. A comprehensive paper or a formal master's thesis, requiring original research, practically guarantees additional experience with research.

For this reason, undergraduates denied admission directly into doctoral programs frequently enter master's programs to gain valuable research (and clinical) competencies. And remember: the majority of clinical psychology doctoral programs prefer master's-level applicants to have completed a thesis (Piotrowski & Keller, 1996).

Whichever avenue you eventually pursue, the procedures are quite similar. Following is a step-by-step guide to help you make the most of your research experience.

Determining Your Interests

The first step is finding a research area that interests you. If you are not interested in the work, it will diminish your energy and enthusiasm and probably your decision to apply to graduate school. A good place to begin is to read through your department brochure or Web site describing faculty interests and current research. If you are out of school, check with a local university. Visit with the Director of Psychology Advising or the Director of Undergraduate Studies in the psychology department (if a large university) or the department chairperson (if a smaller college) to discuss research possibilities. Speak to other students in the major about potential faculty mentors. Look for professors who have a proven track record of scholarly publications.

Once you have a list of faculty interests, you may find someone interesting but not be sure exactly what the research is all about ("I've heard about autism and think I'd like to study it, but I don't really know much about it . . ."). If publications are not provided on the departmental Web site, or if reprints are not posted in the department, then you can go to *PsycLIT* or *PsycINFO* (found in most university libraries; ask at the reference desk) and read what that professor has published in the area over the last 5 to 7 years. This should make it easier to decide which professor you would like to approach to volunteer to do research with. *Do not narrow your choices too quickly!* Find at least two or three professors whose work initially interests you.

Selecting Professors

Next, find out more about that professor as a person. Do you know people who have taken a class with him or her? What did they think? Are there other undergraduate or graduate students working with this professor now? What do they do, and what is it like working under this person? Is the professor easy to get along with? Is the professor helpful to students? Do not be afraid to approach people and ask questions.

Having narrowed the choice to two or three professors whose work interests you and with whom you think you might get along, consider the rank of the professor. There are tenured faculty (a *full* or *associate* professor) and untenured (an *assistant* professor), both with respective advantages and disadvantages.

Full or associate professors have been in the field longer and will probably have colleagues at other universities. If the professor is well known, it gives your letter of recommendation that much more weight. If your professor's reputation in the discipline is strong, with a long list of publications, you are also likely to learn more and increase your own attractiveness as a candidate. However, once a faculty member becomes tenured, he or she is no longer under the same pressure to produce research as when he or she was pursuing tenure. Certainly if these faculty members are still conducting grant-funded research, they are likely to be committed to maintaining their productivity. Regardless, you should establish that tenured faculty are actively engaged in research and are currently publishing their work.

Assistant professors are newer to the field, probably 1 to 7 years post doctorate. They are often in more need of undergraduate help and will likely involve you to your full potential. The possibility of being included on a research presentation or publication as a coauthor may also be increased. New assistant professors, in particular, may not yet have students but may have start-up funds for their research. What they lack in terms of a reputation built on years of publications may be balanced by their energy and their motivation to produce.

One word of caution: some professors maintain large research facilities and employ vast numbers of undergraduates to help them with their data collection and management. If there are 10 or 15 undergraduates working in a lab, the attention given to each individual tends to decrease, as well as the value of the research experience. On the other hand, some large laboratories provide unique research opportunities unavailable elsewhere. The key is to talk to students who have worked there to learn about their experiences and to determine if former students have had success applying to graduate school.

An optimal research context, then, is one in which there is a faculty member or research mentor who has an established reputation in his or her field of inquiry, a record of producing publishable research, similar interests to your own, a history of working successfully with students, a propensity to share authorship credit with students, and the ability to construct discrete research projects. Be guided by these general principles in selecting professors to approach, but do not expect all these qualities to be available to you.

Making Initial Contact

Having chosen a professor with whom you would like to work, it is now time to make yourself known to him or her. You need to schedule an appointment or approach the professor during posted office hours. It is natural for you to feel nervous! However, the more familiar with his or her work you are, the more secure you are likely to feel. Once again, read what the professor has written. Additionally, it helps to remember that you are coming to the professor to offer your services.

A good opening line might be, "Hello, Dr. Jones, my name is Chris Smith. I've been doing some reading on autism and came across several articles you've written. I'm pretty interested and was wondering if I could help with your research projects." As the conversation progresses, let the professor know your long-term goals as well as your immediate desire both to contribute as a member of the research team and to acquire research skills. Let him or her know you are seriously considering graduate study in clinical or counseling psychology—it will increase your appeal.

Negotiating Research Responsibilities

"Well Mr./Ms. Smith, I'd be very interested in speaking with you about helping out with my research . . ." You have made the contact. If the professor does not need help, you have lost nothing and gained the experience. Ask if he or she knows of someone with similar interests who is looking for help, or simply approach the next person on your list.

After the initial contact, your next move is dictated by your professor's needs and your abilities. Regardless of all your wonderful qualities, be prepared to run some of the grunt work! Photocopying needs to be done, literature searches need to be conducted, and at times you might well be expected to do some lab cleanup. You are "low on the totem pole," so approach this with humility. But if you have experience with test administration or statistical analysis, let the professor know, being aware that ultimately your activities will be dictated first by his

or her needs. However, if grunt work is the full extent of your duties, your needs are not being addressed properly. Spending a year doing nothing but photocopying or proofreading would be a waste of time.

Research experience is, above all, an opportunity to learn. Volunteer to be trained to be of more use. For example, learn the computer skills to input data and conduct statistical analyses. Learn to score and, more importantly, to *understand* a Minnesota Multiphasic Personality Inventory-2 (MMPI-2) or a Beck Depression Inventory (BDI-II). Learn how to calibrate and run psychophysiological equipment. Learn what you can about the various equipment or tests in use. And always ask questions about what you do not understand. When it comes time to put your research on your curriculum vitae, these are the responsibilities you will want to list.

Some researchers have a weekly lab group or research meeting with graduate students, undergraduates, or both. These might entail a discussion of the project at hand, or a presentation on another area within psychology, or a training session for new people. In any of these cases, it is an opportunity to learn more about your area of interest. If you have not been invited to these meetings, go ahead and ask about them. Optimize your contact with your professor! Convey your willingness and enthusiasm. Give your professor reason to write an outstanding letter of recommendation.

Finally, there are some instances where undergraduates are solely supervised by graduate students and have little contact with the professor in charge of the project. This can happen if faculty members have a large number of students working with them or if they are well known and are continually approached by masses of students. Being supervised exclusively by a graduate student can be an undesirable situation for a potential applicant. Although there is much to be learned from graduate students—and they are fresh from the application process themselves—a letter of recommendation from a graduate student does not carry the same weight as one from a professor. Moreover, a lack of interaction with the professor means that he or she must depend solely on graduate students for feedback on your work, thus detracting from the value of his or her assessment.

This is *not* to say that you must avoid research opportunities that are primarily supervised by graduate students. Again, find out how undergraduates in prior years have fared coming out of this lab. In sum, personal access to the faculty member is one of several important factors to be considered in your decision on where to volunteer for research experience.

Arranging Credit and Semesters

Most colleges allow students to complete a certain amount of research experience for academic credit. If the opportunity is available, take advantage of it. Some professors may even demand that you sign up for credit, because it institutes a contract between them and you about the number of hours per week required and how long they can count on you to work with them. Generally speaking, multiply the number of course credits by 3, and this will give you the number of weekly hours that you should spend doing research.

Expect to spend two semesters on a project. This demonstrates your commitment and allows ample contact between you and your professor. Thus, it is a good idea to work with someone at least 1 year before you plan to apply to graduate school. For instance, begin research in fall 2001 if you are applying in fall 2011 for a fall 2012 entrance to graduate school.

In consultation with your faculty advisor, consider applying for a university or national grant to fund your research project. These grant monies may be used to purchase equipment, pay postage for surveys, reimburse research participants for their time, and send you to a convention to present your findings. In most colleges and universities, these small grants are called undergraduate research grants, summer research fellowships, or something similar. At the University of Scranton, for example, the summer grants allow students to live on campus free for the summer, provide a tidy stipend, contribute up to $500 for research supplies, and fund travel to a conference in order to present the research. At the national level, Psi Chi and several publishers provide small awards and grants for research. Go to www.psichi.org/awards to access the list.

In terms of research, there is no such thing as too much for a Ph.D. applicant. The longer you have worked on a project and the greater your responsibilities, the more attractive you are as an applicant. Ideally, you would work with two professors over the course of your undergraduate education. This is not necessary, but when schools expect three letters of recommendation, having two letters summarizing two different research experiences is particularly strong. Although they will allocate less attention to research than Ph.D. applicants, Psy.D. applicants are reminded that research is still an important admission criterion.

One word of caution: do not overextend yourself. Be realistic about the amount of time you can commit. Some students juggle two or three research projects at once and end up performing poorly on them all. It is far more important to concentrate your energies and perform solidly on one project than it is to spread yourself too thin. Conduct as much research as your academic studies and other commitments allow.

An ideal time to begin research is during the summer, when you can balance it with a part- or full-time job. Since most undergraduates and some graduate students leave during the summer, professors may be short-staffed during this period. It is a prime opportunity to optimize your usefulness at the outset and increase your chances of picking up desirable skills.

The net result of your research experiences will be skill enhancement and professional identification. Depending on the nature of your project, you will probably have engaged in a literature search, hypothesis generation, experimental design, data collection, statistical analyses, and the write-up.

Presenting and Publishing Research

Presenting or publishing your research is a definite asset. Opportunities for presentation are numerous: a department or university colloquium, a local or regional undergraduate psychology conference, an annual conference of a professional organization, a state or national psychology convention. Participation in research conferences is viewed favorably as an index of your professional identification and commitment. Check with your advisor or mentor about these opportunities and other possibilities for your work to be seen by colleagues.

Publication of your research in a scholarly journal is held in very high regard by graduate admissions committees. As we discuss in Chapter 7, research experience leading to a coauthored publication is the most highly rated final selection criterion for Ph.D. (though not necessarily Psy.D.) admission decisions following the interview. The peer-review process by which journals accept papers for publication gives a seal of collegial affirmation that the research contributes to the scientific understanding of behavior. Although not common, undergraduate publication is slowly becoming more frequent.

If your research project is not quite up to the standards of a competitive, peer-reviewed journal, then consider sending the paper to a journal publishing student research in psychology. One such publication is the *Psi Chi Journal of Undergraduate Research*, which has the dual purpose of fostering the scholarly efforts of undergraduate psychology students and of providing them with a valuable learning experience.

Other publications for student research in psychology are *Modern Psychological Studies, Journal of Psychology and Behavioral Sciences*, and *Journal of Psychological Inquiry*. All these journals publish research in psychology conducted and written by students. Look for their instructions to authors on the Web (puffin.creighton.edu/psy/journal/student-journals.asp), on departmental bulletin boards, or in *Eye on Psi Chi* (the newsletter of Psi Chi).

Of course, though submission to these journals can be instructive, publishing in them does not carry as much weight as publication in established peer-reviewed journals. In fact, recent research suggests that a student publication in an undergraduate journal may be judged neutral or even unfavorably by research-oriented professors in a doctoral program (Ferrari & Hemovich, 2004). So, always aim to publish your research in peer-reviewed, scholarly journals.

Still impressive is a paper/poster presentation at a state, regional, or national meeting. Only between 10% and 20% of undergraduate psychology majors present their research at some type of research conference, whether local, regional, or national (Terry, 1996; Titus & Buxman, 1999).

Most regional and national meetings are listed in each issue of the *American Psychologist, APS Observer*, and *Eye on Psi Chi*. These meetings are also listed on the Psi Chi Web site. Psi Chi members who present papers can receive a certificate recognizing their excellence in research. This award should be duly noted on your curriculum vitae and application. Refer to *Eye on Psi Chi*, ask your local Psi Chi moderator or consult their Web site at www.psichi.org/pdf/postcert.pdf to receive the form entitled "Certificate Recognition Program for Paper Presentations by Psi Chi Members."

Different graduate programs will assess your research experience in different ways, of course. Nonetheless, as an aid to applicants, we reproduce below (with permission) two rating scales employed at different times by one clinical program (University of Rhode Island) over the past dozen years. The first rating scale emphasizes research activity. Examples of relevant activities might include producing honors theses, serving as a research assistant, conducting independent research, coauthoring scientific publications, and developing research skills, such as data analysis and interviewing.

Rating	Criteria
5	Senior author of one or more articles in significant journals in addition to experience that provided a basis for extensive

mastery of one or more directly related research skills.

Rating	Criteria
4	Coauthor of one or more articles in significant journals in addition to experiences providing considerable familiarity with one or more directly relevant research skills.
3	Project leadership or significant participation in research activity (beyond activities connected with course work) serving to provide for considerable development of mastery of one or more relevant research skills.
2	Experience that provides a basis for some familiarity with relevant research skills.
1	Little if any experience according to these criteria.

The second rating scale, now in use at the University of Rhode Island, favors four criteria in evaluating research experience.

1. *Demonstrated research productivity:* sole or co-authorship of research publications, presentation of papers at scientific meetings, other tangible indications of research achievement.
2. *Breadth and quality of experience:* development of one or more research skills, data collection with different populations, work on more than one project.
3. *Research interest:* the strength of interest in research can be inferred from research activity over a sustained period of time and recommendations from research supervisors documenting skills, motivation, participation, and accomplishments.
4. *Individual autonomy:* responsibility for planning, implementing, and carrying out research tasks as a member of a research team or evidence of independent work.

Rankings are based on the aforementioned criteria and assigned as follows:

Rating	Criteria
5	Satisfies all four criteria
4	Satisfies three criteria
3	Satisfies two criteria
2	Satisfies one criterion
1	Evidence of some prior research involvement or interest

Balance is the key. On the one hand, an absence of research experience is usually seen as a serious drawback to an application to a doctoral psychology program. On the other hand, over committing yourself to multiple projects at one time can lead to poor performance and a neglect of clinical experience and GRE preparation. And do not forget, research also provides you with the opportunity to make professional contacts. The professors or graduate students with whom you collaborate are excellent sources of information about the discipline and about applying to graduate schools.

Entrance Examinations

About 90% of doctoral clinical psychology programs (Mayne et al., 1994) and 80% of doctoral counseling psychology programs (Turkson & Norcross, 1996) require you to complete two exams: the Graduate Record Examination (GRE) General Test and the GRE Psychology Subject Test. The two GRE tests are often used to complement each other in admission decisions because the General Test is a measure of broad abilities and the Subject Test is an index of achievement in a specific field of study. The Miller Analogies Test (MAT) is required by fewer programs, about 3% of doctoral programs and 9% of master's programs in psychology (Murray & Williams, 1999; Norcross et al., 2005).

Blanket statements about entrance exams are difficult because not all schools require all tests, and some schools require additional testing (e.g., in the past the University of Minnesota required clinical psychology applicants to take the MMPI—a personality inventory!). Moreover, not all schools weight these test scores equally among the application criteria. Some schools clearly state a minimum score that all applicants must obtain, whereas others state that they have no such criteria. Interestingly, a study showed that even without an imposed cutoff, applicants admitted into its program had GRE scores of 600 or better (Rem, Oren, & Childrey, 1987). This suggests that even if a program does not emphasize entrance exams, (1) scores can still play a major role in the selection of candidates, or (2) applicants with high exam scores are also the applicants considered most desirable on the other admissions criteria.

Consequently, the best assistance that can be offered is a brief description of each test, an overview of minimum and actual GRE scores of incoming graduate students, guidelines for deciding how much preparation will be needed, and some suggestions as to the available study aids for each test.

GRE General Test

Use of GRE scores for admission to clinical and counseling psychology programs continues to be the norm and continues to be controversial (Dollinger, 1989; Ingram, 1983; Sternberg, 1997). The traditional rationale—buttressed by some evidence—is that the GRE is ordinarily more valid than undergraduate GPA in predicting graduate school success (Boudreau et al., 1983; Goldberg & Alliger, 1992). Another rationale is that GRE performance is an "equalizer" among the diverse curriculum requirements and grading practices in thousands of undergraduate institutions. The entrance exam is probably the only standardized measure of all applicants that an admissions committee has. Does a 3.7 GPA and stellar letters of recommendation from a small local college reflect more, the same, or less knowledge than a 3.3 GPA and strong letters of recommendation from an Ivy League university? Since all students take the identical GRE test, the playing field is leveled.

The empirical research indicates that the GRE General Test has modest predictive validity for graduate school performance. A meta-analysis of studies conducted in psychology and counseling departments found that GRE scores predicted about 8% of the variance in graduate school GPA (Goldberg & Alliger, 1992). A later meta-analysis of two dozen studies encompassing more than 5,000 test takers similarly reported that 6% of the variance in graduate-level academic achievement was accounted for by GRE scores (Morrison & Morrison, 1995). These and other studies (e.g., Chernyshenko & Ones, 1999; Kuncel, Hezlett, & Ones, 2001) indicate that GRE General Test scores are generalizably valid in a modest way for all sorts of measures of graduate performance, especially when selection/admission ratios are taken into account. At the same time, Subject Test scores tend to be better predictors than the General Test scores (Kuncel et al., 2001).

Information about the GRE and registering to take it are all online at www.gre.org. Bookmark that site on your computer as you will return to it frequently. At the Web site you can order (with a credit card) test preparation books and download preparation software directly onto your home computer.

The test is similar in format to the Scholastic Aptitude Test (SAT) that most of you took prior to college. The three GRE scales are Verbal Reasoning (V), Quantitative Reasoning (Q), and Analytical Writing (AW). The Verbal and Quantitative scales are multiple-choice in format, and scores on the test are based on the number of correct answers selected.

Most graduate schools rely on the Verbal and Quantitative scores in evaluating candidates.

The Analytical Writing section, in which you write two essays, is delivered on the computer, and you word-process your responses. For the "Present Your Perspective on an Issue" task, you will choose one of two essay topics selected by the computer from a larger pool of topics. For the "Analyze an Argument" task, you do not have a choice of topics; the computer will present you with a single topic for which you provide a critical, logical analysis. Your essays are read and scored by two trained raters using a holistic 6-point scale (scoring guidelines can be found at www.ets.org/gre/revised). Your Analytical Writing (AW) score is reported on a 0–6 scale in half-point increments. On average, students score 4.2 on the AW, with psychology majors scoring slightly higher at 4.4 (ETS, 2007). Since the AW test is relatively recent, many graduate schools are not placing as much emphasis on it as the Verbal and Quantitative scores in admission decisions.

In August 2011, the GRE General Test was extensively revised and introduced a new score scale. In place of the familiar 200 to 800 score range in 10-point increments, the Verbal Reasoning and Quantitative Reasoning scores are now presented on a 130 to 170 scale in 1-point increments. (The Analytical Writing scores will continue to be reported on their 0-6 scale.) The purpose of compressing the reporting metric is to produce scores that don't exaggerate small performance differences among students.

The scale change will cause havoc for several years, as graduate programs will continue to report average scores on the old scale and as applicants struggle to compare scores on the new test with scores on the old test. In fact, we need to report all GRE scores according to the old scale in this book as graduate programs have not yet had any experience with the new scale! The mix of new scores and old scores will persist for a few years as GRE scores are valid and reported for five years. At www.gre.org, you will find useful information on understanding the new scores, using the percentile ranks, and even a video on the new score scale.

Some content revisions have also occurred in the new GRE. On the Quantitative scale, you may now use an on-screen calculator. On the Verbal scale, antonyms and analogies are gone, replaced with additional questions on reasoning skills and reading comprehension. The GRE continues to be a computer adaptive test, meaning that correct answers to early questions lead to more difficult subsequent questions. But in the new GRE the adaptivity will no longer be question by question but section by section, so that within a section, you can skip a question and return to it later.

This 3-hour, 30-minute computer-based test begins with the Analytical Writing section. That's followed, in any order, by two Verbal sections, two Quantitative sections, and one unscored section. Within any section, you can skip a question and come back to it later, if you like. Within any section, you can also revise and edit your answers. All told, you will probably spend about 4 to 5 hours at the testing center.

When you complete all sections of the GRE at the testing center, you will be asked two questions: Do you want to cancel your scores? To which four graduate schools would you like your test scores sent? If you do *not* cancel your scores, then your Verbal and Quantitative scores are immediately presented on the computer screen. Your Analytical Writing score will arrive by mail in another 4 weeks or so. If you cancel your scores, then you are not provided with those scores.

The testing center consists of multiple cubicles, each containing a computer station. The center may be noisy, so many of our students recommend wearing ear plugs or accepting the offered headphones to minimize the extraneous noise and to enhance your concentration. Some test-takers are unnerved by the presence of cameras in the center (or above the cubicle); these exist only for test security purposes. But knowing in advance will probably decrease your anxiety.

The GRE registration booklet and the free tutorial software (POWER PREP, available off of your new favorite, www.gre.org) will familiarize you with the computer-based adaptive format of the Verbal and Quantitative sections. These and other resources will also prepare you for the Analytical Writing section. You should be very familiar with the test format and computer functions before test day!

In deciding how much and what type of preparation you will need for this test, ask yourself several questions:

1. What were my SAT scores? These two tests are highly correlated, so this may be your first clue as to how much preparation is ahead of you.
2. How well have I done on multiple-choice tests in college? There is a certain savvy to taking standardized tests, and this is one way to assess yours.
3. How anxious do I become in a testing situation? A moderate amount of test anxiety is optimal:

too little anxiety can breed indifference, but too much begets interference. If you tend to experience tests with more than moderate discomfort, you might benefit from additional preparation aimed at relaxing yourself and building your confidence.

4. Can I discipline myself to do the necessary studying? Be honest with yourself. If you cannot imagine sitting down regularly and studying independently for the GREs, you might be better off taking a preparatory course offered online or privately in most cities.

Students typically spend an inordinate amount of time worrying about the GREs. The myth exists that clinical applicants need a score of 600 on each of their scales to be considered seriously. This is simply not the case. Many Psy.D. programs do not even require the GREs. On the other hand, many APA-approved Ph.D. programs prefer GREs of 600 or above. The average GRE score (combined Verbal and Quantitative) of first-year graduate students in psychology master's programs is 1053; in doctoral psychology programs, 1183 (Norcross et al., 2005).

However, even these averages mask considerable variation in preferred minimum GRE scores. In our studies of the admission statistics of APA-accredited clinical programs (Mayne et al., 1994; Turkson & Norcross, 1996), we found that the preferred minimum scores differed consistently according to the type of program. As shown in Table 3-4, research-oriented clinical Ph.D. programs preferred the highest GRE scores—about 600 each for the Quantitative and Verbal scales. Psy.D. programs were willing to accept lower (but still not low) minimum GRE scores—about 540 each on the two scales. In between these two poles are the remainder of clinical psychology doctoral programs, which expect a minimum score of 550 to 560 on each of the scales (Turkson & Norcross, 1996).

Remember that these are the *minimum* scores for admission consideration, not the average scores of accepted students. Those scores are higher than the minimums, of course. Please pay more attention to the average scores of incoming students; the minimum required scores are at the lower end of acceptable scores to get in the door.

Table 3-5 provides the *average* GRE scores of incoming clinical psychology students across the practice-research continuum. As seen there, the research-oriented Ph.D. programs demand the highest scores: 676 Quantitative, 607 Verbal, and 672 Psychology Subject Test on average. Students entering the equal-emphasis programs tend to score a bit lower, followed by students enrolling in University-based Psy.D. programs. Our past research indicates that students entering freestanding Psy.D. programs tend to score lower than students entering the other types of programs; however, of late, those programs have been steadily not requiring or not reporting GRE scores. That's why average scores for students in freestanding Psy.D. programs are not reported in Table 3-5; only 22% of those programs reported such scores (Norcross et al., 2010).

The take-home point here is that the more research-oriented the doctoral program, the more stringent the admission requirements in terms of GRE scores and grade point averages. The payoff for the more stringent admission requirements is far more financial assistance, as we detail in Chapter 5.

Even if your scores are lower than 550, you can bolster other areas of your application to overcome low scores. But if your GRE scores are below 500, then most Ph.D. programs will not seriously consider your application. In this case, it will probably be necessary to take them again after completing a preparatory course or after spending time with a study guide. Or you may decide to apply to Psy.D. and master's programs as well.

TABLE 3-4. Minimum GRE Scores Preferred by APA-Accredited Clinical Psychology Programs

	Psy.D. programs		Practice-oriented Ph.D.		Equal-emphasis Ph.D.		Research-oriented Ph.D.		All programs	
Preferred minimum score	M	SD	M	SD	M	SD	M	SD	M	SD
Quantitative scale	544	46	566	58	580	44	598	36	581	46
Verbal scale	533	50	566	58	583	46	598	36	580	48
Psychology subject test	542	49	601	17	581	48	605	43	587	47

Note. Adapted from Mayne, Norcross, & Sayette (1994) and Turkson & Norcross (1996).

TABLE 3-5. Average GRE Scores of Incoming Students in APA-Accredited Clinical Psychology Programs

GRE scores	Freestanding Psy.D. programs		University-based Psy.D. programs		Equal-emphasis Ph.D.		Research-oriented Ph.D.		All programs	
	M	SD	M	SD	M	SD	M	SD	M	SD
Quantitative scale	—	—	600	48	648	43	676	38	652	52
Verbal scale	—	—	550	42	592	43	607	47	591	49
Analytical writing	—	—	4.7	.38	4.9	.39	5.1	.40	4.9	.44
Psychology subject test	—	—	644	17	669	38	683	48	672	43

Note. Adapted from Norcross, Ellis, & Sayette (2010).

Overconfidence can be disastrous here. Even if you obtained 700 SATs, aced every multiple-choice exam in college, and are cool-headed in testing situations, you should still familiarize yourself with the test format and complete the practice test offered in the application booklet. It certainly would not hurt to prepare more, but this should be considered the bare minimum.

Many self-study manuals and software packages are sufficient for a disciplined applicant to ready him or herself for the GRE. The books provide helpful test-taking hints, vocabulary and math reviews, and sample tests that the student can self-administer. Many include actual questions given on past GREs that can provide a real flavor for the material likely to be seen on testing day. The software packages administer sample tests and give helpful hints. Sample questions, practice manuals, and downloadable practice software packages can also be found and ordered on the official GRE Web site at www.gre.com. In addition to the official site, several comprehensive and commercial Internet sites provide valuable tips and full-length practice tests. Some of the material is offered for free; some offered for a price. Visit:

- www.princetonreview.com/gre
- www.kaptest.com/GRE/
- www.mygretutor.com
- www.greguide.com/

We heartily recommend taking an online GRE practice test. A practice GRE test serves as a diagnostic tool to assess your abilities, gauges your competitiveness for admission to graduate programs, and identifies areas that need further improvement (Walfish, 2004). Our favorites are the practice GRE tests at www.kaplan.com and www.princetonreview.

com. These are free and confidential; use the practice test as a starting point.

Lastly, give yourself *at least* 6 weeks of study time if you decide to use a manual or 8 weeks if you do not have a lot of time to devote solely to studying.

Students feeling less confident, more anxious, or "out of the exam business" should contemplate private courses designed to help you prepare for the GRE. They offer a number of benefits beyond those of study guides:

- A structured time several times a week when the material is taught by an impartial instructor who can assess your strengths and weaknesses
- An abundance of study materials and the possibility of individual tutoring
- The chance to take tests under actual test-taking conditions (especially helpful for those with test anxiety)
- Specific work on test-taking skills and the shortcuts that can make problems easier
- Brief introduction to relaxation exercises that can counter test anxiety

The imposed structure on studying and the conscious use of test-taking skills can be very useful. Although these classes cannot guarantee that they will improve your scores, they are undoubtedly the best course of action for some students. Having worked for one of these agencies, we have seen the benefits of this system for many students.

Many students attempt to strengthen their vocabulary for the GRE Verbal section by preparing flashcards or memorizing a vocabulary word each day. The early research on the word-a-day method suggests it can slightly enrich your vocabulary (Prevoznak & Bubka, 1999), but more importantly, it gets you into the swing of GRE preparation and the admissions process. If you are inclined to try this method, consider receiving a word a day from the Web site, www.wordsmith.org, which presents a word with its pronunciation and examples. Or try the vocabulary builders at www.supervoca.com/gre.htm and www. number2.com. They require only a couple of minutes per day.

Scheduling *when* to take your general GRE should be carefully considered. If you do poorly on the test, you can retake it. Consequently, it is prudent to take it at least 6 months before the application deadline, which gives you time to study and prepare for a second administration. For undergraduates planning to apply to graduate school during their senior year, this means taking it during the summer following your junior year or early fall of the senior year. For graduates, this means taking it the spring before you plan to apply. Even if you improve your scores, the current ETS policy is to send to each institution scores from *all* your tests taken during the last 5 years.

We are frequently asked by students in our graduate school workshops if they should retake the GRE General Test if they are dissatisfied with their original scores. Our immediate answer is: it depends. If you studied diligently for the test and performed similarly to the practice tests and your SAT scores, then no—probably do not retake the test. But if any of the following factors apply to you, then retaking the test seems like a good idea (Keith-Spiegel & Wiederman, 2000):

- You were ill the day you took the GRE
- You were distracted by test anxiety
- You did not prepare sufficiently for the test
- You were unfamiliar with or confused by the computer-based format
- Your SAT scores were much higher than your GRE scores
- Your scores on the GRE practice tests were consistently higher than your GRE scores

Should you decide to retake the GRE General Test, please be aware of the probable effects of repeating it. The average score gain for repeaters is about 27 points on the Verbal scale and 30 points on the Quantitative scale. Increases of more than 100 points rarely occur, in only 1 or 2% of repeaters (ETS, 1984).

The vast majority of graduate schools take the highest combination of your various GRE scores. Say you scored 520 Verbal and 600 Quantitative the first time, and 560 Verbal and 580 Quantitative the second time. Most graduate programs will calculate your scores for admission purposes as 560 Verbal and 600 Quantitative.

We have not said much about your score on the third GRE scale: the Analytical Writing (AW) test. That's because only about 35% of psychology graduate programs are using it in their admissions process (Briihl & Wasieleski, 2007). Programs using the AW rated it as medium or low in importance in their admissions decisions. Few programs have minimum or cutoff scores for the AW (Briihl & Wasieleski, 2007). Thus, your GRE scores are still widely calculated as the sum of your Verbal and Quantitative scores. Keep in mind, though, that particular professors who are interested in working with you (especially true at research-oriented Ph.D. programs) may decide to weight your various GRE scores differently than what their program suggests. Consequently, all your scores—including the AW—may come into play.

Your GRE scores can partially determine where to apply. Low scores suggest applying only to institutions whose minimum scores you surpass. In this way, your GREs can help you make realistic decisions as to your chances of being accepted at a given school and ultimately whether to apply there.

GRE Psychology Subject Test

The General Test measures knowledge acquired over a long period of time and not indigenous to any specific field of study. By contrast, the Subject Tests—such as the Psychology Subject Test—assume an undergraduate major or extensive background in the specific subject. Consequently, the test may be relatively difficult if you were not an undergraduate psychology major.

Another difference between the General Test and the Subject Test lies in the mode of administration. The General Test is a computer-based test available year-round at over 600 test centers. The Subject Test, by contrast, continues to be a paper-based test offered three times during the academic year.

Table 3-6 summarizes the differences between the GRE General Test and the GRE Subject Test. These profound test differences will lead to different preparation and test-taking strategies on your part.

The GRE Psychology Test consists of about 205 multiple-choice questions. Each item has five options, from which you select the correct or best response. The total time allotted for the test is 2 hours and 50 minutes.

The GRE Psychology Test yields a total score and two subscores. The possible scores range from 200

TABLE 3-6. Comparison of the GRE General Test and the GRE Psychology Subject Test

	General Test	Psychology Subject Test
Content assessed	Broad knowledge	Specific knowledge in psychology
Test format	Computer	Paper-and-pencil
Administration schedule	Throughout the year	Three times per year (Oct., Nov., & Apr.)
Recommended test date	Summer of junior year Early Fall of senior year	October for Ph.D./Psy.D. applicants November for master's applicants
Administration format	Individual	Group
Test cost (2009–2010)	$160	$140
Repeat policy	May repeat test once per calendar month up to 5 times per year	May repeat test as often as it is offered
Testing time	3 hours, 30 minutes	2 hours, 50 minutes
Scoring procedure	Adaptive: your responses determine difficulty level of subsequent questions in that section	Total items answered correctly minus one-fourth the number answered incorrectly
Skipping questions	Permitted within sctions; computer administers one question at a time	Permitted
Scores provided	3 scores (Verbal Reasoning, Quantitative Reasoning, and Analytical Writing)	1 total score, 2 subscores
Scores range	130–170 for Verbal and Quantitative; 0–6 for Analytical Writing	200–990
Scores mean (*SD*)	To be determined	540 (100)
Recommended preparation	Intense	Moderate

to 990 in 10-point increments. Virtually all graduate programs concentrate on the total score, not on the subscores. The preferred minimum score is 587 for clinical psychology doctoral programs and 541 for counseling psychology doctoral programs (Mayne et al., 1994; Turkson & Norcross, 1996). That is, most programs will expect you to secure a score at or above this number. But here again, as shown in Table 3-4, the preferred minimum ranges from a low of 542 in Psy.D. programs to a high of 605 in research-oriented Ph.D. programs.

The two subscales are an Experimental or natural science orientation (about 40% of the items) and a Social or social science orientation (about 43% of the items). The Experimental subscore covers questions in learning, cognition, perception, comparative psychology, sensation, and physiological psychology. The Social subscore includes about an equal number of questions in personality, clinical, abnormal, developmental, and social psychology.

Percentages of questions devoted to a subject area will vary somewhat from one test administration to another. Nonetheless, one set of investigators

(Waters, Drew, & Ayers, 1988) found these approximate percentages on past tests:

Physiological/comparative psychology	14%
Developmental psychology	12%
Learning and motivation	12%
Sensation and perception	12%
Clinical/abnormal psychology	11%
Personality and social psychology	11%
Cognition and complex human learning	10%
Applied psychology	9%
Research methodology	9%

Scores on the GRE Psychology Test are best predicted by your GRE General Test scores and the number of basic psychology courses completed. The irony is that students can obtain excellent grades in all their psychology courses but still not perform adequately on the Psychology Test if they have not taken the critical courses. A narrow focus on—and many courses in—clinical psychology will probably detract from your score since this one area only accounts for 10 to 12% of the test items. The questions are drawn from courses most commonly offered at the under-graduate level within psychology (ETS, 1995).

A maximum number of "traditional" courses in psychology, as represented in the foregoing list, and a minimum of special topics and "pop" psychology will prepare you best for the GRE Psychology Subject Test. Choose your elective courses for breadth and rigor, not merely your specialized interest.

The GRE Psychology Subject Test is designed to be challenging. Students accustomed to getting 90% correct on in-class exams often worry about the large number of items they miss. The average student answers about half the items correctly, misses about 30%, and omits 20% (Kalat & Matlin, 2000). Because your score is based on the number of questions answered correctly minus one-fourth of the questions answered incorrectly, guessing does *not* lower your score. You are not penalized for guessing; but you are rewarded for eliminating one or two possible answers.

Adequate preparation is essential for this test. We—and others—suggest four steps: (1) obtain online the free ETS *Psychology Test Practice Book* that describes the test structure, content, and instructions and that contains one actual full-length GRE Psychology Test; (2) review a good introductory psychology textbook; (3) volunteer to be a TA (teaching assistant) for the Introduction to Psychology course; and (4) purchase one of the study guides with practice tests. Our favorite study guides are *GRE Psychology with CD-ROM—The Best Test Prep for the GRE* (Kellogg, 2003; published by Research & Education Association), Kaplan GRE Subject Test: Psychology (2010 by Kaplan), Barron's GRE Psychology (2009 by Barron's), and *Cracking the GRE Psychology Subject Test* (2010 by Princeton Review and Random House). If these four steps do not suffice, then private courses in preparing for the psychology test are available.

Miller Analogies Test

A few clinical and counseling psychology doctoral programs request the MAT, a 50-minute test consisting of 100 word analogies. Your score is the total number correct; the mean for students intending to study psychology in graduate school is 50 to 51 (The Psychological Corporation, 1994). As with the GREs, booklets are available to help improve your scores on the test, and it is useful to take practice tests to familiarize and prepare yourself for the actual event. There are states in which the MAT cannot be administered (e.g., New York) because of test disclosure

laws enacted in those states, so be sure to locate the testing center nearest you.

The MATs are rarely required by graduate schools. Because the test can be scheduled at any time, through a network of over 600 testing centers nationwide, consider taking this test after you have received your GRE scores and after you have selected the schools you would like to apply to. You will save time and money if none of the schools that interest you require the test.

Part of the expense of applying to graduate school is the cost of sending test scores. One possible way to reduce costs is to make copies of the test results sent to you and mail them with your application. Any school that is interested in you will request that you have the scores "officially" sent to them. Any school not interested will not need your official scores, and you will have saved the expense of having them forwarded.

Two words of caution must accompany this possibility. First, only do this if you send in your application early. Unless you check with a graduate program before the application deadline to make sure that this procedure will not exclude you as an applicant, you should not send copies. Second, some students send copies of test scores after altering the original document, for example, whiting out poor scores or past scores, putting scores in different columns, and even falsifying scores. *You must never resort to these practices!* These should immediately invalidate your application, and any school that accepts you will need official copies sent anyway.

Finally, low scores on entrance exams do not automatically preclude you from applying to clinical or counseling psychology graduate programs. Rather, low scores mean you will apply to programs that do not emphasize test scores or that accept scores in your range. You can partially compensate in other areas to help offset weak GRE scores. Conversely, at highly competitive programs, strong GRE scores do not guarantee acceptance. We have seen indignant applicants contact us following rejection who did not realize that there were dozens of other applicants with combined Verbal and Quantitative scores above 1400. As with each admission criterion, entrance examinations are only one part of the overall picture of a candidate. The best anyone can do is to make his or her application as attractive as possible.

Extracurricular Activities

An applicant's extracurricular pursuits are accorded less weight than GPAs, GRE scores, research competency, and clinical experience. The research reviewed earlier in this chapter clearly bears this point out. However, extracurricular activities, such as Psi Chi membership and campus involvement, are still considered in evaluating the "total person" of the applicant.

The admission implications are thus proscriptive and prescriptive. Strictly in terms of enhancing your candidacy (not in terms of other goals, such as life satisfaction), you should favor good grades and research experience over extracurricular activities. Involvement in a dozen student organizations will not compensate for meager grades and research; doctoral programs will not accept you because you are coaching the junior high's cheerleading squad. When confronted with time conflicts, recall that admissions committees place a premium on variables other than intense campus commitments.

Having stated the obvious but unpleasant facts, we would also urge you to routinely engage in *some* campus and community pursuits. The reasoning here is that clinical and counseling psychology programs seek well-rounded individuals with diverse interests. The "egghead" or "Mr. Peabody" image is to be avoided in the practice of psychology, where your interpersonal skills are as critical as your scientific preparation. Moderate involvement can also better acquaint you with faculty members, who may serve as sources of recommendations, and with the discipline of psychology itself. You can create professional opportunities by simply being involved in departmental activities. "Familiar faces" are frequently given first shots at clinical or research opportunities.

Applicants frequently learn too late that active involvement outside of the classroom is an indispensable education in and of itself. Consider the following student qualities contained in many letter of recommendation forms:

- Academic performance
- Organizational skills
- Interest/enthusiasm
- Interpersonal skills
- Emotional stability
- Communication skills
- Originality/resourcefulness
- Social judgment
- Responsibility/dependability
- Stress tolerance

Most of these dimensions refer to faculty–student interactions *outside* of the classroom, not to your course grades. Many a bright student has sabotaged his or her educational experience, recommendation letters, and career goal by not becoming involved outside of the classroom.

In your extracurricular activities, try to exhibit the chief personality trait which, interacting with intelligence, relates most to vocational success— namely, conscientiousness (Jensen, 1998). Be responsible, dependable, organized, and persistent. This trait applies to every kind of educational and job success. What's more, you want colleagues and friends to document in their letters of recommendation that you are extraordinarily conscientious.

Four specific suggestions come to mind regarding the type of extracurricular activities to pursue. First, join departmental student organizations, such as the Psychology Club, Psi Chi, and the American Psychological Society's Student Caucus. Second, we heartily recommend that you join the American Psychological Association (APA) and/or the Association for Psychological Science (APS) as a student affiliate. Your APA affiliation brings with it monthly issues of the *American Psychologist*, the flagship journal, and the *Monitor on Psychology*, the association's magazine. Similarly, APS membership includes subscriptions to the monthly journal *Psychological Science* and the *APS Observer*. Student membership in professional associations reflects favorably on your commitment to the discipline, and this affiliation should be recorded on your curriculum vitae. Your psychology advisor might have applications for student affiliation in his or her office; if not, go online to www.apa.org/membership/forstudents.html and www.psychologicalscience.org/join/.

Third, additional campus and community commitments should be guided by your interests. But those associated with human services, social causes, and artistic endeavors seem to be differentially rewarded. These will obviously vary with the locale; examples include Hand-in-Hand, campus ministries, course tutoring, peer advising, homeless shelters, women's centers, BACHUSS, SADD, theater productions, creative writing, Amnesty International, and the like.

A fourth and invaluable extracurricular experience is to attend a regional or national psychology convention. The benefits are many: socializing you into the profession; learning about current research; discovering how students and professors present research; meeting and hearing nationally known psychologists; adding to your growing professional network; attending and perhaps participating in sessions designed for prospective graduate students (e.g., the Psi Chi sessions and workshops); experiencing the intellectual stimulation; and enjoying the interpersonal camaraderie of fellow students and psychologists (Lubin, 1993; Tryon, 1985). For all these reasons, we have never—and we mean *never*—heard a single graduate school applicant express disappointment about attending his or her first psychology convention.

The challenge for most prospective psychologists is to locate and afford travel to one of the regional or national psychology conferences. To locate upcoming conferences in your area, ask your psychology professors, consult the lists regularly published in *Eye on Psi Chi* and *American Psychologist*, and keep an eye open for announcements and posters on departmental bulletin boards. Convention season in psychology is from March to May, when the regional psychological associations hold their annual conventions. These include the Eastern Psychological Association, Midwestern Psychological Association, Rocky Mountain Psychological Association, Western Psychological Association, and Southeastern Psychological Association. The national conventions of APA and APS are annually held in the late spring and summer months. To afford the travel and lodging, consider organizing a convention trip with your fellow students, requesting information on special hotel and registration rates for students, volunteering as a convention assistant, and holding fund-raisers with psychology student organizations to offset your expenses. By hook or crook, definitely plan on expanding your extracurricular horizons by attending a psychology convention.

Extracurricular activities should reflect your active and passionate pursuit of excellence. This is, after all, your chosen profession, your career, your future. Join honor societies, compete for awards, pursue honors, and consider applications for Truman, Rhodes, and Fulbright scholarships. You should be actively investigating undergraduate grants for your research, such as those administered nationally by Psi Chi or those awarded locally in your university. Passivity doesn't cut it in graduate school (or life).

Finally, as part of your preparation, discuss your graduate plans with those people who will be affected by those plans, such as partner, spouse, parents, children, and close friends. The sooner you start discussing your plans, the better. You may move hundreds of miles away and will probably be working 60 hours a week as a graduate student. Your absence—psychological and physical—will likely impact other people close to you. Begin the discussions now, not after you apply (Megargee, 2001).

In this chapter, we reviewed six admission criteria—course work, faculty mentoring, clinical experience, research skills, entrance examinations, and extracurricular activities—and suggested ways to improve in these areas. The material covered in this chapter is concerned with how you as the applicant can improve your credentials or marketability. But the application process goes both ways. In addition to selling yourself, you are also a consumer, evaluating the programs and deciding which ones are for you. In the next two chapters, we help you evaluate characteristics of graduate programs.

CHAPTER 4
GETTING STARTED

U p to this point in the *Insider's Guide*, we have focused on what you can do to enhance your credentials before beginning the application process. At some point, you must take realistic stock and evaluate where you stand as an applicant. Maybe you have taken your GREs. Perhaps you have signed up for some advanced psychology courses and have a satisfactory GPA. You have been supervised in a clinical setting and have begun research. You have reviewed your credentials and found that you have many strengths but also some weaknesses. You either shore up the deficient areas or make a decision to go ahead with what you have and hope to sell it well. In other words, you are ready to get started with the application process.

Process is an appropriate word to describe the endeavor that you are about to begin. The way you approach this task will greatly influence your chances of gaining admission. Sure, you can simply complete an application and passively wait for an interview. And this may work if your credentials are extremely strong. But for most individuals, an informed approach to the process can make all the difference!

Prospective graduate students frequently become nervous about the application process for several reasons. Perhaps the following remarks sound familiar: "Well, I have good recommendations and a 3.3 GPA, but my GREs are low"; "I have good GREs and spent a year working on a suicide hot line, but I don't have a lot of research experience"; "Although my credentials are excellent, all the schools that I applied to only accept 10 out of 250 applicants." Whichever of these situations applies, simply submitting an application

minimizes your chances of acceptance. You can do a great deal to increase your admission probabilities and to decrease your anxiety as you compare yourself to exaggerated standards.

Common Misconceptions

We would like to begin by dispelling three common misconceptions about clinical and counseling psychology programs. The first misconception: there is a strong correlation between a university's undergraduate reputation and the status of its psychology graduate programs. Many of the best undergraduate institutions—Brown, Princeton, and the elite liberal arts colleges, for example—do not even offer graduate studies in clinical or counseling psychology.

A second misconception is that you should apply to a graduate psychology program on the basis of that institution's sports performance. We have met a number of students who have used this selection criterion with unfortunate consequences. Please do not allow your application decisions to rest on whether a university has an excellent football team or whether their basketball team made it to the final Four of the NCAA tournament! Do not scoff at the reality of this practice; careful research has demonstrated that winning a national championship in a visible college sport consistently translates into increased applications to the winning institution (Toma & Cross, 1998).

A third common misconception is that there is an authoritative list of the finest graduate programs in clinical psychology. In reality, unlike business or law schools, there is no definitive ranking of the "best" psychology graduate programs. The quality of a program depends on what *you* are looking to get out of it. The best school for someone seeking to become a psychologist conducting psychoanalytic psychotherapy in private practice is probably not going to be the program of choice for someone who has set his or her heart on becoming a psychophysiological researcher at a medical school. Each person could attend the "best" school for psychology in his or her interests.

What we want to do is to shift the burden from you trying to meet a school's admissions demands to you finding a school that meets *your* needs. Graduate schools are looking for students with direction and passion. This does not mean you have made an irrevocable commitment to an area of research or type of clinical work. It means that you have an idea of the professional work you would like to do and toward which theoretical orientation(s) you lean.

You are selecting an institution because it will mold you in the direction *you* have chosen. Graduate programs will look for this attitude in your statement of purpose. During your interviews, you will be asked about which professors you want to work with and what thoughts you have about their research projects. Even more likely, you will be directly asked, "Why are you applying here instead of someplace else?" By identifying your graduate training goals, you will impress interviewers at your selected programs with your direction and passion.

Acceptance Rates

The most pervasive myth about doctoral psychology programs is that "hardly anyone gets in—only 10%." Like most myths, this one does have a grain of truth. The average acceptance rate for *all* APA-accredited Ph.D. programs in clinical and counseling psychology is, in fact, 10% (Norcross et al., 2004; Norcross et al., 2010). But in a very real way, the 10% figure is misleading and inaccurate on many counts.

Let's begin our foray into acceptance rates by defining the term. "Acceptance rate" refers to the percentage of applicants accepted for admission into a single graduate program, *not* the percentage of the entire applicant pool to all programs accepted for admission in a given year. The clinical doctoral program at University X may accept only 15 of 150 applicants (10%), but many of the applicants to University X not accepted there will be admitted elsewhere. Although only 10% of the applicants to a single doctoral program might be accepted into that *particular* program, about half of the entire applicant pool will be accepted into *some* clinical or counseling doctoral program. And half a chance isn't that bad.

Note, too, that the 10% figure refers only to acceptance rates of APA-accredited programs in clinical or counseling psychology. The acceptance rates at *non*-APA-accredited doctoral programs are double that for APA-accredited programs: 20% for nonaccredited Ph.D. programs and 60% for nonaccredited Psy.D. programs (Norcross et al., 2005). The acceptance rates for master's programs are also much higher than those for doctoral programs. The average acceptance rates for master's programs are 37% in clinical psychology and 63% in counseling psychology (Table 1-3).

In reality, that 10% acceptance figure applies only to APA-accredited Ph.D. programs. As we have already emphasized, Psy.D. programs offer higher acceptance rates—40 to 50% of applicants are admitted on average to any single program (Norcross et al., 2010).

Acceptance rates vary tremendously from doctoral program to doctoral program as a function of the practice-research dimension. As shown in the Reports on Individual Programs following Chapter 8, acceptance rates at research-oriented clinical Ph.D. programs, such as Harvard and Yale, start as low as 2%. And acceptance rates at freestanding Psy.D. programs go as high as 70%.

Table 4-1 summarizes the results of our studies on acceptance rates to APA-accredited clinical psy-

TABLE 4-1. Average Acceptance Rates for APA-Accredited Clinical Psychology Programs

	Freestanding Psy.D.	University-based Psy.D.	Practice-oriented Ph.D.	Equal-emphasis Ph.D.	Research-oriented Ph.D.
Number of applications	227	163	155	160	183
Number of acceptances	108	58	18	16	12
Acceptance rate	50%	40%	16%	14%	7%

Note. Data from Norcross, Ellis, & Sayette (2010).

chology programs as a function of the type of program. All types of programs average between 150 and 250 applications per year. Research-oriented Ph.D. programs accept only 7% of their applicants, on average, whereas the corresponding figures are 14% for equal-emphasis Ph.D. and 16% for practice-oriented Ph.D. programs. University-based Psy.D. programs accept 40% of their applicants on average, and freestanding Psy.D. programs accept 50%. That's quite a range of acceptance rates—7% to 50%—all in APA-accredited doctoral programs in clinical psychology. And that's why we urge caution in tossing around the 10% acceptance rate.

Costs of Applying

Applying to graduate school is an expensive proposition—not only in terms of your valuable time but also in terms of hard money. Application fees average $50 per doctoral program and $35 per master's program (Norcross et al., 2004). Only 7% of graduate schools let you apply for free (Norcross et al., 1996). The fee (in 2011) for the GRE General Test is $160, with a $50 rescheduling fee, and the Psychology Subject Test costs another $140. ETS will electronically transmit your GRE scores free of charge to four graduate schools that you designate in advance; however, each additional score report costs $20 per recipient. Throw in the costs of transcripts, photocopying, postage, and the innumerable telephone calls, and the investment can become quite costly. All told, we estimate that applying to 12 schools will run about $1,000 (and that number can increase depending on the cost of traveling to multiple interviews).

Several students challenged our estimate that the graduate application process would cost them $1,000. They protested that our figure was way too high. So, we encouraged them, like good psychologists, to collect data as they proceeded through the process. Here is the breakdown of costs from one typical applicant (Dennis Reidy) who applied to 13 doctoral programs in 2003:

Taking the GRE tests	$235
Sending GRE scores	$180
Requesting transcripts	$106
Application fees	$455
Mailing applications	$78

That's a total of $1,054 in 2003 dollars, before he traveled to three programs for personal interviews. He now realizes that for anyone considering a national search the $1,000 estimate is conservative.

The good news is that graduate schools are sensitive to financial hardship and that, for many students, the burdensome short-term cost is an excellent long-term investment. Schools build into the application process allowances for students who cannot afford the expense. Even the GRE has a fee waiver for students in dire financial circumstances.

Moreover, think of the application cost as an investment in yourself and in your career. If you gain acceptance into a doctoral program with tuition remission and a stipend for 4 years, your $1,000 can be converted into a $80,000 to $120,000 payback over the course of your graduate school career.

The bottom line in getting started is this: anticipate the costs of applying to graduate school and plan to have the funds (or waivers) available before you begin completing applications.

Starting Early

Let's discuss timing up front. Applications are typically due from the middle week in December to the second week in February. The sooner you begin preparing, the more advantage you can take of an aggressive, early start to the admission process. As mentioned in earlier chapters and in the Time Line (Appendix A), for undergraduates, ideally this would take place the summer of your junior year. For others, this would best occur the summer of the year before you actually plan to attend graduate school. If it is past that point, you are not too late. You can follow the steps we will describe as late as October of your application year.

Applying to graduate school is like planning a political campaign or a military operation. It is impossible to begin too soon or to be too thorough (Megargee, 1990). Recognize this about the application process and *start almost a year before you expect to begin graduate school*. Completing the application materials in the fall semester alone will consume as much time as a 3-credit course!

Virtually all APA-accredited clinical and counseling psychology programs only accept matriculating students for their fall semesters. As mentioned earlier, in order to be accepted for the fall of 2012, most doctoral programs have application deadlines anywhere from mid-December 2011 to February 2012. The typical deadline for doctoral programs in clinical and counseling psychology is January 15 (Norcross et al., 1996). Accordingly, you will need college transcripts, test scores, and letters of recommendation, not to mention time to prepare yourself before the application deadline. You should expect to begin no later than the fall of the year before you intend to attend graduate school. If you are willing to put in the maximum effort to get into a program, expect to begin the spring before that.

The APA has accredited 234 active doctoral programs in clinical psychology, 66 active doctoral programs in counseling psychology, and 8 active doctoral programs in combined psychology throughout the United States and Canada. Toss in nonaccredited doctoral programs and the mass of master's programs in clinical and counseling psychology and you wind up with roughly 700 graduate programs. How does one proceed in whittling this list to a manageable number?

To begin the selection process, ask yourself, "What do I want to do as a psychologist? What kind of research or clinical work do I like? Is there some article I've read or presentation I've heard that intrigues me?" There is a certain advantage if you have already conducted research or completed clinical experience as an undergraduate and know something about the discipline. And, if you have completed an honors project or thesis, you may even have a certain degree of expertise. Or you may decide you would like to try something different now.

For example, suppose you have an interest in suicidology, but you are not sure that you want to do research in that area or exactly what that research would entail. Or you think you'd like to specialize in suicide prevention, but you're not sure how psychologists treat the issue clinically. There are several approaches you can take to familiarize yourself with this area. Ask one of your professors for some readings. Check out a current textbook in the area. Go to a suicide prevention or crisis center and read through their literature. Surf the Web. Then decide whether you like the questions being asked and the methods used to answer them.

In summary, have an idea of the field(s) in which you would like to work, either the ones with which you are already familiar or those you are willing to research. Familiarize yourself with the questions being asked and the methods being used to answer them. Use as many sources as possible to gain information to help you narrow down your interests and educate yourself about them.

In addition to the resources in this book, a number of Internet sites will help you at this stage of the process. You can familiarize yourself with psychology graduate programs in the United States and Canada by accessing a large number of Web sites. Our favorites are:

- www.apa.org/students/
  (APA's site for students includes a list of accredited programs, relevant articles, and other useful materials)
- www.socialpsychology.org/clinical.htm
  (useful page features hyperlinks to 185 departments in the United States offering a Ph.D. in psychology)
- www.clas.ufl.edu/CLAS/american-universities.html#A
  (links for a plethora of American universities)
- www.psychwww.com/resource/deptlist.htm
  (an impressive listing of over 1,000 psychology department Web sites)
- www.petersons.com/gradchannel/
  (brief descriptions of programs offering graduate training in clinical and counseling psychology)
- www.gradschools.com/listings/menus/psych_clinic_menu.html and www.gradschools.com/listings/menus/psych_cmt_menu.html
  (for searching clinical and counseling psychology programs, respectively, with the added ability to search by geographic region)
- www.jobweb.com/students.aspx?folderid=92
  (links to sites about applying to and financing graduate school, and about making the transition to graduate school)

All these—and other—sites enable you to take a virtual tour of graduate programs in professional psychology. Develop an early feel for various departments and begin to sharpen your interests.

Next is the task of putting this knowledge to use. You have interests, and you now need to learn which graduate programs can provide these research or clinical opportunities. Although knowing how much you enjoy research or clinical work may not take a lot of reflection, deciding whether to select a research-oriented, a practice-oriented, or an equal-emphasis program is a question with far-reaching ramifications. This question tends to divide people into three groups: the research oriented (clinical scientists); the practice oriented (practitioners); and the dually committed (scientist–practitioners). The following sections are designed to lead each group in its appropriate direction. These groups tend to follow three rather distinctive career paths in the profession of clinical and counseling psychology (Bernstein & Kerr, 1993; Conway, 1988).

We have repeatedly surveyed the APA-accredited clinical and counseling psychology programs over the past 22 years. Their responses to our questionnaires (e.g., Farry et al., 1995; Mayne et al., 1994; Norcross et al., 1998; Norcross et al., 2004; Norcross,

2005; Norcross et al., 2010; Oliver et al., 2005; Sayette & Mayne, 1990; Sayette et al., 1999; Sayette et al., 2011; Turkson & Norcross, 1996) can serve as the basis for your initial selection of graduate programs. By using their responses, we will lead you through an exercise that will provide you with a list that ranks schools by how closely they meet your expectations and interests.

As you review the Reports on Individual Programs, bear in mind that the listings are alphabetical, not geographical. We list the programs alphabetically as they are on the APA (2010; www.apa.org/ed/accreditation/programs/index.aspx) materials, but sometimes the order is counterintuitive. For example, the University of Arkansas is not listed under "U," but between Arizona State University and Auburn University. Thus, you might need to look under two letters to identify programs of interest.

For the Research Oriented and Dually Committed

This section guides those applicants who are centrally focused on research and those with equal interests in practice and research. We group these two sorts of applicants together because their initial selection of schools will place more emphasis on the research available at each program and secondarily on the clinical work available. This will allow people with an equal emphasis to cast their nets as widely and as efficiently as possible.

One question we asked of each graduate program in our studies was "In which areas of research are your faculty presently working? Do they presently have a grant in that area?" Appendix E lists all the research areas provided by the graduate programs along with the number of faculty interested in these areas and an indication of whether they have a grant. This information provides you with an index of how intensively each program is pursuing this area of research. Thus, a program with three faculty members researching autism that has a grant supporting their work indicates serious involvement on the part of that faculty.

Find your areas of interest in the appendix; underneath them you will see a list of programs doing that type of research. In addition, you will know the number of professors with whom you could potentially work and whether there is grant money supporting this research.

A few words of caution in interpreting this appendix: not all programs were equally comprehensive in completing the survey. Some schools only included core faculty, whereas others included adjunct faculty. This accounts for what seems to be an overrepresentation of some institutions on the list. Also, some schools had research interests combining two different areas and listed a single grant under both.

Appendix B, entitled "Worksheet for Choosing Programs," is used to select programs to which you will eventually apply. Begin by writing your research interest in the far left-hand column. In the next column, marked "Schools," write the list of schools under that heading in Appendix B. In columns 3 and 4, write down the number of faculty in that area at each school and whether they are grant funded. In addition, some schools merely indicated the presence of grant funding and not the total number of grants. Thus, a "1" in the "Grants" column indicated *at least* one grant. A "0" indicates no grants, and numbers greater than 1 indicate multiple grants.

There are two worksheets provided in Appendix B, allowing you to explore different areas of interest. If you have more than two main areas of interest, unless they are closely related, you may find the list becoming exceptionally long. In that case, you may wish either to narrow your areas of interest or to complete this worksheet with the aid of a trusted professor who can help you pare down the list of schools to a manageable number. If you have more than one area of interest, put stars next to the programs that have faculty doing research in both of them.

If your interests lean toward research, then you want to pick programs highly regarded in the area of research you would like to pursue. How do you evaluate the clinical and counseling psychology programs on your list in terms of research? Refer to Table 4-2, which is adapted from the results of the *Social Sciences Citation Index* (SSCI) and *Science Citation Index* (SCI) databases complied for us by Thomson Reuters, Web of Science. More than 225 psychology journals from 2004 to 2008 were analyzed to determine the institutions with the most citations. The goal was to identify the institutions employing faculty members who authored the most frequently referenced articles in psychology and psychiatry journals. These two categories of journals publish the bulk of research conducted by clinical and, albeit to a lesser degree, counseling psychologists. The table lists, in rank order, the frequency with which articles written by members of a particular institution are cited. Only those institutions with an APA-accredited clinical or counseling program are included on this list. It should also be noted that the list only includes those institutions that produced at least 250 papers over the 5-year span; as a result, several smaller institu-

TABLE 4-2. Institutions with Most Citations, Most Papers, Greatest Impact in Psychology/Psychiatry, and Strongest Clinical Faculty Production in Psychology

Citation Rank	Institution[a]	Citations	Papers	Impact (citations per paper)	Faculty Production Rank[b]
1	Harvard University	27,441	3,295	8.33	—
3	University of California, Los Angeles	14,737	1,729	8.52	1
4	University of Pittsburgh	12,539	1,497	8.38	16.5
5	Yale University	11,813	1,583	7.46	21.5
6	University of California, San Diego[c]	11,548	1,541	7.49	46
7	University of Pennsylvania	9,977	1,281	7.79	18.3
9	Duke University	9,539	1,178	8.10	37.25
10	University of Michigan	8,517	1,386	6.15	8
11	University of Washington	8,417	1,174	7.17	7
12	University of North Carolina at Chapel Hill	8,025	1,106	7.26	21.5
13	University of Minnesota	7,380	1,251	5.90	5
14	New York University[d]	6,739	1,130	5.96	—
15	University of Maryland	6,067	1,128	5.38	—
16	Washington University	5,673	771	7.36	60.2
17	University of Iowa	5,630	838	6.72	21.5
18	University of Wisconsin–Madison	5,564	723	7.70	10
21	Indiana University	5,420	1,014	5.35	11.25
23	Emory University	5,005	711	7.04	89.3
25	Boston University	4,844	796	6.09	73.25
26	Rutgers, The State University of New Jersey	4,718	862	5.47	27.5
28	University of Illinois at Chicago	4,558	659	6.92	60.2
29	University of Missouri	4,493	849	5.29	—
30	University of Illinois at Urbana–Champaign	4,441	812	5.47	3
31	Vanderbilt University	4,322	672	6.43	11.25
32	City University of New York	4,179	799	5.23	27.5
33	Pennsylvania State University	4,163	1,031	4.04	11.25
34	Ohio State University	4,145	742	5.59	32.5
36	University of Texas at Austin	4,039	712	5.67	11.25
37	University of Missouri–Columbia[e]	3,838	628	6.11	35.5
38	University of Cincinnati	3,789	421	9.00	89.3
39	University of Massachusetts	3,759	733	5.13	—
40	University of Rochester	3,682	559	6.59	18.3
41	University of Maryland–College Park[f]	3,641	745	4.89	69.3
43	Michigan State University	3,602	648	5.56	37.25
44	University of Florida	3,539	773	4.58	15
45	University of Southern California	3,535	645	5.48	27.5
46	Case Western Reserve University	3,498	421	8.31	69.3
47	University of Texas Southwestern Medical Center at Dallas	3,460	263	13.16	108.3
48	Northwestern University	3,366	639	5.27	21.5
49	University of California, Berkeley	3,270	630	5.19	41
50	University of Colorado at Boulder	3,267	450	7.26	56.3
51	University of Virginia	3,219	611	5.27	44
54	Florida State University	3,098	723	4.28	27.5
56	Arizona State University	3,056	654	4.67	60.2

cont.

TABLE 4-2. *cont.*

Citation Rank	Institution[a]	Citations	Papers	Impact (citations per paper)	Faculty Production Rank[b]
57	University of South Florida	3,002	597	5.03	73.25
58	University of Arizona	2,979	515	5.78	81
59	University of Connecticut	2,975	691	4.31	37.25
60	Virginia Commonwealth University	2,956	411	7.19	108.3
61	University at Buffalo/State University of New York	2,784	540	5.16	46.25
63	University of Miami (Florida)	2,730	469	5.82	32.5
66	Purdue University	2,369	608	3.90	21.5
67	University of Kentucky	2,346	435	5.39	60.2
68	Temple University	2,334	446	5.23	69.3
69	Texas A&M University System	2,260	562	4.02	100.25
71	Indiana University–Purdue University Indianapolis	2,207	329	6.71	157
72	Stony Brook University/State University of New York	2,161	384	5.63	4.
73	Yeshiva University	2,134	268	7.96	—
74	University of Maryland–Baltimore County[f]	2,059	314	6.56	138.5
75	University of Vermont	2,038	319	6.39	73.25
76	University of New Mexico	2,031	328	6.19	89.3
77	University of Alabama System[g]	2,021	462	4.37	18.3
78	University of Oregon	1,975	324	6.10	16.5
79	University of Kansas	1,974	535	3.69	35.5
80	University of Georgia	1,971	512	3.85	6
81	University of Massachusetts–Amherst[h]	1,967	373	5.27	27.5
83	Miami University (Ohio)	1,854	416	4.46	138.5
84	San Diego State University[h]	1,712	335	5.11	46.25
85	University of Utah	1,671	360	4.64	13
88	Wayne State University	1,632	446	3.66	56.3
90	Teachers College, Columbia University	1,507	261	5.77	46.25
92	University at Albany/State University of New York	1,488	377	3.95	56.3
93	University of Nebraska	1,473	499	2.95	—
94	Iowa State University[d]	1,431	313	4.57	—
96	University of Delaware	1,341	281	4.77	100.25
97	University of Arkansas System[i]	1,337	316	4.23	125.3
101	University of South Carolina	1,247	304	4.10	51.3
103	Georgia State University	1,244	322	3.86	125.3
106	University of Oklahoma[d]	1,128	290	3.89	—
107	University of Nebraska–Lincoln[i]	1,127	368	3.06	51.3
108	University of Houston	1,125	299	3.76	51.3
109	University of Tennessee–Knoxville	1,112	379	2.93	46.25
112	Syracuse University	1,095	266	4.12	60.2
115	George Washington University	1,057	270	3.91	108.3
118	Louisiana State University	1,030	328	3.14	37.25
120	Kent State University	989	313	3.16	73.25

cont.

TABLE 4-2. *cont.*

Citation Rank	Institution[a]	Citations	Papers	Impact (citations per paper)	Faculty Production Rank[b]
124	Brigham Young University	935	255	3.67	100.25
125	University of Hawaii System[k]	916	252	3.63	100.25
126	George Mason University	913	260	3.51	150
151	Auburn University	627	251	2.50	96
154	Texas Tech University	616	265	2.32	125.3

Note. Adapted from the results of the Social Sciences Citation Index (SSCI)® and Science Citation Index Expanded (SCIE)® databases (2004-2008) compiled by Thomson Reuters® © Copyright THOMSON REUTERS ® 2009. All rights reserved. Also adapted from Roy, Roberts, and Stewart (2006).

[a]Institutions without APA-accredited programs in clinical or counseling psychology have been omitted from this table.

[b]Faculty production refers to the rank ordering of APA-accredited clinical psychology programs on the basis of the total number of clinical faculty members trained by that program.

[c]San Diego State University and the University of California, San Diego have a joint clinical psychology Ph.D. program.

[d]This university has an APA-accredited counseling psychology program, but does not have an APA-accredited clinical psychology program.

[e]See also, University of Missouri.

[f]See also, University of Maryland.

[g]In addition to the University of Alabama at Tuscaloosa, which has an APA-accredited program in clinical psychology, this system also includes the University of Alabama at Birmingham (UAB) and the University of Alabama in Huntsville.

[h]See also, University of Massachusetts.

[i]In addition to the University of Arkansas, which has an APA-accredited program in clinical psychology, this system also includes four other universities, five community colleges, one college of medicine, two schools of law, one presidential school, one math and science high school, and divisions of agriculture, archeology, and criminal justice.

[j]See also, University of Nebraska.

[k]In addition to the University of Hawaii at Manoa, which has an APA-accredited program in clinical psychology, this system also includes nine other campuses and dozens of educational, training, and research centers across the Hawaiian Islands.

tions with clinical or counseling psychology programs did not make the list. There are many other rankings that you might wish to examine, though our sense is that generally the top programs appear fairly consistently across methods.

Although it has its critics, another popular ranking of clinical psychology programs appears in the recent *U.S. News and World Report*'s ranking: http://grad-schools.usnews.rankingsandreviews.com/best-graduate-schools/top-clinical-psychology-schools/rankings. This listing focuses on clinical psychology rather than all of psychology. While *U.S. News* weighs heavily program reputation, you also might review a recent article that evaluated the scholarly productivity of 166 APA-accredited clinical psychology Ph.D. programs using a number of objective, normative variables (e.g., number of total publications; Stewart, Roberts, & Roy, 2007). These authors also show that rankings based on their analyses reveal a reasonable association with the *U.S. News* rankings. This last

article also provides a nice summary of prior efforts to rank the productivity of psychology departments.

Using Table 4-2, write the citation ranking for each school in column 5, labeled "Citation Rank." Be advised that this ranking reflects the psychology department in general, not just the clinical or counseling program. In fact, about 20% of the institutions on the original list of 75 were deleted because they do not have clinical or counseling psychology programs. Inclusion of these nonclinical influences will affect the ranking of the schools you have selected. Still, this will provide you with a rough idea of where each school stands in terms of its research. Our position is that a school that makes it onto this list is probably a strong research-oriented institution. If the school fails to appear on the table, then it may or may not emphasize psychological research. Recognize that only about 20% of APA-accredited programs appear on this list.

Table 4-2 also contains a column headed "Fac-

55

ulty Production Rank." This number represents the rank ordering of APA-accredited clinical psychology programs on the basis of the total number of clinical faculty members trained by that program (Roy, Roberts & Stewart, 2006). Any program that received a high ranking in this column has an established track record of producing clinical psychologists who, themselves, later assumed clinical psychology faculty positions. Remember that no single measure can ever capture the excellence of graduate education. And, again, only about 50% of APA-accredited clinical programs appear on the list. Still, the list does direct students interested in academic careers to programs that have historically excelled in this domain.

As mentioned, any APA-accredited program must provide both clinical and research training. Thus, it is important also to evaluate the practice opportunities available. As already mentioned, Psy.D. programs by definition emphasize practice and train students to be practitioners. Although it is possible to obtain research training at a Psy.D. program, this is not the primary emphasis of such programs. Consequently, a student with a clear research focus should choose a Ph.D. program. For the research oriented, this column will be used to cross schools off their application list. Look up each school on your list in the Reports on Individual Programs. If any of these schools offer only Psy.D. programs (see Table 2-1), you can delete that program.

The first column under the "Clinical" section of Appendix B is marked "Orientation." Under each program listed in our reports on individual programs, you will see a list of five theoretical orientations:

- Psychodynamic/psychoanalytic
- Radical behavioral/applied behavioral analysis
- Systems/family systems
- Humanistic/existential
- Cognitive/cognitive-behavioral

If you are clearly committed to (or strongly leaning toward) one of these orientations, then it is important that some faculty share that orientation with you. Check each program on your list and see if a suitable percentage of the faculty shares your orientation. If so, mark the "Orientation" column with a "+" sign. If not, mark it with a "−" sign.

If you are unsure of an orientation, or see yourself as integrative or eclectic, then be sure there is a wide variety of faculty orientations. If there is representation among the faculty in four or more of these orientations, that's a good sign. If the total you get when adding up all the percentages in the different

orientations is greater than 100%, this is also a plus. It means some (or most) of the faculty bridge orientations and are integrative themselves. In other words, professors are listed under more than one category. In either case, mark the "Orientation" column with a "+" sign. If the faculty are of one or two orientations and without overlap, then mark this column with a "−" sign.

The second column under "Clinical" is "Res/Clin." Turn to Appendix F, "Specialty Clinics and Practica Sites." This is a list of specialty clinics and practica available at different programs. Specialty clinics focus on a specific clientele, such as depressed or eating-disordered clients. Practica are placements where students will conduct clinical work in their second, third, and/or fourth years of study. Some practica also specialize in a certain clientele. If you have a research interest in a particular population, it is important that the population be available for you to study and that you have the chance to work with that population clinically. For this reason, it is a great help for a researcher to have a specialty clinic or practicum in his or her area.

Look up your research area in Appendix F. If any of the programs on your list in Appendix B has a clinic or practicum in that area, mark the "Res/Clin" column with a plus. You can do likewise using Appendix G, "Program Concentrations and Tracks." Programs offering a formal track or concentration in your area of interest deserve a plus as well.

Again, this is only one indicator and must be kept in perspective. Most programs will have their own psychological training clinic, where clinical populations may be seen or made available for research. Additionally, a faculty member may have a research population readily available in the community. And last, a few programs did not include practica placements off campus in the community, thus underrepresenting their practica opportunities. Still, being informed about a clinic or practicum specializing in your population of interest is certainly an advantage in selecting potential graduate programs.

The third column under the "Clinical" section is marked "Rank." Here, we refer to a program's production of students who go on to distinguished careers as clinicians, as measured by becoming ABPP Diplomates and by election as Fellows in APA's Division of Clinical Psychology or Division of Counseling Psychology. The "ABPP" refers to diplomate status awarded by the American Board of Professional Psychology (www.abpp.org), which certifies excellence in 14 fields of psychology, including clinical psychology and counseling psychology. Applicants for ABPP must have at least 5 years of postdoctoral experience, submit examples of their clinical work, and pass an oral examination. The entrance requirements and performance standards are more rigorous than those involved in licensure and represent excellence in applied psychology. Fellowship in APA is based on evidence of unusual and outstanding performance in psychology.

One study (Robyak & Goodyear, 1984) investigated the graduate school origins of ABPP Diplomates and APA Fellows in clinical and counseling psychology. Although older and larger doctoral programs are obviously favored in such a historical study, the results nonetheless give some indication of institutional reputation and their graduates' accomplishments. Table 4-3 presents the top 25 institutional origins of clinical psychology diplomates and fellows as well as the top 12 institutional origins of counseling psychology diplomates and fellows. Clinical psychology diplomates graduated from 153 different universities; fellows from 92. Counseling psychology diplomates graduated from 55 universities; fellows from 46.

If a school is listed in Table 4-3, place a "+" in the "Rank" column in the "Clinical" section. Though many schools not listed on this table provide fine clinical training, this listing indicates that the program is outstanding in terms of its track record for producing excellent professional psychologists.

Finally, there is a column in Appendix B marked "Self-Rating." The first question we asked each program to answer was, "On a 7-point scale, how research or practice oriented would you rate your program?" (1 = practice emphasis; 4 = equal emphasis; and 7 = research emphasis). You will find the school's rating of itself under each individual listing in the reports on individual programs sections. Mark this number under the "Self-Rating" column.

What you now have is a list of programs that offer research in your area of interest. You also have the number of faculty in the area that you might work with and whether they presently have grant funding. Finally, you have an approximate rank of that school's research standing.

In clinical terms, you have some sense of whether that school will conform to your theoretical orientation, whether it has clinical training or a formal track in your area of interest, how it ranks in terms of producing outstanding clinicians, and whether it rates itself as emphasizing practice or research.

Given the information before you, you may already want to begin crossing programs off your list. If you're research oriented, and the program is a Psy.D. program or rates itself a 1, 2, or 3 (meaning it is practice oriented), you can probably delete that school. Alternatively, if your interests reflect equal research and clinical emphasis and you lean toward a psychodynamic orientation, you may want to cross off a school that rates itself as a 7 (very research oriented) or whose faculty is 100% cognitive or behavioral.

Your revised list of schools can probably satisfy your research and clinical interests. In addition, you have the start of a ranking system, which at this point gives you a rough idea of how well each school conforms to your interests and needs. Unfortunately, this provides you with only half of the information you need to begin writing to schools. The second part of this process asks, "How close do you come to the standards they specify?" This is covered in a later section entitled "Assessing Program Criteria."

For the Practice Oriented

This section gives guidance to those applicants who are centrally focused on psychological practice. These applicants will want to begin to choose their programs based on their theoretical orientation and the availability of practice opportunities.

Begin by turning to Table 2-1, which lists all the APA-accredited Psy.D. programs. With this list, turn to Appendix B, "Worksheet for Choosing Programs." Under the column marked "School," write the names of the programs found in Table 2-1.

In addition to these programs, you may have a specific population in mind that you are especially eager to work with. Perhaps you already have a sense that you want to work with patients suffering from, say, anxiety disorders. In this case, turn to Appendix F. This appendix, "Specialty Clinics and Practica Sites," lists specialty clinics or practica areas available at different programs. Specialty clinics focus on specific clientele, such as depressed or eating-disordered clients. As mentioned in the previous section, practica are placements where a student will conduct clinical work in his or her second, third, and/or fourth year of study, and some practica also specialize in treating a certain clientele. For a practice-oriented student, it would be especially desirable to be in a program with a specialty clinic in his or her particular area of treatment interest. Therefore, write down the names of programs with specialty clinics or practica in your area of interest on your list in Appendix B.

Do likewise for programs that offer a formal track or concentration in your area of interest. This

TABLE 4-3. Institutional Origins of Clinical and Counseling Psychology Diplomates and Fellows

University	Rank order	
	Diplomates	Fellows
Clinical psychology		
New York University	1	2
Columbia University	2	1
University of Chicago	3	3
University of California–Los Angeles	4	14
University of Michigan	5.5	9
University of Iowa	5.5	5
University of Minnesota	7	6
Northwestern University	8	7.5
University of California–Berkeley	9	15.5
Harvard University	10	7.5
Pennsylvania State University	11	17.5
Purdue University	12.5	—
Boston University	12.5	17.5
Ohio State University	14	4
University of Washington	15	5.5
University of Southern California	16	11.5
Duke University	18	—
Stanford University	18	10
University of Texas	18	—
University of Pittsburgh	20	11.5
University of Kansas	21	—
Case Western Reserve University	23.5	—
University of Illinois at Urbana–Champaign	23.5	—
Yale University	23.5	13
University of Pennsylvania	23.5	—
Counseling psychology		
Columbia University	1	2
Ohio State University	2	3
University of Minnesota	3	1
New York University	4	4.5
University of Michigan	5	—
University of Chicago	6	8
Stanford University	7	7
University of Iowa	8	7
University of Texas	9.5	—
University of Wisconsin	9.5	—
Catholic University	11.5	—
Harvard University	11.5	4.5

Note. From Robyak & Goodyear (1984). © 1984 American Psychological Association. Reprinted by permission.

information can be found in Appendix G, "Program Concentrations and Tracks."

A word of caution is in order. Most programs will have their own psychology training clinic where clinical populations may be seen or made available for research. Practica may also be available in a wide range of settings in the community, providing fertile ground for a rich clinical experience. Still, a clinic or practicum specializing in a population that is of special interest to you is a definite plus and an additional piece of information on which to base your decision. If a program both offers a Psy.D. and has a specialty clinic or concentration in your area, put a star next to it.

The next important column for the practice-oriented applicant is marked "Orientation." In the Reports on Individual Programs, you will find each school listed, along with information pertaining to its program. Among that information, you will see a list of five theoretical orientations, followed by the percentage of the faculty that subscribes to that orientation:

- Psychodynamic/psychoanalytic
- Radical behavioral/applied behavioral analysis
- Systems/family systems
- Humanistic/existential
- Cognitive/cognitive-behavioral

If you are clearly committed to (or strongly leaning toward) one of these orientations, then it is important that some portion of the faculty share that orientation with you. Check each program on your list and determine if a suitable percentage of the faculty shares your orientation. If so, mark the "Orientation" column with a "+" sign; if not, mark it with a "–" sign.

If you are unsure of your orientation or see yourself as integrative or eclectic, then be sure there is a wide variety of faculty orientations. If there is representation among the faculty in four of these orientations, that's a good sign. If the total you obtain after adding up all the percentages in the different areas is greater than 100%, this is also advantageous. It means some (or most) of the faculty bridge orientations and are integrative themselves. In either case, mark the "Orientation" column with a "+" sign. If you're integrative and the faculty are of one or two orientations and do not overlap, then mark this column with a "–" sign.

The next column is marked "Res/Clin." As we mentioned previously, even if you are looking for a practice-oriented program, you still will have to conduct some research: a lengthy professional paper or a clinical dissertation at the very least! Consequently, it is important that someone in your program is conducting research in an area that interests you. With this in mind, look through Appendix E and locate area(s) of research that you find interesting. Under each area, you will find a list of schools that have researchers in that field. If any of the schools on your list in Appendix B is listed here, place a "+" in the column marked "Res/Clin."

The third column under "Clinical" is marked "Rank." Here, we refer to a program's production of students who go on to distinguished careers as clinicians, as imperfectly measured by their becoming ABPP Diplomates and by their election as Fellows in APA's Division of Clinical Psychology and Division of Counseling Psychology. The "ABPP" refers to diplomate status awarded by the American Board of Professional Psychology (www.abpp.org), which certifies excellence in 14 fields of psychology, including clinical psychology and counseling psychology. Applicants for ABPP must have at least 5 years of postdoctoral experience, submit examples of their clinical work, and pass an oral examination. The entrance requirements and performance standards are more rigorous than those involved in licensing and represent excellence in applied psychology. The APA Fellowship is based on evidence of unusual and outstanding performance.

One study (Robyak & Goodyear, 1984) investigated the graduate school origins of ABPP Diplomates and APA Fellows in clinical and counseling psychology. Although older and larger doctoral programs are obviously favored in such a historical study, the results nonetheless give some indication of institutional reputation and their graduates' accomplishments. Table 4-3 presents the top 25 institutional origins of these diplomates and fellows as well as the top 12 institutional origins of counseling psychology diplomates and fellows. Because this list indicates programs that have historically produced outstanding clinicians, place a "+" in this column for any program included in Table 4-3. Though many schools not listed in this table offer fine clinical training, the list provides an indication of the Ph.D. programs (Psy.D. programs are too new to be listed) that are likely to offer the sort of clinical training you seek.

Finally, there is a column in Appendix B marked "Self-Rating." In the reports on individual programs you will find each school's rating of itself (1 = practice emphasis; 4 = equal emphasis; and 7 = research emphasis). Mark this number under the "Self-Rating" column. Though Psy.D. programs are practice oriented by definition, they vary on how much research they expect their students to conduct. Thus, their ratings will allow you to guide your expectations of what each program will expect of you. This self-rating will also help you avoid a Ph.D. program with a specialty clinic in your area that is clearly research oriented.

What you now have is a list of programs that are practice oriented and/or that offer a specialty clinic or formal track in your area of interest. You have some sense of whether these schools will conform to your theoretical orientation and whether they have ongoing research in your area of clinical interest. You also have their self-rating of the program's emphasis on practice or research.

Given the information on your worksheet, you may already want to begin crossing programs off your list. If you're practice oriented and a Ph.D. program offers a specialty clinic in your area but rates itself with a 6 or 7 (very research oriented), you may choose to delete that school. Alternatively, if you're very behaviorally oriented, you may want to cross off a school where 100% of the faculty is psychodynamic/psychoanalytic.

Your revised list of schools can provide you with practice-oriented training and possibly special clinical training in your population of choice. In addition, you have the start of a ranking system that at this point gives you a rough idea of how well each school conforms to your interests and needs. Unfortunately, this only provides you with half the information you need to begin writing to schools. The second half of this process is related to how closely you come to the specified standards of these programs. This is covered in the "Assessing Program Criteria" section.

For the Racial/Ethnic Minority Applicant

Before continuing to the assessment of program criteria, it is important to discuss the special case of minority applications. "Minority" in this context refers to racial or ethnic background, although with women comprising 70% of all doctoral students in psychology (Pate, 2001), a few graduate student programs are starting to treat men as minority applicants. Ethnic minority students now account for 21% of master's students in psychology and 27% of doctoral students in psychology (Norcross, Kohout, & Wicherski, 2005).

Nearly every APA-accredited program makes special efforts to recruit minority applicants (Munoz-Dunbar & Stanton, 1999; Rogers & Molina, 2006),

recognizing the need in our society for well-trained minority professionals. Typical methods for recruiting underrepresented groups to clinical and counseling psychology programs are offers of financial aid, the use of personal contacts, funded visits to programs, use of APA's Minority Undergraduate Students of Excellence (MUSE) program, diversity courses, special events, reimbursements of application fees, and preferential screening (Rogers & Molina, 2006; Steinpreis et al., 1992). Programs often make an extra effort to review minority applications to ensure that qualified candidates are given appropriate consideration.

In fact, a study of Psy.D. programs revealed that 82% of them implemented formal minority admissions policies designed to improve racial representation (Young & VandeCreek, 1996). The study found that:

- 94% of the programs gave extra points on ratings of application materials to minority applicants;
- 69% of the programs waived or lowered GRE scores for minority applicants;
- 41% of the programs waived or lowered GPA cutoffs for minority applicants; and
- 21% of the programs interviewed all minority applicants, regardless of the quality of their application materials.

As a consequence, ethnic minorities in the applicant pool are more likely than whites to receive offers of admission (Munoz-Dunbar & Stanton, 1999). Our guidance and the following worksheets in this *Insider's Guide* may thus not accurately reflect a minority applicant's enhanced chances of acceptance. We recommend that you carefully read program descriptions regarding their minority selection procedures and encourage you to apply to programs that are within reach of your credentials.

Several ethnic/racial minority students have written to us over the years and complained that they were neither actively recruited nor accepted for admission into the doctoral psychology programs to which they had applied. So let us be perfectly clear and honest: Most, but not all, doctoral programs have implemented policies (as reviewed above) to recruit and admit underrepresented racial/ethnic minority students. However, that does not mean that all programs will be knocking down your door to interview you. Nor does that mean that most programs will finance your interview. Nor does that mean acceptance is a certainty. Doctoral programs will evaluate all candidates on their GPAs, GREs, letters of recommendation, research experiences, and so on. A modest advantage is just that—an advantage, never a guarantee.

APA is committed to ensuring that the practice of psychology—and the production of psychologists—is in the vanguard of addressing the needs of culturally diverse populations. The APA's Commission on Ethnic Minority Recruitment, Retention, and Training in Psychology produces several valuable publications in this regard. Go to www.apa.org/careers/resources/guides/grad-school.aspx to read APA's guidebook, *For College Students of Color Applying to Graduate & Professional Programs*. Also consult the Web site of *Project 1000*, a national program created to assist students of color applying to graduate school (mati.eas.asu.edu:8421/p1000).

Although the special consideration given minority applicants is advantageous, it also represents a special challenge. One well-qualified minority student we knew was advised by a university career counselor that he would have no problem getting into the doctoral program of his choice. He applied to several very competitive programs, and received acceptances and offers of financial aid across the board. Unfortunately, he skipped the process of matching his interests with the strengths of the program. After a single year, he was looking to transfer to another program that had more faculty conducting research and psychotherapy in his areas of interest.

The moral of the story is: Don't let the potential advantage of being an ethnic/racial minority candidate become a disadvantage. Just because you can get into a program doesn't mean that it is the best program for you. A rigorous approach to the application process is the best approach for everyone.

For the LGBT Applicant

Lesbian, gay, bisexual, and transgendered (LGBT) applicants to doctoral programs can face the same social and interpersonal hurdles as ethnic/racial minority applicants. There is, however, a key difference: There are limited federal protections for members of the LGBT community. This fact may lead lesbian, gay, bisexual, and transgendered students to question whether to disclose their sexual orientation ("come out") in the application process, or even to inquire about the atmosphere of inclusivity toward sexual minorities within a particular program. In this section, we review some research and advice on LGBT applicants' selection of graduate programs and present potential strategies for those who elect to come out during the application process.

Before turning to the specifics, let us emphasize this general point: The burden should not be placed on the potentially stigmatized applicant to disclose sexual orientation. Such a burden promotes silence and fear. Rather, each applicant should choose his/her own path, and program faculty should create an inclusive, welcoming atmosphere for all students. The APA accreditation guidelines require doctoral programs to embrace diversity in their students.

Qualitative research (e.g., APA, 2006; Lark & Croteau, 1998; Rader, 2000) indicates that LGBT psychology students screen prospective graduate schools for their gay affirming (or at least, nonhomophobic) position. The typical criteria used for screening prospective programs are (Biaggio et al., 2003):

- Reports of other LGBT students
- Presence of faculty who are openly lesbian/gay or heterosexual allies
- Availability of specific training on LGBT issues and opportunity to work with LGBT clients
- Sensitivity to diversity on campus (including the presence of LGBT support and advocacy groups)
- Geographic location of the program (frequently avoiding programs in conservative rural areas)
- Size of the educational institution (larger public institutions being relatively more liberal)

In addition, we recommend that LGBT students look for climate indicators favorable to sexual diversity. Screen prospective programs by

- searching departmental and university home pages for the presence of an LGBT student union and faculty teaching and researching on sexuality.
- looking for specific housing policies for LGBT couples (remember, though legally married in one state, another state may not recognize your gay marriage or civil union, and the university may not be legally bound to provide equal access to "married" housing).
- avoiding institutions that require a religious or doctrinal oath and that prohibit LGBT organizations on campus.
- seeking programs with curricula that explicitly integrate LGBT and other diversity issues.
- reviewing APA's list of graduate faculty in psychology interested in lesbian, gay, and bisexual issues (available at www.apa.org/pi/lgbt/resources/survey/ q6-7-table.pdf).
- evaluating the university's mission statement for a formal commitment to diversity of sexual orientation.

- determining if the institution has a coordinator (or office) for lesbian, gay, and bisexual concerns.
- considering the state laws concerning equitable treatment of LGBT, such as civil unions, domestic partnership, adoption, health insurance for partners, and the like.

Homophobia and heterosexism continue to exist in the United States and, unfortunately, also in institutions of higher education. Although the situation has improved considerably in recent decades, some institutions remain "tolerant" as opposed to "affirming" of sexual diversity, whereas other institutions may favor an LGBT student to maintain or expand program diversity.

The question, then, is whether to come out during the application process. On one side, there is the risk of being rejected from a program where some discrimination persists. On the other side, there is the potential advantage of being a member of a minority group in a program that actively pursues diversity. In either case, the alternative to not coming out during the application process is to come out later, or to try to hide your sexual orientation for 4 to 6 years.

If and when to disclose sexual orientation in the admissions process is ultimately a personal decision, and it can occur at different stages in the process: in the application itself, during the interview, upon acceptance to the program, or upon the decision to attend the program. As part of your application, you can indicate your sexual orientation in your research interests (e.g., lesbian health), clinical experiences (e.g., working with gay youth), and/or extracurricular activities (e.g., member of the LGBT alliance on campus). More directly, you can incorporate your sexual identity into your personal statement, especially if it has bearing on your choice of clinical or research work, or your decision to pursue psychology as a career. If you do come out in your personal statement, be sure that this fact is integrated into the overall statement and not simply a dangling fact unconnected to the rest of what you've written.

Some applicants choose to come out during the interview process with a simple but straightforward statement: "As a gay man (or lesbian), it's important to me to be in a gay-friendly environment. Would being gay be a concern in this program?" Though it would be a mistake to over-generalize, such questions are typically met with positive responses about program diversity and discussions of resources for LGBT students. If such questions are met otherwise,

it serves as a key piece of information in your decision process.

Another strategy is to raise sexual orientation at the point at which an offer of admission is tendered. As discussed in subsequent chapters, once an offer is made, an applicant has some latitude in negotiating issues around admission, tuition remission, funding, and so on. This can be the time to indicate that having a gay-affirmative environment is one of the factors in your decision of which program to accept and to inquire about the atmosphere in that program. Still other LGBT students elect not to disclose until they are actually matriculated in the program and have begun coursework.

Whatever path you decide to take, your sexual orientation should not be the defining issue of your application; your composite strengths as a potential doctoral student remain the center of your application. [For additional information, consult the *APAGS Resource Guide for LGBT Students in Psychology* (APA, 2006) and *Graduate Faculty in Psychology Interested in Lesbian, Gay, and Bisexual Issues* (at www.apa.org/pi/lgbt/resources/survey/q6-7-table.pdf).

For the Disabled Applicant

Organized psychology is increasingly aware that diversity extends beyond gender, ethnicity, and sexual orientation to all individual differences, including disability status. Applicants with disabilities confront many of the same prejudices as other minority populations, including obstacles to graduate applications and interviews. According to the National Science Foundation, psychology and the social sciences are slightly more likely to have graduates with some type of disability—about 2%.

APA's Resource Guide for Psychology Graduate Students with Disabilities (www.apa.org/pi/disability/resources/publications/resource-guide.aspx) presents tips on applying to graduate school, requesting fair accommodations, and preparing for a successful experience. The guide also lists national resources on disability issues; our favorite is Dr. Ken Pope's Web site on accessibility in psychology graduate education and practice (at kpope.com). APA has also initiated a Disability Mentoring Program to match psychology students with veteran disabled psychologists (www.apa.org/pi/disability/resources/mentoring/index.aspx).

When and how to disclose a disability is a complex and personal decision, a decision that you must make after sorting through the choices and perhaps discussing them with a knowledgeable mentor. There are eight different occasions during the admissions process when you might choose to disclose (Khubchandani, 2002):

- In your personal statement or application form
- When a prospective graduate school contacts you for an interview
- During the interview
- After the interview but before an offer
- After the offer but before an acceptance
- After you start the graduate program
- After a problem on the job
- Never (disclose)

There are pros and cons for each timing of disclosure, but ultimately your decision will be based on what you know about your own needs and what you have learned about the particular graduate program (Khubchandani, 2002). If and when you do disclose a disability, be straightforward and factual about it only as it affects your specific job functions, as defined by the Americans with Disabilities Act (ADA). Specify the type of accommodation that you will require or the work restrictions that are involved. Don't dwell on your disability; rather, be enthusiastic about your skills and resources. Stress that your disability did not interfere with previous performance or attendance.

Your multiple abilities, not select disabilities, are what count in graduate school. As with ethnicity and sexual orientation, your disability status should not occupy center stage in your application. Assertively request fair accommodation and accessibility as provided by law, to be sure. But help the admissions committee avoid the stereotype of equating you with your disability. Your application should focus squarely on your credentials and accomplishments.

For the International Applicant

APA-accredited programs tend to look favorably upon qualified international students. In fact, fully 8% of counseling psychology doctoral students (Norcross et al., 2009) and 7% of clinical psychology doctoral students (Norcross et al., 2010) are international. Graduate psychology education in the United States is definitely going more global.

The unique challenges for international students revolve around demonstrating equivalent academic preparation, mastery of the English language (if not the native tongue), and beginning the entire process earlier than usual. With regard to credentials, the GRE scores will address your knowledge base. But

submit your graduate school application well before the deadline and anticipate hearing from the graduate admissions committee about the equivalency of your undergraduate and graduate degrees. With regard to mastery of the English language, most graduate schools will require applicants whose native language is not English to take the Test of English as a Foreign Language (TOEFL). The fee for taking TOEFL is currently $140 U.S.

International students need to start the application process earlier because it takes longer and entails more paperwork. In addition to the TOEFL, international applicants will need to arrange for certified transcripts in English from each university attended and for an Affidavit of Support, a document demonstrating they possess adequate funding to meet the costs of at least one full academic year. That Affidavit is required before applying for the student visa (Landi, 2010).

In determining where to apply, the usual criteria pertain to international students, as reviewed in Chapter 5, with a few twists. Search for graduate programs that already feature some international students and perhaps international faculty, that offer special services for international students, and that conduct cross-cultural research. A multicultural learning environment and greater support from training programs improve international students' psychosocial and academic adjustment (Hasan et al., 2008).

We also heartily recommend two detailed guides: *Studying Psychology in the United States: Expert Guidance for International Students* published by the American Psychological Association (Hasan et al., 2008) and *Succeeding as an International Student in the United States and Canada* published by the University of Chicago Press (Lipson, 2008). In addition, consult with the international student offices at the universities to which you are applying.

Assessing Program Criteria

Assessing the criteria clinical and counseling psychology programs use to evaluate applicants is an important step in the process of applying to graduate school. To illuminate this point, we will relate the story of one applicant we knew several years ago. She was an Ivy League graduate, a 3.8 psychology major, who had conducted research with a prominent psychologist. She had fine letters of recommendation and clinical experience with developmentally disabled children, but her GREs were in the low 500s. Thinking that her credentials were excellent, she applied to the most competitive research-oriented programs and one practice-oriented program. She was rejected across the board at these top research schools and just barely made it into what she had mistakenly considered her practice-oriented "safety school." Her mistake was to ignore the fact that all the research-oriented programs to which she applied specified minimum GRE scores of 600 or more. Her application was unsuccessful because she ignored one piece of essential information. She was nearly rejected in the more practice-oriented program she had felt was a "sure thing" because she did not possess the clinical experience they were looking for. And she was lucky that that particular doctoral program did not have GRE requirements beyond her range!

The moral of the story is twofold: (1) Attend closely to the admission standards of each program. If a school sets standards you cannot realistically meet, you need to work very, very hard to get them to make an exception. In other words, think thrice about applying there. (2) Apply to programs with a range of admission criteria, and consider a safety school as one that announces admission requirements that you exceed by a wide margin. This does not guarantee acceptance, but does dramatically increase the probability of making it into their finalist pool.

Now, turn your attention to Appendix C, "Worksheet for Assessing Program Criteria." In Appendix C, you will rate yourself on how well you conform to each school's admission requirements. The aim is that you not waste time and money applying to programs that indicate in no uncertain terms that you do not meet their criteria. There is no reason to feel inadequate because you fall short of these specifications. There may be programs on your list with requirements you do meet or exceed. If you are unable to meet the minimum requirements of any programs on your list, you should seriously consider taking time off to better prepare yourself or apply to less competitive master's programs.

Begin by transferring the name of each school from Appendix B to the "School" column of Appendix C. Simply copy the list from one table to the other. Also copy the number in the "Self-Rating" column from one worksheet to the other. Next, look up the first program on your list in the Reports on Individual Programs. Read through all the information provided just to start familiarizing yourself with that program.

As you begin filling out Appendix C and listing each school's admission criteria, remember that these are simply indications of your strength as an appli-

cant to each school. These scales are not set in stone and do not guarantee that you will be accepted. You may not readily fall into any of the categories listed and will have to make some rough approximations for yourself. Or you may find that you fall between categories and have to add 0.5 point here or subtract 0.5 point there. If you think it is appropriate to modify the categories or scoring systems, by all means do so. *The most important result is not an absolute number but a relative sense of how well you meet each program's admission criteria.*

You may also discover that a graduate program does not require certain entrance examinations, or gives no mean GRE scores, or doesn't list preferred or mandatory courses. In this case, simply score a "0" in the appropriate column. When it comes time to total each school's score, this will neither detract from nor add to your ability to meet their requirements.

Now, go to the respective Reports on Individual Programs and look at the prerequisite courses. You will see two questions pertaining to course preparation prior to applying: "What courses are required for incoming students to have completed prior to enrolling?" and "Are there courses you recommend that are not mandatory?" Underneath each question you will find a list of courses that the particular school assigned to each category. On your list in Appendix C, under the column marked "Courses," score yourself as follows (in this table, "M" indicates "mandatory" and "R" indicates "recommended"):

+2	You have taken all the M and R courses and earned B+ or better in them all.
+1	You have taken all the M courses and/or several of the R courses and earned B+ or better.
0	You have taken all the M courses, but none of the Rs, or earned B– or lower in some M courses.
–1	You have not taken one or two of the M courses, or have earned B– or lower in several of them.
–2	You have not taken several or any of the M courses or have received C or lower in some of the M or R courses.

The next section on each "Program" page is marked GREs and GPA. This section gives mean scores for the GREs and GPAs for each program listed.

On your list, under the columns marked "GRE-V" (verbal), "GRE-Q" (quantitative), and "GRE-S" (psychology subject test), score yourself as follows:

+2   You exceed the school's M score by at least 100 points.

+1   You exceed the school's M score by more than 50 but less than 100 points.

0   You meet the school's M minimum or exceed it by less than 50 points.

−1   You do not meet the school's M score, but are less than 100 points below it.

−2   You are below the M score by 100 points or more.

For GPA, we asked programs for the mean score of their incoming class and asked if that applied to more than one type of GPA. It is not uncommon for programs to look at cumulative or overall GPA (all undergraduate courses taken) and psychology GPA (only psychology courses). Again, it is wise to review the average GPA of incoming students. Under the column marked "GPA," score yourself as follows:

+2   You exceed the school's cumulative GPA by 0.3 points or more.

+1   You exceed the school's cumulative GPA by less than 0.1 point.

0   You meet the school's average GPA.

−1   You do not meet the school's cumulative GPA, but are less than 0.1 below it.

−2   You are below the school's cumulative by more than 0.3 points.

Next, look back to the second column of Appendix C, "Self-Rating." This is how the program rates itself on the practice–research continuum. If a program emphasizes one more than the other, this gives some indication of what it would consider important in an applicant. A program that stresses research will probably desire an applicant to have research experience. Under the "Research" column in Appendix C, rate yourself as follows:

+2   The school rates itself as a 6 or a 7 and you will have completed an honors thesis or will have at least 2 years of experience in psychology research.

+1   The school rates itself as a 4, 5, 6, or 7 and you will have at least 1 year of experience in psychology research.

0   The school rates itself as a 1, 2, or 3.

−1   The school rates itself as a 4 or 5, and you have no research experience.

−2   The school rates itself as a 6 or 7, and you have no research experience.

Similarly, a program emphasizing clinical work will prefer that an applicant enter with some practical experience in human services or health care. Under the "Clinical" column, rate yourself as follows:

+2   The school rates itself as a 1 or a 2, and you will have worked in a full-time (35+ hr./week) clinical position for at least 1 year.

+1   The school rates itself as a 1, 2, 3, or 4 and you will have volunteered part-time (8+ hr./week) at a clinical facility for at least 1 year.

0   The school rates itself as a 5, 6, or 7.

−1   The school rates itself as a 3 or 4, and you have no clinical experience.

−2   The school rates itself as a 1 or 2, and you have no clinical experience.

At this point, you should have completed the first nine columns of Appendix C from "School" to "Clinical."

Additional information provided for each program in the Reports on Individual Programs are "How many students applied in 2009?," "How many applicants were offered admission in 2009?," and "How many admitted students are incoming?" These give a rough estimate of the competitiveness of a program.

In applying to programs, be realistic and reasonable. You may have a sterling application, but when Yale and Harvard accept roughly 2 in 100 applicants, you had best be applying to other places as well.

Bear in mind: Programs accept more applicants than actually end up attending. This makes programs appear more restrictive than they actually are. This is why we added the third item regarding the number of students who will enter the program—a number invariably smaller than the number of accepted students. For example, an applicant gaining acceptance to five programs will ultimately reject four of them. A program planning on an incoming class of six students will accept more than six before gaining their new class. Nonetheless, apply to several schools with a range of competitiveness as a precautionary measure.

In the column marked "Compete" in Appendix C, record the ratio of applications to acceptances. It should be noted that competitiveness is difficult to quantify. Although we have selected the ratio of applicants to acceptances as our measure, other relevant criteria include GRE scores and GPA. Since we have already discussed these criteria, we are using this opportunity to highlight yet another area related to competitiveness.

The last column is marked "Total." Add the numbers under the "Courses," "GRE-V," "GRE-Q," "GRE-S," "GPA," "Research," and "Clinical" columns. This will provide you with a total somewhere between −14 and +14, which is a rough indication of how well you meet each school's admission requirements and expectations.

Now you have a grand list of programs that are performing research or clinical work in the areas you have specified. In addition, you have several indications of how well each school will address your needs and expectations as a graduate student. Finally, you have a rating of yourself as an applicant to each program.

The best way to begin your decision-making process is to select the programs that have admission requirements within your reach. As you look through the "school requirements" part of your list, note any −2s. Unless you can reasonably expect to change these to zeros or better before you complete your applications, you are better off dropping these programs from your list. After that, you will then have to decide for yourself what are reasonable places to apply.

Below is a rating system based on your "Total" column for each program. Although this system may help you decide where to apply, it is by no means definitive. *These are rough approximations*, and ultimately you will have to decide where to apply based on this and any other information to which you are privy. From the "Total" column of Appendix C, evaluate each program as follows:

10 to 14 Your chances are very good. Apply to many of these schools, since your application may be especially strong here.

6 to 9 Your chances are good. These schools are within your reach, as you exceed several of the credentials they value.

114 to 5 Your chances are moderately good here, but be sure to apply to some schools where you rank more highly.

110 to 3 These schools are within your range of abilities. Your application may not be outstanding, but it is somewhere between "adequate" and "more than adequate." Be sure also to apply to several schools in a higher range.

1 to −4 These schools are a stretch for you. Go ahead and apply to a few, but the bulk of your applications should go to schools on which you achieved a higher score.

< −4 These schools are looking for something different from your experience or performance at this time. If you wish to attend a program in this range, take time off or attend a master's program to bolster your research, clinical, and academic performance.

Although this worksheet embodies many of the relevant criteria used by admissions committees, it of course cannot integrate all possible criteria. If a professor has expressed interest in working with you, for example, the worksheet total may underestimate your chances for acceptance. Other useful resources when selecting your list of schools include specific professors, undergraduate psychology advisors, and the Web sites of the respective programs. Graduate students at your local university can also be helpful, and a few large universities have even created notebooks on clinical and counseling psychology graduate programs (Todd & Farinato, 1992). Take advantage of all the available information to augment the data provided in the Reports on Individual Programs.

Using the system in Appendix C, delete some of the schools that list admission criteria outside of your present range. This will enable you to begin the next phase: selecting programs that match your expectations in terms of the training you desire.

For the research-oriented applicant, these decisions may be easiest. Look at the schools remaining on your worksheet. Note the number of faculty interested in your research area(s) and whether any of them are funded. Grant funding is a rough indicator of the intensity of the program's commitment to a particular research area. The premise is that a grant-funded area may offer more opportunities to study the topic and may be more likely to generate research. In addition, grant funding has the potential of making assistantship money available. This by no means suggests that a program that does not have a grant in your area is not conducting current research or will not have money available to you. Additionally, a program with several faculty in an area may simply be "between" grants. Thus, the number of faculty alone also can indicate a school's commitment to this area of research.

Next, check the program's productivity ranking (Table 4-2) and their self-rating as being more practice or research oriented. Again, if you are more research oriented, you may well find yourself crossing those schools off your list that are low on productivity and that are clearly practice oriented. You will discover that this shortens your list but that

September 3, 2012

Director of Admissions
Department of Psychology
Bogus University

Dear Sir or Madam:

I am interested in applying to your Ph.D. (Psy.D.) program in clinical (counseling) psychology for the fall of 2013. Please send me an application and any information you have available concerning your program. Kindly include financial aid information as well.

Thank you for your time and consideration.

Sincerely yours,

Chris Smith

FIGURE 4-1. Sample e-mail requesting application and information.

you still have a number of schools that cover a wide range of desirability. This is exactly where you want to be at this point! What you desire is a list of 15 to 30 programs for which you will secure additional information. Then, you can begin fine-tuning and selecting the 10 to 20 programs to which you will actually apply.

If you are more strongly inclined toward practice, you will find yourself crossing schools off your list that are research oriented, favor theoretical orientations different from your own, or are too restricted for your needs. The programs highlighting clinical work, and especially those sharing your orientation or providing a track or clinic in your area, will be the most desirable.

The applicant who equally emphasizes practice and research training is the most challenged. You want a program that is research oriented, but not at the cost of clinical work. But you also want a program that will offer high-quality clinical training without sacrificing high standards in research. Using your list, find the programs that are moderate or high in productivity and that have a number of people interested in your area. Ensure that they rate themselves as a 4 or 5, indicating that they emphasize practice and research nearly equally. Then, check to see if their theoretical orientation conforms to your own and whether they have a specialty clinic or for-

mal tracks in your area. Again, you are going to find a range of programs, some conforming to your needs better than others. This is exactly what you want at this point in the process.

You are now ready to gather the detailed information necessary to choose among the 15 to 30 programs you will use for your selection pool. If your number of schools does not fall within these parameters, you should consider modifying your list. The Web site, mailing address, and e-mail address of each program are listed with each entry in the Reports on Individual Programs. At this point, all you need is to spend a few hours on the Web. Research demonstrates that Web sites provide more information about graduate programs than direct mailings, especially in areas not directly related to graduate applications (Bartsch, Warren, Sharp, & Green, 2003), so feel comfortable in securing the requisite information online. Upwards of 90% of graduate programs will post their application forms and instructions online.

In a few cases, you might need to send a brief email or letter requesting information and an application. When requesting information, your communciation should be neat, typed, and focused. Figure 4-1 shows a sample letter or e-mail.

Congratulations! You have taken the initial steps in your application process.

C H A P T E R 5
SELECTING SCHOOLS

Between late summer and late fall, you will scan Web sites and download files describing each graduate program. You may also spend time e-mailing a letter similar to the one displayed in Figure 4-1 to a number of graduate programs for information. You are ahead of the game if you begin during late summer, because most applicants will not be starting this process for another 2 to 3 months. This is an opportunity for you to leverage an early start to set yourself apart as an organized and optimal candidate.

When applying for undergraduate study, you probably visited a few colleges to help you decide where to apply. When applying for graduate study, by contrast, visits are rare—at least until you are invited for an interview. The exception may be when you live close to a graduate school of special interest. But otherwise, you will only visit doctoral programs "virtually" through online descriptions until invited for a pre-admission interview.

In order to select programs that best suit your needs and interests, we again return to the questions: What is it I want for myself? What is it I'm interested in doing? And where do I want to do it? A firm commitment to a single practice interest, research area, geographic location, or theoretical orientation is not required at this time; however, the more specific your interests, the more intelligent a choice you are going to make.

In the previous chapter we helped you get started narrowing your choices of potential graduate programs. We did so by identifying your interests, comparing your credentials to those required by graduate programs of interest, and by searching for potential matches with the offerings of graduate programs. In this chapter we will help you by reviewing six critical variables to take into account in narrowing your choices: research interests, clinical opportunities, theoretical orientations, financial aid, program outcomes, and quality of life.

A Multitude of Considerations

Each graduate school applicant is undeniably unique in his or her reasons for applying to particular programs in clinical or counseling psychology. As we advise students and conduct workshops on graduate school admission, we hear a litany of restrictions: "I have to stay close to my spouse in Los Angeles," "It must be a Catholic school," "I can only attend if I receive full financial aid," "The program needs to be gay friendly, or have gay faculty mentors," "I am interested solely in cognitive-behavioral programs," "I would really like to be near the mountains," "The program must have lots of women faculty," and so on. There is obviously no single, definitive list of factors to consider in selecting potential schools. Although we will examine in some detail the six most common considerations, we will be unable to canvass the almost infinite range of reasons for selecting programs to which to apply.

In an ideal world, graduate student aspirants would have sufficient funds and freedom to consider any clinical or counseling psychology program in the country. In the real world, however, you may be limited in your choice by financial, family, and geographic considerations. Although we appreciate these real constraints, we encourage you not to be prematurely limited by your own vision. Try to think broadly and boldly. It is, quite simply, your career at stake.

Geographic location will be a determining factor for some applicants. By this we mean both the area of the country and proximity to significant others in your life, such as parents, spouses/partners, siblings, or lovers. If you do not possess the mobility to relocate to another area of the country, then you might delay applying until your situation changes or apply only to regional schools, even if they are less desirable. Don't spend time, money, and energy on futile missions, in this case applying to programs you will be unable to attend.

At the same time, we heartily encourage you to "get out of town." Far too often students restrict themselves unnecessarily to schools close to their homes or to their undergraduate institution. Yet, graduate programs that better match their needs may be located across the country or four states south. Your future demands that you look around the entire country and Canada.

The gender, ethnicity, or sexual orientation composition of programs may be an influential factor for other applicants. If this is the case for you, obtain updated resource directories from the American Psychological Association and apply accordingly. Three examples are APA's *Graduate Faculty Interested in the Psychology of Women* (http://forms.apa.org/pi/women/gradsearch/), *Directory of Ethnic Minority Professionals in Psychology* (www.apa.org/pubs/books/4070873.aspx), and *Graduate Faculty Interested in Gay, Lesbian, and Bisexual Issues in Psychology* (www.apa.org/pi/lgbt/resources/survey/q6-7-table.pdf). The Reports on Individual Programs also present the percentage of ethnic minority, international, and women students in each clinical, counseling, and combined psychology program. These can be a useful source of direction in your choice.

Our general point is this: think through your personal criteria for applying to certain programs and then proactively secure information about those criteria. Even if your choice of programs is limited, make it an informed choice. Accept as you must the restrictions in the range of potential graduate schools, but do not leave your future to chance!

Research Interests

The Web site for most programs will include a list of psychology faculty members in that department and their current research. You are looking to learn something from the faculty, so our advice is to locate the professors who are experts in your areas of interest. If you are interested in clinical child or pediatric psychology, locate those psychologists active in training and research in that field. If you are interested in clinical health psychology, find the researchers or clinicians tackling that subject. Scan the faculty member's Web page, or the description provided by the department. Read their descriptions carefully. What kind of questions are they asking? Have you asked yourself those same questions? Is this the sort of thing you can envision yourself exploring? Have you read a sample of what they have written?

In selecting professors whose interests parallel your own, you are searching for a good *match*. You are looking for mentors—psychologists who will take you on as an apprentice and teach you about your chosen profession. Indeed, the admission system for virtually all research-oriented Ph.D. programs is explicitly mentor-based: Students are chosen for their interest in working, at least initially, with an individual faculty mentor with a shared research interest.

The more similar your views are, the better the match. For example, if you are practice oriented, psychodynamically disposed, and interested in private practice, you might choose to cross off your list a program with professors who operate exclusively from behavioral orientations and research perspectives. This does not mean your interest has to be pinpoint focused. Knowing you would rather investigate or treat psychodynamically may be enough to narrow your list of schools down to a sufficient range. But it is our experience that the more focused you are, the better fit you will find.

As you review the faculty list and other materials, you should begin to get a sense of whom you would like to work with, and who is going to have the facilities to allow you to research or treat the population in which you are interested. Eventually you should have a list of 10 to 20 programs that have faculty with whom you would like to work and a general idea of what each of them does.

Having created such a list of programs, we suggest that you review the recent articles or books that these professors have written. Most Web sites include a list of each faculty member's recent publications. So examine their bibliographies online, inspect the program homepage, or search the *Psychological Abstracts* on *PsycLIT* for the last 5 to 7 years to locate some recent publications. Then go online and look them up. What methods do they use? What are the specifics of their treatment or research that hold your attention? If you notice yourself quickly getting bored or saying, "So what? OK, so alcoholics tend to smoke more? Who cares?", then you have a valuable piece of information. If you find these articles interesting, you are on the right track. This is a time to get excited about your profession and where you want to attend graduate school!

Here are some additional bits of information you can gather to whittle down your number of applications in terms of research interests. Consult (1) the data in the Reports on Individual Programs in this book, (2) the program's Web page, (3) correspondence with faculty, (4) interviews with professors and/or graduate students at your own school about the programs in question, and (5) the CUR Registry of Undergraduate Researchers and Graduate Schools (at www.cur.org/UGRegistryselect.html). The latter links undergraduate students who have research experience with graduate programs interested in recruiting such students. Get the necessary information and corroborate it, if possible.

When it comes to your research interests, discover if there are medical school or science facilities at your disposal. Library facilities should be a prime consideration, but we have found that medical libraries in particular contain journals and books not usually available elsewhere. More importantly, access to journals online through university computer facilities is essential. An associated medical school or hospital may also offer facilities and populations available for your research. Determine if they are present, and then investigate their relationship to the Psychology Department. In addition, learn more about the research space dedicated to your area. For example, does someone have the equipment you need, lab or research space, funding? If you desire to conduct research in cardiovascular psychophysiology and you have found a professor who has published several articles, determine if he or she has equipment to monitor cardiac responses. If not, there should be equipment available somewhere in the department [or in certain cases (e.g., neuroimaging or genotyping research), there should be resources available somewhere in the university].

We realize that this process requires a great deal of time and energy. It may also provoke anxiety in an already nerve-wracking application process. This is one reason why we advocate an early start. Again, we would emphasize that you can get into a graduate program without doing this extra work. This preparation, however, will give you the edge to get into the program of your choice or to overcome weaknesses in your application.

Clinical Opportunities

Having read articles, chapters, or book by the professors with whom you would like to work, you know better which ones you find interesting. However, if your career interest is primarily practice, it is possible you might determine that the person you're most interested in working with does not have recent publications in your area(s) of interest. Or you know a program has a substance abuse clinic, but you can't figure out which professors treat clients or supervise students there. Your first recourse should be to search the university's Web site to try to locate this information. If it is not on the psychology program's Web page, it may exist somewhere else within the university's Web site. If all else fails, email the department coordinator and ask this person for materials specific to the clinic you would like to work in, or ask to speak with the director of that clinic to determine which faculty are practicing there.

Now, we are going to suggest something that we have found to be powerful in making final decisions about where to apply and of increasing your chances of being accepted there. During early fall of the year you apply, contact a *few* of the professors you have been investigating. E-mail the ones whose interests seem most closely aligned to your own. Practically all program Web sites include faculty e-mail addresses.

There are many reasons to directly contact a faculty member. First, it gives you an opportunity to gain information you probably could not gather in any other way—information about the program, its facilities, and its faculty. Second, these e-mails give you a chance to get to know someone you are genuinely interested in working with. It gives you an opportunity to evaluate how happy you would be in a mentorship with this faculty member. Of course, there must be aspects of this person's research or clinical work that attract you. If you do not know his or her interests or the literature well enough to demonstrate a working knowledge of the individual's contributions, do *not* write to him or her. Professors routinely receive letters from people looking to make contact, and unless you can pique their interest and demonstrate familiarity with their work, you are unlikely to receive a response.

Whether your interests are oriented toward research, practice, or both, you are not looking to take this person, or his or her field, by storm. You seek to make a contribution in this particular area, a contribution made *after* you have taken the time to learn and gain experience under their mentorship.

Or, you are looking to gain experience and clinical training with an experienced practitioner.

Take a moment to look at this relationship from the professor's perspective. If she is a researcher, then she is looking for students to help with that research, for students with the knowledge and drive to help design and run studies. If she is a clinician, then she is looking for individuals eager for supervision who will be able to carry a client load. And that is what you have to offer. You are looking for the best fit between your interests and a program and its faculty.

Contacting a professor is not a necessity. Many students are admitted to excellent programs and then take 1 or 2 years to explore, to figure out what they want and where they fit in. In fact, some programs require students to work with several professors during their initial year before selecting an adviser. Nonetheless, it is to your advantage to spend sufficient time deciding which professors would be best suited for you. Locate programs and professors who seem appropriate; then go ahead and contact a few of them to test the waters.

Figures 5-1 and 5-2 show sample e-mail letters of introduction, the former for research-oriented applicants and the latter for practice oriented. *These are not forms to copy in which you simply insert your own words!* You may want to show a draft of your letter to a mentor to preview how well it is likely to be received. When these emails are professional and succinct, they are generally well-received by potential professors. According to our own students, approximately 75% of these emails receive a response, most within three or four days.

But let us forcefully reiterate the caveats about sending letters of introduction. Do *not* send a formulaic letter; it must be tailored to the faculty member. Do *not* send an email inquiring if the faculty member is accepting new students until you have searched his or her Web site for that information. Do *not* ask

---

September 3, 2012

Dear Dr. Morris:

I am a psychology senior at Babylon University, where I have been working with Dr. Frances Murrow, studying the effects of self-esteem on math anxiety. As I was searching the literature, I read several of your articles concerning the use of relaxation techniques to improve self-esteem and test anxiety.

After reading your article "The Uses of Relaxation in Schools" (December 2010 issue of *School Psychology*), I have a question I hoped you could answer. We used several of the questionnaires that you used in that study. In looking at our data, we have found that participants responded quite differently to the Test Anxiety Questionnaire at various times in the semester. We found that the further into the semester students progressed, the more their anxiety affected their scores. Have you also found this to be true in your research?

On a related matter, I will soon be applying to clinical psychology doctoral programs that offer research experience in anxiety. I read on your program's website that you are taking on new graduate students. I hope to get the chance to meet with you in the future.

Thank you for your time and consideration. I look forward to hearing from you.

Sincerely yours,

Chris Smith

FIGURE 5-1. Sample e-mail of introduction—research oriented.

September 3, 2012

Dear Dr. Morris:

I am a psychology senior at Babylon University, where I recently completed an upper-level course in clinical/counseling psychology. My professor, Dr. Frances Ellis, discussed your social problem-solving program targeted to elementary school children. Dr. Ellis spoke highly about the manner in which you use your clinical findings to derive theoretical models of problem solving and use these models to guide your treatment.

I am interested in learning more about school-based social problem-solving programs. I have been involved in such a project with Dr. Ellis and wish to continue my education in this area. I am preparing applications for Psy.D. programs and would like to learn more about your particular program. Specifically, what opportunities exist for clinical Psy.D. students to work on your social problem-solving program? I would like to help train teachers in imparting social problem-solving skills to students.

I would appreciate any materials that you could send me describing your problem-solving program in greater detail. I am especially interested in the role for Psy.D. students. Thank you for your time and consideration.

Sincerely yours,

Chris Smith

FIGURE 5-2. Sample e-mail of introduction—practice oriented.

about a faculty member's research or clinical inter-ests; those are presented on the Web site. Do *not* email a request to speak with a professor or a grad student before applying; they will contact you if you rise to their finalist pool. Any of these silly mistakes will probably place you on the professor's reject list.

Asking a busy professor to stop what she is doing to send you a letter describing future research direc-tions at this early stage in the process risks irritating her. Indeed, one of the authors was told by a promi-nent faculty member that students who send him a request to elaborate on his current or future research before applying usually are not invited to interview! Keep in mind that even the busiest faculty members are motivated to review the promising graduate appli-cations, and if you are in the mix, there will be ample opportunity to ask your questions as the application process moves along.

Some students have asked whether it is accept-able to send letters to more than one faculty member at the same program. Despite the fact that applicants

may have multiple research and clinical interests, most faculty (ourselves included) have a negative reaction to learning that the same person has written to more than one faculty member. Remember, there is a certain amount of self-interest involved: We're looking for bright, motivated students to collaborate in research and practice. It can be awkward when an admissions committee is discussing an applicant, and two faculty express a desire to work with him/her, only to discover that the applicant has been actively expressing interest in *both* of them. Our advice: Unless a few faculty members share highly overlap-ping research interests, don't write to more than one faculty member in any one graduate program. If you do write to more than one, be open about it in your letters.

What if the professor does not respond within a few weeks? Absence of a response does not mean that you will not be able to work with that individual if you are accepted. Most likely the professor received too many queries to respond. Indeed, at some schools, professors are receiving dozens of e-mails during the months leading up to the application deadline. Later, when your application is reviewed, your e-mail may be read.

If the selected professor does write back, then it may be the beginning of a working relationship. Even if you are not accepted to his or her program or ultimately decide not to attend, you are making professional contacts in your field. There is no guideline as to exactly how to behave from here, since each professor is different. But you should begin getting a sense of whether this is the right person (and program) for you.

If the task of introducing yourself to a professor "cold" seems overly daunting, consider alternatives. Local and regional conferences present prime opportunities for meeting potential mentors and gathering information about graduate programs. Numerous societies hold yearly conferences in which research is presented in specialty areas of psychology. For example, if one of your interests lies in health psychology or behavioral medicine, there is the Society for Behavioral Medicine, the American Psychosomatic Society, and the Society for Psychophysiological Research. If, for another example, your interests lie in psychotherapy, there are the annual conferences of the Society for Psychotherapy Research, the APA Division of Psychotherapy, and the Society for the Exploration of Psychotherapy Integration. Your psychology advisor can probably suggest several societies in each area of psychology.

Student membership in a scientific society brings a number of benefits. For beginners, it will probably provide you access to a directory of members (including contact information), which is an easy way of quickly ascertaining who is doing research in your area. Most scientific organizations will invite you to join their electronic listserve. With membership also typically comes a newsletter or a journal, which can give you a sense of the leaders in the field.

Attending a conference can provide a great deal more information, as we have already emphasized in Chapter 3. If you are interested in particular professors, you may have a chance to see them in action if they are presenting an address or poster. In this way, you can get acquainted with the person and the research without taking the risk of formally introducing yourself. Alternatively, you may approach the professor directly and express your interest in the research or ask your psychology advisor to make the introduction. Many graduate students first met their mentors in these ways.

Try to determine if the department's psychologi-cal clinic serves the surrounding community or only the college community. College students are fine clients with whom to begin, but you will probably desire a greater diversity of populations and disorders. Learn more about the school's affiliated or specialized departmental clinics. Who can work there and when? Who does the supervision? Do you have to be affiliated with a specific professor, or is there a competitive process toward earning that placement? If you're choosing a program in part based on the availability of its clinic, how available will this clinic be to you?

Table 5-1, "Questions to Ask about Psy.D. Programs," contains questions more specific to Psy.D. and practice-oriented Ph.D. applicants. This list was compiled, in part, by surveying the clinical Psy.D. students at the Graduate School of Applied and Professional Psychology at Rutgers University and asking them what questions they had (or wish they had) asked when applying to Psy.D. programs.

Theoretical Orientations

A question related to clinical and research opportunities is whether the graduate program will provide you with training in the desired theoretical orientations. We are *not* recommending that you prematurely affiliate with any theoretical camp; rather, we suggest that you identify those orientations you are interested in learning more about and those you are not. Several programs in the Northeast are strongly committed to a psychoanalytic approach and offer few, if any, training opportunities beyond that. The obvious implication is to avoid applying to programs that will not offer supervised experience in your theoretical approach(es). By the same token, you may scratch programs from your preliminary list that rigidly adhere to, say, a behavioral persuasion if you are disinclined toward behaviorism.

The Reports on Individual Programs provide the approximate percentage of faculty in each program who subscribe to the five most popular theoretical orientations—psychodynamic/psychoanalytic, behavioral analysis/radical behavioral, family systems/systems, existential/phenomenological/humanistic, and cognitive/cognitive-behavioral. Let these figures guide you in ruling out a few programs that fail to address your theoretical predilections or, if you are uncommitted, that neglect exposure to multiple or integrative approaches.

Table 5-2 presents the average percentage of faculty endorsing these five theoretical orientations in APA-accredited clinical and counseling programs.

TABLE 5-1. Questions to Ask about Psy.D. Programs

Is the Psy.D. program freestanding or part of a comprehensive university?

Is the program owned or operated by a for-profit company?

If the program also has a clinical Ph.D. program, are the "best" practicum opportunities available to Psy.D. students or Ph.D. students? Is it possible to take the Ph.D. courses as well? What is the relationship between the Psy.D. and Ph.D. students?

Will the internship occur in the third or fourth year? Do you complete an internship before or after your clinical dissertation?

What percentage of Psy.D. students receive full financial support? What is the annual tuition?

What is the typical debt level of graduating students?

Does the university offer housing for Psy.D. students? If not, how much are the monthly rents locally?

Are there opportunities for live supervision? Do the full-time faculty perform the clinical supervision?

Does the school offer exposure to a variety of theoretical orientations, or is it dominated by one orientation?

Is it possible to gain experience working with . . . ? With families? With groups?

What types of clinical populations are available?

What percentage of the faculty are full-time? What percent are tenured?

Do the faculty have independent practices?

What percentage of first-year students complete the program? How many years does it typically require to complete the program?

What is the size of the incoming class? How many students are in a typical graduate course?

What percentage of students obtain an APA or APPIC-accredited internship?

In general, the cognitive/cognitive-behavioral tradition predominates, accounting for more than half of the faculty members. Radical behaviorism is relatively infrequent, with psychodynamic, systems, and humanistic theories falling in between these two extremes. These global figures do not specifically include the integrative/eclectic orientation, which is the most popular approach of mental health professionals (Norcross & Goldfried, 2005). The fact that the percentages add up to more than 100% indicates that faculty practice across orientations. Note too that the counseling psychology faculty endorse the humanistic/existential orientations much more frequently than do the clinical psychology faculty (28% versus 11%).

These average percentages mask significant differences among programs as a function of their placement along the practice–research continuum. Research-oriented programs, as a rule, have a higher percentage of cognitive-behavioral faculty, while practice-oriented programs have a higher percentage of psychodynamic faculty (Mayne et al., 1994; Sayette et al., 2011). These differences are quite large: Fully 74% of faculty members in research-oriented Ph.D. programs are cognitive-behavioral versus 28% in practice-oriented Psy.D. programs. Only 9% of faculty in research-oriented Ph.D. programs are psychodynamic versus 30% in practice-oriented Psy.D. programs (Norcross et al., 2010).

The upshot is to investigate thoroughly the area

TABLE 5-2. Theoretical Orientations of Faculty in APA-Accredited Clinical and Counseling Psychology Programs

Orientations	% of clinical faculty	% of counseling faculty
Psychodynamic/Psychoanalytic	19	19
Applied behavioral analysis/Radical behavioral	9	13
Family systems/Systems	20	21
Existential/Phenomenological/Humanistic	11	28
Cognitive/Cognitive-behavioral	60	43

Note. Data from Norcross, Ellis, & Sayette (2010) and Norcross, Evans, & Ellis (2010).

of psychology (clinical, counseling) and the type of program (practice-oriented to research-oriented) that regularly provide training in your preferred theoretical orientation(s).

In addition to reviewing the percentages of faculty theoretical orientations in the Reports on Individual Programs, those of you with an intense hankering for training in a particular theoretical orientation may want to peruse specialty directories. A number of professional societies maintain or publish lists of graduate programs that offer training in their theory of choice. The Association for Behavioral and Cognitive Therapies (ABCT), for example, publishes a directory of graduate programs in behavior therapy and experimental clinical psychology (www.aabt.org). The Society for the Exploration of Psychotherapy Integration (SEPI), for another example, has pulled together a list of integrative and eclectic training programs throughout North America (visit http://sepiweb.org/, Norcross & Kaplan, 1995). The APA Division of Humanistic Psychology, for a final example, cosponsors a directory of graduate programs in humanistic and transpersonal psychology (visit www.westga.edu/~psydept/humanisticdirectory). Consult your advisors regarding the existence of specialty directories in your field of interest.

The popularity of theories, as with other professional fads, undergoes transformation over time. Extrapolating from historical trends and expert predictions (Norcross, Hedges, & Prochaska, 2002), cognitive-behavioral, eclectic/integrative, family systems, and multicultural theories will be in the ascendancy in the future. By contrast, classical psychoanalysis, humanistic theories, and existentialism are expected to decline. In an era of managed care, theoretical orientations that emphasize brief problem-focused treatments and document their effectiveness will probably thrive.

Financial Aid

The next question, and it is by no means premature, is the availability of financial aid. Unless you can afford to pay for graduate school on your own or you are prepared to take out substantial loans, you require some idea of the probability of support from the graduate program. This is not a suggestion to avoid schools with scarce financial aid. It is a suggestion not to apply only to schools with scarce financial aid.

APA's (2002) *Ethical Principles of Psychologists and Code of Conduct* requires truth in advertising about graduate programs. Standard 7.02 (Description

of Programs) stipulates that "Psychologists responsible for education and training programs take reasonable steps to ensure that there is a current and accurate description of program content . . . stipends and benefits, and requirements that must be met for satisfactory completion of the program. This information must be made readily available to all interested parties." Not only is it your perfect right to request such information, but it is also the ethical obligation of the graduate psychology program to provide it.

Until quite recently, only a minority of psychology doctoral programs were fully disclosing all of the information requested by the APA Commission on Accreditation (Burgess, Keeley, & Blashfield, 2008). But the APA recently required accredited doctoral programs to publicly post on their Web sites their education outcomes and financial costs to allow for informed decision-making among prospective students. We will discuss where this information is posted and how to access in the next section. For now, please know that a prime objective of this *Insider's Guide* is to present financial aid information in our Reports on Individual Programs.

Figuring the total cost of full-time graduate study must include both academic expenses and living expenses. The academic side includes tuition, fees, supplies, books, and journals. Full-time tuition ranges from a low of $8,000 a year for some in-state Ph.D. students to $25,000 for private, Psy.D. programs. Multiplying the tuition by 4 years gives you some idea of the probable tuition burden. The living side includes rent, transportation, food, clothing, insurance, and entertainment. Health insurance has emerged as a large part of the cost of graduate studies. Some assistantships include health insurance, but others do not. Not surprisingly, most graduate students are relatively poor; at least you will have company in your financial misery (Fretz & Stang, 1980).

Determine the availability of teaching assistantships and research assistantships from the program's home page and the Reports on Individual Programs. In particular, determine the percentage of first-year students who receive assistantships. Is it 100%, 50%, or 0%? Do the assistantships include health insurance? If not, you will either go without insurance or purchase it on your own.

On average, 57% of full-time doctoral students in psychology receive some financial support from the program; the remaining 43% do not. The picture is less encouraging for full-time master's students in psychology: only 23% receive any support (Gehlman, Wicherski, & Kohout, 1995). As you can see, the probability of financial support from the program itself is a very salient consideration in narrowing your choices.

Be wary of online descriptions of doctoral programs that simply declare "all incoming students receive financial aid" unless that same description provides the sources of the aid and the typical monetary stipend. We are aware of several psychology programs that automatically award "fellowships" to every student in the amount of $1,000 but then immediately charge over $20,000 annual tuition! Hence, we have begun to use the phrase *full assistantship* in our Reports on Individual Programs.

These reports provide the percentages of incoming doctoral students who receive full tuition waiver only, full assistantship/fellowship only, and both tuition waiver *and* assistantship for each doctoral program.

Table 5-3 summarizes these data across the practice–research continuum for APA-accredited clinical psychology programs. The continuum moves from the freestanding Psy.D. programs on one end, through the equal-emphasis Ph.D. programs in the middle, to the research-oriented Ph.D. programs on the other end. As seen there, the probability of receiving financial assistance in graduate school is a direct function of the type of program (Norcross et al., 2010). Only 1 to 10% of Psy.D. students, on average, will receive both a tuition waiver and a full assistantship, compared to 89% of students in research-oriented Ph.D. programs in clinical psychology. You don't need to perform a *t* test; that is a large, significant difference. Indeed, the gap in funding between freestanding Psy.D. programs and research-oriented Ph.D. programs seems to be expanding. The equal-emphasis Ph.D. programs tend to fall in between; about 54% of their students receive both a tuition waiver and a full assistantship.

Figure 5-3 graphically illustrates the probability of getting in (acceptance rates) and getting money (percentage of students receiving full support) across the various types of APA-accredited clinical psychology programs. The two graphs demonstrate that higher acceptance rates come at a (tuition and living) cost to the incoming student. More rigorous admission standards and acceptance odds translate into increased probability of substantial financial aid (Kohout, Wicherski, & Pion, 1991; Mayne et al., 1994). In the most extreme comparison, freestanding Psy.D. students are 7 times more likely to gain admission but 50 times less likely to receive full funding (stipend plus tuition waiver) than are students in research-oriented Ph.D. programs (Norcross et al., 2010). An awareness of these trade-offs among the different types of programs will enable you to make informed choices regarding your graduate applications and career trajectories.

There *is* financial aid available from graduate schools to students possessing sterling credentials, and we wish to reaffirm its existence. Nevertheless, the increasing number of acceptances into clinical and counseling psychology doctoral programs during a period of economic downsizing raises difficult questions about internal funding opportunities and federal financial assistance. Our findings (Norcross et al., 2004) on financial aid portend a "pay as you go" expectation for half of all doctoral candidates in clinical and counseling psychology. This is particularly true, as we have seen, in Psy.D. programs. The explicit expectation, as is true in such other practice disciplines as medicine and law, is that graduates will be able to repay their debt after they are engaged in full-time practice. We should note, however, that uncertainties regarding health care—specifically changes in insurance coverage for mental health—in the United States make this expectation difficult to evaluate at the present time.

The debt may be substantial. Research indicates that 77% of recent graduates in clinical and counseling psychology are saddled with debt related to graduate studies (over and above any debt associated with their undergraduate education; Pate & Finno, 2009). Graduates of Psy.D. programs report a median

TABLE 5-3. Percentage of Students Receiving Financial Aid in APA-Accredited Clinical Psychology Programs

	Free-standing Psy.D.	University-based Psy.D.	Equal-emphasis Ph.D.	Research-oriented Ph.D.
Tuition waiver only	0%	1%	3%	0%
Assistantship only	13%	21%	20%	8%
Waiver and assistantship	1%	10%	54%	89%

Note. Data from Norcross, Ellis, & Sayette (2010).

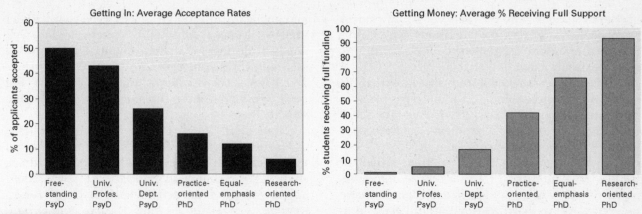

FIGURE 5-3. Getting in and getting money in various types of clinical psychology programs.

debt of $90,000 (Pate & Finno, 2009). In fact, about one-third of recent Psy.D. graduates report more than $120,000 of graduate school debt. The median debt for clinical Ph.D. graduates is $45,000, lower but still substantial.

Figure 5-4 presents the amount of graduate-school debt separately for recent clinical Ph.D. and Psy.D. recipients. These data are based on the *2007 Doctorate Employment Survey* conducted by the APA Center for Workforce Studies (2009).

With a median starting salary of approximately

$60,000 for new psychology doctorates (Pate & Finno, 2009), this debt represents a heavy financial burden for many years. (Go to the Loan Repayment Calculator at www.finaid.org/calculators/ for a sobering look at repayment schedules.)

In large part, the difference in debt between Psy.D.s and Ph.D.s is attributable to the huge differences in financial aid between Vail-model and Boulder-model programs as pictured in Table 5-3. The APA researchers who compiled the debt figures conclude, "It is important to disseminate this infor-

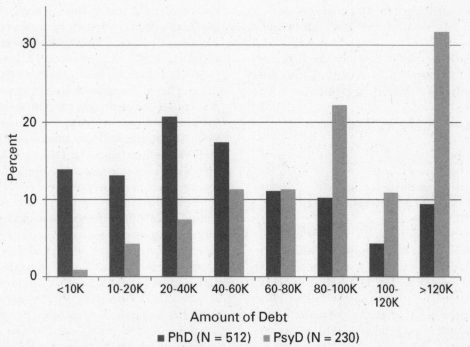

FIGURE 5-4. Amount of graduate debt for recent clinical Ph.D. and Psy.D. recipients.
Source: Doctorate Employment Survey (APA Center for Workforce Studies, 2009)

mation to students who may be considering a career in psychology—so that their decisions can be fully informed" (Kohout & Wicherski, 1999, p. 10). We wholeheartedly agree.

In fact, we conducted a study that looked at the financial assistance offered by various types of Psy.D. programs (Norcross et al., 2004). You may recall from Chapter 2 that Psy.D. programs can be housed in three different settings: (1) in a university's Psychology Department; (2) as a separate school or institute in a university; (3) as a private, freestanding institution without affiliation to a comprehensive university. As you have already learned, Psy.D. programs give proportionally less financial assistance to students than Ph.D. programs. But it gets a bit more complicated because not all Psy.D. programs provide similar amounts of financial assistance. An average of 14% of incoming Psy.D. students to a freestanding program will receive *any* financial support from the program and only 1% of incoming students will receive a full boat (tuition remission plus full assistantship). By contrast, an average of 32% of incoming Psy.D. students to a Psychology Department program will receive some financial support and 10% of incoming students a full boat (see Table 5-3). That's a whopping difference. If you require considerable financial assistance directly from the graduate program, then do not apply to the freestanding Psy.D. programs. Your best bet, financially speaking, will be the university-affiliated Psy.D. programs and, of course, the equal-emphasis and research-oriented Ph.D. programs.

How do students cobble together the necessary funds to pay for doctoral study in clinical and counseling psychology? By a mixture of means:

- university-provided financial assistance
- personal savings
- family support
- graduate school loans
- earnings during graduate school
- federal fellowships or traineeships

Many universities provide Web pages on these sources of funding graduate school. In addition to general information, they often list school- or program-specific scholarships and fellowships available to incoming students. It is worth the added effort to examine the financial aid pages at each school to search for scholarship programs for which you may be eligible.

In addition to aid provided by the school itself, financial assistance is available from external private and public organizations. This funding comes under various names—self-sought, external, independent—to distinguish it from financial aid provided internally by the university. A variety of scholarships and fellowships is offered annually, but you will need to research those that pertain to your circumstances.

Your local Office of Career Services and Office of Financial Assistance should be able to direct you to potential sources of external support for graduate studies. We recommend Princeton Review's (2005) *Paying for Graduate School Without Going Broke*. Another very useful resource is *Financing Graduate School*, a compact paperback authored by Patricia McWade (1996). The subtitle captures the centrality of the topic—*How to Get the Money for Your Master's or Ph.D.* These two books transverse the entire geography of financial aid—grant applications, loan possibilities, federal and state support, and other sources of money for graduate study.

Peterson also offers a free online cram course in financial aid at www.petersons.com/gradchannel/file. asp?id=1080&path=gr.pfs.overview. Be sure to check out the loads of advice and searchable databases on line at www.finaid.com and at www.studentaid. ed.gov/PORTALSWebApp/students/english/gradstudent.jsp.

Federal funding is also available for psychology graduate students, either in the form of training and research grants to institutions, which then fund graduate assistantships, or in the form of fellowships and dissertation grants awarded directly to students (Bullock, 1997). The National Science Foundation (NSF), for example, funds Minority Graduate Fellowships. The National Institutes of Health (NIH) fund psychology student awards through the National Institute of Mental Health, the National Institute on Drug Abuse, the National Institute on Alcohol Abuse and Alcoholism, and the Office of AIDS Research. Check out these programs through their Web pages: www.nsf.gov and www.nih.gov.

Several funding directories are available free of charge from philanthropic and professional organizations. Among the more prestigious (and therefore, more competitive) are the predoctoral fellowships sponsored by the Danforth Foundation, Ford Foundation, and Armed Forces Health Professions Scholarship. The American Psychological Association publishes a searchable database *Directory of Selected Scholarship, Fellowship, and Other Financial Aid Opportunities for Women and Ethnic Minorities in Psychology*, which we highly recommend (www.apa. org/about/awards/index.aspx). The APA Minority Fellowship Program is online at www.apa.org/pi/mfp. APA offers an online list of resources for financial assistance at www.apa.org/ppo/funding/.

As you can anticipate, the Web has literally exploded with interactive sites devoted to securing financial assistance for graduate school. Many of these are useful and recommended, but be wary of and avoid those that charge you for their services. In addition to the APA sites listed above, we would suggest you visit:

- www.gradview.com/financialaid/
- www.scholarships.com
- www.petersons.com/finaid/
- www.finaid.org/otheraid
- collegeapps.about.com/

Explore all these possibilities early and actively.

Student loans are also available for graduate students, but these are monies that must be repaid. The Federal Family Education Loan (FFEL) Program and the William D. Ford Federal Direct Loan (Direct Loan) Program, generally known as Stafford Loans, are available to assist graduate and professional students. Students may borrow up to $8,500 per academic year through the subsidized Stafford Loan. The interest on these loans is subsidized by the federal government and repayment at reasonable interest rates does not begin until 6 months after graduation, or following withdrawal from the program. In addition to this $8,500, up to an additional $12,000 per academic year can be borrowed through the unsubsidized Stafford Loans. The total amount that can be borrowed, including both subsidized and unsubsidized portions, is $20,500 each academic year and $138,500 in total. The in-school interest on the unsubsidized Stafford Loans may be paid quarterly or deferred and repaid when principal repayments begin.

Starting in 2006, the government began offering Graduate PLUS Loans, federally sponsored loans for students attending graduate school at least half time. With a Grad PLUS loan, you may borrow up to the full cost of your education, less other financial aid received including Federal Stafford loans. Graduate students should exhaust their federal Stafford loan eligibility before applying for a Graduate PLUS loan because the Staffords charge lower interest.

Some institutions also award Federal Perkins Loans, a long-term loan program with a 5% interest rate available to graduate students demonstrating financial need. Other state loan programs exist; check these out as well. The bottom line is that every full-time graduate student is eligible for loans to finance his or her education, if necessary.

Speaking of loans reminds us to mention loan repayment options and loan forgiveness programs. We recommend that you visit the U.S. Department of Education Web site, www.ed.gov, which describes student loan types and loan repayment options. Three options that can trim loan payments for graduate students are the graduated repayment plans, income-sensitive repayment plans, and the loan consolidation plans. See the Web site for details, but remember that most student loans only permit a single refinancing or consolidation.

About 30 federal agencies offer loan forgiveness or repayment programs. Clinical and counseling psychologists are eligible for most of these, and we advise you to thoroughly investigate the options. Practitioners working in designated underserved areas as part of the National Health Services Corps (NHSC) are eligible for loan forgiveness (up to $50,000) while receiving a competitive salary. Go to nhsc.bhpr.hrsa.gov for details. Similarly, the NIH Loan Repayment Program will repay up to $35,000 per year in exchange for several years of service. NIH also offers a repayment program for clinical researchers from disadvantaged backgrounds. See www.lrp.nih.gov/ for details. Regularly visit the APA Web site (www.apa.org) for updates on loan forgiveness.

Program Outcomes

The success of a graduate program can be measured in many ways: the knowledge of the graduating students; the quality of the faculty; the careers of the alumni; and so on. As part of their APA accreditation requirements, psychology programs must publicly disclose their education and training outcomes to allow for informed decision-making among prospective students. The required information must all be located in one place on the Web and is frequently entitled *Student Admissions, Outcomes, and Other Data*. These data permit you to directly ascertain several key indicators of a program's success—or *program outcomes*, as they are known in research circles—in selecting graduate programs to which to apply .

Table 5-4 presents the outcomes of the University of Alabama's clinical psychology program for the past seven years in a format prescribed by APA. Similar tables must be available on the Web sites of every APA-accredited program; use our Reports on Individual Programs to find the Web addresses or search for them online. These tables are loaded with

TABLE 5-4. Representative Summary of Education/Training Outcome Data Found on an APA-Accredited Program's Web Site

The following charts contain information about our most recent cohorts of clinical graduate students at the University of Alabama at Tuscaloosa.

Year of entry	2004	2005	2006	2007	2008	2009	2010
Admissions data							
Number of applicants	219	177	171	189	204	191	198
Number accepted for admission	17	17	15	17	23	19	22
Actual size of incoming class	12	12	9	10	16	10	12
Number of incoming students	12	12	9	10	16	10	12
GRE and GPA data	$n = 12$	$n = 12$	$n = 9$	$n = 10$	$n = 16$	$n = 10$	
GRE – Verbal mean score	560	610	600	675	565	620	
GRE – Quantitative mean score	700	660	670	656	680	670	
GRE – Advanced Psy. mean score	640	650	690	676	650	680	
GPA – Average undergraduate	3.8	3.6	3.64	3.6	3.6	3.7	
GPA – Average graduate	*	*	*	3.7	3.9	3.9	
Internship data							
Number of students applying	6	9	14	10	12	11	7
Obtained Internships	6 (100%)	9 (100%)	13 (93%)	9 (90%)	12 (100%)	10 (90%)	7 (100%)
Obtained APPIC member internships	6 (100%)	9 (100%)	13 (93%)	9 (90%)	12 (100%)	10 (90%)	7 (100%)
Obtained APA-accredited internships	6 (100%)	9 (100%)	13 (93%)	9 (90%)	12 (100%)	10 (90%)	7 (100%)

Graduation data

Number of students who took	Total graduates ($N = 67$)	Cumulative
Less than 5 years to complete degree	3 (4%)	3 (4%)
5 years to complete degree	20 (30%)	23 (34%)
6 years to complete degree	26 (39%)	49 (73%)
7 years to complete degree	9 (13%)	58 (87%)
More than 7 years to complete degree	9 (13%)	67 (100%)

Attrition data

Students admitted to the program between 2001 and 2007 = 81

Students who left the program prior to completion of Ph.D. = 6 (7%)

Licensure data

Ph.D. graduates who are currently licensed = 30 (of 34 respondents)

Tuition and fee schedule for graduate students

Full-time rates per semester

Hours	Resident	Nonresident
9–15	$3,950.00	$10,250.00

Enrolled hours over 15 are assessed an overload fee per hour of $305 for graduate residents and $890 for graduate nonresidents.

All students admitted to the clinical program are offered a graduate assistantship, which includes a tuition grant for the academic year.

Note. Adapted with the kind permission of Dr. Beverly E. Thorne, University of Alabama.

valuable information on acceptance rates, GRE and GPA averages, probability of securing an APA-accredited internship, and time to complete the program,. We have compiled most of this information for you in this Insider's Guide, and will walk you through these considerations throughout the book. For now, we direct your attention to three critical measures of program outcome: internship match, attrition rate, and licensure data.

To receive your doctorate in clinical or counseling psychology, you will complete a one-year, full-time internship. The best way to do so is to complete an APA-accredited internship, as many universities, states, and government agencies insist on graduation from both an APA-accredited doctoral program and an APA-accredited internship.

In the past, if you were attending an APA-accredited doctoral program, you would rather easily obtain an APA-accredited internship on match day (when a computer matches applicants to internship sites in February). But in the present, the proliferating number of doctoral programs, particularly large Psy.D. programs, has dramatically increased the number of doctoral students seeking APA-accredited internships. The result is a growing imbalance between the rapidly growing number of internship applicants and the slowly growing number of internship spots. Psy.D. students tend to match at a lower rate than Ph.D. students, in spite of applying to more internship sites than Ph.D. students (Callahan, Collins, & Klonoff, 2010).

In 2011, only 76% of applicants were matched to an internship position on match day. That leaves one-quarter of doctoral psychology students without an APA-accredited internship. That's why it is important for you to select schools that will maximize the probability of you being in that three-quarters, not in that unfortunate one-quarter.

Another index of program quality is the attrition or dropout rate. Doctoral students leave a graduate program prematurely for many reasons, such as pursuing an area other than psychology, health problems, family considerations, financial needs, or program dissatisfaction. But better programs tend to boast higher graduate rates. Be certain that the programs you are considering graduate at least 80% of their students. In other words, avoid any program where 20% or more of its students dropout. That typically spells trouble. The attrition rates during the past 5 years for APA-accredited programs are listed in the respective Reports on Individual Programs as well.

After years of hard work completing a doctoral program and an internship, you naturally expect to pass the national licensure examination in psychology – the Examination for Professional Practice in Psychology (EPPP). But not everyone passes on the first try or even on subsequent tries. If you attend an APA-accredited program, you stand a 77% chance of passing on any single attempt (www.asppb.net). If you attend a non-APA-accredited program, that chance drops to 65%. The better the program, the higher the licensure pass rate.

Thus, as you select potential programs, seriously consider the licensure pass rates of their graduates. These statistics are helpfully presented on the Web site of the Association of State and Provincial Psychology Boards at www.asppb.net. Click on the link for Psychology Licensing Exam Scores by Doctoral Program and you will find a table of pass rate for each program. Graduates of the University of Alabama's clincial program, for example, have recently passed at a 94% clip. That's typical of the smaller, more competitive, Ph.D. programs in the scientist-practitioner (Boulder model) tradition. However, graduates of the less competitive, huge Psy.D. programs, particularly the for-profit institutions, typically score much lower on the EPPP (Graham & Kim, 2011; Templer et al., 2008). Their average licensure pass rates fall in the 55% to 75% range.

One day, while discussing these figures in class, an undergraduate spontaneously yelled, "Why would anyone even THINK about applying to a program where only half the graduates can pass the licensure exam!?" That memorable event led us to formulate the three-quarters rule: Apply only to doctoral programs where three-quarters or more of their students secure an APA-accredited internship, complete their degrees, and pass the licensure examination.

That's our general advice, but you will need to tailor it to your individual situation and goals. On occasion, a couple of our students have entered a doctoral program with an inordinately high attrition rate or a depressingly low licensure pass rate, but they did so with their eyes wide open to the facts. That's precisely our intent in helping you select potential graduate programs: well-informed consumers aware of the facts and the tradeoffs about program outcomes.

Quality of Life

A sixth and final consideration in selecting graduate schools is the quality of student life. It may be difficult to imagine, but occasionally you will want a break from graduate studies, to relax or engage in some nonpsychological pursuit!

You should have a handle on your own needs. Can they be met by the university and surrounding community? Do you want museums, fine dining, and professional theater? Then you probably want to live in or near a city. If not, do you have a car capable of regularly getting you to one? Or do you get away to the mountains, enjoy rock climbing and camping, and find the city distracting? Or do you prefer to work at your office late at night and need a campus that's safe after dark? Then be sure to apply to some rural campuses. Also, consider whether you have friends or family nearby. Having a place to escape to can be important, especially if you do not have the funds to *really* escape. You are not going to base your decisions exclusively on any of these factors. But you can increase the probability of having everything you want by applying to schools you know can provide it all.

The Web is an excellent resource for investigating locations, towns, and cities that are far away and that you may not have the time or finances to visit. Most cities have their own Web pages, which include pictures, maps, lists of attractions, and so on, for potential visitors and residents. Take the time to "virtually" explore the towns and cities of programs on your list. You may find that it is far more (or less) desirable than you had imagined.

The weight accorded to the quality of life in application decisions varies considerably among people. At one extreme are those applicants who give little thought to program location and heavily value the research and clinical opportunities. In the words of one colleague, "I'd live in hell for 4 or 5 years [the time it ordinarily takes to complete a doctorate] to be trained by the best people in my field." At the other extreme are those who will only apply to programs situated near family, friends, or an attractive community. "Five years," they say, "is too long to be away from what I need as a person." We will not be so presumptuous as to advise which position you should adopt for yourself, except to remark that you should carefully weigh personal (location, fit) and professional (reputation, opportunities) considerations.

Putting It All Together

Having seriously reflected on your own interests and having carefully examined the clinical opportunities, research training, theoretical orientations, financial aid, program outcomes, and quality of life of various schools, you are close to completing applications.

Now is the time to put together all the information you have obtained about yourself and graduate programs in the form of a final list of schools—anywhere from 10 to 20, depending on the specificity of your interests and the strength of your credentials. As you make a final list of the applications you are about to complete, make one last check to insure that you are applying to the programs that best fit your needs. You may do this informally by mentally reviewing the program information you have obtained or you may do this systematically by completing Appendix D.

To complete Appendix D, write the name of each graduate program in the first column. In column 2, "School Criteria," write the total you computed for each school in Appendix C. This is an index of your strength as an applicant and should range from about 5 to 15. For each of the next six columns, you can rate your impressions about each program on a 5-point scale. Create these scales in ways that are personally relevant to you. The important thing is to know where each school rates in these areas in terms of your needs and desires. Below are some examples of rating systems you might model your own after.

In the column marked "Research," rate how strongly you feel toward the professors you have singled out as wanting to work with:

1	I do not know enough about them, but their research is in my general interests.
3	I like the specifics of their research but do not know enough about their lab or their personalities.
5	I have been in contact with these professors and am impressed by their facilities and by them personally. I would like to work with them.

In the column marked "Clinical," rate each school according to how its opportunities suit your needs.

1	The school has only a psychological training clinic that treats students, and I want more experience.
3	The school has a fine psychological training clinic, but it has no practica in the community, and getting various populations may be difficult.
5	The school has many excellent clinical opportunities, including a specialty (e.g., eating disorders) clinic or track in my area of interest.

Or, possibly:

1   The school requires students to find their own clinical placements in the community, and I don't like that system.

3   The school has a college counseling center, but I'm not interested in working only with college students.

5   The school has an excellent psychological services clinic, and that's all I need.

"Theoretical Orientation" is the following column:

1   The program avers strict adherence to, and training in, a theoretical orientation that is in contrast to mine.

3   The program offers some courses and supervision in my preferred theoretical orientation.

5   The program provides considerable training in my preferred theoretical orientation plus other opportunities.

Next, consider "Financial Aid":

1   There is no funding for first-year students and no mention of outside means of support, and I need it.

3   I am likely to get at least tuition remission and have the possibility of working part-time for the university. It is likely that I could be a resident advisor and get free housing.

5   For the last 5 years, all first-year students have gotten full stipends and full tuition remission.

Or, possibly:

1   There is no funding for first-year students and no mention of outside means of support.

3   I am likely to get at least tuition remission, though only for the first 2 years.

5   The school guarantees tuition remission for 4 years, and that's all I need.

Under the column marked "Program Outcomes," rate each program on its record of internship match, attrition rate, and licensure pass-rates. For example:

1   This program matches less than 50% of its students with APA-accredited internships

and less than three-quarters of their students pass the licensure exam.

3   This program reports a reasonable attrition rate and about three-quarters of its student match with an APA-accredited internship.

5   This program has a consistent track record of high student success in matching to APA-accredited internships and passing the licensure exam.

And last, rate the "Quality of Life":

1   This program is located in an unattractive area and seems bereft of culture.

3   I am indifferent to the location, and there is culture within the college community.

5   The area is ideal for me, and there are museums, concert halls, and theaters nearby.

Or, possibly:

1   This university is located in an unsafe section of a large city where I don't know anyone.

3   This university is located in a small city, and a friend of mine also attends.

5   This university is located in a small college town, and I have several close relatives and friends there.

Look at your list. Are you applying to programs within a realistic range of admission criteria? Are you applying to at least some programs where you like the faculty, where the clinical facilities are suitable, where the theoretical orientation is compatible, where the program outcomes exceed the three-quarters rule, where financial aid is available, and where you will feel comfortable living? If the answer to all of these is "No," then go back a step. Find at least a few graduate programs where these qualities are present, possibly in abundance, and add them to your list of applications.

"What," you might reasonably ask, "are acceptable ratings in Appendix D for the program outcomes?" Our threshold of quality is expressed in the three-quarters rule (at least three-quarters of the students complete the program, secure an APA-accredited internship, and pass the licensure exam). But you may need to relax this rule if your credentials are a bit weak or if you are applying to a limited number of schools. However you define quality, we implore you not to consider or apply to any programs below your personal line of acceptability. You owe it to yourself and to your future career.

Before moving on to the next chapter of this Insider's Guide and the next step in the application process, take one final moment to celebrate. You deserve it! You have learned much about graduate training in clinical and counseling psychology, inves-

tigated potential graduate programs, assessed your match with those programs, and whittled down your final list. You have already mastered challenges more intense than those associated with many college courses. So, after weeks of arduous and sometimes anxious work, you deserve affirmation and reward. Give them to yourself or, at least, allow us to affirm and reward you from afar.

C H A P T E R   6
APPLYING TO PROGRAMS

You are ready to start completing the applications. You have assessed your interests and have located programs that provide the training and mentorship you desire. You have evaluated your own credentials and have chosen programs that will consider you seriously. You have received applications from these programs by downloading their materials. You have carefully looked at their research offerings, clinical opportunities, theoretical orientations, financial aid, program quality, quality of life, and other variables of importance to you. Your task now is to actually apply to these graduate programs.

You should attack this application process with all the drive and commitment you can muster. The rewards of applying are typically in direct proportion to your exertion. Try to emulate the manic zeal of successful medical school applicants. As they will readily inform you, the application itself reflects directly on your potential as a graduate student. In a real sense, your professional future is at stake.

The "application year," as it is known, will probably be intense. We suggest that you take a lighter course load or work schedule during the fall of your application year. Completing applications, securing letters of recommendation, and writing personal statements constitute more work than a typical college course. We also suggest that you inform friends and family members that you will be more preoccupied and distracted than usual. Position yourself for a busy fall.

A completed application will typically consist of the following elements: application form, curriculum vitae, personal statement, letters of recommenda-

tion, transcripts, entrance examination scores, and an application fee. In this chapter, we trace the requisite steps of compiling, completing, and transmitting these materials in a coordinated fashion. But before we address the nuts and bolts of doing so, let us touch upon the crucial question of how many programs to apply to.

How Many?

The average number of applications made by students to clinical and counseling psychology programs is about 10. The precise number to which you should apply depends on the strength of your credentials and the competitiveness of the prospective programs; more applications are indicated for weaker credentials and more competitive programs.

Our rule of thumb is to apply to *at least* 10 to 12 programs: five "safe" (you clearly meet or exceed their standards); five "target" or "ambitious" programs (your credentials just make or miss their requirements); and perhaps one or two "reach" or "stretch" programs (where you do not approximate their standards but you have a particular hunch, research compatibility, or personal relationship that has a chance of sweeping you into the finalist pool). We have met industrious students who have applied to over 40 programs and confident students who have applied to just four or five.

But don't pull a Missar, as we say at the University of Scranton. David Missar was an exceptional undergraduate and good-humored fellow (who gave us permission to use his story as a lesson for others to learn). He had a sky-high GPA, impressive GREs, a practicum to his credit, and even a coauthored publication. He was feeling a bit too confident in applying to only four doctoral programs, all located around his home town of Washington, DC, which happens to host some of the most competitive programs in the country. Despite his stellar academic credentials, Dave did not receive any acceptances his first year simply because his research interests and strengths did not match those of the clinical faculty and institutions to which he applied. Had he applied to a greater number or a larger variety of programs, he surely would have been accepted somewhere, as he was easily the next year when he corrected his miscalculations.

Web Self-Audit

For all of its wonders, the Web presents ample opportunities for mischief and an anti-professional impression. Photographs of your high-jinks and drinking games on Facebook may entertain fellow students, but probably not the director of clinical training. Cute e-mail addresses, such as bongmeister@gmail. com or hotchick@aol.com, may delight romantic partners, but certainly not the dean of the graduate school.

Before you complete any application is the time to conduct a Web self-audit to assess and probably enhance your internet and telephone presence so that it conveys a professional demeanor. More than one-quarter of employers research potential job candidates on the Web (National Association of Colleges and Employers, 2007), and that number is growing. We know for a fact that many members of graduate admission committees do likewise.

Here's a self-audit checklist used by several career service offices:

- email address: Is it professional and permanent?
- Google yourself: Are you satisfied with what you found?
- social networking site (e.g., Facebook, MySpace): Are your comfortable if a potential graduate mentor were to view your profile, pictures, groups, and friends' comments?
- personal Web site or blog: Does it follow the rule of "if you wouldn't want to read it in the front page of the newspaper, don't put it on the Web?"
- voice mail: Is your message professional and clear?

Take a few moments before submitting applications to evaluate and improve your electronic footprint. What entertains family and friends may alienate academics, who may question your judgment and seriousness.

Application Form

You have a list of 10 to 20 programs in front of you. The deadlines range from mid-December to mid-February. You have used the late summer and fall months to investigate potential programs—the professors, the orientations, the locations, and the costs. It is now time to start writing.

One of the easiest parts is filling out the application itself. When you download an application from the Web, be sure it is on clean, white, high-quality paper. Some students have found it useful to make a copy of the application and complete a first draft on the photocopy. The completed application reflects on you; keep it as professional and neat as possible.

Nearly all graduate programs now request that you submit an application on line. Be careful to scrutinize your materials and catch any errors, including typos, prior to submitting. Proofread the documents several times and try to cut and paste a fully formed personal statement from a word processing file.

Begin completing the application forms at least one month before the earliest deadline. Some applicants, particularly undergraduates in their senior year, wait until the end of the fall semester on the holiday break. *This is too late*—do not wait, lest you be rushed, unprepared, and working on a tight deadline.

Unlike the medical school process, which uses an identical application form for every school, each graduate program in psychology has its own, unique application. Providing the same information over and over again in slightly different formats can become frustrating and time consuming. Several years ago a committee recommended a standardized graduate application form to reduce the paperwork, but comparatively few programs have instituted it. Nonetheless, it provides a good idea of the information that will be requested of you:

- Full name
- Previous and maiden names
- Citizenship status
- Semester of entrance
- Current mailing address
- Permanent home address
- Educational history

- Degree sought
- Field of study
- Relevant courses taken
- Grade point averages
- Academic honors
- Clinical experience
- Special qualifications
- Employment history
- Teaching/research experience
- Career objectives
- Professional references

Submitting applications is worse than filling out income tax returns (Fretz & Stang, 1980). Allow yourself enough uninterrupted time to do it carefully and completely. Illegible handwriting, incorrect spelling, and poor grammar will hurt your chances.

Some additional tips:

- Keep the application forms for each school separated. Individual computer files or paper folders for each program might help. Since the forms are often poorly marked, you may not otherwise know which forms belong to which school.
- Create a spreadsheet to keep track of your multiple applications—the application deadlines, number of recommendations required, what was sent, what was received, and so on. This method helps to organize the blizzard of paperwork, especially if you are applying to more than a few graduate programs.
- Save a hard copy or electronic file of each application. Graduate schools have been known to lose—or misplace—entire forms. A copy and backup file will enable you to quickly resubmit if necessary.

Curriculum Vitae

Curriculum vitae means, literally, "the course of your life." The vitae or CV summarizes your academic and employment history in a structured form.

Both resumes and CVs summarize your credentials, but they differ in several ways. A resume is typically for employment, whereas a CV is for graduate school and academic positions. Resumes are brief, typically on a single page, whereas CVs go on for several pages. Resumes always list objectives, such as "To obtain an entry-level position in . . .", but CVs do not. Resumes frequently present personal interests and hobbies; CVs rarely do.

Figures 6-1 and 6-2 present two possible formats for a CV; you will need to adapt these samples to your individual needs. Although the samples are single-spaced and occupy only one page, CVs are *double-spaced* between entries and occupy several pages.

As a general comment, keep the CV honest and positive. Never fabricate, but perhaps "embellish" appropriately. The line to be drawn here is demarcated by whether you can look an interviewer directly in the eye and factually defend an entry that could subsequently be corroborated by a supervisor, professor, or another person. Structured brevity is the key; lengthy expositions of experiences are best left to personal statements or job descriptions.

Your "academic resume" should be positive, upbeat in tone. Avoid any negative features that might red-flag your application. Save confessions and excruciating honesty for the clergy and psychotherapist. Omit sections that do not apply to you, such as "Presentations" or "Publications" if you have had none at this point in your career.

Let's proceed through the different sections of a CV and offer some additional hints. List your legal name, including any suffixes such as "Jr." Distinguish between a current address and a permanent home address, if this applies to your living circumstances. Note any anticipated changes in your address. Include telephone numbers and e-mail addresses at which program directors or professors can easily reach you. If you share voice mail or an answering machine with other people, insure that they will graciously take a message and reliably transmit that message to you.

Information on your marital status and dependents is definitely optional. Opinions differ widely on whether you should include this material on your CV: the probable positives are that you are being honest and sharing information about yourself; the likely downsides are that the information may be used against you or lead to illegal considerations in admission decisions. The marital status question is now almost moot since approximately half of all graduate students in psychology are married (Pate, 2001).

Regarding education, list degrees as "anticipated" if they have not yet been awarded. Impressive grade point averages may also be listed here. Honors are listed in chronological order, usually excluding those obtained in high school. If you received an award or honor specific to a university (e.g., the Lawrence Lennon Memorial Award), then record what it is for in parentheses following the award. As two examples: Dean's Scholarship, 2009 – 2013 (one-half tuition scholarship for exceptional academic performance) and Lawrence Lennon Memorial Award, 2012 (awarded for superior performance in psychology).

November 2012

CURRICULUM VITAE

Name:	Chris Smith
Address:	15 Easy Street
	Babylon, NY 12345
Telephone:	(516) 555-1212
E-mail:	bear@babu.edu
Citizenship:	United States of America

Education:

H.S. Diploma   Cherry Hill High School, City, State, June 2009
B.S. (anticipated)   Psychology, Babylon University, May 2012

Honors and Awards:

New York State Regents Scholarship, 2009–2012
Dean's List, Babylon University, 2010–2012
Psi Chi, 2011
Babylon University Honors Program, 2009–present
Who's Who Among Students in American Colleges & Universities, 2011

Clinical Experience:

Mental Health Technician, Friendship House, Jackson, Wyoming, June 2010–August 2011. Duties: recreational counseling and supervision of 20 behaviorally and emotionally disturbed children. Supervisor: Doris Day, M.S. 40 hours weekly.
Telephone Counselor, Mesopotamia County Community Crisis Center, Babylon, New York, 2009–2010. Duties: used a crisis intervention model to counsel a wide range of callers. Supervisor: Randal Kaplan, M.A. 4 hours weekly.

Research Experience:

Research Assistant, Babylon University, Department of Psychology, September 2009–June 2010. Duties: word processing, manuscript preparation, and data analyses for Chris Demanding, Ph.D. 15 hours weekly.
Honors Research, Babylon University with Rita Murrow, Ph.D., 2008–2010. Duties: proposed and conducted an original project; data input and analysis using SPSSx; write-up and oral defense.

Professional and Honor Societies:

Psi Chi, International Honor Society in Psychology
American Psychological Association (student affiliate)
Alpha Gamma Epsilon Omega (National Honor Society in Ergonomics)

Presentations and Publications:

Smith, C., & Murrow, F. A. (2010, April). *Self-esteem and math performance: Another look*. Paper presented at the meeting of the Babylon Psychological Association, New York.
Murrow, F. A., & Smith, C. (2011). The effects of self-esteem on math test performance. *Journal of Psychology, 46,* 113–117.

Campus Activities and Leadership:

Psychology Club, member (2010–2011) and president (2009–present)
University Singers, Babylon University, 2009–2011
Hand-in-Hand, participant (2007–2010) and campus coordinator (2011)

References:

Frances Murrow, Ph.D., Associate Professor, Department of Psychology, Babylon University, Babylon, NY 12345. Voice: 516-555-1212; e-mail: murrow@babu.edu
Theodore Demanding, Ph.D., Professor and Chair, Department of Psychology, Babylon University, Babylon, NY 12345. Voice: 516-555-1212; e-mail: les@babu.edu
Doris Day, M.S., Senior Therapist, Children's House, 78 Oak Street, Jackson, WY 12345. Voice: 307-555-1212

FIGURE 6-1. One format for curriculum vitae.

Chris Smith   November 2012

Personal History:

Business Address:	Department of Psychology
	Babylon University
	Babylon, New York 12345
Phone:	(516) 555-1212
Home Address:	1017 Jefferson Avenue
	Cherry Hill, NJ 08002
Phone:	(609) 555-1212
E-mail:	bear@babu.edu
Citizenship:	United States of America

Educational History:

Babylon University, Babylon, New York
Major: Psychology
Degree: B.S. (anticipated), May 2012
Dean's List, 2008–2010
Who's Who Among Students in American Colleges & Universities, 2011
Honors Thesis: Investigation of the relationship between self-esteem and math performance (Chairperson: Rita Murrow, Ph.D.)

Professional Positions:

1. Telephone Counselor, Mesopotamia County Community Crisis Center, Babylon, New York. Part-time position, 2009–2011. Duties: used a crisis intervention model to counsel a wide range of callers. Supervisor: Randal Kaplan, M.A.
2. Mental Health Technician, Friendship House, Jackson, Wyoming. Full-time summer, 2010. Duties: recreational counseling and supervision of 20 behaviorally and emotionally disturbed children. Supervisor: Doris Day, M.S.
3. Research Assistant, Babylon University. Half-time position, 2009–2010. Duties: word processing, manuscript preparation, and data analysis. Supervisor: Chris Demanding, Ph.D.

Membership in Professional Associations:

Psi Chi (International Honor Society in Psychology)
American Psychological Association (student affiliate)
Alpha Gamma Epsilon Omega (National Honor Society in Ergonomics)

Professional Activities:

President, Babylon University Chapter of Psi Chi, 2010–2012
Member of Program Committee, Babylon University Psychology Conference, 2011

Papers Presented:

Smith, C. E., & Murrow, F. A. (2010, April). *Self-esteem and math performance: Another look.* Paper presented at the meeting of the Babylon Psychological Association, New York.

Publication:

Murrow, F. A., & Smith, C. (2011). The effects of self-esteem on math test performance. *Journal of Psychology, 46,* 113–117.

Campus Activities:

Psychology Club, member (2009-2011) and president (present)
University Singers, Babylon University, 2009–2011
Hand-in-Hand, participant (2009–2011) and campus coordinator (2011)

References:

Frances Murrow, Ph.D., Associate Professor, Department of Psychology, Babylon University, Babylon, NY 12345. Voice: 516-555-1212; e-mail: murrow@babu.edu
Theodore Demanding, Ph.D., Professor and Chair, Department of Psychology, Babylon University, Babylon, NY 12345. Voice: 516-555-1212; e-mail: les@babu.edu
Doris Day, M.S., Senior Therapist, Children's Hospital, 78 Oak Street, Jackson, WY 12345. Voice: 307-555-1212

Note. Adapted from Hayes & Hayes (1989) with permission of the authors.

FIGURE 6-2. Another format for curriculum vitae.

Similarly, specify the disciplines of honor societies; for example, Psi Chi (International Honor Society in Psychology), 2012. Clinical experiences and research experiences can be listed together or separately, depending on what will strengthen your CV, but in either case indicate position title, relevant dates, number of hours, duties performed, and the supervisor. Include any presentations or publications in APA style, thereby demonstrating your familiarity with the psychologist's publication manual. The names of references should be listed only after you have obtained their permission to do so. *Never list a reference on a CV or application unless you have already secured that person's agreement to write a letter in support of your application.*

Place the date (month and year) in smaller font on the upper right-hand corner of the CV. In this way, you can submit an addendum if your credentials significantly improve by, say, having a paper accepted for publication or receiving your department's student of the year award.

Lay out the information in an attractive and organized manner. Select a plain font, such as Times Roman or Arial, and a large enough font so that readers don't need to squint. Use a consistent format both within each section and between sections. For example, if you opt to list your clinical experiences from the most recent to the past, then maintain this format in all the other sections.

Here is an idea to enhance the CV for students who have developed specific research or computer competencies. List them on your vitae as a separate section. Computer skills might include proficiency with SPSS, SAS, R, Pascal, Harvard Graphics, Chartmaster, SigmaScan, SigmaPlot, CricketGraph, and Aldus Pagemaker. Research skills might include performing computerized library searching on *PsycLIT* or *Medline*, administering the Wisconsin Card Sorting Test (or another psychological test), or operating an electroencephalograph (EEG). Also include here any special skills, such as certification in the Facial Action Coding System, fluency in foreign languages, or proficiency in American Sign Language. A faculty member screening applications may realize that these competencies are exactly what he or she is looking for in a new graduate assistant or research assistant. So use your CV to highlight your abilities! Omit this optional section if you have none or only one specific competency; in the latter case, describe that qualification in your personal statement.

What should *not* be put on the CV? Eliminate listings of religion, hobbies, pets, favorite books, and items of that kind (Hayes & Hayes, 1989). They are unnecessary; save them for a resume. Nor is a photograph customary.

Padding of all varieties must be avoided. Padding occurs when a reader reacts to the CV as more form than substance ("Who are they trying to fool?!"). Potentially risky is listing professional projects under way—one or two legitimate research projects may pass but any more will probably be considered suspect. Other signs of padding, and therefore sections to exclude, are conventions attended, journals read, and projects you worked on in a nonprofessional capacity.

Pumping up your past on CVs and application forms is common but inadvisable. A survey of 2.6 million job applications discovered that 44% of them contained lies (Kluger, 2002); do not be among the 44%. Once you are caught fibbing on a graduate school application, it is practically impossible to restore your integrity and character at that program. While some of your friends may exhort you to exaggerate your previous positions and to inflate your GPA, we strongly advise honesty.

Proofread the document carefully; review it with an advisor or mentor before you send it. If you are sending any hard copies to graduate schools, then print them on standard-sized white or cream stock. Purchase good quality bond paper for these documents. Avoid onionskin paper, goldenrod color, odd-sized papers, memo pads, green or red ink, and other unconventional materials.

Although much of the information contained in the CV is requested on the application form itself, we believe the inclusion of a CV enhances your application—providing it is properly prepared. A CV denotes a scholarly demeanor, highlights your accomplishments, and communicates familiarity with the workings of academia.

Personal Statements

Another bridge you must cross is writing the statement of purpose. Every program will want to know why you chose clinical or counseling psychology and the area within it that you plan to study. Admissions committees will also want to know how you came to this decision and what sorts of goals you have in mind. These essays, required by more than 95% of doctoral programs, go by different names: statement of goals, personal essays, professional objectives, and personal statements.

Each application will ask the questions in a slightly different way because each program has different expectations and approaches to training.

Read the instructions carefully. You cannot word process one statement and submit it to every program.

Do not misinterpret the meaning of personal in *personal statement*. This essay is not the place to espouse your philosophy of life, to describe your first romance, or to tell the story about your being bitten by the neighbor's dog and subsequently developing an anxiety disorder. Instead, think of the essay as a *professional statement*. Write about your activities and experiences as an aspiring psychologist (Bottoms & Nysse, 1999).

An analysis of 360 essays required as part of the graduate application process demonstrated wide variability in the content requested (Keith-Spiegel, 1991). The most frequent requests were to articulate:

- Career plans
- Clinical experiences
- Interest areas
- Specific faculty of interest
- Research experiences
- Autobiographical statement
- Academic objectives
- Reasons for applying to that particular program
- Educational background

Of late, Psy.D. programs that rarely supply financial assistance have also taken to asking applicants to specify how they will finance their graduate studies. We recommend that you respond directly and list a combination of sources – personal savings, family support, summer work, and student loans, for example. No need to be embarrassed or hesitant in responding. In fact, this question prompts you to realistically consider financing your education, if you opt for a Psy.D. program.

Be attentive to what the program requests. If they stress research, highlight your research interests and experience. If they stress clinical work, highlight the development of these interests and your training experiences to date. Show how you started with a question or a clinical observation, how you pursued that question, and how it developed into a greater understanding of the issues at hand and a need to know more. Demonstrate how this program meets your needs and is the ideal place to continue to pursue knowledge. State the goals you wish to attain with this knowledge, the career path you hope to work toward. If you are committed to the Boulder model, indicate how research is useful and how it is clinically applicable. When you make this connection in your personal statement, you will impress on the admission committee the ideal integration for Boulder-model, Ph.D. programs.

To reiterate: carefully read the question, individualize your response to each program, and respond to all parts of the question posed to you. If the application specifies two pages, then give only two pages, not three. If the application asks for single-spacing and your social security number at the top of the page, then do just that. Follow the instructions in length, content, and format. Graduate selection committees value clarity, focus, and passion in personal statements (Keith-Spiegel, 1991). Clarity and focus are typically construed as indicators of lucid thought, realistic planning, and self-direction, all valuable assets in a graduate student. At the same time, try to communicate a heartfelt commitment to your chosen career. "Passion" is not too strong a term—even relentless, obsessed, committed, fascinated; in short, what we call "catching the fever!" Graduate faculty seek students who find it difficult to distinguish between work and pleasure when it comes to academic tasks (Kieth-Spiegel & Wiederman, 2000).

Many students ask us if they should begin the personal statement with an inspiring quote or a cute metaphor. Our answer; probably not. Instead, organize your statement around a compelling theme that shows and illustrates your best qualities for entry into a graduate program. Stick to that theme and then return to it at the end of your statement.

The personal statement is a prime opportunity to induce a match with the research and clinical interests of a faculty member. Many programs, as we have said, attempt to match faculty with incoming graduate students on the basis of mutual interest, for example, child therapy, GLBT issues, or neuropsychological assessment. This matching strategy is more often employed by research-oriented than practice-oriented programs, but attempt it in all of your personal statements.

To illustrate, consider the clinical admissions process of the University of Ottawa, a program with an equal emphasis on research and practice. Like many programs, they create a finalist pool by eliminating applications with low GPAs and GRE scores. Then each of the clinical faculty members reviews all the finalist applications in order to locate several possible matches. These applicants then receive interviews. As you can see, and as we have repeated throughout this book, gaining admission into competitive doctoral programs is not limited simply to one's credentials but also includes a match in research and clinical interests.

Here, then, are a few general guidelines for writing personal statements that increase the probability of a match:

- Mention at least two and perhaps up to four of your interests. This obviously covers a wider range than a single interest. If the program is research oriented and you hope to work with a prominent researcher, you probably do not want to include more than two research interests. You likely will be competing against many other applicants who specifically want to work with that person and your application might look too diffuse.
- Cast your interests in fairly broad terms—not administering the Wisconsin Card Sorting Test, but neuropsychological assessment; not a mail survey of counseling psychologists, but the characteristics and practices of psychotherapists.
- Nominate at least two professors with whom you would like to work at that particular graduate program. This, too, enhances the chance of a successful match.
- Integrate the program's training philosophy into your personal statement. For example, "I resonate with Babylon University's goal of producing multiculturally competent psychologists to work directly in the community."

A commonly asked question is, "How personal should I get in my personal statement?" Although there is no universally correct answer, some suggestions can be offered. A personal detail, such as describing how growing up with a handicapped or disturbed sibling has affected your life and decision to enter psychology, is appropriate. However, depicting the situation in intimate detail without relating it to its contribution to your own growth may lead an admissions committee to question your judgment. A rule of thumb is to be introspective and self-revealing without sounding exhibitionistic. For example, it is fine for an applicant to state how personal life experiences have contributed to better self-understanding, but it sounds peculiar when the applicant goes into great detail about particular relationships or early life events (Halgin, 1986). Although allusions to your personal psychotherapy in personal statements does not appear to overly stigmatize candidates or lead disproportionately to their rejections (Schaefer, 1995), we recommend against including your personal therapy in written materials.

Many personal statements are ineffective because, first, the student fails to spend time preparing them and, second, the student fails to be "personal" (Osborne, 1996). Therefore, as an applicant you should devote a substantial amount of time thinking, writing, rethinking, and rewriting the personal statement. Your statement should include personal details that relate to your ability to be a successful graduate student and that demonstrate maturity, adaptation, and motivation—the very characteristics sought by admissions committees.

Another question we are frequently asked is, "How distinctive or unique should my personal statement be?" Our answer is: as distinctive or unique as you are. Some applicants labor under the delusion that personal statements should resemble creative

It is my strong desire to attend a doctoral program in clinical psychology. I am seeking a program committed to the Boulder model, training scientist–practitioners able to serve society in a variety of capacities. The program I attend should stress the importance of understanding and integrating the broad field of psychology, as well as providing the knowledge and training specific to clinical psychology.

    After a thorough review of more than 50 programs in clinical psychology, I have chosen to apply to Bogus University for a number of reasons. First, your program is known for producing stellar graduates, and has been repeatedly recommended to me by several psychology faculty. Second, Bogus University allows students to immerse themselves in research early in their graduate careers. Third, I am drawn toward several of your faculty members, including Dr. Babe Ruth for her work in substance abuse and cognitive therapy, and Dr. Ty Cobb for his work in sexual health, stress, and coping. I would be pleased to have either of these faculty members as my mentor. Fourth, the available clinical experiences would allow me to work with a population I find of particular interest, such as adults and families at the Psychological Services Center. And fifth, I am looking to attend school in a scenic area of the country where both my fiancé and I think we would be happy.

FIGURE 6-3. Portion of a sample autobiographical statement.

writing samples that magnify their singular accomplishments or that set the world on fire. Set the bar more realistically and aim for a personal statement that tells your own story clearly and convincingly.

A good idea is to show humility. Even if you have golden research and clinical experiences and 1400 GRE scores, you are still entering as a student. You are coming to learn. Mention the areas you hope to develop during your graduate school experience.

Your personal statement should lead the reader to say, "I want to meet and interview this person." It should leave a memorable, positive impression of your accomplishments and potential. You want a ticket to the dance.

Be prepared to back up the claims you make in your personal statements. If you profess a working knowledge of, say, experiential psychotherapy, then be prepared for questions on the work of Carl Whitaker and Leslie Greenberg. Similarly, if you claim fluency in Spanish, then expect one of the interviews to be conducted entirely in Spanish (Megargee, 1990).

The "to do's" of personal statements are process suggestions and thus difficult to pinpoint, but the "not to do's" are content oriented and easier to delineate (Whitbourne, 1999). We characterize three such "nots" as the three H's: Humor, Hyperbole, and Hard luck stories. Humor rarely works in a formal written statement; so unless you are an unusually gifted satirist, we recommend you avoid jokes and funny stories about your life. Similarly, hyperbole rarely impresses the admissions committee. References to your "overwhelming childhood trauma" and "triumph over undiagnosed learning disabilities" in personal statements cast doubt on the veracity and accuracy of your judgment. Avoid the hyperbolic language of *always*, *never*, and *every* in your statement. And hard luck stories typically come off feebly. Many students financed their undergraduate educations, many survived disastrous relationship choices, and many muddled through three academic majors before discovering their niche in psychology. Avoid making adversity the theme of your statement.

Our advice is supported by an interesting study on the "kisses of death" in the graduate school application process (Appleby & Appleby, 2004). Eighty-eight chairs of graduate admissions committees provided examples of application materials that caused the admissions committee to draw negative conclusions about the applicant. A prevalent theme among these kisses of death was damaging personal statements that were (a) overly altruistic, (b) excessively disclosing, or (c) professionally inappropriate.

Examples of the overly altruistic statements were "I want to help all people live happy lives" and "I want to help people because of how very much I have been helped." Examples of excessive self-disclosure were "being a recovering drug addict daughter of a sexually deviant and alcoholic mother" and excruciating details of an applicant's year-long struggle with painful hemorrhoids! Our favorite example of professional inappropriateness was the applicant who submitted a statement of purpose titled "Statement of Porpoise" that contained drawings of the sea mammal and a description of the applicant frolicking in the ocean with a porpoise on a visit to Florida. As we said, avoid humor, hyperbole, and hard luck in your personal statement.

One way to make your personal statement sparkle is to describe any teaching assistantships or experiences. Talk about how you learned leadership skills and teamwork in this role. Specific examples of how you responsibly handled challenging courses or teaching activities will lead the reader to infer you possess the "right stuff."

Your personal statement should tell a compelling, integrative story of a reflective individual who notes accomplishments without joking or bragging or sobbing. As our colleague Sue Krauss Whitbourne (1999) puts it: Don't say it softly or loudly, just say it clearly!

You will be asked in practically every personal statement and personal interview why you chose to apply to *this* particular graduate program in clinical or counseling psychology. Figure 6-3 presents a *portion* of a sample statement, addressing this ubiquitous question, written by one of our undergraduate students in his successful bid for entry into a clinical psychology doctoral program committed to the scientist–practitioner model. His reasons for applying to "Bogus University" are presented only as a single example; your statements will need to be tailored to your interests and credentials as well as the application instructions. Remember that this is just one part of an entire autobiographical statement.

Nonetheless, his why-I-applied-to-your-program statement illustrates several important points. First, he advances multiple reasons for applying to that particular program. Five reasons sound much more convincing than one or two (though don't overdo it). Second, his reasons for applying to Bogus U. primarily address his professional match with the program (their reputation, faculty members, clinical opportunities) but nicely concludes with a personal touch (geographic location). Third, he mentions two specific faculty and several potential research interests in an attempt to maximize the chances of a match. Fourth, the statement reflects his careful reading and incorporation of the program's self-description; for example, he cites the opportunity to immerse himself early into research and names the Psychological Services Center. Fifth, the statement is systematically organized and clearly written—indicators of an organized and clear-thinking graduate student!

Compose your personal statement as carefully as you would an important term paper. Write several rough drafts and then set it aside for a few days. Avoid slang words on the one hand, and overly technical or elaborate words on the other. Stick to the information requested; avoid too many "ruffles" and lengthy expositions of your own philosophy (Fretz & Stang, 1980). Write as many drafts as necessary until the statement sounds right to you.

Before you finish a draft of your personal statement, have friends read it for grammar, spelling, and typos. Regardless of the content, technical accuracy really makes a difference.

Once it is error free, have one or more faculty members read it and make suggestions. Do *not* give faculty or mentors a rough draft of your personal statement; give them a formal draft once you have reworked it and your peers have reviewed it. Let them know where the statement is going, and they can guide you on form and content. In fact, some faculty ask that you bring in the exact wording of the questions, along with your formal draft, so that their feedback can be pinpoint targeted.

Then, revise it again. Take the critical feedback seriously and rewrite accordingly. You will understandably protest that you have already devoted hours to your statement. One of our students complained that she had spent 10 hours preparing only 500 words! But remind yourself that the extra hour you put in now may mean the difference between acceptance and rejection by a particular program.

As you examine the final draft, perform a mental checklist: Does the statement have a theme or focus? Does it proceed logically and chronologically? Does it come alive with detail and language? Does it avoid the three H's? Does it begin and end with attention-

TABLE 6-1. Professors' Pet Peeves: Avoiding Neutral Letters of Recommendation

Students sometimes are unaware of how the seemingly innocuous things they do and say can annoy their professors. In turn, the professors provide students with less than enthusiastic letters of recommendation. Here are some examples suggested by William W. Nish of Georgia College, reprinted with his kind permission.

Be quick to apply such concise labels as "busy work," "irrelevant," and "boring" to anything you do not like or understand. Not only is this a convenient way of putting the professor down, but also you will not be bothered with the inconvenience of understanding something before you judge it.

Always be ready with reasons why you are an exception to the rules established for the class, such as the dates for submitting written assignments.

Avoid taking examinations at the same time as the rest of the class. Be certain to take it for granted that the professor will give you a make-up exam at your convenience, regardless of your reason for missing the exam.

Be very casual about class attendance. When you see your professor be sure to ask, "Did I miss anything important in class today?" This will do wonders for his or her ego. By all means expect the professor to give a recital of all of the things you missed instead of taking the responsibility for getting the information from another member of the class.

Be consistently late to class and other appointments. This shows other people how much busier you are than they are.

Do not read your assignments in advance of class lecture and discussion. This actually allows you to study more efficiently, for you can take up class time asking about things that are explained in the reading.

Avoid using the professor's office hours or making an appointment. Instead, show up when he or she is frantically trying to finish a lecture before the next class hour and explain that you must see him or her right that minute.

Do not participate in such mundane activities as departmental advising appointments. Instead, wait until the last minute for approval of your schedule, and then expect the professor to be available at your convenience.

grabbing sentences? Does it communicate passion? (Keith-Spiegel & Wiederman, 2000).

For further tips on writing your personal statement, skim Donald Asher's (2008) *Graduate Admissions Essays: How to Write Your Way into the Graduate Program of Your Choice* and visit the following Web sites:

- www.psywww.com/careers/perstmt.htm
- www.accepted.com/grad/personalstatement.aspx
- www.psychologytoday.com/blog/fulfillment-any-age/201101/writing-about-yourself-step-step-guide
- www.indiana.edu/~wts/pamphlets/personal_statement.shtml

We hope that our suggestions in this section guide you in writing your personal statement. It is also our hope that they are not too constraining. This is the part of the application where an admissions committee gets to see you in a more personal, three-dimensional light, an area where "you can be you."

Letters of Recommendation

What do admission committees gain from letters of recommendation? The answer is a personal but objective evaluation of your work from a professional experienced in the field. Admission committees desire a more objective sense of your abilities and experience than what you provide about yourself. Consequently, it is best to have at least two of the people writing your letters be at the doctoral level in psychology or psychology-related disciplines. One fine letter from a master's-level clinician is usually acceptable, but he or she will not be in a position to attest to your ability to complete doctoral studies.

By the same token, bachelor's degree recipients, friends, and relatives should never write letters of recommendation to doctoral programs. They simply do not have the experience or knowledge of what it takes to earn a doctorate. Letters from politicians and your psychotherapists typically are inappropriate as well—they tend to write personal and psychological testimonies instead of academic letters of reference.

Choose people with whom you have worked for a long enough period, preferably for a year or more. That typically excludes a professor with whom you have taken a single class, even if you did get an A. If you wrote a particularly strong paper in the class and the professor knows you a bit better, then he or

she could serve as a reference, but this reference is still not the most desirable. At best this person can say, "This student was always on time, participated in discussions, attended office hours, and tested very well. On this basis I consider him/her an intelligent student and a good candidate for graduate school."

By contrast, admissions committees want to hear something more detailed, like: "This student has worked with me for 1 year. During that time she scored MMPIs, tested participants using a polygraph, analyzed data, and conducted her own honors thesis. She was dependable and worked beyond what was required by the department. Given this student's intelligence, motivation, and responsibility, I think she would make an outstanding doctoral student." Though the above is a strong example, the point is that you want someone to attest to your ability and responsibility.

Table 6-1 lists some of the self-sabotaging things students do to receive neutral letters of recommendation. Although presented for its humor, it also provides sage warnings about interpersonal behaviors that annoy professors.

Other students receive neutral letters of recommendation through no fault of their own. They experience difficulty in securing detailed letters of recommendation because they:

- Transferred from one college to another college before graduating (which occurs, according to the U.S. Department of Education, to almost one-third of all students);
- Attended a mammoth state university where they only took huge lecture classes and never had the same psychology professor twice;
- Switched majors relatively late in their college career and did not get to know their psychology professors well;
- Completed college part-time for 10 or so years and did not acquire close contacts with full-time faculty members.

We are sympathetic to these plights. If you fall into one of these categories, then you need to double your efforts to get involved in clinical experiences, research activities, and departmental matters—and do so quickly.

Most doctoral programs request three letters of recommendation. Try to secure letters that will give the admissions committee the information it desires. At a practice-oriented program, one letter from a clinical supervisor, one letter from a professor, and one from a research advisor would probably prove

November 2012

Leslie Jones, Ph.D.
Department of Psychology
East Coast University
1200 Faculty Building
Hausman, MD 43707

Dear Dr. Jones:

Thank you for agreeing to write a letter of recommendation on my behalf. I hereby waive (or do not waive) my right to inspect the letter of recommendation written for me and sent to the designated schools of my choice. I am applying to (master's, doctoral) programs in clinical (counseling) psychology. My earliest deadline is

_____.

Here are the courses I have taken from you.

Fall 2009	Abnormal Psychology	A–
Spring 2010	Clinical Psychology	B+
Fall 2011	Undergraduate Research	

Here are other activities in which I have participated.

2010–2011	Research Assistant
2009–2010	Vice President of Psi Chi

My latest GRE scores were 156 Verbal, 160 Quantitative, and 5.0 Analytical Writing. My Psychology Subject Test score was 610.

(If applicable:)
In your laboratory in Fall 2011, while participating in undergraduate research, I was involved in several different activities. My responsibilities included entering participant data, conducting telephone screening interviews to determine participant eligibility, and coding several indices of social functioning during a key interaction period in the alcohol administration study. I also participated in the weekly journal club meetings.

Finally, I attach a copy of my current vitae and a list of psychology courses for any additional information that might prove useful. Please feel free to call me at 555-1212 or to e-mail me at Chris_smith@phonyemail.com. Thanks again.

Sincerely yours,

Chris Smith

Encls.

FIGURE 6-4. Sample letter to request a letter of recommendation.

the ideal mix. At a research-oriented program, two letters from research advisors and one from a clinical supervisor or professor would probably be better. All things being equal, it is preferable to have your "research" letters come from faculty. However, if you believe that a letter from an employer would be substantially more helpful than that of a professor with whom you are not well acquainted, then it is probably a good idea to use the employer.

Our general advice was confirmed by an interesting study (Keith-Spiegel & Wiederman, 2000) that asked members of admissions committees to rank sources of recommendation letters. Raters were asked to assume that the letters from these different sources were equally positive so that rating variations were due solely to the referee's characteristics. The most valuable sources of letters of recommendation were (in descending order): (1) A mentor with whom the applicant has done considerable work; (2) the applicant's professor, who is also a well-known and highly respected psychologist; (3) an employer in a job related to the applicant's professional goals; (4) the chair of the academic department in which the applicant is majoring; (5) a professor from another department from whom the applicant has taken a relevant upper-division course. By contrast, a letter from a graduate teaching assistant was rated, essentially, as no help. And a letter from one's personal therapist was rated negatively!

Applicants are naturally tempted to request a recommendation from, for want of a better term, "nice" professors. As long as those professors have worked extensively with you and are highly respected, that is a fine plan of action. But asking nice professors instead of credible, respected professors can result in trouble. Even the kindest, student-centered professors cannot comment on what they do not know directly about you. Avoid securing brief, diffuse letters from friendly folks who say nothing of substance or import. Follow the research and seek positive letters that yield both gravitas (seriousness) and veritas (the truth).

Very important: First ask the person writing the letters whether he or she can write you a good one. Ask this direct and specific question: "Can you write a good letter of recommendation for me?" If the person is hesitant or gives any indication of having reservations, *ask someone else!* A bad letter of recommendation is deadly. Better to have one brief letter from a professor who gave you an "A" than from someone who might express reservations about your abilities. "I don't know" is better than "I know, and I have reservations."

The way you approach professors for a recommendation is an underappreciated topic. Remember, you will ask, "Can you write a good recommendation for me?" If the person responds in the affirmative, we strongly recommend that you provide that person with a letter similar to that shown in 6-4. If you worked in this professor's laboratory and if the lab was fairly large, you might also provide an outline of the various tasks that you conducted while working there. This will help refresh the professor's memory and make for a stronger letter. The person writing a letter of recommendation needs adequate information in order to produce a credible and informative letter. You can be powerful in shaping a professor's letter of recommendation!

Do all of these steps in person. Yes, it is interpersonally anxious to ask someone, "Can you write a good letter of recommendation for me?" And, of course, all of these steps are painstaking and time-consuming. But that is precisely the point: You are demonstrating your interpersonal skills, responsibility, and work ethic to the professor even as you are requesting a letter of recommendation attesting to those very attributes! Thus, ask in person during a formal meeting–not in an e-mail, not by telephone, not in a few minutes before work or class, not by placing a recommendation form in the person's mailbox. Take the initiative and do it directly in real-time (Norcross & Cannon, 2008).

This letter—and the attendant course listing and CV—will promote accuracy and detail. These are essential characteristics of strong letters of recommendation in that the admissions committee looks for positive tone *and* detail. A two-paragraph laudatory letter on the order of "Great student, fine person" simply doesn't make the detailed case for your admission into competitive graduate programs.

What admissions committees also find useless in letters are duplicate and irrelevant information. One set of researchers (Elam et al., 1998) queried members of admissions committees and discovered the five *least* helpful aspects of letters of recommendation:

- Repetition of information from the application (e.g., repeating grades, honors, and scores available elsewhere on the application)
- Unsubstantiated superlatives or vague generalities
- Detailed descriptions of grades in one particular course
- Lack of strong relationship between applicant and letter writer

• Inclusion of irrelevant information, such as religious beliefs or hearsay

Put another way, give your referees sufficient data to render informed and positive letters about your personal characteristics, academic strengths, and interpersonal skills so that they do not resort to filling your recommendations with irrelevant content.

Here's how one doctoral program (University of Rhode Island) attempts to translate the content of recommendation letters into numerical categories.

1   Summary recommendations in all three letters are neutral or negative. Positive and negative assessments are listed. Overall evaluation in all three is neutral.
2   Letters meet criteria between anchor points 1 and 3.
3   Summary recommendations in all three letters are positive and general. Positive statements from all three letters. Statements are general in nature.
4   Letters meet criteria between anchor points 3 and 5.
5   Summary recommendations in all three letters are excellent and detailed. Positive statements from all three letters are very favorable and very detailed in their support.

Note, again, that the emphasis is on positive tone *and* supportive detail. This is the desired result of your extra work in providing references with factual information and assertive requests for letters of recommendation. A "liability letter" is one that communicates limited knowledge of the applicant, leading an admissions committee to conclude that the person was only minimally connected to professors in his or her undergraduate or master's department (Halgin, 1986).

Most universities provide their own form for recommendations as part of the application materials. These forms can be handled in three ways, depending upon the graduate school's instructions and the recommender's preferences. One way is to provide your professor with these forms and stamped envelopes addressed to the schools to which the forms are to be sent. This is a small but crucial precaution—do not take the chance that postage will delay return of the letter. It is also courteous: Your professor is doing you a favor taking considerable time and contemplation to write a good letter. A second way is that the forms are submitted electronically through the graduate program's homepage or admission portal. In this case, you list on your application the names, positions, and e-mail addresses of people writing you letters of recommendation. The graduate schools then directly contact your referees via e-mail and provide them with the URL and a password to electronically submit their letters of recommendation to your application file. Online submission of recommendations streamlines the entire process and has become the rule. A third, less popular way is to provide your professor with these forms; he or she will then complete them and return them to the Office of Career Services/Planning for processing and mailing. The recommendation forms from graduate schools may appear to be quite different at first glance; however, closer inspection will reveal that they all request essentially the same information. The forms typically ask the people writing the letters to note the length of time they have known you and in what capacities. Then the referees are asked to rate your research ability, originality, writing skills, organizational ability, maturity, interpersonal skills, persistence, and similar qualities on a structured grid. Typical forms request an appraisal of the applicant in terms of 10 qualities in comparison with others applying for graduate study whom the referees have known in the applicant's proposed field of study. The rating grid offers responses of top 3%, next 10%, next 20%, middle third, lowest third, and unable to judge. On most forms, an open space is then presented for a narrative description of your strengths and weaknesses. The forms usually conclude with a request for a summary rating: a check mark on a continuum from "not recommended" to "highly recommended" or a numerical value representing an overall ranking of this student to others taught in the past or some similar estimate.

Researchers have identified the most frequent applicant characteristics that recommenders were requested to rate on the forms (Appleby, Keenan, & Mauer, 1999). The resulting list—based on the analysis of 143 recommendation forms—describes the characteristics that psychology graduate programs value in their applicants. In descending order of frequency, the top dozen are as follows:

• Motivated and hardworking
• High intellectual/scholarly ability
• Research skills
• Emotionally stable and mature
• Writing skills
• Speaking skills
• Teaching skills/potential

TABLE 6-2. Summary Table of a Student's Graduate Program Applications

School	Grad program	Deadline	Letter or form	Submission
Midwestern University	PhD clinical	January 1	Letter	Mail directly to grad school
Pacific West University	PhD clinical	January 15	Letter & form	Online
Southern School of Professional Psychology	PhD clinical	February 1	Letter	An e-mail will be sent to you
Northeast University	MS clinical	March 15	Form; letter optional	Either mail or online but online preferred
Regional College	MA psychology	March 22	Letter	Back to me; I include it in my application

- Works well with others
- Creative and original
- Strong knowledge of area of study
- Character or integrity
- Special skills, such as computer or lab

One vital lesson to be learned is that graduate school aspirants should make a concerted effort to behave in ways that allow them to acquire relevant skills (research, writing, speaking, computer) and to be perceived by at least two of their professors as motivated, bright, emotionally stable, capable of working well with others, and possessing integrity (Appleby et al., 1999).

These forms, by law, will contain a waiver statement asking whether you do or do not waive your right to inspect the completed letter of reference. The Family Education Rights and Privacy Act of 1974 (the so-called Buckley Amendment) mandated that students over age 18 be given access to school records unless they waive this right. This is a complicated topic, but we invariably advise applicants to waive their right of access *providing*, as previously discussed, the person writing the letter knows the student well and has unhesitantly agreed to provide a strong recommendation. Do not waive access—or better yet, do not request letters—from persons you do not trust or do not know.

A confidential letter carries more weight. By waiving your right to access, you communicate a confidence that the letters will be supportive, and you express trust in your reference. In fact, over 90% of health profession schools prefer letters of recommendation that are waived by the student (Chapman & Lane, 1997). Our experiences and naturalistic studies (e.g., Ceci & Peters, 1984; Shaffer & Tomarelli, 1981) suggest that professors' honest evaluations will be compromised when you have access to what

they have written. By waiving the right, you are communicating an intent to have the "truth" told. Otherwise, admissions committees may lump the letter with all the other polite and positive testimonials (Halgin, 1986). Worse, admissions committees may suspect that your unwillingness to waive your right means that you are worried that your letters might be weak.

In making your choice of whether to waive or not to waive, be clear about the law. Most students correctly know that if they waive their rights they may never see the letter. However, many students erroneously think that choosing not to waive their rights means that they can see their letter if they do not get accepted or that they have a right to preview the letter before it is sent (Ault, 1993). These are common fallacies, but fallacies nonetheless.

The relevant laws do not dictate that professors must show students the completed letter. One study (Keith-Spiegel, 1991) of college faculty found that 17% never show students their letters of recommendation, 46% usually do not, 8% only to students they know well, 15% only if students ask, and 14% routinely show students their letters. Nor does the law guarantee a student access to letters if the student is rejected from a graduate program; in fact, students may inspect their files at a graduate school only after they have been accepted at and enrolled in that graduate school (Ault, 1993).

Going one step further, contrary to some students' beliefs, faculty do *not* have to write letters of recommendation for students. Letters are a common and voluntary courtesy, not a job requirement.

Why might faculty members decline to write a letter for a student? The single most common reason is that they don't know the student well enough (Keith-Spiegel, 1991). Other frequent reasons given by faculty are that they question the student's motivation level, emotional stability, academic credentials, or professional standards. If faculty defer on your request for a letter, politely inquire about their reasoning and graciously thank them for their candor.

One creative study asked psychologists how they would handle requests for a letter of recommendation from a student exhibiting particular problems (Grote, Robiner, & Haut, 2001). The majority indicated that they would *not* write a letter for a student who was abusing substances or who had shown unethical behavior. For most of the other student problems—interpersonal problems, lack of motivation, paucity of responsibility, marginal clinical skills—psychologists routinely would tell the student about their reservations, then write the letter including the negative information. If faculty members tell you that they have reservations about your behavior, then they will probably include the negative evaluation in their letter of recommendation. Politely inquire if their reservation will in fact appear in the letter. If so, thank them for their candor and withdraw your request for a letter.

The last impression you make on the recommender concerns your organization and preparation. If your recommendation packet is complete and orderly, then the person feels respected and remembers you as a dedicated student. If, on the other hand, your packet is disorganized and incomplete, you frustrate the person and behaviorally remind him or her of your weaknesses. We therefore recommend that you create a summary table of your graduate program applications and place it on the top of the materials you deliver to the referee (along with the aforementioned letter, CV, and various forms). A shortened sample of such a table is provided in Table 6.2. The table will assist and impress the recommender while simultaneously helping you remain organized and on-deadline. Play it safe and provide the reference packet at least 6 weeks before the earliest deadline. Completing your recommendation may not be the top priority of the person you have asked to write it, or he or she may be out of town prior to the deadline. Do not take any chances that a letter will be late. Allow 3 weeks and ask if the letter has been sent. Be politic: do not pester, but do follow up.

If you seek additional information on requesting letters of recommendation, then we suggest the pointers offered by the following Web sites:

- http://gradschool.about.com/od/askingforletters/ht/howletter.htm
- www.writeexpress.com/recommendation-letters.html
- www.uwm.edu/People/ccp2/work/recletter.html
- www.psychwww.com/careers/lettrec.htm
- www.boxfreeconcepts.com/reco/

Transcripts and GRE Scores

A graduate application will not be complete—and probably not even considered by the admissions committee—unless the required academic transcripts and entrance examination scores have been received. Your task here consists of requesting the appropriate organizations to transmit official copies of these materials to the graduate schools of your choice and then ensuring that the schools have received them.

With respect to transcripts, you must request that the Registrar's Office of all attended colleges and universities mail an *official* copy of your transcript directly to the graduate school. An official copy will contain the seal, stamp, and authorized signature of the institution. The cost of transcripts varies from place to place, but it averages $5 per copy. Submit transcript requests at least 1 month before the application deadline. Many universities take several weeks during the semester to process these requests. The college form requesting a transcript will most likely accompany the transcript itself and thereby enter your graduate application file. Accordingly, this request form or mailing address should be typed or printed neatly.

Virtually all graduate programs continue to require hard copies of transcripts mailed from academic institutions. Online transcript exchange has been difficult to establish and is still uncommon. However, online transcripts will become more common with the advent of companies such as the recently formed National Transcript Center to provide secure electronic transmissions among institutions (Fauber, 2006).

A reminder: request an unofficial copy of your own transcript in September or October prior to applying. Inspect it closely for errors and omissions. Horror stories abound regarding erroneous transcript entries misleading admissions committees—an initial grade of I (incomplete) becoming an F (failure), honors credits not registered, unpaid term bills delaying transcripts, and so on. Don't leave it to chance; check it out yourself.

One creative researcher (Landrum, 2003) surveyed graduate admissions directors about the impact of transcripts and withdrawals in the admissions process. Results show that your transcript will get a careful review in practically all programs and will be reviewed by more than one member of the admissions committee in about 87% of the programs. With respect to the effects of course withdrawals (dropping a course after mid-semester) on transcripts, less than 4% of programs indicated that a withdrawal from a single course would hurt an applicant's chance of admission into the graduate program. But more than 20% of the programs indicated that two or more withdrawals hurt a student's entry into their graduate program. Thus, our advice to students contemplating a course withdrawal is that one is probably not hurtful, but that two or more withdrawals, especially from required courses such as statistics and research methods, may well have a negative impact.

With respect to GREs, score reports will automatically be mailed to you and electronically submitted to the four graduate schools you listed when you completed the GRE testing. The mailing date for the score reports is approximately 6 weeks after the test date for paper-based testing (Psychology Subject Test) and 2 weeks for computer-based testing (General Test). Your copy of the score report is intended only for your information; official reports are sent directly by ETS to the score recipients you designate. This procedure—as with the registrar transmitting an official transcript—"is intended to ensure that no questions are raised about the authenticity of a score report" (GRE, 2001, p. 16).

You will probably be applying to more than the four schools you designated for score reports. Toward this end, you will submit an Additional Score Report Request Form online or by snail mail and remit your payment of $23.00 for *each* score recipient listed, charged to your credit card. Or, you can use the Phone Service for Additional Score Reports by dialing 1-888-GRE-SCORE. The charge for additional score reports is $23.00 per score recipient. Your scores will be mailed to you and to the programs within 5 working days. ETS pledges in writing to "make every effort to send your score reports within 10 working days after receipt of your request" (GRE, 2001), but you should allow for at least 1 month. You may have your GRE scores transmitted at any time during the 5-year period after they are initially reported.

Unsolicited Documents

A frequently asked question is, "What if a program doesn't ask for something that I'd like to send?" Some examples are the curriculum vitae, a research paper, and job descriptions. If a graduate program does not want additional documents, it will state so clearly on the application. In that case, do as the program requests. But even then, you may be able to make additional documents a part of your application if you have come to know a professor at the school and have shared any of these documents with him or her. In general, it is a good idea to send a curriculum vitae and/or job descriptions if they are applicable.

If you have relevant work and clinical experiences but can only use one for a letter of reference, then include a curriculum vitae or job description. One benefit is that these allow you to spend less time focusing on the details of these work experiences in your personal statement. You can relate how the experiences influenced you without wasting space explaining exactly what you did.

As a professional, you will need a CV eventually, and we recommend you begin one even if you do not use it in every application. Start a vitae file and toss notes and memos into it regarding assistantship duties, noteworthy activities, committee assignments, professional associations—in short, everything you need to update your vitae (Hayes & Hayes, 1989).

A job description details your duties and responsibilities. When asking a supervisor to write a job description, ask him or her to focus on your specific tasks and how well you performed them rather than asserting how well suited you are to graduate school. This allows you to spend less time describing what you did and how well you did it when writing your personal statement. For example, prior to graduate school, one of us worked with a psychotherapist conducting a social skills group for preadolescents. In his personal statement he was able to focus on how that experience had affected him. By referring to the "enclosed job description," the personal statement did not get bogged down in the details of this experience. Further, if you performed well at this job, having a supervisor's positive assessment allows you to be more modest in your personal statement.

If you have a large number of work experiences, be careful not to overwhelm admissions committees with paperwork. Choose one or two experiences that showcase your credentials and that highlight characteristics not likely tapped by those writing your letters of recommendation. If you send more job descriptions than this, you may weaken their impact and increase the chances that the most laudatory ones will not be read (or at least not carefully).

If you have written an honors thesis or an original research paper and have received faculty feedback that it is well written, then include it. If there is someone whose research corresponds with your own, this may open a door for you. However, if there is a question about your paper's quality, do not send it. A questionable paper may do more harm than good.

Application Fees

Last but unfortunately not least, most schools require application fees. These fees range from $0 to $100 per school, and average $50 for doctoral programs and $35 for master's programs (Norcross et al., 2005). Credits cards are typically used when applying electronically. Or, you can send a personal or a cashier's check (never cash).

If you are in dire financial need or are experiencing trouble meeting application expenses, read the application instructions carefully. There is usually a statement allowing fees to be waived because of financial hardship. Go to the school's application Web site or call and ask how to have the application fee waived. That some students cannot afford the fees is the reason schools make the allowance in the first place. Graduate schools are sensitive to the impoverished status of many applicants, so feel no compunction about requesting a fee waiver if it applies to you.

Check and Recheck

At this point, you have completed the application forms, requested letters of recommendation (and seen to it they were sent), written your personal statement, asked to have transcripts and GREs transmitted, and copied the unsolicited documents you plan to include in your applications. Once again, before you actually submit the material, ask your mentor or a professor to check it for accuracy and clarity. Have friends review it for typos and spelling. All material should look neat and professional. It represents you in a very real way. Anything sloppy or tattered can convey the message that *you* are careless and unprofessional. Submission of materials should reflect a meticulous attention to detail. *Finally, ensure your personal statement is not among those we see each year that carelessly includes the name of a different university when explaining why it is a perfect match for you!*

After all this effort, make certain your applica-

tion is sent on time. In most cases, the application is sent electronically. If a couple of programs request that you send the application the old-fashioned way, we suggest (if you can afford the extra expense) that you send your application via FedEx, UPS, Express, or certified mail. Each of these will allow you to track your materials to ensure they have arrived and to document the name of the person to whom they were delivered. However, our suggestion does not imply that you should wait until the last minute to express mail your application, implying procrastination (not a positive quality in a graduate student). Do use express mail, but do it well ahead of the deadline.

One of the most frustrating experiences in the graduate application process is confirming that the respective programs have, in fact, received all of your materials. Your application, transcripts, GREs, letters of recommendation—all need to be received, processed, and filed correctly by the graduate admissions office. Horror stories abound about application materials being lost or misfiled or sent to the wrong department. It happened to one of us!

Recently, one of our students shared a similar story. The ETS claimed that her GRE scores were electronically transmitted to and downloaded at a major Midwest university. The university, which required two official sets of GRE scores, claimed that they never received either set. The student was caught in the middle between two opposing claims. She telephoned ETS again and the university's graduate admissions office repeatedly. The GREs had to be resent, at the student's expense.

We estimate that 50% of graduate programs will send an e-mail or postcard apprising you of the application materials they have received on your behalf. Another 20% to 25% of graduate programs will post an application status page on their Web site where you can check yourself. That leaves 25% of the graduate programs that you can either blindly trust (which we *do not* recommend) or that you can contact (which we *do* recommend).

Call or e-mail the admissions office and verify that the material has been received. You have invested too much sweat, time, and money to leave the application to chance. Do not rely on graduate schools to keep you apprised; take personal responsibility.

CHAPTER 7
MASTERING THE INTERVIEW

The applications have been electronically submitted or physically mailed and are now out of your hands. Following the short-lived relief of finishing your applications, this period can be a nerve-wracking time. You have sold yourself on paper, and now it is up to the graduate programs to decide which applicants to contact for further consideration and probable interviews.

The doctoral admissions process has been characterized as "multiple hurdles" (King, Beehr, & King, 1986). The initial hurdle in most programs is the GRE and GPA score minimums. The second hurdle is the rating of applications on such criteria as clinical experience, research skills, letters of recommendation, and the like. Being invited for an interview means you have successfully leaped these early hurdles, and this is a great compliment in and of itself. The final and determining hurdle for most programs is the personal interview.

Let's look at this situation from the perspective of graduate programs. APA-accredited clinical psychology programs receive an average of 150 to 225 applicants (Norcross, Ellis, & Sayette, 2010) and APA-accredited counseling psychology programs receive an average of 60 to 120 applicants (Norcross, Evans, & Ellis, 2010). The admissions committee must narrow the entire applicant pool to a smaller number to invite for interviews. Programs ordinarily interview two to three times as many students as they can admit. A research-oriented Ph.D. program will typically invite 20 applicants for interviews, from which 10 to 12 will be tendered an offer to obtain 7 confirmed acceptances. By contrast, a large Psy.D. program may invite 120 applicants for interviews, from which they will accept 90 in order to obtain 50 confirmed acceptances.

Not all programs require personal interviews, and they will most likely state in the application if they do not. Make a note of this so that you do not become distressed when you are not invited. We wonder which is worse: the disappointment of not being asked to interview or the stress of being asked!

Our research on APA-accredited clinical, counseling, and combined psychology programs found that 93% of them required some type of preadmission interview (Oliver et al., 2005). As shown in Figure 7-1, 62% of APA-accredited programs strongly preferred

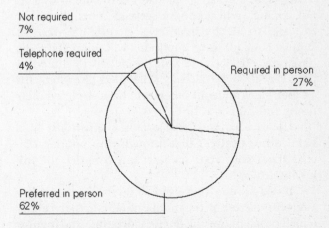

FIGURE 7-1. Preadmission interview policies of APA-accredited programs. Data from Oliver, Norcross, Sayette, Griffin, & Mayne (2005).

an interview in person but were willing to accept a telephone interview. Another 27% of the programs absolutely required a face-to-face interview. Four percent required only a telephone interview. All told, only 7% of programs did not require an interview before admission into the program.

Nearly all clinical and counseling psychology programs, then, require some type of personal interview, be it by phone or in person, prior to acceptance. Since some programs absolutely insist on interviews in person, do *not* apply to distant programs requiring an in-person interview unless you can afford it. Only in rare instances will graduate programs reimburse the applicant for all interview costs, and only 10% of the programs reimburse for some of the costs (Kohout et al., 1991). In other words, more than 80% of the programs expect you to absorb all the interview expenses.

Expect to hear from interested doctoral programs that require interviews from early-January through early March. The contact date will depend in part on the practice-research emphasis of the program: the clinical scientist and scientist-practitioner Ph.D. programs contact finalists earlier and typically finish their admission offers in March, whereas practice-oriented Ph.D. and Psy.D. programs contact finalists later. Programs rarely contact students in the finalist pool after March 30 because offers must go out on April 1, at the latest. It is still possible to be contacted, however, if you are on the alternate or waiting list.

Interview Strategically

The simple situation occurs when you are invited on a couple of interviews, the dates of the interviews do not conflict, and you have set aside enough money to travel to all the interviews. If only life were so simple! Instead, some applicants will not receive any interview offers, some will be invited to interview on a day they are already scheduled elsewhere for an interview, and still others will have depleted their funds and cannot afford interview travel.

How to handle these complex situations? In a word, strategically. Think through your options, discuss them with your mentor, and consider the following strategies.

If you have not received an interview request or a rejection letter by the middle of March, then calmly e-mail or telephone the doctoral program and inquire about the status of your application. If you have been rejected, politely thank the person. You never know: you may apply there again or have professional con-

tact with the people in that program in the future. If your application is still being considered, it is permissible to ask when you might expect a decision. Just be careful not to be rigid or demanding.

If you are offered a personal interview at two doctoral programs on the same day, not to worry. Should you be so blessed, we recommend that you (1) inquire if the programs have alternative interview days (and schedule one program on the alternative day). If not, then (2) ask if you can complete a video-conference interview or telephone interview at the less-preferred program. Remember that approximately two-thirds of programs will accept a telephone interview. If you value both programs equally, then (3) accept the interview at the least expensive program or the program with the higher likelihood of acceptance.

If you have depleted your funds for interview travel, then honestly inform the program and respectfully request a phone interview. Your e-mail might read: "I am very interested in your program and initially planned to attend your interview day on February 15th. Unfortunately, my personal finances do not allow me to travel to Bogus University on that day. I am hopeful that you will permit me to conduct a phone interview on a day that is convenient for you. Thanks very much for understanding; I do wish that I could visit in person." Realize, though, that in some instances, this may harm your chances of gaining admission.

Many applicants obtain strategic information on interview invitations and admission offers from online message boards. The last few years have witnessed an increase in the number and popularity of these message boards devoted to doctoral programs in psychology (Fauber, 2006). Three examples spring to mind: PsychGrad.org, the Student Doctor Network (psychology), and Yahoo Message Board. These and other online boards are particularly valuable for notifying everyone the moment interview invitations are extended and admission offers are delivered. They also provide peer support through the taxing application process. However, we have read much online advice that is questionable, even downright wrong. Thus, use the free online boards to secure strategic information and timely support from peers but be wary of the proffered advice.

The Dual Purpose

The interview provides a critical opportunity for information gathering, not only for the graduate program but also for you. That is, the dual purpose of an interview is for the program to check you out and for you to check out the program. Perhaps right now it seems outrageous to contemplate evaluating a doctoral program—you're probably delighted just to be asked! But a few interviews and an acceptance or two will reorient your perspective.

If you go on more than one interview, these interactions will give you decisive information in choosing which program to attend. You will find out about clinical training, faculty members, student life, program fit, research facilities, and the like. Interviewers will look at your social skills, your emotional stability, your professional maturity, your focus, and your goals. The interviewers may want to see the development of your pursuits, the connection between your research and clinical work, or perhaps your adherence to the Boulder or Vail model. You may be asked pointed questions and will be expected to ask probing questions about the program.

Although the interview often generates anxiety for an applicant, it need not. As with anything else in the application process, the more you prepare, the more confident and less nervous you will feel.

A few basic observations about the interview process will contribute to your preparation. The interview is highly charged for the applicants and programs alike. *Both* wish to be evaluated positively and to achieve the best match. You are not alone in trying to put your best foot forward! Interview styles, moreover, vary tremendously—from a conversational tone to grueling questions, from casual to formal, from mundane content to intrusively personal content. Be prepared for all styles, and remember that all count equally in the final analysis. That final analysis is the program's unenviable task of deciding which of the interviewees they will eventually select for admission.

Rehearsal and Mock Interviews

Rehearse the interview beforehand with your mentor, a professor, a career counselor, or a knowledgeable friend. Although the research-oriented programs are usually less personal and invasive in their interviews, it may behoove you to get accustomed to being asked personal questions without being thrown. Such practice is invaluable, especially for preparing you to think on your feet. Rehearsing also will desensitize you to some degree, take the edge off of your anxiety, and add to your comfort with the process. During the interview you are on stage, selling yourself, and knowing what the interview is all about can only help you.

In keeping with the dual purpose of the interview, rehearsing will also afford you practice in the interview style you seek to convey. A respectful and curious tone—"I am wondering about the chances of receiving an assistantship if I am fortunate enough to be accepted?"—is preferable to a blunt and forceful disposition—"How much will you pay me if I come?" How you phrase a question is important. The interviewer will be more impressed with your eagerness to learn if you ask how many courses in an area are *offered* as opposed to how many are *required* (Megargee, 1990).

Rehearsing should also entail preparation for frequently asked questions of applicants. Table 7-1 presents common interview questions to anticipate and prepare for. *We strongly recommend that you have a concise and thoughtful response ready for each of these*. An "I haven't really given that question much thought" answer hurts. Role-play these questions with a professor or, better yet, undergo a mock interview at your career services center. During this pretend experience, request that the interviewer ask several of the questions in Table 7-1 and videotape the encounter.

The type of doctoral program will naturally influence the content of interview questions. For those of you interviewing at research-oriented Ph.D. programs, don't be surprised if most of the interview questions focus on your research experiences and how your research interests match with particular faculty members there. This also might include discussing past research projects to allow the professor to evaluate how well you think on your feet about research. For those of you interviewing at Psy.D. programs, most of the questions will center on your clinical experiences and interests and how you match that program's training model.

Beneath the dozens and dozens of possible questions that an interviewer could ask you, career experts say they all boil down to only a few basic questions. The people making the final decisions really want to know (Bolles, 2006):

- Why are you *here?* (As opposed to another graduate program; in other words, how well do you fit with us?)
- What can you do for us? (How can your skills, knowledge, and experience enhance our program?)
- What kind of person are you? (Are you reliable and personable? Can we trust you with our research projects and/or our clinic patients?)
- What distinguishes you from 20 other people who can do the same tasks? (What makes you

TABLE 7-1. Common Interview Questions to Anticipate

1. Why do you want to be a psychologist?
2. What qualifications do you have that will make you a successful psychologist?
3. What attracts you to our program?
4. Will you tell me a little about yourself as a person?
5. Do you think your undergraduate grades (or GRE scores) are valid indicators of your academic abilities?
6. What do you see as your strengths and weaknesses?
7. What do you bring into the program? What are your special attributes?
8. Have you ever had personal therapy? If yes, what sort of issues did you work on? If no, why not?
9. What are your research interests? Tell me about your research project/honors thesis.
10. What is your theoretical orientation?
11. Which of our faculty members do you think you would work with?
12. Where else have you applied or interviewed?
13. Can you tell me about a recent clinical encounter? How did you conceptualize or treat your last client?
14. What are your hobbies, avocations, favorite books, and interests outside of psychology?
15. What are your future plans and goals as a psychologist? Where do you want to be in 10 years?
16. How do you work under stress and pressure? Can you give me examples?
17. How will you finance your graduate education?
18. What attracts you to the Boulder (or Vail) model of training?
19. What is your interest in teaching during graduate school? In your career?
20. What questions do you have for me?

different from the other qualified applicants we are interviewing? Do you work better, harder, longer, more thoroughly?)

- Can we get you here? (If we accept you into our program, what is the probability that you will attend? How much will it cost us—in tuition remission or an assistantship, for example?)

Of course, you cannot anticipate all possible questions. Some interviewers pride themselves on avoiding stock questions and instead asking novel questions, thus precluding rehearsed and polished replies. The rationale behind these queries, such as "Who are your heroes?" and "What was the best day in your life?" is that they give a glimpse into your natural response style and tap into spontaneous information processing. One method to handle novel queries is to delay thoughtfully, remark that it is one you have not been asked before, request a moment of contemplation, and then respond forthrightly.

Similar to novel questions are behavior-based interview questions. These are increasingly being asked to assess an applicant's behavioral repertoire and actual experiences. The behavioral questions rely on the familiar psychological dictum, "Past

behavior is the best predictor of future behavior," to glean something about your future behavior in their doctoral program. Six examples are:

- Tell me about an instance when someone asked you to do something that you considered ethically or morally wrong. How did you respond?
- Describe the biggest challenges you faced in the past year and how you handled it.
- Tell me about a work or school situation where you had to do creative problem solving.
- Relate a recent situation in which you had to persuade someone to accept your idea or proposal.
- Present an example when multiple priorities were pulling you in several directions at the same time and how you dealt with it.
- Tell me about an instance when you were unsuccessful in reaching a goal that involved a client, a customer, or a fellow student.

In responding to such questions, follow the *three S's:* Situation, Skills, and Success. First, describe the situation and your challenge or conflict. For example, "I was working with a group of students for a class project and all of us but one student agreed on the way to proceed." Second, identify your skills that helped you to master the situation. For example, "I tried to understand the dissenter's perspective, communicate that understanding back to him, spoke to the faculty member about her preferences, and asked the dissenter for a compromise." Third, communicate a successful ending, both for you and the other party involved in the situation. "The other person appreciated my listening, instead of arguing, and in the end agreed to go with the group decision. He was happy and the project ended with us all learning a lot and earning an A on the project."

Your answers to behavior-based questions will enable you to concretely demonstrate integrity, resilience, creativity, persuasion, and time management as opposed to simply saying you possess those traits. Apply the three S's to similar questions as those presented above involving conflicted relationships, ethical dilemmas, and complicated decisions. Visit Web sites on behavioral and situational interviews to get comfortable and competent in answering such questions; two of our favorite sites are the behavioral interview links off of www.quintcareers.com and www.emurse.com. Practice the three S's in your mock interview and you will be prepared to tackle even the thorniest questions.

Interview Attire

Your interview rehearsal should direct attention to your physical attire, which will be an influential factor in attributions made about you. For men, we recommend a conservative two-piece suit or a jacket and slacks, white or light shirt, and contrasting tie. Three-piece suits and "funeral outfits" are out. Wear shined brown or black shoes that are well maintained; as your parents have probably told you, the way you take care of your shoes communicates a lot about you. Dark socks only; save your white socks for workouts. Hair should be trimmed and neatly groomed. For women, we recommend a pant suit or a suit with a skirt, dark in color or muted plaid, polished pumps or medium heels in matching color. Wear a simple style blouse, white or soft color. Interview professionals suggest a no-distraction hairstyle, tasteful makeup, and clear or light nail polish. One pair of small earrings should suffice. Avoid wearing spikes or stilettos; others may see them as "club attire" and you may suffer from bruised feet or buckling ankles. For both men and women, plan your interview clothes in advance. Try them on, and lay them out well before the interview to assure that they fit, are clean, and are in good repair.

Some applicants prefer to "be themselves" and may still get in without changing their typical appearance. Nevertheless, we recommend that attire should err on the side of conservative and formal; better to be overdressed and loosen a tie or remove a scarf than to be underdressed for the occasion. Avoid flashy colors and loud fashions. Jewelry should be conservative and understated; go light on the perfume and cologne. Leave the piercings at home.

Some applicants complain to us that many faculty interviewers are wearing business casual, and thus ask why they (the applicants) can't wear business casual as well. Our answer is clear: You are an applicant trying to make a stellar impression as a serious, motivated candidate for a competitive graduate program. You are trying to distinguish yourself as one of the premier students, not one of the underdressed herd. We urge you to dress for success in interviews, not in business casual. You can wear casual clothes after you are admitted to the program for most of your graduate life. But during the interview, you never have a second chance to make a first impression.

Questions about the program and other written material should be held in a professional attaché or briefcase. The location and weather will influence your choice of clothing. Reliable answers about expected attire can be provided by graduate students with whom you are staying prior to the interview itself.

Travel Arrangements

While preparing and rehearsing for the interviews, you simultaneously will be making arrangements to travel to the interviews. The costs of travel vary wildly—from a few bucks for parking at a local university on interview day to more than $1,000 for a 3-day jaunt across the nation involving air travel, rental car, and hotel. Our intent in the following paragraphs is to save you hassle and money in getting to the interviews.

As a general rule, you can save a great deal of money by booking early and paying promptly for air travel, but you will probably incur a stiff penalty for making any changes in your reservation. So begin early to locate those bargains. Start by going online to seek the best fares through airlines' Web sites. Airlines typically post special discounted fares on their sites. Before booking, take a quick look at kayak.com, expedia.com, travelocity.com, and other commercial sites that promise the lowest possible fares. Compare the schedules and fares from both sources—the airlines' Web site and commercial Web sites—and then make a decision.

Being flexible in your travel schedule will probably save you money. It may save you money to leave from a different city than the one closest to you. We have saved hundreds of dollars on airfare by simply driving an extra hour to another airport. Or it may save you money to fly to a different city and then drive an hour or two to the interview. Try inserting nearby alternative cities in your computer search and see what fare comes up. One applicant flew out of Washington, DC instead of his home airport of Norfolk, Virginia, and reduced his ticket price from over $1,000 to $278 (Megargee, 2001).

Another way of being flexible is changing when you fly. As most business travelers return home on the weekend, airlines typically offer deep discounts on trips that extend over a Saturday night. The cost of another night at the hotel might save you hundreds in airfare. And consider flying on the "red eye" or "night owl" flights that criss-cross the country overnight. In order to fill otherwise empty seats, airlines frequently offer reduced fares at unpopular (and ungodly) hours (Megargee, 2001).

Booking an airline ticket with multiple destinations (circle trips) can also ease the toll on your credit card. You can fly from Chicago to an interview in Denver and then onto an interview in Dallas before returning to Chicago. This circle ticket often costs less than a separate round trip to each destination.

Build in time for travel delays due to inclement weather. After all, you will be traveling during the months of January, February, and March. Even if your flight is between two uniformly sunny cities in the South, the originating aircraft may be stuck in the snow in the Northeast or grounded because of sleet in the Midwest.

Some doctoral programs coordinate rides from the airport to the university for applicants, but most do not. You are on your own. In advance of your arrival, check out bus and train routes. The university's homepage will typically have public transportation routes and driving directions from the local airport to the campus. If public transportation is unavailable, you will need to rent a car at the airport. You will discover, again, that the rental costs vary widely. And you will, again, investigate the costs early and aggressively to locate the best fare. Rely on the three traditional sources—the rental company's toll-free number, its Web site, and the commercial travel Web sites—for several rental companies.

Renting a car on your own will require at least three things: a valid driver's license; a major credit card in your name; and a chronological age over the minimum, typically 25 years of age. The latter can be a huge hassle if you are still an undergraduate; be aware of the company's age policy in advance. Most companies will charge an extra daily fee for renters age 21 to 24—typically about $25 per day.

Most doctoral programs will extend you an invitation to room with a graduate student in the program the night before the interview. If possible, take advantage of this opportunity. It will allow you to save money, acquire masses of information, and gain a sense of student life and the campus community from people in a position to know. If you reside with a graduate student, ask for a tour the day or night before the interview. Ask to see the psychology building, the training clinic, the library, and some of the labs. If possible, get comfortable with the rooms where the interviews will be held.

Unfortunately, not all programs offer or provide a free place to sleep. In these cases, unless you have a large extended family, you will spend an evening or two in a hotel. Your task here is to secure a safe, convenient location at a reasonable rate. Use the AAA tour book and the Web for preliminary reconnaissance. If you have wheels, you can often save money by staying at one of the less expensive motels on the edge of town or near an Interstate exit. In particular, if you are on a tight budget, be sure to check out places with the code word "Inn" in their names, as in Comfort Inn, Days Inn, Fairfield Inn, Hampton Inn, Hobo Inn, and Red Roof Inn (Megargee, 2001).

Even these inns may have negotiated rates. Ask the person scheduling your interview if the university has negotiated special rates with any local hotels. When booking your room, ask what discounts are available—for students, AAA members, government employees, and so on.

Whether you spend the night in a hotel or with a graduate student, you may well be invited to dinner. Be sociable and friendly, but do not drink heavily or party hearty the night before (even though you may be invited!). Get a solid night's sleep, arise on time, and eat a sensible breakfast.

Although we discussed attire and appearance in the previous section, it is worth a few more sentences as applied to travel. You may well experience delays or cancellations in your flight itinerary or in your driving time to the interview. As a consequence, you may not have that expected hour or two to clean up and change clothes before the interview. Or you may meet other applicants en route and faculty members at the airport. The moral: take only carry-on luggage and do not travel in cutoffs, warm-up suits, or t-shirts unless you are prepared to interview in that outfit. Dress and travel like a professional.

Interview Style

The objective of your interview style is to present yourself as a confident, knowledgeable, and genuine person—an imperfect human, to be sure, but one without major interpersonal deficits or gross psychopathology. Even if you are anxious, try to appear relaxed, calm, confident. Any anxiety you may be experiencing is understandable and should be dealt with maturely. Strive to be as mature and natural as possible.

The interview is designed for the interviewer to get to know you as a person—your interpersonal skills, career goals, and clinical acumen. One of the few empirical studies on the role of the personal interview in the psychology admission process found that the rating of an applicant's clinical potential was the most highly weighted measure among all the interview data. Ratings of verbal skills and research skills also contributed to the prediction equation, but ratings of clinical potential contributed most to discriminating among groups of accepted applicants, alternates, and rejected applicants (Nevid & Gildea, 1984). In one way or another, you must impress the interviewers as someone they would be comfortable sending a member of their own family to for professional treatment.

The following factors have been found to lead to rejection of an applicant during interviews (Fretz, 1976):

• Poor personal appearance
• Overbearing, overaggressive, know-it-all style
• Inability to express yourself clearly—poor voice, diction, grammar
• Inadequate interest and enthusiasm—passive, indifferent
• Lack of confidence and poise—nervousness, appearing ill at ease
• Making excuses, evasiveness, hedging on unfavorable factors in record
• Lack of tact and maturity
• Condemnation of past professors
• Little sense of humor
• Emphasis on whom you know
• Inability to take criticism
• Failure to ask questions about the program

The last point is worth emphasizing. Each interviewer will want to get to know you as a person and will expect you to ask questions. Nothing is tougher on an interviewer than the person who does not ask questions or simply responds "Yes" or "No."

So even if it has been a long day, when the fourth interviewer asks you if you have any questions, don't reply, "No, all my questions have already been answered." And respond to the questions of the fourth interviewer with the same enthusiasm as you showed to the first interviewer (Megargee, 1990).

At the same time that you are conveying clinical potential and a mature interpersonal presence, you want to acquire the factual program information necessary to make informed decisions. Table 7-2 presents questions you can ask when you interview. You should ask some of these questions during the interview, others before, and others after. Some should be asked of professors, because they are best suited to answer them and asking can make you look prepared and informed. Some questions should be asked of first-year students because they have recently been through the process and are closest to your situation. Some questions are better asked of advanced graduate students because they are about to leave and may have less investment in hiding the program's shortcomings.

The best questions to ask are those that indicate initiative, curiosity, and responsibility (Hersh & Poey, 1984). Try to communicate motivation to learn and eagerness to participate in many activities; avoid questions that promote a speculation that you are demanding, complaining, or single-minded.

A caveat: never ask for information that is available in the program description or the graduate catalog. These questions make you appear unprepared for the interview and uninterested in the program.

Alternatively, link your questions to the information provided on the program's Web site. Examples might include: "I read that all of your first-year students receive an assistantship and tuition remission. Is this also true of second-year students?" "Your graduate catalogue lists a Couples Therapy course, a special interest of mine, but it does not indicate if clinical supervision in that area is available." "While reading about your impressive Psychological Services Clinic, I wondered how many of the full-time clinical faculty provide supervision there." And so on.

The intent is to get beyond the gloss and formality of the published program descriptions to the lived and personal experiences of the program participants. Virtually all descriptions of clinical and counseling psychology programs, for example, will allude to ample opportunities for practical experience in

TABLE 7-2. Interview Questions an Applicant Might Ask

Practice

Is training available in different theoretical orientations?

Is the supervision individual or group? Is it live supervision?

Do the full-time faculty conduct the clinical supervision?

What type of supervision will I receive?

When do I actually begin clinical work?

How many practica are offered?

What are your off-campus clinical practica like? Where are they located?

What types of patient populations are available?

Are specialty clinics available?

How many of the full-time faculty are licensed?

Do the faculty have active private practices?

Do faculty serve as clinicians or consultants at local mental health facilities?

Research

How common is it for students to be coauthors on peer-reviewed publications?

What is the student–faculty ratio?

About how many dissertations and master's theses are chaired by each faculty member?

When and how am I assigned an advisor?

Does this person have weekly research meetings?

Could I sit in on a lab meeting?

How many core faculty members are actively involved in research projects (e.g., regularly publishing)?

How many research grants finance graduate students?

If I wanted to change my mentor or advisor, is that allowed?

How many computers are available to graduate students?

Are computers readily available? Is photocopying free?

Is SAS, SPSS, or R available?

What is the relationship with the medical or law school?

Finances

What percentage of students receive full financial support (assistantship plus tuition waiver)?

What types of fellowships are available?

What types of research and teaching assistantships are available?

What is the average amount of a 9-month assistantship?

Who gets tuition remission? What are my chances?

Do the stipends cover the costs of living in this area? How expensive are the rents?

What percentage of students receive funding during the summer?

Do any of the assistantships include health insurance?

What percentage of students have taken out student loans?

Quality of Life

What is it like to live around campus? Is it safe? Expensive?

What is the surrounding city/town like?

Is graduate housing available? Do most students live on campus?

What is the off-campus housing situation like? The neighborhoods?

Where can I go to get a housing application today?

Are there theaters, movies, decent restaurants nearby?

Is there public transportation, or do I need a car?

What are some of the campus events and clubs?

Is the Graduate Student Association active?

Do the students socialize frequently?

How is the student cohesion?

Do students and faculty attend the colloquia?

Can I speak to a couple of graduate students here?

Department and Politics

Do students and faculty have good relationships with each other?

Do graduate students have a role in departmental policy and admission decisions?

In your experience, what are the best and worst features of this program? (ask of graduate students)

What are one or two things you wished you knew before attending this program? (ask of graduate students)

What is the standing of the psychology department within the university?

How do the different branches of psychology interact?

What are the professional goals of the current students?

How many fifth-, sixth-, seventh- . . . year students are there?

Is there a sense of competition or cooperation among the students?

How much emphasis is put on course work and grades?

How common are grades of C?

Do professors tend to collaborate on projects?

Do I get a master's degree along the way? When is this usually done?

Can the program be undertaken on a part-time basis? What percentage of the student body is part-time?

When do I take the qualifying exams? What are they like? How many people fail? Can they be retaken?

Could I see a course schedule for next (or last) year?

Are teaching opportunities available for graduate students?

For applicants who already have a master's: Once accepted, how are transcripts evaluated regarding credits?

Outcomes

Where do your students complete their internships?

What percentage of your students obtains an APPIC or APA-accredited internship?

What is the average length of the program (including internship)?

What percentage of your incoming students eventually earn their doctorates here?

Do dissertations usually get published?

In what type of settings do most of your graduates eventually find employment—academic, private practice, clinics?

off-campus placements. But when you directly ask students, "What is your clinical placement like?" their answers may diverge substantially from the published information. Their responses may indeed be positive, but it is not uncommon to learn that some of the placements are 50 miles away, do not offer any stipend, and are very competitive. To be sure, be tactful in your questioning, but also be assertive in securing crucial data.

Program directors (e.g., Hersh & Poey, 1984) have nominated certain questions to *avoid* asking. These unwittingly annoy interviewers or communicate an undesirable impression: questions regarding the typical length of a graduate-student week, which may indicate fear of hard work or a long week; persistent inquiries regarding an area of interest that the graduate program only minimally provides; questions reflecting resistance to learning the major theoretical orientation offered by that program; and antagonistic questions concentrating on the perceived limitations of the program, be they financial, faculty, or geographical.

Bring your list of questions with you to the interview, but do not constantly have it in plain sight to check off. Your task is to ask the questions of the most appropriate individuals in a respectful manner. On a similar note, many people have PDAs to help organize personal information. Though you might use one to make an important note at the *end* of an interview, keep them away during the interview itself.

On that note, cell phones and beepers should be turned off during the interview. Not on vibrate or silent alert; completely off. Having one beep or buzz will be disruptive, and checking a pager or taking a call would be seen as *extremely* unprofessional and rude. Nobody is as important on interview day as the interviewers.

Extreme ideologies—religious, sociopolitical, or clinical—do not bode well in interviews. One interesting study (Gartner, 1986) mailed mock graduate school applications to professors of clinical psychology. The results showed that professors were more likely to admit an applicant who made no mention of religion than they were to admit an otherwise identical applicant who was identified as a fundamentalist Christian. Do not deny your beliefs, of course, but try to avoid expressions of rigid extremes. Academics favor informed pluralism and critical open-mindedness.

Bernard Lubin (1993), a former national president of Psi Chi and a veteran of conducting admission interviews, enjoins applicants to present themselves as *knowledgeable* and *collaborative* during the interview. Being familiar with the research interests and productivity of the program faculty can go a long way. Carefully reading the program's online material and identifying faculty publications through *PsycLIT* are direct evidence of a mature and scholarly attitude. This leads to presenting yourself as a potential collaborator: welcoming opportunities to work with faculty members and fellow students, displaying an affirming and positive attitude toward interdependent activities.

Our final piece of advice on interview style concerns your nonverbal behavior. Some applicants are so preoccupied with asking questions and trying to impress the interviewer that they neglect the way they present themselves nonverbally. But interviewer impressions of candidate personality depend heavily on nonverbal behaviors (Anderson & Shackleton, 1990). Maintaining eye contact, making changes in posture, and varying facial expressions strongly contribute to an image as a mature and enthusiastic person. The research consistently advises interviewees to keep high levels of eye contact with the interviewer and to display frequent positive facial expressions to maximize their chances of success. (Of course, we don't suggest that you fake your smiles, as that likely won't be persuasive and may even be off-putting!) Your mock and actual interviews should strive for an interpersonally engaging style that creates personal liking and that cultivates an impression of interpersonal and intellectual skill.

Literally hundreds of Web sites offer advice on interviewing skills. Although they are no substitute for live rehearsals and mock interviews, they are a source of considerable information and examples. Some even offer virtual interviews. Our favorite sites are:

- www.quintcareers.com
- www.quintcareers.com/behavioral_interviewing.html
  (specifically on behavioral interviewing)
- www.glencoe.com/sec/careers/career_city/
- www.nextsteps.org

Stressful Questions

This brings us to consider a prominent fear, namely, being placed on the spot with intensely personal questions. You may have heard "war stories" about applicants being asked intimate questions about their families of origin, romantic relationships, and personal history they would prefer not to share.

You should be prepared to answer personal questions about such relationships and self-perceptions. Answering these questions in a straightforward manner contributes to the interviewer's positive evaluation of an applicant.

The nature of these questions varies with the interviewer's style as well as the program's theoretical orientation. Applying to a research-oriented cognitive-behavioral program, however, is no guarantee that you will not be interviewed by a psychodynamic member of their faculty. Questions pertaining to family conflict or to your personal therapy could arise. Anticipating such questions can help you to determine how to handle them most comfortably and to decide how much information you are willing to disclose. Knowing where to set your boundaries will lead to a smoother interview.

Speaking of boundaries, the APA Ethics Code (APA, 2002, p. 1068) does not require students to disclose sensitive information regarding their "sexual history, history of abuse and neglect, psychological treatment, and relationships with parents, peers, and spouses or significant others" unless the training program has clearly identified this requirement ahead of time. Thus, unless the program notified you of such a requirement for the interview, you are not ethically obliged to reveal such personal information. Our advice is to balance your need for privacy with the program's need for information about your personal history and psychological dynamics.

One stressful but popular question concerns your personal weaknesses. Applicants naturally wonder how honest to be about their deficits and try to balance the need for honesty with the need to leave a favorable impression. We have found three strategies useful in approaching this question. One is to minimize an existing limitation: showing your awareness of it but not articulating the full severity or manifestation. If being taken advantage of frequently is your perceived weakness, for example, you might reply on the order of "Occasionally I find myself being taken advantage of by others in small but consistent ways." A second strategy is to turn the weakness into a possible strength. Following the same example, you might remark that "I give to a fault on occasion and notice some people will take advantage of my tendency to look for the best in people." A third possible strategy is to express your awareness of the weakness and your efforts to remediate it; this reply demonstrates both introspective and corrective attitudes. "I've been working to become more conscious of how people, especially personality-disordered clients, can take advantage of me. My overtrusting nature

is slowly giving way as I attend more closely to this relationship pattern." Whatever strategy—or combination of strategies—you elect, the response must be consistent with who you are. A phony or inauthentic response can immediately strike an applicant from further consideration.

One stressful situation necessitates your careful preparation. A few programs and faculty use what is called a stress interview. In this interview, the faculty member intentionally acts inappropriately and tries to intimidate applicants, simply to see how they handle the stress of the situation. This can come in many forms: long silences after you answer questions; asking overly intimate questions; disagreeing violently with your position or answer; feigning disinterest in you as an applicant; or even giving you coffee in one hand, a powdered donut without a napkin in the other, and then handing you an article to browse! Knowing ahead of time that this can happen is crucial, because you can remind yourself that it is not personal but simply part of the process. In a few programs, the professors place all the applicants in an empty room and suggest they speak with each other while the professors observe the interpersonal process: no other directions, no other structure. This all serves to compound the students' anxiety.

Stress interviews are designed to assess how comfortably you behave under such interpersonally challenging conditions. The interviewers deliberately arrange situations or ask questions that you cannot predict, for examples, "How would you redesign a giraffe?" or "Where is Oregon?" The particular answer you give is not as important as the manner in which you answer. Here your interpersonal savvy and presence can triumph. The interviewer is testing your reaction to stress: do you react to stress with humor, anxiety, self-denigration, anger? The stress interview is an ambiguous, semi-projective device.

Our advice is to remain calm and polite, yet assertive. Do not become entangled in a verbal battle or retreat into an apologetic or defensive stance. In the face of an inappropriately personal question, a "I wonder how that question relates to my admission here?" will demonstrate both your personal boundaries and your willingness to broach a difficult topic. In the face of continuing conflict, a polite "we respectfully disagree" can suffice, and leave it at that (Heppner & Downing, 1982).

Practicing stress interviews with professors or peers may sufficiently desensitize you to keep your head and field the situation without too much ego bruising. Another way to prepare yourself is to stay overnight before the interview and take the opportunity to ask graduate students which professors might conduct such an interview, allowing you to know ahead of time that this person is likely to intentionally try to stress you. Foreknowledge and preparation are the best defenses.

Group Interviews

Admission interviews in clinical and counseling psychology differ markedly from one program to another. At one extreme, a few programs invite you for a single, 2-hour interview with a senior faculty member. That's it—no tour, no group interview, no program orientation, and no interaction with current graduate students.

At the other extreme, a number of programs invite selected applicants for an entire admissions weekend. At the University of Pittsburgh, for example, invitees to the clinical psychology program's weekend spend a full day (about 7 hours) interviewing with faculty and graduate students. In addition, there are clinical and research information sessions, laboratory tours, evening parties, and a poster session featuring research projects. Many of the applicants arrive on Friday and leave Sunday morning.

In between these two approaches are intensive 1-day sessions. For instance, at Fordham University's counseling psychology program (Kopala et al., 1995), the interview process entails a brief orientation to the program, individual interviews with a faculty member and a graduate student, a videotaped group experience, an open session with graduate students, and then a closing session with the director of training.

Virtually all programs will arrange for at least one individual interview with a faculty member and for interaction with current doctoral students. A healthy proportion of programs will also include admission interviews featuring multiple candidates in the same room at the same time. This group interview may be conducted in the interest of sheer efficiency, of observing your interpersonal style, or both.

Our advice on your interview style and objectives in these group interviews remains essentially the same as for the individual interviews, but there are a couple of twists. First of all, strive to be pleasant and honest with the other interviewees. Share your experiences, never denigrate their credentials, and treat them like future colleagues (which they may very well be). A negativistic or superior attitude is likely to be held against you in the deliberations of the admission committee.

Second, since it is a group situation, try to present yourself as an admirable facilitator. Don't be a group psychotherapist or a control maniac, but a respectful cofacilitator of the interview process. If you have already asked a few questions about the program, for instance, you might say that you have additional questions but would first like other people to have an opportunity to have their questions answered. As they say in the social psychology literature, try to manifest both a high task orientation and a high social orientation.

Additional Tips

Whether it is an individual interview or a group interview, here are additional tips regarding the interview.

- Arrive at least 15 minutes early on interview day. Find the offices, acclimate to the building, and get settled.
- Be compulsive and double-check your interview schedule. Being late or missing an interview (even when it is not your fault) can reflect poorly on you.
- Greet each interviewer in a friendly, open manner. Your handshake should be firm and your eye contact frequent.
- Demonstrate your active listening skills: wait to answer until the interviewer has completed asking the question and give complete answers to the question posed to you.
- Keep your answers to 1.5 to 2 minutes long. If interested, the interviewer can ask you for details or to expand. If your answer is sufficient, the interviewer can move onto another question or topic.
- Use good grammar and diction. Say "No," not "nah."
- Avoid all irritating hiccups in your answers. On the short list are the irritating "you know," "like," and "okay."
- Always bring extra copies of your CV. Every interviewer may have not received a copy or may have not yet reviewed it, so bring along copies to present and leave with people (Megargee, 1990).
- Take cash along in case you are invited to lunch or dinner with graduate students.
- Conclude each interview by thanking the interviewer for her time and information. Wrap it up with a hand shake and cordial tone.

Our collective experience in conducting interviews also generates a list of *don'ts:*

- Don't call faculty members by their first names until (or if) they offer. The default option is to call them "Dr." or "Professor."
- Don't whine or complain about the interview arrangements. Accept the free housing with gratitude; be agreeable about the food; act flexibly about interview dates. Nobody, including admissions committees, likes a fussbudget.
- Don't accept offers of coffee or other beverages during the interview itself. It tends to be messy, distracting, and awkward for you as the interviewee. Wait until after the interviews are complete and then graciously accept the offer.
- Don't say anything negative about other graduate programs or your previous faculty. It comes off as complaining and negative.
- Don't ask about or negotiate financial assistance before receiving an offer of admission. The nitty-gritty of finances can wait until later.
- And don't ask questions during the interview that are answered in the materials sent to you or posted on the program Web site. We have already made this point earlier in the chapter, but it is important enough to reiterate it here.

Follow these tips and you will relax more during the interview. The more relaxed and prepared you are, the more confident and authentic you will feel.

Telephone Interviews

Two situations may dictate a telephone interview. In the first, you are asked to visit the school for an interview, but you cannot afford to do so. This is no reason to be embarrassed, and the more straightforward you are about it the better. You can request a phone interview in advance if you do not have the resources for an actual visit. (As noted earlier, though, at some institutions failure to visit will place you at a competitive disadvantage.) In the second situation, you receive the dreaded, unannounced phone interview. At least one of your prospective programs will probably call without prior notice and ask to speak with you on the spot.

Luckily, if you anticipate telephone interviews, you have nothing to worry about. One strategy is to rarely or never take a phone interview "cold." Consider telling the caller, "I'm sorry, but I was just leaving for an appointment. Could you leave a number and arrange for me to call you back at a convenient time for you?" This buys you time to review your information on that program and to prepare for the

interview. However, you do not want to communicate disinterest in the program.

Another strategy is to prepare phone cards, palm pilot notes, or computer files. You make index cards or short files for each program to which you applied. On it, record a few reasons for your interest in that graduate program and the name(s) of the professor(s) you are interested in working with, a little about their research areas, and questions you may have about clinical training or facilities (many of the questions in Table 7-2). Figure 7-2 is an example of such a card. Keep these files with you, or on a computer by the phone and in moments you will find the card for a particular school and not be caught unaware! This little extra effort can prevent a serious detraction from your application. If you receive one of these telephone calls and cannot remember which professors are at that school, their areas of research, or their facilities, it tells the interviewer that you are not serious about his or her program. This could place you lower than someone who has this information off the top of his or her head.

A Note of Thanks

Once you have completed an interview, whether by telephone or in person, a brief note of thanks to the interviewer is in order. This gesture serves multiple purposes: it demonstrates your social skills, communicates your gratitude to the faculty and students involved, reaffirms your interest in the program, and keeps your name alive in the admission process. Seldom will such a brief note do so much for you. (Sending flowers, candies, or gifts is not deemed appropriate in these circumstances.)

The "who" and "what" of these thank-you letters are almost entirely dependent on your interview experiences. The "who" should certainly include anyone who has shown you special attention, such as a graduate student you roomed with the night before or after the interview, a professor who personally escorted you around a lab or clinic, or a faculty member who offered an unscheduled interview. Letters to several people are often called for. If the interview was less personal, then at a minimum send the Director of Training a letter of appreciation. A sample letter is displayed in Figure 7-3. An e-mail note of appreciation also may suffice.

The "what" of the letter must be individualized to your particular experiences, but will probably contain at least three components: an expression of gratitude for the interview, an enumeration of your favorable impressions of the program, and a reitera-

University of Alexandria

Reasons for my interest: Great reputation in child psychopathology and psychotherapy; specific professors (Smith, Adams); geographic location; has specialty clinic in behavioral medicine.

Key professors:

Dr. Smith: child psychopathology; substance abuse

I read your May [2009] article in *Journal of Bogus Psychology,* in which you found offspring of alcoholics to be more receptive to the anxiety-reducing effects of alcohol than control subjects. Do you expect to continue this line of research next year? Is an assistantship available?

Dr. Adams: behavioral medicine; psychotherapy

I was impressed that you have a separate clinic in behavioral medicine. What type of clients do you most often treat? What opportunities are there for clinical experience?

Other professors with potential interest:

Dr. Jones: prevention

Dr. Watson: forensic psychology

Program questions: [Refer to Table 7-2 for representative listing]

When do I begin seeing clients in the training clinic?

What percentage of incoming students are financially supported?

What are the research opportunities in child psychopathology?

FIGURE 7-2. Sample telephone card.

tion of your interest in attending that program. Try to personalize each letter by referring to specific topics or experiences; for instance, recall your discussion of potential research studies or mention the friendliness of the graduate students. There is no definitive list of do's and don'ts, but don't send a generic, impersonal letter and don't promote your candidacy. Do sound appreciative and personal. As with all written materials, ensure that your letter communicates an image of sincerity and professionalism. Most of the letters should probably be emailed, but a neat, handwritten note is appropriate if an interview was relatively informal and personal.

The Wait

Once you have completed the interviews and mailed the thank-you letters, it is a waiting game. But not for the programs, which still have a finalist pool of students much larger than they are able to accept! The interview process has probably weeded out a few, but the faculty are left with too many finalists, all of whom have acceptable GPAs, GREs, and letters of recommendation.

What, then, are the *final* selection criteria? This pivotal question was addressed in a study by Keith-Spiegel, Tabachnick, and Spiegel (1994), who had 113 faculty members actively involved in selecting psychology Ph.D. students rate criteria used in making the last cuts in admission decisions. (Results of this study should *not* be generalized to Psy.D. programs.) The faculty members were asked to imagine that they were left with a pool of finalists, three times the size of the number they can accept, all of whom had strong undergraduate GPAs, GRE scores, and letters of recommendation. They then rated 31 variables in terms of importance.

Congruent with this book's advice and earlier studies, the top-rated criteria in clinical programs pertained to student match with the program and its faculty, research experience resulting in a journal article or a paper presentation, and the clarity and focus of the applicant's statement of purpose. Considered to be somewhat to very important in assisting selection committees with their final admission decisions were research assistant experience; reputation of the student's referees; relevant clinical experience; membership in an underrepresented ethnic minority group; knowledge and interest in the pro-

March 16, 2012

Patricia Jones, Ph.D.
Director of Clinical Training
Department of Psychology
University of Western States
13 Orangegrove Drive
Wilksville, CA 98765

Dear Dr. Jones:

I want to thank you for interviewing me for a position in your clinical psychology doctoral program. I enjoyed meeting with your faculty and staff and learning more about the program. My enthusiasm for the program was particularly strengthened as a result of my interactions with Drs. Timothy Hogan, Elizabeth Cannon, and Carole Buchanan.

I want to reiterate my strong interest in attending your program; the University of Western States offers a great deal that appeals to me. Please feel free to call me at (123) 456-7890 or e-mail me at csmith@university.edu if I can provide you with any additional information.

Again, thank you for the interview and your consideration.

Sincerely yours,

Chris Smith

FIGURE 7-3. Sample letter of appreciation to an interviewer.

gram; number of statistics, methodology, and hard science courses completed; prestige of the psychology faculty in the student's undergraduate department; reputation of the undergraduate institution itself; and honors bestowed on the student by that undergraduate institution. Rated as not important or minimally important were such variables as the student's geographic residence, Psi Chi membership, and a close relationship between the student and former graduates of that program.

Demand always exceeds supply in competitive clinical and counseling psychology programs. The three primary criteria used to evaluate applicants by doctoral selection committees—grade point averages, GREs, and letters of recommendation—typically fail to narrow the applicant pool to the small number of slots available. At that point, research skills, clinical experiences, "good match" factors, and writing skills come to the fore (Keith-Spiegel et al., 1994). Bear these considerations in mind as you approach your interview—just as we have in preparing this book.

And now you wait until contacted with the final decision of the admissions committee. Until the week before April 1, it is probably not a good idea to contact a program and ask where you stand. Applicants who make repeated calls or e-mails may appear overly anxious and irritate the staff (Mitchell, 1996). The one exception is if you have received other offers, and the program you would most like to attend has not contacted you—a situation covered in Chapter 8.

This brings us to the last step in the application process and the final chapter of the *Insider's Guide*.

CHAPTER 8
MAKING FINAL DECISIONS

Before April 1, all APA-accredited clinical, coun-seling, and combined psychology programs will make their initial round of acceptance offers. Recall that research-oriented Ph.D. programs will almost always tender their first round of admission offers well before that date, even as early as February. Practice-oriented Ph.D. and Psy.D. programs tend to run later in the admissions season. Do not be surprised to receive a call or email only a few days after your interview.

At that point you will have until April 15th to make your final decision as to where you want to attend graduate school. By APA regulation, you have the right to consider offers until mid-April, at which time an offer may be withdrawn. So you must be thoughtful but decisive in these weeks.

To protect applicants from making hasty, prema-ture decisions, all APA-accredited programs and most others have agreed to allow candidates until April 15 for a decision (or the first Monday after April 15, if April 15 falls on a weekend). This is in accordance with a policy adopted by the Council of Graduate Schools in the United States and endorsed by the Council of Graduate Departments of Psychology. The Resolution Regarding Graduate Scholars, Fellows, Trainees and Assistants (www.cgsnet.org/?tabid=201) reads as follows:

> Acceptance of an offer of financial aid (such as graduate scholarship, fellowship, traineeship, or assistantship) for the next academic year by a pro-spective or enrolled graduate student completes an agreement that both student and graduate school

expect to honor. In that context, the conditions affecting such offers and their acceptance must be defined carefully and understood by all parties.

> Students are under no obligation to respond to offers of financial support prior to April 15; earlier deadlines for the acceptance of such offers violate the intent of this Resolution. In those instances in which the student accepts the offer before April 15 and subsequently desires to withdraw that accep-tance, the student may submit in writing a resigna-tion of the appointment at any time through April 15. However, an acceptance given or left in force after April 15 commits the student not to accept another offer without first obtaining a written release from the institution to which the commit-ment has been made. Similarly, an offer by an insti-tution after April 15 is conditional on presentation by the student of the written release from any pre-viously accepted offer.

As you wait to hear from programs in February and March, carefully check your e-mails and missed calls, particularly if you use an account that receives a large volume of incoming messages. Just last year, two of our undergraduates missed emailed invita-tions to interview at doctoral programs because they were lost among a blizzard of unsolicited e-mails and junk messages. Be vigilant and double check on a daily basis.

Acceptances and Rejections

What do you do when one program makes you an offer and you are still waiting to hear from another program you would prefer to accept? To begin with, *don't say yes to any graduate program until you are certain that this is where you want to go!* Once you say "yes," that is it. You are committed. Saying yes to another program can endanger your acceptance at both places. If you have reservations, do not feel pressured to say yes. Thank the person and say that you have been made other offers and you need a few days to consider this crucial decision.

Only 50 to 70% of the students accepted at a particular APA-accredited program will accept that offer (Norcross et al., 2009). You need not worry about hurting faculty feelings should you decline their offer of admission. Qualified applicants will receive multiple offers. Experienced faculty understand the process. Do not fret about them; focus on what's best for you.

If you have received offers but have not heard from the programs that most interest you, telephone or e-mail them. Explain that you are considering offers but that you do not want to act on them until you know what your status is there. It's OK to say, "I've been accepted at University X and Y, but I am most interested in your program. Can you give me an indication where my application stands, or at least whether it is still being considered?"

The Guidelines for Graduate School Offers and Acceptances, adopted by the Council of University Directors of Clinical Psychology (1993), encourage directors of training (or admissions) to apprise students of their position on the alternate list. Typically, this entails a placement of high, middle, or low on the alternate list. If such a designation is used, the operational definition of "high on the alternate list" is that, in a normal year, the student would receive an offer of admission (but not necessarily funding) prior to the April 15 decision date.

Earlier, we emphasized the point that you should not accept an offer until you are certain that is the program you want to attend. On the other hand, if you have been accepted at three programs, and one of them is obviously less suited to your needs, be considerate of other applicants and decline that offer. The program can then make their offer to someone else who may very much want to attend that school. *Only keep two offers alive at any one time.* Otherwise, a huge logjam or bottleneck effect will occur across the country, with each program waiting for a few students to decide.

As long as there is a possibility that you may attend a certain program, be careful not to decline prematurely. As other students decline at these schools, you may be offered a better financial package if you have not yet made a formal commitment.

When all is said and done, how will you decide which offer to accept? This is a difficult question to answer because of the multiple factors involved and because the final determinant will be how you, as an individual, weigh those various factors.

One study (Walfish, Stenmark, Shealy, & Shealy, 1989) had 201 first-year graduate students rate the reasons for their final selection of a doctoral clinical program. Their average ratings are shown in Table 8-1, where a rating of 1 was "very unimportant" and 5 was "very important." As seen there, the most important factors were the reputation of the program, the amount of clinical supervision, the training facilities, availability of mentors, and the emotional atmosphere of the program. (At highly research-oriented programs, this prioritization may differ, with the match to the individual faculty member assuming increased importance.) We have emphasized throughout the preceding chapters the importance of the first four factors, but not the last.

The emotional and interpersonal ambience of a program should not be underestimated. Seriously consider interactions with faculty and graduate students in your decision. The faculty–student relationship may be the single most important factor in your intellectual and professional development, and this relationship may be formal or informal, distant or close. Concurrently, the vast majority of graduate student time is spent with other students rather than with faculty members. You are likely to retain these personal contacts and professional relationships over the years. Moreover, fellow students are essential sources of encouragement, companionship, and inspiration. You want a good, lasting fit with the program (Scott & Silka, 1974).

In choosing a graduate program, all students place a premium on general factors such as program quality, training opportunities, emotional atmosphere, and financial aid. At the same time, ethnic minority applicants rate the relevance of multicultural factors higher than do white students (Bernal et al., 1999; Toia, Herron, Primavera, & Javier, 1997). These considerations include minority students in the program, presence of minority faculty, research on minority topics, and opportunity to work with multicultural clients. Be particularly attentive to the program's diversity as it relates to your interests and goals.

The expected length of the doctoral program is a fairly important reason for choosing a particular program, as seen in the middle of Table 8-1. You may recall from Chapter 2 that clinical Ph.D. students take an average of 6 years to complete their doctorates,

TABLE 8-1. Student Reasons for Choosing a Clinical Psychology Doctoral Program

Reason	Mean rating	Rank
Reputation of the program	4.29	1
Amount of clinical supervision	4.27	2
Training facilities available	4.21	3
Appropriate mentors available	4.19	4.5
Emotional atmosphere of the program	4.19	4.5
Tuition waiver available	4.10	6
Amount of stipend offered	4.07	7
Theoretical orientation	4.04	8
Diversity of program	4.00	9
Specific specialty training available	3.89	10
Research experience available	3.85	11
Expected length of program	3.82	12
Amount of research supervision	3.80	13
Success of previous graduates	3.79	14
Specificity of the training program	3.66	15
Geographic location	3.60	16
Specific professor to work with	3.57	17
Family/significant others in area	3.00	18
Recreational activities available	2.69	19
Number of minority members in program	2.48	20
Break required during program	2.30	21

Note. From Walfish, Stenmark, Shealy, & Shealy (1989). © 1989 American Psychological Association. Reprinted by permission.

including the 1-year internship. Psy.D. students take an average of 5 years, a consistent difference of 1 to 1.5 years less. On the one hand, the shorter training period favors the Psy.D. programs. But, on the other hand, the financial aid favors the Ph.D. programs. As you have learned, far more Ph.D. students are receiving tuition waivers and assistantship stipends than Psy.D. students, most of whom are footing the entire bill for their doctoral education. Also keep in mind your ultimate career goal: it may take longer to gain your degree if you hope to compete for research and faculty positions, where completing multiple publishable studies will be critical to your success. Use the Reports on Individual Programs to consider the expected length of the program in the context of probable financial aid and your career trajectory. The reasons for choosing a clinical psychology program, as shown in Table 8-1, are largely self-evident, but several reasons *not* listed in that table deserve your consideration. Three of these reasons concern the program's outcomes—attrition rate, internship match, and licensure data – introduced earlier in the book. *Attrition rates* refer to the percentage of

students not completing the program. Attrition has been characterized as a "hidden crisis in graduate education" (Lovitts & Nelson, 2000). Between 20 and 24% of full-time psychology students, on average, formally leave programs without completing their doctorates (Fennell & Kohout, 2002). Our recent data suggest this number is smaller for clinical and counseling psychology programs (Norcross, Ellis, & Sayette, 2010; Norcross, Evans, & Ellis, 2010). Attrition in graduate programs is not solely related to academic ability; life problems, financial difficulties, interpersonal conflicts, and program dissatisfaction enter into the equation. In some cases (e.g., starting a family), the decision is not even related to a "problem." Doctoral programs in which more than 20% of the students fail to graduate should be carefully screened when you make your final decision.

Our Reports on Individual Programs provide the attrition rates for each doctoral program, as reported by that program's director of training. The attrition rate is calculated for the past 7 years as the number of matriculated students who have left the program for any reason divided by the total number of students matriculated in the program. Again, pay close attention to any program in which more than a fifth of students have left the program.

We implored you in Chapter 5 *not* to apply to any doctoral programs below your threshold of quality. In the event one or two questionable programs snuck onto your list, please conduct a final check on the outcomes of that program before accepting an offer. You may recall our three-quarters rule: apply only to doctoral programs where three-quarters or more of their students secure an APA-accredited internship, complete their degrees, and pass the licensure examination. Carefully inspect the Report on Individual Programs in this book, the required outcomes data on the program's Web site, and the national licensure site (www.asppb.net) to acquire these numbers. Determine your own threshold of quality and proceed with your eyes wide open as to the probable consequence of attending that particular program. At the risk of sounding melodramatic, it is literally your career at stake.

Preliminary or qualifying examinations, another consideration in the complexities of your choice, are a series of structured tests that certain programs require at the end of their first or second year. These examinations assume many forms, but they all test a candidate's knowledge of a wide range of areas in psychology—research methodology, learning, development, motivation, history, social, and personality. In some programs, only one attempt may be permitted to pass this examination (Scott & Silka, 1974). You should learn if the program requires "prelims" or "quals," whether multiple attempts are provided, and what percentage of students pass, before you make your final decision. Instead of an exam, many research-oriented clinical programs require submission of a lengthy review paper prior to embarking on a dissertation.

You should now be well acquainted with a program's outcomes and the decision criteria presented in Table 8-1 in your own life and well informed about the program's attractiveness on these criteria. If not, immediately request additional information on any of these for which you lack knowledge prior to making an informed choice of the program to attend.

The Financial Package

Note in Table 8-1 that the sixth and seventh most important selection factors are financial (tuition waiver and stipend amount). For many applicants, the financial aid offered by the school will probably assume an even higher priority in making final deci-

sions. When an offer is made, establish if the program is offering financial assistance. If so, does it cover tuition remission? Is it guaranteed for 4 years? Is it considered taxable at that institution? Does it provide health insurance? If you have a teaching or research assistantship, how many hours per week will it entail? Are you allowed to earn additional outside income?

On average, private universities are more expensive than public or state universities. Typically, the in-state versus out-of-state cost difference that operates in undergraduate education is not as salient in graduate education. That is because (1) once you begin study, you can establish residency there and pay in-state tuition after the first year, and (2) many financial aid packages include a tuition remission.

But graduate training is expensive, and external sources of financial support are slowly drying up. Consider, for instance, the average stipends and accumulated loans for Ph.D. psychology students over the years (Golding, Lang, Eymard, & Shadish, 1988). Back in the 1960s and 1970s the average graduate stipend was higher, and the typical student's accumulated loan lower, than in the 2000s, adjusted for inflation. In fact, the average stipend amount decreased 36% (controlled for inflation) over the past 30 years. About three-quarters of psychology doctoral candidates carry loans. Support is still available but not to the degree it once was—which accounts, in part, for your professors' fond memories of their "good ol' graduate days."

Federal support for graduate training has been eroding in all fields, including psychology. In the 1970s, for instance, almost 30% of Ph.D. recipients in clinical psychology reported that federal grants and traineeships provided the major support for their graduate training (Coyle & Bae, 1987). Thirty years later, federal sources supported less than 4% of full-time graduate students in psychology (Wicherski & Kohout, 2005). Federal sources have slipped as a primary source of support for psychology graduate students and, to compensate for these shrinking resources, students have had to look elsewhere, to personal resources, student loans, and university financial assistance.

Research supports the conclusion that today's graduate students are being asked to shoulder a larger share of their education costs. This is particularly true in Psy.D. programs, which fund proportionally fewer graduate students than Boulder-model Ph.D. programs. Refer to the Reports on Individual Programs for the percentage of a program's students who receive partial or full funding.

Table 8-2 shows the median tuition costs per year for psychology graduate students. The numbers demonstrate that tuition is largely a function of three variables: institution type, state residence, and degree level. Private universities uniformly charge higher graduate tuition than public institutions, just as is the case on the undergraduate level. Tuition at private institutions per academic year is typically two or three times higher than state tuition at public institutions. Psy.D. programs routinely charge between $20,000 and $25,000 per year for tuition. Although your state residence does not influence tuition at private universities, it definitely reduces your tuition at public universities—from a median of $15,847 for nonstate residents to $6,297 for state residents per year. Predictably, too, tuition is higher for doctoral programs than for master's programs. So, your annual tuition can range from $0 if you secure tuition remission, to $6,000 if you are a resident attending your state university, to $22,000 if you attend a Ph.D. program at a private university with no financial assistance, all the way up to $25,000 if you attend a freestanding Psy.D. program.

Table 8-3 presents the assistantship stipends for psychology graduate students in 2010. As seen there, the median 9-month stipends for teaching and research assistantships average about $6,000 for master's students and $13,000 for doctoral students (Mulvey, Wicherski, & Kohout, 2010). Stipends for doctoral students are consistently higher than those for master's students (Fennell & Kohout, 2002).

The typical hours worked per week for an assistantship are 15 to 16. Practically all graduate programs will expect between 10 and 20 hours a week from their research and teaching assistants (Mulvey et al., 2010). Financial considerations include the tuition cost, available stipend, and living costs. The latter cannot be ignored: although tuition costs may be equivalent in New York City and Kansas, the living costs are certainly not.

Once accepted into a doctoral program, you will naturally be eager to learn about the status of your financial assistance, but you will hear from institutions at different times depending on the form of the financial assistance. If it is department-controlled financial assistance, then you will ordinarily hear when you are accepted or shortly thereafter. If it is university financial assistance, not directly controlled by the psychology department or school, then it may well be weeks after you are accepted. Examples in this category are fellowships from the Graduate School, resident assistantships from Student Affairs, or a Graduate Assistantship in the Admission Office. If it is financial assistance from a government agency, such as the National Science Foundation (NSF) or National Institutes of Health (NIH), then you will hear on or before their published notification dates. Finally, if it is financial assistance in the form of loans, then you will hear from the bank, Sally Mae, or the lending institution on their (painfully slow) schedule.

The Alternate List

Your fervent hope is to receive an e-mail or telephone call in February, March, or early April from the director of admissions offering you acceptance into your top-rated program with generous financial aid. But this glorious dream may not happen; instead, the sobering reality is that many applicants will be rejected from several programs, will secure offers from programs lower on their list, or will receive offers without financial assistance. Many will also receive calls informing them that they have been wait listed—that is, placed on the alternate list.

As mentioned previously, ask the director of admissions where you stand on the alternate list—high, middle, or low. For your planning purposes, be politely assertive in probing further: "In typical years, what percentage of students with this position on the alternate list receive an admission offer? What percentage of the students admitted from the alter-

TABLE 8-2. Median Tuition Costs in Psychology by Institution Type and Degree Level

	Institution type		Degree level	
	Public	Private	Doctoral	Master's
State residents	$6,297	$22,700	$6,570	$4,980
Nonstate residents	$15,847	$23,600	$17,934	$10,530

Note. Adapted from 2008 Graduate Study in Psychology (APA Center for Psychology Workforce Studies, 2008).

TABLE 8-3. Median Assistantship Stipends in Psychology by Institution Type and Degree Level

	Doctoral students		Master's students	
	Public	Private	Public	Private
Teaching assistantship	$12,623	$14,000	$6,502	$3,675
Research assistantship	$12,933	$6,425	$6,574	$3,150
Fellowship/scholarship	$15,000	$5,200	$2,000	$2,170
Traineeship	$14,516	$15,000	$6,000	$6,750

Note. Data from Mulvey, Wicherski, & Kohout (2010).

nate list receive funding?" Without answers to these questions, you cannot render an informed decision on your other offers.

The admissions directors will, in all likelihood, arrange for you to be kept abreast of your admissions status until April 15th. They may e-mail you or you may e-mail them on occasion to determine the probability of admission.

When speaking with the program representative at a school you would like to attend try to impress upon him or her three key ideas. First, you are keenly interested in attending that program. Second, express your availability by stating you have not accepted another offer of admission. And third, if you have received another offer, inform the program accordingly; most schools desire people who are attractive to others. Enthusiasm, availability, and attractiveness frequently move students up the alternate list. The tricky part of this process is how frequently an alternate should contact (by telephone or e-mail) the program representative. Too much contact will appear aggressive or desperate; too little, passive or complacent. Strike a balance by asking the program representative how often you may contact him or her without being irritating.

Decision Making

The choice of which admission offer to accept and which program to attend is a momentous one indeed. You, like 86% of students enrolling in graduate programs, will quickly discover that the decision-making process boils down to your sense of fit with a program (Kyle, 2000). A few fortunate souls may receive an early offer with excellent financial aid from their number one program. But most graduate school applicants will ultimately select the program that makes the best offer—an offer that needs to be seri-

ously weighed on a host of the aforementioned and often conflicting considerations.

The "April madness" abounds with such quandaries as: "Should I take Program X with the best training but with no financial aid or Program Y with solid training and half tuition remission for 4 years?"; "Two programs have offered the same money, but the one that I prefer is 600 miles from my partner. What should I do?"; "My top program guaranteed me a teaching assistantship that requires 15 hours a week. My fourth choice is offering tuition remission and a fellowship. Any advice?"

Our advice centers on using systematic decision making. Begin by gathering all the salient data by interviewing program faculty and students, consulting published materials, and speaking with your mentors. Prioritize your primary reasons for selecting one program over another. Then develop a decision-making grid that will assist you in ranking your choices.

Two practical articles describe in detail how to apply decision-making techniques to choosing psychology programs and internships. Jacob's (1987) decision grid asks candidates to evaluate training programs along criteria that are important to them. You weigh those criteria that are more important to you correspondingly higher. You then tally the ratings for each training program to make the final decision. While it may sound a bit over-intellectual, in practice we have found that the decision grid forces students to identify the criteria that they value most highly.

Stewart and Stewart (1996) describe a paired-comparison ranking technique, a method originally traced back to psychophysiological methods developed by Gustav Fechner. The first step of this technique is to select the relevant personal, professional, and practical criteria that you will use in comparing programs to one another. Consult the preceding pages to identify these criteria; conduct an honest self-evaluation to determine which of these lie in your heart. The second step involves prioritizing these selection criteria. Do this by writing the name of each criterion on a single index card or piece of paper, and then forcing yourself to rank them in order. The third step entails generating a list of programs that will be compared to one another. We suggest that you use those programs that have accepted you or which have placed you on their waiting list.

The fourth step of the technique involves the actual pairwise comparison of the programs. Write the names of the graduate programs along one side of a large piece of paper and the selection criteria on the other side. Which of the training programs most clearly satisfies your criteria? Make a choice and allow no ties. For each criterion, put a hash mark across from the program that wins. The hash marks will be counted to determine your choice.

Although the final result will generally agree with what you expected, the more productive outcome of these two decision-making techniques may be that they force you to view your selection decision from multiple perspectives and to prioritize numerous criteria. To be sure, this is a complex method for a complex decision, but one that we and our students have repeatedly found effective for making "impossible" choices more thoughtfully and systematically.

Finalizing Arrangements

An offer of admission must eventually be formalized in writing. Verbal offers and verbal acceptances are binding, but your acceptance of the offer should be in writing at the end of the process. Likewise, assistantships, tuition waivers, and stipends should be guaranteed in the written offer; respectfully insist that the financial arrangements be specified so that misunderstandings do not ensue. Should the offer be "contingent on expected funding," determine the odds of the funding coming through. No position is absolutely certain in life, but some are more certain than others.

Weighing offers, negotiating financial aid, and dealing with rejections make this a heady period. Be careful not to get caught up in the experience and forget the most important point: accept one offer and confirm it in writing!

One of our students (the affable Jean Willi) was offered admission to a prestigious doctoral program, with financial assistance. He carefully considered alternative offers, negotiated with other programs, leading to predictable delays. He awoke one morning in a cold sweat, realizing that he had turned down all other offers but had not formally accepted the offer of admission and financial package from his school of choice. He was in graduate school purgatory! Although the school was understanding and everything eventually worked out for Jean, because he missed the deadline, the school had the option of changing the financial aid package, or even revoking the offer of admission. The moral of the story: don't pull a Willi! Be clear and decisive and put it in writing.

Figure 8-1 presents a representative letter of acceptance. Note that the letter or email should explicitly mention any conditions of your acceptance, including financial assistance. Many graduate programs will accept an email as your formal confirmation, but a few programs still insist upon a snail-mailed letter.

Once you have formally accepted an offer of admission in writing, two matters of etiquette remain: (1) informing other programs who have accepted you, and (2) expressing your appreciation to those mentors who wrote letters of recommendation on your behalf and on their own time. Figure 8-2 offers a sample letter declining an offer of admission. It should be succinct yet polite. Thereafter, send a brief e-mail or thank-you note to those who have assisted you through your graduate application journey. They will be interested in the outcome of your application process and may well join the ensuing celebration!

If Not Accepted

What happens if you are not accepted anywhere? The grim truth is that about one-third of the entire applicant pool to APA-accredited clinical and counseling psychology programs will *not* make it in a given year.

Start by taking time to recover from your disappointment after an emotionally taxing process. Relax a few days and break from the graduate school preoccupation. Seek support from your friends and family members. Remind yourself that many psychologists took several tries to enter graduate school. Most importantly, remember that your worth as a person is not dependent on your academic credentials.

Then, huddle with your mentors and consider these five alternatives:

1. *Consult the APA Education Directorate's Graduate Openings list in late April.* This document contains a list of graduate programs in psychology that still have openings for students in the fall. Although there are no APA-accredited clinical or counseling doctoral programs and only a few nonclinical doc-

March 25, 2012

Annika Jones, Ph.D.
Director, Admissions Committee
Department of Psychology
University of Western States
13 Orangegrove Drive
Wilksville, CA 98765

Dear Dr. Jones:

I am pleased to accept your offer of admission to the University of Western States's Ph.D. program in counseling psychology as a full-time matriculated student beginning in the Fall 2013 term. My acceptance is predicated on the conditions outlined in your letter of March 20th (attached), including full tuition remission for three years. I appreciate your confidence in me and very much look forward to joining the counseling psychology program.

Sincerely yours,

Chris Smith

FIGURE 8-1. Sample letter of acceptance.

toral programs on the list, you may locate other programs of interest to you. To review the listings, go to the APA Web site at www.apa.org/education/grad/graduate-openings.aspx.

2. *Apply to master's programs in clinical or counseling psychology.* Master's degrees are frequent stepping stones to the doctorate in psychology. Although taking your master's at one institution and transferring to another for the doctorate is not as efficient as being admitted directly into a doctoral program, there are advantages nonetheless. One is that the acceptance odds are more favorable—37% for master's programs in clinical psychology and 63% for master's in counseling psychology on average (Table 1-3). A second advantage is that a few years of graduate training in psychology can improve your grade point average, GRE Psychology Subject Test score, clinical acumen, and research skills. A third plus is an opportunity to confirm that psychology is the career for you. A cruel irony of baccalaureate recipients admitted directly into doctoral programs is that they have little direct contact with the field they claim as their lifelong career! A fourth advantage is exposure to twice the number of faculty supervisors and theoretical orientations. A fifth and final advan-

tage is the flexible course offerings—part-time study and, frequently, night courses are available in master's programs (Actkinson, 2000).

Selecting a *quality* master's program in psychology may be a key to eventual admission into a doctoral clinical program. By all means try to avoid master's programs that have come to be pejoratively called "money mills." These programs exhibit most or all of the following features: accepting a very high percentage (80% plus) of applicants; offering courses only in the evening or largely by part-time faculty; providing no funded graduate assistantships; being reluctant or unwilling to state what percentage of their graduates go on to doctoral programs; declaring openly their disinterest in research; requiring little undergraduate preparation in psychology; and communicating greater interest in filling classroom seats than in attracting qualified students.

By contrast, quality terminal master's programs in psychology can be roughly assessed by three criteria: exhibiting few of the aforementioned characteristics of money mills; holding a favorable reputation among the psychological community; and faculty producing published research. Gordon (1990) lists 20 American master's programs ranked highest in

124

March 25, 2012

Annika Jones, Ph.D.
Director, Admissions Committee
Department of Psychology
University of Western States
13 Orangegrove Drive
Wilksville, CA 98765

Dear Dr. Jones:

I was pleased to receive your March 19th letter offering me acceptance to the Psy.D. program in clinical psychology at the University of Western States. I thoroughly enjoyed speaking with you and your colleagues and appreciated your generous offer of admission. Unfortunately, I can only accept one admission offer, and I must regrettably decline your attractive offer. Please extend my genuine thanks and best wishes to the entire Admissions Committee.

Sincerely yours,

Chris Smith

FIGURE 8-2. Sample letter declining an admission offer.

productivity in 15 APA journals; interested students are directed to that article.

In addition to the foregoing research-based article, we heartily recommend that you consult an extensive compilation of master's programs in psychology. The classic is APA's (2011) *Graduate Study in Psychology*, which lists hundreds of master's (and doctoral) programs in psychology throughout the United States and Canada. To order, go to APA's Web site where you can purchase a hard copy or purchase a three-month electronic access.

3. *Apply to doctoral programs that are not accredited by APA.* In general these programs fit into one of two categories. They may be credible institutions that simply have not been around long enough to gain APA approval. Programs cannot apply for accreditation until they have graduated doctoral students, which takes several years. Usually these programs are planning on applying for accreditation as soon as they are eligible.

However, there is a second category of institution not accredited by APA. These programs usually do not conform to APA standards and often do not even attempt to gain accreditation. The quality of these programs is often considerably lower than those of the APA-accredited programs. Because of their sta-

tus, non-APA-accredited programs typically provide greater probabilities for acceptance. If you do apply to such programs, by all means determine why they are not accredited, and whether their students are able to gain admission into credible internships and, later, to become licensed psychologists. You can refer to the most recent edition of APA's *Graduate Study in Psychology* to explore these and other programs.

4. *Decide against a doctorate in clinical or counseling psychology.* If your goal is to become a researcher or a practitioner, psychology is not your only option. Reexamine the other choices listed in Chapter 1 and consult your advisors to see if one of these options is suited to your needs.

5. *Apply again in a year or two to APA-accredited programs.* Knowing the criteria used by graduate schools, take a realistic look at what seem to be the limitations in your application. Many students continue to resubmit the same rejected application year after year to no avail; "doing more of the same" typically results in more of the same misery.

Another year can be an opportunity to remediate your weaknesses. Were your GREs low? Take a professional preparation course and retake the test. Was your GPA a bit low? Then take some additional courses or retake some old courses in which you did not perform your best to improve it. Take some graduate courses in psychology on a nonmatriculating basis to demonstrate your ability. Were you short on research skills? Then take 1 or 2 years and acquire a research position, paid or volunteer, in a psychology or psychiatry department. Did you lack significant clinical experience? Then spend a night or two a week working for a suicide hot line or find a job at a women's shelter. Were your letters of recommendation tepid or brief? Then acquaint yourself better with potential referees so they can write a positive and detailed letter.

Another year can also provide an opportunity to enhance your interview style or to acquire better matches with graduate faculty members. Some applicants find themselves in the position of perennial bridesmaids or best men, not because their credentials were inadequate, but because their interview style or matching potential was a tad weak. Spend the extra months improving your interpersonal presentation and investigating programs that promise to be better fits with your interests.

The so-called gap year is not intended as a vacation or a year off. Instead, it is a year dedicated to improving your credentials and working hard at what interests you. When friends or parents ask what you are doing on your purported "year off," we believe the appropriate response is to proudly reply, "Preparing for my career in clinical/counseling psychology!"

In summary, reread this text and conduct a rigorous self-assessment of where you are and where you want to be. If you're still set on a career in clinical or counseling psychology, be prepared to take the time and energy to make yourself a better applicant. Especially if you are still in college and had planned to go straight on to graduate school, take time to gain some life experiences. Age and experience can work in your favor, and they will certainly help you better define your goals next time through the application process.

Two Final Words

Realism and persistence. Be realistic about your credentials, capacities, and acceptance odds. Some applicants refuse to accept the hard facts of the admission process and tragically resubmit the identically flawed application year after year to no avail. An honest evaluation of your credentials, with the assistance of an experienced professor, will enable you to strengthen your application, select more appropriate programs, or reevaluate your career decisions. This is not to dissuade or discourage you; it is realistic encouragement.

And be persistent! Many successful psychologists have required two or three tries to get into a doctoral program. Thousands of clinical and counseling psychologists have earned a master's degree at one institution before moving on to receive a doctorate at a different university. There is no shame in reaching for the stars; the real loss is not to reach at all.

We hope the information and suggestions contained in this *Insider's Guide* have been helpful to you. We wish you the best success in the application process and in graduate school.

REPORTS ON COMBINED PSYCHOLOGY PROGRAMS

University at Buffalo/State University of New York (Ph.D.)

(counseling/school combined)
Department of Counseling, School, & Educational Psychology
Buffalo, NY 14260
phone#: (716) 645-2484
e-mail: gse-info@buffalo.edu
Web address: http://www.gse.buffalo.edu/programs/cpsp

1	2	3	4	5	6	7
Practice oriented			Equal emphasis			Research oriented

Percentage of faculty subscribing to each of the following orientations:

Psychodynamic/Psychoanalytic	0%
Applied behavioral analysis/Radical behavioral	50%
Family systems/Systems	25%
Existential/Phenomenological/Humanistic	5%
Cognitive/Cognitive-behavioral	25%

Courses required for incoming students to have completed prior to enrolling:

Most students have a B.A. or B.S. in psychology.

Recommended but not mandatory courses:

None

GRE mean

Verbal 560   Quantitative 645   Analytical Writing 5.0

GPA mean

Overall GPA 3.6

Number of applications/admission offers/incoming students in 2008

92

% of students receiving:

Full tuition waiver only: 0%
Assistantship/fellowship only: 0%
Both full tuition waiver & assistantship/fellowship: 100%

Approximate percentage of students who are

Women: 85% **Ethnic Minority:** 40%
International: 0%

Average years to complete the doctoral program (including internship): 5 years

Personal interview

Required in person

Attrition rate in past 7 years: 0%

Percentage of students applying for internship last year accepted into APPIC or APA internships: 86%

Formal tracks/concentrations/specializations: none

Research areas	# Faculty	# Grants
assessment	4	1
ADHD	1	3
family therapy	1	0
health psychology	4	3
multicultural psychology	1	0

rehabilitation psychology	2	0
vocational psychology	2	0

Clinical opportunities

Very diverse, including schools, community agencies, and hospitals in urban, suburban, and rural areas.

University of California–Santa Barbara (Ph.D.)

(clinical/counseling/school)
Department of Counseling, Clinical and School Psychology
Santa Barbara, CA 93106
phone#: (805) 893-3375
e-mail: cosden@education.ucsb.edu
Web address: http://www.education.ucsb.edu/Graduate-Studies/CCSP/CCSP-home.html

1	2	3	4	5	6	7
Practice oriented			Equal emphasis			Research oriented

Percentage of faculty subscribing to each of the following orientations:

Psychodynamic/Psychoanalytic	30%
Applied behavioral analysis/Radical behavioral	20%
Family systems/Systems	40%
Existential/Phenomenological/Humanistic	20%
Cognitive/Cognitive-behavioral	60%
Developmental	30%
Feminist	20%
Solution focused	20%
Positive psychology	20%

Courses required for incoming students to have completed prior to enrolling:

None

Recommended but not mandatory courses:

Human development, personality or abnormal psychology, research design or statistics, biopsychology

GRE mean

Verbal 600   Quantitative 636

GPA mean

Junior/Senior GPA 3.77

Number of applications/admission offers/incoming students in 2009

219 applied/21 admission offers/14 incoming

% of students receiving:

Full tuition waiver only: 0%
Assistantship/fellowship only: 29%
Both full tuition waiver & assistantship/fellowship: 69%

Approximate percentage of incoming students with a B.A./B.S. only: 50% Master's: 50%

Approximate percentage of students who are

Women: 82% **Ethnic Minority:** 60%
International: 3%

Average years to complete the doctoral program (including internship): 6 years

Personal interview
Preferred in person but telephone acceptable

Attrition rate in past 7 years: 7%

Percentage of students applying for internship last year accepted into APPIC or APA internships: 100%

Formal tracks/concentrations/specializations:
counseling, clinical, school

Research areas

ADHD	multicultural issues
autism	neuropsychological
career counseling	assessment
cross-cultural counseling	psychological assessment
child abuse/family violence	psychotherapy
immigrant/refugee youth	school violence/
learning disabilities	safety/bullying
LGBT mental health issues	social justice issues
mental health services for	substance abuse
high-risk families, children	trauma exposure

Clinical opportunities

autism clinic	family therapy
career counseling center	inpatient psychiatric
child abuse community-	hospital
based agency	neuropsychological and
LGBT community-based	personality assessment
agency	school consultation
community-based mental	school interventions
health	university counseling center

Florida State University (Ph.D.)

(counseling/school)
Psychological Services in Education Program
Department of Educational Psychology and
Learning Systems
307 Stone Building
Tallahassee, FL 32306-4453
phone#: (850) 644-8796
e-mail: spfeiffer@fsu.edu
Web address: www.epls.fsu.edu/general/programs.htm

1	2	3	4	5	6	7
Practice oriented		Equal emphasis			Research oriented	

Percentage of faculty subscribing to each of the following orientations:

Psychodynamic/Psychoanalytic	10%
Applied behavioral analysis/Radical behavioral	20%
Family systems/Systems	40%
Existential/Phenomenological/Humanistic	10%
Cognitive/Cognitive-behavioral	100%

Courses required for incoming students to have completed prior to enrolling:
None required; core psychology (e.g., statistics, research) highly recommended

Recommended but not mandatory courses:
Core psychology recommended

GRE mean
Verbal 570   Quantitative 610

Analytical Writing 4.5–5.0

GPA mean
Junior/Senior GPA 3.65

Number of applications/admission offers/incoming students in fall 2009
75 applied/9 admission offers/9 incoming

% of students receiving:
Full tuition waiver only: 0%
Assistantship/fellowship only: 0%
Both full tuition waiver & assistantship/fellowship: 100%

Approximate percentage of incoming students with a B.A./B.S. only: 40%   **Master's:** 60%

Approximate percentage of students who are Women: 60%   **Ethnic Minority:** 20%
International: not reported

Average years to complete the doctoral program (including internship): 6.5 years

Personal interview
Very strongly encouraged following invitation to visit campus as finalist

Attrition rate in past 7 years: 10–15%

Percentage of students applying for internship last year accepted into APPIC or APA internships: 100%

Formal tracks/concentrations/specializations:
counseling and school psychology

Research areas

Research areas	# Faculty	# Grants
career development	3	1
counseling/psychotherapy	4	1
school/community interventions	3	1
gifted/talent development	1	1
rehab counseling	2	1

Clinical opportunities
On-campus: Adult learning and evaluation center (diagnose learning disabilities and prescribe treatments to young adults)
On-campus: Career counseling center
On-campus: Human services center (mental health services to 5-county area)
On-campus: University counseling center; Employee Assistance Program
Community placements: Variety of mental health, medical and behavioral health care agencies

James Madison University (Psy.D.)

(clinical/school)
Department of Graduate Psychology
Harrisonburg, VA 22807-7401
phone#: (540) 568-7857
e-mail: henriqgx@jmu.edu
Web address: www.psyc.jmu.edu/cipsyd/

1	2	3	4	5	6	7
Practice oriented		Equal emphasis			Research oriented	

Percentage of faculty subscribing to each of the following orientations:

Psychodynamic/Psychoanalytic	20%
Applied behavioral analysis/Radical behavioral	0%
Family systems/Systems	40%
Existential/Phenomenological/Humanistic	20%
Cognitive/Cognitive-behavioral	20%

Courses required for incoming students to have completed prior to enrolling:

Students are required to have a master's degree in a psychology-related field.

Recommended but not mandatory courses:

Master's degree and professional experience

GRE mean

Verbal 578   Quantitative 668
Psychology Subject Test 610
Analytical Writing 5

GPA mean

Master's GPA 3.8

Number of applications/admission offers/incoming students in 2009

50 applied/8 admission offers/6 incoming

% of students receiving:

Full tuition waiver only: 0%
Assistantship/fellowship only: 0%
Both full tuition waiver & assistantship/fellowship: 100%

Approximate percentage of incoming students with a B.A./B.S. only: 0%   **Master's:** 100%

Approximate percentage of students who are Women: 86%   **Ethnic Minority:** 25%
International: 15%

Average years to complete the doctoral program (including internship): 3.8 years

Personal interview

Required

Attrition rate in past 7 years: 10%

Percentage of students applying for internship last year accepted into APPIC or APA internships: 100%

Formal tracks/concentrations/specializations: none

Research areas	# Faculty	# Grants
attachment theory	1	0
integrative theory	4	0
beliefs and values	3	1
clinical training processes	3	0
depression and suicide	1	0
biofeedback	1	0
family processes	2	0
international/cultural issues	4	1
parent–child interaction	2	0
social motivation and affect	1	0
social/skill development	4	0
supervision and leadership	1	0
theoretical unification	1	0

Clinical opportunities

child/family therapy	multidisciplinary assessment
counseling and psychological clinic	neuropsychology
forensic assessment	outpatient private practice
inpatient/hospital practice	school assessment
learning disabilities	supervision/leadership

Northeastern University (Ph.D.)

(counseling/school)
Department of Counseling and Applied Educational Psychology
Bouve College of Health Sciences
International Village
Boston, MA 02115
phone#: (617) 373-2708
e-mail: bouvegrad@neu.edu
Web address: www.northeastern.edu/bouve/caep/programs/cpphd.html

---

1	2	**3**	4	5	6	7
Practice oriented		Equal emphasis				Research oriented

Percentage of faculty subscribing to each of the following orientations:

Psychodynamic/Psychoanalytic	10%
Applied behavioral analysis/Radical behavioral	10%
Family systems/Systems	30%
Existential/Phenomenological/Humanistic	20%
Cognitive/Cognitive-behavioral	30%

Courses required for incoming students to have completed prior to enrolling:

We accept students with either a bachelor's or a master's degree

Recommended but not mandatory courses:

None

GRE mean

Verbal 500   Quantitative 500
Analytic Writing not reported

GPA mean

Overall GPA 3.0   Psychology GPA 3.0

Number of applications/admission offers/incoming students in 2009

We are NOT accepting new students—see new programs in counseling and in school

% of students receiving:

Full tuition waiver only: 25%
Assistantship/fellowship only: 0%
Both full tuition waiver & assistantship/fellowship: 75%

Approximate percentage of incoming students with a B.A./B.S. only: 10%   **Master's:** 90%

Approximate percentage of students who are Women: 70%   **Ethnic Minority:** 20%
International: 10%

Average years to complete the doctoral program (including internship): 5.5 years

Personal interview
Required

Attrition rate in past 7 years: 10%

Percentage of students applying for internship last year accepted into APPIC or APA internships: 100%

Formal tracks/concentrations/specializations: school psychology, counseling psychology

Research areas	# Faculty	# Grants
counseling needs of minorities	1	1
early intervention	1	1
eating disorders	3	1
impact of managed care on clinical training	1	0
leadership development	3	1
neuropsychological function	1	0
spatial ability and cognitive transfer	2	0

Clinical opportunities
Students have the opportunity to work with families, adults, college students, and children, chronically ill, child cancer patients, both inpatient and outpatients, etc. Training settings in the Boston area include all manners of ethnic and cultural diversity, medical, mental health, and private care facilities. Virtually all kinds of experience is available to students in a supervised setting.

Pace University (Psy.D.)

(school/clinical)
Department of Psychology
New York, NY 10038
phone#: (212) 346-1531
e-mail: gradnyc@pace.edu
Web address: appsrv.pace.edu/academics/view-programs/
?school=GAS&Cred=DSY&Maj=CSY&Location=nyc+details

1	2	3	4	5	6	7
Practice oriented		Equal emphasis				Research oriented

Percentage of faculty subscribing to each of the following orientations:

Psychodynamic/Psychoanalytic	33%
Applied behavioral analysis/Radical behavioral	0%
Family systems/Systems	22%
Existential/Phenomenological/Humanistic	11%
Cognitive/Cognitive-behavioral	33%

Courses required for incoming students to have completed prior to enrolling:
General psychology, experimental psychology, statistics, developmental psychology, learning, personality, psychopathology

Recommended but not mandatory courses:
None

GRE mean
Verbal + Quantitative 1300
Analytical Writing not reported

GPA mean
Overall GPA 3.6

Number of applications/admission offers/incoming students in 2008
219 applied/74 admission offers/19 incoming

% of students receiving:
Full tuition waiver only: 25% partial tuition waiver
Assistantship/fellowship only: 25%
Both full tuition waiver & assistantship/fellowship: 0%

Approximate percentage of incoming students with a B.A./B.S. only: 88% **Master's:** 12%

Approximate percentage (varies from year to year) of students who are
Women: 85% **Ethnic Minority:** 26%
International: 5%

Average years to complete the doctoral program (including internship): 5.7 years (varies from year to year)

Personal interview
Required in person (on occasion grant telephone interviews)

Attrition rate in past 7 years: 5–10%

Percentage of students applying for internship last year accepted into APPIC or APA internships: 75%

Formal tracks/concentrations/specializations: none

Research areas	# Faculty	# Grants
community psychology	1	0
gender	2	0
infant and early childhood	3	0
instructional psychology	1	1
learning disabilities	1	0
learning	1	0
multicultural and diversity	2	0
posttraumatic stress disorder	1	0
psychometric	3	0

Clinical opportunities
infant and early childhood psychology
psychotherapy and clinical interventions
neuropsychological assessment
many varied opportunities available in the New York City metropolitan area

Utah State University (Ph.D.)

(clinical/counseling/school)
Department of Psychology
Logan, UT 84322-2810
phone#: (435) 797-1460
e-mail: PsyDept@cc.usu.edu
Web address: psychology.usu.edu/Graduate-Programs/
Combined-Program-in-Clinical-Counseling-School-
Psychology-PhD/

1	2	3	4	5	6	7
Practice oriented		Equal emphasis				Research oriented

Percentage of faculty subscribing to each of the following orientations:

Psychodynamic/Psychoanalytic	0%
Applied behavioral analysis/Radical behavioral	10%
Family systems/Systems	10%

Existential/Phenomenological/Humanistic 20%
Cognitive/Cognitive-behavioral 60%

Courses required for incoming students to have completed prior to enrolling:
General psychology, developmental psychology, learning, elementary statistics, personality, physiological, abnormal

Recommended but not mandatory courses:
Introduction to counseling, cognitive psychology, social psychology

GRE mean
Verbal 542 Quantitative 680
Verbal + Quantitative 1222
Analytical Writing not reported

GPA mean
Junior/Senior GPA 3.75

Number of applications/admission offers/incoming students in 2009
99 applied/11 admission offers/7 incoming

% of students receiving:
Full tuition waiver only: 0%
Assistantship/fellowship only: 85%
Both full tuition waiver & assistantship/fellowship: 15%

Approximate percentage of incoming students with a B.A./B.S. only: 86% **Master's:** 14%

Approximate percentage of students who are Women: 80% **Ethnic Minority:** 25%
International: 4%

Average years to complete the doctoral program (including internship): 6 years

Personal interview
Preferred in person but telephone acceptable

Attrition rate in past 7 years: 8%

Percentage of students applying for internship last year accepted into APPIC or APA internships: 100%

Formal tracks/concentrations/specializations: child clinical/school, health/neuropsychology, rural/multicultural

Research areas	# Faculty	# Grants
addiction/substance abuse	1	0
ADHD	1	0
behavioral medicine/health psychology	3	2
child behavior problems	4	2
childhood/adolescent depression	2	0
Native American mental health	1	0
rural mental health	2	1
school behavioral assessment	1	0
acceptance and commitment therapy	1	1
ethics	2	1

Clinical opportunities

behavioral medicine	Head Start
cardiac rehabilitation	minority mental health
chronic mental health	neuropsychology
community mental health	pediatric psychology
disabilities	student counseling center
early intervention	student wellness center
eating disorders	

Yeshiva University (Psy.D.)

(clinical/school)
Ferkauf Graduate School of Psychology
Bronx, NY 10461
phone#: (718) 430-3945
e-mail: givner@aecom.yu.edu
Web address: www.yu.edu/ferkauf/page.
aspx?id=733&ekmensel=242_submenu_290_btnlink

1	2	3	4	5	6	7
Practice oriented		Equal emphasis				Research oriented

Percentage of faculty subscribing to each of the following orientations:
Psychodynamic/Psychoanalytic 50%
Applied behavioral analysis/Radical behavioral 10%
Family systems/Systems 20%
Existential/Phenomenological/Humanistic 0%
Cognitive/Cognitive-behavioral 40%

Courses required for incoming students to have completed prior to enrolling:
Statistics, abnormal psychology, child development

Recommended but not mandatory courses:
None

GRE mean
Verbal 562 Quantitative 670
Analytical Writing 5.0

GPA mean
Overall GPA 3.54

Number of applications/admission offers/incoming students in 2009
150 applied/50 admission offers/24 incoming

% of students receiving:
Full tuition waiver only: 5%
Assistantship/fellowship only: 40%
Both full tuition waiver & assistantship/fellowship: 5%

Approximate percentage of incoming students with a B.A./B.S. only: 85% **Master's:** 15%

Approximate percentage of students who are Women: 85% **Ethnic Minority:** 10%
International: 5%

Average years to complete the doctoral program (including internship): 5.0 years

Personal interview
Required in person

Attrition rate in past 7 years: 5 students in past 7 years

Percentage of students applying for internship last year accepted into APPIC or APA internships: 100%

Formal tracks/concentrations/specializations: child psychotherapy

Research areas	# Faculty	# Grants
ADHD	2	0
adolescence	2	0
assessment	3	0

attachment	3	0	professional issues	3	0
behavioral interventions	3	0	social-emotional correlates	3	1
early childhood	2	0	symbolic play	1	0
fathering	2	0			
learning disabilities	3	0			
multicultural issues	3	1			
nontraditional families	2	0			

Clinical opportunities

bilingual/multicultural	family–school collaboration
child/adolescence	parent training
early childhood	school age

REPORTS ON INDIVIDUAL CLINICAL PSYCHOLOGY PROGRAMS

Adelphi University (Ph.D.)

Derner Institute of Advanced Psychological Studies
Garden City, NY 11530
phone#: (516) 877-4800
fax#: (516) 877-4805
e-mail: jcmuran@adelphi.edu
Web address: derner.adelphi.edu/phd-psychology-program.php

1	2	3	4	5	6	7
Practice oriented		Equal emphasis			Research oriented	

Percentage of faculty subscribing to each of the following orientations:

Psychodynamic/Psychoanalytic	90%
Applied behavioral analysis/Radical behavioral	15%
Family systems/Systems	10%
Existential/Phenomenological/Humanistic	10%
Cognitive/Cognitive-behavioral	20%

Courses required for incoming students to have completed prior to enrolling:
Statistics, experimental methods, developmental psychology, abnormal psychology

Recommended but not mandatory courses:
none

GRE mean
Verbal 600 Quantitative 650
Analytical Writing not reported
Psychology Subject Test 650

GPA mean
Overall GPA 3.50   Psychology GPA 3.60

Number of applications/admission offers/incoming students in 2009
275 applied/44 admission offers/21 incoming

% of students receiving:
Full tuition waiver only: 0%
Assistantship/fellowship only: 100%
Both full tuition waiver & assistantship/fellowship: 0%

Approximate percentage of incoming students with a B.A./B.S. only: 67%   **Master's:** 33%

Approximate percentage of students who are Women: 80%   **Ethnic Minority:** 25%
International: 15%

Average years to complete the doctoral program (including internship): not reported

Personal interview
Required in person

Attrition rate in past 7 years: 7.5%

Percentage of students applying for internship last year accepted into APPIC or APA internships: 90%

Formal tracks/concentrations: none

Research areas	# Faculty	# Grants
developmental	2	2
personality	3	1
personal relationships	1	1
couples & group therapy	2	1
health psychology	1	1
psychoanalysis	8	3
change & psychotherapy process	4	3
therapeutic relationship	2	1
unconscious processes & motivation	1	1
trauma	2	1
diversity	6	3

Clinical opportunities

psychoanalytic psychotherapy
addiction & eating disorders
child, adolescent, and family
couples & group therapy
psychotherapy integration
short-term psychotherapy
neuropsychological assessment

Adler School of Professional Psychology (Psy.D.) (2008 data)

65 East Wacker Place, #2100
Chicago, IL 60601-7203
phone#: (312) 201-5900
admissions: (312) 201-5900 ext 222
e-mail: admissions@adler.edu
Web address: www.adler.edu/academics/4211DoctorofPsychologyinClinicalPsychologyPsyD.asp

1	2	3	4	5	6	7
Practice oriented		Equal emphasis			Research oriented	

Percentage of faculty subscribing to each of the following orientations:

Psychodynamic/Psychoanalytic	10%
Applied behavioral analysis/Radical behavioral	0%
Family systems/Systems	10%
Existential/Phenomenological/Humanistic	40%
Cognitive/Cognitive-behavioral	40%

Courses required for incoming students to have completed prior to enrolling:
Advanced abnormal psychology, general psychology, psychometrics, theories of personality, and others to total 18 credits

Recommended but not mandatory courses:
none

GRE mean
not reported

GPA mean
not reported

Number of applications/admission offers/incoming students in 2007
262 applied/131 admission offers/59 incoming

% of students receiving:
Full tuition waiver only: 0%
Assistantship/fellowship only: 10%
Both full tuition waiver & assistantship/fellowship: 0%

Approximate percentage of incoming students with a B.A./B.S. only: 75%   **Master's:** 25%

Approximate percentage of students who are
Women: 79.6%   **Ethnic Minority:** 28.8%
International: 2%

Average years to complete the doctoral program (including internship): 5.1 years

Attrition rate in past 7 years: 15.5%

Percentage of students applying for internship last year accepted into APPIC or APA internships:
67% APPIC
26% APA/CPA

Formal tracks/concentrations: Adlerian psychotherapy, clinical neuropsychology, child & adolescence, group psychotherapy, primary care psychology, substance abuse treatment, marriage & family

Personal interview
Required in person

Research areas	# Faculty	# Grants
adult human development	1	0
disabled children and coping	2	0
neuropsychology of offenders	4	1
community clinical	1	1

Clinical opportunities

department of corrections — schools
developmental disabilities — hospitals
halfway release programs for sex offenders — community mental health centers

---

University of Alabama at Birmingham (Ph.D.)

Department of Psychology
CH 415
1530 3rd Avenue South
Birmingham, AL 35294-1170
phone#: (205) 934-8723
e-mail: jmilb@uab.edu
Web address: www.psy.uab.edu/medpsych.htm

1	2	3	4	5	6	7
Practice oriented			Equal emphasis			Research oriented

Percentage of faculty subscribing to each of the following orientations:

Psychodynamic/Psychoanalytic	30%
Applied behavioral analysis/Radical behavioral	0%
Family systems/Systems	0%
Existential/Phenomenological/Humanistic	0%
Cognitive/Cognitive-behavioral	70%
Health psychology	100%

Courses required for incoming students to have completed prior to enrolling:
At least 18 credit hours of psychology, including statistics; at least 18 credit hours of life sciences (the number of hours are recommended, not required)

Recommended but not mandatory courses:
Psychopathology, learning, cognitive psychology, social psychology

GRE mean
Verbal 560   Quantitative 670
Analytical Writing & Psychology Subject Test not required for admission

GPA mean
Overall GPA 3.65

Number of applications/admission offers/incoming students in 2009
86 applied/13 admission offers/7 incoming

% of students receiving:
Full tuition waiver only: 0%
Assistantship/fellowship only: 100%
Both full tuition waiver & assistantship/fellowship: 100%

Approximate percentage of incoming students with a B.A./B.S. only: 86%   **Master's:** 14%

Approximate percentage of students who are
Women: 86%   **Ethnic Minority:** 14%
International: 0%

Average years to complete the doctoral program (including internship): 6 years

Personal interview
Preferred in person but telephone acceptable

Attrition rate in past 7 years: 9%

Percentage of students applying for internship last year accepted into APPIC or APA internships: 100%

Formal tracks/concentrations: medical/clinical psychology, neuropsychology, pediatric psychology, geropsychology

Research areas	# Faculty	# Grants
aging	3	6
behavioral medicine	2	2
developmental disabilities	6	16
eating disorders	1	1
neuropsychology	3	2
psychophysiology	1	1
substance abuse	3	5

Clinical opportunities
behavioral medicine
neuropsychology

University of Alabama at Tuscaloosa (Ph.D.)

Department of Psychology
P. O. Box 870348
Tuscaloosa, AL 35487-0348
phone#: (205) 348-1913
e-mail: tabrooksi@as.ua.edu
Web address: psychology.ua.edu/academics/graduate/clinical/clinical.html

1	2	3	4	5	6	7
Practice oriented			Equal emphasis			Research oriented

Percentage of faculty subscribing to each of the following orientations:
Psychodynamic/Psychoanalytic   0%

Applied behavioral analysis/Radical behavioral	10%
Family systems/Systems	10%
Existential/Phenomenological/Humanistic	10%
Cognitive/Cognitive-behavioral	80%

Courses required for incoming students to have completed prior to enrolling:
Undergrad statistics, research methods, abnormal psychology, experimental psychology

Recommended but not mandatory courses:
None

GRE mean
Verbal 620   Quantitative 670
Psychology Subject Test 680
Analytical Writing 4.85

GPA mean
Overall GPA 3.7   Psychology GPA 3.7
Junior/Senior GPA 3.7

Number of applications/admission offers/incoming students in 2009
191 applied/19 admission offers/10 incoming

% of students receiving:
Full tuition waiver only: 0%
Assistantship/fellowship only: 0%
Both full tuition waiver & assistantship/fellowship: 82%

Approximate percentage of incoming students with a B.A./B.S. only: 90%   Master's: 10%

Approximate percentage of students who are Women: 78%   Ethnic Minority: 10% International: 2%

Average years to complete the doctoral program (including internship): 6.5 years

Personal interview
Preferred in person but telephone acceptable

Attrition rate in past 7 years: 10%

Percentage of students applying for internship last year accepted into APPIC or APA internships: 91%

Formal tracks/concentrations: health, child, geropsychology, psychology & law

Research areas	# Faculty	# Grants
adult psychopathology	3	2
affective disorders/depression	1	0
aging	6	5
assessment	2	0
autism	1	2
behavioral medicine	3	2
caregiving	1	2
child clinical	3	4
conduct disorders	2	1
cross-cultural psychology	3	3
diversity in aging	2	2
forensic	4	0
long-term care	3	3
pain management	2	3
professional issues	2	0
psychotherapy process and outcome	3	0
rural mental health	4	2
sleep disorders	1	1
social skills	2	1
violence/abuse	2	2
youth psychopathology	1	0

Clinical opportunities

autism	ADHD
conduct disorder	college student counseling
factitious disorder	family therapy
forensic psychology	state psychiatric hospital
gerontology	youth correctional services
health promotion behavior	state forensic medical
pain management	center
parent–child interaction	PTSD
anxiety	Veterans Medical Center
chronic mental illness	high-risk youth
neuropsychological	elder law
assessment	residential child center
sleep disorders	hospice

University at Albany/State University of New York (Ph.D.)

Department of Psychology
1400 Washington Avenue
Albany, NY 12222
phone#: (518) 442-4820
e-mail: forsyth@albany.edu
Web address: www.albany.edu/psy/grad_studies.shtml

1	2	3	4	5	6	7
Practice oriented		Equal emphasis				Research oriented

Percentage of faculty subscribing to each of the following orientations:

Psychodynamic/Psychoanalytic	0%
Applied behavioral analysis/Radical behavioral	30%
Family systems/Systems	0%
Existential/Phenomenological/Humanistic	0%
Cognitive/Cognitive-behavioral	70%

Courses required for incoming students to have completed prior to enrolling:
18 semester hours in psychology, including classes in statistics and experimental design

Recommended but not mandatory courses: None

GRE mean
Verbal 600   Quantitative 652
Psychology Subject Test 652
Analytical Writing 5.1

GPA mean
Overall GPA 3.5   Psychology GPA 3.7

Number of applications/admission offers/incoming students in 2008
182 applied/6 admission offers/6 incoming

% of students receiving:
Full tuition waiver only: 0%
Assistantship/fellowship only: 0%
Both full tuition waiver & assistantship/fellowship: 100%

Approximate percentage of incoming students with a B.A./B.S. only: 100%   **Master's:** 0%

Approximate percentage of students who are Women: 82%   **Ethnic Minority:** 26% **International:** 2%

Average years to complete the doctoral program (including internship): 6.2 years (past 7 years)/ median = 5.5 years

Personal interview
Preferred in person during March Interview Weekend, but telephone acceptable

Attrition rate in past 7 years: 11.7%

Percentage of students applying for internship last year accepted into APPIC or APA internships: 78%

Formal tracks/concentrations: none

Research areas	# Faculty	# Grants
anxiety disorders	1	1
acceptance & commitment therapy	1	1
autism/developmental disabilities	1	3
behavioral medicine	2	0
children & families	4	2
eating disorders	1	1
emotion regulation/dysregulation	7	5
mindfulness-based interventions	3	2
neuropsychology	1	1
psychopathology	1	0
substance abuse/addiction	2	2

Clinical opportunities

acceptance & commitment therapy
addictive disorders
adolescents
anxiety disorders
autism/developmental disabilities
behavioral medicine/health psychology
children & families
cross-cultural issues
eating disorders
neuropsychology

Alliant International University–Fresno (Psy.D.)

5130 East Clinton Way
Fresno, CA 93727
phone#: (866) 825-5426
e-mail: admissions@alliant.edu
Web address: http://www.alliant.edu/wps/wcm/connect/website/Home/Campuses/Fresno+Campus/Academic+Programs

1	2	3	4	5	6	7

Practice oriented   Equal emphasis   Research oriented

Percentage of faculty subscribing to each of the following orientations:

Psychodynamic/Psychoanalytic	10%
Applied behavioral analysis/Radical behavioral	10%
Family systems/Systems	20%
Existential/Phenomenological/Humanistic	10%
Cognitive/Cognitive-behavioral	50%

Courses required for incoming students to have completed prior to enrolling:
If no BA in psychology or score is below the 80th percentile on the Advanced Psychology GRE, then the following are required: 1) Statistics; 2) Tests & Measurements or Differential Psychology; 3) Abnormal Psychology or Psychopathology; and 4) Experimental Psychology or Physiological Psychology or Learning Theory.

Recommended but not mandatory courses:
Please refer to above.

GRE mean
GRE scores are not used as part of the standard admissions process

GPA mean
Overall Undergraduate GPA: 3.2; Master's GPA: 3.7

Number of applications/admission offers/incoming students in 2008
92 applied/53 admission offers/31 incoming

% of students receiving:
Full tuition waiver only: 0%
Assistantship/fellowship only: 5%
Both full tuition waiver & assistantship/fellowship: 0%

Approximate percentage of incoming students with a B.A./B.S. only: 81%   **Master's:** 19%

Approximate percentage of students who are Women: 81%   **Ethnic Minority:** 29% **International:** 2%

Average years to complete the doctoral program (including internship): 4.0 years

Personal interview
Preferred in person but telephone available

Attrition rate in past 7 years: 1% (annual attrition rate)

Percentage of students applying for internship last year accepted into APPIC or APA internships: 100% of the students who applied for an APA/APPIC internship in 2008-2009 received one. 100% of the students who applied for a CAPIC internship in 2008-2009 received one.

Formal tracks/concentrations: Ecosystemic Clinical Child Psychology Emphasis, Health Psychology Emphasis, Civil Forensic Psychology Emphasis

Research areas	# Faculty	# Grants
family/child development	1	not
psychotherapy delivery/ theory/process/outcomes	4	reported
multicultural/international	2	
neuropsychology	1	
health behaviors/medical conditions & interventions	3	
substance abuse	1	
trauma/PTSD	1	
gender/psychology of women	1	
assessment	1	
LGBT	1	

Clinical opportunities
The settings where students complete the professional training requirements include community mental health

140

centers, clinics, inpatient mental health facilities, medical settings, specialized service centers, rehabilitation programs, residential, or day care programs, forensic/correctional facilities, and educational programs.

Alliant International University– Los Angeles (Ph.D.)

1000 South Fremont Avenue, Unit 5
Alhambra, CA 91803-1360
Phone: (866) 825-5426
e-mail: admissions@alliant.edu
Web address: www.alliant.edu/cspp

1	2	3	4	5	6	7
Practice oriented		Equal emphasis				Research oriented

Percentage of faculty subscribing to each of the following orientations:

Psychodynamic/Psychoanalytic	15%
Applied behavioral analysis/Radical behavioral	0%
Family systems/Systems	15%
Existential/Phenomenological/Humanistic	0%
Cognitive/Cognitive-behavioral	15%
Research	50%

Courses required for incoming students to have completed prior to enrolling:

If no BA in psychology or score is below the 80th percentile on the Advanced Psychology GRE, then the following are required: 1) Statistics; 2) Tests & Measurements or Differential Psychology; 3) Abnormal Psychology or Psychopathology and 4) Experimental Psychology or Physiological Psychology or Learning Theory.

Recommended but not mandatory courses:
Refer to above.

GRE mean
GRE scores are not used as part of the standard admissions process.

GPA mean
Overall Undergraduate GPA: 3.4; Master's GPA: 3.8

Number of applications/admission offers/incoming students in 2008
92 applied/46 admission offers/29 incoming

% of students receiving:
Full tuition waiver only: 0%
Assistantship/fellowship only: 5%
Both full tuition waiver & assistantship/fellowship: 0%

Approximate percentage of incoming students with a B.A./B.S. only: 79% Master's: 21%

Approximate percentage of students who are
Women: 83% Ethnic Minority: 44%
International: 3%

Average years to complete the doctoral program (including internship): 5.3 years

Personal interview
Preferred in person but telephone available

Attrition rate in past 7 years: 1% (annual attrition rate)

Percentage of students applying for internship last year accepted into APPIC or APA internships: 50% of the students who applied for an APA/APPIC internship in 2008–2009 received one. 100% of the students who applied for a CAPIC internship in 2008–2009 received one.

Formal tracks/concentrations: Clinical Health Psychology Emphasis; Family & Couple Clinical Psychology Emphasis; Multicultural Community-Clinical Psychology Emphasis

Research areas	# Faculty	# Grants
psychotherapy delivery/ theory/process/outcomes	5	not reported
multicultural/immigrants	3	
health behaviors/medical conditions & interventions	5	
substance abuse	2	
population psychology	1	
trauma/PTSD	2	
advocacy/social policy/activism	2	
peace psychology	1	
gender/psychology of women	2	
community interventions/service delivery/prevention/social policy	1	
personality/personality disorders/ psychopathology	1	

Clinical opportunities
The types of settings in which students might train include: university and college counseling centers; inpatient psychiatric hospitals; public and private community mental health agencies; medical hospitals or outpatient clinics; physical rehabilitation programs; day treatment programs; substance abuse programs; and residential treatment centers.

Alliant International University– Los Angeles (Psy.D.)

1000 South Fremont Avenue, Unit 5
Alhambra, CA 91803-1360
Phone: (866) 825-5426
e-mail: admissions@alliant.edu
Web address: www.alliant.edu/cspp

1	2	3	4	5	6	7
Practice oriented		Equal emphasis				Research oriented

Percentage of faculty subscribing to each of the following orientations:

Psychodynamic/Psychoanalytic	50%
Applied behavioral analysis/Radical behavioral	0%
Family systems/Systems	30%
Existential/Phenomenological/Humanistic	10%
Cognitive/Cognitive-behavioral	10%

Courses required for incoming students to have completed prior to enrolling:
If no BA in psychology or score is below the 80th percentile on the Advanced Psychology GRE, then the following are required: 1) Statistics; 2) Tests & Measurements or Differential Psychology; 3) Abnormal Psychology or Psychopathology and 4) Experimental Psychology or Physiological Psychology or Learning Theory.

Recommended but not mandatory courses:
Please refer to above.

GRE mean
GRE scores are not used as a part of the standard admissions process.

GPA mean
Overall Undergraduate GPA: 3.3; Master's GPA: 3.8

Number of applications/admission offers/incoming students in 2008
265 applied/113 admission offers/67 incoming

% of students receiving:
Full tuition waiver only: 0%
Assistantship/fellowship only: 5%
Both tuition waiver & assistantship/fellowship: 0%

Approximate percentage of incoming students with a B.A./B.S. only: 81%   **Master's:** 19%

Approximate percentage of students who are Women: 82%   **Ethnic Minority:** 51%
International: 2%

Average years to complete the doctoral program (including internship): 3.9 years

Personal interview
Preferred in person but telephone available

Attrition rate in past 7 years: 1% (annual attrition rate)

Percentage of students applying for internship last year accepted into APPIC or APA internships: 39% of the students who applied for an APA/APPIC internship in 2008-2009 received it. 100% of the students who applied for a CAPIC internship in 2008-2009 received it.

Formal tracks/concentrations: Clinical Health Psychology Emphasis; Family and Couple Clinical Psychology Emphasis; Multicultural Community-Clinical Psychology Emphasis

Research areas	# Faculty	# Grants
family/child/adolescent/ development	2	not reported
interventions/psychotherapy services/theory/process/ outcomes	10	
multicultural/international	3	
neuropsychology	2	
health behaviors/medical conditions & interventions	5	
trauma/PTSD	3	
personality disorders/ psychopathology	2	
assessment	3	
LGBT	2	
professional & training issues in psychology/ethics	3	
positive psychology/resilience	1	

Clinical opportunities
The types of settings in which students might train include: university and college counseling centers; inpatient psychiatric hospitals; public & private community mental health agencies; medical hospitals or outpatient clinics; physical rehabilitation programs; day treatment programs; substance abuse programs; and residential treatment centers.

Alliant International University– San Diego (Ph.D.)

10455 Pomerado Road
San Diego, CA 92131-1799
phone#: (866) 825-5426
e-mail: admissions@alliant.edu
Web address: www.alliant.edu/cspp

1	2	3	4	5	6	7
Practice oriented			Equal emphasis			Research oriented

Percentage of faculty subscribing to each of the following orientations:

Psychodynamic/Psychoanalytic	15%
Applied behavioral analysis/Radical behavioral	31%
Family systems/Systems	38%
Existential/Phenomenological/Humanistic	0%
Cognitive/Cognitive-behavioral	16%

Courses required for incoming students to have completed prior to enrolling:
If no BA in psychology or score is below the 80th percentile on the Advanced Psychology GRE, then the following are required: 1) Statistics; 2) Tests & Measurements or Differential Psychology; 3) Abnormal Psychology or Psychopathology and 4) Experimental Psychology or Physiological Psychology or Learning Theory.

Recommended but not mandatory courses:
Refer to above.

GRE mean
GRE scores are not used as part of the standard admissions process.

GPA mean
Overall UG GPA: 3.4; Master's GPA: 3.7

Number of applications/admission offers/incoming students in 2008
118 applied/60 admission offers/39 incoming

% of students receiving:
Full tuition waiver only: 0%
Assistantship/fellowship only: 5%
Both full tuition waiver & assistantship/fellowship: 0%

Approximate percentage of incoming students with a B.A./B.S. only: 95% **Master's:** 5%

Approximate percentage of students who are Women: 81%   **Ethnic Minority:** 26%
International: 1%

Average years to complete the doctoral program (including internship): 6.1 years

Personal interview
Preferred in person but telephone available

Attrition rate in past 7 years: 1% (annual attrition rate)

Percentage of students applying for internship last year accepted into APPIC or APA internships: 62% of the students who applied for an APA/APPIC internship in 2008–2009 received one. 98% of the students who applied for a CAPIC internship in 2008–2009 received one.

Formal tracks/concentrations: Applied Behavior Analysis Emphasis, Family/Child Psychology Emphasis, Forensic Clinical Psychology Emphasis, Health Psychology Emphasis and Track, Multicultural and International Emphasis, Psychodynamic Emphasis

Research areas	# Faculty	# Grants
family/child/adolescent/ development	4	not reported
psychotherapy delivery/theory/ process/outcomes	5	
multicultural/international	2	
neuropsychology	2	
health behaviors/medical conditions & interventions	4	
trauma/PTSD/stress	2	
gender/psychology of women/male roles	2	
personality/personality disorders/psychopathology	8	
assessment	4	
professional & training issues in psychology/ethics	2	

Clinical opportunities

Students select their practicum and local internship placements from more than 75 agencies. Most of these facilities are within a 25-mile radius of the campus, but some are as far as 80 miles away for the benefit of advanced students who live in Orange County. These agencies have over 350 professional training positions.

Alliant International University– San Diego (Psy.D.)

10455 Pomerado Road
San Diego, CA 92131-1799
phone#: (866) 825-5426
e-mail: admissions@alliant.edu
Web address: www.alliant.edu/cspp

1	2	3	4	5	6	7
Practice oriented		Equal emphasis				Research oriented

Percentage of faculty subscribing to each of the following orientations:

Psychodynamic/Psychoanalytic	35%
Applied behavioral analysis/Radical behavioral	10%
Family systems/Systems	25%
Existential/Phenomenological/Humanistic	5%
Cognitive/Cognitive-behavioral	25%

Courses required for incoming students to have completed prior to enrolling:

If no BA in psychology or score is below the 80th percentile on the Advanced Psychology GRE, then the following are required: 1) Statistics; 2) Tests & Measurements or Differential Psychology; 3) Abnormal Psychology or Psychopathology and 4) Experimental Psychology or Physiological Psychology or Learning Theory.

Recommended but not mandatory courses:
Refer to above.

GRE mean
GRE scores are not used as part of the standard admissions process.

GPA mean
Overall Undergraduate GPA: 3.4; Master's GPA: 3.8

Number of applications/admission offers/incoming students in 2008
175 applied/64 admission offers/44 incoming

% of students receiving:
Full tuition waiver only: 0%
Assistantship/fellowship only: 5%
Both full tuition waiver & assistantship/fellowship: 0%

Approximate percentage of incoming students with a B.A./B.S. only: 91%   Master's: 9%

Approximate percentage of students who are
Women: 79%   Ethnic Minority: 24%
International: 2%

Average years to complete the doctoral program (including internship): 5.1 years

Personal interview
Preferred in person but telephone available

Attrition rate in past 7 years: 1% (annual attrition rate)

Percentage of students applying for internship last year accepted into APPIC or APA internships: 0% of the students who applied for an APA/APPIC internship in 2008-2009 received one. 97% of the students who applied for a CAPIC internship in 2008-2009 received one.

Formal tracks/concentrations: Assessment Emphasis; Family/Child Psychology Emphasis; Forensic Psychology Emphasis; Integrative Psychology Emphasis; Multicultural and International Emphasis; Psychodynamic Emphasis

Research areas	# Faculty	# Grants
family/couples/child/ adolescent/development	7	not reported
interventions/therapy/service delivery/theory/process/ outcomes	10	
multicultural/international	5	
reproductive psychology	1	
chemical dependency	2	
trauma/PTSD	2	
gender/psychology of women	3	
assessment	2	
LGBT	1	
self injury/suicide	2	
professional & training issues in psychology/ethics	2	

Clinical opportunities

There are placements available in more than 75 agencies. Most of these facilities are within a 25-mile radius of the campus, but some are as far as 80 miles away for the benefit of students who live in Orange County. These agencies have over 350 professional training positions.

Alliant International University–San Francisco (Ph.D.)

One Beach Street, Suite 100
San Francisco, CA 94133
phone#: (866) 825-5426
e-mail: admissions@alliant.edu
Web address: www.alliant.edu/cspp

1	2	3	4	5	6	7
Practice oriented		Equal emphasis				Research oriented

Percentage of faculty subscribing to each of the following orientations:

Psychodynamic/Psychoanalytic	30%
Applied behavioral analysis/Radical behavioral	0%
Family systems/Systems	60%
Existential/Phenomenological/Humanistic	20%
Cognitive/Cognitive-behavioral	50%

Courses required for incoming students to have completed prior to enrolling:

If no BA in psychology or score is below the 80th percentile on the Advanced Psychology GRE, then the following are required: 1) Statistics; 2) Tests & Measurements or Differential Psychology; 3) Abnormal Psychology or Psychopathology and 4) Experimental Psychology or Physiological Psychology or Learning Theory.

Recommended but not mandatory courses:
Refer to above.

GRE mean
GRE scores are not used as part of the standard admissions process.

GPA mean
Overall UG GPA: 3.4; Master's GPA: 3.7

Number of applications/admission offers in 2008
86 applied/47 admission offers/24 incoming

% of students receiving:
Full tuition waiver only: 0%
Assistantship/fellowship only: 5%
Both full tuition waiver & assistantship/fellowship: 0%

Approximate percentage of incoming students with a B.A./B.S. only: 83%   Master's: 17%

Approximate percentage of students who are
Women: 77%   Ethnic Minority: 39%
International: 3%

Average years to complete the doctoral program (including pre-doc internship): 6.6 years

Personal interview
Preferred in person but telephone available

Attrition rate in past 7 years: 1% (annual attrition rate)

Percentage of students applying for internship last year accepted into APPIC or APA internships: 85% of the students who applied for an APA/APPIC internship in 2008–2009 received one. 100% of the students who applied for a CAPIC internship in 2008–2009 received one.

Formal tracks/concentrations: Family/Child/Adolescent Psychology; Health Psychology; Multicultural and Community Psychology; Gender Studies (Psychology of Women, Men, and Lesbian/Gay/Bisexual/Transgender)

Research areas	# Faculty	# Grants
family/child/adolescent/ development	2	not reported
psychotherapy delivery/ theory/process/outcomes	5	
multicultural/international	4	
health behaviors/medical conditions & interventions/ neuropsychology	3	
substance abuse	3	
trauma/PTSD/stress/coping	3	
gender/psychology of women/male roles	4	
community interventions/ service delivery evaluation/ prevention/social policy/ activism	4	
personality/personality disorders/ psychopathology	3	
assessment	2	
LGBT	2	
professional & training issues in psychology/ethics	2	
violence/juvenile delinquency/ forensics	3	

Clinical opportunities

Because of CSPP's large network of affiliated agencies, the school can offer professional training placements in community mental health clinics, adult outpatient services, hospitals, neuropsychiatric institutions, infant-parent programs, child and adolescent guidance clinics, college counseling centers, family service agencies, residential treatment centers, forensic settings, pediatric psychology programs, school-based settings, substance abuse treatment centers, and programs serving predominantly African American, Asian American, and Latino populations. The San Francisco campus places students in agencies throughout Alameda, Contra Costa, Marin, San Francisco, San Mateo, Santa Clara, and Solano counties. Additional placements are located in some counties outside the immediate Bay Area, including Napa, Sacramento, Santa Cruz, Sonoma, San Benito, and Yolo counties.

Alliant International University–San Francisco (Psy.D.)

One Beach Street, Suite 100
San Francisco, CA 94133
phone#: (866) 825-5426
e-mail: admissions@alliant.edu
Web address: www.alliant.edu/cspp

1	2	3	4	5	6	7
Practice oriented		Equal emphasis				Research oriented

Percentage of faculty subscribing to each of the following orientations:

Psychodynamic/Psychoanalytic	26%

Applied behavioral analysis/Radical behavioral	0%
Family systems/Systems	21%
Existential/Phenomenological/Humanistic	15%
Cognitive/Cognitive-behavioral	5%

Courses required for incoming students to have completed prior to enrolling:
If no BA in psychology or score is below the 80th percentile on the Advanced Psychology GRE, then the following are required: 1) Statistics; 2) Tests & Measurements or Differential Psychology; 3) Abnormal Psychology or Psychopathology and 4) Experimental Psychology or Physiological Psychology or Learning Theory.

Recommended but not mandatory courses:
Refer to above.

GRE mean
GRE scores are not used as part of the standard admissions process.

GPA mean
Overall UG GPA: 3.3; Master's GPA: 3.8

Number of applications/admission offers in 2008
199 applied/130 admission offers/69 incoming

% of students receiving:
Full tuition waiver only: 0%
Assistantship/fellowship only: 5%
Both full tuition waiver & assistantship/fellowship: 0%

Approximate percentage of incoming students with a B.A./B.S. only: 87%　**Master's:** 13%

Approximate percentage of students who are Women: 79%　**Ethnic Minority:** 36%
International: 4%

Average years to complete the doctoral program (including internship): 4.9 years

Personal interview
Preferred in person but telephone available

Attrition rate in past 7 years: 1% (annual attrition rate)

Percentage of students applying for internship last year accepted into APPIC or APA internships: 62% of the students who applied for an APA/APPIC internship in 2008–2009 received one. 100% of the students who applied for a CAPIC internship in 2008-2009 received one.

Formal tracks/concentrations: Child & Family Psychology Track; Forensic Family/Child Psychology Track; Family/Child Psychology; Gender Studies (Psychology of Women, Men, Gender Roles, and Sexual Orientation); Health Psychology; Multicultural & Community Psychology; Adult Psychotherapy

Research areas	# Faculty	# Grants
family/child/adolescent/ development	10	not reported
psychotherapy delivery/ theory/process/outcomes	14	
multicultural/international/ immigrants	11	
neuropsychology	1	
health behavior/medical conditions & interventions	4	
substance abuse/addictions	4	
trauma/PTSD	2	
gender/psychology of women	2	
community interventions/ prevention/social policy/ activism	4	
personality/personality disorders/psychopathology	4	
assessment	1	
LGBT	1	
professional & training issues in psychology/ethics	3	
forensics	3	

Clinical opportunities
Because of CSPP's large network of affiliated agencies, the school can offer professional training placements in community mental health clinics, hospitals and neuropsychiatric institutions, child guidance clinics, college counseling centers, residential treatment centers, forensic settings, pediatric psychology programs, school-based child treatment settings, and a host of other settings as well. The San Francisco campus places students in agencies throughout Alameda, Contra Costa, Marin, San Francisco, San Mateo, Santa Clara, and Solano counties. Additional placements are located in some counties outside the immediate Bay Area, including Napa, Sacramento, Santa Cruz, Sonoma, San Benito, and Yolo counties.

American University (Ph.D.)
Department of Psychology
Washington, DC 20016
phone#: (202) 885-1726
e-mail: cweissb@american.edu
Web address: www.american.edu/cas/psychology/clinical.cfm

1	2	3	4	5	6	7
Practice oriented			Equal emphasis			Research oriented

Percentage of faculty subscribing to each of the following orientations:

Psychodynamic/Psychoanalytic	0%
Applied behavioral analysis/Radical behavioral	0%
Family systems/Systems	0%
Existential/Phenomenological/Humanistic	15%
Cognitive/Cognitive-behavioral	85%

Courses required for incoming students to have completed prior to enrolling: none

Recommended but not mandatory courses:
psychology major, including experimental psychology, statistics

GRE mean
Verbal 674　Quantitative 627
Psychology Subject Test 685　Analytical Writing 4.43

GPA mean
Overall GPA 3.70　Psychology GPA 3.5

Number of applications/admission offers/incoming students in 2009
216 applied/9 admission offers/ 7 incoming

% of students receiving:
Full tuition waiver only: 0%
Assistantship/fellowship only: 0%
Both full tuition waiver & assistantship/fellowship: 85%

Approximate percentage of incoming students with a B.A./B.S. only: 85.72%   **Master's:** 14.28%

Approximate percentage of students who are Women: 100%   **Ethnic Minority:** 14.28%
International: not reported

Average years to complete the doctoral program (including internship): 6.5 years

Personal interview
Required in person

Attrition rate in past 7 years: 1%

Percentage of students applying for internship last year accepted into APPIC or APA internships: 80%

Formal tracks/concentrations: none

Research areas	# Faculty	# Grants
addiction	2	2
anxiety disorders	1	0
child	1	0
coping	1	0
depression	1	0
eating disorders	1	0
treatment cost effectiveness	1	0
sports psychology	2	0

Clinical opportunities

cognitive-behavior therapy	psychological testing
person-centered therapy	neuropsychological testing
therapy	externships

Antioch University New England (Psy.D.)

Department of Clinical Psychology
40 Avon Street
Keene, NH 03431
phone#: (603) 357-3122
e-mail: rpeterson@antiochne.edu
Web address: www.antiochne.edu/cp/

1	2	**3**	4	5	6	7
Practice oriented		Equal emphasis				Research oriented

Percentage of faculty subscribing to each of the following orientations:

Psychodynamic/Psychoanalytic	30%
Applied behavioral analysis/Radical behavioral	10%
Family systems/Systems	10%
Existential/Phenomenological/Humanistic	10%
Cognitive/Cognitive-behavioral	20%
Integrative	20%

Courses required for incoming students to have completed prior to enrolling:
Undergraduate or graduate degree in psychology is preferred, at a minimum at least 15 credits of relevant coursework is required.

Recommended but not mandatory courses: None

GRE mean
Verbal 550   Quantitative 640

GPA mean
Overall GPA 3.6

Number of applications/admission offers/incoming students in 2008
81 applied/51 admission offers/27 incoming

% of students receiving:
Full tuition waiver only: 0%
Assistantship/fellowship only: 18% (small stipends)
Both full tuition waiver & assistantship/fellowship: 0%

Approximate percentage of incoming students with a B.A./B.S. only: 53%   **Master's:** 47%

Approximate percentage of students who are Women: 81%   **Ethnic Minority:** 6%
International: 2%

Average years to complete the doctoral program (including internship): 7 years

Personal interview
Required in person

Attrition rate in past 7 years: 12.8%

Percentage of students applying for internship last year accepted into APPIC or APA internships: 100%

Formal tracks/concentrations: child clinical, adult psychotherapy, and heath psychology

Research areas	# Faculty	# Grants
community services	2	2
children	2	0
health psychology	1	1
graduate training	2	0
group	1	0
multicultural psychology	1	0
outcome evaluation	2	0
women's issues	2	0

Clinical opportunities

assessment	gay and lesbian
battering/abuse	group therapy
behavioral medicine	health psychology
child clinical psychology	neuropsychology/
cognitive/behavioral therapy	rehabilitation
conduct disorders	personality disorders
community services	psychodynamic
counseling center	rural psychology
family therapy	school based: substance
forensic	abuse, supervision

Argosy University–Atlanta (Psy.D.)

Formerly—Georgia School of Professional Psychology
980 Hammond Drive, Suite 100
Atlanta, GA 30328
phone#: (770) 671-1200 or (888) 671-4777
e-mail: tcbrown@argosy.edu
Web address: www.argosy.edu/colleges/programdetail.aspx?ID=577

1	2	3	4	5	6	7
Practice oriented		Equal emphasis			Research oriented	

Percentage of faculty subscribing to each of the following orientations:

Psychodynamic/Psychoanalytic	35%
Applied behavioral analysis/Radical behavioral	0%
Family systems/Systems	15%
Existential/Phenomenological/Humanistic	15%
Cognitive/Cognitive-behavioral	35%

Courses required for incoming students to have completed prior to enrolling:

General psychology, abnormal psychology, and statistics/research methods

Recommended but not mandatory courses:

Tests and measurement, physiological psychology, and personality theory

GRE mean

Verbal 515   Quantitative 580
Psychology Subject Test not reported
Analytical Writing 4.25

GPA mean

Overall GPA 3.52   Psychology GPA not available
Junior/Senior GPA not available

Number of applications/admission offers/incoming students in 2009

124 applied/43 admission offers/20 incoming

% of students receiving:

Full tuition waiver only: 0%
Assistantship/fellowship only: 20%
Both full tuition waiver & assistantship/fellowship: 0%

Approximate percentage of incoming students with a B.A./B.S. only: 74%   Master's: 26%

Approximate percentage of students who are Women: 70%   Ethnic Minority: 20% International: 5%

Average years to complete the doctoral program (including internship): 5.75 years

Personal interview

On-campus interview strongly preferred; minimal requirement is telephone interview.

Attrition rate in past 7 years: Annual attrition from 7 to 12%

Percentage of students applying for internship last year accepted into APPIC or APA internships: 96%

Formal tracks/concentrations: child/family, adult clinical, health psychology, neuropsychology/geropsychology

Research areas	# Faculty	# Grants
multicultural issues	3	0
neuropsychology	3	0
pediatric psychology	2	0
psychological assessment	4	0
short-term, dynamic therapy	2	0
teenage sexuality	2	0

Clinical opportunities

assessment	health psychology
adult psychotherapy	inpatient and outpatient
child & adolescent	clinical services
psychotherapy	neuropsychology
crisis intervention	rehabilitation medicine
educational assessments	substance abuse
and consultation	rehabilitation
forensic psychology	

Argosy University, Chicago (Psy.D.)

225 N. Michigan, Suite 1300
Chicago, IL 60601
phone#: (312) 777-7600 or (800) 626-4123
e-mail: lhorvath@argosy.edu
Web address: www.argosy.edu/colleges/ProgramDetail.aspx?ID=568

1	2	3	4	5	6	7
Practice oriented		Equal emphasis			Research oriented	

Percentage of faculty subscribing to each of the following orientations:

Psychodynamic/Psychoanalytic	35%
Applied behavioral analysis/Radical behavioral	0%
Family systems/Systems	12%
Existential/Phenomenological/Humanistic	18%
Cognitive/Cognitive-behavioral	35%

Courses required for incoming students to have completed prior to enrolling:

Abnormal psychology, statistics, tests and measures, personality

Recommended but not mandatory courses:

None

GRE mean

Not reported

GPA mean

Overall GPA 3.3 Psychology GPA 3.3
Junior/Senior GPA 3.3

Number of applications/admission offers/incoming students in 2009

246 applied/113 admission offers/55 incoming

% of students receiving:

Full tuition waiver only: 0%
Assistantship/fellowship only: 14%
Both full tuition waiver & assistantship/fellowship: 0%

Approximate percentage of incoming students with a B.A./B.S. only: 61%   Master's: 39%

Approximate percentage of students who are Women: 77%   Ethnic Minority: 27% International: 7%

Average years to complete the doctoral program (including internship): 5.9 years

Personal interview

Required in person
Preferred in person but telephone acceptable (international students only)

Attrition rate in past 7 years: 11.4%

Percentage of students applying for internship last year accepted into APPIC or APA internships: 70%

Formal tracks/concentrations: child/adolescent psychology, client-centered/experiential psychotherapies, diversity/multicultural psychology, family psychology, forensic psychology, health psychology, organizational consulting, psychoanalytic psychology, psychology & spirituality, neuropsychology

Research areas	# Faculty	# Grants
adolescence and delinquency	1	0
behavioral medicine	4	3
diverse students' needs	3	1
eating disorders	1	0
gay men adult development	2	0
international psychology	1	0
parenting	1	0
person-centered interventions	2	0
personality disorders	1	0
play therapy	1	0
romantic relationships	1	0
substance abuse	1	0
therapist development	2	1
therapy of severe mental illness	1	0
trauma recovery	1	0
women's career choices	1	0

Clinical opportunities

behavioral medicine
child and adolescent psychology
chronic mental illness
cognitive-behavioral psychotherapy
community psychology
couples
eating disorders
emergency crisis
ethnic-racial psychology
family psychology
forensic psychology
gay/lesbian/bisexual
gerontology
group therapy
neuropsychology
person-centered and experiential psychotherapy
personality disorders
prevention
psychoanalytic psychotherapy
refugee populations/trauma and torture survivors
rehabilitation
religiously committed clients
school-based programs
sexual abuse
short-term psychotherapy
sports psychology
substance abuse
victim/abuse/battering

Argosy University, Hawaii (Psy.D.)

400 ASB Tower, 1001 Bishop Street
Honolulu, HI 96813
phone#: (808) 536-5555
e-mail: hawaii@argosy.edu
Web address: www.argosy.edu/colleges/programdetail.aspx?ID=627

1	2	3	4	5	6	7
Practice oriented		Equal emphasis				Research oriented

Percentage of faculty subscribing to each of the following orientations:

Psychodynamic/Psychoanalytic	0%
Applied behavioral analysis/Radical behavioral	0%
Family systems/Systems	28%

Existential/Phenomenological/Humanistic	36%
Cognitive/Cognitive-behavioral	36%

Courses required for incoming students to have completed prior to enrolling:
abnormal psychology, tests and measurements, personality, research methods/ statistics

Recommended but not mandatory courses: None

GRE mean
Not reported

GPA mean
Overall 3.7

Number of applications/admission offers/incoming students in 2009
102 applied/87 admission offers/30 incoming

% of students receiving:
Full tuition waiver only: 0%
Assistantship/fellowship only: 5%
Both full tuition waiver & assistantship/fellowship: 0%

Approximate percentage of incoming students with a B.A./B.S. only: 75% **Master's:** 25%

Approximate percentage of students who are Women: 80% **Ethnic Minority:** 54% **International:** 3%

Average years to complete the doctoral program (including internship): 5.72 years (mean); 5.43 (median)

Personal interview
Preferred in person but telephone acceptable

Attrition rate in past 7 years: 1.8%

Percentage of students applying for internship last year accepted into APPIC or APA internships: 87%

Formal tracks/concentrations: child/family, diversity, health psychology

Research areas	# Faculty	# Grants
diversity education	9	0
gay/lesbian relationships	2	0
health psychology	1	0
neuropsychology	2	0
children	3	0

Clinical opportunities

child and adolescent
day treatment and hospice programs
community mental health centers
developmental evaluation clinics
outpatient treatment centers
psychiatric, medical, and veterans hospitals
public and private schools
state courts, prisons
substance abuse
hospitals

Argosy University, Orange County (Psy.D.)

601 South Lewis Street
Orange, CA 92868
phone#: (714) 620-3700
e-mail: gbruss@argosy.edu
Web address: www.argosy.edu/colleges/programdetail.aspx?ID=679

1	2	3	4	5	6	7
Practice oriented			Equal emphasis			Research oriented

Percentage of faculty subscribing to each of the following orientations:
Not reported

Courses required for incoming students to have completed prior to enrolling:
General Psychology; Statistics or Research Methods; Personality Theories or Counseling Theories; Maladaptive Behavior & Psychopathology; Psychological Assessment

Recommended but not mandatory courses: None

GRE mean
N/A

GPA mean
N/A

Number of applications/admission offers/incoming students in 2009
N/A

% of students receiving:
N/A

Approximate percentage of incoming students with a B.A./B.S. only: N/A   **Master's:** N/A

Approximate percentage of students who are Women: N/A   **Ethnic Minority:** N/A **International:** N/A

Average years to complete the doctoral program (including internship): N/A

Personal interview
Preferred in person but telephone acceptable

Attrition rate in past 7 years: N/A

Percentage of students applying for internship last year accepted into APPIC or APA internships: N/A

Formal tracks/concentrations:
Child and Adolescent Psychology
Forensic Psychology

Research areas	# Faculty	# Grants
None reported		

Clinical opportunities
None reported

Argosy University—Phoenix Campus (Psy.D.)

American School of Professional Psychology
2233 West Dunlap Avenue, Suite 150
Phoenix, AZ 85021
phone#: (602) 216-2600
Web address: www.argosy.edu/colleges/programdetail.aspx?ID=971

1	2	3	4	5	6	7
Practice oriented			Equal emphasis			Research oriented

Percentage of faculty subscribing to each of the following orientations:

Psychodynamic/Psychoanalytic	0%
Applied behavioral analysis/Radical behavioral	10%
Family systems/Systems	10%
Existential/Phenomenological/Humanistic	0%
Cognitive/Cognitive-behavioral	42%

Courses required for incoming students to have completed prior to enrolling:
Personality, abnormal psychology, test and measurement, psychological assessment, statistics or research methods.

Recommended but not mandatory courses: none

GRE mean
not reported

GPA mean
Overall 3.62

Number of applications/admission offers/incoming students in 2008-2009
116 applied/63 admission offers/61 incoming

% of students receiving:
Full tuition waiver only: 0%
Assistantship/fellowship only: 0%
Both full tuition waiver & assistantship/fellowship: 0%

Approximate percentage of incoming students with a B.A./B.S. only: 80%   **Master's:** 20%

Approximate percentage of students who are Women: 80%   **Ethnic Minority:** 16% **International:** 1%

Average years to complete the doctoral program (including internship): 5 years

Personal interview
Preferred in person but telephone acceptable

Attrition rate in past 7 years: not reported

Percentage of students applying for internship last year accepted into APPIC or APA internships: 91%

Formal tracks/concentrations: none

Research areas	# Faculty	# Grants
diversity	5	0
learning disability/ADHD	4	0
neuropsychology	2	0
psychopharmacology	1	0
geropsyhcology	2	0
health	2	0

Clinical opportunities
None as a part of the school, but we do offer a diverse array of practicum placement in specialty clinics, including but not limited to sexual offender treatment, substance abuse, pain management, neuropsychology, surgical centers, schools and specialty schools, inpatient and outpatient psychotherapy, HIV/AIDS, and culturally diverse sites.

Argosy University—Schaumburg Campus (Psy.D.)

(American School of Professional Psychology)

999 Plaza Drive, Suite 111
Schaumburg, IL 60173
phone#: (847) 969-4900
e-mail: admissionscnw@argosy.edu
Web address: www.argosy.edu/colleges/programdetail.
aspx?ID=797

1	2	3	4	5	6	7
Practice oriented		Equal emphasis				Research oriented

Percentage of faculty subscribing to each of the following orientations:

Psychodynamic/Psychoanalytic	17%
Applied behavioral analysis/Radical behavioral	0%
Family systems/Systems	17%
Existential/Phenomenological/Humanistic	25%
Cognitive/Cognitive-behavioral	25%

Courses required for incoming students to have completed prior to enrolling:

Abnormal psychology, tests and measurement (or intro to psychological assessment), personality theory, introductory statistics

Recommended but not mandatory courses: none

GRE mean
not required

GPA mean
3.5

Number of applications/admission offers/incoming students in 2008
140/67/40

% of students receiving:
Full tuition waiver only: 0%
Assistantship/fellowship only: 25%

Both full tuition waiver & assistantship/fellowship: 0%

Approximate percentage of incoming students with a B.A./B.S. only: 58% **Master's:** 42%

Approximate percentage of students who are Women: 80% **Ethnic Minority:** 16% **International:** .5%

Average years to complete the doctoral program (including internship): 5.2 years

Personal interview
Required in person

Attrition rate in past 7 years: 4-7%

Percentage of students applying for internship last year accepted into APPIC or APA internships: 86%

Formal tracks/concentrations: Forensic Psychology; Clinical Health Psychology; Child & Family Psychology; Multicultural Psychology, Neuropsychology

Research areas	# Faculty	# Grants
ADHD and child externalizing	1	0
cultural bias in psychological testing	1	0
effectiveness of EFT	1	1
experiential therapy	3	1
family therapy effectiveness	1	0
men's perception of psychotherapy	1	0
multicultural training	2	1
psychotherapy process and outcome	2	1
substance abuse program evaluation	1	1
treatment of domestic violence	2	0
eating disorders and trauma	1	1
treating diverse couples	1	1
spirituality and psychotherapy	1	1
sleep disorders	1	1
pediatric neuropsychology	1	1

Numerous sites available; more than 250 practicum sites in greater Chicago area. Specialization sites include:

child and pediatric psychology · inpatient psychiatric
college counseling center · hospital, adult and
community mental health · adolescent neuro-
correctional psychology · psychological assessment
family and marital counseling · rehabilitation
forensics · severely mentally ill
health and medical psychology · substance abuse

Argosy University–Tampa (Psy.D.)

1403 N. Howard
Tampa, FL 33607
phone#: (813) 463-714
e-mail: jpeterson@argosy.edu
Web address: www.argosy.edu/colleges/programdetail.
aspx?ID=837

1	2	3	4	5	6	7
Practice oriented		Equal emphasis				Research oriented

Percentage of faculty subscribing to each of the following orientations:

Psychodynamic/Psychoanalytic	25%
Applied behavioral analysis/Radical behavioral	25%
Family systems/Systems	25%
Existential/Phenomenological/Humanistic	0%
Cognitive/Cognitive-behavioral	25%

Courses required for incoming students to have completed prior to enrolling:

BA or MA in Psychology or related field OR the following four courses: Introduction to Psychology or Clinical/Counseling Psychology, Statistics/Research Methods or Tests and Measures, Two other psychology courses

Recommended but not mandatory courses: none

GRE mean
N/A: GRE scores are not a mandatory part of our admissions process

GPA mean
3.41

Number of applications/admission offers/incoming students in 2009
194 applied/45 admission offers/21 incoming

% of students receiving:
Full tuition waiver only: 0%
Assistantship/fellowship only: 20%
Both full tuition waiver & assistantship/fellowship: 0%

Approximate percentage of incoming students with a B.A./B.S. only: 70%   **Master's:** 30%

Approximate percentage of students who are Women: 80%   **Ethnic Minority:** 20% **International:** 10%

Average years to complete the doctoral program (including internship): 5.1

Personal interview
Not reported

Attrition rate in past 7 years: 5.3%

Percentage of students applying for internship last year accepted into APPIC or APA internships: 100%

Formal tracks/concentrations: Neuropsychology, Geropsychology, Marriage and Family Psychology, Child Psychology

Research areas	# Faculty	# Grants
psychotherapy with diverse populations	2	0

Clinical opportunities
Multiple practica with specialty populations/services are available: neuropsychology, medical psychology, forensic/correctional populations, schools, anxiety/obsessive-compulsive disorders, college counseling centers, trauma survivors, familty therapy, substance abuse

Argosy University–Twin Cities Campus (Psy.D.)

Clinical Psychology Program
Graduate Admissions
Argosy University/Twin Cities
1515 Central Parkway
Eagan, MN 55121
phone#: (888) 844-2004
e-mail: tcadmissions@argosy.edu
Web address: www.argosy.edu/colleges/programdetail.aspx?ID=186

1	2	3	4	5	6	7
Practice oriented		Equal emphasis				Research oriented

Percentage of faculty subscribing to each of the following orientations:

Psychodynamic/Psychoanalytic	35%
Applied behavioral analysis/Radical behavioral	0%
Family systems/Systems	20%
Existential/Phenomenological/Humanistic	20%
Cognitive/Cognitive-behavioral	25%

Courses required for incoming students to have completed prior to enrolling:
4 psychology courses and 1 statistics course

Recommended but not mandatory courses: none

GRE mean
not reported

GPA mean
3.32 for students applying with a BA; 3.83 for students applying with an MA

Number of applications/admission offers/incoming students in 2008
183 applied/85 admission offers/49 incoming

% of students receiving:
Full tuition waiver only: 0%
Assistantship/fellowship only: 33%
Both full tuition waiver & assistantship/fellowship: 0%

Approximate percentage of incoming students with a B.A./B.S. only: 57%   **Master's:** 43%

Approximate percentage of students who are Women: 69%   **Ethnic Minority:** 12% **International:** 5%

Average years to complete the doctoral program (including internship): 5 year

Personal interview
Required in person

Attrition rate in past 7 years: 64.9%

Percentage of students applying for internship last year accepted into APPIC or APA internships: 79%

Formal tracks/concentrations: forensic psychology, health/neuro psychology, psychology and trauma, child clinical

Research areas	# Faculty	# Grants
properties of Rorschach	2	0
psychotherapy outcome	2	0
attachment disorders	1	0
multicultural competence	2	0

Clinical opportunities
Over 90 practicum sites in the greater Twin Cities area training site network

Mixed feelings

Argosy University–Washington, DC Campus (Psy.D.)

1550 Wilson Boulevard, Suite 600
Washington, DC 22209
phone#: 703-526-5800
e-mail: rbarrett@argosy.edu
Web address: www.argosy.edu/colleges/programdetail.aspx?ID=887

1	2	3	4	5	6	7
Practice oriented		Equal emphasis				Research oriented

Percentage of faculty subscribing to each of the following orientations:

Psychodynamic/Psychoanalytic	57%
Applied behavioral analysis/Radical behavioral	0%
Family systems/Systems	21%
Existential/Phenomenological/Humanistic	36%
Cognitive/Cognitive-behavioral	64%

Courses required for incoming students to have completed prior to enrolling:
Statistics or research methods, abnormal psychology, plus two other psychology courses (excluding introductory psychology)

Recommended but not mandatory courses: None

GRE mean
not reported

GPA mean
Overall 3.25

Number of applications/admission offers/incoming students in 2008
345 applied/166 admission offers/83 incoming

% of students receiving:
Full tuition waiver only: 0%
Assistantship/fellowship only: 11%
Both full tuition waiver & assistantship/fellowship: 11%

Approximate percentage of incoming students with a B.A./B.S. only: 51%   **Master's:** 45%

Approximate percentage of students who are Women: 81.5%   **Ethnic Minority:** 31%
International: not reported

Average years to complete the doctoral program (including internship): 5 years

Personal interview
Preferred in person but telephone acceptable

Attrition rate in past 7 years: 4% Annual
Percentage of students applying for internship last year accepted into APPIC or APA internships: 90%

Formal tracks/concentrations: forensic concentration, child and family concentration, health and neuropsychology concentration, diversity concentration

Research areas	# Faculty	# Grants
cognitive attributions	1	0
multicultural competence	4	
psychotherapy integration	2	
eating disorders	2	
social psychology	1	
forensic psychology	3	
GLBT issues	2	
child and family	4	
CBT cognitive schemas	3	
geopolitical conflict		1
trauma and PTSD	1	0

Clinical opportunities

anxiety disorders/OCD	sexual orientation
child abuse	school mental health
children's hospitals	substance abuse
forensic hospitals/prisons	university counseling
gerontology	center
neuropsychology	community mental health
posttraumatic stress disorder	centers

University of Arizona (Ph.D.)

Department of Psychology
Psychology Building
Tucson, AZ 85721
phone#: (520) 621-7447
e-mail: psychology@email.arizona.edu

Web address: psychology.arizona.edu/programs/
g_each/clinical.php

1	2	3	4	5	6	7
Practice oriented		Equal emphasis			Research oriented	

Percentage of faculty subscribing to each of the following orientations:

Psychodynamic/Psychoanalytic	0%
Applied behavioral analysis/Radical behavioral	10%
Family systems/Systems	35%
Existential/Phenomenological/Humanistic	5%
Cognitive/Cognitive-behavioral	50%

Courses required for incoming students to have completed prior to enrolling:
B.A. or B.S. in psychology; abnormal psychology; statistics and methods.

Recommended but not mandatory courses:
Social, biological psychology, cognitive, and developmental

GRE mean
Verbal 620 Quantitative 700
Psychology Subject Test 700

GPA mean
Overall GPA 3.65

Number of applications/admission offers/incoming students in 2008
210 applied/12 admission offers/9 incoming

% of students receiving:
Full tuition waiver only: 0%
Assistantship/fellowship only: 0%
Both full tuition waiver & assistantship/fellowship: 100%

Approximate percentage of incoming students with a B.A./B.S. only: 90%   **Master's:** 10%

Approximate percentage of students who are Women: 75%   **Ethnic Minority:** 22%
International: 20%

Average years to complete the doctoral program (including internship): 6 years

Personal interview
Preferred in person but telephone acceptable

Attrition rate in past 7 years: 6%

Percentage of students applying for internship last year accepted into APPIC or APA internships: 100%

Formal tracks/concentrations: none

Research areas	# Faculty	# Grants
clinical neuropsychology	3	3
depression	2	3
family systems	2	4
health psychology	6	6
mental health policy	1	1
sleep disorders	1	2
treatment outcome	3	4

Clinical opportunities

empirically supported treatments	sleep disorders
individual, couple, and family therapy	neuropsychology/ rehabilitation
depression, addiction, neurological disorders	gerontology
	behavioral medicine
	community psychology

Arizona State University (Ph.D.)

Department of Psychology
Tempe, AZ 85287-1104
phone#: (480) 965-7598
e-mail: psygrad@asu.edu
Web address: http://psychology.clas.asu.edu/clinical

1	2	3	4	5	**6**	7
Practice oriented		Equal emphasis				Research oriented

Percentage of faculty subscribing to each of the following orientations:

Psychodynamic/Psychoanalytic	0%
Applied behavioral analysis/Radical behavioral	0%
Family systems/Systems	30%
Existential/Phenomenological/Humanistic	0%
Cognitive/Cognitive-behavioral	70%

Courses required for incoming students to have completed prior to enrolling:
B.A. in psychology or equivalent

Recommended but not mandatory courses: None

GRE mean
Verbal 625   Quantitative 688
Analytical Writing 5.08

GPA mean
Overall GPA 3.79

Number of applications/admission offers/incoming students in 2009
163 applied/13 admission offers/6 incoming

% of students receiving:
Full tuition waiver only: 0%
Full assistantship/fellowship only: 0%
Both full tuition waiver & assistantship/fellowship: 100%

Approximate percentage of incoming students with a B.A./B.S. only: 90%   **Master's:** 10%

Approximate percentage of students who are Women: 75%   **Ethnic Minority:** 27%
International: 20%

Average years to complete the doctoral program (including internship): 6.6 years

Personal interview
Preferred in person, but telephone acceptable

Attrition rate in past 7 years: 4%

Percentage of students applying for internship last year accepted into APPIC or APA internships: 100%

Formal tracks/concentrations: child clinical, community/ prevention, health

Research areas

	# Faculty	# Grants
behavioral medicine/health psychology	8	5
child clinical	7	8
community psychology	7	5
family interactions	5	3
hispanic studies	3	1
minority mental health	5	1
personality assessment	1	0
prevention	6	4
substance abuse	3	2

Clinical opportunities

behavioral analysis	individual therapy
behavioral medicine	intellectual and academic assessment
child clinical psychology	
child health psychology	marital/couples therapy
family therapy	parenting groups
geropsychology	prevention programs

University of Arkansas (Ph.D.)

Department of Psychology
216 Memorial Hall
Fayetteville, AR 72701
phone#: (479) 575-4256
e-mail: psycapp@uark.edu
Web address: www.uark.edu/depts/psyc/clinical.htm

1	2	3	4	**5**	6	7
Practice oriented		Equal emphasis				Research oriented

Percentage of faculty subscribing to each of the following orientations:

Psychodynamic/Psychoanalytic	0%
Applied behavioral analysis/Radical behavioral	30%
Family systems/Systems	50%
Existential/Phenomenological/Humanistic	0%
Cognitive/Cognitive-behavioral	100%

Courses required for incoming students prior to enrolling:
Core courses in the science of psychology.

Courses recommended but not mandatory:
18 semester hours in psychology including statistics, learning, and experimental psychology

GRE mean
Verbal 581   Quantitative 649
Analytical Writing 5.28

GPA mean
Overall GPA 3.77

Number of applications/admission offers/incoming students in 2008
96 applied/9 admission offers/6 incoming

% of students receiving:
Full tuition waiver only: 0%
Assistantship/fellowship only: 0%
Both full tuition waiver & assistantship/fellowship: 100%

Approximate percentage of incoming students with a B.A./B.S. only: 100%   **Master's:** 0%

Approximate percentage of students who are
Women: 70%   **Ethnic Minority:** 15%
International: 0%

Average years to complete the doctoral program (including internship): 6 years

Personal interview
For invited applicants only

Attrition rate in past 7 years: 7%

Percentage of students applying for internship last year accepted into APPIC or APA internships: 100%

Formal tracks/concentrations: none

Research areas	# Faculty	# Grants
aggression & victimization	3	1
child and family interventions	2	0
anxiety disorders	4	2
experimental psychopathology	5	2
family, parent, couples relationships	3	0
pseudoscience in clinical psychology	1	0
multicultural psychology	2	1
substance abuse/addictions	3	2

Clinical opportunities

child/family clinic
community mental health
developmental pediatrics
school-based mental health
substance abuse

neuropsychological assessment
minority mental health
college student mental health

Auburn University (Ph.D.)

Department of Psychology
226 Thach
Auburn, AL 36849
phone#: (334) 844-6471
e-mail: shapisk@ auburn.edu
Web address: media.cla.auburn.edu/psychology/gs/clinical/index.cfm

1	2	3	4	5	6	7
Practice oriented		Equal emphasis			Research oriented	

Percentage of faculty subscribing to each of the following orientations:

Psychodynamic/Psychoanalytic	5%
Applied behavioral analysis/Radical behavioral	15%
Family systems/Systems	60%
Existential/Phenomenological/Humanistic	20%
Cognitive/Cognitive-behavioral	100%

Courses required for incoming students to have completed prior to enrolling:
Strong foundation in theoretical or experimental psychology and quantitative methods; evidence of previous research and/or applied experience

Recommended but not mandatory courses:
History of Psychology

GRE mean
Verbal + Quantitative 1200

GPA mean

Overall GPA 3.7

Number of applications/admission offers/incoming students in 2008
160 applied/13 admission offers/7 incoming

% of students receiving:
Full tuition waiver only: 0%
Assistantship/fellowship only: 0%
Both full tuition waiver & assistantship/fellowship: 100%

Approximate percentage of incoming students with a B.A./B.S. only: 85%   **Master's:** 15%

Approximate percentage of students who are
Women: 80%   **Ethnic Minority:** 22%
International: 5%

Average years to complete the doctoral program (including internship): 6 years

Personal interview
Required in person

Attrition rate in past 7 years: 17%

Percentage of students applying for internship last year accepted into APPIC or APA internships: 88%

Formal tracks/concentrations: clinical child psychology

Research areas	# Faculty	# Grants
anxiety disorders	2	0
child clinical/psychopathology	4	1
developmental disabilities	1	1
pediatric obesity	1	0
personality assessment	1	0
sexuality/deviation/dysfunction	1	1
marital relations	1	1

Clinical opportunities

anxiety disordersdisorders in adolescence
ADHD/LD
pediatric obesity
posttraumatic stress disorder
substance abuse

autism spectrum disorder
marital discord and relationships
primary care
veterans and their family

Azusa Pacific University (Psy.D.)

Department of Psychology
901 East Alosta Avenue
Azusa, CA 91702-7000
phone#: (626) 815-5008
e-mail: kakers@apu.edu
Web address: www.apu.edu/bas/graduatepsychology/psyd

1	2	3	4	5	6	7
Practice oriented		Equal emphasis			Research oriented	

Percentage of faculty subscribing to each of the following orientations:

Psychodynamic/Psychoanalytic	42%
Applied behavioral analysis/Radical behavioral	0%
Family systems/Systems	58%
Existential/Phenomenological/Humanistic	25%
Cognitive/Cognitive-behavioral	33%

Courses required for incoming students to have completed prior to enrolling:

Master's level courses: child abuse (7 hours), family therapy, human sexuality/sex therapy, introduction to clinical practice, intro to psychological testing, psychopathology, psychotherapy and cultural diversity, theories of personality and psychotherapy.

Bachelor's level courses: Abnormal psychology, human growth and development, theories of personality, introduction to statistics

Recommended but not mandatory courses: none

GRE mean
Verbal 495   Quantitative 557
Analytical Writing 4.7

GPA mean
Overall GPA Master's 3.7   Bachelor's 3.34

Number of applications/admission offers/incoming students in 2009
106 applied/40 admission offers/26 incoming

% of students receiving:
Full tuition waiver only: 0%
Assistantship/fellowship only: 11%
Both full tuition waiver & assistantship/fellowship: 0%

Approximate percentage of incoming students with a B.A./B.S. only: 76%   **Master's:** 24%

Approximate percentage of students who are Women: 68%   **Ethnic Minority:** 35%
International: 3%

Average years to complete the doctoral program (including internship): 5 years

Personal interview
Preferred in person but telephone acceptable

Attrition rate in past 7 years: 14%

Percentage of students applying for internship last year accepted into APPIC or APA internships: 85%

Formal tracks/concentrations: family psychology, forensic psychology

Research areas	# Faculty	# Grants
family psychology	2	0
diversity/multiculturalism	2	0
child and adolescent	2	1
counseling skills	2	1
psychological assessment	2	0
forensics	3	1
homelessness/HIV	1	0
moral development	2	1
religion/spirituality	4	1
school-based interventions	2	1
neuropsychology	1	0

Clinical opportunities

behavior medicine
children and family
chronically mentally ill
community clinics
forensics
general population
geriatric

HIV/AIDS
inpatient: acute and
  chronic
school-based
substance abuse
university counseling

Baylor University (Psy.D.)
Department of Psychology
P.O. Box 97334
Waco, TX 76798-7334
phone#: (254) 296-9344; (254) 710-2417
e-mail: Gary_Elkins@baylor.edu
Web address: www.baylor.edu/psychologyneuroscience/
index.php?id=72649

1	2	3	4	5	6	7
Practice oriented		Equal emphasis				Research oriented

Percentage of faculty subscribing to each of the following orientations:

Psychodynamic/Psychoanalytic	15%
Applied behavioral analysis/Radical behavioral	0%
Family systems/Systems	15%
Existential/Phenomenological/Humanistic	15%
Cognitive/Cognitive-behavioral	55%

Courses required for incoming students to have completed prior to enrolling: none

Recommended but not mandatory courses:
developmental psychology, psychopathology, theory of counseling and psychotherapy, statistics, biopsychology, personality, social, learning perception/cognitive, human development, research methods

GRE mean
Verbal 642   Quantitative 727
Analytical Writing Data not available

GPA mean
Overall GPA 3.56   Psychology GPA 3.53
Junior/Senior GPA 3.7

Number of applications/admission offers/incoming students in 2009
134 applied/7 admission offers/7 incoming

% of students receiving:
Full tuition waiver only: 0%
Assistantship/fellowship only: 0%
Both full tuition waiver & assistantship/fellowship: 100%

Approximate percentage of incoming students with a B.A./B.S. only: 71%   **Master's:** 29%

Approximate percentage of students who are Women: 69%   **Ethnic Minority:** 14%
International: Data not available

Average years to complete the doctoral program (including internship): 5 years

Personal interview
Required in person

Attrition rate in past 7 years: 8.77%

Percentage of students applying for internship last year accepted into APPIC or APA internships: 100%

Formal tracks/concentrations: none

Research areas	# Faculty	# Grants
behavioral medicine	1	0
child psychopathology	2	0
cognitive therapy	3	0
depression	3	0
group therapy	1	0
personality assessment	3	0

Clinical opportunities

alcohol and drug dependence	mood disorders
anxiety disorders	neuropsychology
behavioral medicine	personality disorder
child psychotherapy	play therapy
community psychology	rural psychology
crisis intervention	schizophrenia/psychoses
eating disorders	school/educational
family therapy	sexual offenders
gerontology	suicide prevention
group dynamics	suicide risk assessment
group therapy	and treatment
health psychology	victim/battering/abuse
impulse control	

Binghamton University/State University of New York (Ph.D.)

Department of Psychology
Vestal Parkway East
Binghamton, NY 13902-6000
phone#: (607) 777-2334
e-mail: clinpsyc@binghamton.edu
Web address: www2.binghamton.edu/psychology/
graduate/clinical-psychology/index.html

1	2	3	4	5	6	7
Practice oriented		Equal emphasis				Research oriented

Percentage of faculty subscribing to each of the following orientations:

Psychodynamic/Psychoanalytic	10%
Applied behavioral analysis/Radical behavioral	10%
Family systems/Systems	0%
Existential/Phenomenological/Humanistic	0%
Cognitive/Cognitive-behavioral	80%

Courses required for incoming students prior to enrolling:

Equivalent of a psychology major, with knowledge of experimental psychology and research methods

Courses recommended but not mandatory:

Physiological psychology

GRE mean

Verbal 611   Quantitative 621
Analytical Writing 5.0   Psychology Subject Test 630

GPA mean

Overall GPA 3.7

Number of applications/admission offers/incoming students in 2009

215 applied/10 admission offers/6 incoming

% of students receiving:

Full tuition waiver only: 0%

Assistantship/fellowship only: 0%
Both full tuition waiver & assistantship/fellowship: 100%

Approximate percentage of students who are

Women: 77%   **Ethnic Minority:** 14%
International: 5%

Average years to complete the doctoral program (including internship): 6.25 years

Personal interview

Strongly preferred in person but telephone possible

Attrition rate in past 7 years: 13%

Percentage of students applying for internship last year accepted into APPIC or APA internships: 100%

Formal tracks/concentrations: none

Research areas	# Faculty	# Grants
adult psychopathology	8	2
anxiety disorders	2	1
assessment	4	0
autism spectrum disorders	1	1
behavioral medicine	1	1
child clinical	2	2
depression	1	1
developmental disabilities	1	2
hypnosis	1	1
learning disabilities	1	1
marital process and therapy	1	1
memory construction	2	0
neuropsychology	1	2
pain management	1	1
pediatric psychology	1	1
personality disorders	1	1
posttraumatic stress disorder/trauma	2	0
prevention	3	1
psychophysiology	2	0
social skills	1	0
substance abuse	1	1

Clinical opportunities

adolescent delinquency	disorders of childhood
adult psychopathology	family therapy
anxiety disorders	learning disabilities
autism spectrum disorders	neuropsychology
behavioral medicine	pain management
conduct disorder	psychotherapy supervision
correctional facility	schizophrenia
couples therapy	school consultation
depression	substance abuse

Biola University (Ph.D.)

Rosemead School of Psychology
13800 Biola Avenue
La Mirada, CA 90639
phone#: (562) 903-4752
e-mail: admissions@biola.edu
Web address: www.rosemead.edu/programs/phd.cfm

1	2	3	4	5	6	7
Practice oriented		Equal emphasis				Research oriented

Percentage of faculty subscribing to each of the following orientations:

Psychodynamic/Psychoanalytic	54%
Applied behavioral analysis/Radical behavioral	0%
Family systems/Systems	15%
Existential/Phenomenological/Humanistic	8%
Cognitive/Cognitive-behavioral	23%

Courses required for incoming students to have completed prior to enrolling:

Statistics, experimental psychology, abnormal psychology, personality, learning

Recommended but not mandatory courses:

Social psychology, history of psychology, physiological psychology, biology/zoology, developmental psychology

GRE mean

Verbal + Quantitative 1275
Analytical Writing not reported

GPA mean

3.6

Number of applications/admission offers/incoming students in 2009

153 applied/13 admission offers & 4 waitlist admission offers/10 incoming

% of students receiving:

Full tuition waiver only: 2%
Assistantship/fellowship only: 60%
Both full tuition waiver & assistantship/fellowship: 0%

Approximate percentage of incoming students with a B.A./B.S. only: 78%   **Master's:** 32%

Approximate percentage of students who are Women: 67%   **Ethnic Minority:** 35%
International: 25%

Average years to complete the doctoral program (including internship): 6 years

Personal interview

Required in person

Attrition rate in past 7 years: 10%

Percentage of students applying for internship last year accepted into APPIC or APA internships: 86%

Formal tracks/concentrations: none

Research areas	# Faculty	# Grants
cross-cultural adjustment	4	0
grief	1	0
neuropsychology	1	0
object relations	4	0
parenting behaviors	3	0
spirituality	4	2

Clinical opportunities

cultural and individual diversity
family/child
individual outpatient/inpatient
therapy and spirituality

Biola University (Psy.D.)
Rosemead School of Psychology

13800 Biola Avenue
La Mirada, CA 90639
phone#: (562) 903-4752
e-mail: admissions@biola.edu
Web address: www.rosemead.edu/programs/psyd.cfm

1	2	3	4	5	6	7

Practice oriented   Equal emphasis   Research oriented

Percentage of faculty subscribing to each of the following orientations:

Psychodynamic/Psychoanalytic	54%
Applied behavioral analysis/Radical behavioral	0%
Family systems/Systems	15%
Existential/Phenomenological/Humanistic	8%
Cognitive/Cognitive-behavioral	23%

Courses required for incoming students to have completed prior to enrolling:

statistics, experimental psychology, abnormal psychology, personality, learning

Recommended but not mandatory courses:

social psychology, history of psychology, physiological psychology, biology/zoology, developmental psychology

GRE mean

Verbal + Quantitative 1100
Analytical Writing not reported

GPA mean

3.5

Number of applications/admission offers/incoming students in 2009

153 applied/27 admission offers & 5 waitlist admission offers/18 incoming

% of students receiving:

Full tuition waiver only: 5%
Assistantship/fellowship only: 60%
Both full tuition waiver & assistantship/fellowship: 0%

Approximate percentage of incoming students who entered with a B.A./B.S. only: 60%   **Master's:** 40%

Approximate percentage of students who are Women: 65%   **Ethnic Minority:** 25%
International: 12%

Average years to complete the doctoral program (including internship): 6 years

Personal interview

Required in person

Attrition rate in past 7 years: 10%

Percentage of students applying for internship last year accepted into APPIC or APA internships: 77%

Formal tracks/concentrations: none

Research areas	# Faculty	# Grants
cross-cultural adjustment	4	0
gender issues	2	1
grief	1	0
neuropsychology	1	1
object relations	4	0

parenting behaviors	3	0
spirituality	4	2

Clinical opportunities

cultural and individual diversity	individual outpatient/inpatient
family/child	therapy and spirituality

Boston University (Ph.D.)

Department of Psychology
64 Cummington Street
Boston, MA 02215
phone#: (617) 353-2587
e-mail: nclement@bu.edu
Web address: www.bu.edu/psych/graduate/clinical/

1	2	3	4	5	6	7
Practice oriented			Equal emphasis			Research oriented

Percentage of faculty subscribing to each of the following orientations:

Psychodynamic/Psychoanalytic	10%
Applied behavioral analysis/Radical behavioral	0%
Family systems/Systems	17%
Existential/Phenomenological/Humanistic	5%
Cognitive/Cognitive-behavioral	70%
Neuropsychology	17%
Eclectic	10%

Courses required for incoming students to have completed prior to enrolling:
Statistics, abnormal/clinical psychology, experimental

Recommended but not mandatory courses:
Broad liberal arts and science

GRE mean
Verbal + Quantitative 1320
Analytical Writing 5.0

GPA mean
Overall GPA 3.77

Number of applications/admission offers/incoming students in 2009
614 applied/17 admission offers/8 incoming

% of students receiving:
Full tuition waiver only: 0%
Assistantship/fellowship only: 0%
Both full tuition waiver & assistantship/fellowship: 96%

Approximate percentage of incoming students with a B.A./B.S. only: 62% **Master's:** 38%

Approximate percentage of students who are Women: 62% **Ethnic Minority:** 50%
International: 13%

Average years to complete the doctoral program (including internship): 6.5 years

Personal interview
Required in person

Attrition rate in past 7 years: 4%

Percentage of students applying for internship last year accepted into APPIC or APA internships: 100%

Formal tracks/concentrations: adult clinical, child clinical, neuropsychology

Research areas	# Faculty	# Grants
affective disorders	2	1
anxiety disorders	7	5
behavioral genetics	1	1
community psychology	1	0
emotion	3	0
family	2	1
gender	1	0
gerontology	2	2
minority	1	0
neuropsychology	2	2
personality disorders	1	0
schizophrenia	1	0
substance abuse/addiction	3	2
victim/abuse	1	0
women's emotional health	1	1
eating disorders	1	1

Clinical opportunities

adolescents	family therapy
affective disorders	gerontology
anxiety disorders	motivational interviewing
behavioral medicine	neuropsychology
cognitive behavioral therapy	PTSD
community psychology	substance/alcohol use
eating disorders	

Bowling Green State University (Ph.D.)

Department of Psychology
Bowling Green, OH 43403
phone#: (419) 372-2306
e-mail: pwatson@bgsu.edu
Web address: www.bgsu.edu/departments/psych/page31041.html

1	2	3	4	5	6	7
Practice oriented			Equal emphasis			Research oriented

Percentage of faculty subscribing to each of the following orientations:

Psychodynamic/Psychoanalytic	20%
Applied behavioral analysis/Radical behavioral	0%
Family systems/Systems	30%
Existential/Phenomenological/Humanistic	20%
Cognitive/Cognitive-behavioral	65%

Courses required for incoming students to have completed prior to enrolling: none

Recommended but not mandatory courses:
science, math, statistics, introductory and advanced psychology courses, abnormal, psychology lab courses

GRE mean
Verbal 572   Quantitative 682
Analytical Writing not used for admissions decisions

GPA mean
Overall GPA 3.80   Psychology GPA 3.86

Number of applications/admission offers/incoming students in 2009
166 applied/19 admission offers/10 incoming

% of students receiving:
Full tuition waiver only: 0%
Assistantship/fellowship only: 0%
Both full tuition waiver & assistantship/fellowship: 100%

Approximate percentage of students who are Women: 79%   **Ethnic Minority:** 8%
International: 7%

Average years to complete the doctoral program (including internship): 5.5 years

Personal interview
Preferred in person but telephone acceptable

Attrition rate in past 7 years: 2%

Percentage of students applying for internship last year accepted into APPIC or APA internships: 100%

Formal tracks/concentrations: health psychology, child clinical psychology, community psychology

Research areas	# Faculty	# Grants
alcohol and substance abuse	1	0
child clinical psychology	2	1
community psychology	1	1
family	2	0
health psychology	2	1
psychology of religion	2	1

Clinical opportunities

health psychology	community mental health
child clinical psychology	developmental disabilities
community psychology	school-based assessment/
family	intervention

Brigham Young University (Ph.D.)

Department of Psychology
284 TLRB
Provo, UT 84602
phone#: (801) 422-4050
e-mail: bruce_carpenter@byu.edu
Web address: http://psychology.byu.edu/Clinical/Home.dhtml

1	2	3	4	5	6	7
Practice oriented		Equal emphasis				Research oriented

Percentage of faculty subscribing to each of the following orientations:
Psychodynamic/Psychoanalytic   20%
Applied behavioral analysis/Radical behavioral   0%
Family systems/Systems   10%
Existential/Phenomenological/Humanistic   20%
Cognitive/Cognitive-behavioral   50%
Interpersonal   30%

Courses required for incoming students prior to enrolling:
psychological statistics, research design, abnormal psychology, personality, learning or cognition, tests and measurements

Courses recommended but not mandatory:
Additional coursework in areas of interest may be helpful

GRE mean
Verbal 580   Quantitative 670
Analytical Writing Data 5.0

GPA mean
Overall GPA not reported   Upper-Division Coursework GPA 3.80

Number of applications/admission offers/incoming students in 2009
58 applied/10 admission offers/9 incoming

% of students receiving tuition waiver & assistantship/ fellowship:
All 1st-year students receive assistantships and a waiver for part of their tuition. All 2nd-, 3rd-, and 4th-year students are funded in work settings, which are coordinated by the department, and they also receive a waiver for part of their tuition.

Approximate percentage of incoming students with a B.A./B.S. only: 80%   **Master's:** 20%

Approximate percentage of students who are Women: 39%   **Ethnic Minority:** 27%
International: 14%

Average years to complete the doctoral program (including internship): 5.5 years

Personal interview
In-person interview preferred, but telephone possible

Attrition rate in past 7 years: 9%

Percentage of students applying for internship last year accepted into APPIC or APA internships: 94%

Formal tracks/concentrations: neuropsychology, child/adolescent

Research areas	# Faculty	# Grants
autism: emotional regulation, neuroimaging	2	2
cardiac/respiratory distress/ QOL, neuroimaging	1	1
child/adolescent development	2	1
child/adolescent psychotherapy	1	1
clinical assessment	3	1
cognitive-behavioral therapy	1	0
dementia: neuroimaging	1	1
eating disorders: assessment, treatment, process	1	1
group therapy: process and outcome	3	0
health psychology/behavioral medicine	1	1
individual therapy: process, outcome	3	3
measurement	1	1
neuropsychology	3	3
obsessive compulsive disorder: neuroimaging	1	1
psychopathology	1	0
traumatic brain injury & neuroimaging	1	1

Clinical opportunities

adolescent residential treatment facilities	private practices
	residential facilities for

community mental health
centers
neuropsychology
rehabilitation units
private general hospitals—
behavioral medicine,
psychiatric units

eating disorders
school districts
state hospital
state prison
university counseling
centers—Utah and
Hawaii

University of British Columbia (Ph.D.)

Department of Educational and Counseling Psychology,
and Special Education
2125 Main Mall
Vancouver, British Columbia V6T 1Z4, Canada
phone#: (604) 822-0242
e-mail: lynn.miller@ubc.edu
Web address: ecps.educ.ubc.ca/

1	2	3	4	5	6	7
Practice oriented		Equal emphasis				Research oriented

Percentage of faculty subscribing to each of the following orientations:

Psychodynamic/Psychoanalytic	5%
Applied behavioral analysis/Radical behavioral	0%
Family systems/Systems	60%
Existential/Phenomenological/Humanistic	60%
Cognitive/Cognitive-behavioral	50%

Courses required for incoming students to have completed prior to enrolling:

Ph.D. applicants are required to have completed courses
equivalent to the M.A. in Counseling offered by the
department. Please check the Web site.

Recommended but not mandatory courses:

We encourage more methods courses (a methods certificate
can be additionally earned).

GRE mean

Verbal 556   Quantitative 510

GPA mean

Overall 3.5

Number of applications/admission offers/incoming students in 2008

29 applied/10 admission offers/10 incoming

% of students receiving:

Full tuition waiver only: 0% (This was a one year change in
UBC policy. Expected to be full tuition waiver in future)
Assistantship/fellowship only: 100%
Both full tuition waiver & assistantship/fellowship: 0%

Approximate percentage of incoming students with a B.A./B.S. only: 0%   Master's: 100%

Approximate percentage of students who are Women: 80%   Ethnic Minority: 20% International: 30%

Average years to complete the doctoral program (including internship): 4.8 years

Personal interview

Preferred candidate visits and telephone encouraged; no
interview required

Attrition rate in past 7 years: 2%

What percentage of students applying for internship last year was accepted into APPIC or APA internships? 25%

Formal tracks/concentrations: not reported

Research areas	# Faculty	# Grants
aboriginal approaches to healing	3	7
anxiety in other cultures	2	2
Asian approaches to counseling	1	2
assessment in rehabilitation	1	1
counseling process	1	0
ethics	1	0
career development	4	4
infertility	1	0
stress and coping	1	2
trauma	3	3
women's sexuality	2	1

Clinical opportunities

Not reported

University at Buffalo/State University of New York (Ph.D.)

Department of Psychology
Park Hall
Buffalo, NY 14260
phone#: (716) 645-3651
e-mail: stiffany@buffalo.edu
Web address: http://www.psychology.buffalo.edu/graduate/
phd/clinical

1	2	3	4	5	6	7
Practice oriented		Equal emphasis				Research oriented

Percentage of faculty subscribing to each of the following orientations:

Applied behavioral analysis/Radical behavioral	25%
Family systems/Systems	0%
Existential/Phenomenological/Humanistic	0%
Cognitive/Cognitive-behavioral	75%

Courses required for incoming students prior to enrolling:

Research methods, statistics

Courses recommended but not mandatory:

Good science background, abnormal psychology, cognitive
psychology, social psychology, developmental psychology

GRE mean

Verbal 530   Quantitative 630   Analytical Writing 4.88
Psychology Subject Test 680

GPA mean

3.81

Number of applications/admission offers/incoming students in 2009

157 applied/13 admission offers/4 incoming

% of students receiving:

Full tuition waiver only: 0%
Assistantship/fellowship only: 0%
Both full tuition waiver & assistantship/fellowship: 100%

Approximate percentage of incoming students with a B.A./B.S. only: 100%   **Master's:** 0%

Approximate percentage of students who are Women: 70%   **Ethnic Minority:** 20%
International: 6%

Average years to complete the doctoral program (including internship): 6 years

Personal interview
Telephone required

Attrition rate in past 7 years: .08%

Percentage of students applying for internship last year accepted into APPIC or APA internships: 80%

Formal tracks/concentrations: none

Research areas	# Faculty	# Grants
addictions	4	8
anxiety disorders	2	1
attention-deficit disorder	2	10
behavioral medicine	3	3
childhood risk of psychopathology	3	1
depression	1	0
assessment/psychometrics	1	1

Clinical opportunities
addiction
ADHD
anxiety disorders
child/adolescent externalizing behavior
depression
parent training
personality disorders
psychological services center

University of California–Berkeley (Ph.D.)

Department of Psychology
Berkeley, CA 94720-1650
phone#: (510) 642-2055
e-mail: psychapp@berkeley.edu
Web address: psychology.berkeley.edu/graduate/cl_program.html

1	2	3	4	5	**6**	7
Practice oriented		Equal emphasis				Research oriented

Percentage of faculty subscribing to each of the following orientations:
Psychodynamic/Psychoanalytic — 0%
Applied behavioral analysis/Radical behavioral — 0%
Family systems/Systems — 30%
Existential/Phenomenological/Humanistic — 0%
Cognitive/Cognitive-behavioral — 70%

Courses required for incoming students to have completed prior to enrolling: None

Recommended but not mandatory courses:
Research design and methods, breadth in psychology

GRE mean
Verbal 595   Quantitative 725
Psychology Subject Test not required

Analytical Writing 5.0

GPA mean
Overall GPA 3.66

Number of applications/admission offers/incoming students in 2008
295 applied/8 admission offers/6 incoming

% of students receiving:
Full tuition waiver only: 0%
Assistantship/fellowship only: 0%
Both full tuition waiver & assistantship/fellowship: 100%

Approximate percentage of incoming students with a B.A./B.S. only: 80%   **Master's:** 20%

Approximate percentage of students who are Women: 72%   **Ethnic Minority:** 28%
International: 1%

Average years to complete the doctoral program (including internship): 6.5 year

Personal interview
Preferred in person but telephone acceptable

Attrition rate in past 7 years: 1/35 or 2.86%

Percentage of students applying for internship last year accepted into APPIC or APA internships: 100%

Formal tracks/concentrations: none

Research areas	# Faculty	# Grants
ADHD externalizing behavior	1	2
depression	1	1
emotion and aging	1	1
emotion and marriage	1	1
emotion and dementia	1	1
emotion, cognition, and schizophrenia	1	2
insomnia	1	2
bipolar disorder	2	2
temperament, internalizing, and externalizing behavior	1	1
culture and mental health	1	1
stigma and mental illness	1	1

Clinical opportunities
Not reported

University of California–Los Angeles (Ph.D.)

Department of Psychology
1285 Franz Hall, Box 951563
Los Angeles, CA 90095-1563
phone#: (310) 825-2617
e-mail: gradadm@psych.ucla.edu
Web address: www.psych.ucla.edu/graduate/areas-of-study/clinical-psychology/clinical-psychology

1	2	3	4	5	6	**7**
Practice oriented		Equal emphasis				Research oriented

Percentage of faculty subscribing to each of the following orientations:
Psychodynamic/Psychoanalytic — 0%
Applied behavioral analysis/Radical behavioral — 0%

Family systems/Systems	25%
Existential/Phenomenological/Humanistic	0%
Cognitive/Cognitive-behavioral	75%

Courses required for incoming students prior to enrolling:
Elementary statistics; two of the following: learning, physiological, or perception/information processing; two of the following: developmental, social, or personality/abnormal; one course in biology or zoology; two physical science courses (physics and/or chemistry) although a course in anthropology, philosophy, or sociology may be substituted for one of the physical science courses; at least one math course, preferably calculus or probability; advanced statistics

Courses recommended but not mandatory:
Research design and methods, psychology research labs, independent research courses; a broad background in the mathematical, biological and social sciences

GRE mean
Verbal 661   Quantitative 763
Analytical Writing 5.0   Psychology Subject Test 749

GPA mean
Overall GPA 3.77

Number of applications/admission offers/incoming students in 2009
399 applied/18 admission offers/10 incoming

% of students receiving:
Full tuition waiver only: 0%
Assistantship/fellowship only: 0%
Both full tuition waiver & assistantship/fellowship: 80%–90%

Approximate percentage of incoming students with a B.A./B.S. only: 100%   **Master's:** 0%

Approximate percentage of students who are Women: 70%   **Ethnic Minority:** 10%
International: 0%

Average years to complete the doctoral program (including internship): 6.1 years

Personal interview
Preferred in person but telephone acceptable

Attrition rate in past 7 years: 4.5%

Percentage of students applying for internship last year accepted into APPIC or APA internships: 100%

Formal tracks/concentrations: no formal tracks, but there is focused training in severe adult psychopathology, child/adolescent psychopathology, clinical-health psychology, minority mental health, and couples and families

Research areas	# Faculty	# Grants
anxiety disorders and treatment	2	7
family issues	5	5
marital and couple relationships and treatments	2	5
medical issues	2	7
minority mental and physical health issues	3	5

mood disorders	4	5
schizophrenia	2	6
school mental health	2	3
substance use disorders	1	3

Clinical opportunities

adoptions, families	developmental disabilities/ autism
child and adult affective disorders	family/child
child and adult anxiety disorders	major mental illness, psychosis
community psychology, community mental health	minority populations
couples/marital	psychotherapy supervision
	school mental health

Carlos Albizu University–Miami Campus (Psy.D.)

2173 NW 99th Avenue
Miami, FL 33172-2209
phone#: (305) 593-1223, ext. 124
e-mail: gspecter@albizu.edu
Web address: mia.albizu.edu/web/academic_programs/psychology/doctor_of_psychology_in_clinical_psychology.asp

1	2	3	4	5	6	7
Practice oriented		Equal emphasis				Research oriented

Percentage of faculty subscribing to each of the following orientations:

Psychodynamic/Psychoanalytic	20%
Applied behavioral analysis/Radical behavioral	0%
Family systems/Systems	10%
Existential/Phenomenological/Humanistic	20%
Cognitive/Cognitive-behavioral	50%

Courses required for incoming students to have completed prior to enrolling:
Research methodology, abnormal psychology, and statistics

Recommended but not mandatory courses: none

GRE mean
not required for admission

GPA mean
3.42

Number of applications/admission offers/incoming students in 2008
214 applied/75 admission offers/60 incoming

% of students receiving:
Full tuition waiver only: 0%
Assistantship/fellowship only: 5%
Both full tuition waiver & assistantship/fellowship: 0%

Approximate percentage of incoming students with a B.A./B.S. only: 60% **Master's:** 40%

Approximate percentage of students who are Women: 77%   **Ethnic Minority:** 78%
International: 0.5%

Average years to complete the doctoral program (including internship): 5.1 years

Personal interview
Preferred in person but telephone acceptable

Attrition rate in past 7 years: 3.1%

Percentage of students applying for internship last year accepted into APPIC or APA internships: 96%

Formal tracks/concentrations: child psychology, neuropsychology, forensic psychology and general practice

Research areas	# Faculty	# Grants
children and adolescents	3	2
depression	3	0
elderly	1	0
forensic psychology	1	0
multicultural issues	6	0
neuropsychology	2	0
positive psychology	1	0
psychotherapy	6	0
health psychology	2	0

Clinical opportunities
In-house training clinic where students work with multi-ethnic populations of various ages, including children.

Carlos Albizu University–San Juan Campus (Ph.D.) (2008 data)

P.O. Box 9023711
San Juan, PR 00902-3711
Phone#: (787) 725-6500, ext. 1129
E-mail: ssayers@albizu.edu
Web address: sju.albizu.edu/code/doctoral_programs/
phd_in_clinical_psychology.asp

1	2	3	**4**	5	6	7
Practice oriented		Equal emphasis			Research oriented	

Percentage of faculty subscribing to each of the following orientations:

Psychodynamic/Psychoanalytic	25%
Applied behavioral analysis/Radical behavioral	12%
Family systems/Systems	12%
Existential/Phenomenological/Humanistic	12%
Cognitive/Cognitive-behavioral	37%
Integrative	12%

Courses required for incoming students to have completed prior to enrolling:
Experimental psychology and laboratory, physiological psychology and laboratory, abnormal psychology, introductory statistics, personality theories

Recommended but not mandatory courses: none

GRE mean:
not reported

GPA mean:
not reported

Number of applications/admission offers/incoming students in 2007:
32 applied/26 admission offers/26 incoming

% of students receiving:

Full tuition waiver only: 0%
Assistantship/fellowship only: 0%
Both full tuition waiver & assistantship/fellowship: 0%

Approximate percentage of incoming students who entered with a B.A./B.S. only: 92%   **Master's:** 8%

Approximate percentage of students who are Women: 76%   **Ethnic Minority:** 99%
International: 0%

Average years to complete the doctoral program (including internship): 7 years

Personal interview:
Required in person

Attrition rate in past 7 years: 16%

Percentage of students applying for internship last year accepted into APPIC or APA internships: 16%

Formal tracks/concentrations: none

Research areas	# Faculty	# Grants
attention-deficit disorder	2	1
child abuse and neglect	1	0
elderly	2	1
high risk children/adolescents	4	1
HIV/AIDS	1	0
impulsion-aggressive children	3	0
instrument validation	2	0
social skills	2	1
sport psychology	1	0

Clinical opportunities
domestic violence program

Carlos Albizu University–San Juan Campus (Psy.D.) (2008 data)

San Juan, PR 00902-3711
phone#: (787) 725-6500, ext. 1552
e-mail: galtieri@prip.edu
Web address: sju.albizu.edu/code/doctoral_programs/
psyd_in_clinical_psychology.asp

1	2	**3**	4	5	6	7
Practice oriented		Equal emphasis			Research oriented	

Percentage of faculty subscribing to each of the following orientations:

Psychodynamic/Psychoanalytic	0%
Applied behavioral analysis/Radical behavioral	10%
Family systems/Systems	30%
Existential/Phenomenological/Humanistic	10%
Cognitive/Cognitive-behavioral	50%

Courses required for incoming students to have completed prior to enrolling:
Experimental psychology and laboratory, physiological psychology and laboratory, abnormal psychology, introductory statistics, personality theories

Recommended but not mandatory courses: none

GRE mean
not required for admission

GPA mean
3.25

Number of applications/admission offers/incoming students in 2007
60 applied/47 admission offers/44 incoming

% of students receiving:
Full tuition waiver only: 0%
Assistantship/fellowship only: 10%
Both full tuition waiver & assistantship/fellowship: 10%

Approximate percentage of incoming students with a B.A./B.S. only: not reported **Master's:** not reported

Approximate percentage of students who are Women: 70% **Ethnic Minority:** 100%
International: not reported

Average years to complete the doctoral program (including internship): 6 years

Personal interview
Required in person

Attrition rate in past 7 years: 10%

Percentage of students applying for internship last year accepted into APPIC or APA internships: 18%

Formal tracks/concentrations: none

Research areas	# Faculty	# Grants
health and well-being in elderly	2	0
sexual behavior	2	0
sport anxiety	2	0
forensic	3	0

Clinical opportunities

domestic violence	sexual disorders
forensic psychology	sports psychology
program for sexual abuse victims	victims of crime
	family individual
sex abuse therapy for children victims of abuse and their families	couples

---

Case Western Reserve University (Ph.D.)

Department of Psychological Sciences
Mather Memorial Building
11220 Bellflower Road
Cleveland, OH 44106
phone#: (216) 368-2686 (800) 368-2685
e-mail: cwrupsych@gmail.com
Web address: psychology.case.edu/clinical/jimwelcome.html

1	2	3	4	5	6	7
Practice oriented		Equal emphasis			Research oriented	

Percentage of faculty subscribing to each of the following orientations:
Psychodynamic/Psychoanalytic 50%
Applied behavioral analysis/Radical behavioral 5%
Family systems/Systems 25%
Existential/Phenomenological/Humanistic 5%
Cognitive/Cognitive-behavioral 50%

Courses required for incoming students to have completed prior to enrolling:
General undergraduate psychology courses

Recommended but not mandatory courses:
psychology major

GRE mean
Verbal + Quantitative 1229

GPA mean
Overall GPA 3.66

Number of applications/admission offers/incoming students in 2009
120 applied/9 admission offers/5 incoming

% of students receiving:
Full tuition waiver only: 100%
Assistantship/fellowship only: 0%
Both full tuition waiver & assistantship/fellowship: 67%

Approximate percentage of incoming students with a B.A./B.S. only: 100% **Master's:** 0%

Approximate percentage of students who are Women: 100% **Ethnic Minority:** 0%
International: 0%

Average years to complete the doctoral program (including internship): 6.8 years

Personal interview
Preferred in person but telephone acceptable

Attrition rate in past 7 years: 19%

What percentage of students applying for internship last year was accepted into APPIC or APA internships? 100%

Formal tracks/concentrations: child/pediatric psychology, adult psychology

Research areas	# Faculty	# Grants
aging	2	1
behavioral medicine/health psychology	1	1
chronic mental illness	1	0
developmental disabilities	1	1
learning disabilities	1	1
memory	2	0
parent–child interaction	2	0
personality disorders	1	6
self-psychology	1	0
temperament	1	1

Clinical opportunities

ADHD	juvenile bipolar disorder
affective disorders	obsessive–compulsive disorders
aging and dementia	
anxiety disorders	personality disorders
gerontology/Alzheimer's	schizophrenia/psychosis

Catholic University of America (Ph.D.)

Department of Psychology

620 Michigan Avenue, NE
Washington, DC 20064
phone#: (202) 319-5729
e-mail: cua-psychology@cua.edu
Web address: psychology.cua.edu/graduate/phdclprog.cfm

1	2	3	4	5	6	7
Practice oriented		Equal emphasis			Research oriented	

Percentage of faculty subscribing to each of the following orientations:

Psychodynamic/Psychoanalytic — 29%
Applied behavioral analysis/Radical behavioral — 14%
Family systems/Systems — 57%
Existential/Phenomenological/Humanistic — 43%
Cognitive/Cognitive-behavioral — 86%
Integrative — 86%

Courses required for incoming students to have completed prior to enrolling:

Statistics and research methods; in addition to coursework, research experience is required.

Recommended but not mandatory courses:

Abnormal psychology; personality; developmental psychology; social psychology

GRE mean

Verbal 653   Quantitative 725
Psychology Subject Test 706
Analytical Writing 4.75

GPA mean

Overall GPA 3.80

Number of applications/admission offers/incoming students in 2009

128 applied/13 admission offers/6 incoming

% of students receiving:

Tuition waiver only: 17%
Assistantship/fellowship only: 0%
Both tuition waiver & assistantship/fellowship: 83%

Approximate percentage of incoming students with a B.A./B.S. only: 100%   Master's: 0%

Approximate percentage of students who are Women: 75%   Ethnic Minority: 23% International: 0%

Average years to complete the doctoral program (including internship): 6 years (median)

Personal interview

Required in person

Attrition rate in past 7 years: 4.6%

Percentage of students applying for internship last year accepted into APPIC or APA internships: 100%

Formal tracks/concentrations: Adult clinical; Children, family, and cultures.

Research areas	# Faculty	# Grants
adolescence	4	2
adult psychopathology	3	1
anxiety	3	1
anxiety disorders	3	1
assessment	1	1
attachment	1	1
child clinical	4	3
cognition	3	1
community context	2	2
couples	1	1
developmental	3	2
developmental psychopathology	4	3
emotions	2	1
emotion regulation	3	1
ethics/risk management	1	0
family	4	2
interpersonal processes	2	1
language development	1	1
military families	2	0
mindfulness	2	0
mood disorders	2	2
parent training	1	0
parent–child interactions	4	2
psychotherapy integration	2	0
psychotherapy outcome	3	0
psychotherapy practice	3	0
psychotherapy process	2	0
self-efficacy	2	0
social anxiety	2	0
sport psychology	1	0
stress and coping	5	2
suicide	2	1
veterans mental health care	1	1
violence	1	1

Clinical opportunities

adult psychotherapy
assessment batteries
child and adult assessment
couple therapy
family therapy
minority mental health
neuropsychology
neuropsychological assessment

University of Central Florida (Ph.D.)

4000 Central Florida Blvd, Psychology Building
Orlando, Florida, 32816-1390
phone#: (407) 823-4344
e-mail: psyinfo@mail.ucf.edu
Web address: psychology.cos.ucf.edu/graduate_degrees_clinicalphd.php

1	2	3	4	5	6	7
Practice oriented		Equal emphasis			Research oriented	

Percentage of faculty subscribing to each of the following orientations:

100% Equal Emphasis

Courses required for incoming students to have completed prior to enrolling:

A minimum of 18 semester hours of undergraduate psychology courses is required prior to matriculation.

Recommended but not mandatory courses:

Research experience is heavily weighted during admissions

GRE mean

Quantitative 615   Verbal 548

Psychology Subject Test not reported
Analytical Writing not reported

GPA mean
Overall GPA 3.6

Number of applications/admission offers/incoming students in 2009
165 applied/9 admission offers/6 incoming

% of students receiving:
Full tuition waiver only: 0%
Assistantship/fellowship only: 0%
Both full tuition waiver & assistantship/fellowship: 100%

Approximate percentage of incoming students with a B.A./B.S. only: 100%   **Master's:** 0%

Approximate percentage of students who are Women: 72%   **Ethnic Minority:** 18%   **International:** 0%

Average years to complete the doctoral program (including internship): 6 years

Personal interview
Required in person

Attrition rate in past 7 years: 4%

Percentage of students applying for internship last year accepted into APPIC or APA internships: 100%

Formal tracks/concentrations: Clinical—Child, Adult

Research areas	# Faculty	# Grants
alcohol and substance abuse	1	—
child/pediatric psychology	1	—
developmental psychopathology	1	—
ADHD/cognition	1	—
eating behavior and body image	2	—
multicultural	1	—
prevention	1	—
schizophrenia	1	—

Clinical opportunities

children's learning clinic	family
clinical neuroscience	substance use
eating, appearance, & health	

Central Michigan University (Ph.D.)

Department of Psychology
Mt. Pleasant, MI 48859
phone#: (989) 774-6463
e-mail: Reid.Skeel@cmich.edu
Web address: www.cmich.edu/chsbs/x20739.xml

1	2	3	**4**	5	6	7
Practice oriented			Equal emphasis			Research oriented

Percentage of faculty subscribing to each of the following orientations:

/Psychoanalytic	10%
oral analysis/Radical behavioral	10%
/Systems	25%

Existential/Phenomenological/Humanistic   10%
Cognitive/Cognitive-behavioral   70%

Courses required for incoming students to have completed prior to enrolling:
none

Recommended but not mandatory courses:
statistics, experimental psychology, developmental psychology, abnormal psychology, personality theory, measurement theory

GRE mean
Verbal 622   Quantitative 671
Analytical Writing 5.2

GPA mean
Overall GPA 3.91   Psychology GPA N/A

Number of applications/admission offers/incoming students in 2009
157 applied/9 admission offers/5 incoming

% of students receiving:
Full tuition waiver only: 0%
Assistantship/fellowship only: 0%
Both full tuition waiver & assistantship/fellowship: 100%

Approximate percentage of incoming students with a B.A./B.S. only: 100%   **Master's:** 0%

Approximate percentage of students who are Women: 60%   **Ethnic Minority:** 0%   **International:** 0%

Average years to complete the doctoral program (including internship): 6 years

Personal interview
Interview not required

Attrition rate in past 7 years: 3%

Percentage of students applying for internship last year accepted into APPIC or APA internships: 100%

Formal tracks/concentrations/specializations: none

Research areas	# Faculty	# Grants
anxiety disorders	1	1
assessment	1	0
children	1	2
diversity and sexual deviance	1	0
health psychology	1	1
neuropsychology	1	1
severe psychopathology	1	1
violence and aggression	1	0

Clinical opportunities

adult clinical	parent–child
behavior therapy	interaction therapy
child clinical	psychodynamic therapy
cognitive-behavioral therapy	psychological assessment
forensic psychology	school-based interventions
neuropsychology/ rehabilitation	

Chestnut Hill College (Psy.D.)

Department of Professional Psychology
9601 Germantown Avenue

Philadelphia, PA 19118-2693
phone#: (215)-248-7020
e-mail: mashettj@chc.edu
Web address: www.chc.edu/sgs_programs_faculty.
aspx?id=377

1	2	3	4	5	6	7
Practice oriented		Equal emphasis				Research oriented

Percentage of faculty subscribing to each of the following orientations:

Psychodynamic/Psychoanalytic	40%
Applied behavioral analysis/Radical behavioral	0%
Family systems/Systems	30%
Existential/Phenomenological/Humanistic	10%
Cognitive/Cognitive-behavioral	20%

Courses required for incoming students to have completed prior to enrolling:
General psychology, abnormal psychology, statistics, at least one other psychology class

Recommended but not mandatory courses:
Developmental psychology, research design

GRE mean
Verbal 602 Quantitative 520
Analytical Writing 4.6
Psychology Subject Test not reported

GPA mean
Overall GPA 3.6

Number of applications/admission offers/incoming students in 2008
161 applied/47 admission offers/21 incoming

% of students receiving:
Full tuition waiver only: 0%
Assistantship/fellowship only: 10%
Both full tuition waiver & assistantship/fellowship: 0%

Approximate percentage of incoming students with a B.A./B.S. only: 52%   Master's: 48%

Approximate percentage of students who are Women: 70%   Ethnic Minority: 10% International: 2%

Average years to complete the doctoral program (including internship): 6.5 years

Personal interview
Required in person

Attrition rate in past 7 years: 7.1%

Percentage of students applying for internship last year accepted into APPIC or APA internships: 67%

Formal tracks/concentrations: psychological assessment, family therapy

Research areas	# Faculty	# Grants
step-families	1	1

Clinical opportunities
not reported

Chicago School of Professional Psychology (Psy.D.)
325 N Wells
Chicago, IL 60610
phone#: (312) 329-6666
e-mail: admissions@thechicagoschool.edu
Web address: www.thechicagoschool.edu/chicago/Our_
Programs/PsyD_in_Clinical_Psychology_Generalist_Track

1	2	3	4	5	6	7
Practice oriented		Equal emphasis				Research oriented

Percentage of faculty subscribing to each of the following orientations:

Psychodynamic/Psychoanalytic	46%
Family systems/Systems	38%
Existential/Phenomenological/Humanistic	50%
Cognitive/Cognitive-behavioral	50%

Courses required for incoming students to have completed prior to enrolling:
18 hours in psychology, including statistics, lifespan/human development, abnormal psychology

Recommended but not mandatory courses: none

GRE mean
Verbal + Quantitative 1110
Analytical Writing Data not available

GPA mean
Overall GPA 3.46

Number of applications/admission offers/incoming students in 2008
578 applied/229 admission offers/118 incoming

% of students receiving:
Full tuition waiver only: 0%
Assistantship/fellowship only: 2%
Both full tuition waiver & assistantship/fellowship: 0%

Approximate percentage of incoming students with a B.A./B.S. only: 80%   Master's: 20%

Approximate percentage of students who are Women: 84%   Ethnic Minority: 14% International: 5%

Average years to complete the doctoral program (including internship): 5 years

Personal interview
Required in person

Attrition rate in past 7 years: 2006 = 6% attrit, 94% retained; 2007 = 5% attrit, 95% retained; 2008=4% attrit, 96% retained

Percentage of students applying for internship last year accepted into APPIC or APA internships: 98%

Formal tracks/concentrations: child/ adolescent, health, multicultural/community, forensic, industrial/organizational

Research areas	# Faculty	# Grants
behavioral intervention	1	0

diversity and cultural competence training	9	1
forensic psychology	2	0
latino early education	1	0
multigenerational health	1	0
pediatric obesity	1	0
trauma	1	0

Clinical opportunities

child and adolescent
college counseling center
community mental health
community psychology
correctional/forensic settings
creative and expressive arts
cross-cultural/international
early education/head start/ infants
forensic
health
inner city and rural populations

inpatient/outpatient/ partial hospitalization
mental health administration
private and group practice
organizational
school based intervention
sexual orientation and gender identity
teaching
veterans

University of Cincinnati (Ph.D.)

Department of Psychology
429 Dyer Hall
Cincinnati, OH 45221-0376
phone#: (513) 556-5377
e-mail: Paula.Shear@uc.edu
Web address: www.artsci.uc.edu/collegedepts/psychology/grad/phd/clinical.aspx

1	2	3	4	5	6	7
Practice oriented		Equal emphasis			Research oriented	

Percentage of faculty subscribing to each of the following orientations:

Family systems/Systems	27%
Cognitive/Cognitive-behavioral	73%

Courses required for incoming students prior to enrolling:
Preference given to applicants with coursework in psychology

Courses recommended but not mandatory:
Abnormal, statistics, and research methods

GRE mean
Verbal 530   Quantitative 620
Analytical Writing 4.5
Psychology Subject Test (optional) 740

GPA mean
Overall GPA 3.7

Number of applications/admission offers/incoming students in 2009
221 applied/8 admission offers/6 incoming

% of students receiving:
Full tuition waiver only: 0%
Assistantship/fellowship only: 0%
Both full tuition waiver & assistantship/fellowship: 100%

Approximate percentage of incoming students with a B.A./B.S. only: 100%   **Master's:** 0

Approximate percentage of students who are Women: 73%   **Ethnic Minority:** 16%
International: 0

Average years to complete the doctoral program (including internship): 6 years

Personal interview
In person interview strongly preferred for invited candidates

Attrition rate in past 7 years: 8.7%

Percentage of students applying for internship last year accepted into APPIC or APA internships: 100%

Formal tracks/concentrations: human factors, neuropsychology, heath psychology, general clinical

Research areas	# Faculty	# Grants
addictive behaviors	4	5
adolescence	4	4
child clinical	5	4
health psychology	10	6
neuropsychology	6	5
serious mental illness	2	1

Clinical opportunities

addictive behaviors
child & adolescent clinical psychology
clinical neuropsychology

community mental health
developmental disorders
health psychology
serious mental illness

Clark University (Ph.D.)

Frances L. Hiatt School of Psychology
950 Main Street
Worcester, MA 01610
phone#: (508) 793-7269
e-mail: jcordova@clarku.edu
Web address: http://www.clarku.edu/departments/psychology/grad/clinical.cfm

1	2	3	4	5	6	7
Practice oriented		Equal emphasis			Research oriented	

Percentage of faculty subscribing to each of the following orientations:

Psychodynamic/Psychoanalytic	20%
Applied behavioral analysis/Radical behavioral	40%
Family systems/Systems	40%
Existential/Phenomenological/Humanistic	20%
Cognitive/Cognitive-behavioral	60%

Courses required for incoming students to have completed prior to enrolling:
Statistics, research methods, abnormal psychology

Recommended but not mandatory courses:
Psychology major, substantial research experience

GRE mean
Verbal 620   Quantitative 650
Psychology Subject Test 680

GPA mean
Overall GPA 3.5

Number of applications/admission offers/incoming students in 2009
144 applied/10 admission offers/4 incoming

% of students receiving:
Tuition waiver only: 0%
Assistantship/fellowship only: 0%
Both tuition waiver & assistantship/fellowship: 100%

Approximate percentage of incoming students with a B.A./B.S. only: 75%   **Master's:** 25%

Approximate percentage of students who are Women: 75%   **Ethnic Minority:** 25%
International: 0%

Average years to complete the doctoral program (including internship): 7 years

Personal interview
Required in person

Attrition rate in past 7 years: 7.7%

Percentage of students applying for internship last year accepted into APPIC or APA internships: 83%

Formal tracks/concentrations/specializations:
Not reported

Research areas	# Faculty	# Grants
adult psychopathology	2	0
affective disorders	1	0
assessment/diagnosis/classification	1	0
child abuse and children at-risk	1	1
child clinical/child psychopathology	2	1
family research/therapy	3	2
gender roles/sex differences	1	1
motivation	1	1
parent–child interaction	2	1
prevention	4	2
psychotherapy process and outcome	1	1
social learning	1	0

Clinical opportunities

child therapy/assessment   preventive interventions
couples/family therapy   school-based interventions

University of Colorado at Boulder (Ph.D.)

Department of Psychology
345 UCB
Boulder, CO 80309-0345
phone#: (303) 492-8805
e-mail: whisman@colorado.edu
Web address: psych.colorado.edu/~clinical/

1	2	3	4	5	6	7

Practice oriented   Equal emphasis   Research oriented

Percentage of faculty subscribing to each of the following orientations:
Psychodynamic/Psychoanalytic   22%
Applied behavioral analysis/Radical behavioral   33%

Family systems/Systems   56%
Existential/Phenomenological/Humanistic   44%
Cognitive/Cognitive-behavioral   78%

Courses required for incoming students to have completed prior to enrolling:
Psychology or the equivalent (30 semester hours in psychology)

Recommended but not mandatory courses:
Psychopathology/abnormal, statistics, research methods, psychological assessment, psychotherapy, developmental, social/personality, biological psychology

GRE mean
Verbal 627   Quantitative 733
Psychology Subject Test 710
Analytical Writing 4.83

GPA mean
Overall GPA 3.6

Number of applications/admission offers/incoming students in 2009
197 applied/6 admission offers/3 incoming

% of students receiving:
Full tuition waiver only: 0%
Assistantship/fellowship only: 0%
Both full tuition waiver & assistantship/fellowship: 100%

Approximate percentage of incoming students with a B.A./B.S. only: 91%   **Master's:** 9%

Approximate percentage of students who are Women: 77% **Ethnic Minority:** 15% **International:** 4%

Average years to complete the doctoral program (including internship): 6 years

Personal interview
Required in person

Attrition rate in past 7 years: 3%

Percentage of students applying for internship last year accepted into APPIC or APA internships: 100%

Formal tracks/concentrations: behavioral genetics certification, joint clinical psychology/neuroscience Ph.D.

Research areas	# Faculty	# Grants
adult psychopathology	5	3
affective disorders	5	4
assessment/diagnosis/classification	4	1
child clinical	6	3
developmental	2	2
family research	4	4
genetics	3	3
personality disorders	1	1
prevention	3	2
psychotherapy outcome/process	4	4
substance abuse	2	2
violence/abuse	1	0

Clinical opportunities

assessment   interpersonal
behavioral activation therapy   psychotherapy
behavior therapy   marital/couple therapy
cognitive therapy   mindfulness

family therapy	psychodynamic
group therapy	psychotherapy

University of Colorado at Colorado Springs

Department of Psychology
1420 Austin Bluffs Parkway
Colorado Springs, CO 80918
phone#: 719-255-4500
e-mail: ddubois@uccs.edu
Web address: www.uccs.edu/~psych/pages/phd.htm

1	2	3	**4**	5	6	7
Practice oriented			Equal emphasis			Research oriented

Percentage of faculty subscribing to each of the following orientations:

Psychodynamic/Psychoanalytic	20%
Applied behavioral analysis/Radical behavioral	20%
Family systems/Systems	20%
Existential/Phenomenological/Humanistic	0%
Cognitive/Cognitive-behavioral	40%

Courses required for incoming students to have completed prior to enrolling:

"a sufficient background in psychology" no specific courses

Recommended but not mandatory courses:

statistics, research methods or experimental psychology

GRE mean

Verbal 524 Quantitative 644
Analytical Writing not reported
Psychology Subject Test 590

GPA mean

3.52

Number of applications/admission offers/incoming students in 2009

21 applied/9 admission offers/5 incoming

% of students receiving:

Full tuition waiver only: 0%
Assistantship/fellowship only: 100%
Both full tuition waiver & assistantship/fellowship: 0%

Approximate percentage of incoming students with a B.A./B.S. only: 80%   Master's: 20%

Approximate percentage of students who are Women: 100%   Ethnic Minority: 17% International: 0%

Average years to complete the doctoral program (including internship): not reported

Personal interview

Required in person

Attrition rate in past 7 years: 6%

Percentage of students applying for internship last year accepted into APPIC or APA internships: 100%

Formal tracks/concentrations: geropsychology

Research areas	# Faculty	# Grants
program evaluation	2	2
trauma	1	2
cognitive evolution	1	0
geriatric neuropsychology	1	0
behavioral gerontology	1	0
adolescent psychology	1	0
psychology & the law	1	0
cognitive psy	1	1
social psychology	1	1
clinical geropsychology	3	1
child clinical	1	0
lifespan development	1	0
evolutionary psychology	1	1

Clinical opportunities

geropsychology
aging families and caregiver programs
assisted living placements
developmental disabilities
behavioral medicine
integrated health care
memory and cognitive assessment
neuropsychological assessments

Concordia University (Ph.D.) (2008 data)

Department of Psychology, PY 119-2
7141 Sherbrooke Street West
Montreal, Quebec H4B 1R6 Canada
phone#: (514) 848-2424 ext. 2205
e-mail: Shirley.Black@concordia.ca
Web address: psychology.concordia.ca/Grads/admissionsPhD.html

1	2	3	4	**5**	6	7
Practice oriented			Equal emphasis			Research oriented

Percentage of faculty subscribing to each of the following orientations:

Psychodynamic/Psychoanalytic	15%
Applied behavioral analysis/Radical behavioral	0%
Family systems/Systems	25%
Existential/Phenomenological/Humanistic	0%
Cognitive/Cognitive-behavioral	60%

Courses required for incoming students to have completed prior to enrolling:

honors (B.A./B.S.) in psychology

Recommended but not mandatory courses:

GRE mean

Verbal 496   Quantitative 641
Psychology Subject Test 697
(Note: GRE's are recommended, but optional.)

GPA mean

Overall GPA 3.81
(Note: Based on Concordia's scale of 4.3)

Number of applications/admission offers/incoming students in 2007

246 applied/28 admission offers/19 incoming

% of students receiving:
Full tuition waiver only: 0%
Assistantship/fellowship only: 78%
Both full tuition waiver & assistantship/fellowship: 22%

Approximate percentage of incoming students with a B.A./B.S. only: 95%   **Master's:** 5%

Approximate percentage of students who are Women: 89%   **Ethnic Minority:** 22%
International: Data not available

Personal interview
Preferred in person but telephone acceptable

Attrition rate in past 7 years: 2%

Percentage of students applying for internship last year accepted into APPIC or APA internships: 60%

Formal tracks/concentrations: behavioral neuroscience, clinical health, human development/developmental processes, cognitive science

Research areas	# Faculty	# Grants
anxiety	2	3
behavioral medicine	1	1
developmental/infancy	8	10
developmental psychopathology	3	5
gender roles	2	1
health psychology	1	0
major mental disorder/ psychopathology	2	1
neuropsychology	2	5
neuroscience/psychobiology	9	12
perception/cognition	4	5
social competence	1	1

Clinical opportunities
adult
child/adolescent
cognitive/cognitive-behavioral
couples
family
psychodynamic

University of Connecticut (Ph.D.)

Department of Psychology
406 Babbidge Road, Unit 1020
Storrs, CT 06269-1020
phone#: (860) 486-2057 (Admissions information)
e-mail: psychgrad@uconn.edu
Web address: web.uconn.edu/psychology/academics/graduate/phd_clinical.html

1	2	3	4	5	6	7
Practice oriented		Equal emphasis				Research oriented

Percentage of faculty subscribing to each of the following orientations:
Psychodynamic/Psychoanalytic   20%
Applied behavioral analysis/Radical behavioral   20%
Family systems/Systems   33%
Existential/Phenomenological/Humanistic   8%
Cognitive-behavioral   90%

Courses required for incoming students to have completed prior to enrolling: none

Recommended but not mandatory courses:
abnormal, research methods

GRE mean
Verbal 623   Quantitative 720
Analytical Writing 5.2   Psychology Subject Test 712

GPA mean
Overall GPA 3.57

Number of applications/admission offers/incoming students in 2009
359 applied/10 admission offers/6 incoming

% of students receiving:
Full tuition waiver only: 0%
Assistantship/fellowship only: 0%
Both full tuition waiver & assistantship/fellowship: 100%

Approximate percentage of incoming students with a B.A./B.S. only: 66%   **Master's:** 33%

Approximate percentage of students who are Women: 85% **Ethnic Minority:** 13% **International:** 4%

Average years to complete the doctoral program (including internship): 5.6 years

Personal interview
Preferred in person but telephone acceptable

Attrition rate in past 7 years: 6%

Percentage of students applying for internship last year accepted into APPIC or APA internships: APPIC 100%; **APA** 100%

Formal tracks/concentrations: child clinical, neuropsychology, health psychology

Research areas	# Faculty	# Grants
adult psychopathology	5	4
aging	1	0
anxiety disorders	2	1
autism	4	3
child psychopathology	7	4
developmental psychopathology	7	4
domestic violence	1	1
health psychology	3	3
multicultural psychology	2	1
neuropsychological assessment	3	2
trauma	4	3
depression	4	2

Clinical opportunities
autistic children
childhood psychopathology
chronic mental illness
health psychology
multicultural psychology
neuroimaging
neuropsychological assessment
traumatic brain injury
traumatic stress disorders
anxiety disorders
substance abuse
depression

University of Delaware (Ph.D.)

Department of Psychology
Newark, DE 19716
phone#: (302) 831-8724

e-mail: lcohen@psych.udel.edu
Web address: http://www.psych.udel.edu/graduate/detail/category/clinical_science

1	2	3	4	5	6	7
Practice oriented		Equal emphasis				Research oriented

Percentage of faculty subscribing to each of the following orientations:

Psychodynamic/Psychoanalytic	11%
Applied behavioral analysis/Radical behavioral	0%
Family systems/Systems	55%
Existential/Phenomenological/Humanistic	0%
Cognitive/Cognitive-behavioral	89%

Courses required for incoming students to have completed prior to enrolling: None

Recommended but not mandatory courses:
Statistics, biopsychology, abnormal psychology, history and systems, cognitive, developmental, research design

GRE mean
Verbal 675   Quantitative 670
Analytical Writing 5.0

GPA mean
Overall GPA 3.92

Number of applications/admission offers/incoming students in 2009
165 applied/6 admission offers/4 incoming

% of students receiving:
Full tuition waiver only: 0%
Assistantship/fellowship only: 0%
Both full tuition waiver & assistantship/fellowship: 100%

Approximate percentage of incoming students with a B.A./B.S. only: 100%   Master's: 0%

Approximate percentage of students who are
Women: 77%   Ethnic Minority: 17%   International: 5%

Average years to complete the doctoral program (including internship): 6 years

Personal interview
Required in person

Attrition rate in past 7 years: 14%

Percentage of students applying for internship last year accepted into APPIC or APA internships: 100%

Formal tracks/concentrations: clinical-developmental

Research areas	# Faculty	# Grants
anxiety, stress, and coping	3	1
attachment theory	2	2
child clinical	4	3
developmental risk	5	3
emotions	2	1
foster care	1	2
psychophysiology	3	1
psychotherapy research	2	0
couples research	1	1

Clinical opportunities

anxiety disorders	family therapy
child assessment	child maltreatment
conduct disorder	depression
developmental disabilities/ autism	couples therapy
	coping with cancer

University of Denver (Ph.D.)
Department of Psychology
University Park
Denver, CO 80208
phone#: (303) 871-3803
e-mail: phoughta@nova.psy.du.edu
Web address: www.du.edu/psychology/research/child_clinical.htm

1	2	3	4	5	6	7
Practice oriented		Equal emphasis				Research oriented

Percentage of faculty subscribing to each of the following orientations:

Psychodynamic/Psychoanalytic	9%
Applied behavioral analysis/Radical behavioral	0%
Family systems/Systems	16%
Existential/Phenomenological/Humanistic	0%
Cognitive/Cognitive-behavioral	100%

Courses required for incoming students prior to enrolling: None

Courses recommended but not mandatory:
Statistics

GRE mean
Verbal + Quantitative 1391
Analytical Writing not reported

GPA mean
Overall GPA 3.7

Number of applications/admission offers in 2008
250 applied/10 admission offers/7 incoming

% of students receiving:
Full tuition waiver only: 0%
Assistantship/fellowship only: 0%
Both full tuition waiver & assistantship/fellowship: 100%

Approximate percentage of incoming students with a B.A./B.S. only: 90%   Master's: 10%

Approximate percentage of students who are
Women: 82%   Ethnic Minority: 18%   International: 0%

Average years to complete the doctoral program (including internship): 6 years

Personal interview
Preferred in person but telephone acceptable

Attrition rate in past 7 years: 6%

Percentage of students applying for internship last year accepted into APPIC or APA internships: 100%

Formal tracks/concentrations: child clinical

Research areas	# Faculty	# Grants
adolescent psychopathology	4	3
behavioral genetics	2	2
child psychopathology	2	2
close relationships	2	5
community	2	1
developmental disabilities	1	1
eating disorders	1	0
family	1	1
marital	1	4
neuropsychology	1	1
poverty	2	1
prevention	2	1
psychotherapy	2	1
sexual abuse	2	2
trauma	1	1

Clinical opportunities

developmental disorders
family
inpatient adolescents
marital/couples
minority/cross-cultural

neuropsychology
pediatrics
trauma treatment
outpatient children,
    adolescents, and adults

University of Denver (Psy.D.)

Graduate School of Professional Psychology
2460 South Vine Street
Denver, CO 80208-0208
phone#: (303) 871-3736
e-mail: gsppinfo@du.edu
Web address: www.du.edu/gspp/degree-programs/clinical-psychology/overview/index.html

1	2	3	4	5	6	7
Practice oriented		Equal emphasis			Research oriented	

Percentage of faculty subscribing to each of the following orientations:

Psychodynamic/Psychoanalytic	40%
Applied behavioral analysis/Radical behavioral	20%
Family systems/Systems	20%
Existential/Phenomenological/Humanistic	10%
Cognitive/Cognitive-behavioral	10%

Courses required for incoming students prior to enrolling:
Statistics, learning, personality, experimental, child, abnormal, history of psychology

Courses recommended but not mandatory:
Physiological psychology

GRE mean
Verbal 550   Quantitative 550
Psychology Subject Test 660
Analytical 4.5

GPA mean
Overall GPA 3.5

Number of applications/admission offers/incoming students in 2009
379 applied/79 admission offers/39 incoming

incoming % of students receiving:
Full tuition waiver only: 2%
Assistantship/fellowship only: 35%
Both full tuition waiver & assistantship/fellowship: 5%

Approximate percentage of incoming students with a B.A./B.S. only: 60%   **Master's:** 39%

Approximate percentage of students who are Women: 76%   **Ethnic Minority:** 11%   **International:** 5%

Average years to complete the doctoral program (including internship): 4 years

Personal interview
Required in-person in Denver, Colorado

Attrition rate in past 7 years: 6%

Percentage of students applying for internship last year accepted into APPIC or APA internships: 95%

Formal tracks/concentrations: child clinical, forensic psychology, international disaster psychology, sport and performance psychology, student-chosen specialty

Research areas	# Faculty	# Grants
behavioral medicine/therapy	1	0
cognitive issues	1	0
couples and family therapy	2	0
forensic issues	2	0
multicultural issues	1	0

Clinical opportunities

assessment
behavioral medicine
cognitive therapy
group therapy
hypnosis

international disaster
    psychology
psychodynamic/
    psychoanalytic therapy
psychotherapy supervision

DePaul University (Ph.D.)

Department of Psychology
2219 North Kenmore
Chicago, IL 60614
phone#: (312) 362-8000
e-mail: gradpsych@depaul.edu
Web address: http://las.depaul.edu/psy/Programs/GraduatePrograms/ClinicalPsychology/index.asp

1	2	3	4	5	6	7
Practice oriented		Equal emphasis			Research oriented	

Percentage of faculty subscribing to each of the following orientations:

Psychodynamic/Psychoanalytic	0%
Applied behavioral analysis/Radical behavioral	8%
Family systems/Systems	46%
Existential/Phenomenological/Humanistic	0%
Cognitive/Cognitive-behavioral	46%

Courses required for incoming students prior to enrolling:
24 semester hours in psychology, 3 semester hours of statistics, and 3 semester hours in experimental psychology

Courses recommended but not mandatory:
science, computer, and math courses

GRE mean
Verbal 602   Quantitative 660
Analytical Writing not reported
Psychology Subject Test 624

GPA mean
Overall GPA 3.40

Number of applications/admission offers/incoming students in 2009
284 applied/13 admission offers/6 incoming

% of students receiving:
Full tuition waiver only: 0%
Assistantship/fellowship only: 0%
Both full tuition waiver & assistantship/fellowship: 100%

Approximate percentage of incoming students with a B.A./B.S. only: 83%   **Master's:** 17%

Approximate percentage of students who are Women: 59%   **Ethnic Minority:** 43%   **International:** 4%

Average years to complete the doctoral program (including internship): 7 years

Personal interview
Preferred in person but telephone acceptable

Attrition rate in past 7 years: 5%

Percentage of students applying for internship last year accepted into APPIC or APA internships: 100%

Formal tracks/concentrations: child clinical, community clinical

Research areas	# Faculty	# Grants
adolescent depression	2	2
child abuse and neglect	1	1
chronic fatigue syndrome	1	3
disability	2	2
HIV/AIDS adolescent prevention	1	3
minority mental health	4	1
parent–child interaction	1	1
program evaluation	4	1
smoking cessation	1	1
social support	2	1
teenage pregnancy	2	1
violence prevention	3	3

Clinical opportunities

assessment	group therapy
child and adolescent	minority/diversity
community psychology	empirically supported
family therapy	interventions

University of Detroit–Mercy (Ph.D.)
Department of Psychology
4001 W. McNichols Road
Detroit, MI 48221-3038
phone#: (313) 578-0570
e-mail: dauphivb@udmercy.edu
Web address: http://liberalarts.udmercy.edu/programs/depts/psychology/graduate/pycphd/index.htm

1	2	3	4	5	6	7
Practice oriented		Equal emphasis				Research oriented

Percentage of faculty subscribing to each of the following orientations:

Psychodynamic/Psychoanalytic	75%
Applied behavioral analysis/Radical behavioral	10%
Family systems/Systems	10%
Existential/Phenomenological/Humanistic	10%
Cognitive/Cognitive-behavioral	25%

Courses required for incoming students prior to enrolling:
Statistics, experimental, research methods, personality, abnormal psychology, research course

Courses recommended but not mandatory:
Physiological psychology

GRE mean
Verbal 492   Quantitative 640
Analytical Writing 4.85

GPA mean
Overall GPA 3.6

Number of applications/admission offers/incoming students in 2009
80 applied/15 admission offers/9 incoming

% of students receiving:
Full tuition waiver only: 0%
Assistantship/fellowship only: 100%
Both full tuition waiver & assistantship/fellowship: 100%
(all students in first 2 years of program)

Approximate percentage of incoming students with a B.A./B.S. only: 90%   **Master's:** 10%

Approximate percentage of students who are Women: 80%   **Ethnic Minority:** 10%   **International:** 30%

Average years to complete the doctoral program (including internship): 6 years

Personal interview
Required in person

Attrition rate in past 7 years: 1%

Percentage of students applying for internship last year accepted into APPIC or APA internships: 85%

Formal tracks/concentrations: none

Research areas	# Faculty	# Grants
alcohol abuse	1	1
critical incident response	2	0
helping behavior	1	0
identity development	2	0
intellectual assessment using human figure drawings	1	0
marital and family relationships	2	0
perception and eye movement	1	1
posttraumatic stress disorder	2	0
psychiatric diagnosis, ethnicity, and clinical judgment	1	0
psychotherapy process and outcome	4	0

self-esteem/body image	2	0
spirituality	3	0

Clinical opportunities
Practicums and internships are completed at one of over 30 agencies in the metropolitan area

Drexel University (Ph.D.)
Department of Psychology
Main Campus Office
3141 Chestnut Street
Philadelphia, PA 19104
phone: (215) 762-4021
e-mail: evan.forman@drexel.edu
Web address: http://drexel.edu/psychology/academics/graduate/clinical/

1	2	3	4	**5**	6	7
Practice oriented		Equal emphasis				Research oriented

Percentage of faculty subscribing to each of the following orientations:
Psychodynamic/Psychoanalytic	0%
Applied behavioral analysis/Radical behavioral	0%
Family systems/Systems	5%
Existential/Phenomenological/Humanistic	0%
Cognitive/Cognitive-behavioral	95%

Courses required for incoming students to have completed prior to enrolling: none

Recommended but not mandatory courses:
foundational courses in psychology

GRE mean
Verbal 634   Quantitative 629
Psychology Subject Test 733
Analytical Writing 5

GPA mean
Overall GPA 3.64

Number of applications/admission offers/incoming students in 2009
347 applied/16 admission offers/13 incoming

% of students receiving:
Full tuition waiver only: 0%
Assistantship/fellowship only: 0%
Both full tuition waiver & assistantship/fellowship: 100% (1st-year class)**
**All students in subsequent years currently receive at least a tuition waiver and additional support.

Approximate percentage of incoming students with a BA/BS only: 82% Master's: 18%

Approximate percentage of students who are Women: 86% Ethnic Minority: 14% International: 8%

Average years to complete the doctoral program (including internship): 5 years

Personal interview
Preferred in person but telephone acceptable

Attrition rate in past 7 years: 2.7%

Percentage of students applying for internship last year accepted into APPIC or APA internships: 91%

Formal tracks/concentrations: health, forensic, neuropsychology

Research areas	# Faculty	# Grants
acceptance and mindfulness	2	1
anxiety disorders	2	0
at-risk youth	2	2
behavioral medicine/health psychology	7	2
cognitive behavior therapy	5	1
cognitive psychology	2	2
depression	2	1
drug policy	1	1
eating disorders	1	1
forensic interventions	2	2
forensic mental health assessment	3	1
human-computer interaction	1	0
insomnia	1	0
juvenile justice	1	1
memory	1	0
neuroimaging	3	0
neuropsychological assessment	2	0
neuropsychology	2	0
neurorehabilitation	3	2
obesity	2	2
problem-solving therapy	2	1
psychopathy	1	0
psychotherapy research	4	1
stressful life events	1	0
women's health	3	0
written emotional expression	1	0

Clinical Opportunities
forensic	CBT
health	adult
neuropsychology	child and family

Duke University (Ph.D.)
Department of Psychology & Neuroscience
Durham, NC 27708
phone#: (919) 660-5716
e-mail: morrell@duke.edu
Web address: pn.aas.duke.edu/graduate/clinical

1	2	3	4	5	**6**	7
Practice oriented		Equal emphasis				Research oriented

Percentage of faculty subscribing to each of the following orientations:
Psychodynamic/Psychoanalytic	15%
Applied behavioral analysis/Radical behavioral	0%
Family systems/Systems	15%
Existential/Phenomenological/Humanistic	0%
Cognitive/Cognitive-behavioral	70%

Courses required for incoming students to have completed prior to enrolling:
Statistics

Recommended but not mandatory courses:
Personality, Research Methods

GRE mean
Verbal 636   Quantitative 700
Analytical Writing 5.2

GPA mean
Overall GPA 3.73

Number of applications/admission offers/incoming students in 2009
238 applied/10 admission offers/6 incoming

% of students receiving:
Full tuition waiver only: 0%
Assistantship/fellowship only: 0%
Both full tuition waiver & assistantship/fellowship: 100%

Approximate percentage of incoming students with a B.A./B.S. only: 94%   **Master's:** 6%

Approximate percentage of students who are Women: 85% **Ethnic Minority:** 30% **International:** 1%

Average years to complete the doctoral program (including internship): 5.5 years

Personal interview
Required in person

Attrition rate in past 7 years: 5%

Percentage of students applying for internship last year accepted into APPIC or APA internships: 92%

Formal tracks/concentrations: child clinical, adult clinical, health psychology

Research areas	# Faculty	# Grants
adolescent treatment	3	2
affective disorders	3	2
behavioral genomics	2	2
behavioral medicine	4	6
conduct disorders	2	3
developmental psychopathology	3	3
prevention of substance abuse	3	3
eating disorders	3	3
pediatric neuropsychology	1	1
social cognition	3	2
stress and coping	4	4

Clinical opportunities

affective disorders	cognitive behavior therapy
behavioral cardiology	dialectical behavior therapy
behavioral medicine	eating disorders
behavior disorders of children	family therapy
child abuse	pediatric psychology
child and adolescent CBT	

Duquesne University (Ph.D.)

Department of Psychology
Pittsburgh, PA 15282-1753
phone#: (412)-396-6522
e-mail: psychology@duq.edu
Web address: www.duq.edu/psychology/graduate/program-gr.cfm

1	2	3	4	5	6	7
Practice oriented		Equal emphasis			Research oriented	

Percentage of faculty subscribing to each of the following orientations:

Psychodynamic/Psychoanalytic	65%
Applied behavioral analysis/Radical behavioral	0%
Family systems/Systems	18%
Existential/Phenomenological/Humanistic	91%
Cognitive/Cognitive-behavioral	18%

Courses required for incoming students to have completed prior to enrolling: none

Recommended but not mandatory courses:
general breadth, development, social, abnormal, personality, research methods

GRE mean
Verbal 588
Quantitative 674
Analytical Writing not reported
Psychology Subject Test not reported

GPA mean
Overall GPA 3.54

Number of applications/admission offers/incoming students in 2008
85 applied/7 admission offers/7 incoming

% of students receiving:
Full tuition waiver only: 0%
Assistantship/fellowship only: 0%
Both full tuition waiver & assistantship/fellowship: 100%

Approximate percentage of incoming students with a B.A./B.S. only: not reported   **Master's:** not reported

Approximate percentage of current students who are Women: 50% **Ethnic Minority:** 19.5% **International:** 21%

Average years to complete the doctoral program (including internship): 7.9 years

Personal interview
Required in person

Attrition rate in past 7 years: not reported

Percentage of students applying for internship last year accepted into APPIC or APA internships: 80%

Formal tracks/concentrations: none

Research areas	# Faculty	# Grants
Please note: our research is qualitative	not reported	not reported

Clinical opportunities
Psychology Clinic (offers psychotherapy to Duquesne's students, faculty and staff as well as the public)

Eastern Michigan University (Ph.D.)

Department of Psychology
Ypsilanti, MI 48197
phone#: (734) 487-1155
e-mail: ellen.koch@emich.edu
Web address: www.emich.edu/psychology/programs-grad.html

1	2	3	4	5	6	7
Practice oriented			Equal emphasis			Research oriented

Percentage of faculty subscribing to each of the following orientations:
Psychodynamic/Psychoanalytic 10%
Applied behavioral analysis/Radical behavioral 20%
Family systems/Systems 20%
Existential/Phenomenological/Humanistic 10%
Cognitive/Cognitive-behavioral 40%

Courses required for incoming students to have completed prior to enrolling:
Statistics, experimental psychology, 20 undergraduate credits in psychology

Recommended but not mandatory courses:
Abnormal, personality, learning, history and systems

GRE mean
Verbal 565 Quantitative 722
Analytical Writing 4.94
Psychology Subject Test not required

GPA mean
Overall GPA 3.41

Number of applications/admission offers/incoming students in 2009
139 applied/10 admission offers/8 incoming

% of students receiving:
Full tuition waiver only: 0%
Assistantship/fellowship only: 0%
Both full tuition waiver & assistantship/fellowship: 100%

Approximate percentage of incoming students with a B.A./B.S. only: 66%   Master's: 33%

Approximate percentage of students who are Women: 60%   Ethnic Minority: 15%   International: 5%

Average years to complete the doctoral program (including internship): 6 years

Personal interview
In person interview highly preferred

Attrition rate in past 7 years: 13%

Percentage of students applying for internship last year accepted into APPIC or APA internships: 78%

Formal tracks/concentrations: Applied Behavioral Analysis

Research areas	# Faculty	# Grants
anxiety disorders (PTSD)	2	0
child and family	3	1
neuropsychology	2	1
personality disorders	1	1
substance abuse	1	0
applied behavioral analysis	2	0
behavioral medicine	1	0
sexual deviance	1	0
multicultural issues	2	0

Clinical opportunities
anxiety disorders and PTSD   inpatient hospital for
depression   children and adolescents

personality disorders   veterans
neuropsychology evaluations   college students
traumatic brain injury
behavioral medicine clinic—
    chronic pain and migraine

Emory University (Ph.D.)

Department of Psychology
Kilgo Circle
Atlanta, GA 30322
phone#: (404) 727-7438
e-mail: lcraigh@emory.edu
Web address: psychology.emory.edu/clinical/index.html

1	2	3	4	5	6	7
Practice oriented			Equal emphasis			Research oriented

Percentage of faculty subscribing to each of the following orientations:
Psychodynamic/Psychoanalytic 10%
Applied behavioral analysis/Radical behavioral 10%
Family systems/Systems 20%
Existential/Phenomenological/Humanistic 0%
Cognitive/Cognitive-behavioral 40%

Courses required for incoming students to have completed prior to enrolling:
None

Recommended but not mandatory courses:
methodology, psychopathology, personality

GRE mean
Verbal 650   Quantitative 650   Analytical 680
Analytical Writing 5.5

GPA mean
Overall GPA 3.5

Number of applications/admission offers/incoming students in 2009
230 applied/8 admission offers/5 incoming

% of students receiving:
Full tuition waiver only: 0%
Assistantship/fellowship only: 0%
Both full tuition waiver & assistantship/fellowship: 100%

Approximate percentage of incoming students with a B.A./B.S. only: 98%   Master's: 2%

Approximate percentage of students who are Women: 80% Ethnic Minority: 20% International: 20%

Average years to complete the doctoral program (including internship): 6 years

Personal interview
Required (in person upon invitation from faculty)

Attrition rate in past 7 years: 0.2%

Percentage of students applying for internship last year accepted into APPIC or APA internships: 100%

Formal tracks/concentrations: none

Research areas	# Faculty	# Grants
adolescent psychopathology	2	1
attention-deficit disorder	1	1
behavioral genetics	2	1
eating disorders	1	0
infant development	1	1
neuropsychology	1	0
personality and personality disorders	2	2
schizophrenia	1	1

Clinical opportunities

assessment	interpersonal therapy
behavior therapy	neuropsychology
cognitive/behavior therapy	psychodynamic therapy

Fairleigh Dickinson University (Ph.D.)

School of Psychology T-WH1-01
Teaneck–Hackensack Campus
1000 River Road
Teaneck, NJ 07666
phone#: (201) 692-2445
e-mail: mcgrath@fdu.edu
Web address: view.fdu.edu/default.aspx?id=6280

1	2	3	4	5	6	7
Practice oriented			Equal emphasis			Research oriented

Percentage of faculty subscribing to each of the following orientations:

Psychodynamic/Psychoanalytic	55%
Applied behavioral analysis/Radical behavioral	9%
Family systems/Systems	18%
Existential/Phenomenological/Humanistic	18%
Cognitive/Cognitive-behavioral	55%

Courses required for incoming students to have completed prior to enrolling:

18 credits in psychology with statistics, developmental, experimental, social preferred

Recommended but not mandatory courses:

Psychopathology, physiological, assessment

GRE mean

Verbal 614   Quantitative 682   Analytical 5
Psychology Subject Test 678
Analytical Writing N/A

GPA mean

Overall GPA 3.76

Number of applications/admission offers/incoming students in 2008

220 applied/35 admission offers/16 incoming

% of students receiving:

Full tuition waiver only: 0%
Assistantship/fellowship only: 100% (can be taken as tuition remission)
Both full tuition waiver & assistantship/fellowship: 0%

Approximate percentage of incoming students with a B.A./B.S. only: 73%   **Master's:** 27%

Approximate percentage of students who are Women: 81%   **Ethnic Minority:** 18%   **International:** 2%

Average years to complete the doctoral program (including internship): 5.5 years

Personal interview

Required in person

Attrition rate in past 7 years: 3%

Percentage of students applying for internship last year accepted into APPIC or APA internships: 85%

Formal tracks/concentrations: none

Research areas	# Faculty	# Grants
assessment	5	1
behavioral medicine	3	0
child clinical	2	0
community psychology	2	0
eating disorders	1	1
ethical issues	2	0
forensic	2	1
minority issues	2	0
relationship	4	0
sexual abuse	3	0
statistics	2	0
stress—disasters	1	0
women's studies	2	0

Clinical opportunities

anxiety disorders	gerontology
assessment	minority populations
behavioral medicine	neuropsychology
community psychology	substance abuse
family therapy	

University of Florida (Ph.D.)

Department of Clinical and Health Psychology
Box 100165 University of Florida Health Science Center
Gainesville, FL 32610
phone#: (352) 265-0294
e-mail: jhj@phhp.ufl.edu
Web address: chp.phhp.ufl.edu/programs/doctoral/index.html

1	2	3	4	5	6	7
Practice oriented			Equal emphasis			Research oriented

Percentage of faculty subscribing to each of the following orientations:

Psychodynamic/Psychoanalytic	0%
Applied behavioral analysis/Radical behavioral	15%
Family systems/Systems	60%
Existential/Phenomenological/Humanistic	20%
Cognitive/Cognitive-behavioral	85%

Courses required for incoming students to have completed prior to enrolling:

Statistics, abnormal

Recommended but not mandatory courses:

Undergraduate courses in experimental, developmental, social, personality, physiological, perception

GRE mean
Verbal 610 Quantitative 700
Analytical Writing 5.0
Psychology Subject Test not reported

GPA mean
3.8

Number of applications/admission offers/incoming students in 2009
358 applied/21 admission offers/13 incoming

% of students receiving:
Full tuition waiver only: 0%
Assistantship/fellowship only: 0%
Both full tuition waiver & assistantship/fellowship: 95% all students; 100% incoming

Approximate percentage of incoming students with a B.A./B.S. only: 85%　**Master's:** 15%

Approximate percentage of students who are Women: 75%　**Ethnic Minority:** 30%　**International:** 6%

Average years to complete the doctoral program (including internship): 6.1 years

Personal interview
Preferred in person but telephone acceptable

Attrition rate in past 7 years: 3.7%

Percentage of students applying for internship last year accepted into APPIC or APA internships: 100%

Formal tracks/concentrations: clinical health psychology, clinical child/pediatric psychology, neuropsychology, neurorehabilitation, and clinical neuroscience

Research areas	# Faculty	# Grants
anxiety disorders and emotions	2	2
child clinical psychology	3	1
clinical/medical psychology	3	3
functional neuroimaging	2	3
neuropsychology	6	4
obesity treatment	2	2
pain	2	3
pediatric psychology	2	4
rural health	1	1

Clinical opportunities

ADHD
clinical child psychology
forensic psychology
inpatient consultation/liaison
learning disabilities
medical/health psychology
neuropsychology

pain and stress
parent training
pediatric consultation
rural behavioral health
cognitive behavior therapy
weight loss

Florida Institute of Technology (Psy.D.)

School of Psychology
150 West University Boulevard
Melbourne, FL 32901
phone#: (321) 674-8105
e-mail: relmore@fit.edu
Web address: cpla.fit.edu//clinical/index.htm

1	2	3	4	5	6	7
Practice oriented		Equal emphasis				Research oriented

Percentage of faculty subscribing to each of the following orientations:

Psychodynamic/Psychoanalytic	10%
Applied behavioral analysis/Radical behavioral	10%
Family systems/Systems	20%
Existential/Phenomenological/Humanistic	20%
Cognitive/Cognitive-behavioral	40%

Courses required for incoming students to have completed prior to enrolling:
Statistics, learning, personality, physiological psychology, abnormal psychology, social psychology

Recommended but not mandatory courses:
Data not available

GRE mean
Verbal + Quantitative 1054
Analytical Writing 4.5

GPA mean
Overall GPA 3.63

Number of applications/admission offers/incoming students in 2009
154 applied/47 admission offers/21 incoming

% of students receiving:
Full tuition waiver only: 0%
Assistantship/fellowship only: 58%
Both full tuition waiver & assistantship/fellowship: 0%

Approximate percentage of incoming students with a B.A./B.S. only: 60%　**Master's:** 40%

Approximate percentage of students who are Women: 78%　**Ethnic Minority:** 16%　**International:** 1%

Average years to complete the doctoral program (including internship): 5 years

Personal interview
Preferred

Attrition rate in past 7 years: 10%

Percentage of students applying for internship last year accepted into APPIC or APA internships: 90%

Formal tracks/concentrations: family/child psychology, neuropsychology, clinical health psychology, forensic psychology

Research areas	# Faculty	# Grants
aging	1	2
eating disorders	1	0
family psychology	2	0
health psychology	3	0
neuropsychology	2	1
personality assessment	3	0
sexual abuse	1	1
supervision	1	0
PTSD (Vietnam veterans)	1	0

Clinical opportunities

behavioral medicine/
　health psychology

sexual abuse (offenders
　and victims)

family and marital therapy
forensic settings
neuropsychology

Vietnam veterans
(posttraumatic stress
syndrome)

Florida State University (Ph.D.)

Department of Psychology
Tallahassee, FL 32306-1051
phone#: (850) 644-2499
e-mail: grad-info@psy.fsu.edu
Web address: www.psy.fsu.edu/clinical/index.htm

1	2	3	4	5	6	**7**
Practice oriented		Equal emphasis				Research oriented

Percentage of faculty subscribing to each of the following orientations:

Psychodynamic/Psychoanalytic — 0%
Applied behavioral analysis/Radical behavioral — 0%
Family systems/Systems — 0%
Existential/Phenomenological/Humanistic — 0%
Cognitive/Cognitive-behavioral — 100%

Courses required for incoming students to have completed prior to enrolling:

Undergraduate degree

Recommended but not mandatory courses: None

GRE mean

Verbal 653   Quantitative 723
Analytical Writing 4.9

GPA mean

Junior/Senior GPA 3.9

Number of applications/admission offers/incoming students in 2009

Not reported

% of students receiving:

Full tuition waiver only: 0%
Assistantship/fellowship only: 0%
Both full tuition waiver & assistantship/fellowship: 100%

Approximate percentage of incoming students with a B.A./B.S. only: 80%   Master's: 20%

Approximate percentage of students who are

Women: 81%   Ethnic Minority: 23%   International: 2%

Average years to complete the doctoral program (including internship): 7 years

Personal interview

Preferred in person but telephone acceptable

Attrition rate in past 7 years: 5%

Percentage of students applying for internship last year accepted into APPIC or APA internships: 100%

Formal tracks/concentrations/specializations: none

Research areas	# Faculty	# Grants
addictive behavior	2	1
anxiety	1	4
conduct disorder and antisocial	1	1
bulimia nervosa	3	3
developmental psychopathology	3	3
early intervention	2	1
epidemiological psychology	1	1
prediction of criminal behavior	1	0
problematic social interactions	1	1
suicide	1	0

Clinical opportunities

adolescent delinquency
anxiety disorders
behavioral health
child problems

juvenile felony offenders
migrant workers
state psychiatric hospital

Fordham University (Ph.D.)

Department of Psychology
441 East Fordham Road
Bronx, NY 10458
phone#: (718) 817-3775
fax#: (718) 817-3785
e-mail: dct@fordham.edu
Web address: www.fordham.edu/academics/programs_at_
fordham_/psychology_departmen/academic_programs/
graduate/phd_in_clinical_psyc/

1	2	3	4	5	6	7
Practice oriented		Equal emphasis				Research oriented

Percentage of faculty subscribing to each of the following orientations:

Psychodynamic/Psychoanalytic — 15%
Applied behavioral analysis/Radical behavioral — 10%
Family systems/Systems — 15%
Existential/Phenomenological/Humanistic — 10%
Cognitive/Cognitive-behavioral — 50%

Courses required for incoming students to have completed prior to enrolling:

Statistics, research methods in psychology, introductory psychology

Recommended but not mandatory courses:

An undergraduate background in psychology is expected, but not required.

GRE mean

Verbal + Quantitative: 1385

GPA mean

3.58

Number of applications/admission offers/incoming students in 2009

502 applied/19 admission offers/11 incoming

% of students receiving:

Full tuition waiver only: 20%
Assistantship/fellowship only: 0%
Both full tuition waiver & assistantship/fellowship: 80%

Approximate percentage of incoming students with a B.A./B.S. only: 80%   Master's: 20%

Approximate percentage of students who are

Women: 66%   Ethnic Minority: 35%   International: 10%

Average years to complete the doctoral program (including internship): 6.8 years

Personal interview
Strongly recommended

Attrition rate in past 7 years: 10%

Percentage of students applying for internship last year accepted into APPIC or APA internships: 88%

Formal tracks/concentrations: child/family, health/neuropsychology, forensic, spirituality

Research areas	# Faculty	# Grants
adolescent development	1	0
assessment	3	0
attachment relationships in couples	1	0
clinical child psychology	2	1
family systems	1	0
health psychology/behavioral medicine	3	2
MMPI	3	0
neuropsychology	1	2
parent–child relationships	2	0
personality disorders	2	1
prevention	1	0
social support	2	0
stress and coping	2	1
substance abuse	2	1

Clinical opportunities
Clinical externships available at numerous inpatient and outpatient specialty clinics in the New York metropolitan area. Appropriate training sites can be found in any area including highly specialized.

Forest Institute of Professional Psychology (Psy.D.)

2885 West Battlefield Road
Springfield, MO 65807
phone#: (417) 823-3477 or (800) 424-7793
e-mail: admissions@forest.edu
Web address: www.forest.edu

1	2	3	4	5	6	7
Practice oriented		Equal emphasis				Research oriented

Percentage of faculty subscribing to each of the following orientations:

Psychodynamic/Psychoanalytic	40%
Applied behavioral analysis/Radical behavioral	10%
Family systems/Systems	20%
Existential/Phenomenological/Humanistic	10%
Cognitive/Cognitive-behavioral	20%

Courses required for incoming students to have completed prior to enrolling:
18 hours of psychology, abnormal psychology, statistics, development, biological sciences

Recommended but not mandatory courses:
General psychology, history and systems, theories of personality

GRE mean
Verbal 550   Quantitative 470
Analytical Writing Data not available

GPA mean
Not reported

Number of applications/admission offers/incoming students in 2009
Not reported

% of students receiving:
Full tuition waiver only: 0%
Assistantship/fellowship only: 6%
Both full tuition waiver & assistantship/fellowship: 0%

Approximate percentage of incoming students with a B.A./B.S. only: 54%   **Master's:** 46%

Approximate percentage of students who are Women: 60%   **Ethnic Minority:** 15%
International: not reported

Average years to complete the doctoral program (including internship): 5 years

Personal interview
Required in person

Attrition rate in past 7 years: 4%

Percentage of students applying for internship last year accepted into APPIC or APA internships: 91%

Formal tracks/concentrations: marriage & family therapy, child & adolescent psychology, forensic psychology, neuropsychology

Research areas	# Faculty	# Grants
diversity	1	1
healthy marriages	1	1

Clinical opportunities

child therapy	neuropsychology (adult
corrections/forensics	and child/adolescent)
integrated healthcare	pain management
marriage and family therapy	underserved populations

Fuller Theological Seminary (Ph.D.)

(Part of Fuller Theological Seminary)
180 North Oakland Avenue
Pasadena, CA 91101
phone#: (626) 584-5500
e-mail: lwagener@fuller.edu
Web address: www.fuller.edu/academics/school-of-psychology/department-of-clinical-psychology/doctor-of-philosophy.aspx

1	2	3	**4**	5	6	7
Practice oriented		Equal emphasis				Research oriented

Percentage of faculty subscribing to each of the following orientations:

Psychodynamic/Psychoanalytic	20%
Applied behavioral analysis/Radical behavioral	10%
Family systems/Systems	30%

Existential/Phenomenological/Humanistic	10%
Cognitive/Cognitive-behavioral	30%

Courses required for incoming students to have completed prior to enrolling:

6 courses in psychology and a B.A. from an accredited school

Recommended but not mandatory courses:

Courses in the areas of abnormal, developmental, experimental, physiological, social psychology, statistics, tests and measures, learning, motivation, and personality

GRE mean

Verbal + Quantitative 1180

GPA mean

Psychology GPA 3.6

Number of applications/admission offers/incoming students in 2009

111 applied/70 admission offers/40 incoming

% of students receiving:

Full tuition waiver only: 0%
Assistantship/fellowship only: 10%
Both full tuition waiver & assistantship/fellowship: 0%

Approximate percentage of incoming students with a B.A./B.S. only: 76%   Master's: 24%

Approximate percentage of students who are

Women: 70%   Ethnic Minority: 35%   International: 6%

Average years to complete the doctoral program (including internship): 6 years

Personal interview

Preferred in person but telephone acceptable

Attrition rate in past 7 years: not reported

Percentage of students applying for internship last year accepted into APPIC or APA internships: 77% in APA internships, 92% in APPIC

Formal tracks/concentrations: Family (Ph.D. & Psy.D.), Leadership (Psy.D. only)

Research areas	# Faculty	# Grants
biopsychosocial	3	2
child clinical	3	1
cognition	1	0
cross-cultural psychology	2	0
depression	1	0
developmental	3	1
family	2	1
group processes	1	0
health psychology/behavioral medicine	3	0
marriages	4	0
neuropsychology	2	0
posttraumatic stress disorders	2	0
relaxation/biofeedback	1	0
religion	7	0
stress and coping	1	0
substance abuse	1	0

Clinical opportunities

assessment	interpersonal
child/adolescent therapy	psychotherapy
chronic mental illness	marital/couples therapy

family therapy	neuropsychology/
forensic population	rehabilitation
gerontology	supervision
group therapy	victim/battering
inpatient adult population	

Fuller Theological Seminary (Psy.D.)

(Part of Fuller Theological Seminary)
180 North Oakland Avenue
Pasadena, CA 91101
phone#: (626) 584-5500
e-mail: lwagener@fuller.edu
Web address: www.fuller.edu/academics/school-of-psychology/department-of-clinical-psychology/doctor-of-psychology.aspx

1	2	3	4	5	6	7
Practice oriented			Equal emphasis			Research oriented

Percentage of faculty subscribing to each of the following orientations:

Psychodynamic/Psychoanalytic	20%
Applied behavioral analysis/Radical behavioral	10%
Family systems/Systems	30%
Existential/Phenomenological/Humanistic	10%
Cognitive/Cognitive-behavioral	30%

Courses required for incoming students to have completed prior to enrolling:

6 courses in psychology and a B.A. from an accredited school

Recommended but not mandatory courses:

Courses in the areas of abnormal, developmental, experimental, physiological, social psychology, statistics, tests and measures, learning, motivation, and personality

GRE mean

Verbal + Quantitative 1180

GPA mean

Psychology GPA 3.6

Number of applications/admission offers/incoming students in 2009

111 applied/70 admission offers/40 incoming

% of students receiving:

Full tuition waiver only: 0%
Assistantship/fellowship only: 10%
Both full tuition waiver & assistantship/fellowship: 0%

Approximate percentage of incoming students with a B.A./B.S. only: 76%   Master's: 24%

Approximate percentage of students who are

Women: 70%   Ethnic Minority: 35%   International: 6%

Average years to complete the doctoral program (including internship): 6 years

Personal interview

Preferred in person but telephone acceptable

Attrition rate in past 7 years: not reported

Percentage of students applying for internship last year accepted into APPIC or APA internships: 77% in APA internships, 92% in APPIC

Formal tracks/concentrations: Family (Ph.D. & Psy.D.), Leadership (Psy.D. only)

Research areas	# Faculty	# Grants
biopsychosocial	3	2
child clinical	3	1
cognition	1	0
cross-cultural psychology	2	0
depression	1	0
developmental	3	1
family	2	1
group processes	1	0
health psychology/behavioral medicine	3	0
marriages	4	0
neuropsychology	2	0
posttraumatic stress disorders	2	0
relaxation/biofeedback	1	0
religion	7	0
stress and coping	1	0
substance abuse	1	0

Clinical opportunities

assessment
child/adolescent therapy
chronic mental illness
family therapy
forensic population
gerontology
group therapy
inpatient adult population
interpersonal psychotherapy
marital/couples therapy
neuropsychology/ rehabilitation
supervision
victim/battering

Gallaudet University (Ph.D.)

Department of Psychology
8th and Florida Avenue, NE
Washington, DC 20002-3695
phone#: (202) 651-5647
e-mail: Patrick.Brice@Gallaudet.edu
Web address: www.gallaudet.edu/x718.xml

1	2	3	4	5	6	7

Practice oriented   Equal emphasis   Research oriented

Percentage of faculty subscribing to each of the following orientations:

Psychodynamic/Psychoanalytic	40%
Applied behavioral analysis/Radical behavioral	0%
Family systems/Systems	0%
Existential/Phenomenological/Humanistic	0%
Cognitive/Cognitive-behavioral	60%

Courses required for incoming students to have completed prior to enrolling:
Major or minor in undergraduate psychology including statistics and experimental psychology, abnormal, and child development

Recommended but not mandatory courses:
Social psychology, personality, learning, cognition, perception

GRE mean
Verbal 430   Quantitative 535

Psychology Subject Test is not required
Analytical Writing 4.3

GPA mean
Overall GPA 3.62   Psychology GPA 3.63

Number of applications/admission offers/incoming students in 2009
25 applied/8 admission offers/7 incoming

% of students receiving:
Full tuition waiver only: 0%
Assistantship/fellowship only: 100%
Both full tuition waiver & assistantship/fellowship: 0%

Approximate percentage of incoming students with a B.A./B.S. only: 71%   **Master's:** 29%

Approximate percentage of students who are Women: 86%   **Ethnic Minority:** 29% **International:** 14%   **Deaf or Hard of Hearing:** 43% **Hearing:** 57%

Average years to complete the doctoral program (including internship): 7 years

Personal interview
Preferred in person but telephone acceptable

Attrition rate in past 7 years: 13%

Percentage of students applying for internship last year accepted into APPIC or APA internships: 100%

Formal tracks/concentrations: none

Research areas	# Faculty	# Grants
adult development issues	1	0
assessment of attachment in deaf persons	2	1
assessment of attention in deaf children	2	1
assessment of depression in deaf clients	1	0
cognitive processing and memory in deaf persons	1	0
ethics in mental health and deafness	1	0
neuropsychological assessment of deaf clients	2	0
parental involvement with education of ethnic minority deaf children	1	1
cognitive behavioral treatment	1	0

Clinical opportunities
Assessment and therapy with deaf and hard-of-hearing clients through our multidisciplinary mental health clinic. More than 60 externship programs available in Washington, D.C. metropolitan area.

George Fox University (Psy.D.)

Graduate Department of Clinical Psychology
School of Behavioral and Health Sciences
414 N Meridian Street
Newberg, OR 97132-2697
phone#: 800-631-0921 x2263
e-mail: psyd@georgefox.edu
Web address: psyd.georgefox.edu

1	2	3	4	5	6	7
Practice oriented		Equal emphasis				Research oriented

Percentage of faculty subscribing to each of the following orientations:

Psychodynamic/Psychoanalytic	10%
Applied behavioral analysis/Radical behavioral	10%
Family systems/Systems	10%
Existential/Phenomenological/Humanistic	10%
Cognitive/Cognitive-behavioral	50%

Courses required for incoming students prior to enrolling:

18 semester hours or the equivalent (no specific courses required)

Courses recommended but not mandatory:

Psychopathology (abnormal psychology), developmental, statistics, social, experimental, personality, psychobiology

GRE mean

Verbal + Quantitative 1099
Analytical Writing not used

GPA mean

Overall GPA 3.48

Number of applications/admission offers/incoming students in 2008

75 applied/34 admission offers/24 incoming

% of students receiving:

Full tuition waiver only: 0%
Partial tuition waiver only: 20%
Assistantship/fellowship only: 25%
Both full tuition waiver & assistantship/fellowship: 0%

Approximate percentage of incoming students with a B.A./B.S. only: 70%   Master's: 30%

Approximate percentage of students who are Women: 70% Ethnic Minority: 21% International: 0%

Average years to complete the doctoral program (including internship): 5.2 years

Personal interview

Preferred in person but telephone acceptable with special circumstances.

Attrition rate in past 7 years: 5%

Percentage of students applying for internship last year accepted into APPIC or APA internships: 78%

Formal tracks/concentrations: None

Research areas	# Faculty	# Grants
adjudicated youth/adults	1	0
child and geriatric memory	1	0
clinical supervision	1	0
coping skills in high-risk junior high students	1	1
marriage relationships	1	1
memory assessment	1	1
school consultation	1	1
pain management	1	1
shame	1	0
spirituality and mental health	1	1
Stroop effect	1	1
values and psychologist training	1	0

Clinical opportunities

addictions
adolescent residential
assessment
child psychopathology
community mental health
corrections
emergency room consultation
geriatrics
health psychology
inpatient hospital consultation
Native American setting
neuropsychology
out-patient hospital consultation/treatment
pain management
primary health care setting
public school setting
rural psychology
spirituality in psycho-therapeutic intervention

George Mason University (Ph.D.)

Department of Psychology 3F5
4400 University Drive
Fairfax, VA 22030-4444
phone#: (703) 993-1384
e-mail: psycgrad@gmu.edu
Web address: psychology.gmu.edu/clinical/

1	2	3	4	5	6	7
Practice oriented		Equal emphasis				Research oriented

Percentage of faculty subscribing to each of the following orientations:

Psychodynamic/Psychoanalytic	10%
Applied behavioral analysis/Radical behavioral	0%
Family systems/Systems	10%
Existential/Phenomenological/Humanistic	20%
Cognitive/Cognitive-behavioral	80%
Community	0%

(Total is greater than 100% because several faculty subscribe to more than one orientation.)

Courses required for incoming students to have completed prior to enrolling:

Statistics, abnormal psychology, any laboratory science course

Recommended but not mandatory courses:

Tests and measurements/psychometrics, personality, social

GRE mean

Verbal 640   Quantitative 708
Analytical Writing not reported

GPA mean

Overall GPA 3.77

Number of applications/admission offers/incoming students in 2009

176 applied/10 admission offers/5 incoming

% of students receiving:

Full tuition waiver only: 0%
Assistantship/fellowship only: 0%
Both full tuition waiver & assistantship/fellowship: 100%

Approximate percentage of incoming students with a B.A./B.S. only: 80%   Master's: 20%

Approximate percentage of students who are
Women: 75% **Ethnic Minority:** 25%
International: 5%

Average years to complete the doctoral program (including internship): 6 years

Personal interview
Required in person (phone interview possible)

Attrition rate in past 7 years: 15%

Percentage of students applying for internship last year accepted into APPIC or APA internships: 90%

Formal tracks/concentrations: none

Research areas	# Faculty	# Grants
social psychological aspects of adjustment	4	0
cognition and affect	4	0
domestic violence	1	0
criminal behavior	1	1
gay and lesbian issues	1	0
personality	1	1
positive human functioning	3	1
prevention	3	2
program evaluation	3	2
psychotherapy/counseling process	1	0
self-efficacy	1	0
social anxiety	1	0
stress and coping	2	0

Clinical opportunities
child and adult assessment
cognitive-behavioral psychotherapy
community consultation/ education
group/marriage/ family psychotherapy
individual adult psychotherapy
program evaluation

George Washington University (Ph.D.)

Department of Psychology
2125 G Street, NW
Washington, DC 20052
phone#: (202) 994-6320
e-mail: ghowe@gwu.edu
Web address: www.gwu.edu/~clinpsyc

1	2	3	4	5	6	7
Practice oriented		Equal emphasis				Research oriented

Percentage of faculty subscribing to each of the following orientations:

Psychodynamic/Psychoanalytic	0%
Applied behavioral analysis/Radical behavioral	10%
Family systems/Systems	30%
Existential/Phenomenological/Humanistic	10%
Cognitive/Cognitive-behavioral	60%

Courses required for incoming students to have completed prior to enrolling:
The equivalent of a major in psychology, statistics, research methods (or experimental course), basic psychology theory courses (from neuropsychology, physiological psychology, abnormal psychology, social psychology, learning and cognition, developmental psychology, community psychology)

Recommended but not mandatory courses: None

GRE mean
Verbal 632   Quantitative 698
Analytical Writing 5.13

GPA mean
Overall GPA 3.68

Number of applications/admission offers/incoming students in 2009
275 applied/5 admission offers/4 incoming

% of students receiving:
Full tuition waiver only: 0%
Assistantship/fellowship only: 0%
Both full tuition waiver & assistantship/fellowship: 100%

Approximate percentage of incoming students with a B.A./B.S. only: 100%   **Master's:** 0%

Approximate percentage of students who are
Women: 75% **Ethnic Minority:** 25% **International:** 0%

Average years to complete the doctoral program (including internship): 6.5 years

Personal interview
Preferred in person but telephone acceptable

Attrition rate in past 7 years: 7.5%

Percentage of students applying for internship last year accepted into APPIC or APA internships: 100%

Formal tracks/concentrations: none

Research areas	# Faculty	# Grants
adolescence	3	2
AIDS	1	2
anxiety disorders	1	1
behavioral medicine	1	0
child	2	1
community	6	1
depression	2	2
family	2	1
health	1	0
minority mental health	4	3
relaxation/biofeedback	1	0
stress	3	1

Clinical opportunities
adolescent problems
AIDS
adolescent delinquency
affective disorders/depression
anxiety disorders
assessment
behavioral medicine
child assessment and therapy
conduct disorder
developmental disabilities/ autism
dissociative disorder
eating disorders
family therapy
health
hyperactivity
impulse control/aggression
marital/couples therapy
minority/cross-cultural
neuropsychology/ rehabilitation
obsessive–compulsive disorder
personality disorders
psychodynamic/ psychoanalytic therapy
schizophrenia/psychoses
substance abuse

185

logy   victim/battering abuse

George Washington University (Psy.D.)

Center for Professional Psychology
1922 F Street NW, Suite 103
Washington, DC 20052
phone#: 202-994-1835
e-mail: psyd@gwu.edu
Web address: www.gwu.edu/~psyd/index.htm

1	2	3	4	5	6	7
Practice oriented		Equal emphasis				Research oriented

Percentage of faculty subscribing to each of the following orientations:

Psychodynamic/Psychoanalytic	80%
Applied behavioral analysis/Radical behavioral	0%
Family systems/Systems	10%
Existential/Phenomenological/Humanistic	0%
Cognitive/Cognitive-behavioral	10%

Courses required for incoming students to have completed prior to enrolling:
B.A./B.S.

Recommended but not mandatory courses:
Psychodynamic/psychoanalytic theory, personality, development, psychodynamic/psychoanalytic therapy, cognitive development and a course in statistics

GRE mean
Verbal 556   Quantitative 626   Analytical 641
Analytical Writing 5.2

GPA mean
Overall GPA 3.5

Number of applications/admission offers/incoming students in 2009
337 applied/admission offers (not reported)/36 incoming

% of students receiving:
Full tuition waiver only: 0%
Assistantship/fellowship only: 33%
Both full tuition waiver & assistantship/fellowship: 0%

Approximate percentage of incoming students with a B.A./B.S. only: 63%   Master's: 17%

Approximate percentage of students who are Women: 76% Ethnic Minority: 28% International: 10%

Average years to complete the doctoral program (including internship): 4.3 years

Personal interview
Required in person

Attrition rate in past 7 years: not reported

Percentage of students applying for internship last year accepted into APPIC or APA internships: 98%

Formal tracks/concentrations: adult, child, assessment

Research areas	# Faculty	# Grants
adult psychopathology	4	0
child clinical	2	1
child development	2	2
community intervention	3	1
group process	3	0
infant and early childhood research	1	1
intellectual assessment	3	0
personality assessment	3	0

Clinical opportunities

assessment	family therapy
clinical intervention	learning disorders
with children	psychotherapy
clinical outcome studies	schizophrenia
developmental disorders	

University of Georgia (Ph.D.)

Department of Psychology
Athens, GA 30602
phone#: (706) 542-1787
e-mail: gradpsych@uga.edu
Web address: psychology.uga.edu/graduate/programs/clinical/

1	2	3	4	5	6	7
Practice oriented		Equal emphasis				Research oriented

Percentage of faculty subscribing to each of the following orientations:

Psychodynamic/Psychoanalytic	0%
Applied behavioral analysis/Radical behavioral	0%
Family systems/Systems	10%
Existential/Phenomenological/Humanistic	0%
Cognitive/Cognitive-behavioral	100%

Courses required for incoming students to have completed prior to enrolling: None

Recommended but not mandatory courses:
Abnormal, statistics

GRE mean
Verbal + Quantitative 1272

GPA mean
Overall GPA 3.77

Number of applications/admission offers/incoming students in 2008
210 applied/16 admission offers/9 incoming

% of students receiving:
Full tuition waiver only: 0%
Assistantship/fellowship only: 0%
Both full tuition waiver & assistantship/fellowship: 100%

Approximate percentage of incoming students with a B.A./B.S. only: 100%   Master's: 0%

Approximate percentage of students who are Women: 89% Ethnic Minority: 33% International: 11%

Average years to complete the doctoral program (including internship): 5.25 years

Personal interview
Preferred in person but telephone acceptable

Attrition rate in past 7 years: 4.7%

Percentage of students applying for internship last year accepted into APPIC or APA internships: 100%

Formal tracks/concentrations: child, neuropsychology

Research areas	# Faculty	# Grants
adolescence	3	10
adult psychopathology	4	2
affective disorder/depression	1	1
African Americans	1	0
aggression	3	0
aggression against sexual minorities	1	0
aging/gerontology	2	2
alcohol use and stress	1	1
anxiety disorders	1	0
battering	1	0
cardiovascular function	1	1
child clinical/child psychopathology	3	1
depression	1	1
developmental psychopathology	3	3
eating disorders	1	1
emotions	1	0
family/therapy/systems	2	0
gender issues	1	0
interpersonal processes	1	0
marriage/couples	1	3
neuropsychology	1	1
pain management/control	1	1
parent–child interaction	2	5
pediatric psychology	1	5
personality	1	0
prevention	1	5
schizophrenia/psychoses	1	0
stress and coping	2	0
substance abuse	3	11
suicide	1	0
violence/abuse/victim–offender	5	0

Clinical opportunities

affective disorders/depression	1
anxiety disorders	2
assessment	2
behavior therapy	1
eating disorders	1
neuropsychology	1
pediatric psychology	5
personality disorders	2
stress management	1
victim/battering/abuse	1

Georgia State University (Ph.D.)

Department of Psychology
University Plaza
P.O. Box 5010
Atlanta, GA 30303
phone#: (404) 413-6200
e-mail: ffloyd@gsu.edu
Web address: www2.gsu.edu/~wwwpsy/ClinProg.htm

1	2	3	4	5	6	7
Practice oriented			Equal emphasis			Research oriented

Percentage of faculty subscribing to each of the following orientations:

Psychodynamic/Psychoanalytic/Interpersonal	10%
Applied behavioral analysis/Radical behavioral	0%
Family systems/Systems	15%
Existential/Phenomenological/Humanistic	0%
Cognitive/Cognitive-behavioral	45%
Clinical Neuropsychology	45%

Courses required for incoming students to have completed prior to enrolling:
Research methods, psychological statistics, and two additional Junior/Senior-level psychology courses

Recommended but not mandatory courses:
Abnormal psychology

GRE mean
Verbal 566   Quantitative 672

GPA mean
Overall GPA 3.48

Number of applications/admission offers/incoming students in 2009
372 applied/18 admission offers/10 incoming

% of students receiving:
Full tuition waiver only: 0%
Assistantship/fellowship only: 0%
Both full tuition waiver & assistantship/fellowship: 100%

Approximate percentage of incoming students with a B.A./B.S. only: 90%   **Master's:** 10%

Approximate percentage of students who are Women: 80% **Ethnic Minority:** 40% **International:** 0%

Average years to complete the doctoral program (including internship): 6 years

Personal interview
Preferred in person but telephone acceptable

Attrition rate in past 7 years: 8%

Percentage of students applying for internship last year accepted into APPIC or APA internships: 100%

Formal tracks/concentrations: general clinical, neuropsychology, clinical/community psychology

Research areas	# Faculty	# Grants
ACT	1	0
alcohol and aggression	1	1
acquired brain injuries	3	1
anxiety disorders—children	1	1
autism	1	1
couples therapy	1	0
crime and delinquency	2	1
culture, mental health and therapy	3	1
early brain injury and visiospatial and attention skills	1	0
emotion and executive functioning	3	0
empowerment	1	0
developmental neuropsychology	3	2

families and developmental disabilities	1	1
functional neuroimaging	3	1
gender issues	1	1
HIV and families	1	1
HIV prevention	1	3
male parenting	1	1
mood disorders—children	1	1
multicultural issues	3	0
pediatric psychology	1	2
reading/dyslexia	1	4
treatment of anxiety disorders	1	1

Clinical opportunities

adjustment problems of childhood, adolescence, and adulthood
anxiety disorders
behavioral assessment
child abuse
chronic health conditions
clinical-community psychology
clinical neuropsychology and treatment
developmental disabilities
family violence
health psychology
:vention

individual, couples, family, and group therapy
inpatient therapy
multicultural assessment and therapy
neuropsychological assessment
personality assessment
personality disorders
psychopathology of childhood
psychosocial rehabilitation
psychotherapy supervision
violence prevention

No-weekends (handwritten)

University of Hartford (Psy.D.)

Graduate Institute of Professional Psychology
200 Bloomfield Ave.
West Hartford, CT 06105
phone#: (860) 768-4778
Director: John G. Mehm, Ph.D.
e-mail for admissions questions: viereck@hartford.edu
Web address: www.hartford.edu/gipp

1	2	3	4	5	6	7
Practice oriented		Equal emphasis				Research oriented

Percentage of faculty subscribing to each of the following orientations:

Psychodynamic/Psychoanalytic	40%
Applied behavioral analysis/Radical behavioral	0%
Family systems/Systems	40%
Existential/Phenomenological/Humanistic	15%
Cognitive/Cognitive-behavioral	60%

Courses required for incoming students prior to enrolling:

abnormal, social, personality, developmental, cognitive, physiological, research methods/experimental psychology, statistics

Recommended but not mandatory courses:
Psychology major

GRE mean
Verbal 535   Quantitative 630
Psychology Subject Test 645
Analytical Writing 4.5

Number of applications/admission offers/incoming students in 2009
229 applied/54 admission offers/24 incoming

% of students receiving:
Full tuition waiver only: 0%
Assistantship/fellowship only: 58%
Both full tuition waiver & assistantship/fellowship: 0%

Approximate percentage of incoming students with a B.A./B.S. only: 70%   Master's: 30%

Approximate percentage of students who are
Women: 84%   Ethnic Minority: 18%   International: 5%

Average years to complete the doctoral program (including internship): 5.2 years

Personal interview
Required in person (unless international students)

Attrition rate in past 7 years: 3%

Percentage of students applying for internship last year accepted into APPIC or APA internships: 88%

Formal tracks/concentrations: child & adolescent proficiency

Research areas	# Faculty	# Grants
child/adolescent	2	2
community treatment	2	0
intimate partner violence	1	1
clinical supervision/mentoring	1	0
psychological assessment	1	0
applied behavior analysis	1	0
substance abuse	1	0
stigma of mental illness	1	1

Clinical opportunities

acute psychiatry/mental health
anxiety disorders
depression
hospital-based psychology departments
chronic mental illness
children, adolescents, and families

forensics
community mental health centers
counseling centers
residential schools

Harvard University

Department of Psychology
33 Kirkland Street
Cambridge, MA 02138
phone#: (617) 495-3810
e-mail:cir@wjh.harvard.edu
Web address: www.isites.harvard.edu/
icb/icb.do?keyword=k3007&pageid=icb.
page19735&pageContentId=icb.
pagecontent44048&view=view.do&viewParam_
name=clinical.html#a_icb_pagecontent44048

1	2	3	4	5	6	7
Practice oriented		Equal emphasis				Research oriented

Percentage of faculty subscribing to each of the following orientations:

Psychodynamic/Psychoanalytic	0%
Applied behavioral analysis/Radical behavioral	0%
Family systems/Systems	0%
Existential/Phenomenological/Humanistic	0%
Cognitive/Cognitive behavioral	100%

Courses required for incoming students to have completed prior to enrolling:
None required.

Recommended but not mandatory courses:
Abnormal Psychology
Developmental Psychology
Cognitive Neuroscience
Introductory Neuroscience
Statistics
Other science and mathematics courses

GRE mean
Verbal 688   Quantitative 748
Analytical Writing 5.13
Psychology Advanced Test 763

GPA mean
Overall GPA 3.73

Number of applications/admission offers/incoming students in 2009
178 applied/4 admission offers

% students receiving:
Full tuition waiver only: 0%
Assistantship/fellowship only: 0%
Both full tuition waiver & assistantship/fellowship 100%

Approximate percentage of incoming students with a BA/BS only: 100%   **Master's** 0%

Approximate percentage of students who are Women: 78% **Ethnic Minority:** 13% **International:** 9%

Average years to complete the doctoral program (including internship): 7 years

Personal interview
Preferred in person but telephone acceptable

Attrition rate in past 7 years: 3%

Percentage of students applying for internship last year accepted in to APPIC or APA internships: 100%

Formal tracks/concentrations: Clinical Psychology (Clinical Science emphasis)

Research areas	# Faculty	# Grants
anxiety disorders	3	0
bipolar disorder	1	1
child & adolescent psychotherapy	1	4
child psychopathology (1)	2	1
child psychopathology (2)	1	3
cultural variations in child	1	0
development & dysfunction depression	3	4
personality disorders	1	0
schizophrenia/psychosis	1	1
substance abuse	1	0
suicide/self-injury	2	4

Clinical opportunities
depression clinic
bipolar clinic
OCD clinic & institute
asian clinic
victims of violence clinic
adolescent inpatient and assessment unit
adult developmental disabilities clinic
geriatric clinic
behavioral health partial program
eating disorders clinic
cognitive behavior therapy program
dialectical behavior therapy program
behavioral neurology unit
center for anxiety and related disorders
judge baker children's center
prevention and recovery in early psychosis (PREP) program

University of Hawaii at Manoa (Ph.D.)

Clinical Studies Program
Department of Psychology
2430 Campus Road
Honolulu, HI 96822
phone#: (808) 956-8414
e-mail: gradpsy@hawaii.edu
Web address: www.psychology.hawaii.edu/pages/graduate_programs/clinical.html

1	2	3	4	5	6	7
Practice oriented			Equal emphasis			Research oriented

Percentage of faculty subscribing to each of the following orientations:

Psychodynamic/Psychoanalytic	0%
Behavioral	50%
Family systems/Systems	15%
Existential/Phenomenological/Humanistic	0%
Cognitive/Cognitive-behavioral	85%

Courses required for incoming students prior to enrolling:
Psychology major or approximately 5–10 selected psychology courses

Recommended but not mandatory courses: None

GRE mean
Verbal 610   Quantitative 700
Psychology Subject Test not required
Analytical Writing 5.0

GPA mean
Overall GPA 3.5

Number of applications/admission offers/incoming students in 2008
125 applied/10 admission offers/10 incoming

% of students receiving:
Full tuition waiver only: 0%
Assistantship/fellowship only: 0%
Both full tuition waiver & assistantship/fellowship: 90%

Approximate percentage of incoming students with a B.A./B.S. only: 60%   **Master's:** 40%

Approximate percentage of students who are Women: 90% **Ethnic Minority:** 30% **International:** 30%

Average years to complete the doctoral program (including internship): 8 years

Personal interview
Telephone required

Attrition rate in past 7 years: 11%

Percentage of students applying for internship last year accepted into APPIC or APA internships: 100%

Formal tracks/concentrations: none

Research areas	# Faculty	# Grants
anxiety	1	1
assessment	7	2
behavioral medicine	1	0
childhood clinical	3	4
cross-cultural	2	1
data-based case management	2	0
depression	2	0
eating disorders	2	1
ethnic minority	2	2
health care compliance	2	0
mental health systems	5	6
neurocognitive assessment	1	0
schizophrenia	5	1
substance use prevention	1	3
treatment outcome	4	4

Clinical opportunities

assessment	dual diagnoses
behavioral medicine	eating disorders
case and system consultation	neuropsychology
child clinical	rehabilitation psychology
cross-cultural	severely mentally ill
developmental disabilities	substance use prevention

Hofstra University (Ph.D.)

(clinical)
Department of Psychology
Hempstead, NY 11549
phone#: (516) 463-5662
e-mail: Psyjtc@hofstra.edu
Web address: www.hofstra.edu/Academics/Colleges/HCLAS/PSY/phdcp

1	2	3	4	5	6	7
Practice oriented		Equal emphasis				Research oriented

Percentage of faculty subscribing to each of the following orientations:

Psychodynamic/Psychoanalytic	2%
Applied behavioral analysis/Radical behavioral	45%
Family systems/Systems	3%
Existential/Phenomenological/Humanistic	0%
Cognitive/Cognitive-behavioral	50%

Courses required for incoming students to have completed prior to enrolling:
Statistics, research design, psychology lab

Recommended but not mandatory courses:
Psychopathology/Abnormal Psychology, History or Systems of Psychology, Physiological Psychology or Sensation/Perception Tests and Measurements

GRE mean
Verbal 583   Quantitative 681
Psychology Subject Test 669
Analytical Writing 5.0

GPA mean
Overall GPA 3.64

Number of applications/admission offers/incoming students in 2009
211 applied/24 admission offers/14 incoming

% of students receiving:
Full tuition waiver only: 21%
Assistantship/fellowship only: 79%
Both full tuition waiver & assistantship/fellowship: 0%

Approximate percentage of incoming students with a B.A./B.S.only: 75%   **Master's:** 25%

Approximate percentage of students who are Women: 70% **Ethnic Minority:** 20% **International:** 10%

Average years to complete the doctoral program (including internship): 5.5 years

Personal interview
Required in person

Attrition rate in past 7 years: 10.9%

Percentage of students applying for internship last year accepted into APPIC or APA internships: 78%

Formal tracks/concentrations/specializations: none

Research areas	# Faculty	# Grants
addictive behaviors (smoking, obesity, etc.)	3	1
anger disorders	2	0
attitudes and attitude change	1	0
behavior analysis	3	0
behavior modification (in industry, professional sports, depression, anxiety, social skills)	2	0
biofeedback	1	0
body image	2	0
communication of emotions	1	0
cross-cultural psychology	2	0
depression	1	0
family process/therapy	1	0
human error	1	0
infant/toddler development	1	0
normal and abnormal personalities	2	0
prevention of childhood disorders	2	0
psychotherapy for anger, guilt, fear, and anxiety	1	2
quantitative research methods	2	0
rational-emotive/behavior therapy for marital therapy	1	0
schizophrenia	2	1
self-report validity	1	0
sexual dysfunctions	1	0
verbal behavior	1	0
work attitudes and scholarly activities	1	0

Clinical opportunities

Professional services are offered to the community at the Hofstra University Psychological Evaluation and Research Clinic. Our specialty clinics include the Institute for the Study and Treatment of Anger and Aggression, The Phobia and Trauma Clinic, The Parent-Child Psychotherapy Services Clinic, The Anxiety & Depression Clinic and the Acceptance and Treatment Therapy Clinic. We place externs throughout the New York City metro area.

University of Houston (Ph.D.)

Department of Psychology
126 Heyne Building
Houston, TX 77204-5022
phone#: (713) 743-8500
e-mail: jvincent@uh.edu
Web address: www.Psychology.uh.edu/
GraduatePrograms/Clinical/

1	2	3	4	5	6	7
Practice oriented		Equal emphasis				Research oriented

Percentage of faculty subscribing to each of the following orientations:

Psychodynamic/Psychoanalytic	6%
Applied behavioral analysis/Radical behavioral	5%
Family systems/Systems	20%
Existential/Phenomenological/Humanistic	0%
Cognitive/Cognitive-behavioral	100%

Courses required for incoming students prior to enrolling: None

Recommended but not mandatory courses:

Statistics, history and systems, physiological psychology, abnormal, experimental, social, developmental, methods

GRE mean

Verbal 592   Quantitative 686   Analytical/Writing 664

GPA mean

Overall GPA 3.6

Number of applications/admission offers/incoming students in 2009

270 applied/21 admission offers/14 incoming

% of students receiving:

Full tuition waiver only: 0%
Assistantship/fellowship only: 10%
Both full tuition waiver & assistantship/fellowship: 100%

Approximate percentage of incoming students with a B.A./B.S. only: 85.8%   Master's: 14.2%

Approximate percentage of students who are

Women: 82.67%   Ethnic Minority: 16.7%
International: 3%

Average years to complete the doctoral program (including internship): 5.5 years

Personal interview : Preferred in person but telephone acceptable

Attrition rate in past 7 years: 1.2%

Percentage of students applying for internship last year accepted into APPIC or APA internships: 100%

Formal tracks/concentrations: clinical neuropsychology, adult behavior disorders, child-family

Research areas	# Faculty	# Grants
adult psychopathology	6	3
affective disorder/depression	2	2
anxiety disorder	3	3
child clinical	3	2
chronic mental illness	3	1
cross-cultural	3	2
family research/therapy	3	2
forensic psychology	2	1
marriage/couples	2	1
neuropsychology	4	4
parent–child interaction	2	1
schizophrenia/psychoses	2	1
social skills	4	3

Clinical opportunities

adolescent suicide	health psychology
Alzheimer's/dementia	interpersonal
anxiety disorders	psychotherapy
child custody evaluation	learning disabilities
child victimization	multicultural
clinical assessment	post traumatic stress
cognitive therapy	disorder
conduct disorder	rehabilitation
couples therapy	neuropsychology
domestic violence	schizophrenia/psychoses
family therapy	traumatic brain injury
forensic psychology	stroke

Howard University (Ph.D.)

Department of Psychology
525 Bryant Street, NW
Washington, DC 20059
phone#: (202) 806-6805
e-mail: dso@howard.edu
Web address: www.coas.howard.edu/psychology/clinical

1	2	3	4	5	6	7
Practice oriented		Equal emphasis				Research oriented

Percentage of faculty subscribing to each of the following orientations:

Psychodynamic/Psychoanalytic	20%
Applied behavioral analysis/Radical behavioral	0%
Family systems/Systems	20%
Existential/Phenomenological/Humanistic	20%
Cognitive/Cognitive-behavioral	40%

Courses required for incoming students to have completed prior to enrolling:

Psychology major, including the following: statistics, abnormal psychology, experimental psychology, developmental psychology

Recommended but not mandatory courses:

Psychological testing or statistics II

GRE mean
Verbal 520   Quantitative 667
Analytical Writing not reported

GPA mean
3.82

Number of applications/admission offers/incoming students in 2009
140 applied/5 admission offers/3 incoming

% of students receiving:
Full tuition waiver only: 0%
Assistantship/fellowship only: 0%
Both full tuition waiver & assistantship/fellowship: 67%

Approximate percentage of incoming students with a B.A./B.S. only: 67%   **Master's:** 33%

Approximate percentage of students who are Women: 71% **Ethnic Minority:** 100% **International:** 6%

Average years to complete the doctoral program (including internship): 6.5 years

Personal interview
required in person

Attrition rate in past 7 years: 8%

Percentage of students applying for internship last year accepted into APPIC or APA internships: 86%

Formal tracks/concentrations: adult, child

Research areas	# Faculty	# Grants
adolescent development	2	0
behavioral medicine	3	2
clinical training	4	2
family therapy	2	0
minority mental health	4	2
neuropsychology	2	1
psychophysiology	1	1
suicide prevention	1	0

Clinical opportunities

anxiety disorders	family
behavioral medicine	minority
child violence prevention	neuropsychology
community psychology,	schizophrenia
program development	victim/battering/trauma
crisis intervention	various health psychology
substance use disorders	& primary care settings

Idaho State University (Ph.D.)

Psychology Department
Box 8112
Idaho State University
Pocatello ID 83209
phone#: (208) 282-2462
e-mail: robemark@isu.edu
Web address: www.isu.edu/psych/clinicalprogram
.shtml

1	2	3	4	5	6	7
Practice oriented		Equal emphasis			Research oriented	

Percentage of faculty subscribing to each of the following orientations:

Psychodynamic/Psychoanalytic	15%
Applied behavioral analysis/Radical behavioral	33%
Family systems/Systems	33%
Existential/Phenomenological/Humanistic	100%
Cognitive/Cognitive-behavioral	100%

Courses required for incoming students to have completed prior to enrolling:
Psychology major or its equivalent. The stronger the major, the better, i.e., methodology courses plus undergraduate courses in the major areas: history and systems, developmental, cognitive/learning, social, physiological, and personality. The methodology courses are mandatory.

Recommended but not mandatory courses: None

GRE mean
Verbal 579   Quantitative 691
Analytical Writing 5.1
Psychology Subject Test 668

GPA mean
Overall GPA 3.85

Number of applications/admission offers/incoming students in 2009
46 applied/8 admission offers/6 incoming

% of students 2009-10 receiving:
Full tuition waiver only: 0%
Assistantship/fellowship only: 58% (all of whom receive non-resident tuition waivers)
Both full tuition waiver & assistantship/fellowship: 38%

Approximate percentage of incoming students with a B.A./B.S. only: 79%   **Master's:** 21%

Approximate percentage of students who are Women: 58%   **Ethnic Minority:** 8% **International:** 13%

Average years to complete the doctoral program (including internship): 6.1 years

Personal interview
Preferred in person, but telephone acceptable

Attrition rate in past 7 years: 7%

Percentage of students applying for internship last year accepted into APPIC or APA internships: 100%

Formal tracks/concentrations: none

Research areas	# Faculty	# Grants
addictions	3	1
behavioral pharmacology	1	1
developmental psychopathology	1	1
parent–child interaction therapy	1	0
trauma	2	1
working memory	1	0
person perception	1	1
developmental psychobiology	1	2
sexual decision-making	2	2
goal setting	1	1

Clinical opportunities

cognitive behavioral treatments	neuropsychological
for anxiety & trauma	evaluations

family systems therapy
parent–child interaction therapy
relapse prevention group therapy (addictions)

sexual dysfunction
couples therapy

University of Illinois at Chicago (Ph.D.)

Department of Psychology
1007 West Harrison
Chicago, IL 60680
phone#: (312) 996-3036
e-mail: robinm@uic.edu
Web address: http://portal.psch.uic.edu/Clinical/Default.aspx

1	2	3	4	5	6	7
Practice oriented		Equal emphasis			Research oriented	

Percentage of faculty subscribing to each of the following orientations:

Psychodynamic/Psychoanalytic	0%
Applied behavioral analysis/Radical behavioral	5%
Family systems/Systems	15%
Existential/Phenomenological/Humanistic	20%
Cognitive/Cognitive-behavioral	80%
Community psychology	10%

Courses required for incoming students prior to enrolling: None

Recommended but not mandatory courses:

Statistics, science courses, independent research (for psychology majors), other research experience

GRE mean

Verbal + Quantitative = 1309
Analytical Writing not reported

GPA mean

Junior/Senior GPA 3.77

Number of applications/admission offers/incoming students in 2009

241 applied/14 admission offers/10 incoming

% of students receiving:

Full tuition waiver only: 0%
Assistantship/fellowship only: 0%
Both full tuition waiver & assistantship/fellowship: 100%

Approximate percentage of incoming students with a B.A./B.S. only: 50% Master's: 50%

Approximate percentage of students who are Women: 70.3% Ethnic Minority: 0.8% International: 2.7%

Average years to complete the doctoral program (including internship): 8 years

Personal interview

Preferred in person but telephone acceptable

Attrition rate in past 7 years: 15%

Percentage of students applying for internship last year accepted into APPIC or APA internships: 25%

Formal tracks/concentrations: none

Research areas	# Faculty	# Grants
AIDS	2	2
alcohol relapse, models of relapse	1	1
anxiety	3	1
cognitive deficits in schizophrenia	1	4
community psychology	1	1
depression	2	0
eating disorders and obesity	1	0
health behavior change	4	1
neurobehavioral and genetic aspects of autism	1	4
tobacco use, etiology, prevention and cessation	3	5

Clinical opportunities

adjustment reactions
anxiety and depression
health-related behaviors
HIV prevention

preventive intervention with youth
smoking cessation
weight reduction

University of Illinois at Urbana–Champaign (Ph.D.)

Department of Psychology
Psychology Building
603 East Daniel Street
Champaign, IL 61820
phone#: (217) 333-2169
e-mail: gradstdy@s.psych.uiuc.edu
Web address: www.psychology.illinois.edu/about/divisions/clinicalcommunity/

1	2	3	4	5	6	7
Practice oriented		Equal emphasis			Research oriented	

Percentage of faculty subscribing to each of the following orientations:

Psychodynamic	100%
Applied behavioral analysis/Radical behavioral	0%
Family systems/Systems	100%
Existential/Phenomenological/Humanistic	0%
Cognitive/Cognitive-behavioral	100%

Courses required for incoming students to have completed prior to enrolling: None

Recommended but not mandatory courses:

Psychology major, undergraduate statistics

GRE mean

Verbal 603   Quantitative 671
Psychology Subject Test 688
Analytical Writing 4.8

GPA mean

Overall GPA 3.83

Number of applications/admission offers/incoming students in 2009

159 applied/12 admission offers/4 incoming

% of students receiving:

Full tuition waiver only: 0%

Assistantship/fellowship only: 0%
Both full tuition waiver & assistantship/fellowship: 100%

Approximate percentage of incoming students with a B.A./B.S. only: 100% **Master's:** 25%

Approximate percentage of students who are Women: 76% **Ethnic Minority:** 31% **International:** 12%

Average years to complete the doctoral program (including internship): 7 years

Personal interview
Telephone required

Attrition rate in past 7 years: 13%

Percentage of students applying for internship last year accepted into APPIC or APA internships: 80%

Formal tracks/concentrations: none

Research areas	# Faculty	# Grants
behavior genetics	2	2
clinical neuropsychology	2	4
clinical psychophysiology	3	8
community psychology	5	4
research/program evaluation	4	3
cultural-community mental health	2	2
electrophysiological and hemodynamic neuroimaging	3	8
intervention research	2	2
emotion and psychopathology	5	10
minority mental health	5	5
indigenous mental health/wellness	2	2
psychotherapy/systems	1	1
schizophrenia	2	5
suicide	1	1
women's issues	3	2

Clinical opportunities

anxiety
child assessment
change assessment
community & economic development
community-based organizations
consultation
community intervention
culturally-competent therapy and consultation
depression
diverse populations
family interventions
forensic evaluations
group therapy
human/health care systems
individual adult psychotherapy
inpatient assessment
minority mental health
neighborhood/community organization
neuropsychological assessment, children, adolescents, adults
school consultation
school and educational settings and policy

Illinois Institute of Technology (Ph.D.)

Department of Psychology
IIT Center, LS252
Chicago, IL 60616
phone#: (312) 567-3500, (312) 567-3506
e-mail: sher@iit.edu
Web address: www.iit.edu/psych/admission/graduate/clinical/index.shtml

1	2	3	4	5	6	7
Practice oriented			Equal emphasis			Research oriented

Percentage of faculty subscribing to each of the following orientations:

Psychodynamic/Psychoanalytic	0%
Applied behavioral analysis/Radical behavioral	0%
Family systems/Systems	10%
Existential/Phenomenological/Humanistic	0%
Cognitive/Cognitive-behavioral	90%

Courses required for incoming students to have completed prior to enrolling:
18 credits in psychology including experimental and statistics

Recommended but not mandatory courses: None

GRE mean
Verbal 568   Quantitative 600
Analytical Writing Data not available

GPA mean 3.23

Number of applications/admission offers/incoming students in 2009
123 applied/24 admission offers/13 incoming

% of students receiving:
Full tuition waiver only: 0%
Assistantship/fellowship only: 100%
Both full tuition waiver & assistantship/fellowship: 23%

Approximate percentage of incoming students with a B.A./B.S. only: 77% **Master's:** 23%

Approximate percentage of first-year students who are Women: 70% **Ethnic Minority:** 8% **International:** 8%

Average years to complete the doctoral program (including internship): 5.5 years

Personal interview
Preferred in person but telephone acceptable

Attrition rate in past 7 years: 5%

Percentage of students applying for internship last year accepted into APPIC or APA internships: 88%

Formal tracks/concentrations: general clinical, combined rehab/clinical

Research areas	# Faculty	# Grants
ADHD	1	0
affective disorders	1	1
child behavior	2	1
family	1	0
health	1	1
marital	1	1
pediatric	2	1
severe mental illness	2	1
social support	1	0
rehabilitation	2	1
acceptance and commitment therapy	1	0

Clinical opportunities

affective disorders
child
family
health/behavioral medicine
marital/couples
minority/cross-cultural
neuropsychology
pain
severe mental illness

Immaculata University (Psy.D.)

Department of Graduate Psychology
Immaculata, PA 19345-0500
phone#: (610) 647-4400, ext. 3503
e-mail: jyalof@immaculata.edu
Web address: www.immaculata.edu/academics/
departments/graduatepsychology/psydclinicalpsych

1	2	3	4	5	6	7
Practice oriented		Equal emphasis				Research oriented

Percentage of faculty subscribing to each of the following orientations:

Psychodynamic/Psychoanalytic	20%
Applied behavioral analysis/Radical behavioral	0%
Family systems/Systems	0%
Existential/Phenomenological/Humanistic	20%
Cognitive/Cognitive-behavioral	30%
Integrative/Transtheoretical	30%

Courses required for incoming students to have completed prior to enrolling:

Currently there are two tracks 1) MA or equivalent post baccalaureate, or 2) bachelor's degree

Recommended but not mandatory courses: None

GRE mean
A calculated mean is not used.

GPA mean
A calculated mean is not used.

GPA mean
MA minimum of 3.0; BA minimum of 3.3

Number of applications/admission offers/incoming students in 2009
120/applied/57 admission offers/34 incoming

% of students receiving:
Full tuition waiver only: 0%
Assistantship/fellowship only: 0%
Both full tuition waiver & assistantship/fellowship: 0%

Approximate percentage of incoming students with a B.A./B.S. only: 38% Master's: 62%

Approximate percentage of students who are
Women: 88% Ethnic Minority: 9% (among new PsyD admits) International: not reported

Average years to complete the doctoral program (including internship): 6 years

Personal interview
Required

Attrition rate in past 7 years: 11%

Percentage of students applying for internship last year accepted into APPIC or APA internships: 25% APA; 75% on APPIC for 08-09

Formal tracks/concentrations: Advanced Proficiency Certificates: Psychological Testing, Psychodynamic, Neuropsychology, Integrative Therapy Human and Cultural Diversity, Drug and Alcohol

Research areas	# Faculty	# Grants
child, adolescent	6	0
development	10	0
existential-humanistic	2	
diversity	4	NO
psychotherapy process	5	
family therapy	2	0
positive psychology	3	0
neuropsychology	3	0
personality assessment	4	0
school psychology	2	0
geriatric	1	0
ethics	2	0

Clinical opportunities
—

Indiana State University (Psy.D.)

Department of Psychology
Root Hall
Terre Haute, IN 47809
phone#: (812) 237-4314
e-mail: Cari.Riggs@indstate.edu
Web address: www.indstate.edu/psychology/psydprog.htm

1	2	3	4	5	6	7
Practice oriented		Equal emphasis				Research oriented

Percentage of faculty subscribing to each of the following orientations:

Psychodynamic/Psychoanalytic	15%
Applied behavioral analysis/Radical behavioral	0%
Family systems/Systems	15%
Existential/Phenomenological/Humanistic	5%
Cognitive/Cognitive-behavioral	70%

Courses required for incoming students prior to enrolling:
Abnormal psychology, personality, experimental psychology, statistics, learning or cognition (24 credits in undergraduate psychology)

Recommended but not mandatory courses:
Physiological psychology

GRE mean
Verbal + Quantitative 1222

GPA mean
3.77

Number of applications/admission offers/incoming students in 2009
155 applied/9 admission offers/9 incoming

% of students receiving:
Full tuition waiver only: 0%
Assistantship/fellowship only: 0%
Both full tuition waiver & assistantship/fellowship: 100%

Approximate percentage of incoming students with a B.A./B.S. only: 89% Master's: 11%

Approximate percentage of students who are
Women: 78% Ethnic Minority: 0% International: 0%

Average years to complete the doctoral program (including internship): 5.5 years

Personal interview
Preferred in person but telephone acceptable

Attrition rate in past 7 years: 11.6%

Percentage of students applying for internship last year accepted into APPIC or APA internships: 88%

Formal tracks/concentrations: Generalist clinical program with opportunities to emphasize child, health, forensics

Research areas	# Faculty	# Grants
adult psychopathology	2	0
affective disorders/depression	2	0
assessment	2	0
behavioral medicine	2	1
child clinical psychopathology	1	0
clinical judgment	1	0
eating disorders	1	1
friendship/relationships/intimacy	1	0
gender roles	2	0
personality disorders	1	0
professional training	1	0
stress and coping	2	0
substance abuse	1	1
women's studies	2	0

Clinical opportunities

ADHD assessment/treatment   forensic psychology
behavioral medicine   rural psychology

Indiana University—Bloomington (Ph.D.)

Department of Psychological and Brain Sciences
1101 E. 10th Street
Bloomington, IN 47405
phone#: (812) 855-2311
e-mail: shiricha@indiana.edu
Web address: http://psych.indiana.edu/graduate/courses/clinical.asp

1	2	3	4	5	6	7
Practice oriented		Equal emphasis			Research oriented	

Percentage of faculty subscribing to each of the following orientations:

Psychodynamic/Psychoanalytic	0%
Applied behavioral analysis/Radical behavioral	0%
Family systems/Systems	100%
Existential/Phenomenological/Humanistic	0%
Cognitive/Cognitive-behavioral	100%

Note: Our faculty doesn't really have particular "orientations" ... empirical science" commitment.

... ired for incoming students to have ... or to enrolling:
Psychology major

Recommended but not mandatory courses:
Basic sciences, math

GRE mean
Verbal: 606   Quantitative: 673

GPA mean
Overall GPA: 3.87

Number of applications/admission offers/incoming students in 2009
84 applied/6 admission offers/3 incoming

% of students receiving:
Full tuition waiver only: 0%
Assistantship/fellowship only: 0%
Both full tuition waiver & assistantship/fellowship: 100%

Approximate percentage of incoming students with a B.A./B.S. only: 100%   **Master's:** 0%

Approximate percentage of students who are Women: 69%   **Ethnic Minority:** 38%   **International:** 7%

Average years to complete the doctoral program (including internship): 6 years

Personal interview
Preferred in person but telephone acceptable

Attrition rate in past 7 years: 10%

Percentage of students applying for internship last year accepted into APPIC or APA internships: 83%

Formal tracks/concentrations: none

Research areas	# Faculty	# Grants
antisocial behavior	3	2
behavioral genetics	3	4
childhood/temperament/family	1	2
developmental psychopathology	4	4
eating disorders	1	0
health psychology	2	2
internalizing disorders	2	1
marital violence	1	1
mathematical models of causality	2	1
schizophrenia	2	4
sexuality and reproduction	1	3
social information processing and social interaction	3	1
stress	1	1
substance abuse	4	4

Clinical opportunities

anxiety disorders
assessment of health-related family adjustment problems
child and family therapy
depression
marital violence/marital therapy
neuropsychology

obsessive–compulsive disorder
schizophrenia
school/Head Start consultation
health psychology
smoking cessation

Indiana University of Pennsylvania (Psy.D.)

Department of Psychology
Clinical Psychology Program
201 Uhler Hall
Indiana, PA 15705-1068
phone#: (724) 357-4519
e-mail: goodwin@iup.edu
Web address: www.iup.edu/psychology/psyd/

1	2	3	4	5	6	7
Practice oriented			Equal emphasis			Research oriented

Percentage of faculty subscribing to each of the following orientations:

Psychodynamic/Psychoanalytic	10%
Applied behavioral analysis/Radical behavioral	10%
Family systems/Systems	20%
Existential/Phenomenological/Humanistic	20%
Cognitive/Cognitive-behavioral	40%

Courses required for incoming students to have completed prior to enrolling:
Personality, statistics or methods, abnormal psychology, learning, social psychology

Recommended but not mandatory courses:
6 credits in other areas of psychology

GRE mean
Verbal 530   Quantitative 610
Psychology Subject Test 590

GPA mean
Overall GPA 3.5   Psychology GPA 3.6
Junior/Senior GPA 3.0

Number of applications/admission offers/incoming students in 2009
110 applied/39 admission offers/9 incoming

% of students receiving:
Full tuition waiver only: 0%
Assistantship/fellowship only: 0%
Both full tuition waiver & assistantship/fellowship: 100%
(partial-to-full tuition and stipend)

Approximate percentage of incoming students with a B.A./B.S. only: 78%   Master's: 22%

Approximate percentage of students who are
Women: 89%   Ethnic Minority: 11%   International: 0%

Average years to complete the doctoral program (including internship): 5 years

Personal interview
Required in person

Attrition rate in past 7 years: 10%

Percentage of students applying for internship last year accepted into APPIC or APA internships: 50%

Formal tracks/concentrations: child and behavioral medicine

Research areas	# Faculty	# Grants
behavioral medicine	2	0
clinical judgment	1	0
death and dying	1	0
ethical issues	2	0
family therapy	1	0
gender roles	1	0
minority mental health	3	0
parent–child	4	1
prevention	1	0
professional issues	5	1
psychopathology	3	0
women's studies	2	0
violence prevention	1	0
youth psychopathology	1	0

Clinical opportunities
assessment	intake interviews
behavioral medicine	stress and habit disorders
child and family therapy	

Indiana University–Purdue University Indianapolis (Ph.D.)
Clinical Ph.D. Program
402 North Blackford Street, LD124
Indianapolis, IN 46202-3275
phone#: (317) 274-6945
e-mail: gradpsy@IUPUI.edu
Web address: http://www.psych.iupui.edu/
ClinicalPsychology/Overview/

1	2	3	4	5	6	7
Practice oriented			Equal emphasis			Research oriented

Percentage of faculty subscribing to each of the following orientations:

Psychodynamic/Psychoanalytic	0%
Applied behavioral analysis/Radical behavioral	6%
Family systems/Systems	0%
Existential/Phenomenological/Humanistic	6%
Cognitive/Cognitive-behavioral	88%

Courses required for incoming students to have completed prior to enrolling:
Tests and measurements, statistics, physiology, abnormal psychology

Recommended but not mandatory courses: None

GRE mean
Verbal 610   Quantitative 683
Analytical Writing 4.75

GPA mean
Overall GPA greater than 3.67

Number of applications/admission offers/incoming students in 2009
53 applied/7 admission offers/4 incoming

% of students receiving:
Full tuition waiver only: 0%
Assistantship/fellowship only: 0%
Both full tuition waiver & assistantship/fellowship: 100%

Approximate percentage of incoming students with a B.A./B.S. only: 75%   Master's: 25%

Approximate percentage of students who are
Women: 100%   Ethnic Minority: 50%
International: 25%

Average years to complete the doctoral program (including internship): 6 years

Personal interview
Required in person

197

Attrition rate in past 7 years: 4%

Percentage of students applying for internship last year accepted into APPIC or APA internships: 80%

Formal tracks/concentrations: none

Research areas	# Faculty	# Grants
health psychology	6	1
severe mental illness	2	3

Clinical opportunities

adaptive educational services (students with disabilities)
adult behavioral medicine (community cancer care)
crisis intervention unit (Wishard) hospice
pediatric behavioral medicine
severe mental illness
women's prison—female offenders with psychiatric and medical problems
health psychology

University of Indianapolis (Psy.D.)

School of Psychological Sciences
1400 East Hanna Avenue
Good Hall Room 109
Indianapolis, IN 46227-3697
phone#: (317) 788-3353
e-mail: psych@uindy.edu
Web address: psych.uindy.edu/doctoral.php

1	2	3	4	5	6	7

Practice oriented   Equal emphasis   Research oriented

Percentage of faculty subscribing to each of the following orientations:

Psychodynamic/Psychoanalytic	15%
Applied behavioral analysis/Radical behavioral	15%
Family systems/Systems	15%
Existential/Phenomenological/Humanistic	15%
Cognitive/Cognitive-behavioral	40%

Courses required for incoming students prior to enrolling:
18 credit hours of psychology

Recommended but not mandatory courses:
Abnormal, child/development, statistics, personality, brain and behavior

GRE mean
Verbal 550   Quantitative 646
Psychology Subject Test 657
Analytical Writing 4.7

GPA mean
Overall GPA 3.64

Number of applications/admission offers/incoming students in 2009
208 applied/49 admission offers/25 incoming

% of students receiving:
Full tuition waiver only: 4%
Assistantship/fellowship only: 20%
Both full tuition waiver & assistantship/fellowship: 0%

Approximate percentage of incoming students with a B.A./B.S. only: 60%   **Master's:** 40%

Approximate percentage of students who are Women: 88%   **Ethnic Minority:** 8%   **International:** 5%

Average years to complete the doctoral program (including internship): 5 years

Personal interview
Preferred in person but telephone acceptable

Attrition rate in past 7 years: 4%

Percentage of students applying for internship last year accepted into APPIC or APA internships: 91%

Formal tracks/concentrations: child and adolescent psychology, health psychology/behavioral medicine, adult psychopathology and psychotherapy

Research areas	# Faculty	# Grants
child/family psychology	2	1
clinical supervision	1	0
forensics	1	0
geropsychology	2	1
multicultural mental health	2	1
neuro/health/stress/rehab	3	1
parent–child relationships	1	1
positive psychology	1	0
posttraumatic stress disorders	1	0
psychology of women	2	0
schizophrenia/psychosis	2	1

Clinical opportunities

psychotherapy
assessment
behavioral medicine/health psychology
child psychology
neuropsychological assessment
medical centers
outpatient practices
community mental health centers
schools
shelters
hospitals (VA, psychiatric, general)
correctional facilities
university counseling centers
advanced traineeships (supervision, leadership)

University of Iowa (Ph.D.)

Department of Psychology
E11 Seashore Hall
Iowa City, IA 52242-1407
phone#: (319) 335-2436
e-mail: psych-clinical@uiowa.edu
Web address: www.psychology.uiowa.edu/research/clinical-psychology

1	2	3	4	5	6	7

Practice oriented   Equal emphasis   Research oriented

Percentage of faculty subscribing to each of the following orientations:

Psychodynamic/Psychoanalytic	0%
Applied behavioral analysis/Radical behavioral	10%
Family systems/Systems	10%
Existential/Phenomenological/Humanistic	10%
Cognitive/Cognitive-behavioral/Third wave	100%

Courses required for incoming students prior to enrolling: None

Recommended but not mandatory courses:
Undergraduate psychology major, statistics, abnormal, laboratory research, strong science background

GRE mean (accepted)
Verbal 613   Quantitative 692
Analytical Writing 5.1
Psychology Subject Test not required

GPA mean
Overall GPA 3.7

Number of applications/admission offers/incoming students in 2009
111 applied/11 admission offers/3 incoming

% of 2009 incoming students receiving:
Full tuition waiver only: 0%
Assistantship/fellowship and partial tuition waiver: 33%
Assistantship/fellowship and full tuition waiver: 67%

Approximate percentage of 2009 incoming students with a B.A./B.S. only: 100%   **Master's:** 0%

Approximate percentage of all current students who are: Women: 75%   **Ethnic Minority:** 18%
International: 12%

Average years to complete the doctoral program (including internship): 7.3 years (7.0 without 1 19-year outlier)

Personal interview
Preferred in person but telephone acceptable

Attrition rate in past 7 years: 9.7%

Percentage of students applying for internship last year accepted into APPIC or APA internships: 100%

Formal tracks/concentrations: adult psychopathology, clinical health, neuropsychology, personality

Research areas	# Faculty	# Grants
assessment	3	1
couples therapy	1	0
domestic violence/child abuse	2	1
depression	2	1
health psychology/beh'l medicine	2	3
personality disorders	1	1
quantitative models of psychopathology	2	0

Clinical opportunities
adult psychopathology
child abuse
child psychiatry/pediatrics
cognitive-behavioral therapy
couples therapy
custody assessment
depression
eating disorders
health psychology/behavioral medicine
learning disability assessment
pre-/postpartum psychopathology
neuropsychology

Jackson State University (Ph.D.)
Department of Psychology
Clinical Psychology Ph.D. Program

P.O. Box 17550
Jackson, MS 39217-0350
phone#: (601) 979-2371
e-mail: bryman.e.williams@jsums.edu
Web address: http://sites.jsums.edu/psychology/graduate/

1	2	3	4	5	6	7
Practice oriented		Equal emphasis				Research oriented

Percentage of faculty subscribing to each of the following orientations:
Psychodynamic/Psychoanalytic	10%
Applied behavioral analysis/Radical behavioral	0%
Family systems/Systems	0%
Existential/Phenomenological/Humanistic	0%
Cognitive/Cognitive-behavioral	90%

Courses required for incoming students to have completed prior to enrolling:
24 hours of previous coursework in psychology is required

Recommended but not mandatory courses:
Experimental, learning, statistics, physiological, abnormal

GRE mean
Verbal 496   Quantitative 560
Analytical Writing 4.0

GPA mean
Undergraduate GPA 3.42
Junior/Senior GPA 3.56
Master's GPA 3.86

Number of applications/admission offers/incoming students in 2009
48 applied/6 admission offers/6 incoming

% of students receiving:
Full tuition waiver only: 5%
Assistantship/fellowship only: 80%
Both full tuition waiver & assistantship/fellowship: 5%

Approximate percentage of incoming students with a B.A./B.S. only: 84%   **Master's:** 16%

Approximate percentage of students who are Women: 90%   **Ethnic Minority:** 64%
International: Not reported

Average years to complete the doctoral program (including internship): 6.5 years

Personal interview
Preferred in person but telephone acceptable

Attrition rate in past 7 years: 16.4%

Percentage of students applying for internship last year accepted into APPIC or APA internships: 86%

Formal tracks/concentrations: none

Research areas	# Faculty	# Grants
alcohol/substance abuse	2	0
childhood obesity	1	0
chronic pain/headache	3	1
depression	1	0
health care disparities	3	0
HIV/AIDS	3	3

posttraumatic stress disorder	1	0
psychological assessment	6	0
stigma	2	0

Clinical opportunities

behavioral medicine	inpatient psychiatric
campus counseling center	neuropsychiatric rehab
forensic	outpatient pediatric
inpatient pediatric	outpatient psychiatric

John F. Kennedy University (Psy.D.)

Graduate School of Professional Psychology
100 Ellinwood Way, Pleasant Hill, CA 94523
phone#: 800-696-5358
e-mail: proginfo@jfku.edu
Web address: www.jfku.edu/Programs-and-Courses/
College-of-Graduate-Professional-Studies/Department-
of-Clinical-Psychology/Programs/Doctor-of-Psychology-
PsyD-Program.html

1	2	**3**	4	5	6	7
Practice oriented		Equal emphasis				Research oriented

Percentage of faculty subscribing to each of the following orientations:

Psychodynamic/Psychoanalytic	35%
Applied behavioral analysis/Radical behavioral	0%
Family systems/Systems	25%
Existential/Phenomenological/Humanistic	10%
Cognitive/Cognitive-behavioral	30%
Cultural Diversity Focus	100%

Courses required for incoming students to have completed prior to enrolling:

Theories of personality, statistics, and a diversity related course

Recommended but not mandatory courses: None

GRE mean
Not reported

GPA mean
Overall GPA 3.25

Number of applications/admission offers/incoming students in 2009
146 applied/84 admission offers/30 incoming

% of students receiving:
Full tuition waiver only: 0%
Assistantship/fellowship only: 0%
Both full tuition waiver & assistantship/fellowship: 0%

Approximate percentage of incoming students with a B.A./B.S. only: 83%   Master's: 17%

Approximate percentage of students who are Women: 83%   Ethnic Minority: 40%   International: 3%

Average years to complete the doctoral program (including internship): 5 years

Personal interview
Required

Attrition rate in past 7 years: 6%

Percentage of students applying for internship last year accepted into APPIC or APA internships: 42%
(58% were accepted into CAPIC internships)

Formal tracks/concentrations: none

Research areas	# Faculty	# Grants
multiculturalism	10	0
LGBT policy	3	0
psychological games	1	0
psychology of immigration	1	0
disability psychology	1	0
community psychology	2	0
neuro/health	1	0
self care	1	0

Clinical opportunities
We place our students in dozens of community clinics, hospitals, etc.

University of Kansas (Ph.D.)

Clinical Child Psychology Program
2010 Dole Human Development Center
University of Kansas
1000 Sunnyside Avenue
Lawrence, KS 66045
Phone #: (785) 864-4226
e-mail: ccpp@ku.edu
Web address: www.ku.edu/~clchild

1	2	3	4	**5**	6	7
Practice oriented		Equal emphasis				Research oriented

Percentage of faculty subscribing to each of the following orientations:

Psychodynamic/Psychoanalytic	5%
Applied behavioral analysis/Radical behavioral	5%
Family systems/Systems	25%
Existential/Phenomenological/Humanistic	5%
Cognitive/Cognitive-behavioral	60%

Courses required for incoming students prior to enrolling:
Major in psychology or a minimum of 15–18 hours including: research methods, statistics, developmental/child psychology, developmental psychopathology (abnormal child psychology) or Psychology Subject Test

Recommended but not mandatory courses: None

GRE mean
Verbal 638   Quantitative 683
Analytical Writing Data not available

GPA mean
Overall GPA 3.68

Number of applications/admission offers/incoming students in 2009
107 applied/7 admission offers/4 incoming

% of students receiving:
Full tuition waiver only: 0%
Assistantship/fellowship only: 0%
Both full tuition waiver & assistantship/fellowship: 100%

Approximate percentage of incoming students with a B.A./B.S. only: 75%   **Master's:** 25%

Approximate percentage of students who are Women: 60%   **Ethnic Minority:** 39%   **International:** 0%

Average years to complete the doctoral program (including internship): 6.5 years

Personal interview
Preferred in person but telephone acceptable; by invitation

Attrition rate in past 7 years: 0%

Percentage of students applying for internship last year accepted into APPIC or APA internships: 100%

Formal tracks/concentrations: clinical child psychology, pediatrics

Research areas	# Faculty	# Grants
children with chronic illness	2	1
disasters and children	2	1
domestic violence	1	1
ethnicity/cultural issues	4	0
health promotion	2	1
school-based services for serious emotional disorders	2	1
stress & coping	2	1
anxiety in children	1	
violence and children (bullying)	2	1

Clinical opportunities

community mental health center
early in-home intervention
intensive services for serious emotional disorders
pediatric psychology
child abuse treatment agency

University of Kansas (Ph.D.)

Department of Psychology
Lawrence, KS 66045-7556
Phone #: (785) 864-4121
e-mail: rhiggins@ku.edu
Web address: www.psych.ku.edu/clinprog/

1	2	3	4	5	6	7
Practice oriented		Equal emphasis				Research oriented

Percentage of faculty subscribing to each of the following orientations:

Psychodynamic/Psychoanalytic	10%
Applied behavioral analysis/Radical behavioral	0%
Family systems/Systems	10%
Existential/Phenomenological/Humanistic	30%
Cognitive/Cognitive-behavioral	70%

Courses required for incoming students to have completed prior to enrolling:
Bachelor's degree in psychology or minimum of 15 credit hours of psychology coursework

Recommended but not mandatory courses:
Psychological research, statistics, research methods, abnormal psychology, personality, brain & behavior, social psychology, cognitive psychology

GRE mean
Verbal 608   Quantitative 703
Analytical Writing 4.91
Psychology Subject Test 735

GPA mean
Overall GPA 3.76

Number of applications/admission offers/incoming students in 2009
118 applied/10 admission offers/6 incoming

% of students receiving:
Full tuition waiver only: 0%
Assistantship/fellowship only: 0%
Both full tuition waiver & assistantship/fellowship: 100%

Approximate percentage of incoming students with a B.A./B.S. only: 83.3%   **Master's:** 16.4%

Approximate percentage of students who are Women: 84%   **Ethnic Minority:** 27%   **International:** 4%

Average years to complete the doctoral program (including internship): 6.5 years

Personal interview
Preferred in person but telephone acceptable

Attrition rate in past 7 years: 6%

Percentage of students applying for internship last year accepted into APPIC or APA internships: 87.5%

Formal tracks/concentrations: general adult, clinical health

Research areas	# Faculty	# Grants
stress & cardiovascular health	1	0
women's sexuality	1	0
outcome assessment in clinical settings	1	0
geriatric neuropsychology	1	1
anxiety disorders	2	1
multiple sclerosis	1	1
depression	3	1
adult psychopathology	1	0
health/positive emotion	1	0
health/pain management	1	1
marital & family assessment & treatment	1	0

Clinical opportunities

dialectical behavior therapy
behavioral medicine—
    pediatrics
behavioral medicine—
    pain/oncology
behavioral medicine—
    telemedicine
behavioral medicine—
    neuropsychology/
    rehabilitation
anxiety disorders
forensic evaluation
cognitive-behavior therapy
weight loss
smoking cessation
general adult

Kent State University (Ph.D.)

Department of Psychology
Kent, OH 44242
phone#: (330) 672-7670
e-mail: ndochert@kent.edu

Web address: www.kent.edu/cas/psychology/graduate/clinical/index.cfm

1	2	3	4	5	6	7
Practice oriented		Equal emphasis				Research oriented

Percentage of faculty subscribing to each of the following orientations:

Psychodynamic/Psychoanalytic	15%
Applied behavioral analysis/Radical behavioral	10%
Family systems/Systems	15%
Existential/Phenomenological/Humanistic	0%
Cognitive/Cognitive-behavioral	60%

Courses required for incoming students to have completed prior to enrolling: None

Recommended but not mandatory courses:
Prefer 15–20 hours in psychology, including 1–2 statistics courses and at least 1 psychology class that has a lab associated with it

GRE mean
Verbal 578   Quantitative 677
Analytical Writing not used

GPA mean
Overall GPA 3.7

Number of applications/admission offers/incoming students in 2009
250 applied/13 admission offers/10 incoming

% of students receiving:
Full tuition waiver only: 0%
Assistantship/fellowship only: 0%
Both full tuition waiver & assistantship/fellowship: 100%

Approximate percentage of incoming students with a B.A./B.S. only: 90%   Master's: 10%

Approximate percentage of students who are
Women: 80% Ethnic Minority: 20% International: 10%

Average years to complete the doctoral program (including internship): 6 years

Personal interview
Preferred in person but telephone acceptable

Attrition rate in past 7 years: 8%

Percentage of students applying for internship last year accepted into APPIC and APA internships: 100%

Formal tracks/concentrations: Adult Psychopathology; Assessment; Child/Family; Health; General

Research areas	# Faculty	# Grants
anxiety and depression	2	1
eating disorders	1	0
alcohol abuse	1	1
neuropsychology	1	2
cardiovascular health	1	1
child & family	2	1
child health	1	1
adolescent	1	1
MMPI	1	1
schizophrenia	1	1
stress and trauma	1	1

Clinical opportunities
adult psychotherapy	child/family therapy
eating disorders	marital therapy
anxiety disorders	adult and child assessment
severe mental illness	forensic assessment
health consultation	neuropsychological
palliative care	assessment

University of Kentucky (Ph.D.)
Department of Psychology
Kastle Hall
Lexington, KY 40506-0044
phone#: (859) 257-9640
e-mail: mkkell@email.uky.edu
Web address: www.as.uky.edu/academics/departments_programs/Psychology/Psychology/graduate/trainingprograms/clinical.pages/default.aspx

1	2	3	4	5	6	7
Practice oriented		Equal emphasis				Research oriented

Percentage of faculty subscribing to each of the following orientations:

Psychodynamic/Psychoanalytic	0%
Applied behavioral analysis/Radical behavioral	10%
Family systems/Systems	10%
Existential/Phenomenological/Humanistic	10%
Cognitive/Cognitive-behavioral	100%

Courses required for incoming students prior to enrolling:
Experimental methodology, statistics

Recommended but not mandatory courses:
Abnormal psychology, tests & measures, personality

GRE mean
Verbal 660   Quantitative 645
Analytical 5.0
Psychology Subject Test not reported

GPA mean
Overall GPA 3.86

Number of applications/admission offers/incoming students in 2009
277 applied/9 admission offers/6 incoming

% of students receiving:
Full tuition waiver only: 0%
Assistantship/fellowship only: 0%
Both full tuition waiver & assistantship/fellowship: 100%
First 4 years in program, in-state tuition is not always waived.

Approximate percentage of incoming students with a B.A./B.S. only: 100%   Master's: 0%

Approximate percentage of students who are
Women: 75% Ethnic Minority: 16% International: 0%

Average years to complete the doctoral program (including internship): 6.3 years

Personal interview
Strongly preferred in person but telephone acceptable

Attrition rate in past 7 years: 16%

Percentage of students applying for internship last year accepted into APPIC or APA internships: 88%

Formal tracks/concentrations: neuropsychology, behavioral medicine

Research areas	# Faculty	# Grants
adolescent development	3	3
adult psychopathology	4	1
assessment/diagnosis/classification	3	0
behavioral medicine	2	1
child clinical	2	1
developmental psychopathology	1	1
eating disorders	1	1
neuropsychology	2	1
pain	1	1
personality assessment	3	1
personality disorders	2	0
psychoneuroimmunology	1	1
psychophysiology	2	1
substance abuse	4	3
violence/agression	1	2

Clinical opportunities

assessment
behavioral medicine
child
chronic mental illness
cognitive-behavioral therapies
community mental health
dialectical behavior therapy
neuropsychology
orofacial pain

La Salle University (Psy.D.)

Department of Psychology
Philadelphia, PA 19141
phone#: (215) 951-1350
e-mail: PsyD@lasalle.edu
Web address: www.lasalle.edu/admiss/grad/doc_psych/index.php

1	2	3	**4**	5	6	7
Practice oriented			Equal emphasis			Research oriented

Percentage of faculty subscribing to each of the following orientations:

Psychodynamic/Psychoanalytic	0%
Applied behavioral analysis/Radical behavioral	10%
Family systems/Systems	10%
Existential/Phenomenological/Humanistic	0%
Cognitive/Cognitive-behavioral	80%

Courses required for incoming students to have completed prior to enrolling:
Developmental psychology, personality, statistics, research methods, tests and measurements

Recommended but not mandatory courses:
Abnormal psychology & physiological psychology

GRE mean
Verbal 560   Quantitative 620
Psychology Subject Test 650
Analytical Writing 5.0

GPA mean
Overall GPA 3.54

Number of applications/admission offers/incoming students in 2009
216 applied/96 admission offers/22 incoming

% of students receiving:
Full tuition waiver only: 0%
Assistantship/fellowship only: 27%
Both full tuition waiver & assistantship/fellowship: 0%

Approximate percentage of incoming students with a B.A./B.S. only: 70%   **Master's:** 30%

Approximate percentage of students who are Women: 68%   **Ethnic Minority:** 4%   **International:** 9%

Average years to complete the doctoral program (including internship): 5 years

Personal interview
Required in person

Attrition rate in past 7 years: 18%

Percentage of students applying for internship last year accepted into APPIC or APA internships: 89%

Formal tracks/concentrations: general clinical practice, clinical-child and family psychology, clinical health psychology, sport-performance psychology

Research areas	# Faculty	# Grants
mindfulness interventions	2	1
anxiety/PSTD	3	0
post partum depression	1	1
child/adolescent internalizing disorders	1	0
suicide prevention	1	0
medical adherence	1	0
health psychology	2	1
social problem solving	1	0

Clinical opportunities

anxiety disorders/PSTD
anger dyscontrol
sexual offenders
(intellectually disabled)
behavioral medicine—
  health promotion
mood disorders/post
  partum depression
child and adole...
  services
adult assessmen...

yes

University of La Verne (Psy.D.)

Program in Clinical-Community Psychology
1950 Third Street
La Verne, CA 91750
phone#: (909) 593-3511 ext. 4414
e-mail: jkernes@laverne.edu
Web address: sites.laverne.edu/psychology/psyd-program/

1	2	**3**	4	5	6	7
Practice oriented			Equal emphasis			Research oriented

Percentage of faculty subscribing to each of the following orientations:

Psychodynamic/Psychoanalytic	50%
Applied behavioral analysis/Radical behavioral	0%
Family systems/Systems	50%
Existential/Phenomenological/Humanistic	50%
Cognitive/Cognitive-behavioral	50%

Courses required for incoming students prior to enrolling:
Statistics, research methods, physiological psychology, and abnormal psychology. In addition, one course from: history & systems, social psychology, personality, human development, and clinical or community psychology.

Recommended but not mandatory courses: None

GRE mean
Verbal + Quantitative: not reported
Analytical Writing not reported
Psychology Subject Test not reported

GPA mean
Overall GPA 3.5

Number of applications/admission offers/incoming students in 2009
Not reported

% of students receiving:
Full tuition waiver only: 0%
Assistantship/fellowship only: 33%
Both full tuition waiver & assistantship/fellowship: 0%

Approximate percentage of incoming students with a B.A./B.S. only: 83%   **Master's:** 17%

Approximate percentage of students who are Women: 70% **Ethnic Minority:** 35%
International: 10%

Average years to complete the doctoral program (including internship): 5 years

Personal interview
Required for admission

Attrition rate in past 7 years: not reported

Percentage of students applying for internship last year accepted into APPIC or APA internships: not reported

Formal tracks/concentrations: forensic psychology, geropsychology, multicultural psychology

Research areas	# Faculty	# Grants
multiculturalism	7	2
clinical forensics	2	0
community psychology	12	0
psychotherapy services	3	0
gender issues & sexuality	2	0
values and moral development	2	0

Clinical opportunities

children and adolescents	families
clinical forensics	HIV/AIDS
college counseling center	substance abuse

Loma Linda University (Ph.D.)
Department of Psychology
Loma Linda, CA 92350
phone#: (909) 558-8577 (Central Office)
e-mail: dvermeersch@llu.edu
Web address: http://llu.edu/science-technology/grad/psychology/programs/phd.page

1	2	3	4	5	6	7
Practice oriented			Equal emphasis			Research oriented

Percentage of faculty subscribing to each of the following orientations:

Psychodynamic/Psychoanalytic	10%
Applied behavioral analysis/Radical behavioral	10%
Family systems/Systems	0%
Existential/Phenomenological/Humanistic	30%
Cognitive/Cognitive-behavioral	50%

Courses required for incoming students to have completed prior to enrolling:
Bachelors or masters degree in psychology or related field

Recommended but not mandatory courses:
computer literacy, math, research methods, sociology, biology, history and systems, learning, personality, statistics, social psychology, developmental psychology, psychobiology

GRE mean
Verbal 524   Quantitative 608   Analytical Writing 4.6

GPA mean
Those entering with a bachelors degree, 3.62;
Those entering with a masters degree, 3.71

Number of applications/admission offers/incoming students in 2009
38/14/11

% of students receiving:
Full tuition waiver only: 0%
Assistantship/fellowship only: 0%
Both full tuition waiver & assistantship/fellowship: 0%

Approximate percentage of incoming students with a B.A./B.S. only: 65%   **Master's:** 35%

Approximate percentage of students who are Women: 64%   **Ethnic Minority:** 64%
International: Not reported

Average years to complete the doctoral program (including internship): Approximately 6.5 years

Personal interview
Preferred in person but telephone acceptable

Attrition rate in past 7 years: approximately 10%

Percentage of students applying for internship last year accepted into APPIC or APA internships: 86%

Formal tracks/concentrations: clinical health psychology, pediatric health psychology, neurospsychology, cultural/social psychology

Research areas	# Faculty	# Grants
health psychology	6	3

clinical neuropsychology	2	0
pediatric health psychology	1	2
psychobiology	2	2
psychology and religion	2	0
psychotherapy outcome	1	0
statistics methods	3	0

Clinical opportunities

primary care	pediatric behavioral
medical/hospital	medicine
clinical neuropsychology	forensic
adult behavioral medicine	university/college
obesity treatment	counseling center
community outpatient	

Loma Linda University (Psy.D.)

Department of Psychology
Loma Linda, CA 92350
phone#: (909) 558-8577 (central office)
e-mail: aarechiga@llu.edu
Web address: www.llu.edu/science-technology/
psychology/programs/psyd.page?

1	2	**3**	4	5	6	7

Practice oriented   Equal emphasis   Research oriented

Percentage of faculty subscribing to each of the following orientations:

Psychodynamic/Psychoanalytic	10%
Applied behavioral analysis/Radical behavioral	10%
Family systems/Systems	0%
Existential/Phenomenological/Humanistic	30%
Cognitive/Cognitive-behavioral	50%

Courses required for incoming students to have completed prior to enrolling:
Bachelor's or master's degree in psychology or relevant field

Recommended but not mandatory courses:
computer literacy, math, sociology, biology, History and systems, learning, personality, statistics, social psychology, developmental psychology, psychobiology

GRE mean
Verbal 556   Quantitative 637   Analytical Writing 4.9

GPA mean
3.35

Number of applications/admission offers/incoming students in 2009
Not reported

% of students receiving:
Full tuition waiver only: 0%
Assistantship/fellowship only: 0%
Both full tuition waiver & assistantship/fellowship: 0%

Approximate percentage of incoming students with a B.A./B.S. only: 80%   Master's: 20%

Approximate percentage of students who are
Women: 90%   Ethnic Minority: 30%
International: not reported

Average years to complete the doctoral program (including internship): 5.5 years

Personal interview
Preferred in person but telephone acceptable

Attrition rate in past 7 years: 10%

Percentage of students applying for internship last year accepted into APPIC or APA internships: 78%

Formal tracks/concentrations: clinical health psychology, pediatric health psychology, neuropsychology, forensic psychology, family, culture psychology

Research areas	# Faculty	# Grants
health psychology	6	3
clinical neuropsychology	2	0
pediatric health psychology	1	2
psychobiology	2	2
psychology and religion	2	0
psychotherapy outcome	1	0
statistics methods	3	0

Clinical opportunities

primary care	obesity treatment
medical/hospital	community outpatient
clinical neuropsychology	pediatric behavioral
adult behavioral	medicine
medicine	forensic

Long Island University (Ph.D.)

Department of Psychology
University Plaza
Brooklyn, NY 11201
phone#: (718) 488-1164
e-mail: nicholas.papouchis@liu.edu
Web address: www2.brooklyn.liu.edu/psych/phdprogram/
index.html

1	2	3	**4**	5	6	7

Practice oriented   Equal emphasis   Research oriented

Percentage of faculty subscribing to each of the following orientations:

Psychodynamic/Psychoanalytic	70%
Applied behavioral analysis/Radical behavioral	5%
Family systems/Systems	20%
Existential/Phenomenological/Humanistic	30%
Cognitive/Cognitive-behavioral	25%

Courses required for incoming students to have completed prior to enrolling:
Experimental, statistics, abnormal, developmental, personality

Recommended but not mandatory courses:
Social, history and systems, physiological psychology, learning

GRE mean
Verbal 625   Quantitative 625   Analytical 625
Psychology Subject Test 625   Analytical Writing 5.00

GPA mean
Overall GPA 3.55   Psychology GPA 3.60

205

Number of applications/admission offers/incoming students in 2008
230 applied/23 admission offers/16 incoming

% of students receiving:
Full tuition waiver only: 0%
Both full tuition waiver & assistantship/fellowship: 20%
Half tuition waiver & assistantship: 80%

Approximate percentage of incoming students with a B.A./B.S. only: 60%   **Master's:** 38%

Approximate percentage of students who are Women: 70% **Ethnic Minority:** 20% **International:** 10%

Average years to complete the doctoral program (including internship): 6.2 years

Personal interview
Required in person

Attrition rate in past 7 years: 2%

Percentage of students applying for internship last year accepted into APPIC or APA internships: 100%

Formal tracks/concentrations: Not reported

Research areas	# Faculty	# Grants
aging and mental health	1	1
cultural/cross-cultural	4	1
developmental issues	4	1
developmental psychopathology	2	0
forensic issues	2	0
health psychology	1	1
neuropsychology	1	1
projective techniques	2	0
psychotherapy process	3	1
sociodevelopment	1	1
socioemotional development	1	0
trauma	1	1

Clinical opportunities

behavioral clinics
child clinics and child
   hospital settings
college counseling
community mental health

forensic units
homeless shelters
hospital inpatient/
   outpatient
neuropsychology

Long Island University–C.W. Post Campus (Psy.D.)

Department of Psychology
College of Liberal Arts and Sciences
Brookville, NY 11548
phone#: (516) 299-2090
e-mail: eva.feindler@liu.edu
Web address: www.liu.edu/CWPost/Academics/Schools/
CLAS/Dept/Psychology/PsyD2.aspx

1	2	3	4	5	6	7
Practice oriented		Equal emphasis				Research oriented

Percentage of faculty subscribing to each of the following orientations:
Psychodynamic/Psychoanalytic   50%

Applied behavioral analysis/Radical behavioral   12%
Family systems/Systems   0%
Existential/Phenomenological/Humanistic   0%
Cognitive/Cognitive-behavioral   38%

Courses required for incoming students to have completed prior to enrolling:
A minimum of 18 credit hours of psychology, including courses in Statistics, Research Design or methods, Personality and Abnormal Psychology

Recommended but not mandatory courses:
Not reported

GRE mean
Verbal 593   Quantitative 638
Psychology Subject Test 661
Analytical Writing 4.8

GPA mean
3.53

Number of applications/admission offers/incoming students in 2009
267 applied/43 admission offers/20 incoming

% of students receiving:
Full tuition waiver only: 0%
Assistantship/fellowship only: 50% (100% who apply for aid, receive some sort of aid)
Both full tuition waiver & assistantship/fellowship: 0%

Approximate percentage of incoming students with a B.A./B.S. only: 75%   **Master's:** 25%

Approximate percentage of students who are Women: 75%   **Ethnic Minority:** 35% **International:** 6%

Average years to complete the doctoral program (including internship): 5.5 years

Personal interview
Required in person

Attrition rate in past 7 years: 1%

Percentage of students applying for internship last year accepted into APPIC or APA internships: 100%

Formal tracks/concentrations: Family Violence, Serious & Persistent Mental Illness, Developmental Disabilities

Research areas	# Faculty	# Grants
anger management	1	0
attachment	1	1
developmental disabilities	1	0
marital violence	2	0
parent training	1	1
professional discipline	1	0
schizophrenia	1	0
trauma	1	1

Clinical opportunities
adult difficulties as follows:
   behavior modification for habit control
   behavior patterns
   depression
   domestic violence
   eating disorders and compulsive
   marital and relationship therapy

yes

phobias and anxiety disorders
child and family difficulties as follows:
   academic and school-related problems
   aggressive behavior/anger management
   developmental difficulties (treatment)
   family conflicts/family therapy
   family violence
   hyperactivity/low attention span
   parent/child conflicts
   socialization difficulties
group therapy as follows:
   anger management for children and adults
   assertiveness training
   parent training
   social skills for children
   stress management
individual psychotherapy
psychological assessment as follows:
   achievement and intelligence testing
   emotional and behavioral assessment
   neuropsychological assessment
   personality assessment
short-term and psychodynamic therapy

Louisiana State University (Ph.D.)
Declined to participate.

University of Louisville (Ph.D.)
Department of Psychological and Brain Sciences
Louisville, KY 40292
phone#: (502) 852-6775
e-mail: j.woodruff-borden@louisville.edu
Web address: http://louisville.edu/psychology/doctorate/clinical-psychology/

1 2 3 4 **5** 6 7
Practice oriented / Equal emphasis / Research oriented

Percentage of faculty subscribing to each of the following orientations:
Psychodynamic/Psychoanalytic — 0%
Interpersonal-ego relations — 10%
Applied behavioral analysis/Radical behavioral — 0%
Family systems/Systems — 0%
Existential/Phenomenological/Humanistic — 0%
Cognitive/Cognitive-behavioral — 80%
Eclectic — 10%

Courses required for incoming students to have completed prior to enrolling: none

Recommended but not mandatory courses:
history, abnormal, personality, social, statistics, physiological, learning

GRE mean
Verbal 568 Quantitative 621
Analytical Writing Data not available

GPA mean
Junior/Senior GPA 3.6

Number of applications/admission offers/incoming students in 2009
99 applied/9 admission offers/9 incoming

% of students receiving:
Full tuition waiver only: 0%
Assistantship/fellowship only: 0%
Both full tuition waiver & assistantship/fellowship: 100%

Approximate percentage of incoming students with a B.A./B.S. only: 80% Master's: 20%

Approximate percentage of students who are Women: 62% Ethnic Minority: 12% International: 2%

Average years to complete the doctoral program (including internship): 6 years

Personal interview
Preferred in person but telephone acceptable

Attrition rate in past 7 years: 12%

Percentage of students applying for internship last year accepted into APPIC or APA internships: 84%

Formal tracks/concentrations: none

Research areas	# Faculty	# Grants
anxiety disorders	2	0
health/behavioral medicine	3	1
chronic mental illness	2	0
forensic psychology	1	0
gerontology/aging	3	1
stress and coping	2	0

Clinical opportunities
affective disorders — gerontology/aging
anxiety disorders — health psycholo...
child clinical psychology — interpersonal p...
developmental disabilities — psychosis

yes

Loyola University Maryland (Psy.D.)
Department of Psychology
Baltimore, MD 21210-2699
phone#: (410) 617-2175
e-mail: jlating@loyola.edu
Web address: www.loyola.edu/psychology/programs/psyd/overview.html

1 2 **3** 4 5 6 7
Practice oriented / Equal emphasis / Research oriented

Percentage of faculty subscribing to each of the following orientations:
Psychodynamic/Psychoanalytic — 15%
Applied behavioral analysis/Radical behavioral — 10%
Family systems/Systems — 5%
Existential/Phenomenological/Humanistic — 10%
Cognitive/Cognitive-behavioral — 65%

Courses required for incoming students prior to enrolling:
social psychology, statistics or research methods, abnormal psychology, personality theory, tests and measurements, learning theory or cognitive psychology

Recommended but not mandatory courses: None

GRE mean
Verbal 580   Quantitative 660   Analytical 740
Analytical Writing 5.0

GPA mean
Overall GPA 3.52

Number of applications/admission offers/incoming students in 2009
322 applied/27 admission offers/21 incoming

% of students receiving:
Full tuition waiver only: 0%
Assistantship/fellowship only: 40%
Both full tuition waiver & assistantship/fellowship: 0%

Approximate percentage of incoming students with a B.A./B.S. only: 71%   **Master's:** 29%

Approximate percentage of students who are Women: 76%   **Ethnic Minority:** 24%   **International:** 5%

Average years to complete the doctoral program (including internship): 5.5 years

Personal interview
Required in person

Attrition rate in past 7 years: 6%

Percentage of students applying for internship last year accepted into APPIC or APA internships: 93%

Formal tracks/concentrations: none

Research areas	# Faculty	# Grants
child psychopathology	5	0
domestic violence	1	0
ethics and legal issues	2	0
gambling	1	0
gerontology	2	0
health psychology	3	0
homophobia	1	0
multicultural	3	0
neuropsychology	2	0
nonverbal communication	1	0
posttraumatic stress disorder	4	0
psychotherapy outcomes	1	0
sexuality	2	0
spirituality	2	0
social psychology	1	0
trichotillomania	1	0
women's issues	2	0

Clinical opportunities

adult inpatient / juvenile forensics
behavioral medicine / outpatient private practice
child and family / prison settings
eating disorders / stress and anxiety

Loyola University of Chicago (Ph.D.)
Department of Psychology
Graduate Enrollment Services
820 North Michigan Avenue
Chicago, IL 60611
phone#: (773) 508-2974

e-mail: jhamilt@luc.edu
Web address: www.luc.edu/psychology/clinical.shtml

1	2	3	4	5	6	7
Practice oriented		Equal emphasis				Research oriented

Percentage of faculty subscribing to each of the following orientations:
Psychodynamic/Psychoanalytic 22%
Applied behavioral analysis/Radical behavioral 0%
Family systems/Systems 22%
Existential/Phenomenological/Humanistic 0%
Cognitive/Cognitive-behavioral 55%

Courses required for incoming students prior to enrolling:
Research methods/experimental and statistics plus any 6 other psychology courses (24 hours, total)

Recommended but not mandatory courses: None

GRE mean
Verbal 605   Quantitative 700
Analytical Writing 5.17

GPA mean
Overall GPA 3.73

Number of applications/admission offers/incoming students in 2008
310 applied/11 admission offers/6 incoming

% of students receiving:
Full tuition waiver only: 0%
Assistantship/fellowship only: 0%
Both full tuition waiver & assistantship/fellowship: 100%

Approximate percentage of incoming students with a B.A./B.S. only: 90%   **Master's:** 10%

Approximate percentage of students who are Women: 80%   **Ethnic Minority:** 33%   **International:** 7%

Average years to complete the doctoral program (including internship): 6 years

Personal interview
Preferred in person but telephone acceptable

Attrition rate in past 7 years: 6%

Percentage of students applying for internship last year accepted into APPIC or APA internships: 83%

Formal tracks/concentrations: clinical child, neuropsychology

Research areas	# Faculty	# Grants
adolescence	6	5
adult psychopathology	1	0
clinical-child/psychopathology	7	4
community psychology	3	0
death/bereavement	1	0
developmental psychopathology	4	3
disabilities	1	2
emerging adulthood	1	0
ethical issues	1	0
extracurricular activities	1	1
minority mental health	3	3

pediatric psychology	1	2
prevention	3	2
psychotherapy	4	1

Clinical opportunities

assessment (child and adult)
eating disorders
family psychology
health psychology
HIV/AIDS
neuropsychological
   assessment (child and adult)

personality disorders
psychotherapy (child and adult)
substance abuse
victims of abuse

University of Maine (Ph.D.)

Department of Psychology
5742 Little Hall
Orono, ME 04469-5742
phone#: (207) 581-2038
e-mail: Doug.Nangle@umit.maine.edu
Web address: www.umaine.edu/psychology/graduate-program/clinical-graduate-program/

1	2	3	4	5	6	7
Practice oriented		Equal emphasis				Research oriented

Percentage of faculty subscribing to each of the following orientations:

Psychodynamic/Psychoanalytic	0%
Applied behavioral analysis/Radical behavioral	20%
Family systems/Systems	0%
Existential/Phenomenological/Humanistic	0%
Cognitive/Cognitive-behavioral	80%

Courses required for incoming students prior to enrolling:

At least three to four advanced undergraduate psychology courses; background in natural sciences and mathematics

Recommended but not mandatory courses:

Learning, developmental, cognition

GRE mean

Verbal 565   Quantitative 615
Psychology Subject Test No Longer Required
Analytical Writing 5.0

GPA mean

Overall GPA 3.79

Number of applications/admission offers/incoming students in 2009

95 applied/6 admission offers/4 incoming

% of students receiving:

Full tuition waiver only: 0%
Assistantship/fellowship only: 0%
Both full tuition waiver & assistantship/fellowship: 100% for 1st-year students, 100% of the 2nd- to 4th-year students

Approximate percentage of incoming students with a B.A./B.S. only: 80%   **Master's:** 20%

Approximate percentage of students who are Women: 80%   **Ethnic Minority:** 0%   **International:** 5%

Average years to complete the doctoral program (including internship): 5.5 years

Personal interview

Much preferred in person but telephone interviews sometimes arranged

Attrition rate in past 7 years: 18.5%

Percentage of students applying for internship last year accepted into APPIC or APA internships: 100%

Formal tracks/concentrations: general clinical, developmental

Research areas	# Faculty	# Grants
ADHD	1	0
anxiety disorders	2	1
behavioral medicine	1	1
depression	1	0
forensic psychology	2	1
psychotherapy outcome	3	0
social development	1	1
social skills	2	2
women's health	1	0

Clinical opportunities

ADHD clinic
anxiety disorders clinic
behavioral-developmental
   pediatrics
intervention
behavioral medicine
body dysmorphic disorder
   clinic
community mental health
crisis services—outpatient

health psychology
juvenile offenders
pediatric obesity
PTSD in children
residential program for
   children at risk
social skills interventions
   for violent/aggressive
   youth

Marquette University (Ph.D.)

Psychology Department
P.O. Box 1881
Milwaukee, WI 53201-1881
phone#: (414) 288-3487
e-mail: stephen.saunders@marquette.edu
Web address: www.marquette.edu/psyc/graduate.shtml

1	2	3	4	5	6	7
Practice oriented		Equal emphasis				Research oriented

Percentage of faculty subscribing to each of the following orientations:

Psychodynamic/Psychoanalytic	10%
Applied behavioral analysis/Radical behavioral	20%
Family systems/Systems	40%
Existential/Phenomenological/Humanistic	40%
Cognitive/Cognitive-behavioral	70%

Courses required for incoming students prior to enrolling:

Research methods, statistics, developmental, abnormal, personality, social, cognition, neuroscience

Recommended but not mandatory courses:

History and systems

GRE mean
Verbal 560   Quantitative 670   Analytical Writing N/A

GPA mean
Overall GPA 3.61

Number of applications/admission offers/incoming students in 2009
137 applied/14 admission offers/7 incoming

% of students receiving:
Full tuition waiver only: 10%
Assistantship/fellowship only: 0%
Both full tuition waiver & assistantship/fellowship: 90%

Approximate percentage of incoming students with a B.A./B.S. only: 85%   **Master's:** 15%

Approximate percentage of students who are Women: 65%   **Ethnic Minority:** 20%   **International:** 5%

Average years to complete the doctoral program (including internship): 6.5 years

Personal interview
Preferred in person but telephone acceptable

Attrition rate in past 7 years: 9%

Percentage of students applying for internship last year accepted into APPIC or APA internships: 75%

Formal tracks/concentrations: child/family, adult

Research areas	# Faculty	# Grants
adjustment to major trauma	1	0
adult development	1	0
ADHD	1	0
Alzheimer's disease	1	0
autism/Aspergers	1	0
body esteem	1	0
child development	3	1
child–parent relationships	3	1
depression/anxiety	2	0
family conflict	2	1
fear conditioning	1	0
friendships/relationships	2	0
group dynamics	1	0
help-seeking for mental illness	2	1
Latino mental health	1	0
lesbian/gay/bisexual/transgender	1	0
memory problems	1	2
mental imagery	1	0
minority mental health	2	0
multicultural psychology	3	0
neuropsychology	3	0
organizational behavior	1	0
pediatric psychology	1	0
psychosocial aspects of medical illness	1	0
psychotherapy process	3	0
psychotherapy outcomes	3	0
social stigmatization	1	1
stigma: mental illness	2	0
treatment utilization	2	0

Clinical opportunities

ADHD clinic	adolescent psychotherapy
adult neuropsychology	child psychotherapy
child neuropsychology	group therapy

pediatric neuropsychology
child and adolescent medical health
adult psychotherapy
trauma
family/couples therapy
pain clinic (pediatric)

Marshall University (Psy.D.)

Department of Psychology
Huntington, WV 25755
phone#: (304) 696-2785
e-mail: Marianna Linz – linz@marshall.edu, Okey Napier – okey.napier@marshall.edu
Web address: www.marshall.edu/wpmu/psych/psyd-program/

1	2	3	4	5	6	7
Practice oriented		Equal emphasis				Research oriented

Percentage of faculty subscribing to each of the following orientations:

Psychodynamic/Psychoanalytic	33%
Applied behavioral analysis/Radical behavioral	10%
Family systems/Systems	10%
Existential/Phenomenological/Humanistic	0%
Cognitive/Cognitive-behavioral	60%

Courses required for incoming students to have completed prior to enrolling:
Statistics, research methods, personality, psychometrics, and abnormal

Recommended but not mandatory courses: None

GRE mean
Verbal 525   Quantitative 547
Psychology Subject Test not reported
Analytical Writing not reported

GPA mean
Overall GPA 3.86

Number of applications/admission offers/incoming students in 2009
50 applied/15 admission offers/10 incoming

% of students receiving:
Full tuition waiver only: 0%
Assistantship/fellowship only: 0%
Both full tuition waiver & assistantship/fellowship: 75%

Approximate percentage of incoming students with a B.A./B.S. only: 70%   **Master's:** 30%

Approximate percentage of students who are Women: 85%   **Ethnic Minority:** 0%   **International:** 2%

Average years to complete the doctoral program (including internship): 5 years

Personal interview
Preferred in person but telephone acceptable

Attrition rate in past 7 years: 1%

Percentage of students applying for internship last year accepted into APPIC or APA internships: 50%

Formal tracks/concentrations: non

Research areas	# Faculty	# Grants
depression/suicide	1	0
common factors in psychotherapy	1	0
rural mental health	2	1
women's health	1	0
GLBT ISSUES	1	
learning disabilities	1	0
animal behavior	1	0
poverty	1	0
meta analysis	1	0
racial identity development	1	0

Clinical opportunities

school-based health centers
university training clinic
juvenile correctional facility
adult correctional facility
inpatient psychiatric—adult

medical school practice
community mental health
rural community
 (mandatory)

University of Maryland, Baltimore County (Ph.D.)

Department of Psychology
1000 Hilltop Circle
Baltimore, MD 21250
phone#: (410) 455-2567
e-mail: psycdept@umbc.edu
Web address: www.umbc.edu/psyc/hsp_clinical.html

1	2	3	4	**5**	6	7
Practice oriented			Equal emphasis			Research oriented

Percentage of faculty subscribing to each of the following orientations:

Psychodynamic/Psychoanalytic	10%
Applied behavioral analysis/Radical behavioral	10%
Family systems/Systems	30%
Existential/Phenomenological/Humanistic	0%
Cognitive/Cognitive-behavioral	80%

Courses required for incoming students to have completed prior to enrolling:
Psychological statistics, abnormal psychology, experimental psychology

Recommended but not mandatory courses:
Personality, physiological, developmental

GRE mean
Verbal 581   Quantitative 684
Psychology Subject Test 656

GPA mean
Overall GPA 3.62

Number of applications/admission offers/incoming students in 2009
77 applied/16 admission offers/6 incoming

% of students receiving:
Full tuition waiver only: 0%
Assistantship/fellowship only: 0%
Both full tuition waiver & assistantship/fellowship: 100%

Approximate percentage of incoming students with a B.A./B.S. only: 80%   **Master's:** 20%

Approximate percentage of students who are Women: 83%   **Ethnic Minority:** 20%   **International:** 5%

Average years to complete the doctoral program (including internship): 7 years

Personal interview
Preferred in person but telephone acceptable

Attrition rate in past 7 years: 13%

Percentage of students applying for internship last year accepted into APPIC or APA internships: 100%

Formal tracks/concentrations: behavioral medicine; community and applied social psychology; child clinical

Research areas	# Faculty	# Grants
addictive disorders	2	3
behavioral medicine	3	3
cardiovascular/cerebrovascular disease	1	1
community psychology	4	2
domestic violence	1	0
interpersonal processes	1	0
psychology of religion	1	0
suicide	1	0

Clinical opportunities

addictive disorders
applied behavior analysis
domestic abuse
emergency mental health
 services
family therapy
forensic psychology
severe and chronic mental
 illness

medical liaison
neuropsychology
pediatric psychology
prevention
rehabilitation psychology
school-based mental
 health services

University of Maryland College Park (Ph.D.)

Department of Psychology
Biology–Psychology Building
College Park, MD 20742-4411
phone#: (301) 405-5890
e-mail: jcoldren@psyc.umd.edu
Web address: http://www.bsos.umd.edu/psyc/clinicalpsyc/

1	2	3	4	5	**6**	7
Practice oriented			Equal emphasis			Research oriented

Percentage of faculty subscribing to each of the following orientations:

Psychodynamic/Psychoanalytic	0%
Applied behavioral analysis/Radical behavioral	0%
Family systems/Systems	0%
Existential/Phenomenological/Humanistic	0%
Cognitive/Cognitive-behavioral	100%

Courses required for incoming students to have completed prior to enrolling:
B.A. or B.S. in psychology or related areas

Recommended but not mandatory courses: Statistics, Abnormal Psychology, laboratory courses in psychology

211

GRE mean
Verbal 648   Quantitative 735
Analytical Writing not reported

Number of applications/admission offers/incoming students in 2009
246 applied/12 admission offers/4 incoming

% of students receiving:
Full tuition waiver only: 0%
Assistantship/fellowship only: 0%
Both full tuition waiver & assistantship/fellowship: 100%

Approximate percentage of incoming students with a B.A./B.S. only: 90%   **Master's:** 10%

Approximate percentage of students who are Women: 98%   **Ethnic Minority:** 30%   **International:** 0%

Average years to complete the doctoral program (including internship): 6 years

Personal interview
Required in person

Attrition rate in past 7 years: 7

Percentage of students applying for internship last year accepted into APPIC or APA internships: 100%

Formal tracks/concentrations: none

Research areas	# Faculty	# Grants
addictive behaviors	3	4
depression	1	0
behavioral undercontrol	2	1
personality and physiology	1	0
psychotherapy outcome	2	2
serious mental illnesses	2	2

Clinical opportunities
...tunities in in-house training clinic and
...npatient, outpatient, and specialized settings

NO

Marywood University (Psy.D.)

Department of Psychology and Counseling
Scranton, PA 18509
phone #: (570) 348-6226
e-mail: renjilian@marywood.edu
Web address: www.marywood.edu/psych-couns/psyd/

1	2	3	4	5	6	7
Practice oriented		Equal emphasis				Research oriented

Percentage of faculty subscribing to each of the following orientations:
Psychodynamic/Psychoanalytic   34%
Applied behavioral analysis/Radical behavioral   0%
Family systems/Systems   0%
Existential/Phenomenological/Humanistic   17%
Cognitive/Cognitive-behavioral   83%

Courses required for incoming students to have completed prior to enrolling:
Statistics, research methods, abnormal psychology; at least 18 credits in psychology

Recommended but not mandatory courses: none

GRE mean
Verbal 548   Quantitative 630
Psychology Subject Test 666
Analytical Writing 5.1

GPA mean
Overall GPA 3.8

Number of applications/admission offers/incoming students in 2009
62 applied/16 admission offers/7 incoming

% of students receiving:
Full tuition waiver only: 0%
Full assistantship/fellowship only: 0%
Both full tuition waiver & assistantship/fellowship: 4%
Remaining 96% of students receive a $3,800 scholarship

Percentage of incoming students with a B.A./B.S. only: 72%   **Master's:** 28%

Percentage of students who are Women: 100%   **Ethnic Minority:** 29%   **International:** 0%

Average years to complete (including internship): 5 years (3 years for post-master's admission)

Personal interview
Preferred in person but telephone acceptable

Attrition rate in past 7 years: 4.9%

Percentage of students applying for internship last year accepted into APPIC or APA internships: 100%

Formal tracks/concentrations: none

Research areas	# Faculty	# Grants
attention deficit disorder	1	0
malingering	1	0
psychology and media	2	0
clinical training and supervision	4	0
positive psychology	1	0
multicultural issues	2	0
stress, anxiety and coping	3	0
aggression in boys	1	0
outcome assessment in mental health	1	0
cognitive approaches to self-esteem change	1	0
technology and education	3	0

Clinical opportunities
on-site outpatient mental health
inpatient psychiatry
inpatient behavioral medicine
outpatient childhood disorders
university counseling center
community mental health
inpatient geriatric

University of Massachusetts at Amherst (Ph.D.)

Department of Psychology
135 Hicks Way-Tobin Hall
Amherst, MA 01003
phone#: (413) 545-0662
e-mail: dscherer@psych.umass.edu

Web address: www.umass.edu/psychology/clinical/

1	2	3	4	5	6	7
Practice oriented			Equal emphasis			Research oriented

Percentage of faculty subscribing to each of the following orientations:

Psychodynamic/Psychoanalytic	15%
Applied behavioral analysis/Radical behavioral	0%
Family systems/Systems	5%
Existential/Phenomenological/Humanistic	0%
Cognitive/Cognitive-behavioral	40%
Integrative	40%

Courses required for incoming students to have completed prior to enrolling:
An undergraduate background in psychology which, at a minimum, consists of statistics, methods, and 3 advanced subjects in psychology

Recommended but not mandatory courses: none

GRE mean
Verbal 640   Quantitative 670

GPA mean
Overall GPA 3.53

Number of applications/admission offers/incoming students in 2008
190 applied/10 admission offers/5 incoming

% of students receiving:
Full tuition waiver only: 0%
Assistantship/fellowship only: 0%
Both full tuition waiver & assistantship/fellowship: 100%

Approximate percentage of incoming students who a B.A./B.S. only: 70%   Master's: 30%

Approximate percentage of students who are Women: 79.5%   Ethnic Minority: 33% (last 7 years)   International: 12.8%

Average years to complete the doctoral program (including internship): 6 years

Personal interview
In person strongly recommended, but telephone possible

Attrition rate in past 7 years: 5%

Percentage of students applying for internship last year accepted into APPIC or APA internships: 90%

Formal tracks/concentrations: child/family concentration, adult

Research areas	# Faculty	# Grants
child, adolescent, family	7	1
aging/gerontology	2	0
developmental psychopathology	1	0
stress/coping	1	1
psychotherapy process	2	0
psychotherapist's development	2	0
psychological assessment	1	1
psychotherapy research	1	0
substance abuse	1	0
adoption	1	1

Clinical opportunities
child and adolescent therapy
cognitive-behavior therapy
cultural diversity experience
gerontology
psychoanalytic therapy
psychotherapy supervision
psychological/
 neuropsychological
 assessment
college counseling
outpatient medical settings
inpatient medical settings
residential treatm

University of Massachusetts at Boston (Ph.D.)
Department of Psychology
Boston, MA 02125-3393
phone#: (617) 287-6340
e-mail: linda.curreri@umb.edu
Web address: www.umb.edu/cla/psychology/phd_program/522

1	2	3	4	5	6	7
Practice oriented			Equal emphasis			Research oriented

Percentage of faculty subscribing to each of the following orientations:

Psychodynamic/Psychoanalytic	27%
Applied behavioral analysis/Radical behavioral	0%
Family systems/Systems	19%
Existential/Phenomenological/Humanistic	27%
Cognitive/Cognitive-behavioral	27%

Courses required for incoming students to have completed prior to enrolling:
statistics; 6 courses total in psychology

Recommended but not mandatory courses:
development, abnormal, personality, research methods

GRE mean
Verbal 620   Quantitative 698
Psychology Subject Test 659
Analytical Writing 4.95

GPA mean
Overall GPA 3.53   Psychology GPA 3.70
Junior/Senior GPA 3.7

Number of applications/admission offers/incoming students in 2009
296 applied/10 admission offers/8 incoming

% of students receiving:
Full tuition waiver only: 0%
Assistantship/fellowship only: 0%
Both full tuition waiver & assistantship/fellowship: 100%

Approximate percentage of incoming students with a B.A./B.S. only: 63%   Master's: 37%

Approximate percentage of students who are Women: 100% Ethnic Minority: 63% International: 25%

Average years to complete the doctoral program (including internship): 6.5 years

Personal interview
Required in person

213

Attrition rate in past 7 years: 0%

Percentage of students applying for internship last year accepted into APPIC or APA internships: 88%

Formal tracks/concentrations: none

Research areas	# Faculty	# Grants
cross-cultural	3	2
family	1	1
media and psychology	1	0
severe psychopathology	1	1
trauma	2	1
anxiety and emotions	1	1
health psychopathology	1	2
developmental psychopathology	2	1
neurobehavioral	2	3

Clinical opportunities

Students do practica at all the major teaching hospitals and mental health centers in the greater Boston area. They do _____ clinical internships in Boston and across the

Massachusetts School of Professional Psychology (Psy.D.)

221 Rivermoor Street
Boston, MA 02132
phone#: (617) 327-6777
toll free (888) 664-MSPP
e-mail: admissions@mspp.edu
Web address: www.mspp.edu/academics/degree-programs/psyd/default.asp

1	2	**3**	4	5	6	7
Practice oriented			Equal emphasis			Research oriented

Percentage of faculty subscribing to each of the following orientations:

Psychodynamic/Psychoanalytic	50%
Applied behavioral analysis/Radical behavioral	0%
Family systems/Systems	19%
Existential/Phenomenological/Humanistic	12%
Cognitive/Cognitive-behavioral	19%

Courses required for incoming students prior to enrolling:

Abnormal and two out of the following six courses: developmental psychology, social psychology, personality theories, behavioral statistics, tests and measurements, physiological psychology

Recommended but not mandatory courses:
All psychology related

GRE mean
Verbal 540   Quantitative 603
Analytical Writing 4.5

GPA mean
Overall GPA 3.45

Number of applications/admission offers/incoming students in 2009
405 applied/170 admission offers/86 incoming

% of students receiving:
Full tuition waiver only: 0%
Assistantship/fellowship only: 45%
Both full tuition waiver & assistantship/fellowship: 0%

Approximate percentage of incoming students with a B.A./B.S. only: 60%   **Master's:** 40%

Approximate percentage of students who are Women: 75% **Ethnic Minority:** 12% **International:** 12%

Average years to complete the doctoral program (including internship): 4.5 years

Personal interview
Required in person

Attrition rate in past 7 years: 2.2%

Percentage of students applying for internship last year accepted into APPIC or APA internships: 100%

Formal tracks/concentrations: health psychology, forensic psychology, childhood, adolescence and family

Research areas: a wide variety; **# Faculty:** 38;   **# Grants:** 97

Clinical opportunities
We have 220 sites per year in diverse areas. If your area is not covered, we will find a site. Optional specialty tracks in health and forensic psychology are available.

McGill University (Ph.D.) (2008 data)

Department of Psychology
1205 Avenue Docteur Penfield
Montreal, Quebec H3A 1B1, Canada
phone#: (514) 398-6124
e-mail: gradsec@psych.mcgill.ca
Web address: www.psych.mcgill.ca/grad/program/clinical_program.htm

1	2	3	4	5	**6**	7
Clinically oriented			Equal emphasis			Research oriented

Percentage of faculty subscribing to each of the following orientations:

Psychodynamic/Psychoanalytic	20%
Applied behavioral analysis/Radical behavioral	0%
Family systems/Systems	0%
Existential/Phenomenological/Humanistic	0%
Cognitive/Cognitive-behavioral	80%

Courses required for incoming students to have completed prior to enrolling:
Courses in the biological, cognitive and social bases of behavior as well as statistics.

Recommended but not mandatory courses: none

GRE mean
Verbal and Quantitative 660; Do not require GREs for non-native speakers of English
Analytical Writing Data not available

GPA mean
Overall GPA 3.7

Number of applications/admission offers/incoming students in 2007
180 applied/5 admission offers/4 incoming

% of students receiving:
Full tuition waiver only: 0%
Assistantship/fellowship only: 100%
Both full tuition waiver & assistantship/fellowship: 0%

Approximate percentage of incoming students with a B.A./B.S. only: 95% Master's: 5%

Approximate percentage of students who are
Women: 66% Ethnic Minority: 10% International: 20%

Average years to complete the doctoral program (including internship): 6 years

Personal interview
Telephone required

Attrition rate in past 7 years: not reported

Percentage of students applying for internship last year accepted into APPIC or APA internships: 100%

Formal tracks/concentrations: none

Research areas	# Faculty	# Grants
aggression	1	1
aging (including Alzheimer's)	2	1
assessment/diagnosis	2	0
attention-deficit disorder	1	1
behavior therapy	1	0
behavioral genetics	1	1
behavioral medicine	2	2
child	1	1
child psychopathology	1	1
cognitive information processing	1	0
depression	2	2
developmental	1	1
eating disorders	1	1
emotion	1	1
family	2	1
gender	1	1
health psychology	2	2
interpersonal relations	2	2
memory	2	1
neuropsychology	1	1
olfaction	1	1
personality	1	1
personality assessment	2	0
psychopathology	2	2
psychopharmacology	2	1
psychophysiology	2	1
psychotherapy process/outcome	1	1
sexual dysfunction	1	1
stress	1	1
substance abuse	1	1

Clinical opportunities
The McGill University Psychology Internship Consortium is closely associated with our graduate program in clinical psychology. The Consortium consists of departments of psychology in 3 university teaching hospitals, a children's hospital, and a psychiatric hospital.

The University of Memphis (Ph.D.)
Department of Psychology
Memphis, TN 38152
phone#: (901) 678-3015
e-mail: l.robinson@mail.psyc.memphis.edu
Web address: http://www.memphis.edu/psychology/graduate/Clinical/index.php

1	2	3	4	5	6	7
Practice oriented		Equal emphasis				Research oriented

Percentage of faculty subscribing to each of the following orientations:
Psychodynamic/Psychoanalytic	0%
Applied behavioral analysis/Radical behavioral	0%
Family systems/Systems	30%
Existential/Phenomenological/Humanistic	20%
Cognitive/Cognitive-behavioral	50%

Courses required for incoming students to have completed prior to enrolling:
A minimum of 18 semester hours in undergraduate psychology courses, including courses in Quantitative Methods (psychological statistics), and experimental design. Students lacking some or all of these prerequisite courses, but presenting an exceptional undergraduate record, may nevertheless be granted graduate admission. However, students may be asked to remove such deficiencies before or during their first academic year.

Recommended but not mandatory courses: none

GRE mean
Verbal 560 Quantitative 670
Analytical Writing not reported

GPA mean
Overall GPA 3.63

Number of applications/admission offers/incoming students in 2009
153 applied/11 admission offers/10 incoming

% of students receiving:
Full tuition waiver only: 0%
Assistantship/fellowship only: 0%
Both full tuition waiver & assistantship/fellowship: 100%

Approximate percentage of incoming students with a B.A./B.S. only: 89% Master's: 11%

Approximate percentage of students who are
Women: 72% Ethnic Minority: 23% International: 5%

Average years to complete the doctoral program (including internship): 6.5 years

Personal interview
Interview required

Attrition rate in past 7 years: 11.6%

Percentage of students applying for internship last year accepted into APPIC or APA internships: 75%

Formal tracks/concentrations: behavioral medicine, psychotherapy research, child clinical

Research areas	# Faculty	# Grants
behavioral medicine	4	3
child clinical	3	5
psychotherapy research	5	4

Clinical opportunities

addiction	family therapy
affective disorders	gambling
anxiety disorders	inpatient psychology
behavioral medicine	minority/cross-cultural
cancer and emotional adjustment	
school/educational	
developmental disabilities/autism	
child/adolescent	
eating disorders	

University of Miami (Ph.D.)

Department of Psychology
P.O. Box 249229
Coral Gables, FL 33124
phone#: (305) 284-2814
e-mail: inquire@psy.miami.edu
Web address: www.psy.miami.edu/graduate

1	2	3	4	5	6	7
Practice oriented		Equal emphasis			Research oriented	

Percentage of faculty subscribing to each of the following orientations:

Psychodynamic/Psychoanalytic	10%
Applied behavioral analysis/Radical behavioral	0%
Family systems/Systems	30%
Existential/Phenomenological/Humanistic	10%
Cognitive/Cognitive-behavioral	80%

Courses required for incoming students to have completed prior to enrolling:

statistics, experimental psychology/research methods

Recommended but not mandatory courses:

strong science background

GRE mean

Verbal 620   Quantitative 710
Analytical Writing Data not available

GPA mean

Overall GPA 3.7

Number of applications/admission offers/incoming students in 2009

340 applied/21 admission offers/14 incoming

% of students receiving:

Full tuition waiver only: 0%
Assistantship/fellowship only: 0%
Both full tuition waiver & assistantship/fellowship: 100%

Approximate percentage of incoming students with a B.A./B.S. only: 90%   Master's: 10%

Approximate percentage of students who are Women: 70% Ethnic Minority: 30% International: 2%

Average years to complete the doctoral program (including internship): 6 years

Personal interview

Required in person

Attrition rate in past 7 years: 8%

Percentage of students applying for internship last year accepted into APPIC or APA internships: 100%

Formal tracks/concentrations: adult clinical, child clinical, health clinical, pediatric health

Research areas	# Faculty	# Grants
AIDS	6	2
adult psychopathology	6	2
affective disorders	3	1
cancer	4	1
cardiovascular disease	4	2
child clinical psychology	6	2
child psychopathology	5	2
diabetes	3	2
family therapy	2	1
health psychology	14	2
hypertension	3	1
pediatric psychology	3	2
psychoneuroimmunology	6	2
stress and coping	9	2
trauma	4	2

Clinical opportunities

abuse	family therapy
AIDS	group therapy
behavioral medicine	long-term care
conduct disorder	marital therapy
developmental disabilities/ autism	minority/cross-cultural neuropsychology
diabetes	pediatrics
eating disorders	substance abuse

Miami University (Ph.D.)

Department of Psychology
Oxford, OH 45056
phone#: (513) 529-2400
e-mail: turnerpr@muohio.edu
Web address: www.units.muohio.edu/psychology/category/
research-areas/clinical

1	2	3	4	5	6	7
Practice oriented		Equal emphasis			Research oriented	

Percentage of faculty subscribing to each of the following orientations:

Psychodynamic/Psychoanalytic	8%
Applied behavioral analysis/Radical behavioral	0%
Family systems/Systems	17%
Existential/Phenomenological/Humanistic	25%
Cognitive/Cognitive-behavioral	17%
Developmental/Developmental Psychopathology	33%

Courses required for incoming students prior to enrolling:

1 course in statistics

Recommended but not mandatory courses: None

GRE mean
Verbal 620   Quantitative 700   Analytical Writing 5
Psychology Subject Test 765

GPA mean
Overall GPA 3.76

Number of applications/admission offers/incoming students in 2009
154 applied/8 admission offers/6 incoming

% of students receiving:
Full tuition waiver only: 0%
Assistantship/fellowship only: 0%
Both full tuition waiver & assistantship/fellowship: 100%

Approximate percentage of incoming students with a B.A./B.S. only: 80%   **Master's:** 20%

Approximate percentage of students who are Women: 55%   **Ethnic Minority:** 10%   **International:** 4

Average years to complete the doctoral program (including internship): 6 years

Personal interview
Preferred in person but telephone acceptable

Attrition rate in past 7 years: .075%

Percentage of students applying for internship last year accepted into APPIC or APA internships: 71%

Formal tracks/concentrations: trauma and resilience, child, family, and school-based mental health, adult psychotherapy research

Research areas	# Faculty	# Grants
action research	2	1
anxiety disorders	3	1
bullying youth	3	2
child psychopathology	6	4
consultation/school improvement	3	2
dating violence	3	1
dating violence prevention	1	1
dreams	1	0
early childhood mental health	1	1
eating disorders	1	0
family research	3	1
fetal alcohol spectrum disorders	1	0
immigration/acculturation	2	0
interparental conflict & violence	3	2
narrative methodologies	2	0
parent–child boundary dissolution	1	1
personality disorders	3	0
program development/program evaluation	2	2
psychotherapy process	3	0
PTSD and juvenile delinquency	1	1
school-based mental health	4	3
school–family community partnership	4	3
training/technical assistance	2	1
trauma recovery	4	1

Clinical opportunities

adult psychotherapy
anxiety disorders
assessment with adults
assessment with children
group psychotherapy with adults
group psychotherapy with children
attachment disorders
attention-deficit/hyperactivity disorder
child psychotherapy
college student counseling
community mental health
conduct disorder
consultation
cross-cultural psychology
depression
developmental disabilities
family therapy
hyperactivity
juvenile delinquency
inpatient mental health
parent-child therapy
posttraumatic stress disorder in adults
posttraumatic stress disorder in children
prevention
rural mental health
school-based mental health

University of Michigan (Ph.D.)

Department of Psychology
530 Church Street
Ann Arbor, MI 48109-1109
phone#: (734) 764-6332
e-mail: psych.saa@umich.edu
Web address: www.lsa.umich.edu/psych/areas/clinical/

1	2	3	4	5	**6**	7
Practice oriented		Equal emphasis			Research oriented	

Percentage of faculty subscribing to each of the following orientations:
Psychodynamic/Psychoanalytic	11%
Applied behavioral analysis/Radical behavioral	22%
Family systems/Systems	67%
Existential/Phenomenological/Humanistic	11%
Cognitive/Cognitive-behavioral	67%

Courses required for incoming students to have completed prior to enrolling: none

Recommended but not mandatory courses:
Basic course work in psychology

GRE mean
Verbal 572   Quantitative 654
Analytical Writing 5.1

GPA mean
Overall GPA 3.74

Number of applications/admission offers/incoming students in 2008
274 applied/10 admission offers/7 incoming

% of students receiving:
Full tuition waiver only: 0%
Assistantship/fellowship only: 0%
Both full tuition waiver & assistantship/fellowship: 100%

Approximate percentage of incoming students with a B.A./B.S. only: 43%   **Master's:** 57%

Approximate percentage of students who are Women: 57% **Ethnic Minority:** 29% **International:** 14%

Average years to complete the doctoral program (including internship): 5 years

Personal interview
Preferred in person but telephone in unusual circumstances

Attrition rate in past 7 years: 3%

Percentage of students applying for internship last year accepted into APPIC or APA internships: 90%

Formal tracks/concentrations: none

Research areas	# Faculty	# Grants
autism	1	2
adult depression	1	1
childhood depression	1	
child abuse/neglect	1	
childhood illness/family coping	1	1
childhood loss	2	2
chronic illness and coping (adult)	1	
family systems	4	1
family violence	1	2
health psychology	1	
neuropsychology	2	2
peer relations/social skills in children	3	3
personality disorders	1	
schizophrenia	1	
sleep	1	
social competence in children	2	
stress	1	
psychophysiology	1	
culture and mental health	2	

Clinical opportunities
adult
child and family

Michigan State University (Ph.D.)

Department of Psychology
East Lansing, MI 48824
phone#: (517) 355-9562
e-mail: psygrad@msu.edu
Web address: psychology.msu.edu/clinical/

1	2	3	4	5	6	7
Practice oriented		Equal emphasis				Research oriented

Percentage of faculty subscribing to each of the following orientations:

Psychodynamic/Psychoanalytic	40%
Applied behavioral analysis/Radical behavioral	0%
Family systems/Systems	40%
Existential/Phenomenological/Humanistic	0%
Cognitive/Cognitive-behavioral	40%
Feminist	10%

Courses required for incoming students prior to enrolling:
12 hours of psychology courses at the bachelor's level

Recommended but not mandatory courses:
Quantitative methods, research design, advanced competence with the use of computer programs (SPSS, SYSTAT, etc.)

GRE mean
Verbal 602   Quantitative 680
Psychology Subject Test 675
Analytical Writing 5.0

GPA mean
Overall GPA 3.77

Number of applications/admission offers/incoming students in 2009
119 applied/7 admission offers/5 incoming

% of incoming students receiving:
Full tuition waiver only: 0%
Assistantship/fellowship only: 0%
Both full tuition waiver & assistantship/fellowship: 100%

Approximate percentage of incoming students who entered with a B.A./B.S. only: 80%   **Master's:** 20%

Approximate percentage of students who are Women: 85% **Ethnic Minority:** 30% **International:** 7%

Average years to complete the doctoral program (including internship): 6.5 years

Personal interview
Preferred in person but telephone acceptable

Attrition rate in past 7 years: 20%

Percentage of students applying for internship last year accepted into APPIC or APA internships: 100%

Formal tracks/concentrations: none

Research areas	# Faculty	# Grants
affective and cognitive psychophysiology	1	0
antisocial behavior	1	2
attachment research	2	0
autism	2	1
behavior genetics	3	4
bullying in schools	1	0
culture and mental health	2	0
eating disorders	1	2
domestic violence	2	2
family research/systems	3	1
neuroimaging/neuropsych pediatric disorders	1	1
racial and sexual harassment	1	0
personality psychopathology	1	1

Clinical opportunities

assessment (child, adult, aging, ADHD, clinical neuropsychology)	gerontology/aging
	intimate partner violence
	loss and trauma group therapy
couples therapy	
depression and anxiety	minority/cross-cultural
eating disorders	play therapy
family therapy	

University of Minnesota (Ph.D.)

Department of Psychology
N218 Elliot Hall, 75 East River Road
Minneapolis, MN 55455
phone#: (612) 625-2546
e-mail: cspr@umn.edu
Web address: www.psych.umn.edu/areas/clinical/index.htm

1	2	3	4	5	6	7
Practice oriented		Equal emphasis			Research oriented	

Percentage of faculty subscribing to each of the following orientations:

Psychodynamic/Psychoanalytic	17%
Applied behavioral analysis/Radical behavioral	17%
Family systems/Systems	0%
Existential/Phenomenological/Humanistic	0%
Cognitive/Cognitive-behavioral	83%

Courses required for incoming students to have completed prior to enrolling:
statistics, abnormal psychology

Recommended but not mandatory courses: none

GRE mean
Verbal 636.75   Quantitative 705.75
Analytical Writing 5.5

GPA mean
Overall GPA 3.71

Number of applications/admission offers/incoming students in 2009
165 applied/12 admission offers/7 incoming

% of students receiving:
Full tuition waiver only: 0%
Assistantship/fellowship only: 0%
Both full tuition waiver & assistantship/fellowship: 100%

Approximate percentage of incoming students with a B.A./B.S. only: 100%   Master's: 0%

Approximate percentage of students who are Women: 70% Ethnic Minority: 24% International: 10.8%

Average years to complete the doctoral program (including internship): 6 years

Personal interview
Interview not required

Attrition rate in past 7 years: 2%

Percentage of students applying for internship last year accepted into APPIC or APA internships: 89%

Formal tracks/concentrations/specializations: adult psychopathology, developmental psychopathology

Research areas
affective disorders	molecular genetics
antisocial/psychopathic personality	personality assessment
	personality disorders
anxiety disorders	psychopharmacology
behavioral genetics	psychophysiology/
cross-cultural psychology	neuroimaging
developmental	responses to extreme stress
psychopathology	schizophrenia
eating disorders	substance abuse

Clinical opportunities
ADHD	long-term
affective disorders	psychodynamic
antisocial personality disorders	psychotherapy
anxiety disorders	neuropsychology
behavior therapy	obsessive–compulsive

childhood disorders and therapy	disorder
cognitive therapy	panic disorder
community psychology	post-traumatic stress disorder
conduct disorder	psychopathic personality
crisis intervention	psychotic disorders
eating disorders	schizophrenia
family therapy	substance abuse
forensic psychology	

University of Mississippi (Ph.D.)
Department of Psychology
University, MS 38677
phone#: (662) 915-5186
e-mail: pygross@olemiss.edu
Web address: www.olemiss.edu/depts/psychology/grad/clinical

1	2	3	4	5	6	7
Practice oriented		Equal emphasis				Research oriented

Percentage of faculty subscribing to each of the following orientations:

Psychodynamic/Psychoanalytic	0%
Applied behavioral analysis/Radical behavioral	29%
Family systems/Systems	14%
Existential/Phenomenological/Humanistic	14%
Cognitive/Cognitive-behavioral	71%

(some faculty not easily categorized, e.g. applied behavioral/behavioral)

Courses required for incoming students prior to enrolling:
statistics, lab course

Recommended but not mandatory courses:
physiological psychology, abnormal psychology, developmental psychology, and some grounding in biology/physiology/chemistry

GRE mean
Verbal 572   Quantitative 655
Verbal + Quantitative 1227
Psychology Subject Test 653
Analytical Writing N/A

GPA mean
Overall GPA 3.72   Psychology GPA 3.5
Junior/Senior GPA 3.5

Number of applications/admission offers/incoming students in 2009
applied not reported/15 admission offers/8 incoming

% of students receiving:
Full tuition waiver only: 0%
Assistantship/fellowship only: 0%
Both full tuition waiver & assistantship/fellowship: 100%

Approximate percentage of incoming students with a B.A./B.S. only: 87.5%   Master's: 12.5%

Approximate percentage of students who are Women: 84%   Ethnic Minority: 20%   International: 0%

219

Average years to complete the doctoral program (including internship): 6 years

Personal interview
Preferred in person but telephone acceptable

Attrition rate in past 7 years: 8%

Percentage of students applying for internship last year accepted into APPIC or APA internships: 100%

Formal tracks/concentrations: none

Research areas	# Faculty	# Grants
behavior problems in children	3	0
community psychology	2	0
compliance	1	0
computer-based research	1	1
emotion	2	1
posttraumatic stress disorder	1	0
psychological assessment	2	0
race relations	1	0
rape	2	0
rural mental health	2	0
smoking cessation/addiction/ substance abuse	1	1
social skills/competence	2	0

Clinical opportunities

child/adolescent	family/marital therapy
children's social skills	health psychology
chronic mental illness	mental retardation
clinical assessment	posttramatic stress disorder
community mental health	sexual aggression
consultation	smoking cessation
eating disorders	substance abuse/alcohol abuse

University of Missouri–Columbia (Ph.D.)

Department of Psychology
210 McAlester Hall
Columbia, MO 65211
phone#: (573) 882-0838
e-mail: gradpsych@missouri.edu
Web address: psychology.missouri.edu/grad

1	2	3	4	5	**6**	7
Practice oriented		Equal emphasis				Research oriented

Percentage of faculty subscribing to each of the following orientations:

Psychodynamic/Psychoanalytic	0%
Applied behavioral analysis/Radical behavioral	5%
Family systems/Systems	15%
Existential/Phenomenological/Humanistic	0%
Cognitive/Cognitive-behavioral	75%

Courses required for incoming students to have completed prior to enrolling: None

Recommended but not mandatory courses:
Other sciences, statistics/mathematics

GRE mean
Verbal + Quantitative 1222
Analytical Writing 4.3

Psychology Subject Test 640

GPA mean
Overall GPA 3.66   Psychology GPA 3.75
Junior/Senior GPA 3.76

Number of applications/admission offers/incoming students in 2009
145 applied/11 admission offers/6 incoming

Percent of students receiving:
Full tuition waiver only: 0%
Assistantship/fellowship only: 0%
Both full tuition waiver & assistantship/fellowship: 100%

Approximate percentage of incoming students with a B.A./B.S. only: 86%   **Master's:** 14%

Approximate percentage of students who are Women: 72%   **Ethnic Minority:** 14% **International:** 8%

Average years to complete the doctoral program (including internship): 7.5 years

Personal interview
Preferred in person but telephone acceptable

Attrition rate in past 7 years: 8.8%

Percentage of students applying for internship last year accepted into APPIC or APA internships: 100%

Formal tracks/concentrations: clinical adult, clinical child

Research areas	# Faculty	# Grants
addictions	5	~10
anxiety disorders (child)	2	1
autism/devel. disorders	1	0
multisystemic therapy	1	1
personality disorders	1	2
schizophrenia	1	1
treatment dissemination	2	1
neuroscience	2	1

Clinical opportunities

adult, outpatient and inpatient	research protocol
child, outpatient and inpatient	assessment and
health psychology	prevention
medical center	state hospital
rehabilitation psychology	VA hospital

University of Missouri–Kansas City (Ph.D.)

Department of Psychology
5100 Rockhill Road
Kansas City, MO 64110
phone#: (816)-235-1318
e-mail: psychology@umkc.edu
Web address: cas.umkc.edu/psychology/GCPhD.asp

1	2	3	4	5	6	**7**
Practice oriented		Equal emphasis				Research oriented

Percentage of faculty subscribing to each of the following orientations:

Psychodynamic/Psychoanalytic	0%
Applied behavioral analysis/Radical behavioral	0%

Family systems/Systems 0%
Existential/Phenomenological/Humanistic 0%
Cognitive/Cognitive-behavioral 100%

Courses required for incoming students to have completed prior to enrolling:
A B.A./B.S. in psychology is preferred but not required. At least 9 credits of psychology, including research methods and statistics

Recommended but not mandatory courses:
At least two of the following: abnormal, biopsychology, child, cognitive, learning, motivation, personality, sensation and perception, social psychology

GRE mean
Verbal 530   Quantitative 710
Psychology Subject Test not reported
Analytical Writing 5.0

GPA mean
Overall GPA 3.74

Number of applications/admission offers/incoming students in 2009
83 applied/5 admission offers/4 incoming

% of students receiving:
Full tuition waiver only: 0%
Assistantship/fellowship only: 0%
Both full tuition waiver & assistantship/fellowship: 100% (if enrolled at least 9 credit hours)

Approximate percentage of incoming students with a B.A./B.S. only: 78%   **Master's:** 22%

Approximate percentage of students who are Women: 88% **Ethnic Minority:** 11% **International:** 0%

Average years to complete the doctoral program (including internship): 5.5 years

Personal interview
Telephone required

Attrition rate in past 7 years: 7%

Percentage of students applying for internship last year accepted into APPIC or APA internships:
Not reported

Formal tracks/concentrations: health and life sciences

Research areas	# Faculty	# Grants
emotional social development	2	1
eating disorders/obesity	2	0
smoking cessation/cardiovascular disease	3	2
HIV	2	3
serious mental illness	1	1
attention and emotion	1	0
sensory and cognitive neuroscience	1	1
community psychology	1	1
neuropsychology (multiple sclerosis)	1	1

Clinical opportunities

chronic pain   pre-surgery evaluation
psychiatry   behavioral anxiety
substance abuse   treatment
veterans   primary care

University of Missouri–St. Louis (Ph.D.)
Department of Psychology
One University Blvd.
St. Louis, MO 63121
phone#: (314) 516-5382
e-mail: ann_steffen@umsl.edu
Web address: www.umsl.edu/divisions/artscience/psychology/clinical/index.html

1	2	3	4	5	6	7

Practice oriented   Equal emphasis   Research oriented

Percentage of faculty subscribing to each of the following orientations:
Psychodynamic/Psychoanalytic 12%
Applied behavioral analysis/Radical behavioral 0%
Family systems/Systems 0%
Existential/Phenomenological/Humanistic 12%
Cognitive/Cognitive-behavioral 76%

Courses required for incoming students to have completed prior to enrolling:
A total of 24 undergraduate credits: psychological statistics, research methods in psychology

Recommended but not mandatory courses:
Personality, social psychology, learning and motivation, history and systems, physiological psychology, developmental

GRE mean for Fall 2009 class
Verbal 622   Quantitative 675
Psychology Subject Test 718
Analytical Writing 4.8

GPA mean
Overall GPA 3.79   Psychology GPA 3.78

Number of applications/admission offers/incoming students in 2009
120 applied/14 admission offers/6 incoming

% of students receiving:
Full tuition waiver only: 0%
Assistantship/fellowship only: 0%
Both full tuition waiver & assistantship/fellowship: 100%

Approximate percentage of incoming students with a B.A./B.S. only: 85%   **Master's:** 15%

Approximate percentage of students who are Women: 80% **Ethnic Minority:** 10% **International:** 10%

Average years to complete the doctoral program (including internship): 6.0 years

Personal interview
Preferred in person but telephone acceptable

Attrition rate in past 7 years: 15%

Percentage of students applying for internship last year accepted into APPIC or APA internships: 100%

Formal tracks/concentrations: behavioral medicine, trauma studies, women and gender studies

Research areas

	# Faculty	# Grants
behavioral medicine	2	1
clinical geropsychology	1	1
multicultural issues	1	1
psychology of religion	1	0
women & sexuality	1	2
trauma studies	2	2

Clinical opportunities

adults & couples
assessment
behavioral medicine
  interventions
children/adolescents &
  families
older adults
treatment of PTSD/trauma
  across the lifespan

University of Montana (Ph.D.)

Department of Psychology
32 Campus Drive
Missoula, MT 59812-1584
phone#: (406) 243-4521
e-mail: david.schuldberg@umontana.edu
Web address: psychweb.psy.umt.edu/www/graduate_clinical.asp

1	2	3	4	5	6	7
Practice oriented		Equal emphasis				Research oriented

Percentage of faculty subscribing to each of the following orientations:

Psychodynamic/Psychoanalytic	64%
Applied behavioral analysis/Radical behavioral	9%
Family systems/Systems	36%
Existential/Phenomenological/Humanistic	45%
Cognitive/Cognitive-behavioral	91%
Eclectic	9%

Courses required for incoming students to have completed prior to enrolling: None

Recommended but not mandatory courses:
Research methods, statistics, abnormal psychology, personality, physiological psychology

GRE mean (for current entering class)
Verbal 517   Quantitative 573
Psychology Subject Test (Required) 639
Analytical Writing not reported

GPA mean
Overall (Undergraduate) GPA 3.48   Graduate GPA for students entering with M.A.: 3.93

Number of applications/admission offers/incoming students in 2009
108 applied/12 admission offers/7 incoming

% of (all, not just entering) students receiving:
Full tuition waiver only: 0%
Assistantship/fellowship only: 36%
Both partial fee waiver & assistantship/fellowship: 50%
Note: The above does not include students on internship and ABD.

Approximate percentage of incoming students with a B.A./B.S. only: 57%   **Master's:** 43%

Approximate percentage of students who are Women: 77%   **Ethnic Minority:** 28%   **International:** 0%

Average years to complete the doctoral program (including internship): 6.3 years

Personal interview
Preferred in person but telephone acceptable

Attrition rate in past 7 years: 12.8%

Percentage of students applying for internship last year accepted into APPIC or APA internships: 75%

Formal tracks/concentrations: Child, adolescent, family clinical emphasis; neuropsychology emphasis

Research areas	# Faculty	# Grants
assessment	4	1
behavioral medicine/health psychology	4	0
child psychopathology	3	1
closed-head injury	1	0
cross-cultural (Native American)	2	1
depression	1	0
gender issues	2	1
malingering	1	0
neuropsychology	1	0
nonlinear dynamic systems	1	0
psychotherapy process and outcome	3	0
schizophrenia	1	0
sexuality	1	0
substance abuse	2	1
health care systems	2	0
LGBT health	2	0
elderly	0	0
intimate partner violence	2	1
resilience	1	0
PTSD	3	2
mindfulness	1	0
borderline personality disorder/dialectical behavior therapy	1	1
parent–child relationships	1	0
memory	1	0

Clinical opportunities

adolescent and child
anxiety disorders
assessment
attachment disorder
borderline personality disorder
community health
couples/family
depression
domestic violence
functional analytic therapy
motivational interviewing
neuropsychology
pain management
prison populations
rural psychology
schizophrenia/psychoses
substance abuse
trauma
Inpatient treatment
LGBT populations
mindfulness-based
  interventions

University of Nebraska–Lincoln (Ph.D.)

Department of Psychology
238 Burnett Hall
Lincoln, NE 68588-0308
phone#: (402) 472-3229

e-mail: jlongwel@unlnotes.unl.edu
Web address: www.unl.edu/psypage/grad/clinical.shtml

1	2	3	**4**	5	6	7
Practice oriented			Equal emphasis			Research oriented

Percentage of faculty subscribing to each of the following orientations:
Psychodynamic/Psychoanalytic	0%
Applied behavioral analysis/Radical behavioral	10%
Family systems/Systems	10%
Existential/Phenomenological/Humanistic	10%
Cognitive/Cognitive-behavioral	85%

Courses required for incoming students to have completed prior to enrolling:
Psychology major preferred

Recommended but not mandatory courses:
Methodology and quantitative courses

GRE mean
Verbal 610   Quantitative 650
Analytical Writing Data not available
Psychology Subject Test not required

GPA mean
Overall GPA 3.65

Number of applications/admission offers/incoming students in 2009
215 applied/10 admission offers/10 incoming

% of students receiving:
Full tuition waiver only: 0%
Assistantship/fellowship only: 0%
Both full tuition waiver & assistantship/fellowship: 100%

Approximate percentage of incoming students with a B.A./B.S. only: 80%   Master's: 20%

Approximate percentage of students who are Women: 70%   Ethnic Minority: 20%   International: 5%

Average years to complete the doctoral program (including internship): 5.5 years

Personal interview
Preferred in person but telephone acceptable

Attrition rate in past 7 years: 4%

Percentage of students applying for internship last year accepted into APPIC or APA internships: 100%

Formal tracks/concentrations: adult/general, child and family, forensic

Research areas	# Faculty	# Grants
anxiety disorders	1	0
child abuse/family violence	2	2
child/adolescence	3	2
serious mental illness	1	1
forensic	1	2
psychology and law	1	2
psychopathology	3	2
trauma/PTSD	2	1

Clinical opportunities

anxiety disorders
child abuse/family violence
serious mental illness
forensic/threat assessment

minority/diversity issues
neuropsychology
substance abuse
pediatric psychology

University of Nevada–Las Vegas (Ph.D.)
Department of Psychology
Las Vegas, NV 89154
phone#: (702) 895-0716
e-mail: psyunlv@unlv.nevada.edu
Web address: psychology.unlv.edu/html/clinical_program.html

1	2	3	4	**5**	6	7
Practice oriented			Equal emphasis			Research oriented

Percentage of faculty subscribing to each of the following orientations:
Psychodynamic/Psychoanalytic	5%
Applied behavioral analysis/Radical behavioral	5%
Family systems/Systems	5%
Existential/Phenomenological/Humanistic	5%
Cognitive/Cognitive-behavioral	80%

Courses required for incoming students to have completed prior to enrolling:
Statistics, abnormal psychology, experimental psychology

Recommended but not mandatory courses:
Standardized testing, child behavior disorders, motivation and learning, history of psychology

GRE mean
Verbal 566   Quantitative 604
Psychology Subject Test 620

GPA mean
Overall GPA 3.74

Number of applications/admission offers/incoming students in 2009
120 applied/11 admission offers/6 incoming

% of students receiving:
Full tuition waiver only: 0%
Assistantship/fellowship only: 0%
Both full tuition waiver & assistantship/fellowship: 100%

Approximate percentage of incoming students with a B.A./B.S. only: 82%   Master's: 18%

Approximate percentage of students who are Women: 84%   Ethnic Minority: 22%   International: 0%

Average years to complete the doctoral program (including internship): 6 years

Personal interview
Preferred in person but telephone acceptable

Attrition rate in past 7 years: 2%

Percentage of students applying for internship last year accepted into APPIC or APA internships: 100%

Formal tracks/concentrations: none

Research areas	# Faculty	# Grants
child externalizing disorders	1	1
child internalizing disorders	1	0
descriptive experience sampling	2	0
women's health/sexuality	1	0
eating disorders/multicultural issues	1	0
social skills	1	0
neuropsychology	1	1
statistics	1	0

Clinical opportunities
Achievement Center (childhood externalizing disorders)
UNLV School Refusal and Anxiety Disorders Clinic
Center for Individual, Couple, and Family Counseling
(university-based counseling)
Student counseling and psychological services

University of Nevada–Reno (Ph.D.)
Department of Psychology
Clinical Psychology Program
MSS 298
Reno, NV 89557-0298
phone#: (775) 682-8701
e-mail: follette@unr.edu
Web address: www.unr.edu/psych/clinical/

1	2	3	4	5	6	7
Practice oriented		Equal emphasis			Research oriented	

Percentage of faculty subscribing to each of the following orientations:
Psychodynamic/Psychoanalytic 0%
Applied behavioral analysis/Radical behavioral 40%
Family systems/Systems 15%
Existential/Phenomenological/Humanistic 0%
Cognitive/Cognitive-behavioral 45%

Courses required for incoming students to have completed prior to enrolling: None

Recommended but not mandatory courses:
personality, abnormal/psychopathology, statistics, experimental design, history of psychology, behavior principles, behavior analysis

GRE mean
Verbal 526   Quantitative 606
Psychology Subject Test 700

GPA mean
Overall GPA 3.6   Psychology GPA 3.85

Number of applications/admission offers/incoming students in 2009
114 applied/8 admission offers/3 incoming

% of students receiving:
Full tuition waiver only: 0%
Assistantship/fellowship only: 0%
Both full tuition waiver & assistantship/fellowship: 100%

Approximate percentage of incoming students with a B.A./B.S. only: 66%   Master's: 34%

Approximate percentage of students who are
Women: 66%   Ethnic Minority: 0%   International: 33%

Average years to complete the doctoral program (including internship): 7.3 years

Personal interview
Preferred in person but telephone acceptable

Attrition rate in past 7 years: 7%

Percentage of students applying for internship last year accepted into APPIC or APA internships: 95%

Formal tracks/concentrations: none

Research areas	# Faculty	# Grants
aging	1	2
anxiety disorders	2	0
behavior analysis	3	0
behavioral assessment	3	0
behavioral health	2	0
couples	2	0
drug and alcohol abuse	2	1
gerontology	1	2
health care administration	1	1
incest survivors	2	0
minority mental health	1	0
mood disorders	1	0
prevention	4	2
sexual offenders	1	1
social skills	3	0
suicide	1	0
treatment development	3	1
verbal behavior	4	0

Clinical opportunities
AIDS — gerontology
anxiety disorders — health care administration
behavioral health care — incest survivors
couples — personality disorders
depression — posttraumatic stress disorder
drug and alcohol abuse

University of New Mexico (Ph.D.)
Department of Psychology
MSCO3 2220
Albuquerque, NM 87131-0001
phone#: (505) 277-4121
e-mail: erickson@unm.edu (director),
advising@unm.edu (graduate office) or
tbryant@unm.edu (coordinator)
Web address: psych.unm.edu/clinical.html

1	2	3	4	5	6	7
Practice oriented		Equal emphasis			Research oriented	

Percentage of faculty subscribing to each of the following orientations:
Psychodynamic/Psychoanalytic 0%
Applied behavioral analysis/Radical behavioral 33%
Family systems/Systems 11%
Existential/Phenomenological/Humanistic 11%
Cognitive/Cognitive-behavioral 78%

Courses required for incoming students to have completed prior to enrolling:

statistics, research methods, psychology major or equivalent course work

Recommended but not mandatory courses:

basic science courses, laboratory courses, supervised research

GRE mean

Verbal + Quantitative 1199
Analytical Writing 4.7
Psychology Subject Test 656

GPA mean

Overall GPA 3.65

Number of applications/admission offers/incoming students in 2008

133 applied/11 admission offers/7 incoming

% of students receiving:

Full tuition waiver only: 0%
Assistantship/fellowship only: 0%
Both full tuition waiver & assistantship/fellowship: 100%

Approximate percentage of incoming students with a B.A./B.S. only: 81% Master's: 18%

Approximate percentage of students who are Women: 83% Ethnic Minority: 16% International: 0%

Average years to complete the doctoral program (including internship): 7 years

Personal interview

Preferred in person

Attrition rate in past 7 years: 7.6

Percentage of students applying for internship last year accepted into APPIC or APA internships: 80%

Formal tracks/concentrations: none

Research areas	# Faculty	# Grants
eating disorders	2	0
minority/cultural issues	2	1
health psychology	2	2
neuropsychology	2	0
pediatric psychology	1	0
clinical child psychology	1	0
substance abuse	6	4
neuroimaging and clinical neuroscience	3	3
trauma prevention	1	0

Clinical opportunities

inpatient/outpatient psychotherapy
behavioral medicine
VA healthcare system
child outpatient assessment, consultation, and therapy
forensic settings/domestic violence
multicultural counseling
neuropsychological assessment
rural mental health
neuroimaging
pediatric psychology assessment, consultation, therapy
personality assessment
substance abuse treatment
anxiety disorder treatment
borderline personality disorder treatment

The New School (Ph.D.)

(formerly listed as New School University)
New School for Social Research, Department of Psychology
80 Fifth Avenue, 7th floor
New York, NY 10011
phone#: (212) 229-5727
e-mail: SteeleM@newschool.edu
Web address: www.newschool.edu/nssr/subpage.aspx?id=9888

1	2	3	4	5	6	7
Practice oriented		Equal emphasis				Research oriented

Percentage of faculty subscribing to each of the following orientations:

Psychodynamic/Psychoanalytic	90%
Applied behavioral analysis/Radical behavioral	0%
Family systems/Systems	0%
Existential/Phenomenological/Humanistic	0%
Cognitive/Cognitive-behavioral	10%

Courses required for incoming students to have completed prior to enrolling:

1 course in each of the following: personality, social, developmental; psychopathology; 1 course in assessment of individual differences; 1 course in statistics; 1 research methods course

Recommended but not mandatory courses:

Undergraduate major in psychology recommended, but not mandatory

GRE mean

Verbal 525   Quantitative 590
Psychology Subject Test 595
Analytical Writing not reported

GPA mean

GPA 3.63

Number of applications/admission offers/incoming students in 2009

29 applied/16 admission offers/16 incoming
Note: Only applications from New School University master's students in psychology are considered for enrollment.

% of students receiving:

Full tuition waiver only: 7%
Assistantship/fellowship only: 20%
Both full tuition waiver & assistantship/fellowship: 2% (approximately 33% of students receive a partial tuition waiver)

Approximate percentage of incoming students with a B.A./B.S. only: 0%   Master's: 100%

Approximate percentage of students who are Women: 77% Ethnic Minority: 13% International: 14%

Average years to complete the doctoral program (including internship): 5.5 years

Personal interview

Required in person

Attrition rate in past 7 years: 4%

Percentage of students applying for internship last year accepted into APPIC or APA internships: 77%

Formal tracks/concentrations: Scientist–Practitioner training model

Research areas	# Faculty	# Grants
assessment/diagnosis	2	1
child clinical	1	1
developmental	1	0
emotions	1	0
memory	2	1
moral development	1	0
narrative methodologies	2	0
personality assessment	1	0
prevention	2	1
psychoanalysis	2	0
psychopathology	2	0
psychotherapy process & outcome	3	1

Clinical opportunities
New School–Beth Israel Center for Training and Research
Variety of clinical settings

University of North Carolina at Chapel Hill (Ph.D.)

Department of Psychology
Davie Hall 013A
Chapel Hill, NC 27514
phone#: (919) 962-5082
fax#: (919) 962-2537
e-mail: mitch.prinstein@unc.edu
Web address: www.unc.edu/depts/clinpsy/

1	2	3	4	5	6	7

Practice oriented   Equal emphasis   Research oriented

Percentage of faculty subscribing to each of the following orientations:
Psychodynamic/Psychoanalytic   0%
Applied behavioral analysis/Radical behavioral   0%
Family systems/Systems   0%
Existential/Phenomenological/Humanistic   0%
Cognitive/Cognitive-behavioral   100%

Courses required for incoming students to have completed prior to enrolling:
A psychology major or its equivalent (8 or more courses).

Recommended but not mandatory courses: None

GRE mean
Verbal + Quantitative 1350
Analytical Writing not reported
Psychology Subject Test not reported

GPA mean
Psychology GPA 3.5   Junior/Senior GPA 3.5

Number of applications/admission offers/incoming students in 2009
450 applied/12 admission offers/9 incoming

% of students receiving:

Full tuition waiver only: 0%
Assistantship/fellowship only: 0%
Both full tuition waiver & assistantship/fellowship: 100%

Approximate percentage of incoming students with a B.A./B.S. only: 85%   **Master's:** 15%

Approximate percentage of students who are Women: 71%   **Ethnic Minority:** 28%
International: not reported

Average years to complete the doctoral program (including internship): 6 years

Personal interview
Preferred in person but telephone acceptable

Attrition rate in past 7 years: 7%

Percentage of students applying for internship last year accepted into APPIC or APA internships: 100%

Formal tracks/concentrations: adult clinical, clinical child and adolescent

Research areas	# Faculty	# Grants
schizophrenia	1	2
anxiety disorders	1	0
couples therapy/research	1	2
behavioral medicine/health psychology	1	2
pediatric bipolar disorder	1	2
adolescent substance use	1	1
adolescent peer relationships	1	1
adolescent depression and suicidality	1	1
ethnic minority youth; health disparities	2	0
family functioning and health risk behaviors	1	1
eating disorders	1	0

Clinical opportunities
couples therapy   child assessment
anxiety disorders   health/pediatric psychology
adult therapy and assessment   eating disorders
child behavior therapy   developmental disabilities
child bipolar treatment

University of North Carolina at Greensboro (Ph.D.)

Department of Psychology
263 Eberhart Building
Greensboro, NC 27402-6170
phone#: (336) 256-1022
e-mail: ada@uncg.edu
Web address: www.uncg.edu/psy/grad/clinical/index.html

1	2	3	4	5	6	7

Practice oriented   Equal emphasis   Research oriented

Percentage of faculty subscribing to each of the following orientations:
Psychodynamic/Psychoanalytic   0%
Applied behavioral analysis/Radical behavioral   12%
Family systems/Systems   62%
Existential/Phenomenological/Humanistic   0%
Cognitive/Cognitive-behavioral   100%

Courses required for incoming students to have completed prior to enrolling:
Equivalent of undergraduate major in psychology, which should include statistics and 4 other courses in psychology

Recommended but not mandatory courses:
Physiological psychology, abnormal psychology, statistics, learning, cognitive psychology

GRE mean
Verbal 580   Quantitative 710
Psychology Subject Test not required
Analytical Writing 5.0

GPA mean
Overall GPA 3.8

Number of applications/admission offers/incoming students in 2009
256 applied/10 admission offers/6 incoming

% of students receiving:
Full tuition waiver only: 0%
Assistantship/fellowship only: 0%
Both full tuition waiver & assistantship/fellowship: 100%

Approximate percentage of incoming students with a B.A./B.S. only: 84%   **Master's:** 16%

Approximate percentage of students who are Women: 84%   **Ethnic Minority:** 33%
International: not reported

Average years to complete the doctoral program (including internship): 6 years

Personal interview
Required in person

Attrition rate in past 7 years: 8.8%

Percentage of students applying for internship last year accepted into APPIC or APA internships: 67%

Formal tracks/concentrations: clinical child specialization, ADHD specialization

Research areas	# Faculty	# Grants
ADHD	1	2
behavioral analysis	1	0
behavioral assessment	1	0
children's internalizing disorder	1	0
children's social relationships	2	2
depression	1	0
personality disorders	1	0
schizophrenia	1	1

Clinical opportunities
preschool intervention program
University-based community clinic
University counseling center

University of North Dakota (Ph.D.)

Department of Psychology
Box 8380
Grand Forks, ND 58202
phone#: (701) 777-3451
e-mail: alan.king@und.edu

Web address: www.und.edu/dept/psych/clinicaladmission.html

1	2	3	4	5	6	7
Practice oriented		Equal emphasis				Research oriented

Percentage of faculty subscribing to each of the following orientations:

Psychodynamic/Psychoanalytic	10%
Applied behavioral analysis/Radical behavioral	10%
Family systems/Systems	0%
Existential/Phenomenological/Humanistic	5%
Cognitive/Cognitive-behavioral	75%

Courses required for incoming students to have completed prior to enrolling:
Psychology courses (at least 18 hours) in developmental, abnormal, statistics, experimental or research methods. One semester of college algebra and a year of biological science.

Recommended but not mandatory courses:
A background in social and natural sciences

GRE mean
Verbal + Quantitative 1256
Analytical Writing 4.7
Psychology Subject Test 691

GPA mean
Overall GPA 3.73

Number of applications/admission offers/incoming students in 2009
110 applied/20 admission offers/7 incoming

% of students receiving:
Full tuition waiver only: 0%
Assistantship/fellowship only: 0%
Both full tuition waiver & assistantship/fellowship: 100%

Approximate percentage of incoming students with a B.A./B.S. only: 90%   **Master's:** 10%

Approximate percentage of students who are Women: 75%   **Ethnic Minority:** 25%   **International:** 1%

Average years to complete the doctoral program (including internship): 5.5 years

Personal interview
Preferred in person but telephone acceptable

Attrition rate in past 7 years: 6%

Percentage of students applying for internship last year accepted into APPIC or APA internships: 100%

Formal tracks/concentrations: none

Research areas	# Faculty	# Grants
adult psychopathology	6	0
self-harm behavior	1	1
suicidality	1	1
anxiety disorders	1	0
applied behavioral analysis	2	0
behavioral medicine	2	0
community psychology	2	0
cross-cultural psychology	2	1

friendship/relationships	2	0
gender roles	2	0
minority mental health	2	0
pain management/control	1	0
personality assessment	2	0
personality disorders	3	0
psychophysiology	1	0
relaxation/biofeedback	1	0
rural psychology	2	2
stress and coping	6	0
substance abuse	1	0
women's studies	2	0

Clinical opportunities

affective disorders	minority/cross-cultural
anxiety disorders	obsessive–compulsive
assessment	disorder
behavioral medicine	personality disorders
community psychology	rural psychology
interpersonal psychotherapy	substance abuse
marital/couples therapy	victim/battering abuse

University of North Texas (Ph.D.)

Clinical Psychology Program
Department of Psychology
1155 Union Cir. #311280
Denton, TX 76203-1280
phone#: (940) 565-2631
e-mail: amy.mayfield@unt.edu
Web address: www.psyc.unt.edu/graduate-programs/clinical-psychology

1	2	3	4	5	6	7
Practice oriented			Equal emphasis			Research oriented

Percentage of faculty subscribing to each of the following orientations:

Psychodynamic/Psychoanalytic	25%
Applied behavioral analysis/Radical behavioral	0%
Family systems/Systems	25%
Existential/Phenomenological/Humanistic	37%
Cognitive/Cognitive-behavioral	37%

Courses required for incoming students to have completed prior to enrolling:

statistics, plus three of the following: experimental psychology or research methods, learning, perception, motivation, cognition, psychological measurement, physiological psychology, research thesis

Recommended but not mandatory courses:
See above

GRE mean
Verbal 553   Quantitative 648
Analytical Writing not reported
Psychology Subject Test not reported

GPA mean
3.83

Number of applications/admission offers/incoming students in 2008
151 applied/14 admission offers/8 incoming

% of students receiving:
Full tuition waiver only: 0%
Assistantship/fellowship only: 0%
Both full tuition waiver & assistantship/fellowship: 100%

Approximate percentage of incoming students with a B.A./B.S. only: 88%   **Master's:** 12%

Approximate percentage of students who are Women: 77%   **Ethnic Minority:** 26%   **International:** 6%

Average years to complete the doctoral program (including internship): 6 years

Personal interview
Required in person

Attrition rate in past 7 years: 10.5%

Percentage of students applying for internship last year accepted into APPIC or APA internships: 88%

Formal tracks/concentrations: none

Research areas	# Faculty	# Grants
abuse	2	0
AIDS	2	0
affect management	1	0
aging	1	1
children	1	1
disaster intervention	2	0
forensics	3	1
malingering	2	0
multicultural	1	0
neuropsychology	1	0
posttraumatic stress disorder	2	0
schizophrenia	2	0
stress	2	1

Clinical opportunities

children, adolescent and adults	forensic psychology
	psychopathy
depression	posttraumatic stress
anxiety	disorder

University of North Texas and University of North Texas Health Sciences Center (Consortium)

University of North Texas
Department of Psychology
Terrill Hall, Rm 369
1155 Union Circle #311280
Denton, TX 76203
phone#: (940) 369-8135
e-mail: frank.collins@unt.edu
Web address: http://www.psyc.unt.edu/clinicalhealthpsychology/CHPBMindex.html

1	2	3	4	5	6	7
Practice oriented			Equal emphasis			Research oriented

Percentage of faculty subscribing each of the following orientations:

Psychodynamic/Psychoanalytic	0%
Applied behavioral analysis/Radical behavioral	14%

Family systems/Systems 0%
Existential/Phenomenological/Humanistic 0%
Cognitive/Cognitive behavioral 86%

Courses required for incoming students to have completed prior to enrolling: not reported

Recommended but not mandatory courses:
not reported

GRE mean
Quantitative 570   Verbal 489   Analytical Writing N/A
Psychology Subject Test N/A

GPA mean
Overall GPA 3.41

Number of applications/admissions offers/incoming students in 2009
34 applied/admission offers unknown/0 incoming

% students receiving:
Full tuition waiver only: 0%
Assistantship/fellowship only 90%
Both full tuition waiver AND assistantship/fellowship 0%

Approximate percentage of incoming students with a B.A./B.S. only: 50%   **Master's** 50%

Approximate percentage of students who are Women: 67%   **Racial/ethnic minorities:** 20%
International students: 0%

Average years to complete the doctoral program (including internship): 7.1 years

Personal interview
Preferred in person but telephone acceptable

Attrition rate in past 7 years: 9%

Percentage of students applying for internship last year accepted into APPIC or APA internships: 89%

Formal tracks/concentrations: Clinical Health Psychology

Research areas	# Faculty	# Grants
health disparities	2	1
sleep	1	1
nicotine	1	0
psychoneuroimmunology	1	0
cardiovascular disease	2	1
HIV/AIDS	1	1

Clinical opportunities
UNT Health Sciences Center

Northern Illinois University (Ph.D.)
Department of Psychology
DeKalb, IL 60115
phone#: (815) 753-0772
e-mail: mlovejoy@niu.edu
Web address: http://www.niu.edu/psyc/graduate/clinical/index.shtml

1	2	3	4	5	6	7
Practice oriented		Equal emphasis			Research oriented	

Percentage of faculty subscribing to each of the following orientations:
Psychodynamic/Psychoanalytic 22%
Applied behavioral analysis/Radical behavioral 44%
Family systems/Systems 33%
Existential/Phenomenological/Humanistic 22%
Cognitive/Cognitive-behavioral 89%
Interpersonal 22%
Integrative 33%

Courses required for incoming students prior to enrolling: None

Recommended but not mandatory courses:
Statistics, research methods, laboratory course, history

GRE mean
Verbal 526   Quantitative 654
Analytical Writing 4.5

GPA mean
Overall GPA 3.78

Number of applications/admission offers/incoming students in 2009
166 applied/15admission offers/9 incoming

% of students receiving:
Full tuition waiver only: 0%
Assistantship/fellowship only: 0%
Both full tuition waiver & assistantship/fellowship: 100%

Approximate percentage of incoming students with a B.A./B.S. only: 88%   **Master's:** 12%

Approximate percentage of students who are Women: 80%   **Ethnic Minority:** 25%   **International:** 4%

Average years to complete the doctoral program (including internship): 7.4

Personal interview
Preferred in person but telephone acceptable

Attrition rate in past 7 years: 16%

Percentage of students applying for internship last year accepted into APPIC or APA internships: 67%

Formal tracks/concentrations: none

Research areas	# Faculty	# Grants
adolescents	3	0
adult psychopathology	4	0
anxiety disorders	3	1
child sexual abuse	3	1
couples	3	0
developmental psychopathology	4	0
diversity	4	0
emotion/emotion regulation	4	0
infants and preschool age children	2	0
intimate partner violence	4	0
mood disorders	2	0
parenting	4	0
personality disorders	3	0
physical abuse	3	0
prevention	1	0
psychometrics	3	0
school-age children	1	0
sexual aggression	3	0

temperament	1	0
trauma	3	1

Clinical opportunities

ADHD clinic
anxiety disorders
behavior management and
  progress monitoring
  (learning and behavior
  problems)
child psychotherapy
cognitive assessment
consultation and multi-
  disciplinary assessment

family therapy
forensic evaluation
individual psychotherapy
parent training
personality assessment
school settings
developmental disabilities
developmental assessment
victims/battering/abuse

Northwestern University (Ph.D.)

Department of Psychology
102 Swift Hall, 2029 Sheridan Road
Evanston, IL 60208-2710
phone#: (847) 491-5190
e-mail: malissie-collins@northwestern.edu
Web address: www.wcas.northwestern.edu/psych/

1	2	3	4	5	6	**7**
Practice oriented		Equal emphasis				Research oriented

Percentage of faculty subscribing to each of the following orientations:

Psychodynamic/Psychoanalytic	10%
Applied behavioral analysis/Radical behavioral	0%
Family systems/Systems	10%
Existential/Phenomenological/Humanistic	0%
Cognitive/Cognitive-behavioral	80%

Courses required for incoming students to have completed prior to enrolling: None

Recommended but not mandatory courses:
Psychology major, undergraduate statistics

GRE mean
Verbal + Quantitative 1487
Analytical Writing 5

GPA mean
Overall GPA 3.42

Number of applications/admission offers/incoming students in 2009
92 applied/4 admission offers/3 incoming

% of students receiving:
Full tuition waiver only: 0%
Assistantship/fellowship only: 0%
Both full tuition waiver & assistantship/fellowship: 100%

Approximate percentage of incoming students with a B.A./B.S. only: 33%   **Master's:** 67%

Approximate percentage of students who are Women: 56%   **Ethnic Minority:** 13% **International:** 6%

Average years to complete the doctoral program (including internship): 6 years

Personal interview
not reported

Attrition rate in past 7 years: 10%

Percentage of students applying for internship last year accepted into APPIC or APA internships: 100%

Formal tracks/concentrations: none

Research areas	# Faculty	# Grants
anxiety	2	1
behavioral genetics	1	0
cognitive functioning	2	1
depression	3	0
personality	4	2
psychotherapy	1	0

Clinical opportunities

anxiety disorders
couples
crisis intervention
depression

diagnostic interviewing
family
neuropsychology
personality disorders

Northwestern University, Feinberg School of Medicine (Ph.D.)

Department of Psychiatry and Behavioral Sciences
Division of Psychology
Abbott Hall, Suite 1205
710 North Lakeshore Drive
Chicago, IL 60611
Phone #: (312) 908-5190
e-mail: f-sales@northwestern.edu
Web address: http://psychiatry.northwestern.edu/
index.php/edu-psychology/doctoral-program-in-clinical-psychology/

1	2	3	**4**	5	6	7
Practice oriented		Equal emphasis				Research oriented

Percentage of faculty subscribing to each of the following orientations:

Psychodynamic/Psychoanalytic	30%
Applied behavioral analysis/Radical behavioral	10%
Family systems/Systems	0%
Existential/Phenomenological/Humanistic	10%
Cognitive/Cognitive-behavioral	40%

Courses required for incoming students to have completed prior to enrolling:
Statistics and research design, experimental, abnormal

Recommended but not mandatory courses: None

GRE mean
Verbal 650   Quantitative 640
Psychology Subject Test 650
Analytical Writing not reported

GPA mean
3.52

Number of applications/admission offers/incoming students in 2009
239 applied/10 admission offers/5 incoming

% of students receiving:
Full tuition waiver only: 0%
Assistantship/fellowship only: 0%
Both full tuition waiver & assistantship/fellowship: 0%
(Note: Half or 3/4 tuition: 100%)

Approximate percentage of incoming students with a B.A./B.S. only: 80%   **Master's:** 20%

Approximate percentage of students who are Women: 88%   **Ethnic Minority:** 12%   **International:** 6%

Average years to complete the doctoral program (including internship): 6.4 years

Personal interview
Required in person

Attrition rate in past 7 years: .03%

Percentage of students applying for internship last year accepted into APPIC or APA internships: 100%

Formal tracks/concentrations: neuropsychology, general adult clinical, child clinical

Research areas	# Faculty	# Grants
adolescent/adult depression	3	1
child mental health	2	1
mental health services and policy	2	1
neuropsychology	3	1
psycholegal studies (youth in criminal justice system)	2	1

Clinical opportunities
adult, adolescent, and child outpatient clinics
chronic mental illness
neuropsychology (adult and pediatric)
student mental health

Nova Southeastern University (Ph.D.)

Center for Psychological Studies
3301 College Avenue
Fort Lauderdale, FL 33314
phone#: 800-541-6682, ext. 25790 (954) 262-5790
e-mail: gradschool@nova.edu
Web address: cps.nova.edu/programs/phd/index.html

1	2	3	4	5	6	7
Practice oriented		Equal emphasis			Research oriented	

Percentage of faculty subscribing to each of the following orientations:
Psychodynamic/Psychoanalytic   8%
Applied behavioral analysis/Radical behavioral 12%
Family systems/Systems   8%
Existential/Phenomenological/Humanistic   14%
Cognitive/Cognitive-behavioral   58%

Courses required for incoming students to have completed prior to enrolling:
18 credits in psychology and 3 credits in statistics

Recommended but not mandatory courses:
Courses in statistics, psychology, biology

GRE mean
Verbal 558   Quantitative 662
Psychology Subject Test 620
Analytical Writing 4.5

GPA mean
Overall GPA 3.47

Number of applications/admission offers/incoming students in 2008
155 applied/35 admission offers/20 incoming

% of students receiving:
Full tuition waiver only: 0%
Assistantship/fellowship only: not reported
Both full tuition waiver & assistantship/fellowship: 0%

Approximate percentage of incoming students with a B.A./B.S. only: 91%   **Master's:** 9%

Approximate percentage of students who are Women: 88%   **Ethnic Minority:** 26%   **International:** 2%

Average years to complete the doctoral program (including internship): 5.6 years

Personal interview
Required in person

Attrition rate in past 7 years: 7.5%

Percentage of students applying for internship last year accepted into APPIC or APA internships: 100%

Formal tracks/concentrations: forensic psychology, health psychology, neuropsychology, psychodynamic psychotherapy, child, adolescent, and family psychology, multicultural/diversity, trauma

Research areas	# Faculty	# Grants
ADHD	2	1
alcohol/substance abuse	3	5
anxiety disorders	1	0
behavior therapy	14	2
biofeedback	1	1
child/adolescent depression	6	0
child/adolescent psychotherapy	12	2
child neuropsychology	2	0
community mental health	4	0
cross-cultural counseling	4	0
domestic/interpersonal violence	3	1
forensic psychology	3	2
gerontology	1	0
health psychology	6	2
long-term mental illness	2	0
MMPI-2	1	0
neuropsychology	4	2
posttraumatic stress disorder	8	0
psychoanalysis	2	0
survivors of sexual abuse/assault	2	0
trauma and victimization	8	0

Clinical opportunities
anxiety disorders
behavioral modification
biofeedback
child/adolescent assessment and treatment
child/adolescent depression
interpersonal violence
multilingual services
neuropsychological assessment and evaluation
pain management

community support services
crisis assessment and
intervention
depression
family and multifamily
therapy
forensic evaluation and
testimony
group therapy

parenting skills training
psychodynamic
psychotherapy
psychological consultation
psychological testing
serious emotional
disturbance
stress management
substance abuse

Nova Southeastern University (Psy.D.)

Center for Psychological Studies
3301 College Avenue
Fort Lauderdale, FL 33314
phone#: 800-541-6682, ext. 25790; (954) 262-5790
e-mail: gradschool@nova.edu
Web address: cps.nova.edu/programs/psyd/index.html

1	2	**3**	4	5	6	7
Practice oriented		Equal emphasis			Research oriented	

Percentage of faculty subscribing to each of the following orientations:

Psychodynamic/Psychoanalytic   8%
Applied behavioral analysis/Radical behavioral   12%
Family systems/Systems   8%
Existential/Phenomenological/Humanistic   14%
Cognitive/Cognitive-behavioral   58%

Courses required for incoming students to have completed prior to enrolling:

18 credits in psychology and 3 credits in statistics

Recommended but not mandatory courses:

Courses in statistics, psychology, biology

GRE mean

Verbal 507   Quantitative 629
Psychology Subject Test 629
Analytical Writing 4.3

GPA mean

Overall GPA 3.44

Number of applications/admission offers/incoming students in 2008

256 applied/121 admission offers/75 incoming

% of students receiving:

Full tuition waiver only: 0%
Assistantship/fellowship only: 0%
Both full tuition waiver & assistantship/fellowship: 0%

Approximate percentage of incoming students with a B.A./B.S. only: 91%   Master's: 9%

Approximate percentage of students who are Women: 80%   Ethnic Minority: 26%   International: 2%

Average years to complete the doctoral program (including internship): 5 years

Personal interview

Required in person

Attrition rate in past 7 years: 7.5%

Percentage of students applying for internship last year accepted into APPIC or APA internships: 94%

Formal tracks/concentrations: forensic psychology, health psychology, neuropsychology, psychodynamic psychotherapy, child, adolescent, and family psychology, multicultural/diversity, trauma

Research areas	# Faculty	# Grants
ADHD	2	1
alcohol/substance abuse	3	5
anxiety disorders	1	0
behavior therapy	14	0
biofeedback	1	1
child/adolescent depression	6	0
child/adolescent psychotherapy	12	2
child neuropsychology	2	0
community mental health	4	0
cross-cultural counseling	4	0
domestic/interpersonal violence	3	1
forensic psychology	3	2
gerontology	1	0
health psychology	6	2
long-term mental illness	2	0
MMPI-2	1	0
neuropsychology	4	2
posttraumatic stress disorder	8	0
psychoanalysis	2	0
survivors of sexual abuse/assault	2	0
trauma and victimization	8	0

Clinical opportunities

anxiety disorders
behavioral modification
biofeedback
child/adolescent assessment
and treatment
child/adolescent traumatic
stress and depression
community support services
crisis assessment and
intervention
depression
family and multifamily
treatment
forensic evaluation and
testimony
group therapy

interpersonal violence
multilingual services
neuropsychological
assessment and
evaluation
pain management
parenting skills and training
psychodynamic
psychotherapy
psychological consultation
psychological testing
serious emotional
disturbance
stress management
substance abuse

Ohio State University (Ph.D.)

Department of Psychology
108 Psychology Building
1835 Neil Avenue Mall
Columbus, OH 43210
phone#: (614) 292-4112
e-mail: emery.33@osu.edu
Web address: www2.psy.ohio-state.edu/programs/clinical/

1	2	3	4	5	6	7
Practice oriented		Equal emphasis			Research oriented	

Percentage of faculty subscribing to each of the following orientations:

Psychodynamic/Psychoanalytic	0%
Applied behavioral analysis/Radical behavioral	0%
Family systems/Systems	0%
Existential/Phenomenological/Humanistic	0%
Cognitive/Cognitive-behavioral	100%

Courses required for incoming students prior to enrolling:

Experimental psychology, abnormal psychology, statistics, personality

Recommended but not mandatory courses: None

GRE mean
Verbal 619   Quantitative 726
Analytical Writing 4.9

GPA mean
Psychology GPA 3.65

Number of applications/admission offers/incoming students in 2009
239 applied/15 admission offers/7 incoming

% of students receiving:
Full tuition waiver only: 0%
Assistantship/fellowship only: 0%
Both full tuition waiver & assistantship/fellowship: 100%

Approximate percentage of incoming students with a B.A./B.S. only: 100%   Master's: 0%

Approximate percentage of students who are
Women: 81% Ethnic Minority: 18% International: 13%

Average years to complete the doctoral program (including internship): 5.5 years

Personal interview
Preferred in person but telephone acceptable

Attrition rate in past 7 years: 11%

Percentage of students applying for internship last year accepted into APPIC or APA internships: 100%

Formal tracks/concentrations: adult clinical, child clinical, health

Research areas	# Faculty	# Grants
anxiety disorders	2	1
cardiovascular health	3	4
child psychopathology	3	4
childhood mood disorders	2	4
depression	3	1
oncology	1	3
pediatric neuropsychology	2	3
personality	1	0
psychoneuroimmunology	2	5
psychosocial aspects of pediatric oncology	2	3

Clinical opportunities
anxiety disorder	family
child and adolescent psychopathology	gerontology
	health psychology
childhood mood disorders	neuropsychology
crisis intervention	oncology

depressive disorders
eating disorders

psycho-education evaluations
sex therapy

Ohio University (Ph.D.)
Department of Psychology
Athens, OH 45701-2979
phone#: (740) 593-1707
e-mail: psychology@ohio.edu
Web address: www.ohioupsychology.edu/Graduate-Clinical-General.html

1	2	3	4	5	6	7
Practice oriented		Equal emphasis			Research oriented	

Percentage of faculty subscribing to each of the following orientations:

Psychodynamic/Psychoanalytic	30%
Applied behaviotral analysis/Radical behavioral	0%
Family systems/Systems	30%
Existential/Phenomenological/Humanistic	30%
Cognitive/Cognitive-behavioral	80%

Courses required for incoming students to have completed prior to enrolling:
27 quarter hours of undergraduate psychology, experimental psychology, statistics

Recommended but not mandatory courses:
Computer science, abnormal psychology, personality

GRE mean:
Verbal 556   Quantitative 639
Psychology Subject Test 637

GPA mean
Overall GPA 3.60

Number of applications/admission offers/incoming students in 2009
131applied/13 admission offers/9 incoming

% of students receiving:
Full tuition waiver only: 0%
Assistantship/fellowship only: 0%
Both full tuition waiver & assistantship/fellowship: 100%

Approximate percentage of incoming students with a B.A./B.S. only: 80%   Master's: 20%

Approximate percentage of students who are
Women: 75% Ethnic Minority: 20% International: 12%

Average years to complete the doctoral program (including internship): 5.9 years

Personal interview
Preferred in person but telephone acceptable

Attrition rate in past 7 years: 10.8%

Percentage of students applying for internship last year accepted into APPIC or APA internships: 80%

Formal tracks/concentrations: child clinical, clinical health

Research areas

	# Faculty	# Grants
adult psychopathology and psychotherapy	2	0
family and child	2	2
health psychology	4	6
sexual assault	1	1
neuropsychology	1	1

Clinical opportunities

adult inpatient and outpatient
child and family (including school-based mental health)
neuropsychological assessment
pain management and cardiac rehabilitation
substance abuse
primary care patients
pediatric
veterans

Oklahoma State University (Ph.D.)

Department of Psychology
116 North Murray Hall
Stillwater, OK 74078
phone#: (405) 744-7494
e-mail: thad.leffingwell@okstate.edu
Web address: psychology.okstate.edu/index.php?option=com_content&view=article&id=80&Item=27#cp

1	2	3	4	5	6	7
Practice oriented			Equal emphasis			Research oriented

Percentage of faculty subscribing to each of the following orientations:

Psychodynamic/Psychoanalytic	0%
Applied behavioral analysis/Radical behavioral	0%
Family systems/Systems	10%
Existential/Phenomenological/Humanistic	0%
Cognitive/Cognitive-behavioral	90%

Courses required for incoming students to have completed prior to enrolling:

Statistics, experimental psychology

Recommended but not mandatory courses:

Abnormal psychology, history and systems

GRE mean

Verbal 528   Quantitative 643
Psychology Subject Test not reported
Analytical Writing 4.5

GPA mean

Overall GPA 3.26

Number of applications/admission offers/incoming students in 2009

76 applied/7 admission offers/4 incoming

% of students receiving:

Full tuition waiver only: 0%
Assistantship/fellowship only: 0%
Both full tuition waiver & assistantship/fellowship: 100%

Approximate percentage of incoming students with a B.A./B.S. only: 100%   Master's: 0%

Approximate percentage of students who are

Women: 75%   **Ethnic Minority:** 25%
International: not reported

Average years to complete the doctoral program (including internship): 5 years

Personal interview

No preference given

Attrition rate in past 7 years: 10%

Percentage of students applying for internship last year accepted into APPIC or APA internships: 100% (94% in last six years)

Formal tracks/concentrations: child clinical, behavioral medicine/health psychology

Research areas

	# Faculty	# Grants
anxiety disorders	1	0
health psychology	2	0
pediatric psychology	2	1
substance abuse	2	0
depression	1	0
child/parenting	1	0

Clinical opportunities

anxiety/mood disorder
trauma
behavioral medicine
family therapy
marital therapy
pediatric psychology
substance abuse
geropsychology

University of Oregon (Ph.D.)

Department of Psychology
Eugene, OR 97403
phone#: (541) 346-5060
e-mail: gradsec@psych.uoregon.edu
Web address: psychweb.uoregon.edu/graduates/intellectualcommunities/clinical

1	2	3	4	5	6	7
Practice oriented			Equal emphasis			Research oriented

Percentage of faculty subscribing to each of the following orientations:

Psychodynamic/Psychoanalytic	0%
Applied behavioral analysis/Radical behavioral	20%
Family systems/Systems	20%
Existential/Phenomenological/Humanistic	0%
Cognitive/Cognitive-behavioral	55%

Courses required for incoming students to have completed prior to enrolling:

Good background in psychology; some direct services experience

Recommended but not mandatory courses:

Research, statistics or math background

GRE mean

high 600 or 700 range or higher
Analytical Writing 5.23
Psychology Subject Test not reported

GPA mean
Cumulative undergraduate GPA should be above 3.0

Number of applications/admission offers/incoming students in 2009
200 applied/4 admission offers/4 incoming

% of students receiving:
Full tuition waiver only: 0%
Assistantship/fellowship only: 0%
Both full tuition waiver & assistantship/fellowship: 100%

Approximate percentage of incoming students with a B.A./B.S. only: 75%   **Master's:** 25%

Approximate percentage of students who are Women: 87%   **Ethnic Minority:** 43% **International:** 1%

Average years to complete the doctoral program (including internship): 5 years

Personal interview
Preferred in person but telephone acceptable under special circumstances

Attrition rate in past 7 years: 0%

Percentage of students applying for internship last year accepted into APPIC or APA internships: 100%

Formal tracks/concentrations: please visit departmental website at http://psychweb.uoregon.edu

Research areas	# Faculty	# Grants
affective disorders	3	2
anxiety disorders	2	2
cultural psychology	1	1
developmental psychopathology	4	1
life stress	2	1
neuropsychology	2	2
infant mental health	2	1

Clinical opportunities
anxiety disorders
behavioral genetics
infant, child, family, and adult assessment
cognitive therapy
depression
marital
neuropsychology
infant mental health

University of Ottawa (Ph.D.)
School of Psychology
Lamoureux Hall
145 Jean-Jacques Lussier
Ottawa, Ontario K1N 6N5, Canada
phone#: (613) 562-5801
e-mail: psyco@uottawa.ca
Web address: www.socialsciences.uottawa.ca/psy/eng/prog2_future_students.asp?id=clin

1	2	3	4	5	6	7
Practice oriented			Equal emphasis			Research oriented

Percentage of faculty subscribing to each of the following orientations:
Psychodynamic/Psychoanalytic 5%
Applied behavioral analysis/Radical behavioral 0%
Family systems/Systems 5%

Existential/Phenomenological/Humanistic 5%
Cognitive/Cognitive-behavioral 85%

Courses required for incoming students to have completed prior to enrolling:
Canadian Honors B.A. degree or its equivalent (60 credits in psychology, plus research experience similar to honors thesis)

Recommended but not mandatory courses:
History and systems

GRE mean
GRE is not required for admission

GPA mean
Overall GPA 8 on a scale of 10 required for admission

Number of applications/admission offers/incoming students in 2009
169 applied/18 admission offers/15 incoming

% of students receiving:
Full tuition waiver only: 0%
Assistantship/fellowship only: 0%
Both full tuition waiver & assistantship/fellowship: 100%

Approximate percentage of incoming students with a B.A./B.S. only: 80%   **Master's:** 20%

Approximate percentage of students who are Women: 90%   **Ethnic Minority:** not reported **International:** 2%

Average years to complete the doctoral program (including internship): 6.6 years after BA; 6.1 years after MA

Personal interview
Interview not required

Attrition rate in past 7 years: 4%

Percentage of students applying for internship last year accepted into APPIC or APA internships: 93%

Formal tracks/concentrations: neuroscience specialization

Research areas	# Faculty	# Grants
adult	9	4
child and family	6	3
community/consultation	4	3

Clinical opportunities
anxiety
community psychology
consultation
couples therapy
depression
geropsychology
pain management
parent training
posttraumatic stress disorders
sex therapy

Pacific Graduate School of Psychology (Ph.D.)
Department of Clinical Psychology
935 East Meadow
Palo Alto, CA 94303
phone#: (800) 818-6136
e-mail: admissions@paloaltou.edu
Web address: www.paloaltou.edu/phd-clinical-psychology

1	2	3	4	5	6	7
Practice oriented			Equal emphasis			Research oriented

Percentage of faculty subscribing to each of the following orientations:

Psychodynamic/Psychoanalytic	10%
Applied behavioral analysis/Radical behavioral	10%
Family systems/Systems	10%
Existential/Phenomenological/Humanistic	10%
Cognitive/Cognitive-behavioral	60%

Courses required for incoming students to have completed prior to enrolling: None

Recommended but not mandatory courses:
Statistics, research methods, personality or abnormal, developmental psychology, physiological psychology; a solid academic background

GRE mean
Verbal + Quantitative 1100
Analytical Writing 4.5

GPA mean
Undergraduate GPA 3.33

Number of applications/admission offers/incoming students in 2009
Not reported

% of students receiving:
Full tuition waiver only: 0%
Assistantship/fellowship only: 35%
Both full tuition waiver & assistantship/fellowship: 0%

Approximate percentage of incoming students with a B.A./B.S. only: 75%   Master's: 25%

Approximate percentage of students who are
Women: 90%   Ethnic Minority: 33%   International: 6%

Average years to complete the doctoral program (including internship): 6.5 years

Personal interview
Interview not required

Attrition rate in past 7 years: 8%

Percentage of students applying for internship last year accepted into APPIC or APA internships: 80%

Formal tracks/concentrations: neuropsychology, forensics, child and family, health, community and diversity, psychology and the Law (J.D./Ph.D.), joint MBA/Ph.D.

Research areas	# Faculty	# Grants
adult psychopathology	1	1
aging	1	0
assessment	4	0
bereavement	1	0
children	4	0
culture	5	0
forensics	3	0
health psychology	4	1
LGBT	1	1
minority aging	2	0
neuropsychology	3	1
neuropsychology & aging	2	0
psychology & law	2	0
psychotherapy	5	1
substance abuse	2	0

Clinical opportunities

AIDS	forensics
assessment	VA Palo Alto
child psychology	inpatient services
family	older adults program
health psychology	shyness program
minority	LGBTQ
neuropsychology	

Pacific Graduate School of Psychology-Stanford Psy.D. Consortium (Psy.D.)

1791 Arastradero Road
Palo Alto, CA, 94304
phone#: (800) 818-6136
e-mail: Bruce Arnow, Ph.D. (arnow@stanford.edu) or Jim Breckenridge, Ph.D. (jbreckenridge@pgsp.edu)
Web address: www.paloaltou.edu/program_stanford_psyd_home.php

1	2	3	4	5	6	7
Practice oriented			Equal emphasis			Research oriented

Percentage of faculty subscribing to each of the following orientations:

Psychodynamic/Psychoanalytic	15%
Applied behavioral analysis/Radical behavioral	0%
Family systems/Systems	15%
Existential/Phenomenological/Humanistic	10%
Cognitive/Cognitive-behavioral	60%

Courses required for incoming students to have completed prior to enrolling:
Abnormal Psychology, Statistics, Biopsychology, Developmental
(*These requirements can be waived if students obtain a score of 650 or higher on the Psych GRE*)

Recommended but not mandatory courses:
Research Methods

GRE mean
Verbal 612   Quantitative 658
Psychology Subject Test 694 (n=16; Psych GRE is not required)
Analytical Writing 4.8

GPA mean
Overall undergraduate GPA 3.6

Number of applications/admission offers/incoming students in 2009
209 applied/50 admission offers/30 incoming

% of students receiving:
Full tuition waiver only: 0%
Assistantship/fellowship only: 57%
Both full tuition waiver & assistantship/fellowship: 0%

Approximate percentage of incoming students with a B.A./B.S. only: 83%   Master's: 17%

**Approximate percentage of students who are
Women:** 87% **Ethnic Minority:** 43% **International:** 10%

**Average years to complete the doctoral program
(including internship):** 5.3 years

Personal interview
Required. In person preferred but telephone/webcam
acceptable

Attrition rate in past 7 years: 10.75%

**Percentage of students applying for internship last
year accepted into APPIC or APA internships:** 86%

Formal tracks/concentrations: Child emphasis

Research areas	# Faculty	# Grants
anxiety disorders	5	3
depression	2	2
eating disorders	2	1
terrorism	2	2
medical illness/comorbidity	2	1
substance abuse	2	0
trauma & abused children	2	0
cultural diversity	2	1

Clinical opportunities

adolescent psychotherapy
behavioral medicine
borderline personality
    disorders (DBT)
child psychotherapy
college counseling
community mental health
cross-cultural counseling
HIV
domestic violence
homeless
LGBT
family
geropsychology
mood disorders
    (depression and
    bipolar spectrum)
post traumatic stress
    disorder (inpatient and
    outpatient)

neuropsychological
    assessment
pain management
    (inpatient and
    outpatient)
rehabilitation psychology
    (blind, brain injury, and
    spinal cord injury)
serious mental illness
    (inpatient unit and
    outpatient)
veteran populations (VA
    Palo Alto healthcare
    system and San Francisco
    VA)
substance abuse

Pacific University (Psy.D.)

School of Professional Psychology
222 SE 8th Avenue, Suite 563
Hillsboro, OR 97123
phone#: (503) 352-7322
e-mail: cdunlap@pacificu.edu (Admissions)
Web address: www.pacificu.edu/spp/clinical/index.cfm

1	2	3	4	5	6	7
Practice oriented			Equal emphasis			Research oriented

**Percentage of faculty subscribing to each of the
following orientations:**

Psychodynamic/Psychoanalytic	16%
Applied behavioral analysis	0%
Family systems/Systems	4%
Existential/Phenomenological/Humanistic	4%
Cognitive/Cognitive-behavioral	76%

**Courses required for incoming students to have
completed prior to enrolling:**
A strong undergraduate background in psychology

Recommended but not mandatory courses:
4 of the 7 following courses: introduction, personality,
abnormal, experimental, physiological, social, behavioral
statistics

GRE mean for incoming students in 2009
Verbal 507   Quantitative 562
Psychology Subject Test not reported
Analytical Writing 4.4

GPA mean for incoming students in 2009
Overall GPA 3.54

**Number of applications/admission offers/incoming
students in 2009**
197 applied/104 admission offers/53 incoming

% of students receiving:
Full tuition waiver only: 0%
Assistantship/fellowship only: 23%
Both full tuition waiver & assistantship/fellowship: 0%

**Approximate percentage of incoming students with a
B.A./B.S. only:** 79% **Master's:** 21%

**Approximate percentage of students who are
Women:** 81% **Ethnic Minority:** 13% **International:** 0%

**Average years to complete the doctoral program
(including internship):** 5.5 years

Personal interview
Required in person

Attrition rate in past 7 years: 16%

**Percentage of students applying for internship last
year accepted into APPIC or APA internships:** 83.3%

Formal tracks/concentrations: Latino Bilingual; Forensic;
Neuropsychology; Child/Adolescent; Organizational
Consulting; Health

Research areas	# Faculty	# Grants
anxiety disorders	1	0
behavioral health	2	1
behavior therapy	7	0
child psychopathology	5	0
dynamic psychotherapy	2	0
forensic psychology	3	1
gestalt therapy	1	0
integrative approaches	3	0
neuropsychology	2	0
organizational behavior	5	0
posttraumatic stress disorders	1	0
psychology of women	1	0
psychotherapy with minorities	4	0
single case research	2	0
training, supervision and consultation	3	1

Clinical opportunities
Psychological Service Center in downtown Portland
47 community sites

University of Pennsylvania (Ph.D.)

Department of Psychology
3720 Walnut Street
Philadelphia, PA 19104-6241
phone#: (215) 898-4712
e-mail: cingulli@psych.upenn.edu
Web address: www.psych.upenn.edu/graduate/resareas/cppp

1	2	3	4	5	6	7
Practice oriented		Equal emphasis				Research oriented

Percentage of faculty subscribing to each of the following orientations:

Psychodynamic/Psychoanalytic	5%
Applied behavioral analysis/Radical behavioral	0%
Family systems/Systems	0%
Existential/Phenomenological/Humanistic	10%
Cognitive/Cognitive-behavioral	85%

Courses required for incoming students to have completed prior to enrolling: None

Recommended but not mandatory courses:
Statistics

GRE mean
Verbal 683 Quantitative 751
Psychology Subject Test 786
Analytical Writing 5.6

GPA mean
Overall GPA 3.78

Number of applications/admission offers/incoming students in 2009
265 applied/7 admission offers/4 incoming

% of students receiving:
Full tuition waiver only: 0%
Assistantship/fellowship only: 0%
Both full tuition waiver & assistantship/fellowship: 100%

Approximate percentage of incoming students with a B.A./B.S. only: 100% **Master's:** 0%

Approximate percentage of students who are Women: 50% **Ethnic Minority:** 11% **International:** 19%

Average years to complete the doctoral program (including internship): 6 years

Personal interview
Required in person

Attrition rate in past 7 years: 15%

Percentage of students applying for internship last year accepted into APPIC or APA internships: 75%

Formal tracks/concentrations: none

Research areas	# Faculty	# Grants
anxiety disorders	2	5
depression	3	4
family/community	1	0
psychodynamic treatment	1	1
psychopharmacology	3	3
substance abuse	1	1

Clinical opportunities

assessment and diagnostic interviewing	psychodynamic therapy
behavioral therapy of anxiety disorders	serious mental illness
cognitive-behavioral therapy of depression and anxiety	group therapy

Pennsylvania State University (Ph.D.)

Department of Psychology
417 Bruce V. Moore Building
University Park, PA 16802
phone#: (814) 863-1751
e-mail: mgn1@psu.edu
Web address: psych.la.psu.edu/graduate/programAreas/clinicalProgram.html

1	2	3	4	5	6	7
Practice oriented		Equal emphasis				Research oriented

Percentage of faculty subscribing to each of the following orientations:

Psychodynamic/Psychoanalytic	20%
Applied behavioral analysis/Radical behavioral	0%
Family systems/Systems	20%
Existential/Phenomenological/Humanistic	10%
Cognitive/Cognitive-behavioral	50%

Courses required for incoming students prior to enrolling:
No course requirements. Broad psychology background preferred.

Recommended but not mandatory courses:
Statistics and methodology

GRE mean:
Verbal 647 Quantitative 684
Analytical Writing Data not available

GPA mean
Overall GPA 3.80

Number of applications/admission offers/incoming students in 2008
550 applied with 22 admitted

% of students receiving:
Full tuition waiver only: 0%
Assistantship/fellowship only: 0%
Both full tuition waiver & assistantship/fellowship: 100%

Approximate percentage of incoming students with a B.A./B.S. only: 100% **Master's:** 0%

Approximate percentage of students who are Women: 75% **Ethnic Minority:** 23%
International: 2 students

Average years to complete the doctoral program (including internship): 7.6 years

Personal interview
Preferred in person but telephone acceptable

Attrition rate in past 7 years: 22%

Percentage of students applying for internship last year accepted into APPIC or APA internships: 100%

Formal tracks/concentrations: child and adult

Research areas	# Faculty	# Grants
adult psychopathology	5	1
affective disorders	2	0
anxiety disorders	3	3
behavioral medicine	2	0
child clinical/child psychopathology	3	2
cognition/information processing	2	0
cross-cultural psychology	1	1
developmental/childhood and adolescence	2	1
developmental disabilities	3	1
emotions	5	1
family research/therapy	2	1
hypnosis	1	0
neuropsychology	2	1
parent–child interactions	3	2
personality assessment	3	1
personality development	1	0
personality disorders	2	0
psychoanalysis/psychodynamics	2	0
psychophysiology	7	0
psychotherapy process and outcome	4	3
relaxation/biofeedback	2	1
rural psychology	1	1
violence/abuse	3	0

Clinical opportunities
Since we serve as a mental health center for this area, we offer a broad range of clinical experiences involving a variety of psychopathologies. The only significant area in which we do not offer experience in our clinic is with drug and alcohol dependence.

Pepperdine University (Psy.D.)

Department of Psychology
Graduate School of Education and Psychology
6100 Center Drive
Los Angeles, CA 90045
phone#: (866) 503-5461, (310) 568-5607
e-mail: Cheryl.Saunders@pepperdine.edu
Web address: gsep.pepperdine.edu/doctorate-clinical-psychology/

1	2	3	4	5	6	7
Practice oriented		Equal emphasis				Research oriented

Percentage of faculty subscribing to each of the following orientations:

Psychodynamic/Psychoanalytic	58%
Applied behavioral analysis/Radical behavioral	1%
Family systems/Systems	42%
Existential/Phenomenological/Humanistic	15%
Cognitive/Cognitive-behavioral	65%

Courses required for incoming students prior to enrolling:
Applicants for doctoral study should possess a master's degree in psychology or a closely related field that reflects a master's-level foundation of knowledge in the following domains: biological aspects of behavior; cognitive and affective aspects of behavior; social aspects of behavior; psychological measurement; research methodology; and techniques of data analysis.

Recommended but not mandatory courses: None

GRE mean
Verbal 541   Quantitative 639
Psychology Subject Test 647
Analytical Writing 4.82

GPA mean
Overall GPA 3.43   Master's GPA 3.91

Number of applications/admission offers/incoming students in 2009
135 applied/42 admission offers/28 incoming

% of students receiving:
Full tuition waiver only:
Partial scholarship: 70%
Assistantship/fellowship only: 10%
Both tuition waiver & assistantship/fellowship: 0%

Approximate percentage of incoming students with a B.A./B.S. only: 0%   **Master's:** 100%

Approximate percentage of students who are Women: 87%   **Ethnic Minority:** 31%   **International:** 0%

Average years to complete the doctoral program (including internship): 5.1 years

Personal interview
Preferred in person but telephone acceptable

Attrition rate in past 7 years: 2.7%

Percentage of students applying for internship last year (2009) accepted into APPIC or APA internships: 93%

Formal tracks/concentrations: psychodynamic psychotherapy, cognitive-behavioral therapy, marital and family therapy, cultural-ecological and community-clinical interventions, forensic assessment (subspecialty)

Research areas	# Faculty	# Grants
ADHD	1	2
autism	1	0
clinic-based research	4	1
clinical application of neuroscience (theoretical scholarship)	3	1
	2	0
clinical supervision	5	0
community-based interventions	1	0
couple/marital therapy	1	0
ethnic minority trauma recovery	4	2
family psychology	1	0
forensic psychology	1	0
influence of the media on multicultural development of children	1	0
multicultural mental health	1	0
positive psychology	3	0

posttraumatic stress disorder	6	3
professional ethics	1	0
program evaluation	4	0
psychiatric diagnosis	4	0
psychological assessment	2	0
psychology, religion& spirituality	5	3
psychotherapy effectiveness with Latinos	1	0
psychotherapy with diverse and disadvantaged populations, e.g., foster youth	1	0
psychotherapy training, process, outcome, clinic-based research	10	2
reducing the stigma of mental illness	1	0
social justice issues	2	0

Clinical opportunities

adolescence
ADHD
AIDS
Alzheimer's disease
adoption
aging
assessment
autism
behavior therapy
behavioral medicine (general medical & oncology)
child clinical
cognitive behavioral therapy
community psychology
dialectical behavior therapy (DBT)
chronically mentally ill
eating disorders
existential-humanistic
⌐py

group
homeless population
inpatient
marital/family/systemic psychotherapy
mindfulness-based therapies
multicultural/crosscultural psychology
neuropsychological testing
neuropsychology
posttraumatic stress disorder
psychodynamic psychotherapy
rehabilitation
religion and spirituality
schizophrenia
school psychology
substance abuse
veteran population

No-required

Philadelphia College of Osteopathic Medicine (Psy.D.)

Department of Psychology
4190 City Avenue
Philadelphia, PA 19131-1695
phone#: 215-871-6442
e-mail: StephanieF@pcom.edu
Web address: www.pcom.edu/Academic_Programs/aca_
psych/PsyD_in_Clinical_Psychology/psyd_in_clinical_
psychology.html

1	2	3	4	5	6	7
Practice oriented		Equal emphasis				Research oriented

Percentage of faculty subscribing to each of the following orientations:

Psychodynamic/Psychoanalytic	0%
Applied behavioral analysis/Radical behavioral	0%
Family systems/Systems	0%
Existential/Phenomenological/Humanistic	0%
Cognitive/Cognitive-behavioral	100%

Courses required for incoming students to have completed prior to enrolling:
personality, psychopathology or abnormal psychology, statistics/research, and developmental psychology

Recommended but not mandatory courses:
none

GRE mean
GRE not required for admission

GPA mean
Overall GPA 3.8

Number of applications/admission offers/incoming students in 2009
125 applied/44 admission offers/29 incoming

% of students receiving:
Full tuition waiver only: 0%
Assistantship/fellowship only: 2%
Both full tuition waiver & assistantship/fellowship: 0%

Approximate percentage of incoming students with a B.A./B.S. only: 0%   Master's: 100%

Approximate percentage of students who are Women: 77% Ethnic Minority: 23% International: 1.5%

Average years to complete the doctoral program (including internship): 6.6 years

Personal interview
Required in person

Attrition rate in past 7 years: 4.7%

Percentage of students applying for internship last year accepted into APPIC or APA internships: 100%

Formal tracks/concentrations: none

Research areas	# Faculty	# Grants
clinical health psychology in primary care	3	2
evidence based practices	12	0
anxiety disorders	7	0
cognitive distortions	1	0
critical incident stress management and debriefing	1	0
cognitive behavioral treatment of stress-related medical disorders	3	0
patient non-adherence to medical advice	1	0
anger	1	0
coping with chronic medical illnesses	2	1
personality disorders	1	0
pain management	1	0
somatization disorder	1	0
child and adolescent anxiety disorders	1	0
psychotherapy outcome & process research	2	0
memory and aging	1	0
psychological assessment	3	0
cognitive behavioral therapy for adult ADHD	1	0
personality assessment	3	0

social information processing in the development of children's aggressive behavior	1	0
impact of parental psychopathology on children	1	1
CBT treatment of mood & anxiety	7	0
multicultural issues	4	0
crisis/trauma	1	0
childhood sexual abuse	1	0
supervision/clinical training	1	0
eating disorders	1	0
serious mental illnesses	1	0
dialectic behavior therapy in inpatient hospital and forensic settings	1	0
psychiatric rehabilitation	1	0
forensic assessment and treatment	1	0
mental health services research; program evaluation	1	0
professional development and psychologist self-care	1	0
ethics	1	0

Clinical opportunities

culturally diverse, underserved primary care
outpatient cognitive behavior therapy clinic
internal medicine
family medicine
geriatric medicine

University of Pittsburgh (Ph.D.)

Department of Psychology
Psychology Graduate Office
Sennott Square, 3rd Floor
210 South Bouquet Street
Pittsburgh, PA 15260
phone#: (412) 624-4502
e-mail: psygrad@pitt.edu
Web address: www.psychology.pitt.edu/graduate/clinical/index.php

1	2	3	4	5	6	7

Practice oriented   Equal emphasis   Research oriented

Percentage of faculty subscribing to each of the following orientations:

Psychodynamic/Psychoanalytic	0%
Applied behavioral analysis/Radical behavioral	0%
Family systems/Systems	20%
Existential/Phenomenological/Humanistic	0%
Cognitive/Cognitive-behavioral	80%

Courses required for incoming students to have completed prior to enrolling: None

Recommended but not mandatory courses:
Abnormal psychology, research methods, statistics; background in biology, math, & computer science

GRE mean
Verbal 680   Quantitative 743
Psychology Subject Test 775
Analytical Writing 5.63

GPA mean
Overall GPA 3.97

Number of applications/admission offers/incoming students in 2009
216 applied/8 admission offers/4 incoming

% of students receiving:
Full tuition waiver only: 0%
Assistantship/fellowship only: 0%
Both full tuition waiver & assistantship/fellowship: 100%

Approximate percentage of incoming students with a B.A./B.S. only: 95%   Master's: 5%

Approximate percentage of students who are
Women: 88%   Ethnic Minority: 10%   International: 6%

Average years to complete the doctoral program (including internship): 7 years

Personal interview
Preferred in person but telephone acceptable

Attrition rate in past 7 years: 4%

Percentage of students applying for internship last year accepted into APPIC or APA internships: 100%

Formal tracks/concentrations: adult psychopathology, developmental psychopathology, health psychology

Research areas	# Faculty	# Grants
adult psychopathology	8	19
mood disorders/depression	7	22
at-risk adolescents	8	28
attention-deficit disorder	1	2
autism	3	16
behavioral genetics	4	11
behavioral medicine/ health psychology	14	38
cancer/behavioral oncology	1	3
cardiovascular behavioral medicine	4	13
child & family psychopathology	14	45
chronic disease	2	6
emotion	5	19
eating disorders	1	4
neuroimaging	7	27
neuropsychology	7	27
prevention	3	9
program evaluation	2	3
psychoneuroimmunology	3	9
psychopharmacology	3	8
psychophysiology	5	16
schizophrenia	1	1
social cognition/cognition	4	10
social support	1	4
statistics	2	2
stress and coping	4	15
substance abuse/addictions	8	21
weight management	1	4

Clinical opportunities

adolescent treatment
affective disorders/depression
anxiety disorders
attention-deficit disorder
inpatient
minority populations
neuropsychological assessment
obsessive-compulsive

241

autism
behavioral medicine
child treatment
cognitive-behavioral therapy
conduct disorder
chronic severe mental
   illness
eating disorders
emergency room assessment
family therapy
gay/lesbian
group therapy

pain management
parent training
pediatric
personality disorders
schizophrenia
smoking cessation
substance abuse
suicide prevention
veterans medical center
victim/violence/
   sexual abuse
weight management

Ponce School of Medicine (Psy.D.) (2008 data)

Clinical Psychology Doctoral Program
P.O. Box 7004
Ponce, PR 00732
phone#: (787) 813-5700
e-mail: jpons@psm.edu
Web address: www.psm.edu/Academic%20Affair%20&%20Programs/programs/PsyD/index.htm

1	2	**3**	4	5	6	7
Practice oriented		Equal emphasis			Research oriented	

Percentage of faculty subscribing to each of the following orientations:

Psychodynamic/Psychoanalytic   33%
Applied behavioral analysis/Radical behavioral   0%
Family systems/Systems   33%
Existential/Phenomenological/Humanistic   0%
Cognitive/Cognitive-behavioral   33%

Courses required for incoming students to have completed prior to enrolling:

developmental psychology, statistics, experimental psychology or research methods, abnormal

Recommended but not mandatory courses:
personality psychology, physiological psychology

GRE mean
Most of our students take the Spanish version of the GRE – EXADEP

GPA mean
Overall GPA 3.49

Number of applications/admission offers/incoming students in 2007
91 applied/33 mission offers/30 incoming

% of students receiving:
Full tuition waiver only: 0%
Assistantship/fellowship only: 5%
Both full tuition waiver & assistantship/fellowship: 5%

Approximate percentage of incoming students with a B.A./B.S. only: 85%   Master's: 15%

Approximate percentage of students who are
Women: 74% Ethnic Minority: 100% International: 3%

Average years to complete the doctoral program (including internship): not reported

Personal interview
Required in person

Attrition rate in past 7 years: 8%

Percentage of students applying for internship last year accepted into APPIC or APA internships: 26%

Formal tracks/concentrations: health psychology, neuropsychology

Research areas	# Faculty	# Grants
adaptation and normalization of tests	4	1
HIV stigma and health disparities	3	2
fear conditioning and extinction	1	1

Clinical opportunities
general community hospital
community mental health clinics

Purdue University (Ph.D.)

Department of Psychological Sciences
703 Third Street
West Lafayette, IN 47907-2081
phone#: (765) 494-6996
e-mail: (secretary) dlbatta@psych.purdue.edu, (director) rollock@psych.purdue.edu
Web address: www.psych.purdue.edu/index.php/clinic.html

1	2	3	4	5	**6**	7
Practice oriented		Equal emphasis			Research oriented	

Percentage of faculty subscribing to each of the following orientations:

Psychodynamic/Psychoanalytic   10%
Applied behavioral analysis/Radical behavioral   10%
Family systems/Systems   10%
Existential/Phenomenological/Humanistic   0%
Cognitive/Cognitive-behavioral   90%

Courses required for incoming students to have completed prior to enrolling:
While no specific courses are absolutely required, the most competitive students have rigorous, broad coursework in psychology, especially methodology and statistics, as well as undergraduate research experience (e.g., research assistantship or undergraduate independent thesis research; preferably, though not necessarily, in psychological sciences).

Recommended but not mandatory courses:
The most competitive students also show a strong record of coursework in mathematics (calculus preferable), natural sciences, other social sciences.

GRE mean
Preference is given to students with a combined 1200 GRE Verbal and Quantitative.
[Means based on incoming students from 2007, 2008, 2009; n = 7]
Verbal: 609   Quantitative: 671

GPA mean
[Mean based on incoming students from 2007, 2008, 2009; n = 7]   3.50

Number of applications/admission offers/incoming students in 2009
130 applied/4 admission offers/2 incoming

% of incoming students receiving:
Full tuition waiver only: 0%
Assistantship/fellowship only: 0%
Both full tuition waiver & assistantship/fellowship: 100%

Approximate percentage of incoming students with a B.A./B.S. only: 100%   Master's: 0%

Approximate percentage of students who are (of all 22 students enrolled during 2008–2009):
Women: 63.6% Ethnic Minority: 36.4% International: 4.5%

Average years to complete the doctoral program (including internship): 7.1 years

Personal interview
A small number of the most promising applicants are invited to take part in a day-long series of face-to-face personal interviews and tours during a Program-designated Interview Day. This typically is held in late January or February. Telephone interviews are acceptable under extenuating circumstances.

Attrition rate in past 7 years: 20.45%

Percentage of students applying for internship last year accepted into APPIC or APA internships:
3 out of 4 = 75%

Formal tracks/concentrations: not reported

Research areas	# Faculty	# Grants
adolescence	1	1
anger, aggression, & antisocial behavior	3	1
anxiety disorders	1	0
ethnicity minority/cultural issues	2	0
family processes & child/ adolescent development	2	2
marital/intimate partner violence	2	0
personality and psychopathology	3	1
personality assessment (adult)	1	0
social skills deficits and pathology (adult)	2	0

Clinical opportunities
ADHD, oppositional defiant disorders (ODD), conduct disorders (CD) and other disruptive behavior problems (child)
anxiety (adult & child)
assessment (neuropsychological; adult & child)
assessment (general clinical; child & adult)
depression (adult & child)
family and adolescence
project headstart consultations
personality disorders (adult)
other opportunities specific to individual student clinical and research interests can be developed from a variety of other local and regional service providers.

Regent University (Ph.D.)
Doctoral Program in Clinical Psychology
CRB 154
1000 Regent University Drive
Virginia Beach, VA 23464
phone#: (800) 373-5504 ext. 4498
e-mail: stepbru@regent.edu
Web address: www.regent.edu/psyd

1	2	3	4	5	6	7
Practice oriented		Equal emphasis				Research oriented

Percentage of faculty subscribing to each of the following orientations:
Psychodynamic/Psychoanalytic	30%
Applied behavioral analysis/Radical behavioral	20%
Family systems/Systems	40%
Existential/Phenomenological/Humanistic	30%
Cognitive/Cognitive-behavioral	60%

Courses required for incoming students to have completed prior to enrolling:
18 hours of psychology (undergraduate)

Recommended but not mandatory courses:
Statistics, research methods, personality theories, human growth and development, abnormal psychology, social psychology, physiological psychology

GRE mean
Verbal and Quantitative: 1142
Analytical Writing 3.5

GPA mean
3.68

Number of applications/admission offers/incoming students in Fall, 2009
88 applied/37 admission offers/18 incoming

% of students receiving:
Full tuition waiver only: 0%
(100% of incoming students received Partial tuition waiver)
Assistantship/fellowship only: 13%
Both full tuition waiver & assistantship/fellowship: 13%

Approximate percentage of incoming students with a B.A./B.S. (Honors) only: 80%   Master's: 20%

Approximate percentage of students who are
Women: 68%   Ethnic Minority: 18% International: 4%

Average years to complete the doctoral program (including internship): 5.4 years

Personal interview
Required in person

Attrition rate in past 7 years: 7%

Percentage of students applying for internship last year accepted into APPIC or APA internships: 74%

Formal tracks/concentrations: marital & family psychology, clinical child psychology, health psychology, religion, consulting psychology

Research areas	# Faculty	# Grants
ADHD	1	1
consultation to religious and community organizations by clinicians	4	3
personality, religion, and adjustment	1	1
marital functioning and spirituality	2	1
sexual and religious identity	1	3
God image & emotional adjustment	1	1

Clinical opportunities

behavioral medicine	military mental health and VA
child mental health settings	
Christian counseling centers	neuropsychology
forensic settings	psychiatric hospitals

University of Rhode Island (Ph.D.)

Department of Psychology
10 Chafee Road
Kingston, RI 02881
phone#: (401) 874-2193
e-mail: efschroeder@uri.edu
Web address: http://www.uri.edu/artsci/psy/clinical_welcome.shtml

1	2	3	4	5	6	7

Practice oriented   Equal emphasis   Research oriented

Percentage of faculty subscribing to each of the following orientations:

Psychodynamic/Psychoanalytic	0%
Applied behavioral analysis/Radical behavioral	0%
Family systems/Systems	33%
Existential/Phenomenological/Humanistic	11%
Cognitive/Cognitive-behavioral	66%
Feminist	11%

Courses required for incoming students to have completed prior to enrolling:
Background in undergraduate psychology

Recommended but not mandatory courses:
Psychological tests and measurements

GRE mean
Verbal 560   Quantitative 620
Analytical Writing not reported
Psychology Subject Test not reported

GPA mean
Undergraduate GPA 3.6

Number of applications/admission offers/incoming students in 2009
239 applied/9 admission offers/6 incoming

% of students receiving:
Full tuition waiver only: 22%
Assistantship/fellowship only: 78%

Approximate percentage of incoming students with a B.A./B.S. only: 50%   **Master's:** 50%

Approximate percentage of students who are Women: 78%   **Ethnic Minority:** 32% **International:** 8%

Average years to complete the doctoral program (including internship): 6.6 years

Personal interview
Required in person

Attrition rate in past 7 years: 14%

Percentage of students applying for internship last year accepted into APPIC or APA internships: 100%

Formal tracks/concentrations: neuropsychology, child/family/developmental psychology, applied methodology, multicultural psychology, health psychology

Research areas	# Faculty	# Grants
behavioral medicine/health psychology	4	7
child clinical	1	0
community psychology	1	1
family research	2	0
multicultural issues	1	0
criminal/juvenile justice/ forensic psychology	2	3

Clinical opportunities

child therapy	marriage and couples therapy
community psychology	
family therapy	group therapy
health psychology	multicultural therapy
individual psychotherapy	

University of Rochester (Ph.D.)

Department of Psychology
Meliora Hall
Rochester, NY 14627-0266
Phone#: (585) 275-8704
e-mail: maryann.gilbert@rochester.edu
Web address: www.psych.rochester.edu/graduate/clinical/

1	2	3	4	**5**	6	7

Practice oriented   Equal emphasis   Research oriented

Percentage of faculty subscribing to each of the following orientations:

Psychodynamic/Psychoanalytic	37%
Applied behavioral analysis/Radical behavioral	10%
Family systems/Systems	1%
Existential/Phenomenological/Humanistic	5%
Cognitive/Cognitive-behavioral	48%

Courses required for incoming students to have completed prior to enrolling:
Equivalent of psychology major

Recommended but not mandatory courses:
None

GRE mean
Verbal 653   Quantitative 735
Analytical Writing 5.4

GPA mean
Overall GPA 3.8

Number of applications/admission offers/incoming students in 2009
201 applied/5 admission offers/4 incoming

% of students receiving:
Full tuition waiver only: 0%
Assistantship/fellowship only: 0%
Both full tuition waiver & assistantship/fellowship: 100%

Approximate percentage of students who are
Women: 84% **Ethnic Minority:** 13% **International:** 10%

Average years to complete the doctoral program (including internship): 7 years

Personal interview
Required in person

Attrition rate in past 7 years: 9%

Percentage of students applying for internship last year accepted into APPIC or APA internships: 88%

Formal tracks/concentrations: developmental psychopathology

Research areas	# Faculty	# Grants
attention-deficit disorder	1	0
autism	2	2
child abuse	1	6
depression	1	1
marriage	1	1
motivation	1	5

Clinical opportunities
attention-deficit disorder
autism
child maltreatment/abuse
psychodynamic therapy
smoking prevention

child and adolescent
outpatient psychiatry
inpatient psychiatric
hospital

Roosevelt University (Psy.D.)
Department of Psychology
430 S. Michigan Avenue
Chicago, IL 60605
phone#: (312)-341-3760
e-mail: camcbride@roosevelt.edu
Web address: www.roosevelt.edu/CAS/Programs/
Psychology/PsyD.aspx

1	2	**3**	4	5	6	7

Practice oriented   Equal emphasis   Research oriented

Percentage of faculty subscribing to each of the following orientations:
Psychodynamic/Psychoanalytic 42%
Applied behavioral analysis/Radical behavioral 1%
Family systems/Systems 17%
Existential/Phenomenological/Humanistic 17%
Cognitive/Cognitive-behavioral 42%

Courses required for incoming students to have completed prior to enrolling:
Abnormal, research methods or statistics

Recommended but not mandatory courses:

Personality theory, tests and measurement

GRE mean
Verbal 530   Quantitative 621
Psychology Subject Test not reported
Analytical Writing 4.1

GPA mean
Overall GPA 3.52

Number of applications/admission offers/incoming students in 2008
135 applied/31 admission offers/20 incoming

% of students receiving:
Full tuition waiver only: 5%
Assistantship/fellowship only: 0%
Both tuition waiver & assistantship/fellowship: 30%
(6 students each year receive waiver of 1/2 tuition and 1/2 of the yearly stipend)

Approximate percentage of incoming students with a B.A./B.S. only: 75% **Master's:** 25%

Approximate percentage of students who are
Women: 75% **Ethnic Minority:** 25% **International:** 0%

Average years to complete the doctoral program (including internship): 6 years

Personal interview
Required in person

Attrition rate in past 7 years: 8%

Percentage of students applying for internship last year accepted into APPIC or APA internships: 100%

Formal tracks/concentrations: none

Research areas	# Faculty	# Grants
assessment	3	0
children and adolescents	4	1
health psychology	4	1
neuropsychology	3	0
group psychotherapy/psychodrama	1	0
social cognition	1	0
learning theory/clinical applications	1	0
college teaching	1	0

Clinical opportunities
children and families
adult chronic psychiatric
  hospitals
behavioral medicine
torture survivors
neuropsychology (child,
  adolescent, adult)

therapeutic day schools
veteran's administration
  hospitals
jail/prison populations
anxiety disorders
eating disorders

Rosalind Franklin University of Medicine and Science (Ph.D.)
(2008 data)
Department of Psychology
3333 Green Bay Road
North Chicago, IL 60064
phone#: (847) 578-3305
e-mail: patricia.rigwood@rosalindfranklin.edu

Web address: www.rosalindfranklin.edu/dnn/CHP/
Psychology/Doctorate/tabid/1696/Default.aspx

1	2	3	4	5	6	7
Practice oriented			Equal emphasis			Research oriented

Percentage of faculty subscribing to each of the following orientations:

Psychodynamic/Psychoanalytic	5%
Applied behavioral analysis/Radical behavioral	5%
Family systems/Systems	15%
Existential/Phenomenological/Humanistic	5%
Cognitive/Cognitive-behavioral	70%

Courses required for incoming students to have completed prior to enrolling:
Statistics and biological/physiological psychology

Recommended but not mandatory courses:
abnormal psychology, developmental psychology, social psychology

GRE mean
Verbal 513   Quantitative 600
Psychology Subject Test 668
Analytical Writing 4.2

GPA mean
Overall GPA 3.42

Number of applications/admission offers/incoming students in 2007
68 applied/21 admission offers/12 incoming

% of students receiving:
Full tuition waiver only: 0%
Assistantship/fellowship only: 0%
Both full tuition waiver & assistantship/fellowship: 55%

Approximate percentage of incoming students with a B.A./B.S. only: 50%   Master's: 50%

Approximate percentage of students who are Women: 71%   Ethnic Minority: 14%   International: 0%

Average years to complete the doctoral program (including internship): 7 years

Personal interview
Preferred in person but telephone acceptable

Attrition rate in past 7 years: not reported

Percentage of students applying for internship last year accepted into APPIC or APA internships: 82%

Formal tracks/concentrations: neuropsychology, health psychology, psychopathology

Research areas	# Faculty	# Grants
aging	1	1
anxiety disorders	1	1
cancer	1	0
diabetes	1	0
epilepsy/neuropsychology	1	2
pain	1	1
psychopathy	1	0
risk behaviors in adolescents	1	0
schizophrenia	1	0
sports concussion	1	0

Clinical opportunities
anxiety disorders	neuropsychiatric
behavioral medicine	neuropsychological

Rutgers, The State University of New Jersey (Ph.D.)
Department of Psychology
Graduate School of Arts and Sciences
New Brunswick, NJ 08903
e-mail: tewilson@rci.rutgers.edu
Web address: psych.rutgers.edu/graduate/clinical/index.html

1	2	3	4	5	6	7
Practice oriented			Equal emphasis			Research oriented

Percentage of faculty subscribing to each of the following orientations:

Psychodynamic/Psychoanalytic	0%
Applied behavioral analysis/Radical behavioral	14%
Family systems/Systems	6%
Existential/Phenomenological/Humanistic	0%
Cognitive/Cognitive-behavioral	80%

Courses required for incoming students to have completed prior to enrolling:
A major in psychology or equivalent courses

Recommended but not mandatory courses: none

GRE mean
Verbal 670   Quantitative 700
Psychology Subject Test 710
Analytical Writing not reported

GPA mean
Overall GPA 3.77

Number of applications/admission offers/incoming students in 2009
296 applied/7 admission offers/3 incoming

% of students receiving:
Full tuition waiver only: 0%
Assistantship/fellowship only: 0%
Both full tuition waiver & assistantship/fellowship: 100%

Approximate percentage of incoming students with a B.A./B.S. only: 100%   Master's: 0%

Approximate percentage of students who are Women: 66%   Ethnic Minority: 33%   International: 0%

Average years to complete the doctoral program (including internship): 6 years

Personal interview
Preferred in person but telephone acceptable

Attrition rate in past 7 years: 0.03%

Percentage of students applying for internship last year accepted into APPIC or APA internships: 100%

Formal tracks/concentrations: none

Research areas	# Faculty	# Grants
applied behavioral analysis	2	0
autism	1	1
behavioral medicine	5	1
eating disorders	1	0
marriage/couples	2	1
philosophical issues	1	0
prevention	2	1
psychopathology	1	1
psychotherapy process and outcome	5	1
somatization disorders	1	0
substance abuse	3	1

Clinical opportunities

adolescent delinquency
affective disorders
alcohol use disorders
anxiety disorders
assessment
behavioral medicine
community psychology
depression
developmental disabilities
eating disorders
family therapy
minority
obsessive–compulsive disorder
personality disorders
somatization disorders
substance abuse
Tourette's

Rutgers, The State University of New Jersey (Psy.D.)

Graduate School of Applied and Professional Psychology
152 Frelinghuysen Road
Piscataway, NJ 08854-8085
phone#: (848) 445-3980
e-mail: clinpsyd@rci.rutgers.edu
Web address: gsappweb.rutgers.edu/programs/clinical/index.php

1	2	3	4	5	6	7

Practice oriented   Equal emphasis   Research oriented

Percentage of faculty subscribing to each of the following orientations:

Psychodynamic/Psychoanalytic	30%
Applied behavioral analysis/Radical behavioral	10%
Family systems/Systems	20%
Existential/Phenomenological/Humanistic	10%
Cognitive/Cognitive-behavioral	30%

Courses required for incoming students to have completed prior to enrolling:

Statistics, abnormal psychology, and the biological bases of psychology

Recommended but not mandatory courses:

Students also should have taken 1 and preferably 2 courses in 1 of the following: cognitive psychology, psychology of perception, conditioning and learning, developmental psychology, psychology of personality and social psychology. We prefer that 1 of the above have a laboratory component.

GRE mean

Verbal 640   Quantitative 680
Psychology Subject Test 710

GPA mean

Overall GPA 3.69

Number of applications/admission offers/incoming students in 2009

413 applied/28 admission offers/18 incoming

% of students receiving:

Full tuition waiver only: 0%
Scholarships: 95%
Both full tuition waiver & assistantship/fellowsh

yes, stretch

Approximate percentage of incoming stude
B.A./B.S. only: 72%%   Master's: 28%

Approximate percentage of students who are
Women: 50%   Ethnic Minority: 16.7%   International: 11%

Average years to complete the doctoral program (including internship) 5.8 years

Personal interview
Preferred in person but telephone acceptable

Attrition rate in past 7 years: 5%

Percentage of students applying for internship last year accepted into APPIC or APA internships: 100%

Formal tracks/concentrations: community psychology, sports psychology

Research areas	# Faculty	# Grants
adolescence	3	1
adoption	1	1
anxiety depressive disorders	3	1
applied and behavioral analysis	1	1
autism	1	1
community	2	1
developmental disabilities	3	2
diagnosis and classification	2	0
dissociative disorders	1	0
eating disorders	1	1
empirically supported treatment research	2	1
ethical issues	1	0
family/marriage/couples	3	1
feminist theory and psychology	1	0
mental health policy	2	1
mind/body/health	1	1
multicultural issues	2	0
organizational psychology	1	0
personality disorders	2	0
philosophy and psychology	2	0
program design and evaluation	1	0
psychiatric disabilities	1	1
psychoanalytic theory	4	1
psychology and the arts	1	0
psychophysiological disorders	1	0
psychotherapy process and outcome	3	1
severe mental illness	2	1
social learning theory	1	1
substance abuse	4	2

Clinical opportunities (see website for listing of practicum sites)

adolescent delinquency
affective disorders
anxiety disorders
infancy/postpartum
interpersonal psychotherapy

assessment
behavioral medicine
community psychology
conduct disorder
developmental disabilities
dissociative disorder
eating disorders
family therapy
forensic psychology
group therapy
hyperactivity
hypnosis
impulse control

marital/couples therapy
minority
neuropsychology
obsessive–compulsive
  disorder
organizational psychology
personality disorders
psychodynamic/
  psychoanalytic therapy
schizophrenia
school psychology
substance abuse
victim/abuse

Sam Houston State University (Ph.D.)

Department of Psychology and Philosophy
Huntsville, TX 77341-2210
phone#: (936) 294-1210
e-mail: maconroy@shsu.edu
Web address: www.shsu.edu/clinpsy

1	2	3	4	5	6	7

Practice oriented   Equal emphasis   Research oriented

Percentage of faculty subscribing to each of the following orientations:

Psychodynamic/Psychoanalytic   0%
Applied behavioral analysis/Radical behavioral   0%
Family systems/Systems   17%
Existential/Phenomenological/Humanistic   17%
Cognitive/Cognitive-behavioral   66%

Courses required for incoming students to have completed prior to enrolling: none

Recommended but not mandatory courses: none

GRE mean
Verbal 573   Quantitative 601
Psychology Subject Test not required
Analytical Writing not reported

GPA mean
Overall GPA 3.59

Number of applications/admission offers/incoming students in 2008
102 applied/13 admission offers/8 incoming

% of students receiving:
Full tuition waiver only: 0%
Assistantship/fellowship only: 100%
Both full tuition waiver & assistantship/fellowship: 0%

Approximate percentage of incoming students with a B.A./B.S. only: 62%   Master's: 38%

Approximate percentage of students who are Women: 83%   Ethnic Minority: 22%   International: 3%

Average years to complete the doctoral program (including internship): 6 years

Personal interview
Preferred in person but telephone acceptable

Attrition rate in past 7 years: 19%

Percentage of students applying for internship last year accepted into APPIC or APA internships: 100%

Formal tracks/concentrations: forensic

Research areas	# Faculty	# Grants
juvenile justice	1	1
violence risk	2	0
witness preparation/testimony	1	0
family psychology	1	0
addictive behavior	1	1
advanced data analytic methodology	1	0
trauma	1	0
behavioral medicine	1	0
health psychology: chronic pain, fatigue	1	0
neurobehavioral functioning	1	0
person perception	1	0
jury decision making	1	0
social influences	1	0
relationship commitment and success	1	0
social emotions	1	0
forensic assessment	4	0
stereotyping and prejudice	1	1
blame & responsibility attribution	1	1
personality and individual differences	1	1
psychotherapy	1	1
diversity	2	0
law enforcement psychology	1	0

Clinical opportunities
assessment & treatment:
  children, adolescents,
  adults, couples, & families
neuropsychological settings

hospital practice
correctional settings
forensic evaluations for
  the courts

San Diego State University/University of California–San Diego (Ph.D.)

Joint doctoral program in clinical psychology
San Diego, CA 92182
phone#: (619) 594-2246
e-mail: eklonoff@sunstroke.sdsu.edu
Web address: www.psychology.sdsu.edu/doctoral/

1	2	3	4	5	6	7

Practice oriented   Equal emphasis   Research oriented

Percentage of faculty subscribing to each of the following orientations:

Psychodynamic/Psychoanalytic   5%
Applied behavioral analysis/Radical behavioral   30%
Family systems/Systems   10%
Existential/Phenomenological/Humanistic   5%
Cognitive/Cognitive-behavioral   50%

Courses required for incoming students to have completed prior to enrolling:
psychology major or 18 semester hours in psychology including: personality, abnormal, social, statistics, testing, experimental with lab, physiological.

Recommended but not mandatory courses:
advanced courses in perception and learning, biology, mathematics, linguistics, computer science, medical physics

GRE mean
Verbal 619   Quantitative 712
Psychology Subject Test 715
Analytical Writing not reported

GPA mean
Overall GPA 3.59   Psychology GPA 3.80

Number of applications/admission offers/incoming students in 2008
375 applied/17 admission offers/15 incoming

% of students receiving:
Full tuition waiver only: 0%
Assistantship/fellowship only: 0%
Tuition full waiver & assistantship/fellowship: 100%

Approximate percentage of incoming students with a B.A./B.S. only: 80%   **Master's:** 20%

Approximate percentage of students who are Women: 73%   **Ethnic Minority:** 27%
International: not reported

Average years to complete the doctoral program (including internship): 6 years

Personal interview
Preferred in person but telephone acceptable

Attrition rate in past 7 years: 2%

Percentage of students applying for internship last year accepted into APPIC or APA internships: 100%

Formal tracks/concentrations: behavioral medicine/ health psychology, experimental psychopathology, neuropsychology

Research areas	# Faculty	# Grants
AIDS	7	1
aging	8	1
Alzheimer's/dementia	6	0
anxiety	4	1
applied behavioral analysis	4	0
autism	2	0
bereavement	2	0
biofeedback	1	0
cancer disparities	4	0
cancer prtevention	2	2
cardiovascular disease	4	1
child, marriage, and family	5	0
childhood brain damage	2	0
chronic disease	4	1
cognition and memory	13	0
cognitive psychology/therapy	2	0
community psychology	1	0
cross-cultural psychology	10	0
decision making	1	0
depression	3	2
developmental neuropsychology	7	0
developmental psychopathology	3	0
ethnicity and health	2	0
exercise	2	1
gender and health	2	0
gender issues	2	0
information processing	4	0
interpersonal psychology	1	0
neuropsychological testing	2	1
nutrition	3	0
pain	2	0
posttraumatic stress disorder	1	0
problem solving	1	0
psychological testing	4	0
psychology of humor	1	0
psychopathology	3	0
psychopharmacology	6	2
psychophysiology	5	0
psychotherapy process and outcome	4	0
schizophrenia/psychosis	7	2
sexuality	1	0
sleep	4	0
smoking	7	1
social skills training	1	0
social support	2	0
statistics	4	0
stress and coping	13	0
substance abuse	12	5
women's health	3	0

Clinical opportunities

anxiety disorders   cognitive therapy
behavioral medicine   neuropsychology
child and family therapy   school psychology

Seattle Pacific University (Ph.D.)

Clinical Psychology Department
3307 Third Avenue West, Suite 107
Seattle, WA 98119
phone#: (206) 281-2839
e-mail: clinicalpsyc@spu.edu
Web address: spu.edu/depts/spfc/clinicalpsych/

1	2	3	4	5	6	7
Practice oriented		Equal emphasis				Research oriented

Percentage of faculty subscribing to each of the following orientations:
Psychodynamic/Psychoanalytic   33%
Applied behavioral analysis/Radical behavioral   33%
Family systems/Systems   50%
Existential/Phenomenological/Humanistic   16%
Cognitive/Cognitive-behavioral   83%

Courses required for incoming students to have completed prior to enrolling:
Statistics and 5 from among: abnormal, developmental, experimental, physiological, social, learning, motivation, personality, cognitive, tests and measurement

Recommended but not mandatory courses:
See above

GRE mean
Verbal 531   Quantitative 634
Psychology Subject Test not reported
Analytical Writing not reported

GPA mean
Overall GPA 3.60

Number of applications/admission offers/incoming students in 2009
112 applied/23 admission offers/15 incoming

% of students receiving:
Full tuition waiver only: 0%
Assistantship/fellowship only: 0%
Both full tuition waiver & assistantship/fellowship: 0%

Approximate percentage of incoming students with a B.A./B.S. only: 66%　**Master's:** 33%

Approximate percentage of students who are Women: 80%　**Ethnic Minority:** 14%　**International:** 0%

Average years to complete the doctoral program (including internship): 6 years

Personal interview
Preferred in person but telephone acceptable

Attrition rate in past 7 years: 1%

Percentage of students applying for internship last year accepted into APPIC or APA internships: 77%

Formal tracks/concentrations: none

Research areas	# Faculty	# Grants
gender and psychology	3	1
developmental psychopathology	3	3
psychology of religion	3	1
child and adolescent development	3	1
health psychology	2	0
family psychology	2	0
ethnicity and psychology	2	0
career and life development	2	0
treatment program evaluation	2	1
mental disorder in women	2	2
program and policy development	2	1
hypnosis	2	0
biofeedback	1	1
child social and emotional development	1	1
conduct problems in young children	1	1
attention and self-regulation	1	1
severe mental disorders	1	1
cognitive models of psychopathology	1	1
addictive behavior	1	1
evaluation of career interventions	1	0
counseling process and outcome	1	0
relationships in ministry	1	0
disaster psychology	1	0
relationship between couples	1	0
multisystemic interventions	1	0
interventions for chronic pain	1	0
gender differences in health and illness	2	0
psychodynamic psychotherapy	1	0
supervision/ethics	1	0
psychophysiology of stress	1	0
exercise and quality of life	1	0
self-psychology and self-esteem	1	0
prejudice and intergroup relations	1	0
leadership and executive development	1	0
developmental disabilities	1	0
psychologies of peace and war	1	0
ethnic identity, ethnic memories, and ethnic conflict	1	0
Pacific NW Native American communities	1	0

Clinical opportunities

behavioral medicine/consult	juvenile rehabilitation
neuropsychology	serious mental illness
rehabilitation medicine	latino/a mental health
child and adolescent mental health	autism/autism spectrum
	Christian counseling
university counseling center	foster care
cancer care	family therapy
corrections	community mental health

Simon Fraser University (Ph.D.)
Department of Psychology
Burnaby, British Columbia V5A 1S6, Canada
Phone#: (778) 782-3354
e-mail: turner@sfu.ca
Web address: www.psyc.sfu.ca/grad/index.php?topic=clin_overview

1	2	3	4	5	6	7
Practice oriented			Equal emphasis			Research oriented

Percentage of faculty subscribing to each of the following orientations:

Psychodynamic/Psychoanalytic	15%
Applied behavioral analysis/Radical behavioral	0%
Family systems/Systems	35%
Existential/Phenomenological/Humanistic	0%
Cognitive/Cognitive-Behavioral	85%

Courses required for incoming students to have completed prior to enrolling:
Undergraduate degree (BA, BSc or equivalent) with an honor's or major in psychology

Recommended but not mandatory courses:
Psychology honors program; advanced undergraduate courses across all substantive areas of psychology

GRE mean
Verbal 574　Quantitative 647
Psychology Subject Test 719
Analytical Writing 5.0

GPA mean
Overall GPA 3.98
Psychology GPA 4.07

Number of applications/admission offers/incoming students in 2009
136 applied/14 admission offers/6 incoming

% of students receiving:
Full tuition waiver only: 0%
Assistantship/fellowship only: 100%
Both full tuition waiver & assistantship/fellowship: 0%

Approximate percentage of incoming students with a B.A./B.S. only: 87.5%   **Master's:** 12.5%

Approximate percentage of students who are Women: 80%   **Ethnic Minority:** not reported **International:** not reported

Average years to complete the doctoral program (including internship): 6.5 years

Personal interview
In person if possible, but telephone acceptable

Attrition rate in past 7 years: 5%

Percentage of students applying for internship last year accepted into APPIC or APA internships: 100%

Formal tracks/concentrations: clinical program (general), clinical child, clinical forensic, clinical neuropsychology

Research areas	# Faculty	# Grants
behavioral medicine	1	1
child clinical	4	9
child psychopathology	4	6
cognition	4	4
depression	3	1
developmental	6	7
family	3	3
forensic	4	9
neuropsychology	2	3
psychopathology	8	7
sex offenders	2	2
stress and coping	1	1
violence and abuse	6	7

University of South Carolina (Ph.D.)

Department of Psychology
Columbia, SC 29208
Phone#: (803) 777-2312
E-mail: marthab@mailbox.sc.edu
Web address: www.cas.sc.edu/psyc/grad_psyccc/ccprog.html

1	2	3	4	5	6	7
Practice oriented		Equal emphasis			Research oriented	

Percentage of faculty subscribing to each of the following orientations:

Psychodynamic/Psychoanalytic	10%
Applied behavioral analysis/Radical behavioral	10%
Family systems/Systems	40%
Existential/Phenomenological/Humanistic	0%
Cognitive/Cognitive-behavioral	40%

Recommended but not mandatory courses:
18 hours in psychology, including statistics

Recommended but not mandatory courses:
Research methods, learning, biopsychology, abnormal, social, developmental, personality

GRE mean
Verbal 599   Quantitative 682
Psychology Subject Test 673
Analytical Writing 4.8

GPA mean
Overall GPA 3.64   Psychology GPA not available
Junior/Senior GPA not available

Number of applications/admission offers/incoming students in 2008
106 applied/11 admission offers/8 incoming

% of students receiving:
Full tuition waiver only: 0%
Assistantship/fellowship only: 0%
Both full tuition waiver & assistantship/fellowship: 100%

Approximate percentage of incoming students with a B.A./B.S. only: 67%   **Master's:** 33%

Approximate percentage of students who are Women: 63% **Ethnic Minority:** 13% **International:** 3.6%

Average years to complete the doctoral program (including internship): 6 years

Personal interview
Preferred in person but telephone acceptable

Attrition rate in past 7 years: 8%

Percentage of students applying for internship last year accepted into APPIC or APA internships: 67%

Formal tracks/concentrations: children, adolescents, and families

Research areas	# Faculty	# Grants
child/family	4	14
citizen participation	1	1
community coalition development	2	3
marital relationships	1	0
neuropsychology	2	2
prevention (racism/cross-cultural)	3	4
self-perception in minority youth	2	2
violence/rape/battering	2	0

Clinical opportunities
Our program can be used to develop a variety of unique areas of expertise in the field of Psychology; however, currently there are two major dimensions to our program: (a) Children, Adolescents, and Families and (b) Social and Cultural Aspects of Health. Faculty members often contribute to more than one area through their teaching and research.

University of South Dakota (Ph.D.)

Department of Psychology
Vermillion, SD 57069
phone#: (605) 677-5353
e-mail: byutrzen@usd.edu
Web address: www.usd.edu/arts-and-sciences/psychology/clinical-psychology/index.cfm

1	2	3	4	5	6	7
Practice oriented		Equal emphasis			Research oriented	

Percentage of faculty subscribing to each of the following orientations:

Psychodynamic/Psychoanalytic	33%
Applied behavioral analysis/Radical behavioral	0%
Family systems/Systems	33%

| Existential/Phenomenological/Humanistic | 11% |
| Cognitive/Cognitive-behavioral | 100% |

Courses required for incoming students to have completed prior to enrolling:
18 semester hours in psychology within a distribution among standard coursework in general and experimental

Recommended but not mandatory courses:
Research design, statistics, history/systems, learning/memory, abnormal, physiological

GRE mean (past 7 years)
Verbal 533   Quantitative 607
Psychology Subject Test 621
Analytical Writing not available

GPA mean (past 7 years)
3.65

Number of applications/admission offers/incoming students in 2009
47 applied/7 admission offers/7 incoming

% of students receiving:
Full tuition waiver only: 0%
Assistantship/fellowship only: 100%
(all students on assistantships also receive tuition reduction to 1/3 of in-state tuition costs)
Both full tuition waiver & assistantship/fellowship: 0%

Approximate percentage of incoming students with a B.A./B.S. only: 80%   Master's: 20%

Approximate percentage of students who are Women: 70%   Ethnic Minority: 15%   International: 13%

Average years to complete the doctoral program (including internship): 6.7 years (Median = 5.9 years)

Personal interview
Interviews are by invitation and are required.

Attrition rate in past 7 years: 9%

Percentage of students applying for internship last year accepted into APPIC or APA internships: 73%

Formal tracks/concentrations: clinical disaster psychology

Research areas	# Faculty	# Grants
child clinical	3	0
cross-cultural	7	0
depression	2	0
disaster mental health	4	1
ethics	1	0
family violence	2	0
psychosis/serious mental illness	2	0
rural community psychology	6	0
substance abuse	2	2

Clinical opportunities
crisis intervention/disaster
  mental health
minority/cross-cultural
  (specific emphasis in
  American Indian mental
  health)
rural/community
  mental health
substance abuse
severe and persistent
  mental illness
forensic/sex offenders

University of South Florida (Ph.D.)
Department of Psychology
4202 Fowler Avenue, PCP 4118G
Tampa, FL 33620
phone#: (813) 974-2492
e-mail: phares@cas.usf.edu
Web address: http://psychology.usf.edu/grad/clinical/

1	2	3	4	5	6	7
Practice oriented		Equal emphasis			Research oriented	

Percentage of faculty subscribing to each of the following orientations:
Psychodynamic/Psychoanalytic	0%
Applied behavioral analysis/Radical behavioral	9%
Family systems/Systems	9%
Existential/Phenomenological/Humanistic	9%
Cognitive/Cognitive-behavioral	73%

Courses required for incoming students prior to enrolling: None

Recommended but not mandatory courses:
Research design, statistics, abnormal psychology

GRE mean
Verbal 607   Quantitative 691
Psychology Subject Test not required
Analytical Writing 4.6

GPA mean
Junior/Senior GPA 3.79

Number of applications/admission offers/incoming students in 2009
240 applied/17 admission offers/11 incoming

% of students receiving:
Full tuition waiver only: 0%
Assistantship/fellowship only: 0%
Both full tuition waiver & assistantship/fellowship: 100%

Approximate percentage of incoming students with a B.A./B.S. only: 73%   Master's: 27%

Approximate percentage of students who are Women: 64% Ethnic Minority: 27% International: 0%

Average years to complete the doctoral program (including internship): 6.8 years (median = 6.0 years)

Personal interview
Preferred in person but telephone acceptable

Attrition rate in past 7 years: 6%

Percentage of students applying for internship last year accepted into APPIC or APA internships: 100%

Formal tracks/concentrations: health psychology, personality/psychopathology, clinical neuropsychology, addictive behaviors, clinical child psychology

Research areas	# Faculty	# Grants
child/adolescent	4	2
depression	2	2
eating disorders	2	1
emotions	2	2

family dysfunction	1	0
health psychology	5	8
neuropsychology	2	0
personality assessment	1	0
psychosocial oncology	2	8
substance abuse/addictions	3	5
suicidality	1	2

Clinical opportunities

ADHD	intellectual assessment
adult and child clinical assessment	learning disorders assessment
adult neuropsychology	oppositional defiant disorder
anxiety—child and adult	
child and adolescent disorders	psychosocial oncology
depression/anxiety	selective mutism
eating disorders	substance abuse
family dysfunction	survivors of torture
health psychology	weight management

University of Southern California (Ph.D.)

Doctoral Program in Psychological Clinical Science
Department of Psychology
3620 McClintock, SGM 501
Los Angeles, CA 90089-1061
phone#: (213) 740-2203
e-mail: margolin@usc.edu
Web address: college.usc.edu/psyc/graduate/clinical_program_ove.cfm

1	2	3	4	5	6	7

Practice oriented — Equal emphasis — Research oriented

Percentage of faculty subscribing to each of the following orientations:

Psychodynamic/Psychoanalytic	0%
Applied behavioral analysis/Radical behavioral	27%
Family systems/Systems	27%
Existential/Phenomenological/Humanistic	9%
Cognitive/Cognitive-behavioral	100%

Courses required for incoming students to have completed prior to enrolling: None

Recommended but not mandatory courses:

Elementary statistics*, research methods* or experimental psychology, and courses in neuroscience, philosophy, biology, mathematics, physical sciences, and social sciences. This list consists of courses recommended by at least one faculty reviewer. Courses marked with an asterisk (*) are strongly recommended.

GRE mean
Verbal 664   Quantitative 736
Analytical Writing 5.0

GPA mean
Overall GPA 3.69

Number of applications/admission offers/incoming students in 2009
271 applied/8 admission offers/5 incoming

% of students receiving:
Full tuition waiver only: 0%
Assistantship/fellowship only: 0%
Both full tuition waiver & assistantship/fellowship: 100%

Approximate percentage of incoming students with a B.A./B.S. only: 100%   Master's: 0%

Approximate percentage of students who are
Women: 60%   Ethnic Minority: 20%   International: 0%

Average years to complete the doctoral program (including internship): 6.0 years

Personal interview
Strongly preferred

Attrition rate in past 7 years: 7%

Percentage of students applying for internship last year accepted into APPIC or APA internships: 100%

Formal tracks/concentrations: child and family, clinical/aging. We also have a dual degree (Ph.D./MPH) program in which students can pursue a Master's in Public Health if admitted by the MPH program after being admitted to the Ph.D.

Research areas	# Faculty	# Grants
adult psychopathology	5	0
affective disorders/depression/ mood disorders	4	0
alcohol and substance use/abuse	3	0
behavioral genetics	2	1
child psychopathology	5	0
childhood victimization	4	1
clinical aging	4	5
cognitive behavioral therapy/ assessment	2	0
community psychology	1	2
culturally informed treatment	4	2
ethnicity/culture and intervention	4	2
genetic, biological, and social influences on the development and course of psychopathology	2	0
health psychology	3	3
marital/family	2	0
prevention	2	0
psychological reactions to extreme trauma	1	
psychology applied to school settings	2	0

Clinical opportunities

alcohol/substance abuse interventions group therapy*	correctional psychology/ prisons*
assessment/testing	marital/couples
child/adolescent community mental health	minority/cross-cultural/ multicultural
cognitive/cognitive- behavioral therapy	neuropsychological assessment*
culture and treatment	parent-child interaction/ parent-training
culturally informed treatment	personality disorders
family therapy/systems	schizophrenia/psychosis/ serious mental illness*
geropsychology	
individual adult	underserved populations

*external clinical practicum sites, including opportunities

that are available to students wishing to do work beyond program requirements

Southern Illinois University (Ph.D.)

Department of Psychology
Life Science Building II, Room 281
Carbondale, IL 62901
phone#: (618) 453-3564 (graduate program secretary)
e-mail: dollngr@siu.edu
Web address: psychology.siuc.edu/grad/clinical.htm

1	2	3	4	5	6	7
Practice oriented			Equal emphasis			Research oriented

Percentage of faculty subscribing to each of the following orientations:

Psychodynamic/Psychoanalytic	0%
Applied behavioral analysis/Radical behavioral	0%
Family systems	10%
Existential/Phenomenological/Humanistic	0%
Cognitive/Cognitive-behavioral	90%

Courses required for incoming students prior to enrolling: None

Recommended but not mandatory courses:

History and systems, tests and measurements, abnormal psychology, personality, learning, developmental, physiological/neuroscience, statistics, social psychology

GRE mean

Verbal 584, Quantitative 655 (over last 5 years of incoming students)

GPA mean

3.79 over last 5 years

Number of applications/admission offers/incoming students in 2009

108 applied/11 admission offers/6 incoming

% of students receiving:

Full tuition waiver only: 0%
Assistantship/fellowship only: 0%
Both full tuition waiver & assistantship/fellowship: 100%

Approximate percentage of incoming students with a B.A./B.S. only: 85%   Master's: 15% (average over multiple years)

Approximate percentage of students who are Women: 70%   Ethnic Minority: 20%   International: 15%

Average years to complete the doctoral program (including internship): 7.5 years

Personal interview

No preference given
(Note: Short-listed applicants are invited to an open house in February.)

Attrition rate in past 7 years: 11%

Percentage of students applying for internship last year accepted into APPIC or APA internships: 90%

Formal tracks/concentrations: child and adult

Research areas	# Faculty	# Grants
abortion issues	1	0
abuse	1	0
AIDS attitudes	1	0
adolescent issues	2	0
anxiety disorders	3	0
assessment	8	0
behavioral genetics	1	0
behavioral medicine	2	0
child clinical	3	0
child sexual abuse	1	0
clinical judgment	1	0
community psychology	1	0
delinquency	1	1
depression	2	0
family systems	1	0
gender roles	1	0
learning disabilities	2	1
marital	1	0
pediatric psychology	1	0
personality (five-factor model)	3	0
personality assessment	4	0
psychology of religion	1	0
relationships	2	0
sleep (child)	1	0
smoking	1	many
stress, coping, and social support	1	0

Clinical opportunities

family therapy	severe psychopathology
forensic psychology	sexual abuse
juvenile corrections	substance abuse
neuropsychology/rehabilitation	

Southern Methodist University (Ph.D.)

Department of Psychology
PO Box 750442
Dallas, TX 75275-0442
phone#: (214) 768-4924
e-mail: rhampson@smu.edu
Web address: smu.edu/psychology/html/graduate.html

1	2	3	4	5	6	7
Practice oriented			Equal emphasis			Research oriented

Percentage of faculty subscribing to each of the following orientations:

Psychodynamic/Psychoanalytic	0%
Applied behavioral analysis/Radical behavioral	0%
Family systems/Systems	20%
Existential/Phenomenological/Humanistic	0%
Cognitive/Cognitive-behavioral	80%

Courses required for incoming students to have completed prior to enrolling: Abnormal Psychology, Developmental Psychology, Research Methods/Statistics

Recommended but not mandatory courses: None

GRE mean

Verbal 665
Quantitative 670

Analytical Writing 5.0

GPA mean
Overall GPA 3.71

Number of applications/admission offers/incoming students in 2010
91 applied/8 admission offers/4 incoming

% of students receiving:
Full tuition waiver only: 0%
Assistantship/fellowship only: 0%
Both full tuition waiver & assistantship/fellowship: 100%

Approximate percentage of incoming students with a B.A./B.S. only: 90%   **Master's:** 10%

Approximate percentage of students who are Women: 90%   **Ethnic Minority:**25%   **International:** 5%

Average years to complete the doctoral program (including internship): 5.5 years

Personal interview: Required in person

Attrition rate in past 7 years: 10%

Percentage of students applying for internship last year accepted into APPIC or APA internships: 100%

Formal tracks/concentrations/specializations: none

Research areas	# Faculty	# Grants
family	5	2
health	3	1
psychopathology	3	2
cognitive	1	0
quantitative	1	0

Clinical opportunities
assessment
anxiety disorders
couples therapy
External practica include a wide variety of community counseling centers, VA, Federal prisons, Children's Medical Center, Parkland Hospital Consult/Liaison, Presbyterian Hospital, neuropsychology

University of Southern Mississippi (Ph.D.)
Department of Psychology
Box 5025 Southern Station
Hattiesburg, MS 39406-5025
phone#: (601) 266-4588
e-mail: david.marcus@usm.edu
Web address: http://www.usm.edu/psy/department/ClinicalPsychology.html

1	2	3	4	**5**	6	7
Clinically oriented		Equal emphasis				Research oriented

Percentage of faculty subscribing to each of the following orientations:

Psychodynamic/Psychoanalytic	12%
Applied behavioral analysis/Radical behavioral	13%
Family systems/Systems	0%
Existential/Phenomenological/Humanistic	0%
Cognitive/Cognitive-behavioral	75%

Courses required for incoming students to have completed prior to enrolling:
Statistics, Research methods

Recommended but not mandatory courses:
Abnormal Psychology

GRE mean
Verbal 570   Quantitative 665
Analytical Writing not reported

GPA mean
Overall GPA 3.75

Number of applications/admission offers/incoming students in 2009
101 applied/10 admission offers/5 incoming

% of students receiving:
Full tuition waiver only: 0%
Assistantship/fellowship only: 0%
Both full tuition waiver & assistantship/fellowship: 100%

Approximate percentage of incoming students with a B.A./B.S. only: 80%   **Master's:** 20%

Approximate percentage of students who are Women: 70%   **Ethnic Minority:** 20%   **International:** 8%

Average years to complete the doctoral program (including internship): 5.5 years

Personal interview
Required in person or phone interviews

Attrition rate in past 7 years: 18%

Percentage of students applying for internship last year accepted into APPIC or APA internships: 83%

Formal tracks/concentrations: adult, child

Research areas	# Faculty	# Grants
adult clinical	5	3
child clinical	3	2

Clinical opportunities
adult clinical
child clinical

Spalding University (Psy.D.)
School of Professional Psychology
845 South Third Street
Louisville, KY 40203
phone#: (502) 585-7127
e-mail: bbeauchamp@spalding.edu
Web address: www.spalding.edu/academics/psychology/about-the-psy-d-program/

1	2	**3**	4	5	6	7
Practice oriented		Equal emphasis				Research oriented

Percentage of faculty subscribing to each of the following orientations:

Psychodynamic/Psychoanalytic	10%
Applied behavioral analysis/Radical behavioral	10%

255

Family systems/Systems	10%
Existential/Phenomenological/Humanistic	20%
Cognitive/Cognitive-behavioral	50%

Courses required for incoming students to have completed prior to enrolling:
18 hours of undergraduate work.

Recommended but not mandatory courses:
Undergraduate research

GRE mean
Verbal 515   Quantitative 580
Psychology Subject Test not required

GPA mean
Overall GPA 3.6

Number of applications/admission offers/incoming students in 2009
132 applied/55 admission offers/33 incoming

% of students receiving:
Full tuition waiver only: 0%
Assistantship/fellowship only: 17%
Both full tuition waiver & assistantship/fellowship: 0%

Approximate percentage of incoming students with a B.A./B.S. only: 65%   **Master's:** 35%

Approximate percentage of students who are Women: 73%   **Ethnic Minority:** 15%   **International:** 7%

Average years to complete the doctoral program (including internship): 5.5 years

Personal interview
Preferred in person but telephone acceptable

Attrition rate in past 7 years: 11%

Percentage of students applying for internship last year accepted into APPIC or APA internships: 83%

Formal tracks/concentrations: forensic psychology; health psychology; adult psychology; child, adolescent, and family psychology

Research areas	# Faculty	# Grants
child development	1	0
forensic	1	0
program evaluation	2	2
sports psychology	1	0
trauma	1	0
health	1	0
spirituality	1	0
substance abuse	1	0
bias	1	0
teaching psychology	1	0

Clinical opportunities
family/systems psychology
health psychology

St. John's University (Ph.D.)
Department of Psychology
8000 Utopia Parkway
Jamaica, NY 11439
phone#: (718) 990-6369
e-mail: nevidj@stjohns.edu
Web address: www.stjohns.edu/academics/graduate/liberalarts/departments/psychology/programs/phd_cp

1	2	3	**4**	5	6	7
Practice oriented			Equal emphasis			Research oriented

Percentage of faculty subscribing to each of the following orientations:

Psychodynamic/Psychoanalytic	30%
Applied behavioral analysis/Radical behavioral	0%
Family systems/Systems	10%
Existential/Phenomenological/Humanistic	0%
Cognitive/Cognitive-behavioral	60%

Courses required for incoming students to have completed prior to enrolling:
Statistics, experimental laboratory

Recommended but not mandatory courses: None

GRE mean
Verbal 629   Quantitative 707
Psychology Subject Test 699
Analytical Writing 5.17

GPA mean
Overall GPA 3.70   Psychology GPA 3.78

Number of applications/admission offers/incoming students in 2009
287 applied/22 admission offers/12 incoming

% of incoming students receiving:
Full tuition waiver only: 0%
Assistantship/fellowship only: 0%
Both full tuition waiver & assistantship/fellowship: 100%
(92% of students are given partial support)

Approximate percentage of incoming students with a B.A./B.S. only: 66%   **Master's:** 34%

Approximate percentage of students who are Women: 76%   **Ethnic Minority:** 30%   **International:** 0%

Average years to complete the doctoral program (including internship): 6.2 years

Personal interview
Preferred in person but telephone acceptable

Attrition rate in past 7 years: 9%

Percentage of students applying for internship last year accepted into APPIC or APA internships: 100%

Formal tracks/concentrations: child clinical

Research areas	# Faculty	# Grants
anxiety disorders	2	0
autism	1	1
bilingualism	2	0
child abuse	1	2
gender issues	2	0
health psychology	2	1
minority mental health	5	1

moral development	3	0
intervention	1	1
schizophrenia	1	0
smoking cessation	1	0
stress management	1	1

Clinical opportunities

clinical child psychology	medical centers
cognitive-behavioral therapy	municipal hospitals
neuropsychological assessment	outpatient clinics
psychodynamic/	research institutes
psychoanalytic therapy	

Saint Louis University (Ph.D.)

Department of Psychology
221 North Grand Boulevard
St. Louis, MO 63103
phone#: (314) 977-4272
e-mail: psyclini@slu.edu
Web address: www.slu.edu/x13073.xml

1	2	3	4	5	6	7
Practice oriented			Equal emphasis			Research oriented

Percentage of faculty subscribing to each of the following orientations:

Psychodynamic/Psychoanalytic	15%
Applied behavioral analysis/Radical behavioral	0%
Family systems/Systems	25%
Existential/Phenomenological/Humanistic	15%
Cognitive/Cognitive-behavioral	80%

Courses required for incoming students to have completed prior to enrolling:

Statistics, abnormal psychology, and 6 upper division psychology courses

Recommended but not mandatory courses:

Personality, learning, social psychology, physiological psychology, developmental psychology, tests and measurement

GRE mean

Verbal 532   Quantitative 615
Analytical Writing 4.6

GPA mean

Overall GPA 3.7

Number of applications/admission offers/incoming students in 2008

205 applied/14 admission offers/8 incoming

% of students receiving:

Full tuition waiver only: 0%
Assistantship/fellowship only: 0%
Tuition full waiver & assistantship/fellowship: 100% for first year

Approximate percentage of incoming students with a B.A./B.S. only: 85%   Master's: 15%

Approximate percentage of students who are

Women: 70%   Ethnic Minority: 20%   International: 10%

Average years to complete the doctoral program (including internship): 6 years

Personal interview
Preferred in person but telephone acceptable

Attrition rate in past 7 years: 5%

Percentage of students applying for internship last year accepted into APPIC or APA internships: 90%

Formal tracks/concentrations: none

Research areas	# Faculty	# Grants
abuse/violence	2	1
adjustment	2	0
anxiety	2	0
assessment	2	0
child/adolescent	2	1
community	1	0
depression	2	0
eating disorders	1	1
ethical issues	2	0
family	3	0
minority issues	1	0
neuropsychology	1	0
personality disorders	2	0
professional issues	2	0
sport psychology	1	0
stress and coping	2	0

Clinical opportunities

anxiety	hyperactivity
assessment	learning disabilities
clinical neuropsychology	marital
eating disorders and obesity	parent skills training
ethnic diversity	personality disorders
family therapy	psychodynamic therapy
health psychology	victims of abuse and assault

Stony Brook University/State University of New York (Ph.D.)

Department of Psychology
Stony Brook, NY 11794-2500
phone#: (631) 632-7830
e-mail: k.d.oleary@sunysb.edu
Web address: www.psychology.sunysb.edu/psychology/index.php?graduate/areasofstudy/clinical

1	2	3	4	5	6	7
Practice oriented			Equal emphasis			Research oriented

Percentage of faculty subscribing to each of the following orientations:

Psychodynamic/Psychoanalytic	45%
Applied behavioral analysis/Radical behavioral	82%
Family systems/Systems	64%
Existential/Phenomenological/Humanistic	36%
Cognitive/Cognitive-behavioral	91%

Courses required for incoming students to have completed prior to enrolling: None

Recommended but not mandatory courses:
Statistics, experimental with lab, abnormal psychology, research methods

GRE mean Applicants Accepted for Academic Year 2009–2010
Verbal 625   Quantitative 728   Analytical Writing 5.5

GPA mean
Overall GPA 3.82

Number of applications/admission offers/incoming students in 2009–2010
317 applied/9 admission offers/4 incoming

% of students receiving:
Full tuition waiver only: 0%
Assistantship/fellowship only: 0%
Both full tuition waiver & assistantship/fellowship: 100%

Approximate percentage of incoming students with a B.A./B.S. only: 75%   **Master's:** 25%

Approximate percentage of students who are Women: 75%   **Ethnic Minority:** 33%
International: not reported

Average years to complete the doctoral program (including internship): 6 years

Personal interview
Prefer in person but telephone acceptable

Attrition rate in past 7 years: 18%

Percentage of students applying for internship last year accepted into APPIC or APA internships: 100%

Formal tracks/concentrations: close relationship concentration

Research areas	# Faculty	# Grants
affective disorders	1	2
anxiety disorders	1	2
attachment/close relationships/	1	0
developmental disabilities	0	2
marriage/spousal abuse	2	5
parent–child interactions	1	1
psychotherapy outcome/integration	1	1

Clinical opportunities

center	student counseling center
	various community
pital	agencies

Suffolk University (Ph.D.)

Department of Psychology
41 Temple St., 6th Floor
Boston, MA 02114-4280
phone#: (617) 573-8293
e-mail: phd@suffolk.edu
Web address: www.suffolk.edu/college/7093.html

1	2	3	**4**	5	6	7
Practice oriented		Equal emphasis			Research oriented	

Percentage of faculty subscribing to each of the following orientations:

Psychodynamic/Psychoanalytic	7%
Applied behavioral analysis/Radical behavioral	0%
Family systems/Systems	21%
Existential/Phenomenological/Humanistic	7%
Cognitive/Cognitive-behavioral	64%

Courses required for incoming students to have completed prior to enrolling:
5 courses in psychology

Recommended but not mandatory courses:
Statistics and research methods highly preferred

GRE mean
Verbal 610   Quantitative 638   Analytical 730
Psychology Subject Test 730
Analytical Writing 5

GPA mean
Overall GPA 3.58

Number of applications/admission offers/incoming students in 2009
252 applied/24 admissions offers/13 incoming

% of students receiving:
Full tuition waiver only: 15%
Assistantship/fellowship only: 85%
Both full tuition waiver & assistantship/fellowship: 0%

Approximate percentage of incoming students with a B.A./B.S. only: 47%   **Master's:** 53% (include Ph.D.s)

Approximate percentage of students who are Women: 80%   **Ethnic Minority:** 15%   **International:** 4%

Average years to complete the doctoral program (including internship): 6.5 years

Personal interview
Required; may occur in person or by telephone

Attrition rate in past 7 years: 1.6%

Percentage of students applying for internship last year accepted into APPIC or APA internships: 92%

Formal tracks/concentrations: child, neuropsychology, general

Research areas
See web site for specific research areas

Clinical opportunities

adult inpatient and outpatient	forensic
community mental health	neuropsychological
child and adolescent	assessment
inpatient and outpatient	schools
college/university counseling	
center	

Syracuse University (Ph.D.)

Department of Psychology
430 Huntington Hall
Syracuse, NY 13244-2340

phone#: (315) 443-2760
e-mail: kemaster@syr.edu
Web address: psychweb.syr.edu/graduate/Clinical.html

1	2	3	4	**5**	6	7
Practice oriented		Equal emphasis				Research oriented

Percentage of faculty subscribing to each of the following orientations:

Psychodynamic/Psychoanalytic	0%
Applied behavioral analysis/Radical behavioral	0%
Family systems/Systems	0%
Existential/Phenomenological/Humanistic	20%
Cognitive/Cognitive-behavioral	80%

Courses required for incoming students prior to enrolling:

15 credits of psychology courses, statistics, laboratory course

Recommended but not mandatory courses:

Numerous laboratory courses, research experience, science courses

GRE mean

Verbal 590   Quantitative 740

GPA mean

Overall GPA 3.5   Psychology GPA 3.7

Number of applications/admission offers/incoming students in 2009

117 applied/10 admission offers/3 incoming

% of students receiving:

Full tuition waiver only: 0%
Assistantship/fellowship only: 0%
Both full tuition waiver & assistantship/fellowship: 100%

Approximate percentage of incoming students with a B.A./B.S. only: 100%   Master's: 0%

Approximate percentage of students who are Women: 100%   Ethnic Minority: 33%   International: 0%

Average years to complete the doctoral program (including internship): 6 years

Personal interview

Preferred in person but telephone acceptable

Attrition rate in past 7 years: 28%

Percentage of students applying for internship last year accepted into APPIC or APA internships: 100%

Formal tracks/concentrations: health psychology with special research emphasizes on cardiovascular disorders, HIV/AIDS, and addictions

Research areas	# Faculty	# Grants
psychophysiology	3	2
sexual health, AIDS prevention	2	4
substance abuse	3	6

Clinical opportunities

addictions	crisis intervention
anxiety disorders	family
behavioral medicine	neuropsychology

community psychology   school/educational
couples

Teachers College–Columbia University (Ph.D.)

Department of Clinical Psychology
525 West 120th Street
New York, NY 10027
phone#: (212) 678-3267
fax#: (212) 678-4048
e-mail: farber@tc.edu
Web address: www.tc.columbia.edu/academic/ccp/Clinical/index.asp?id=Doctor+of+Philosophy&Info=ph%2ED%2E+Program+Description#DoctorofPhilosophy

1	2	3	**4**	5	6	7
Practice oriented		Equal emphasis				Research oriented

Percentage of faculty subscribing to each of the following orientations:

Psychodynamic/Psychoanalytic	60%
Applied behavioral analysis/Radical behavioral	0%
Family systems/Systems	0%
Existential/Phenomenological/Humanistic	0%
Cognitive/Cognitive-behavioral	40%

Courses required for incoming students prior to enrolling:

Statistics and 9 credits from among: experimental psychology, personality, history and systems, developmental psychology, or social psychology

Recommended but not mandatory courses:

Abnormal psychology

GRE mean

Verbal 660   Quantitative 680
Psychology Subject Test 680
Analytical Writing 4.9

GPA mean

Overall GPA 3.7

Number of applications/admission offers/incoming students in 2009

340 applied/8 admission offers/7 incoming

% of students receiving:

Full tuition waiver only: 10%
Assistantship/fellowship only: 0%
Both full tuition waiver & assistantship/fellowship: 10%
(80% of students receive a partial tuition wavier)

Approximate percentage of incoming students with a B.A./B.S. only: 25%   Master's: 75%

Approximate percentage of students who are Women: 70%   Ethnic Minority: 20%   International: 20%

Average years to complete the doctoral program (including internship): 7 years

Personal interview

Required in person

259

Attrition rate in past 7 years: 1.4%

Percentage of students applying for internship last year accepted into APPIC or APA internships: 90%

Formal tracks: child clinical

Research areas	# Faculty	# Grants
altruism	1	0
geriatrics	1	0
psychotherapy research	3	1
risk and resilience	2	1
spirituality	1	1
trauma, stress and coping	2	1
bipolarity in families	1	1

Clinical opportunities
child therapy
psychodynamic/psychoanalytic therapy

Temple University (Ph.D.)
Department of Psychology
1701 N. 13th Stree
Philadelphia, PA 19122-6085
phone#: (215) 204-7326
e-mail: rfauber@temple.edu
Web address: www.temple.edu/psychology/clinical/index.htm

1	2	3	4	5	6	7
Practice oriented		Equal emphasis			Research oriented	

Percentage of faculty subscribing to each of the following orientations:

Psychodynamic/Psychoanalytic	0%
Applied behavioral analysis/Radical behavioral	20%
Family systems/Systems	20%
Existential/Phenomenological/Humanistic	10%
Cognitive/Cognitive-behavioral	100%

Courses required for incoming students prior to enrolling:
B.A. or B.S. degree and at least 4 minimally 3-credit courses in psychology (including 1 research methods course) and statistics

Recommended but not mandatory courses:
1 natural sciences laboratory course

GRE mean
Verbal + Quantitative 1400

GPA mean
Overall GPA 3.7

Number of applications/admission offers/incoming students in 2008
375 applied/20 admission offers/10 incoming

% of students receiving:
Full tuition waiver only: 0%
Assistantship/fellowship only: 0%
Both full tuition waiver & assistantship/fellowship: 100%

Approximate percentage of incoming students with a B.A./B.S. only: 90%   **Master's:** 10%

Approximate percentage of students who are Women: 84%   **Ethnic Minority:** 12%   **International:** 6%

Average years to complete the doctoral program (including internship): 6 years

Personal interview
Required in person

Attrition rate in past 7 years: 5%

Percentage of students applying for internship last year accepted into APPIC or APA internships: 100%

Formal tracks/concentrations: none

Research areas	# Faculty	# Grants
adult anxiety disorders/treatment	1	2
child anxiety disorders/treatment	1	2
childhood externalizing problems	1	1
adolescent and adult mood disorders	1	2
prenatal development and risk for schizophrenia	1	0
neuropsychology of everyday action & dementia & schiz.	1	1
aggression and intermittent explosive disorder	1	1
relationship difficulties/ couples therapy	1	0

Clinical opportunities
anxiety disorders in children
adult social phobia and generalized anxiety disorder
bipolar spectrum disorders and depression
conduct disorder and depression
clinical neuropsychology
specialty clinics in a large urban area
couples and family therapy

University of Tennessee (Ph.D.)
Department of Psychology
Austin Peay Psychology Building
Knoxville, TN 37996-0900
phone#: (865) 974-2165
e-mail: mhunsber@utk.edu
Web address: web.utk.edu/~clinical/

1	2	3	4	5	6	7
Practice oriented		Equal emphasis			Research oriented	

Percentage of faculty subscribing to each of the following orientations:

Psychodynamic/Psychoanalytic	30%
Applied behavioral analysis/Radical behavioral	0%
Family systems/Systems	10%
Existential/Phenomenological/Humanistic	0%
Cognitive/Cognitive-behavioral	60%

Courses required for incoming students to have completed prior to enrolling: None

Recommended but not mandatory courses: None

GRE mean
Verbal 604   Quantitative 634
Psychology Subject Test not reported
Analytical Writing not reported

GPA mean
Overall GPA 3.74

Number of applications/admission offers/incoming students in 2009
185 applied/14 admission offers/9 incoming

% of students receiving:
Full tuition waiver only: 0%
Assistantship/fellowship only: 0%
Both full tuition waiver & assistantship/fellowship: 100%

Approximate percentage of incoming students with a B.A./B.S. only: 50%   **Master's:** 50%

Approximate percentage of students who are Women: 77%   **Ethnic Minority:** 12.5%   **International:** 2%

Average years to complete the doctoral program (including internship): 5.7 years

Personal interview
Preferred in person but telephone acceptable

Attrition rate in past 7 years: 5%

Percentage of students applying for internship last year accepted into APPIC or APA internships: 100%

Formal tracks/concentrations: none

Research areas	# Faculty	# Grants
family/relationship	7	5
adult psychopathology	—	1
developmental psychopathology	3	1
therapy	5	2
health	2	1

Clinical opportunities

romantic relationships (adolescent and adult)	therapy with cancer patients
hypnosis	substance abuse (adolescents and adults)
borderline personality disorder development	conduct disorder
	relationship violence

Texas A&M University (Ph.D.)

Department of Psychology
College Station, TX 77843-4235
phone#: (979) 845-2581
e-mail: d-snyder@tamu.edu
Web address: psychology.tamu.edu/AOS.php?ID=1

1	2	3	4	5	6	7
Practice oriented		Equal emphasis				Research oriented

Percentage of faculty subscribing to each of the following orientations:

Psychodynamic/Psychoanalytic	20%
Applied behavioral analysis/Radical behavioral	0%
Family systems/Systems	15%
Existential/Phenomenological/Humanistic	15%
Cognitive/Cognitive-behavioral	50%

Courses required for incoming students prior to enrolling:

Introductory statistics, abnormal, and at least 3 other psychology courses including a course in a core basic experimental area

Recommended but not mandatory courses:
Advanced research-based seminars

GRE mean
Verbal 600   Quantitative 650
Analytical Writing not required

GPA mean
Overall GPA 3.5

Number of applications/admission offers/incoming students in 2009
180 applied/10 admission offers/7 incoming

% of students receiving:
Full tuition waiver only: 0%
Assistantship/fellowship only: 0%
Both full tuition waiver & assistantship/fellowship: 100%

Approximate percentage of incoming students with a B.A./B.S. only: 70%   **Master's:** 30%

Approximate percentage of students who are Women: 60%   **Ethnic Minority:** 30%   **International:** 10%

Average years to complete the doctoral program (including internship): 5 years

Personal interview
Preferred in person but telephone acceptable

Attrition rate in past 7 years: 12%

Percentage of students applying for internship last year accepted into APPIC or APA internships: 100%

Formal tracks/concentrations: none

Research areas	# Faculty	# Grants
addictive disorders	1	1
aging	2	1
anxiety disorders	3	1
assessment	3	0
child behavior disorders	4	3
health psychology	2	1
marital/family studies	5	3
psychopathology	2	1
psychotherapy	7	2

Clinical opportunities

community	neuropsychology
family	rural psychology
forensic	substance abuse

University of Texas at Austin (Ph.D.)

Department of Psychology
1 University Station A8000
Austin, TX 78712
phone#: (512) 471-3393
e-mail: gradoffice@psy.utexas.edu
Web address: www.psy.utexas.edu/psy/clinical/index.html

1	2	3	4	5	6	7
Practice oriented		Equal emphasis			Research oriented	

Percentage of faculty subscribing to each of the following orientations:

Psychodynamic/Psychoanalytic	0%
Applied behavioral analysis/Radical behavioral	0%
Family systems/Systems	0%
Existential/Phenomenological/Humanistic	25%
Cognitive/Cognitive-behavioral	75%

Courses required for incoming students to have completed prior to enrolling:
None

Recommended but not mandatory courses:
Abnormal psychology, neuroscience, research methods, statistics

GRE mean
Verbal + Quantitative 1369
Analytical Writing not reported

GPA mean
Overall GPA 3.63

Number of applications/admission offers/incoming students in 2009
277 applicants/9 offers/5 incoming

% of students receiving:
Full tuition waiver only: 0%
Assistantship/fellowship only: 0%
Both full tuition waiver & assistantship/fellowship: 100%

Approximate percentage of incoming students with a B.A./B.S. only: 80% Master's: 20%

Approximate percentage of students who are
Women: 73% Ethnic Minority: 24% International: 5%

Average years to complete the doctoral program (including internship): 7 years

Personal interview
Required

Attrition rate in past 7 years: 8%

Percentage of students applying for internship last year accepted into APPIC or APA internships: 100%

Formal tracks/concentrations: none

Research areas	# Faculty	# Grants
addictions	1	1
anxiety	1	0
behavior genetics & adolescent psychopathology	1	0
depression	1	1
developmental disabilities/autism	1	0
health psychology	1	1
multicultural psychology	1	0
neurological disorders (animal models)	1	
neurobiology of aging	1	1
neuropsychology	2	1
positive psychology/well-being	1	0
sexual dysfunction	1	1
stress and coping	1	1

Clinical opportunities

addictions/recovery	diverse student populations
ADHD	hoarding
anxiety disorders	marital
assessment	military/veterans
behavioral medicine	neuropsychology
child/family	obsessive–compulsive
child/adolescent/adult	disorder
severe mental illness	personality disorders
community	sleep psychology
crisis intervention	student counseling center
depression	survivors of torture

University of Texas Southwestern Medical Center at Dallas (Ph.D.)

Division of Psychology
5323 Harry Hines Boulevard
Dallas, Texas 75390-9044
phone#: (214) 648-5277
e-mail: ClinicalPsychologyProgram@UTSouthwestern.edu
Web address: www.utsouthwestern.edu/graduateschool/clinicalpsychology.html

1	2	3	4	5	6	7
Practice oriented		Equal emphasis			Research oriented	

Percentage of faculty subscribing to each of the following orientations:

ynamic/Psychoanalytic	35%
Applied behavioral analysis/Radical behavioral	5%
Family systems/Systems	20%
Existential/Phenomenological/Humanistic	5%
Cognitive/Cognitive-behavioral	35%

Courses required for incoming students to have completed prior to enrolling:
Learning (can be experimental psychology, cognitive psychology or behavioral psychology), statistics

Recommended but not mandatory courses:
Developmental, physiological, experimental

GRE mean
Verbal + Quantitative 1250
Analytical Writing not reported
Psychology Subject Test not reported

GPA mean
Overall GPA 3.6

Number of applications/admission offers/incoming students in 2009
150 applied/9 admission offers for class of 7/7 incoming

% of students receiving:
Full tuition waiver only: 0%
Assistantship/fellowship: 100% (in 3rd year through end of 4th year)
Both full tuition waiver & assistantship/fellowship: 0%

Approximate percentage of incoming students with a B.A./B.S. only: 70%   **Master's:** 30%

Approximate percentage of students who are Women: 70%   **Ethnic Minority:** 29%   **International:** 10%

Average years to complete the doctoral program (including internship): 4.5 years

Personal interview
Required in person

Attrition rate in past 5 years: 7.4%

Percentage of students applying for internship last year accepted into APPIC or APA internships: 100%

Formal tracks/concentrations: health psychology, child, neuropsychology

Research areas	# Faculty	# Grants
Alzheimer's	1	1
child depression	3	3
community mental health	1	0
cultural issues in psychology	2	0
depression	3	3
developmental psychology	1	1
health psychology	3	3
health services research	1	1
learning disabilities	1	0
neurobiological aspects of psychological disorders	2	
neuropsychological profiles	2	2
pain management	1	1
pediatric psychology	1	1
rehabilitation psychology	1	1
sleep disorders	1	1

Clinical opportunities

affective disorders
behavioral psychology
clinical child
community mental health
developmental disabilities
family therapy
forensic psychology
health/medical psychology
inpatient psychiatry
neuropsychology

outpatient psychotherapy
personality disorders
primary care clinic consultation
psychiatric emergency care
rehabilitation psychology
sleep disorders
vocational assessment/ counseling

Texas Tech University (Ph.D.)

Department of Psychology
P.O. Box 42501
Lubbock, TX 79409
phone#: (806) 742-3711
fax#: (806) 742-0818
e-mail: kay.hill@ttu.edu or lee.cohen@ttu.edu
Web address: www.depts.ttu.edu/psy/graduate/clinical/overview.php

1	2	3	4	5	6	7
Practice oriented		Equal emphasis			Research oriented	

Percentage of faculty subscribing to each of the following orientations:

Behavioral	87.5%
Cognitive-Behavioral	87.5%
Cognitive	12.5%
Cognitive–Interpersonal	25%
Existential/Humanistic/Phenomenological	25%
Family systems/Systems	37.5%
Interpersonal	25%
Personal Construct/Narrative	12.5%
Psychodynamic/Psychoanalytic	12.5%

Courses required for incoming students prior to enrolling:
18 semester hours of psychology

Recommended but not mandatory courses:
Statistics, abnormal, developmental, physiological psychology, and a research course such as experimental design or independent research with a faculty member

GRE mean
Verbal 568   Quantitative 657
Analytical Writing 4.6

GPA mean
Overall GPA 3.75

Number of applications/admission offers/incoming students in 2009
123 applied/7 admission offers/6 incoming

% of students receiving:
Full tuition waiver only: 0%
Assistantship/fellowship only: 0%
Both tuition waiver & assistantship/fellowship: 100%

Approximate percentage of incoming students with a B.A./B.S. only: 100%   **Master's:** 0%

Approximate percentage of students who are Women: 100%   **Ethnic Minority:** 0%   **International:** 0%

Average years to complete the doctoral program (including internship): 6 years

Personal interview
In-person interviews strongly encouraged but telephone interviews acceptable

Attrition rate in past 7 years: 9%

Percentage of students applying for internship last year accepted into APPIC or APA internships: 100%

Formal tracks/concentrations: none

Research areas	# Faculty	# Grants
addictions	1	1
behavioral assessment	1	0
behavioral medicine	1	1
behavioral parent training	1	0
child depression and anxiety	1	0
child maltreatment and abuse	1	0
cognitive-behavioral therapies	3	0
community interventions	1	0
eating disorders	1	0
ethics/regulatory issues	1	0

ethnic minority/cultural issues	1	2
health psychology	2	0
high-risk patients/suicide	2	2
high-risk youth	1	0
informant discrepancies/rater biases in child assessment	1	0
MMPI/MMPI-2	1	0
neuropsychological assessment	1	0
nicotine dependence/withdrawal	1	1
personal meaning-making processes	1	0
single subject design, time series regression, dynamic factor analysis	2	0
Spanish-speaking families	1	1
suicide	2	0
teachers' evaluations of children's problems	2	0
trauma	2	0

Clinical opportunities

Extensive opportunities with diverse populations are available

---

University of Toledo (Ph.D.)

Department of Psychology
2801 West Bancroft Street
Toledo, OH 43606-3390
phone#: (419) 530-2721
e-mail: DNowak@UTNet.utoledo.edu
Web address: www.psychology.utoledo.edu/showpage.
asp?name=clinical_program

1	2	3	4	5	6	7
Practice oriented			Equal emphasis			Research oriented

Percentage of faculty subscribing to each of the following orientations:

Psychodynamic/Psychoanalytic	67%
Applied behavioral analysis/Radical behavioral	0%
Family systems/Systems	17%
Existential/Phenomenological/Humanistic	0%
Cognitive/Cognitive-behavioral	67%
Neuropsychology	0%

Courses required for incoming students to have completed prior to enrolling:
Statistics and research methods

Recommended but not mandatory courses: None

GRE mean
Verbal 557   Quantitative 638
Analytic Writing 4.9
Psychology Subject Test 655

GPA mean
Psychology GPA 3.7

Number of applications/admission offers/incoming students in 2009
116 applied/7 admission offers/6 incoming

% of students receiving:
Full tuition waiver only: 0%
Assistantship/fellowship only: 0%
Both full tuition waiver & assistantship/fellowship: 100%

Approximate percentage of incoming students with a B.A./B.S. only: 90%   **Master's:** 10%

Approximate percentage of students who are Women: 74%   **Ethnic Minority:** 24%   **International:** 15%

Average years to complete the doctoral program (including internship): 5.1 years

Personal interview
In person (although international students can interview by telephone)

Attrition rate in past 7 years: 5%

Percentage of students applying for internship last year accepted into APPIC or APA internships: 89%

Formal tracks/concentrations: cognitive-behavioral, psychodynamic, family and systems, or child and adolescent

Research areas	# Faculty	# Grants
child/adolescent psychopathology	3	0
public mental health	2	1
program evaluation	2	1
psychotherapy research	3	1
anxiety and depression	2	0
cognitive behavioral therapy	2	0
psychological assessment	2	1
media violence	1	0
children and violence	1	0
diversity & Multicultural Issues	2	0

Clinical opportunities

cognitive behavioral therapy	psychological assessment
child & adolescent therapy	chronic mental illness
psychodynamic therapy	anxiety and depression
family & couple therapy	in-house clinic and externships

University of Tulsa (Ph.D.)

Department of Psychology
Tulsa, OK 74104
phone#: (918) 631-2894
e-mail: michael-bass@utulsa.edu
Web address: www.utulsa.edu/academics/colleges/Henry-Kendall-College-of-Arts-and-Sciences/Departments-and-Schools/Department-of-Psychology/Programs-of-Study/Graduate%20and%20Professional%20Programs-Clinical%20Psychology.aspx

1	2	3	4	6	7
Practice oriented			Equal emphasis		Research oriented

Percentage of faculty subscribing to each of the following orientations:

Psychodynamic/Psychoanalytic	5%
Applied behavioral analysis/Radical behavioral	5%
Family systems/Systems	0%
Existential/Phenomenological/Humanistic	0%
Cognitive/Cognitive-behavioral	90%

Courses required for incoming students prior to enrolling:

18 hours of psychology including abnormal psychology, statistics or research methods, and basic core psychology courses

Recommended but not mandatory courses:
Advanced courses in psychology core

GRE mean
Verbal 580   Quantitative 685
Analytical Writing 4.8

GPA mean
GPA 3.68

Number of applications/admission offers/incoming students in 2009
49 applied/12 admission offers/7 incoming
Masters – 12 applications/5 offers/4 incoming

% of students receiving:
Full tuition waiver only: 0%
Assistantship/fellowship only: 0%
Both full tuition waiver & assistantship/fellowship 100% of Ph.D. (50 % for all enrolled clinical students)

Approximate percentage of incoming students with a B.A./B.S. only: 67% **Master's:** 33%

Approximate percentage of incoming MA and PhD students who are Women: 90% **Ethnic Minority:** 20%
International: 0%

Average years to complete the doctoral program (including internship): 5 years

Personal interview
Held on interview day for all Ph.D. candidates

Attrition rate in past 7 years: 16%

Percentage of students applying for internship last year accepted into APPIC or APA internships: 100%

Formal tracks/concentrations: clinical

Research areas	# Faculty	# Grants
life-span development	2	1
neuropsychology	1	1
personality disorders/personality	2	0
posttraumatic stress disorder	3	2
stress	4	2
pain/health	1	2

Clinical opportunities
Practicum program is community-based with access to over 22 general and specialty clinics; opportunities to conduct research and clinical work in both experimental and applied settings; opportunities for multi-disciplinary collaboration through several institutes

---

Uniformed Services University of Health Sciences (Ph.D.)

4301 Jones Bridge Road
Bethesda, MD 20814-4799
phone#: (301) 295-3270
e-mail: mfeuerstein@usuhs.edu
Web address: www.usuhs.mil/mps/clinindex.html

1	2	3	4	5	6	7
Practice oriented		Equal emphasis			Research oriented	

Percentage of faculty subscribing to each of the following orientations:

Psychodynamic/Psychoanalytic	10%
Applied behavioral analysis/Radical behavioral	0%
Family systems/Systems	10%
Existential/Phenomenological/Humanistic	20%
Cognitive/Cognitive-behavioral	70%

Courses required for incoming students prior to enrolling:
experimental, abnormal, statistics; biological psychology preferred not required

Recommended but not mandatory courses:
Basic undergraduate sequence of courses in psychology, and some course work related to the biological sciences (e.g. biology, chemistry) and research design/statistics

GRE mean
Verbal 580   Quantitative 618
Analytical Writing 5.0

GPA mean
GPA 3.62

Number of applications/admission offers/incoming students in 2009
51 applied/10 admission offers/7 incoming

% of students receiving:
Full tuition waiver only: 0%
Assistantship/fellowship only: 0%
Both full tuition waiver & assistantship/fellowship: 100%

Approximate percentage of incoming students with a B.A./B.S. only: 70% **Master's:** 30%

Approximate percentage of students who are Women: 73% **Ethnic Minority:** 5%
International: none—must be a United States citizen

Average years to complete the doctoral program (including internship): 5 years (includes 1 year internship)

Personal interview
Preferred in person but telephone acceptable

Attrition rate in past 7 years: 5%

Percentage of students applying for internship last year accepted into APPIC or APA internships: 100%

Formal tracks/concentrations: military clinical psychology, medical clinical psychology

Research areas	# Faculty	# Grants
cancer survivorship	1	0
drug abuse and behavioral toxicology	1	3
mood disorders	1	2
neuropsychology	1	1
obesity and eating disorders	1	1
occupational health psychology	1	3
stress and pain in the workplace	-	-
sexual dysfunction	1	0
stress and animal models	1	3
stress and cardiovascular disease	2	4

Clinical opportunities

children and adolescent	substance abuse
medical centers	VA hospitals
military teaching hospitals	unique military settings

University of Utah (Ph.D.)

Department of Psychology
380 S 1530 E, Room 502
Salt Lake City, UT 84112
phone#: (801) 581-6126
e-mail: mary.looser@psych.utah.edu
Web address: www.psych.utah.edu/researchareas/clinical/

1	2	3	4	5	6	7
Practice oriented		Equal emphasis			Research oriented	

Percentage of faculty subscribing to each of the following orientations:

Psychodynamic/Psychoanalytic	4%
Applied behavioral analysis/Radical behavioral	0%
Family systems/Systems	11%
Existential/Phenomenological/Humanistic	4%
Cognitive/Cognitive-behavioral	80%

Courses required for incoming students to have completed prior to enrolling:

Undergraduate degree in psychology or its equivalent, including statistics, research design and abnormal

Recommended but not mandatory courses:

Advanced statistics and research design

GRE mean

Verbal 592   Quantitative 690
Psychology Subject Test 710
Analytical Writing 5.25

GPA mean

Junior/Senior GPA 3.46

Number of applications/admission offers/incoming students in 2009

121 applied/5 admission offers/5 incoming

% of students receiving:

Full tuition waiver only: 0%
Assistantship/fellowship only: 0%
Both full tuition waiver & assistantship/fellowship: 100%

Approximate percentage of incoming students with a B.A./B.S. only: 100%   Master's: 0%

Approximate percentage of students who are Women: 60%   Ethnic Minority: 0%
International: Data not available

Average years to complete the doctoral program (including internship): 7 years

Personal interview

Required in person

Attrition rate in past 7 years: 25%

Percentage of students applying for internship last year accepted into APPIC or APA internships: 100%

Formal tracks/concentrations: adult clinical, child/adolescent/family, health psychology/behavioral medicine, clinical neuropsychology

Research areas	# Faculty	# Grants
adolescent/child psychology	3	3
adult psychopathology	1	0
behavioral medicine/health psychology	1	1
family/couple research	1	1
forensic	1	0
minority mental health	1	1
neuropsychology	1	0
personality assessment	1	0
sexuality	2	1

Clinical opportunities

adolescent/child assessment and psychotherapy	inpatient psychiatry
behavioral medicine/ health psychology	interpersonal psychotherapy
anxiety disorders	minority mental health
CBT	pediatric psychology
clinical neuropsychology	personality disorders
depression	rational-emotive therapy
family therapy	sex therapy/sexuality
homeless/disadvantaged population	substance abuse treatment

Vanderbilt University–Departments of Psychology and Psychology and Human Development (Ph.D.)

111 21st Avenue South
Nashville, TN 37203
phone#: (615) 322-0080
e-mail: j.a.bachorowski@vanderbilt.edu or
bruce.compas@vanderbilt.edu
Web address: www.vanderbilt.edu/psychological_sciences/graduate/programs/clinical.php

1	2	3	4	5	6	7
Practice oriented		Equal emphasis			Research oriented	

Percentage of faculty subscribing to each of the following orientations:

Psychodynamic/Psychoanalytic	0%
Applied behavioral analysis/Radical behavioral	5%
Family systems/Systems	0%
Existential/Phenomenological/Humanistic	0%
Cognitive/Cognitive-behavioral	95%

Courses required for incoming students to have completed prior to enrolling: None

Recommended but not mandatory courses:

Introduction to psychology; abnormal or psychopathology; biological bases of behavior; research methods; statistics

GRE mean

Verbal 630   Quantitative 720
Analytical Writing not reported

GPA mean

Overall GPA 3.5   Psychology GPA 3.8

Number of applications/admission offers/incoming students in 2009
301 applied/14 admission offers/6 incoming

% of students receiving:
Full tuition waiver only: 0%
Assistantship/fellowship only: 0%
Both full tuition waiver & assistantship/fellowship: 100%

Approximate percentage of incoming students with a B.A./B.S. only: 95%   **Master's:** 5%

Approximate percentage of students who are Women: 85%   **Ethnic Minority:** 20%
International: 5%

Average years to complete the doctoral program (including internship): 6 years

Personal interview
On invitation only

Attrition rate in past 7 years: 10%

Percentage of students applying for internship last year accepted into APPIC or APA internships: 100%

Formal tracks/concentrations: child, adolescent, and family, adult psychopathology

Research areas	# Faculty	# Grants
anxiety	7	2
autism	2	1
depression	8	5
eating	2	2
emotion	9	2
ethics and professional practice	1	0
gender issues	2	0
health disparities	2	2
health psychology	5	3
imaging	6	5
intervention	4	3
neuropsychology	4	3
personality	1	1
prevention	3	2
psychopathology	12	5
psychopathy	1	0
psychopharmacology	2	2
psychophysiology	6	2
schizophrenia	2	2
statistics	2	1
substance abuse	3	0
vocal communication	1	0

Clinical opportunities

affective disorders	neuropsychology
aggression/conduct	pediatric psychology
anxiety disorders	personality disorders
behavioral medicine	schizophrenia
child and family	substance abuse
developmental disabilities	

University of Vermont (Ph.D.)
Department of Psychology
John Dewey Hall
Burlington, VT 05405

phone#: (802) 656-2670
e-mail: rex.forehand@uvm.edu
Web address: www.uvm.edu/~psych/
graduate/?Page=clinical/clinical_overview.
html&SM=clinicalsubmenu.html

1	2	3	4	5	6	7
Practice oriented		Equal emphasis			Research oriented	

Percentage of faculty subscribing to each of the following orientations:

Psychodynamic/Psychoanalytic	0%
Applied behavioral analysis/Radical behavioral	0%
Family systems/Systems	10%
Existential/Phenomenological/Humanistic	0%
Cognitive/Cognitive-behavioral	90%

Courses required for incoming students to have completed prior to enrolling:
Psychology major or equivalent including general psychology, statistics, research design, and at least 3 other psychology courses

Recommended but not mandatory courses: None

GRE mean
Verbal 533   Quantitative 623
Psychology Subject Test not reported
Analytical Writing not reported

GPA mean
Overall GPA 3.50

Number of applications/admission offers/incoming students in 2009
180 applied/5 admission offers/3 incoming

% of students receiving:
Full tuition waiver only: 0%
Assistantship/fellowship only: 33%
Both full tuition waiver & assistantship/fellowship: 67%

Approximate percentage of incoming students with a B.A./B.S. only: 100%   **Master's:** 0%

Approximate percentage of students who are Women: 100%   **Ethnic Minority:** 0%   **International:** 0%

Average years to complete the doctoral program (including internship): 5.4 years

Personal interview
In person interview required

Attrition rate in past 7 years: 3%

Percentage of students applying for internship last year accepted into APPIC or APA internships: 100%

Formal tracks/concentrations: none

Research areas	# Faculty	# Grants
adolescent treatment	1	1
anxiety disorders	1	3
depression disorders	2	2
child and adolescent psychopathology	4	2
conduct disorders	1	0

health psychology(AIDS)	1	1
lesbian/gay issues	1	0
prevention	3	3
sex offenders/abuse	2	0
sexual dysfunctional	1	0

Clinical opportunities

adolescent psychotherapy	family therapy
anxiety disorders	HIV/AIDS
behavioral medicine	mental retardation
childhood disorders	refugees
chronically mentally ill	prevention
depression	substance abuse
eating disorders	

University of Victoria (Ph.D.)
(2008 data)

Department of Psychology
Victoria, British Columbia V8W 3P5, Canada
phone#: (250) 721-7525
e-mail: ptaylor@uvic.ca
Web address: web.uvic.ca/psyc/graduate/clinical_
psychology.php

1	2	3	4	5	6	7
Practice oriented		Equal emphasis				Research oriented

Percentage of faculty subscribing to each of the following orientations:

Psychodynamic/Psychoanalytic	12%
Applied behavioral analysis/Radical behavioral	0%
Family systems/Systems	25%
Existential/Phenomenological/Humanistic	12%
Cognitive/Cognitive-behavioral	100%
Interpersonal	25%

Courses required for incoming students to have completed prior to enrolling:

"A"-level grades for 1 full year of course work in at least 4 areas: social psychology, biological psychology, cognitive psychology, developmental, cultural psychology, abnormal

Recommended but not mandatory courses:

Additional special topics in clinical psychology selections

GRE mean
Verbal 630   Quantitative 630
Analytical Writing 4.8

GPA mean
Overall GPA 8.0   Psychology GPA 8.3

Number of applications/admission offers/incoming students in 2007
101 applied/8 admission offers/4 incoming

% of students receiving:
Full tuition waiver only: 0%
Assistantship/fellowship only: 100%
Both full tuition waiver & assistantship/fellowship: 0%

Approximate percentage of incoming students with a B.A./B.S. only: 100%   Master's: 0%

Approximate percentage of students who are
Women: 75% Ethnic Minority: 25% International: 15%

Average years to complete the doctoral program (including internship): 7 years

Personal interview
Preferred in person but telephone acceptable

Attrition rate in past 7 years: 8%

Percentage of students applying for internship last year accepted into APPIC or APA internships: 90%

Formal tracks/concentrations: clinical life span
psychology emphasis, clinical neuropsychology emphasis

Research areas	# Faculty	# Grants
addictions	1	1
attention-deficit disorder	1	1
couples treatment	1	1
childhood sexual abuse	1	1
cognitive disorders in the elderly	1	1
cross-cultural psych	1	1
epilepsy	1	1
families and disabilities	1	1
families and divorce	1	1
fetal alcohol syndrome	1	1
traumatic brain injury	2	2

Clinical opportunities

adolescent and adult forensic	pediatric and adult
adult psychiatric	neuropsychology
adult rehabilitation	young adult counselling
child and adult mental health	couples, family and group
child and adult inpatient	treatment

University of Virginia–Department of Human Services (Ph.D.)

Curry Programs in Clinical and School Psychology
Curry School of Education
P.O. Box 400270
Charlottesville, VA 22904-4270
phone#: (434) 924-7472
e-mail: clin-psych@virginia.edu
Web address: curry.virginia.edu/academics/degrees/
doctor-of-philosophy/ph.d.-in-clinical-and-school-
psychology

1	2	3	4	5	6	7
Practice oriented		Equal emphasis				Research oriented

Percentage of faculty subscribing to each of the following orientations:

Psychodynamic/Psychoanalytic	13%
Applied behavioral analysis/Radical behavioral	0%
Family systems/Systems	25%
Existential/Phenomenological/Humanistic	13%
Cognitive/Cognitive-behavioral	50%

Courses required for incoming students to have completed prior to enrolling: None

Recommended but not mandatory courses:
Undergraduate statistics, child development, learning, abnormal, physiological psychology/biopsychology, social

GRE mean
Verbal 660   Quantitative 700
Psychology Subject Test 730
Analytical Writing 5.0

GPA mean
Overall GPA 3.6   Psychology GPA 3.8
Junior/Senior GPA 3.6

Number of applications/admission offers/incoming students in 2009
141 applied/6 admission offers/5 incoming

% of students receiving:
Full tuition waiver only: 0%
Assistantship/fellowship only: 0%
Both full tuition waiver & assistantship/fellowship: 100%

Approximate percentage of incoming student with a B.A./B.S. only: 88%   **Master's:** 12%

Approximate percentage of students who are Women: 83%   **Ethnic Minority:** 23%   **International:** 3%

Average years to complete the doctoral program (including internship): 5.3 years

Personal interview
Preferred in person but telephone acceptable

Attrition rate in past 7 years: 3%

Percentage of students applying for internship last year accepted into APPIC or APA internships: 100%

Formal tracks/concentrations: school psychology (NASP approved), forensic psychology, family therapy, child clinical

Research areas	# Faculty	# Grants
child clinical	4	0
school interventions	4	2
cognitive/learning disorders	2	0
forensic psychology	2	0
incarcerated populations	2	1
multicultural	2	0
multiproblem families	1	0
parenting behavior	2	0
youth mentoring	2	2
youth violence	3	2

Clinical opportunities

child and family assessment and intervention
school psychology; school interventions
couples and family therapy
adult assessment and therapy
crisis intervention
forensic psychology
special education (ld, autism spectrum disorders, mr)
medical consultation
neuropsychology
parenting/parent–child interaction
systems consultation
youth and adult correctional facilities
youth and adult inpatient facilities

University of Virginia–Department of Psychology

College of Arts and Sciences
P.O. Box 400400
Charlottesville, VA 22904-4477
phone#: (434) 982-4750
e-mail: psy-dept@virginia.edu
Web address: www.virginia.edu/psychology/research/areas.php#clinical

1	2	3	4	5	**6**	7

Practice oriented   Equal emphasis   Research oriented

Percentage of faculty subscribing to each of the following orientations:

Psychodynamic/Psychoanalytic	25%
Applied behavioral analysis/Radical behavioral	0%
Family systems/Systems	25%
Existential/Phenomenological/Humanistic	0%
Cognitive/Cognitive-behavioral	50%

Courses required for incoming students prior to enrolling:
B.A. in psychology or equivalent

Recommended but not mandatory courses:
Abnormal psychology, statistics

GRE mean
Verbal 700   Quantitative 710   Analytical 730
Psychology Subject Test 690
Analytical Writing not reported

GPA mean
Overall GPA 3.6

Number of applications/admission offers/incoming students in 2009
263 applied/9 admission offers/5 incoming

% of students receiving:
Full tuition waiver only: 0%
Assistantship/fellowship only: 0%
Both full tuition waiver & assistantship/fellowship: 100%

Approximate percentage of incoming students with a B.A./B.S. only: 62%   **Master's:** 38%

Approximate percentage of students who are Women: 75%   **Ethnic Minority:** 25%   **International:** 9%

Average years to complete the doctoral program (including internship): 6 years

Personal interview
Preferred in person but telephone acceptable

Attrition rate in past 7 years: 17%

Percentage of students applying for internship last year accepted into APPIC or APA internships: 100%

Formal tracks/concentrations: none

Research areas	# Faculty	# Grants
adult psychopathology	3	3
anxiety/obsessive–compulsive disorders	1	0

behavioral genetics	2	1
child clinical/psychopathology	4	4
community psychology	3	3
developmental adolescence	3	3
epidemiology	2	1
family research/systems	2	2
minority mental health	2	2
neuropsychology	1	1
personality disorders	1	1
prevention	2	2
violence/abuse/victim–offender	2	2

Clinical opportunities

anxiety disorders
behavioral medicine
community psychology
depression
family therapy
forensic psychology
marital/couples therapy

neuropsychology
obsessive–compulsive
   disorder
pediatric psychology
psychology/law
schizophrenia/psychosis
victim/battering/abuse

Virginia Commonwealth University (Ph.D.)

Department of Psychology
806 West Franklin Street
Richmond, VA 23284-2018
phone#: (804) 828-1158 (admissions)
e-mail: clin-psy@vcu.edu
Web address: www.psychology.vcu.edu/clinical/index.shtml

1	2	3	4	5	6	7
Practice oriented		Equal emphasis				Research oriented

Percentage of faculty subscribing to each of the following orientations:

Psychodynamic/Psychoanalytic	15%
Applied behavioral analysis/Radical behavioral	0%
Family systems/Systems	30%
Existential/Phenomenological/Humanistic	0%
Cognitive/Cognitive-behavioral	100%
Interpersonal	20%

Courses required for incoming students to have completed prior to enrolling: None

Recommended but not mandatory courses:

It is recommended that applicants complete at least 18 hours of psychology including general psychology, experimental psychology and statistics. Applicants should also have substantial research experience in an identified area of _____ h interest.

Verbal 596   Quantitative 729
Psychology Subject Test not required
Analytical Writing 4.9

GPA mean:
Overall GPA 3.6

Number of applications/admission offers/incoming students in 2009
176 applied/12 admission offers/7 incoming

% of students receiving:
Full tuition waiver only: 0%

Assistantship/fellowship only: 0%
Both full tuition waiver & assistantship/fellowship: 100% for first 3 years of doctoral program

Approximate percentage of incoming students with a B.A./B.S. only: 75%   Master's: 25%

Approximate percentage of students who are Women: 88% Ethnic Minority: 21% International: 4%

Average years to complete the doctoral program (including internship): 6 years

Personal interview
In person interview strongly recommended, telephone interview may be acceptable in extenuating circumstances

Attrition rate in past 7 years: 8%

Percentage of students applying for internship last year accepted into APPIC or APA internships: 85%

Formal tracks/concentrations: child/adolescent, behavioral medicine

Research areas	# Faculty	# Grants
adolescent	5	4
anxiety	2	1
behavioral medicine	5	3
child clinical/pediatric	5	4
community	5	3
divorce	1	0
forensic psychology	1	1
minority/cross-cultural	2	1
pregnancy issues	1	1
psychopathology	1	1
psychophysiology	2	0
psychotherapy	3	3
stress and coping	2	0
substance abuse	1	1

Clinical opportunities

assessment and testing
clinical health psychology,
   inpatient and outpatient
   medical settings
child and adult anxiety
child pediatric
children of divorce, intensive
   co-parenting therapy, child
   custody evaluations
chronic mental illness
community psychology
correctional psychology

inpatient
neuropsychological
   assessments
poly-trauma treatment
   and treatment of
   psychological aspects of
   spinal cord injury
pain management
school
substance abuse
unipolar mood disorder

Virginia Consortium Program in Clinical Psychology (Psy.D.)

(College of William & Mary, Eastern Virginia Medical School, Norfolk State University, & Old Dominion University)
Higher Education Center
1881 University Drive, Suite 239
Virginia Beach, VA 23453
phone#: (757) 368-1820
e-mail: exoneill@odu.edu
Web address: www.sci.odu.edu/vcpcp

1	2	3	4	5	6	7
Practice oriented			Equal emphasis			Research oriented

Percentage of faculty subscribing to each of the following orientations:

Psychodynamic/Psychoanalytic	31%
Applied behavioral analysis/Radical behavioral	13%
Family systems/Systems	28%
Existential/Phenomenological/Humanistic	7%
Cognitive/Cognitive-behavioral	31%

Courses required for incoming students prior to enrolling: B.A. in psychology or equivalent

Recommended but not mandatory courses:
Strong background in psychology; statistics

GRE mean
Verbal 603   Quantitative 639
Psychology Subject Test not required
Analytical Writing 5.0

GPA mean
Undergraduate GPA 3.93

Number of applications/admission offers/incoming students in:
2008: 249 applied/14 admission offers/10 incoming

% of students receiving:
Full tuition waiver only: 0%
Assistantship/fellowship only: 0%
Both tuition waiver & assistantship/fellowship: 100%
(significant tuition reduction but not a complete waiver)

Approximate percentage of incoming students (2008) with a B.A./B.S. only: 80%   **Master's:** 20%

Approximate percentage of students (2008) who are:
Women: 79% **Ethnic Minority:** 29% **International:** 0%

Average years to complete the doctoral program (including internship): 4.5 years

Personal interview
Required in person

Attrition rate in past 7 years: 2.9%

Percentage of students applying for internship last year accepted into APPIC or APA internships: 80%

Formal tracks/concentrations: neuropsychology

Research areas	# Faculty	# Grants
ADHD	1	0
adjustment to medical illness	2	0
adolescent therapy	3	0
anxiety disorders	3	0
assessment	4	0
attribution	1	0
behavioral medicine	3	0
biofeedback	2	0
cardiovascular behavioral medicine	1	1
child abuse prevention	2	0
child development	1	0
clinical neuropsychology	2	0
cognitive-behavioral therapy	2	0
community psychology	1	0
competency issues	1	0
compliance	1	0
consultation	1	0
couples	2	0
depression	5	0
developmental psychopathology	1	0
drug use, prevention	1	1
eating disorders	2	1
effects of humor in psychotherapy	1	0
emotion regulation in children	1	0
ethical issues	1	0
evaluation of preschoolers	1	0
family therapy	5	0
feminism	1	0
gay and lesbian issues	1	0
gender	2	0
health psychology	3	0
high risk infants	1	0
HIV	1	0
interpersonal behavior, theory	2	0
interventions for minorities	1	0
intimate relationships	2	0
learning disability identification	1	0
marital/sexual issues	2	0
minority issues	2	0
MMPI, MMPI-2, MMPI-A	1	2
moral development	1	0
multicultural lifestyles	3	0
multimodal behavior therapy	1	0
objective personality assessment	3	0
pain management	1	0
parent-child interactions	1	1
parenting	2	0
pediatric psychology	2	0
prevention	1	0
professional issues	2	0
program evaluation	2	0
psychodynamic	2	0
psychology of religion	1	0
psychopathology	3	0
psychophysiology	1	0
psychotherapy w/children, adolescents	4	0
psychotherapy with adults	2	0
race issues	2	0
rehabilitation psychology	1	0
schizophrenia	1	0
self-disclosure	1	0
sleep disorders	2	1
sleep pharmacology	1	0
stress and coping	3	0
supervision	2	0
trauma	1	0
women's issues	4	0

Clinical opportunities
Over 50 public and private agencies that serve adults, adolescents, and children

Virginia Polytechnic Institute and State University (Ph.D.)
Department of Psychology
Williams Hall

Blacksburg, VA 24061-0436
phone#: (540) 231-6581
e-mail: rswinett@vt.edu
Web address: www.psyc.vt.edu/graduate/clinical

1	2	3	4	5	6	7
Practice oriented			Equal emphasis			Research oriented

Percentage of faculty subscribing to each of the following orientations:

Psychodynamic/Psychoanalytic	0%
Applied behavioral analysis/Radical behavioral	5%
Family systems/Systems	20%
Existential/Phenomenological/Humanistic	0%
Cognitive/Cognitive-behavioral	95%

Courses required for incoming students to have completed prior to enrolling:
Research methods, statistics, learning, electives

Recommended but not mandatory courses:
Abnormal psychology, social psychology, developmental psychology, personality

GRE mean
Verbal 600   Quantitative 700
Analytical Writing not reported
Psychology Subject Test not reported

GPA mean
Overall GPA 3.6

Number of applications/admission offers/incoming students in 2009
152 applied/10 admission offers/7 incoming

% of students receiving:
Full tuition waiver only: 0%
Assistantship/fellowship only: 0%
Both full tuition waiver & assistantship/fellowship: 100%

Approximate percentage of incoming students with a B.A./B.S. only: 80%   Master's: 20%

Approximate percentage of students who are
Women: 80%   Ethnic Minority: 15%   International: 10%

Average years to complete the doctoral program (including internship): 6 years

Personal interview
Preferred in person but telephone acceptable

Attrition rate in past 7 years: 15%

Percentage of students applying for internship last year accepted into APPIC or APA internships: 50%

Formal tracks/concentrations: none

Research areas	# Faculty	# Grants
affective disorders/depression	2	0
anxiety disorders	3	1
attention-deficit disorder	1	0
autism	2	0
behavioral medicine	3	2
child clinical	4	2
marriage/couples	1	0
minority mental health	1	1
neuropsychology	2	1
pain management	2	0
parent–child interaction	2	2
pediatric psychology	3	3
prevention	4	3
psychotherapy outcome	2	2
shyness	1	0
social skills	3	0
stress and coping	1	1
substance abuse	1	2

Clinical opportunities
ADHD	gerontology
affective disorders	marital/couples therapy
anxiety disorders	neuropsychology
behavioral medicine	prevention in the
child clinical	community
conduct disorder	substance abuse
consultation	systems management
data management systems	

University of Washington (Ph.D.)
Department of Psychology
Seattle, WA 98195
phone#: (206) 543-8687
e-mail: resmith@u.washington.edu
Web address: www.psych.uw.edu/psych.php#p=233

1	2	3	4	5	6	7
Practice oriented			Equal emphasis			Research oriented

Percentage of faculty subscribing to each of the following orientations:

Psychodynamic/Psychoanalytic	0%
Applied behavioral analysis/Radical behavioral	10%
Family systems/Systems	20%
Existential/Phenomenological/Humanistic	0%
Cognitive/Cognitive-behavioral	70%

Courses required for incoming students to have completed prior to enrolling: None

Recommended but not mandatory courses:
Abnormal/psychopathology, biological bases of behavior, developmental, statistics, learning & motivation, social

GRE median
Verbal 625   Quantitative 745
Analytical Writing not required
Psychology Subject Test not reported

GPA mean
Overall GPA 3.67

Number of applications/admission offers/incoming students in 2009
439 applied/10 admission offers/8 incoming

% of students receiving:
Full tuition waiver only: 0%
Assistantship/fellowship only: 0%
Both full tuition waiver & assistantship/fellowship: 100%

Approximate percentage of incoming students with a B.A./B.S. only: 100%   **Master's:** 0%

Approximate percentage of students who are Women: 82%   **Ethnic Minority:** 21%   **International:** 0.1%

Average years to complete the doctoral program (including internship): 6.5 years

Personal interview
Final candidates based on telephone interviews invited to campus for an interview

Attrition rate in past 7 years: 3%

Percentage of students applying for internship last year accepted into APPIC or APA internships: 85%

Formal tracks/concentrations: adult clinical, child clinical

Research areas	# Faculty	# Grants
anxiety disorders	3	1
autism	1	1
child emotional development	3	3
cognitive therapy	4	2
depression	3	1
minority	5	4
psychology process	1	1
spouse abuse	2	1
substance abuse	3	3
suicide	1	1

Clinical opportunities

anxiety disorders	pediatric psychology
autism	personality disorders
community psychology	psychoeducational (coping
couples	skills) training
family	rehabilitation medicine
minority	substance abuse
neuropsychology	

Washington State University (Ph.D.)

Department of Psychology
P.O. Box 644820
Pullman, WA 99164-4820
phone#: (509) 335-2631
e-mail: psychhelpdesk@wsu.edu
Web address: www.wsu.edu/psychology/
graduateprograms/clinical

1	2	3	**4**	5	6	7
Practice oriented		Equal emphasis			Research oriented	

Percentage of faculty subscribing to each of the following orientations:

Psychodynamic/Psychoanalytic	23%
Applied behavioral analysis/Radical behavioral	0%
Family systems/Systems	23%
Existential/Phenomenological/Humanistic	8%
Cognitive/Cognitive-behavioral	100%

Courses required for incoming students to have completed prior to enrolling: None

Recommended but not mandatory courses:
Abnormal, social, developmental, personality, statistics, research methods

GRE mean
Verbal + Quantitative 1205
Analytical Writing not required

GPA mean
Overall GPA 3.75

Number of applications/admission offers/incoming students in 2009
198 applied/8 admission offers/6 incoming

% of students receiving:
Full tuition waiver only: 0%
Assistantship/fellowship only: 0%
Both full tuition waiver & assistantship/fellowship: 100%

Approximate percentage of incoming students with a B.A./B.S. only: 67%   **Master's:** 33%

Approximate percentage of students who are Women: 67%   **Ethnic Minority:** 33%   **International:** 33%

Average years to complete the doctoral program (including internship): 5 years

Personal interview
Preferred in person but telephone acceptable

Attrition rate in past 7 years: 12%

Percentage of students applying for internship last year accepted into APPIC or APA internships: 100%

Formal tracks/concentrations: none

Research areas	# Faculty	# Grants
adult psychopathology	5	6
behavioral medicine/health psychology	5	8
child clinical	4	4
neuropsychology	1	1

Clinical opportunities

adult and child inpatient	adult and child
adult and child neuro-	psychotherapy
psychological assessment	health psychology

Washington University in St. Louis (Ph.D.)

Department of Psychology
Campus Box 1125
One Brookings Drive
St. Louis, MO 63130-4899
phone#: (314) 935-6520
e-mail: toltmann@artsci.wustl.edu
Web address: www.psych.wustl.edu/clinical/

1	2	3	4	5	**6**	7
Practice oriented		Equal emphasis			Research oriented	

Percentage of faculty subscribing to each of the following orientations:
Psychodynamic/Psychoanalytic   0%

Applied behavioral analysis/Radical behavioral		0%
Family systems/Systems		10%
Existential/Phenomenological/Humanistic		10%
Cognitive/Cognitive-behavioral		80%

Courses required for incoming students to have completed prior to enrolling:
24 credits of psychology and 30 credits in the physical, biological, and social sciences; experimental (with laboratory), and quantitative methods

Recommended but not mandatory courses:
History and systems

GRE mean
Verbal 640   Quantitative 720
Psychology Subject Test 700
Analytical Writing 5.0

GPA mean
Overall GPA 3.43   Psychology GPA 3.7
Junior/Senior GPA 3.6

Number of applications/admission offers/incoming students in 2009
151 applied/12 admission offers/7 incoming

% of students receiving:
Full tuition waiver only: 0%
Assistantship/fellowship only: 0%
Both full tuition waiver & assistantship/fellowship: 100%

Approximate percentage of incoming students with a B.A./B.S. only: 70%   Master's: 30%

Approximate percentage of students who are
Women: 72%   Ethnic Minority: 36%   International: 12%

Average years to complete the doctoral program (including internship): 6 years

Personal interview
Required in person

Attrition rate in past 7 years: 18%

Percentage of students applying for internship last year accepted into APPIC or APA internships: 100%

Formal tracks/concentrations: none

Research areas	# Faculty	# Grants
aging/gerontology	3	5
neuropsychology	4	7
psychopathology	4	0
psychological treatment	3	5

Clinical opportunities
psychological services center
practicum agencies in St. Louis area

University of Waterloo (Ph.D.)
Department of Psychology
Waterloo, Ontario N2L 3G1 Canada
phone#: (519) 888-4567, ext. #33659
e-mail: jmoakman@uwaterloo.ca
Web address: www.psychology.uwaterloo.ca/gradprog/programs/phd/clinical/index.html

1	2	3	4	5	6	7
Practice oriented			Equal emphasis			Research oriented

Percentage of faculty subscribing to each of the following orientations:

Psychodynamic/Psychoanalytic	33%
Applied behavioral analysis/Radical behavioral	22%
Family systems/Systems	33%
Existential/Phenomenological/Humanistic	44%
Cognitive/Cognitive-behavioral	100%

Courses required for incoming students prior to enrolling:
Basic statistics, research design, research courses, undergraduate thesis or equivalent

Recommended but not mandatory courses:
History of psychology

GRE mean
Verbal 670   Quantitative 740   Analytical 5.5
Psychology Subject Test not required
Analytical Writing not reported

GPA mean
Overall GPA 3.7

Number of applications/admission offers/incoming students in 2009
137 applied/5 admission offers/3 incoming

% of students receiving:
Full tuition waiver only: 0%
Assistantship/fellowship only: 100%
Both full tuition waiver & assistantship/fellowship: 0%

Approximate percentage of incoming students with a B.A./B.S. only: 66%   Master's: 34%

Approximate percentage of students who are
Women: 82%   Ethnic Minority: 28%   International: 4%

Average years to complete the doctoral program (including internship): 6.5 years

Personal interview
Preferred in person, but telephone interview acceptable

Attrition rate in past 7 years: 17.3%

Percentage of students applying for internship last year accepted into APPIC or APA internships: 100%

Formal tracks/concentrations: none

Research areas	# Faculty	# Grants
social anxiety	1	3
human sexuality	1	0
obsessive–compulsive disorder	2	0
depression	2	2
anxiety disorders	1	3
reading	1	0
cognitive development	1	1
culture	1	0
marital functioning	1	1
marital communication	1	1
close relationships	1	5
emotion	1	5

motivation		1	5
couples		1	0

Clinical opportunities

child/adolescent/adult	school/educational
hypnosis	marital relationships
neuropsychology	

Wayne State University (Ph.D.)

Department of Psychology
5057 Woodward Avenue, 7th Floor
Detroit, MI 48202
phone#: (313) 577-2800
e-mail: aallen@wayne.edu
Web address: www.clas.wayne.edu/unit-inner.
asp?UnitD=2-&WebPageID=307&site=candle

1	2	3	4	5	6	7
Practice oriented		Equal emphasis				Research oriented

Percentage of faculty subscribing to each of the following orientations:

Psychodynamic/Psychoanalytic	10%
Applied behavioral analysis/Radical behavioral	0%
Family systems/Systems	20%
Existential/Phenomenological/Humanistic	0%
Cognitive/Cognitive-behavioral	60%

Courses required for incoming students to have completed prior to enrolling:
12 semester hour) in psychology, including experimental (with laboratory) and statistical methods

Recommended but not mandatory courses:
Undergraduate courses in mathematics and life sciences

GRE mean
Verbal 600   Quantitative 640
Analytical Writing 5.0

GPA mean
Overall GPA 3.8

Number of applications/admission offers/incoming students in 2009
145 applied/13 admission offers/8 incoming

% of students receiving:
Full tuition waiver only: 10%
Assistantship/fellowship only: 30%
Both full tuition waiver & assistantship/fellowship: 50% (1st-year students: 100%)

Approximate percentage of incoming students with a B.A./B.S. only: 90%   **Master's:** 10%

Approximate percentage of students who are Women: 70% **Ethnic Minority:** 10% **International:** 10%

Average years to complete the doctoral program (including internship): 6.5 years

Personal interview
Required in person

Attrition rate in past 7 years: 0%

Percentage of students applying for internship last year accepted into APPIC or APA internships: 90%

Formal tracks/concentration: health, child clinical, clinical neuropsychology, community

Research areas	# Faculty	# Grants
	not reported	not reported

Clinical opportunities

behavioral medicine	early intervention
community psychology	gerontology
neuropsychology	substance abuse
cross-cultural mental health	rehabilitation

West Virginia University (Ph.D.)

Department of Psychology
1124 Life Sciences Building
Morgantown, WV 26506-6040
phone#: (304) 293-2001, ext. # 31628
e-mail: debra.swinney@mail.wvu.edu
Web address: psychology.wvu.edu/future_students/graduate_programs/doctoral_programs/ph_d__in_clinical_psychology

1	2	3	4	5	6	7
Practice oriented		Equal emphasis				Research oriented

Percentage of faculty subscribing to each of the following orientations:

Psychodynamic/Psychoanalytic	0%
Applied behavioral analysis/Radical behavioral	50%
Family systems/Systems	0%
Existential/Phenomenological/Humanistic	0%
Cognitive/Cognitive-behavioral	50%

Courses required for incoming students to have completed prior to enrolling:
12 hours of undergraduate course work in Psychology, including Research Methods

Recommended but not mandatory courses:
Psychology major or related field, research, clinical experience

GRE mean
Verbal + Quantitative 1234
Psychology Subject Test 688
Analytical Writing 4.5

GPA mean
Overall GPA 3.64

Number of applications/admission offers/incoming students in 2009
121 applied/10 admission offers/10 incoming

% of students receiving:
Full tuition waiver only: 0%
Assistantship/fellowship only: 0%
Both full tuition waiver & assistantship/fellowship: 100%

Approximate percentage of incoming students with a B.A./B.S. only: 90%   **Master's:** 10%

Approximate percentage of incoming students who are
Women: 80% **Ethnic Minority:** 10% **International:** 10%

Average years to complete the doctoral program (including internship): 5 years

Personal interview
Preferred in person but telephone acceptable

Attrition rate in past 7 years: 13%

Percentage of students applying for internship last year accepted into APPIC or APA internships: 88%

Formal tracks/concentrations: clinical, clinical child, clinical health psychology, life span developmental, behavior analysis

Research areas	# Faculty	# Grants
anxiety disorders	2	0
behavioral dentistry	1	1
behavioral medicine	3	1
cardiovascular reactivity	1	0
child behavior disorders	1	0
developmental psychopathology	1	0
ethnic minority issues	1	0
forensics	2	1
gerontology	2	1
pain	1	0
posttraumatic stress disorder	1	0
suicide	1	1

Clinical opportunities

anxiety disorders (adults and children)
behavioral dentistry
behavioral medicine (adults and adolescents)
forensic psychology
gerontology
parent training
primary care service provision
school interventions

Western Michigan University (Ph.D.)

Department of Psychology
Kalamazoo, MI 49008
phone#: (269) 387-4330
e-mail: Kimberly.feenstra@wmich.edu
Web address: www.wmich.edu/psychology/grad/clinical/index.html

1	2	3	4	5	6	7
Practice oriented		Equal emphasis				Research oriented

Percentage of faculty subscribing to each of the following orientations:

Psychodynamic/Psychoanalytic	0%
Applied behavioral analysis/Radical behavioral	71%
Family systems/Systems	29%
Existential/Phenomenological/Humanistic	0%
Cognitive/Cognitive-behavioral	86%

Courses required for incoming students to have completed prior to enrolling:
Psychology major at an accredited institution

Recommended but not mandatory courses:

Basic course in behavior principles/behavior theory

GRE mean
Verbal + Quantitative 1226
Analytical Writing: not reported
Psychology Subject Test not required

GPA mean
Undergraduate GPA 3.62
Psychology GPA 3.64

Number of applications/admission offers/incoming students in 2009
125 applied/7 admission offers/5 incoming

% of students receiving:
Full tuition waiver only: 0%
Assistantship/fellowship only: 0%
Both full tuition waiver & assistantship/fellowship: 100%

Approximate percentage of incoming students with a B.A./B.S. only: 80% **Master's:** 20%

Approximate percentage of students who are
Women: 68% **Ethnic Minority:** 16% **International:** 5%

Average years to complete the doctoral program (including internship): 6 years

Personal interview
Preferred in person but telephone acceptable

Attrition rate in past 7 years: 11%

Percentage of students applying for internship last year accepted into APPIC or APA internships: 80%

Formal tracks/concentrations: none

Research areas	# Faculty	# Grants
AIDS prevention/education	1	0
anxiety disorders/PTSD	1	1
behavioral medicine	1	1
behavioral pediatrics	2	0
child injury & maltreatment	1	0
conceptual analysis of behavior therapy	4	0
depression	3	1
habit behaviors (tics, trichotilamania)	1	0
interpersonal victimization	1	0
multimedia-based treatment	2	2
psychotherapy process & outcome	4	0
sexual deviations and dysfunctions	1	1

Clinical opportunities
2 years training in in-house clinic under close faculty supervision
1 year external practicum in community setting
Focus on evidence-based practices

Wheaton College (Psy.D.)

Department of Psychology
Wheaton, IL 60187-5593
phone#: (630) 752-5104
e-mail: robert.gregory@wheaton.edu
Web address: www.wheaton.edu/psychology/graduate/overview/index.html

1	2	3	4	5	6	7
Practice oriented		Equal emphasis				Research oriented

Percentage of faculty subscribing to each of the following orientations:

Psychodynamic/Psychoanalytic	28%
Applied behavioral analysis/Radical behavioral	0%
Family systems/Systems	33%
Existential/Phenomenological/Humanistic	0%
Cognitive/Cognitive-behavioral	39%

Courses required for incoming students to have completed prior to enrolling:

personality, physiological psychology, abnormal psychology, research methods, statistics

Recommended but not mandatory courses

developmental, cognition, social

GRE mean

Verbal 545   Quantitative 630
Psychology Subject Test not reported
Analytical Writing 4.8

GPA mean

Overall GPA 3.5

Number of applications/admission offers/incoming students in 2008

71 applied/27 admission offers/20 incoming

% of students receiving:

Full tuition waiver only: 0%
Assistantship/fellowship only: 100%
Both full tuition waiver & assistantship/fellowship: 0%

Approximate percentage of incoming students with a B.A./B.S. only: 60%   Master's: 40%

Approximate percentage of students who are Women: 80% Ethnic Minority: 5% tInternational: 10%

Average years to complete the doctoral program (including internship): 5 years

Personal interview

Required in person

Attrition rate in past 7 years: 9.7%

Percentage of students applying for internship last year accepted into APPIC or APA internships: 89%

Formal tracks/concentrations: none

Research areas	# Faculty	# Grants
spirituality/psychology integration	4	1
marriage & family	4	0
gender & sexuality	3	1
older adult and aging	1	0
meta-analysis	1	0
parent training (multicultural)	1	0
rural psychology	2	0
child & adolescent	3	1

Clinical opportunities

Chicago and the suburban area have a great variety of offerings including hospitals, public and private agencies, community-based services, school-based services and private practice.

Wichita State University (Ph.D.)

Department of Psychology
Wichita, KS 67260-0034
phone#: (316) 978-3170
e-mail: ddorr@cox.net
Web address: webs.wichita.edu/?u=PSYCHOLOGY&p=/
graduate/clinical/clinicalphd/

1	2	3	4	5	6	7
Practice oriented		Equal emphasis				Research oriented

Percentage of faculty subscribing to each of the following orientations:

Psychodynamic/Psychoanalytic	20%
Applied behavioral analysis/Radical behavioral	10%
Family systems/Systems	25%
Existential/Phenomenological/Humanistic	10%
Cognitive/Cognitive-behavioral	35%

Courses required for incoming students to have completed prior to enrolling:

Most successful applicants have an undergraduate degree in psychology with course work in statistics, research methods, and history and systems in psychology

Recommended but not mandatory courses:

See above

GRE mean

Verbal 526   Quantitative 604
Analytical Writing 4.3
Psychology Subject Test not reported

GPA mean

Overall GPA 3.5

Number of applications/admission offers/incoming students in 2009

57 applied/6 admission offers/5 incoming

% of students receiving:

Full tuition waiver only: 0%
Assistantship/fellowship only: 0%
Both full tuition waiver & assistantship/fellowship: 0%
(All of our students receive a Teaching Assistantship and partial tuition remission)

Approximate percentage of incoming students with a B.A./B.S. only: 80%   Master's: 20%

Approximate percentage of students who are Women: 93%   Ethnic Minority: 11%   International: 0%

Average years to complete the doctoral program (including internship): 6 years

Personal interview

Required in person

Attrition rate in past 7 years: 15%

Percentage of students applying for internship last year accepted into APPIC or APA internships: 100%

Formal tracks/concentrations: none

277

Research areas	# Faculty	# Grants
antisocial behavior in children	2	2
personal relationships	1	0
teen pregnancy prevention	1	2
acceptance commitment therapy	1	0
MMPI-2	1	0
self help	1	5
teaching excellence	1	1

Clinical opportunities
...rs

yes

Widener University (Psy.D.)

Institute for Graduate Clinical Psychology
One University Place
Graduate Clinical Psychology
Chester, PA 19013
phone#: (610) 499-1206
e-mail: graduate.psychology@widener.edu
Web address: www.widener.edu/academics/
collegesandschools/humanserviceprofessions/
clinicalpsychology

1	2	3	4	5	6	7
Practice oriented			Equal emphasis			Research oriented

Percentage of faculty subscribing to each of the following orientations:

Psychodynamic/Psychoanalytic	40%
Applied behavioral analysis/Radical behavioral	0%
Family systems/Systems	20%
Existential/Phenomenological/Humanistic	20%
Cognitive/Cognitive-behavioral	20%

Courses required for incoming students to have completed prior to enrolling:
Psychopathology or abnormal psychology, experimental psychology or research methods, statistics

Recommended but not mandatory courses: None

GRE mean
Verbal 592   Quantitative 639
Analytical Writing 4.78

GPA mean
Overall GPA 3.32

Number of applications/admission offers/incoming students in 2009
269 applied/55 admission offers/33 incoming

% of students receiving:
Full tuition waiver only: 0%
Assistantship/fellowship only: 0%
Both full tuition waiver & assistantship/fellowship: 0%

Approximate percentage of incoming students with a B.A./B.S. only: 75%   **Master's:** 25%

Approximate percentage of entering students who are Women: 70%   **Ethnic Minority:** 28%   **International:** 1%

Average years to complete the doctoral program (including internship): 5 years

Personal interview
Required in person

Attrition rate in past 7 years: 8%

Percentage of students applying for internship last year accepted into APPIC or APA internships: 100%

Formal tracks: biofeedback, neuropsychology, school psychology

Research areas	# Faculty	# Grants
assessment/diagnosis	5	0
early childhood	3	1
learning disabilities	3	0
problem solving	4	1
stress and coping	5	2

Clinical opportunities

assessment	health psychology
biofeedback	human sexuality
brief intervention	group therapy
cognitive behavioral	neuropsychology
couples therapy	organizational psychology
cross-cultural & diversity	psychoanalytic psychology
family therapy	school psychology
forensic psychology	

University of Windsor (Ph.D.)

Department of Psychology
Windsor, Ontario N9B 3P4, Canada
phone#: (519) 253-3000
fax#: (519) 973-7021
e-mail: bzakoor@uwindsor.ca
Web address: www.uwindsor.ca/psychology/graduate/
ClinicalInfo

1	2	3	4	5	6	7
Practice oriented			Equal emphasis			Research oriented

Percentage of faculty subscribing to each of the following orientations:

Psychodynamic/Psychoanalytic	20%
Applied behavioral analysis/Radical behavioral	5%
Family systems/Systems	15%
Existential/Phenomenological/Humanistic	25%
Cognitive/Cognitive-behavioral	35%

Courses required for incoming students to have completed prior to enrolling:
Honor's B.A. in psychology or its equivalent: 18-20 semester psychology courses including introductory psychology, basic and intermediate statistics, and laboratory courses in learning and experimental methods; Honor's B.A. thesis or its equivalent

Recommended but not mandatory courses: None

GRE mean
Verbal – 80th percentile   Quantitative – 63rd percentile
Analytical Writing – 66th percentile
Psychology Subject Test – 92nd percentile

GPA mean
3.52

Number of applications/admission offers/incoming students in 2009
159 applied/28 admission offers/13 incoming

% of students receiving:
Full tuition waiver only: 20%
Assistantship/fellowship only: 20%
Both full tuition waiver & assistantship/fellowship: 80%

Approximate percentage of incoming students with a B.A./B.S. only: 92% **Master's:** 8%

Approximate percentage of students who are
Women: 84% **Ethnic Minority:** not reported
International: 15%

Average years to complete the doctoral program (including internship): 6.5 years

Personal interview
Telephone interview required

Attrition rate in past 7 years: 7%

Percentage of students applying for internship last year accepted into APPIC or APA internships: 88%

Formal tracks/concentrations: adult clinical, child clinical, clinical neruopsychology

Research areas	# Faculty	# Grants
addiction	2	1
child research	4	3
community psychology	2	2
eating disorders	2	1
gambling behavior	1	3
health psychology	3	5
neuropsychological	4	4
psychotherapy research	3	2

Clinical opportunities
psychological service center
student counseling centre
practica and internships in the Windsor and Detroit areas

Wisconsin School of Professional Psychology (Psy.D.)

9120 West Hampton Avenue
Milwaukee, WI 53225
phone#: (414) 464-9777
e-mail: admissions@wspp.edu
Web address: www.wspp.edu

1	2	3	4	5	6	7
Practice oriented		Equal emphasis			Research oriented	

Percentage of faculty subscribing to each of the following orientations:
Psychodynamic/Psychoanalytic — data not available
Applied behavioral analysis/Radical behavioral — data not available
Family systems/Systems — data not available
Existential/Phenomenological/Humanistic — data not available
Cognitive/Cognitive behavioral — data not available

Courses required for incoming students to have completed prior to enrolling:
Developmental Psychology
Statistics
Abnormal Psychology
Research Methods and Design

Recommended but not mandatory courses: N/A

GRE mean
Quantitative 520   Verbal 500
Analytical Writing data not available
Psychology Advanced Test 520

GPA mean
Overall GPA 3.5

Number of applications/admission offers/incoming students in 2009
20 applied/admission offers/14 incoming

% of students receiving:
Full tuition waiver only: 0%
Assistantship/fellowship only: 0%
Both full tuition waiver AND assistantship/fellowship: 0%

Approximate percentage of incoming students with a B.A./B.S. only: 86% **Master's** 14%

Approximate percentage of students who are:
Women: 82%   Ethnic Minority: 10%   International: 0%

Average years to complete the doctoral program (including internship): 6 years

Personal interview
Preferred in person but telephone acceptable

Attrition rate in past 7 years: 21%

Percentage of students applying for internship last year into APPIC or APA-accredited internships: 100%

Formal tracks/concentrations: Adult Track; Child Track

Research areas	# Faculty	# Grants
data not available		

Clinical opportunities
Behavioral medicine
Outpatient mental health clinic (children and adolescents as well as adults)

University of Wisconsin–Madison (Ph.D.)

Department of Psychology
W. J. Brogden Psychology Building
1202 West Johnson Street
Madison, WI 53706
phone#: (608) 262-2079
e-mail: dgooding@.wisc.edu
Web address: glial.psych.wisc.edu/index.php/psych.
gradprospective/psychgradabout/168

1	2	3	4	5	6	7
Practice oriented		Equal emphasis			Research oriented	

Percentage of faculty subscribing to each of the following orientations:

Psychodynamic/Psychoanalytic	0%
Applied behavioral analysis/Radical behavioral	0%
Family systems/Systems	0%
Existential/Phenomenological/Humanistic	0%
Cognitive/Cognitive-behavioral	100%
Motivational/Interviewing	25%
Child	25%

Courses required for incoming students prior to enrolling:
Psychology major or related field training

Recommended but not mandatory courses: None

GRE mean
Verbal + Quantitative 1330
Analytical Writing not reported
Psychology Subject Test not reported

GPA mean
Overall GPA 3.55

Number of applications/admission offers/incoming students in 2008-09
156 applied/5 admission offers/3 incoming

% of students receiving:
Full tuition waiver only: 0%
Assistantship/fellowship only: 0%
Both full tuition remission (out of state portion only) & assistantship/fellowship: 100%

Approximate percentage of incoming students with a B.A./B.S. only: 100% **Master's:** 0%

Approximate percentage of students who are Women: 73% **Ethnic Minority:** 17% **International:** 10%

Average years to complete the doctoral program (including internship): 7 years

Personal interview
Preferred in person but telephone acceptable

Attrition rate in past 7 years: not reported

Percentage of students applying for internship last year accepted into APPIC or APA internships: 100%

Formal tracks/concentrations: not reported

Research areas	# Faculty	# Grants
affective disorders	6	6
developmental psychopathology	3	3
health	3	3
personality disorders: psychopathy	1	1
schizophrenia and other psychotic disorders	1	0
substance abuse	1	1

Clinical opportunities

addictive disorders
assessment (IQ, objective, psychophysiological, neuropsychological)
assessment of forensic populations
cognitive therapy for affective and anxiety disorders
families/couples therapy
brief dynamic psychotherapy
assessment of schizophrenia and at-risk populations
assessment of childhood psychopathology
affective neuroscience
therapy with criminal offenders
mood and anxiety disorders

University of Wisconsin–Milwaukee (Ph.D.)

Department of Psychology
P.O. Box 413
Milwaukee, WI 53201
phone#: (414) 229-4746
e-mail: que@uwm.edu
Web address: www.graduateschool.uwm.edu/students/prospective/areas-of-study/psychology/#phd

1	2	3	4	5	6	7
Practice oriented		Equal emphasis			Research oriented	

Percentage of faculty subscribing to each of the following orientations:

Psychodynamic/Psychoanalytic	0%
Applied behavioral analysis/Radical behavioral	20%
Family systems/Systems	10%
Existential/Phenomenological/Humanistic	0%
Cognitive/Cognitive-behavioral	70%

Courses required for incoming students to have completed prior to enrolling:
B.A. or B.S. in psychology or equivalent

Recommended but not mandatory courses:
B.A. or B.S. in psychology or undergraduate courses in psychological statistics, a laboratory course in research methodology, and an advanced laboratory course in psychology

GRE mean
Verbal 605 Quantitative 684
Verbal + Quantitative 1289
Psychology Subject Test 690
Analytical Writing not reported

GPA mean
Overall GPA 3.66 Psychology GPA 3.69
Junior/Senior GPA 3.68

Number of applications/admission offers/incoming students in 2008
121 applied/11 admission offers/7 incoming

% of students receiving:
Full tuition waiver only: 0%
Assistantship/fellowship only: 0%
Both full tuition waiver & assistantship/fellowship: 100%

Approximate percentage of incoming students with a B.A./B.S. only: 80% **Master's:** 20%

Approximate percentage of students who are Women: 54% **Ethnic Minority:** 22% **International:** 0%

Average years to complete the doctoral program (including internship): 6.25 years

Personal interview
Preferred in person but telephone acceptable

Attrition rate in past 7 years: 5%

Percentage of students applying for internship last year accepted into APPIC or APA internships: 86%

Formal tracks/concentrations: NIMH Program of Excellence Curriculum in Scientifically Validated Psychosocial Interventions

Research areas	# Faculty	# Grants
alcohol and substance abuse	1	0
anxiety/impulse control disorders	4	7
child psychology	3	1
developmental disabilities	1	1
emotion regulation	2	1
health psychology/behavioral medicine	2	0
learning disabilities	1	0
mood disorders	1	2
multicultural issues	1	0
neuropsychology	2	1
psychotherapy/behavior therapy research	3	9

Clinical opportunities

acceptance and commitment therapy
behavioral activation for depression
behavior therapy
behavioral medicine
child and adult neuropsychology
child development
developmental disabilities/ autism
empirically supported interventions
family violence
functional analytic psychotherapy
inpatient psychiatric
learning disability
OC spectrum disorders (Tourette Syndrome, Trichotillomania)
premature infants and their families—stress
prolonged exposure for PTSD

The Wright Institute (Psy.D.)

2728 Durant Avenue
Berkeley, CA 94704
phone#: (510) 841-9230
e-mail: info@wi.edu
Web address: www.wi.edu/program.html

1	2	3	4	5	6	7
Practice oriented		Equal emphasis				Research oriented

Percentage of faculty subscribing to each of the following orientations:

Cognitive-behavioral/ACT/DBT	25%
Existential/Phenomenological/Humanistic	10%
Family systems/Systems	15%
Integrationist	20%
Psychodynamic	30%

Courses required for incoming students to have completed prior to enrolling:
Human Development, Statistics, Theories of Personality or Abnormal Psychology

Recommended but not mandatory courses:
Biological Psychology or Psychobiology or Behavioral Neuroscience or Physiological Psychology

GRE mean
GRE scores not used in admission decisions

GPA mean
Overall GPA 3.4   Psychology GPA 3.3

Number of applications/admission offers/incoming students in 2009
297/120/60

% of students receiving:
Full tuition waiver only: 0%
Assistantship/fellowship only: 19%
Both full tuition waiver & assistantship/fellowship: 0%

Approximate percentage of incoming students with a B.A./B.S. only: 66%   **Master's:** 34%

Approximate percentage of students who are Women: 67%   **Ethnic Minority:** 25%   **International:** 1.5%

Average years to complete the doctoral program (including internship): 5.3 years

Personal interview
Preferred in person but telephone acceptable

Attrition rate in past 7 years: 5.9%

Percentage of students applying for internship last year accepted into APPIC or APA internships:
Most students plan to have professional careers in California, and many also have family and other responsibilities that make it impossible for them to relocate for a year in order to complete an APA accredited internship in another state. Thus, the majority of students choose a California Psychology Internship Council (CAPIC) internship. CAPIC has established training criteria and has been approving internships for nearly 20 years. 38% will be in APPIC or APA internships; 56% will be in CAPIC internships.

Formal tracks/concentrations: none

Research areas	# Faculty	# Grants
adolescence	2	0
autism	2	0
chronic illness	1	0
couples and family	3	0
cross-cultural psychology	3	0
evolutionary psychology	1	1
gender studies	3	0
infant/parent psychotherapy outcome	2	0
integrationism	2	0
jail and prison facilities	2	0
narrative therapy	4	0
step-families	1	0
stress-related somatic difficulties	1	0
substance abuse	2	0

Clinical opportunities

ACT
AIDS/HIV
affect disorders
altruism
assessment
autism
group therapy
men's issues
neuropsychology
pediatric/developmental
personality disorders
primary care/health care

brief and long-term therapy
child/adolescent assessment
child/adolescent
   psychopathology
couples therapy
crisis intervention
DBT
empirically supported
   treatments
ethnic minority
family therapy
forensic populations
GLBTIQ

program development/
   evaluation
psychodynamic
public policy/advocacy
rehabilitation psychology
schizophrenia
social justice
substance abuse
university counseling
women's issues

Wright State University (Psy.D.)

School of Professional Psychology
3640 Colonel Glenn Highway
Dayton, OH 45435
phone#: (937) 775-3492
e-mail: sopp1@wright.edu
Web address: www.wright.edu/sopp/

1	2	3	4	5	6	7
Practice oriented		Equal emphasis				Research oriented

Percentage of faculty subscribing to each of the following orientations:

Psychodynamic/Psychoanalytic	40%
Applied behavioral analysis/Radical behavioral	0%
Family systems/Systems	20%
Existential/Phenomenological/Humanistic	10%
Cognitive/Cognitive-behavioral	30%

Courses required for incoming students to have completed prior to enrolling:

Abnormal Psychology, Physiological Psychology, Research Methods, Statistics

Recommended but not mandatory courses:

Human Development, Personality, Theory of Tests & Measurements

GRE mean

Verbal + Quantitative 1090

GPA mean

Overall GPA 3.7
Psychology GPA 3.6

Number of applications/admission offers/incoming students in 2009

150 applied/45 admission offers/25 incoming

% of students receiving:

Full tuition waiver only: 0%
Partial tuition waiver: 100%
Assistantship/fellowship only: 0%

Both full tuition waiver & assistantship/fellowship: 0%

Approximate percentage of incoming students with a B.A./B.S. only: 84% Master's: 16%

Approximate percentage of students who are Women: 76% Ethnic Minority: 28% Disabled: 4% International: 0%

Average years to complete the doctoral program (including internship): 5 years

Personal interview

Preferred in person but telephone acceptable

Attrition rate in past 7 years: 6%

Percentage of students applying for internship last year accepted into APPIC or APA internships: 88%

Formal tracks/concentrations: none

Research areas	# Faculty	# Grants
chronic illness	1	0
cross-cultural psychology	3	0
gender studies	3	0
infant/parent psychotherapy outcome	2	0
jail and prison facilities	1	0
neurogerontology	1	0
parenting	3	0
stress-related somatic difficulties	1	0

Clinical opportunities

AIDS/HIV
affect disorders
assessment
brief and long-term therapy
child/adolescent assessment
child/adolescent
   psychopathology
couples therapy
crisis intervention
empirically supported
   treatments
ethnic minority
family therapy
forensic populations
geropsychology

GLBT
group therapy
men's issues
neuropsychology
pediatric/developmental
personality disorders
program development/
   evaluation
psychodynamic
public policy/advocacy
rehabilitation psychology
schizophrenia
substance abuse
university counseling
women's issues

University of Wyoming (Ph.D.)

Department of Psychology
Dept 3415, 1000 E University Ave
Laramie, WY 82071
phone#: (307) 766-6303
e-mail: psyc.uw@uwyo.edu
Web address: www.uwyo.edu/PSYCHOLOGY/graduate/
Clinical%20Psychology.html

1	2	3	4	5	6	7
Practice oriented		Equal emphasis				Research oriented

Percentage of faculty subscribing to each of the following orientations:

Psychodynamic/Psychoanalytic	0%
Applied behavioral analysis/Radical behavioral	14%
Family systems/Systems	0%
Existential/Phenomenological/Humanistic	0%
Cognitive/Cognitive-behavioral	86%

Courses required for incoming students to have completed prior to enrolling: None

Recommended but not mandatory courses:

Statistics, 30–45 psychology credits, research experience

GRE mean
Verbal + Quantitative 1272
Psychology Subject Test 678
Analytical Writing 4.9

GPA mean
Overall GPA 3.5   Psychology GPA 3.7
Junior/Senior GPA 3.8

Number of applications/admission offers/incoming students in 2009
88 applied/8 admission offers/5 incoming

% of students receiving:
Full tuition waiver only: 0%
Assistantship/fellowship only: 0%
Both full tuition waiver & assistantship/fellowship: 100%

Approximate percentage of incoming students with a B.A./B.S. only: 80%   **Master's:** 20%

Approximate percentage of students who are Women: 80% **Ethnic Minority:** 40% **International:** 0%

Average years to complete the doctoral program (including internship): 7 years

Personal interview
Preferred in person but telephone acceptable

Attrition rate in past 7 years: 5%

What percentage of students applying for internship last year was accepted into APPIC or APA internships? 100%

Formal tracks/concentrations: integrated behavioral health focus

Research areas	# Faculty	# Grants
anxiety	2	1
depression	3	2
HIV/AIDS prevention	1	1
mental retardation	2	1
Native American mental health	2	1
primary care	2	1
psychology and the law	2	1
substance abuse	1	1
trauma/posttraumatic stress disorder	1	2
ADHD	1	0
schizophrenia	1	0

Clinical opportunities
adult/child inpatient and residential
trauma/PTSD
developmental disabilities
empirically supported psychotherapies
mood/anxiety disorders
primary/interdisciplinary care
rural/community health care

Xavier University (Psy.D.)

Department of Psychology
3800 Victory Parkway
Cincinnati, OH 45207-6511
phone#: (513) 745-3533
e-mail: maybury@xavier.edu
Web address: www.xavier.edu/psychology-doctorate/

1	2	3	4	5	6	7
Practice oriented		Equal emphasis				Research oriented

Percentage of faculty subscribing to each of the following orientations:

Psychodynamic/Psychoanalytic	40%
Applied behavioral analysis/Radical behavioral	0%
Family systems/Systems	20%
Existential/Phenomenological/Humanistic	0%
Cognitive/Cognitive-behavioral	60%

Courses required for incoming students prior to enrolling:
Minimum 18 semester hours including the following: statistics, research methods, abnormal, testing, social

Recommended but not mandatory courses:
Anatomy and physiology, calculus

GRE mean
Verbal + Quantitative 1200

GPA mean
Overall GPA 3.7

Number of applications/admission offers/incoming students in 2009
237 applied/44 offers/28 incoming

% of students receiving:
Full tuition waiver only: 0%
Assistantship/fellowship only: 42% (includes partial tuition remission)
Both full tuition waiver & assistantship/fellowship: 0%

Approximate percentage of incoming students with a B.A./B.S. only: 85%   **Master's:** 17%

Approximate percentage of students who are Women: 89% **Ethnic Minority:** 11%
International: not reported

Average years to complete the doctoral program (including internship): 5.5 years

Personal interview
Interview not required

Attrition rate in past 7 years: 8%

Percentage of students applying for internship last year accepted into APPIC or APA internships: 69%

Formal tracks/concentrations: children/adolescents & their families, older adults, individuals with severe mental illness

Research areas	# Faculty	# Grants
cognitive/behavioral	5	1
geropsychology	2	0
psychoanalytic	4	0
social/experimental	1	0
statistician	2	0

Clinical opportunities
college-related concerns
Xavier University psychology services center
local agencies and hospitals

Yale University (Ph.D.)

Department of Psychology
P.O. Box 208205
New Haven, CT 06520-8205
Phone #: (203) 432-4500
E-mail: alan.kazdin@yale.edu
Web address: www.yale.edu/psychology/clinical.html

1	2	3	4	5	6	7
Practice oriented			Equal emphasis			Research oriented

Percentage of faculty subscribing to each of the following orientations:

Psychodynamic/Psychoanalytic	0%
Applied Behavioral Analysis/Radical Behavioral	0%
Family Systems/Systems	0%
Existential/Phenomenological/Humanistic	14%
Cognitive/Cognitive-behavioral	100%

Courses required for incoming students prior to enrolling: none

Recommended but not mandatory courses:
broad psychology background, undergraduate psychology

GRE mean
Verbal: 667   Quantitative: 750
Analytical Writing 5.3
Psychology Subject Test not reported

GPA mean
Overall GPA: 3.62

Number of applications/admission offers/incoming students in 2009
326 applied/4 admission offers/3 incoming

% of students receiving:
Full tuition waiver only: 0%
Assistantship/fellowship only: 0%
Both full tuition waiver & assistantship/fellowship: 100%

Approximate percentage of incoming students with a B.A./B.S. only: 100%   **Master's:** 0%

Approximate percentage of students who are Women: 81%   **Ethnic minority:** 33% **International:** 5%

Average years to complete the doctoral program (including internship): 6 years

Personal interview: No preference given

Attrition rate in past 7 years: 18%

Percentage of students applying for internship last year accepted into APPIC or APA internships: 100%

Formal tracks/concentrations: none

Research areas	# Faculty	# Grants
adult psychopathology	5	0
anxiety disorders	2	1
behavior genetics	1	0
cognitive processes	3	0
depression/suicidality	3	1
disruptive behavior disorders	1	0
developmental psychopathology	2	0
eating disorders	2	0
health psychology	2	2
longitudinal epidemiology	1	0
public health/social policy	1	1

Clinical opportunities

adolescents	eating and weight disorders
anxiety and mood disorders	health psychology
child psychotherapy	substance abuse
conduct disorders	

Yeshiva University (Ph.D.)

Ferkauf Graduate School of Psychology
Jack and Pearl Resnick Campus
1300 Morris Park Ave
Bronx, NY 10461
phone#: (718) 430-3856
e-mail: Sonia.Suchday@einstein.yu.edu
Web address: www.yu.edu/Ferkauf/page.
aspx?id=705&ekmensel=242_submenu_282_btnlink

1	2	3	4	5	6	7
Practice oriented			Equal emphasis			Research oriented

Percentage of faculty subscribing to each of the following orientations:

Psychodynamic/Psychoanalytic	0%
Applied behavioral analysis/Radical behavioral	0%
Family systems/Systems	0%
Existential/Phenomenological/Humanistic	0%
Cognitive/Cognitive-behavioral	100%

Courses required for incoming students to have completed prior to enrolling:
Minimum of 15 credits in psych, statistics, abnormal, experimental, personality, or physiological psychology

Recommended but not mandatory courses:
Courses in related fields such as mathematics, natural sciences, social sciences, public health

GRE mean
Verbal 560   Quantitative 630
Psychology Subject Test 650
Analytical Writing 4.9

GPA mean
Overall GPA 3.5

Number of applications/admission offers/incoming students in 2009
120 applied/31 admission offers/17 incoming

% of students receiving:
Full tuition waiver only: 1%
Assistantship/fellowship only: 33%
Both full tuition waiver & assistantship/fellowship: 0%

Approximate percentage of incoming students with a B.A./B.S. only: 82%   **Master's:** 18%

Approximate percentage of students who are Women: 80%   **Ethnic Minority:** 14% **International:** 4%

Average years to complete the doctoral program (including internship): 5.5 years

Personal interview
Required in person

Attrition rate in past 7 years: 2%

Percentage of students applying for internship last year accepted into APPIC or APA internships: 78%

Formal tracks/concentrations: none

Research areas	# Faculty	# Grants
cardiovascular psychology	1	0
acculturation and global health	2	3
neuropsychology	2	2
multiple sclerosis	1	3
obesity	1	0
asthma	1	1
psychosocial oncology	1	2
migraines	1	3
diabetes	1	1

Clinical opportunities

behavioral medicine	asthma and anxiety
cardiovascular psychology	neuropsychology
weight management and related disorders	geropsychology

Yeshiva University (Psy.D.)

Department of Psychology
Ferkauf Graduate School of Psychology
1300 Morris Park Avenue
Bronx, NY 10461
phone#: (718) 430-3850
e-mail: gill@aecom.yu.edu
Web address: www.yu.edu/ferkauf/clinic.
aspx?id=6244&ekmensel=242_submen_280_btnlink

1	2	3	4	5	6	7
Practice oriented		Equal emphasis				Research oriented

Percentage of faculty subscribing to each of the following orientations:

Psychodynamic/Psychoanalytic	40%
Applied behavioral analysis/Radical behavioral	5%
Family systems/Systems	10%
Existential/Phenomenological/Humanistic	5%
Cognitive/Cognitive-behavioral	40%

Courses required for incoming students to have completed prior to enrolling:
Statistics, abnormal, experimental, physiological psychology, personality

Recommended but not mandatory courses: None

GRE mean
Verbal 550   Quantitative 670
Analytical Writing 5.0
Psychology Subject Test 660

GPA mean
Overall GPA 3.5   Psychology GPA 3.5

Number of applications/admission offers/incoming students in 2009
253/72/27

% of students receiving:
Full tuition waiver only: 0%
Assistantship/fellowship only: 80%
Both full tuition waiver & assistantship/fellowship: 0%

Approximate percentage of incoming students with a B.A./B.S. only: 77%   **Master's:** 23%

Approximate percentage of students who are Women: 96%   **Ethnic Minority:** 11%   **International:** 11%

Average years to complete the doctoral program (including internship): 5 years

Personal interview
Required in person

Attrition rate in past 7 years: 2%

Percentage of students applying for internship last year accepted into APPIC or APA internships: 70%

Formal tracks/concentrations: geropsychology, psychodynamics, CBT, mental health counseling

Research areas	# Faculty	# Grants
anxiety disorders	1	0
depression	2	0
early childhood intervention	1	0
ethnicity and identity	2	0
family therapy	1	0
forensics	1	0
gero-psychology	1	1
parenting styles	1	0
psychoanalytic therapy	5	0
psychotherapy process and outcome	3	0
sleep disorders/nightmares	1	0
stress and coping	4	1
trauma	2	0

Clinical opportunities

anxiety disorders	interpersonal therapy
cognitive behavior therapy	marital/couples
depression	parent training
family therapy	psychodynamic therapy
geriatrics	psychoeducational assessment

York University–Adult Clinical Program (Ph.D.)

Department of Psychology
Toronto, Ontario M3J 1P3, Canada
phone#: (416) 736-5115
e-mail: clindir@yorku.ca
Web address: www.yorku.ca/gradpsyc/field2.html

1	2	3	4	5	6	7
Practice oriented		Equal emphasis				Research oriented

Percentage of faculty subscribing to each of the following orientations:

Psychodynamic/Psychoanalytic	5%
Applied behavioral analysis/Radical behavioral	0%
Family systems/Systems	5%

Existential/Phenomenological/Humanistic	37%
Cognitive/Cognitive-behavioral	32%
Neuropsychology	21%

Courses required for incoming students to have completed prior to enrolling:

Physiological/neuropsychology, organizational/social/groups, research design and statistical analysis, learning/perception/emotion/motivation, personality/abnormal/individual differences

Recommended but not mandatory courses:

Multicultural psychology, tests and measurements, health psychology

GRE mean

Verbal 601   Quantitative 697
Psychology Subject Test 709
Analytical Writing 5.1

GPA mean

Overall GPA N/A

Number of applications/admission offers/incoming students in 2009

128 applied/10 admission offers/8 incoming

% of students receiving:

Full tuition waiver only: N/A
Assistantship/fellowship only: 100% incoming students; N/A all other
Both full tuition waiver & assistantship/fellowship: N/A

Approximate percentage of incoming students with a B.A./B.S. only: 75%   Master's: 25%

Approximate percentage of students who are
Women: 100%   **Ethnic Minority:** not reported
International: not reported

Average years to complete the doctoral program (including internship): 6 years

Personal interview

Preferred in person but telephone acceptable

Attrition rate in past 7 years: 1/68 dropped out; 3/68 withdrew in good standing; 7/58 left after MA

Percentage of students applying for internship last year accepted into APPIC or APA internships: 100%

Formal tracks/concentrations: adult clinical psychology, diploma in health psychology, neuroscience

Research areas	# Faculty	# Grants
major depression	2	2
eating disorders	1	1
psychopathology/psychotherapy	2	2
health—cardiovascular disease	1	2
psychosocial oncology	1	1
relationship research—couples therapy	1	1
psychotherapeutic process	3	3
cognitive neuropsychology of memory	2	2
narrative processes	1	1
clinical neuropsychology	1	1
cognitive rehabilitation	1	1
motivation, expectations, psychotherapy	1	1
pain	1	1
schizophrenia and neuropsychology	2	2

Clinical opportunities

anxiety disorders	geriatric
depression	schizophrenia
psychopathology assessment	health psychology
eating disorders	neuropsychological
forensic	assessment/rehab

REPORTS ON INDIVIDUAL COUNSELING PSYCHOLOGY PROGRAMS

University of Akron (Ph.D.)
Department of Counseling and Department of Psychology
Akron, OH 44325-4301
phone#: (330) 972-7280 or (330) 972-7777
e-mail: shardin@uakron.edu
Web address: www.uakron.edu/psychology/academics/
collaborative-program-in-counseling-psychology/index.dot

1	2	3	**4**	5	6	7
Practice oriented			Equal emphasis			Research oriented

Percentage of faculty subscribing to each of the following orientations:
Psychodynamic/Psychoanalytic 10%
Applied behavioral analysis/Radical behavioral 0%
Family systems/Systems 10%
Existential/Phenomenological/Humanistic 40%
Cognitive/Cognitive-behavioral 40%

Courses required for incoming students to have completed prior to enrolling:
The program has 2 tracks: 1 track (Department of Psychology) admits students with a bachelor's degree in psychology; the other track (Department of Counseling) admits students with a master's degree in counseling.

Recommended but not mandatory courses:
quantitative methods, personality

GRE mean
Verbal + Quantitative 1100 recommended
Analytical Writing not reported

GPA mean
Overall GPA 3.45

Number of applications/admission offers/incoming students in 2009
85 applied/15 admission offers/10 incoming

% of students receiving:
Full tuition waiver only: 0%
Assistantship/fellowship only: 0%
Both full tuition waiver & assistantship/fellowship: 100%

Approximate percentage of incoming students with a B.A./B.S. only: 60%   Master's: 40%

Approximate percentage of students who are
Women: 75%   Ethnic Minority: 10%
International: not reported

Average years to complete the doctoral program (including internship): 7 years

Personal interview
No preference given

Attrition rate in past 7 years: 10%

Percentage of students applying for internship last year accepted into APPIC or APA internships: 70%

Formal tracks/concentrations: none

Research areas	# Faculty	# Grants
multicultural	2	0
personality assessment	2	0
suicide	2	0
vocational counseling	2	0
women's issues	3	0

Clinical opportunities
child study and family therapy
community mental health center
college counseling center

University at Albany/State University of New York (Ph.D.)
Department of Educational and Counseling Psychology
ED 220
Albany, NY 12222
phone#: (518) 442-5040
e-mail: mfriedlander@uamail.albany.edu
Web address: www.albany.edu/counseling_psych

1	2	3	**4**	5	6	7
Practice oriented			Equal emphasis			Research oriented

Percentage of faculty subscribing to each of the following orientations:
Psychodynamic/Psychoanalytic 15%
Family systems/Systems 15%
Existential/Phenomenological/Humanistic 20%
Cognitive/Cognitive-behavioral 50%

Courses required for incoming students to have completed prior to enrolling:
Preparation in basic psychology (18 credits minimum, including statistics)

Recommended but not mandatory courses: abnormal, developmental, personality

GRE mean
Verbal + Quantitative 1150
Analytical Writing not reported
Psychology Subject Test not considered

GPA mean
Overall GPA 3.6   Psychology GPA 3.8

Number of applications/admission offers/incoming students in 2009
124 applied/14 admission offers/7 incoming

% of students receiving:
Full tuition waiver only: 0%
Assistantship/fellowship only: 0%
Both full tuition waiver & assistantship/fellowship: 100%

Approximate percentage of incoming students who entered with a B.A./B.S. only: 45%   Master's: 55%

Approximate percentage of students who are
Women: 68% Ethnic Minority: 34% International: 15%

Average years to complete the doctoral program (including internship): 6.5 years

Personal interview
Preferred in person but telephone acceptable

Attrition rate in past 7 years: 2%

Percentage of students applying for internship last year accepted into APPIC or APA internships: 80%

Formal tracks/concentrations: none

Research areas	# Faculty	# Grants
career development	1	1
cross-cultural	3	2
family dynamics	1	0
family therapy	1	1
methodology	1	0
prevention	1	0
process	1	0
social justice	3	1
spirituality	1	0
supervision	2	0
women's issues	1	0

Clinical opportunities

small and large college and university counseling centers
community agencies
county mental health clinics
adolescent residential treatment centers
neuropsychology rehabilitation center
state psychiatric center
private psychiatric center
various units at VA hospital, including neuropsychology, outpatient, day treatment, substance abuse

---

Arizona State University (Ph.D.)

Division of Psychology and Education
Arizona State University
Tempe, AZ 85287-0611
phone#: (480) 965-8733
e-mail: ccp@asu.edu
Web address: sls.asu.edu/cp/phd/

1	2	3	4	5	6	7
Practice oriented			Equal emphasis			Research oriented

Percentage of faculty subscribing to each of the following orientations:

Psychodynamic/Psychoanalytic	20%
Applied behavioral analysis/Radical behavioral	0%
Family systems/Systems	10%
Existential/Phenomenological/Humanistic	30%
Cognitive/Cognitive-behavioral	40%

Courses required for incoming students to have completed prior to enrolling: None

Recommended but not mandatory courses:
Psychology or related background

GRE mean
Verbal 590   Quantitative 610
Analytical Writing not reported

GPA mean
Overall GPA 3.36   Junior/Senior GPA 3.69

Number of applications/admission offers/incoming students in 2009
129 applied/7 admission offers/6 incoming

% of students receiving:
Full tuition waiver only: 0%
Assistantship/fellowship only: 0%
Both full tuition waiver & assistantship/fellowship: 100%

Approximate percentage of incoming students with a B.A./B.S. only: 50%   Master's: 50%

Approximate percentage of students who are Women: 66%   Ethnic Minority: 50%   International: 0%

Average years to complete the doctoral program (including internship): 5 years

Personal interview
Required in person

Attrition rate in past 7 years: 6%

Percentage of students applying for internship last year accepted into APPIC or APA internships: 100%

Formal tracks/concentrations: none

Research areas	# Faculty	# Grants
career development	3	1
cognitive appraisal	1	0
cognitive-behavioral interventions	1	1
consultation	2	0
counseling process	4	0
counseling the gifted and talented	2	1
counseling women and minorities	5	1
culture sensitivity training	4	1
experimental methodology	2	0
family enrichment	1	0
gender issues in counseling	2	0
group counseling	1	0
health psychology	1	0
HIV	1	0
international issues	1	0
interpersonal therapy	3	0
psychology of women	2	0
retention	4	1
social psychological counseling	2	0
training and supervision	4	0
values and decision making	1	0

Clinical opportunities
varied

Auburn University (Ph.D. in Counseling Psychology)

Department of Special Education, Rehabilitation, and Counseling/School Psychology
Auburn, AL 36849-5218
phone#: (334) 844-7676
e-mail: pipesrb@auburn.edu
Web address: education.auburn.edu/academic_departments/serc/academicprograms/counpsych.html

1	2	3	4	5	6	7
Practice oriented			Equal emphasis			Research oriented

Percentage of faculty subscribing to each of the following orientations:

Psychodynamic/Psychoanalytic	33%
Applied behavioral analysis/Radical behavioral	0%
Family systems/Systems	0%
Existential/Phenomenological/Humanistic	67%
Cognitive/Cognitive-behavioral	33%

Courses required for incoming students to have completed prior to enrolling: None; however 3-4 courses are expected as a minimum

Recommended but not mandatory courses: Several (non-specified) courses in psychology are recommended.

GRE mean:
Verbal + Quantitative 1082
Psychology Subject Test not required
Analytical Writing not reported

GPA mean
Overall GPA 3.7 (Undergraduate)

Number of applications/admission offers/incoming students in 2009
78 applied/11 admission offers/7 attending

% of students receiving:
Full tuition waiver only: 0%
Assistantship/fellowship only: 0%
Both full tuition waiver & assistantship/fellowship: 100%

Approximate percentage of incoming students with a B.A./B.S. only: 57%; **Master's:** 43%

Approximate percentage of students who are Women: 83%   **Ethnic Minority:** 24%   **International:** 3%

Average years to complete the doctoral program (including internship): 6.6 years

Personal interview
Preferred in person but telephone acceptable

Attrition rate in past 7 years: 11%

Percentage of students applying for internship last year accepted into APPIC or APA internships: 100%

Formal tracks/concentrations: none

Research areas	# Faculty	# Grants
professional issues/ethics	1	0
psychometrics	1	0
substance abuse prevention	0	1

Clinical opportunities
mental health center (outpatient)
substance abuse unit (inpatient and outpatient)
university counseling centers
rehabilitation

Ball State University (Ph.D.)

Department of Counseling Psychology
Muncie, IN 47306
phone#: (765) 285-8040
fax#: (765) 285-2067

e-mail: SBOWMAN@BSU.EDU
Web address: www.bsu.edu/counselingpsychology

1	2	3	4	5	6	7
Practice oriented		Equal emphasis				Research oriented

Percentage of faculty subscribing to each of the following orientations:

Psychodynamic/Psychoanalytic	15%
Applied behavioral analysis/Radical behavioral	0%
Family systems/Systems	35%
Existential/Phenomenological/Humanistic	20%
Cognitive/Cognitive-behavioral	30%

Courses required for incoming students to have completed prior to enrolling:
Counseling theories, counseling techniques, practicum, one other counseling course

Recommended but not mandatory courses: None

GRE mean
Verbal + Quantitative 1123
Analytical Writing not reported

GPA mean
Overall master's GPA 3.8

Number of applications/admission offers/incoming students in 2009
80 applied/13 admission offers/10 incoming

% of students receiving:
Full tuition waiver only: 0%
Assistantship/fellowship only: 0%
Both full tuition waiver & assistantship/fellowship: 100%

Approximate percentage of incoming students with a B.A./B.S. only: 0%   **Master's:** 100%

Approximate percentage of students who are Women: 69%   **Ethnic Minority:** 10%   **International:** 30%

Average years to complete the doctoral program (including internship): 4.6 years

Personal interview
Preferred in person but telephone acceptable

Attrition rate in past 7 years: 9%

Percentage of students applying for internship last year accepted into APPIC or APA internships: 91%

Formal tracks/concentrations: couples and family, counseling health psychology, diversity in counseling psychology, social justice, vocational psychology

Research areas	# Faculty	# Grants
behavioral medicine	2	0
career/vocational	4	0
child/adolescent	2	0
clinical judgment	1	0
multicultural	4	1
organizational/EAP	1	0
social psychology applications	3	0
rehabilitation	2	1
women's identity	2	0

291

Clinical opportunities

BSU Practicum Clinic   Muncie Community Schools
Cancer Center   Local youth-oriented
University counseling center   programs

Boston College (Ph.D.)

Department of Counseling, Developmental and
Educational Psychology
School of Education
Chestnut Hill, MA 02167
phone#: (617) 552-4710 or (617) 552-4214
e-mail: gsoe@bc.edu
Web address: www.bc.edu/schools/lsoe/academics/
departments/cdep/graduate/counsel.html

1	2	3	4	5	6	7
Practice oriented		Equal emphasis				Research oriented

Percentage of faculty subscribing to each of the following orientations:

Psychodynamic/Psychoanalytic   50%
Applied behavioral analysis/Radical behavioral   0%
Family systems/Systems   20%
Existential/Phenomenological/Humanistic   10%
Cognitive/Cognitive-behavioral   20%

Courses required for incoming students to have completed prior to enrolling:

For applicants without a master's degree, we require at least 18 credit hours of undergraduate psychology

Recommended but not mandatory courses:

Statistics, abnormal, developmental, personality

GRE mean

Verbal 613   Quantitative 741
Analytical Writing 5.33

GPA mean

Overall GPA 3.45

Number of applications/admission offers/incoming students in 2009

271 applied/7 admission offers/6 incoming

% of students receiving:

Full tuition waiver only: 0%
Assistantship/fellowship only: 0%
Both full tuition waiver & assistantship/fellowship: 100%

Approximate percentage of incoming students with a B.A./B.S. only: 14%   Master's: 86%

Approximate percentage of students who are Women: 85% Ethnic Minority: 35% International: 10%

Average years to complete the doctoral program (including internship): 6.45 years; Modal: 5years

Personal interview

Preferred in person

Attrition rate in past 7 years: 7%

Percentage of students applying for internship last year accepted into APPIC or APA internships: 87%

Formal tracks/concentrations: none

Research areas	# Faculty	# Grants
Adolescent & young adult development	3	2
career development	1	1
gender roles	2	1
schools and agencies	6	3
multicultural	1	1

Clinical opportunities

acute psychiatric
college counseling center
community mental health
inpatient adult unit
inpatient child
hospital inpatient

school based mental health clinic
violence prevention/ intervention
VA hospital
hospital outpaitient

Brigham Young University (Ph.D.)

Department of Counseling Psychology and
Special Education
Provo, UT 84602-5093
phone#: (801) 422-3859
e-mail: aaron_jackson@byu.edu
Web address: education.byu.edu/cpse/phd

1	2	3	4	5	6	7
Practice oriented		Equal emphasis				Research oriented

Percentage of faculty subscribing to each of the following orientations:

Psychodynamic/Psychoanalytic   30%
Applied behavioral analysis/Radical behavioral   0%
Family systems/Systems   0%
Existential/Phenomenological/Humanistic   35%
Cognitive/Cognitive-behavioral   35%

Courses required for incoming students to have completed prior to enrolling:

Abnormal, personality, developmental, research methods, statistics

Recommended but not mandatory courses:

GRE mean

Verbal 590   Quantitative 652
Analytical Writing 4.9

GPA mean

Overall GPA 3.64

Number of applications/admission offers/incoming students in 2009

54 applied/7 admission offers/7 incoming

% of students receiving:

Full tuition waiver only: 0%
Assistantship/fellowship only: 100%
Both full tuition waiver & assistantship/fellowship: 0%

Approximate percentage of incoming students with a B.A./B.S. only: 71%   Master's: 29%

Approximate percentage of students who are Women: 66%   Ethnic Minority: 27% International: 6%

Average years to complete the doctoral program (including internship): 5 years

Personal interview
Preferred in person but telephone acceptable

Attrition rate in past 7 years: 4%

Percentage of students applying for internship last year accepted into APPIC or APA internships: 86%

Formal tracks/concentrations: none

Research areas	# Faculty	# Grants
crisis intervention	1	1
mental health and spirituality	6	3
mental health in schools	3	2
multicultural counseling	2	2
Native American vocational development	1	1
outcome research	3	3
women's issues	2	1

Clinical opportunities
Spanish-speaking
Practicum in Hawaii

University of British Columbia (Ph.D.)

Department of Educational and Counseling Psychology, and Special Education
2125 Main Mall
Vancouver, British Columbia V6T 1Z4, Canada
phone#: (604) 822-8539
e-mail: lynn.miller@ubc.edu
Web address: www.grad.ubc.ca/prospective-students/
graduate-degree-programs/phd-counselling-psychology

1	2	3	4	5	6	7
Practice oriented			Equal emphasis			Research oriented

Percentage of faculty subscribing to each of the following orientations:

Psychodynamic/Psychoanalytic	5%
Applied behavioral analysis/Radical behavioral	0%
Family systems/Systems	60%
Existential/Phenomenological/Humanistic	60%
Cognitive/Cognitive-behavioral	50%

Courses required for incoming students to have completed prior to enrolling:
Ph.D. applicants are required to have completed courses equivalent to the M.A. in Counseling offered by the department. Please check the Web site.

Recommended but not mandatory courses:
Yes. We encourage more methods courses (a methods certificate can be additionally earned).

GRE mean
Verbal 556   Quantitative 510

GPA mean
Overall 3.5

Number of applications/admission offers/incoming students in 2008
29 applied/10 admission offers/10 incoming

% of students receiving:
Full tuition waiver only: 0% (This was a one-year change in UBC policy. Expected to be full tuition waiver in future)
Assistantship/fellowship only: 100%
Both full tuition waiver & assistantship/fellowship: 0%

Approximate percentage of incoming students with a B.A./B.S. only: 0%   **Master's:** 100%

Approximate percentage of students who are Women: 80%   **Ethnic Minority:** 20%   **International:** 30%

Average years to complete the doctoral program (including internship): 4.8 years

Personal interview
Preferred candidate visits and telephone encouraged; no interview required

Attrition rate in past 7 years: 2%

What percentage of students applying for internship last year was accepted into APPIC or APA internships? 25%

Formal tracks/concentrations: not reported

Research areas	# Faculty	# Grants
aboriginal approaches to healing	3	7
anxiety in other cultures	2	2
Asian approaches to counseling	1	2
assessment in rehabilitation	1	1
counseling process	1	0
ethics	1	0
career development	4	4
infertility	1	0
stress and coping	1	2
trauma	3	3
women's sexuality	2	1

Clinical opportunities
Not reported

Colorado State University (Ph.D.)

Department of Psychology
Fort Collins, CO 80523
phone#: (970) 491-6363
e-mail: jmoran@lamar.colostate.edu
Web address: www.colostate.edu/Depts/Psychology/
counseling/

1	2	3	4	5	6	7
Practice oriented			Equal emphasis			Research oriented

Percentage of faculty subscribing to each of the following orientations:

Psychodynamic/Psychoanalytic	0%
Applied behavioral analysis/Radical behavioral	0%
Family systems/Systems	0%
Existential/Phenomenological/Humanistic	0%
Cognitive/Cognitive-behavioral	70%

Courses required for incoming students to have completed prior to enrolling: none

Recommended but not mandatory courses:
learning, personality, history and systems, developmental, abnormal, statistics

GRE mean
Verbal 595   Quantitative 695
Psychology Subject Test not required
Analytical Writing 4.8

GPA mean
Overall GPA 3.87

Number of applications/admission offers/incoming students in 2008
195 applied/8 admission offers/5 incoming

% of students receiving:
Full tuition waiver only: 0%
Assistantship/fellowship only: 50%
Both full tuition waiver & assistantship/fellowship: 0%
Both half tuition waiver & assistantship/fellowship: 100%

Approximate percentage of incoming students with a B.A./B.S. only: 100%   **Master's:** 0%

Approximate percentage of students who are Women: 80%   **Ethnic Minority:** 40%   **International:** 0%

Average years to complete the doctoral program (including internship): 5 years

Personal interview
No interview required

Attrition rate in past 7 years: 5%

Percentage of students applying for internship last year accepted into APPIC or APA internships: 90%

Formal tracks/concentrations: none

Research areas	# Faculty	# Grants
ADHD	1	0
adolescents	3	5
aggression (anger research and reduction)	1	0
aging/geriatrics	3	1
anxiety (reduction)	1	0
assessment (including multicultural)	3	1
body image beating disturbances child	1	0
cognitive	5	1
college teaching	1	0
educational outcomes	1	1
emotional disorders	1	0
ethics	1	0
health psychology	8	4
interpersonal relationships	1	0
learning disabilities	1	0
men	1	0
multicultural	6	3
parent–child interaction	1	0
psychopathology	3	0
psychotherapy process	1	0
stress and coping processes	2	0
substance abuse	4	3
supervision and training	2	0
violence/abuse	2	0
vocational psychology	2	0
women	3	1

Clinical opportunities

family stress center	juvenile detention facility
neuropsychology practice	Counseling Center
university counseling center	substance abuse program
community college counseling	University Health Center
primary care	

University of Denver (Ph.D.)

College of Education
Denver, CO 80208
phone#: (303) 871-2482
e-mail: jevaldez@du.edu
Web address: www.du.edu/education/academicPrograms/cnp/

1	2	3	4	5	6	7
Practice oriented		Equal emphasis				Research oriented

Percentage of faculty subscribing to each of the following orientations:

Psychodynamic/Psychoanalytic	25%
Applied behavioral analysis/Radical behavioral	0%
Family systems/Systems	15%
Existential/Phenomenological/Humanistic	25%
Cognitive/Cognitive-behavioral	35%

Courses required for incoming students to have completed prior to enrolling: None

Recommended but not mandatory courses:
Learning, personality, statistics

GRE mean
Verbal 600   Quantitative 600
Analytical Writing 4.7

GPA mean
Overall GPA 3.5

Number of applications/admission offers/incoming students in 2008
71 applied/11 admission offers/8 incoming

% of students receiving:
Full tuition waiver only: 30%
Assistantship/fellowship only: 60%
Both full tuition waiver & assistantship/fellowship: 10%

Approximate percentage of incoming students with a B.A./B.S. only: 0%   **Master's:** 100%

Approximate percentage of students who are Women: 86%   **Ethnic Minority:** 22%

Average years to complete the doctoral program (including internship): 5 years

Personal interview
Preferred in person but telephone acceptable

Attrition rate in past 7 years: not reported

Percentage of students applying for internship last year accepted into APPIC or APA internships: 100%

Formal tracks/concentrations: none

Research areas	# Faculty	# Grants
PTSD	1	1
social support	1	1
ethics	1	0
group counseling	1	0
multicultural counseling	1	1
job satisfaction in work settings	1	1

Clinical opportunities

placements working with racial/ethnic minorities
counseling centers
hospital settings
mental health centers
Veteran Administration Hospital
conducting counseling groups
psychological/neuro-psychological assessment

University of Florida (Ph.D.)

Department of Psychology
Gainesville, FL 32611
phone#: (352) 392-0601
e-mail: heesack@ufl.edu
Web address: www.psych.ufl.edu/index.php/counselingpsychology

1	2	3	4	5	6	7
Practice oriented			Equal emphasis			Research oriented

Percentage of faculty subscribing to each of the following orientations:

Psychodynamic/Psychoanalytic	0%
Applied behavioral analysis/Radical behavioral	0%
Family systems/Systems	25%
Existential/Phenomenological/Humanistic	25%
Cognitive/Cognitive-behavioral	50%

Courses required for incoming students to have completed prior to enrolling:
Undergraduate 4-year degree in psychology or related field

Recommended but not mandatory courses:
Statistics, research design/methods, personality, abnormal

GRE mean
Verbal 573   Quantitative 667
Analytical Writing not reported
Psychology Subject Test not used

GPA mean
Overall GPA 3.8   Psychology GPA 3.9
Junior/Senior GPA 3.8

Number of applications/admission offers/incoming students in 2009
157 applied/7 admission offers/5 incoming

% of students receiving:
Full tuition waiver only: 0%
Assistantship/fellowship only: 0%

Both full tuition waiver & assistantship/fellowship: 100%

Approximate percentage of incoming students with a B.A./B.S. only: 100%   **Master's:** 0%

Approximate percentage of students who are Women: 57%   **Ethnic Minority:** 24%   **International:** 16%

Average years to complete the doctoral program (including internship): 6 years

Personal interview
Preferred in person but telephone acceptable

Attrition rate in past 7 years: 10%

Percentage of students applying for internship last year accepted into APPIC or APA internships: 100%

Formal tracks/concentrations: none

Research areas	# Faculty	# Grants
Addictions	1	0
health psychology	1	2
constructivist psychology	1	0
forensics	1	0
gender and emotion	1	1
mental health of minority clients	1	0
personality and mental health	1	0
sexual orientation	1	0
vocational psychology	1	0
women	1	0

Clinical opportunities

anxiety disorder clinic
career counseling center
community mental health
crisis intervention center
domestic violence clinic
family medical practice
forensics hospital
hospice
nursing facility
pediatric/psychiatric assessment and treatment
prison
rural health care clinic
sexual offender
substance abuse clinic
university counseling center

Fordham University (Ph.D.)

Division of Psychological and Educational Services
Graduate School of Education
113 West 60th Street
New York, NY 10023
phone#: (212) 636-6460
e-mail: mjackson@fordham.edu
Web address: www.fordham.edu/academics/colleges__graduate_s/graduate__profession/education/divisions/psychological__educa/counseling_psycholog/index.asp

1	2	3	4	5	6	7
Practice oriented			Equal emphasis			Research oriented

Percentage of faculty subscribing to each of the following orientations:

Psychodynamic/Psychoanalytic	35%
Applied behavioral analysis/Radical behavioral	20%
Family systems/Systems	16%
Existential/Phenomenological/Humanistic	60%
Cognitive/Cognitive-behavioral	100%

Courses required for incoming students to have completed prior to enrolling:
15 credits in psychology, developmental, experimental, abnormal, personality

Recommended but not mandatory courses:
Qualitative research methods

GRE mean
Verbal 574   Quantitative 610
Analytical Writing 4.4

GPA mean
Overall GPA 3.7

Number of applications/admission offers/incoming students in 2009
103 applied/21 admission offers/12 incoming

% of students receiving:
Full tuition waiver only: 0%
Assistantship/fellowship only: 50%
Both full tuition waiver & assistantship/fellowship: 1%

Approximate percentage of incoming students with a B.A./B.S. only: 50%   **Master's:** 50%

Approximate percentage of students who are Women: 66%   **Ethnic Minority:** 33%   **International:** 11%

Average years to complete the doctoral program (including internship): 7 years

Personal interview
Preferred in person but telephone acceptable

Attrition rate in past 7 years: 8%

Percentage of students applying for internship last year accepted into APPIC or APA internships: 84%

Formal tracks/concentrations: none

Research areas	# Faculty	# Grants
career development	3	1
criminal behavior	1	1
health psychology	2	1
multicultural counseling	5	0
supervision	3	2

Clinical opportunities
college counseling centers
community mental health centers
on-campus clinical/research center
psychological services institute

University of Georgia (Ph.D.)
Department of Counseling and Human Development Services
Athens, GA 30602
phone#: (706) 542-1812
e-mail: edelgado@uga.edu
Web address: www.coe.uga.edu/chds/academic-programs/counseling-psychology/

1	2	3	4	5	6	7
Practice oriented		Equal emphasis				Research oriented

Percentage of faculty subscribing to each of the following orientations:

Psychodynamic/Psychoanalytic	20%
Applied behavioral analysis/Radical behavioral	0%
Family systems/Systems	20%
Existential/Phenomenological/Humanistic	10%
Cognitive/Cognitive-behavioral	50%

Courses required for incoming students to have completed prior to enrolling:
Research methods, statistics, interpersonal relationships, individual assessment, vocational development, theories of counseling, individual counseling practicum, group counseling, multicultural counseling (master's degree required)

Recommended but not mandatory courses: None

GRE mean
Verbal + Quantitative 1100
Analytical Writing 3.5

GPA mean
Overall GPA undergraduate 3.0 Graduate 3.5

Number of applications/admission offers/incoming students in 2009
82 applied/15 admission offers/9 incoming

% of students receiving:
Full tuition waiver only: 0%
Assistantship/fellowship only: 0%
Both full tuition waiver & assistantship/fellowship: 100%

Approximate percentage of incoming students with a B.A./B.S. only: 0%   **Master's:** 100%

Approximate percentage of students who are Women: 70%   **Ethnic Minority:** 43%   **International:** 2%

Average years to complete the doctoral program (including internship): 4 years

Personal interview
In person

Attrition rate in past 7 years: 8%

Percentage of students applying for internship last year accepted into APPIC or APA internships: 91%

Formal tracks/concentrations: marriage and family therapy, supervision, psychological assessment (learning disabilities), preparing future faculty

Research areas	# Faculty	# Grants
accident trauma	1	1
African American Psychology	1	1
attributions and therapy	2	0
Assessment (rural)	1	1
empowering schools	2	1
juvenile delinquency/aggression	2	2
minority male adolescents	1	1
Latino Psychology	1	0

multicultural counseling	3	2
preventing violence and aggression in schools	2	3
school counselor education	2	0
substance abuse	1	1
young adult development	2	0

Clinical opportunities

adolescents
college students
departmental captive clinic
homeless shelter
Learning disabilities assessment
Rural assessment

juvenile offenders
school-age children
supervision
college counseling center
People with developmental disability

Georgia State University (Ph.D.)

Department of Counseling and Psychological Services
Atlanta, GA 30303
phone#: (404) 413-8010
e-mail: jashby2@gsu.edu
Web address: education.gsu.edu/cps/781.html

1	2	3	4	5	6	7
Practice oriented		Equal emphasis				Research oriented

Percentage of faculty subscribing to each of the following orientations:

Psychodynamic/Psychoanalytic	33%
Applied behavioral analysis/Radical behavioral	0%
Family systems/Systems	0%
Existential/Phenomenological/Humanistic	33%
Cognitive/Cognitive-behavioral	33%

Courses required for incoming students to have completed prior to enrolling:
M.A. in counseling or clinical psychology

Recommended but not mandatory courses: None

GRE mean
Verbal 550   Quantitative 600
Psychology Subject Test not reported
Analytical Writing 4.9

GPA mean
Overall GPA 3.6

Number of applications/admission offers/incoming students in 2009
66 applied/8 admission offers/7 incoming

% of students receiving:
Full tuition waiver only: 0%
Assistantship/fellowship only: 0%
Both full tuition waiver & assistantship/fellowship: 100%

Approximate percentage of incoming students with a B.A./B.S. only: 0%   **Master's:** 100%

Approximate percentage of students who are Women: 80%   **Ethnic Minority:** 40%   **International:** 8%

Average years to complete the doctoral program (including internship): 5 years

Personal interview
Preferred in person but telephone acceptable

Attrition rate in past 7 years: 0.05%

Percentage of students applying for internship last year accepted into APPIC or APA internships: 100%

Formal tracks/concentrations: none

Research areas	# Faculty	# Grants
career development	1	0
forensics	1	0
gender/multicultural	2	0
stress/coping	2	1
traumatology	1	0
rehabilitation	1	0
consultation	1	1

Clinical opportunities

behavioral medicine
college counseling
forensic

multicultural counseling
stress management

University of Houston (Ph.D.)

Counseling Psychology Program
Houston, TX 77004-5874
phone#: (713) 743-5019
e-mail: epsy@uh.edu
Web address: www.coe.uh.edu/academic-programs/counseling-psychology-ph/index.php

1	2	3	4	5	6	7
Practice oriented		Equal emphasis				Research oriented

Percentage of faculty subscribing to each of the following orientations:

Psychodynamic/Psychoanalytic	25%
Applied behavioral analysis/Radical behavioral	0%
Family systems/Systems	25%
Existential/Phenomenological/Humanistic	25%
Cognitive/Cognitive-behavioral	25%

Courses required for incoming students to have completed prior to enrolling: None

Recommended but not mandatory courses: None

GRE mean
Verbal 530   Quantitative 620
Analytical Writing 4.5

GPA mean
Overall master's GPA 3.5

Number of applications/admission offers/incoming students in 2009
58 applied/11 admission offers/9 incoming

% of students receiving:
Full tuition waiver only: 0%
Assistantship/fellowship only: 14%
Both full tuition waiver & assistantship/fellowship: 90%

Approximate percentage of incoming students with a B.A./B.S. only: 30%   **Master's:** 70%

Approximate percentage of students who are
Women: 85% **Ethnic Minority:** 34% **International:** 0%

Average years to complete the doctoral program
(including internship): 6 years

Personal interview
Preferred in person but telephone acceptable

Attrition rate in past 7 years: 10%

Percentage of students applying for internship last
year accepted into APPIC or APA internships: 100%

Formal tracks/concentrations: none

Research areas	# Faculty	# Grants
adult attachment/adult survivors of childhood trauma	1	0
career counseling	2	0
cross-cultural counseling	1	—
children/adolescents disorders	1	1
gender identity in men	1	0
mental health policy	1	0
racial identity	2	1
group therapy	1	1

Clinical opportunities

child guidance center
family therapy
crisis intervention program
university counseling
   center
VA hospital
substance abuse
gerontology

chronic inpatient
behavioral medicine
forensics
posttraumatic stress
   disorder
school districts
medical schools
pediatric hospitals

Howard University (Ph.D.) (2008 data)

School of Education
2441 Fourth Street, NW
Washington DC 20059
phone#: (202) 806-7351 or (202) 806-7350
e-mail: adferguson@howard.edu
Web address: www.howard.edu/schooleducation/
Departments/HDPES/CPsychology/index.htm

1	2	3	**4**	5	6	7
Clinically oriented			Equal emphasis			Research oriented

Percentage of faculty subscribing to each of the
following orientations:

Psychodynamic/Psychoanalytic	0%
Applied behavioral analysis/Radical behavioral	0%
Family systems/Systems	0%
Existential/Phenomenological/Humanistic	50%
Cognitive/Cognitive-behavioral	50%

Courses required for incoming students to have
completed prior to enrolling:
Equivalent of Howard University Counseling Psychology
master's (48–52 credit hours) or undergraduate degree in
psychology.

Recommended but not mandatory courses:
Evaluated on a case-by-case basis based on above criteria.

GRE mean
Verbal 477.5   Quantitative 535
Analytical 506.5
Analytical Writing not reported

GPA mean
Overall master's GPA 3.8

Number of applications/admission offers/incoming
students in 2005
12 applied/5 admission offers/4 incoming

% of students receiving:
Full tuition waiver only: 2%
Assistantship/fellowship only: 2%
Both full tuition waiver & assistantship/fellowship: 2%

Approximate percentage of incoming students with a
B.A./B.S. only: 0%   **Master's:** 100%

Approximate percentage of students who are
Women: 95%   **Ethnic Minority:** 100%
International: not reported

Average years to complete the doctoral program
(including internship): 5 years

Personal interview
Required in person; but telephone acceptable for overseas
candidates

Attrition rate in past 7 years: not reported

Percentage of students applying for internship last
year accepted into APPIC or APA internships: 75%

Formal tracks/concentrations: none

Research areas	# Faculty	# Grants
addiction among African American and Bedouin Arabs	3	1
hope in counseling	1	0
multicultural competencies	1	1
racism stress	1	1
spirituality in counseling	2	0
videotapes in training	1	1
worldview, racial identity and self-efficacy	1	0

Clinical opportunities
Howard University (HU) Cancer Center
HU Center on Sickle Cell Anemia
HU Genome Center
HU Student Counseling Center

University of Illinois at Urbana–Champaign (Ph.D.)

Department of Educational Psychology
Champaign, IL 61820
phone#: (888) 843-3779
e-mail: hneville@uiuc.edu
Web address: education.illinois.edu/edpsy/areasofstudy/
counseling/index.html

1	2	3	4	5	**6**	7
Practice oriented			Equal emphasis			Research oriented

Percentage of faculty subscribing to each of the following orientations:

Psychodynamic/Psychoanalytic	0%
Applied behavioral analysis/Radical behavioral	0%
Family systems/Systems	0%
Existential/Phenomenological/Humanistic	0%
Cognitive/Cognitive-behavioral	0%
Eclectic	100%

Courses required for incoming students to have completed prior to enrolling: None

Recommended but not mandatory courses:
Undergraduate psychology degree

GRE mean
Verbal 560   Quantitative 655
Analytical Writing not reported

GPA mean
Overall GPA 3.557

Number of applications/admission offers/incoming students in 2009
91 applied/5 admission offers/4 incoming

% of students receiving:
Full tuition waiver only: 0%
Assistantship/fellowship only: 0%
Both full tuition waiver & assistantship/fellowship: 100%

Approximate percentage of incoming students who entered with a B.A./B.S. only: 75%   **Master's:** 25%

Approximate percentage of students who are Women: 75%   **Ethnic Minority:** 50%
International: not reported

Average years to complete the doctoral program (including internship): 6.5 years

Personal interview
Preferred in person but telephone acceptable

Attrition rate in past 7 years: not reported

Percentage of students applying for internship last year accepted into APPIC or APA internships: 100%

Formal tracks/concentrations: none

Research areas	# Faculty	# Grants
cancer control	1	1
cancer survivorship	1	1
eating disorders	1	0
ethnic/racial identity	2	0
Latina populations	1	1
personality assessment	1	1
racial and sexual violence	2	0
racism	2	3
vocational psychology	2	1

Clinical opportunities

child/adolescent	VA medical center
health psychology	medical/hospital
mental health counseling	community mental health
rehabilitation counseling	
undergraduate counseling	

Indiana University (Ph.D.)

Department of Counseling and Educational Psychology
Wright Education Building, Room 4003
Bloomington, IN 47405
phone#: (812) 856-8300
e-mail: cep@indiana.edu
Web address: http://education.indiana.edu/Default.
aspx?alias=education.indiana.edu/cep

1	2	3	**4**	5	6	7
Practice oriented			Equal emphasis			Research oriented

Percentage of faculty subscribing to each of the following orientations:

Psychodynamic/Psychoanalytic	0%
Applied behavioral analysis/Radical behavioral	0%
Family systems/Systems	30%
Existential/Phenomenological/Humanistic	30%
Cognitive/Cognitive-behavioral	40%

Courses required for incoming students to have completed prior to enrolling: None

Recommended but not mandatory courses:
Statistics and research methods

GRE mean
Verbal 600   Quantitative 614
Analytical Writing 4.81

GPA mean
Overall Undergraduate GPA 3.48
Overall Graduate GPA 3.87

Number of applications/admission offers/incoming students in 2009
11

% of students receiving:
Full tuition waiver only: 0%
Assistantship/fellowship only: 0%
Both full tuition waiver & assistantship/fellowship: 50%

Approximate percentage of incoming students with a B.A./B.S. only: 30%   **Master's:** 70%

Approximate percentage of incoming students who are Women: 75%   **Ethnic Minority:** 10%   **International:** 15%

Average years to complete the doctoral program (including internship): 4 years

Personal interview
Preferred in person but telephone acceptable

Attrition rate in past 7 years: 0%

Percentage of students applying for internship last year accepted into APPIC or APA internships: 100%

Formal tracks/concentrations: none

Research areas	# Faculty	# Grants
at-risk youth	0	2
elementary school counseling	0	1
group counseling	2	0
marriage/family counseling	2	3

299

multicultural counseling	3	1
women's vocational behavior	1	0
substance abuse and prevention	1	1

Clinical opportunities
Not reported

University of Iowa (Ph.D.)

Division of Psychological and Quantitative Foundations
Iowa City, IA 52242
phone#: (319) 335-5578
e-mail: william-liu@uiowa.edu
Web address: www2.education.uiowa.edu/pq/counspsy/
prospective-students/curriculum-phd.aspx

1	2	3	4	5	6	7
Practice oriented		Equal emphasis				Research oriented

Percentage of faculty subscribing to each of the following orientations:

Psychodynamic/Psychoanalytic	25%
Applied behavioral analysis/Radical behavioral	0%
Family systems/Systems	25%
Existential/Phenomenological/Humanistic	0%
Cognitive/Cognitive-behavioral	50%

Courses required for incoming students to have completed prior to enrolling:
None

Recommended but not mandatory courses:
As much core psychology as possible

GRE mean
Verbal 519   Quantitative 625
Analytical Writing 5.0

GPA mean
Overall GPA 3.58

Number of applications/admission offers/incoming students in 2009
90 applied/10 admission offers/10 incoming

% of students receiving:
Full tuition waiver only: 0%
Assistantship/fellowship only: 40%
Both full tuition waiver & assistantship/fellowship: 60%

Approximate percentage of incoming students with a B.A./B.S. only: 40%   Master's: 60%

Approximate percentage of students who are Women: 67%   Ethnic Minority: 35%   International: 2%

Average years to complete the doctoral program (including internship): 7 years

Personal interview
Interview required

Attrition rate in past 7 years: 10%

Percentage of students applying for internship last year accepted into APPIC or APA internships: 100%

Formal tracks/concentrations: none

Research areas	# Faculty	# Grants
child/adolescent health	1	1
college student suicide	1	0
ethics	2	1
multicultural	2	1
psychosocial oncology	2	1
public health	2	0
men	3	0
spirituality	2	0
mood and anxiety disorders	1	0
career	1	1

Clinical opportunities

community mental health	university counseling
hospitals	centers
specialty settings	VA medical center
prisons	women's center
public schools	homeless shelter

Iowa State University (Ph.D.)

Department of Psychology
Ames, IA 50011-3180
phone#: (515) 294-1743
e-mail: dvogel@iastate.edu
Web address: www.psychology.iastate.edu/index.
php?id=22

1	2	3	4	5	6	7
Practice oriented		Equal emphasis				Research oriented

Percentage of faculty subscribing to each of the following orientations:

Psychodynamic/Psychoanalytic	15%
Applied behavioral analysis/Radical behavioral	0%
Family systems/Systems	0%
Existential/Phenomenological/Humanistic	25%
Cognitive/Cognitive-behavioral	60%

Courses required for incoming students to have completed prior to enrolling:
A minimum of 15 credits in psychology, including statistics, psychological measurement, abnormal, developmental, social, and research methods

Recommended but not mandatory courses:
most successful applicants have a diversified psychology major

GRE mean
Verbal 560   Quantitative 700
Psychology Subject Test 690
Analytical Writing 5.0

GPA mean
Overall GPA 3.5   Psychology GPA 3.8
Junior/Senior GPA 3.8

Number of applications/admission offers/incoming students in 2009
38 applied/7 admission offers/4 incoming

% of students receiving:
Full tuition waiver only: 0%

Assistantship/fellowship only: 0%
Both full tuition waiver & assistantship/fellowship: 100%

Approximate percentage of incoming students with a B.A./B.S. only 50% **Master's:** 50%

Approximate percentage of students who are Women: 71% **Ethnic Minority:** 19%
International: 15%

Average years to complete the doctoral program (including internship): 5.5 years

Personal interview
Preferred in person but telephone acceptable

Attrition rate in past 7 years: 4%

Percentage of students applying for internship last year accepted into APPIC or APA internships: 100%

Formal tracks/concentrations: None

Research areas	# Faculty	# Grants
adult attachment	1	0
families/couples	2	1
discrimination	1	0
ethics and legal issues	1	0
forgiveness	1	1
gender roles	1	0
group therapy process/outcome	1	0
health psychology	1	1
help-seeking	1	0
multiculturalism	3	0
personality	1	0
psychology and religion	1	0
social support	1	0
stereotypes/stigma	1	0
supervision	1	0
women in science	1	1
vocational interest assessment	2	0

Clinical opportunities

ADHD assessment clinic	private group practices
community mental health center	university counseling center
corrections unit	VA medical center
mental health unit	Veteran's home

University of Kansas (Ph.D.)

Department of Psychology and Research in Education
Counseling Psychology Program
Lawrence, KS 66045
phone#: (785) 864-3931
e-mail: preadmit@ku.edu
Web address: soe.ku.edu/cpsy

1	2	3	**4**	5	6	7
Practice oriented		Equal emphasis			Research oriented	

Percentage of faculty subscribing to each of the following orientations:

Psychodynamic/Psychoanalytic	20%
Applied behavioral analysis/Radical behavioral	0%
Family systems/Systems	20%

Existential/Phenomenological/Humanistic	20%
Cognitive/Cognitive-behavioral	40%

Courses required for incoming students to have completed prior to enrolling: None

Recommended but not mandatory courses:
Basic courses in psychology (e.g., social, personality, abnormal, experimental, learning)

GRE mean
Verbal 528   Quantitative 535
Psychology Subject Test not required
Analytical Writing 4.9

GPA mean 3.51

Number of applications/admission offers/incoming students in 2009
63 applied/8 admission offers/5 incoming

% of students receiving:
Full tuition waiver only: 0%
Assistantship/fellowship only: 12%
Both full tuition waiver & assistantship/fellowship: 75%

Approximate percentage of incoming students with a B.A./B.S. only: 60% **Master's:** 40%

Approximate percentage of students who are Women: 80% **Ethnic Minority:** 20% **International:** 20%

Average years to complete the doctoral program (including internship): 6.1 years

Personal interview
Required in person or by phone

Attrition rate in past 7 years: 10%

Percentage of students applying for internship last year accepted into APPIC or APA internships: 78%

Formal tracks/concentrations: none

Research areas	# Faculty	# Grants
creativity	1	1
positive psychology	3	1
therapy outcome and process	1	0
vocational decision making	1	0
women and science careers	3	1

Clinical opportunities
Not reported

University of Kentucky (Ph.D.)

Department of Educational, School, and Counseling Psychology
Lexington, KY 40506-0017
phone#: (859) 257-7404
e-mail: RRemer@uky.edu
Web address: www.uky.edu/Education/EDP/counphd.html

1	2	3	4	5	**6**	7
Practice oriented		Equal emphasis			Research oriented	

Percentage of faculty subscribing to each of the following orientations:

Psychodynamic/Psychoanalytic 0%
Applied behavioral analysis/Radical behavioral 0%
Family systems/Systems 20%
Existential/Phenomenological/Humanistic 80%
Cognitive/Cognitive-behavioral 80%

Courses required for incoming students to have completed prior to enrolling: None

Recommended but not mandatory courses:
Prefer master's degree in behavioral science

GRE mean
Verbal + Quantitative 1100
Analytical Writing 5.0

GPA mean
Overall GPA 3.4   Psychology GPA 3.6
Junior/Senior GPA 3.5

Number of applications/admission offers/incoming students in 2009
48 applied/8 admission offers/5 incoming

% of students receiving:
Full tuition waiver only: 0%
Assistantship/fellowship only: 45%
Both full tuition waiver & assistantship/fellowship: 25%

Approximate percentage of incoming students with a B.A./B.S. only: 0%   **Master's:** 100%

Approximate percentage of students who are Women: 80%   **Ethnic Minority:** 25%   **International:** 0%

Average years to complete the doctoral program (including internship): 5.1 years

Personal interview
Preferred in person, but alternative (videotape, telephone) negotiable in exceptional circumstances

Attrition rate in past 7 years: 5%

Percentage of students applying for internship last year accepted into APPIC or APA internships: 100%

Formal tracks/concentrations: Each student required to create a specialization.

Research areas	# Faculty	# Grants
behavioral	2	1
family	2	0
gender	3	1
multicultural	4	0

Clinical opportunities

community mental health	residential treatment facility
counseling center	rural mental health centers
federal prison	VA hospital

———————————————

Lehigh University (Ph.D.)
Counseling Psychology
Bethlehem, PA 18015-4792
phone#: (610) 758-3250

e-mail: agia@lehigh.edu
Web address: www.lehigh.edu/education/cp/academic_programs/doctor_cp.html

1	2	3	4	5	**6**	7
Practice oriented		Equal emphasis				Research oriented

Percentage of faculty subscribing to each of the following orientations:

Psychodynamic/Psychoanalytic 25%
Applied behavioral analysis/Radical behavioral 0%
Family systems/Systems 25%
Existential/Phenomenological/Humanistic 25%
Cognitive/Cognitive-behavioral 25%

Courses required for incoming students to have completed prior to enrolling: Psychology related courses preferred

Recommended but not mandatory courses:
Psychology related

GRE mean
Verbal 531   Quantitative 531
Analytical Writing – not reported

GPA mean
Overall GPA 3.67

Number of applications/admission offers/incoming students in 2009
103 applied/10 admission offers/6 incoming

% of students receiving:
Full tuition waiver only: 0%
Assistantship/fellowship only: 15%
Both full tuition waiver & assistantship/fellowship: 75%

Approximate percentage of incoming students with a B.A./B.S. only: 33%   **Master's:** 67%

Approximate percentage of students who are Women: 90%   **Ethnic Minority:** 50%   **International:** 0

Average years to complete the doctoral program (including internship): 7 years

Personal interview:
Preferred in person but telephone acceptable

Attrition rate in past 7 years: 8%

Percentage of students applying for internship last year accepted into APPIC or APA internships: 100%

Formal tracks/concentrations: none

Research areas	# Faculty	# Grants
cross-cultural	4	1
family systems	2	—
supervision/training	2	1
vocational psychology	1	1

Clinical opportunities
counseling centers, mental health agencies, hospitals

Louisiana Tech University (Ph.D.)

Department of Psychology and Behavioral Sciences
P.O. Box 10048
Ruston, LA 71272
phone#: (318) 257-4315
e-mail: dthomas@latech.edu
Web address: www.latech.edu/tech/education/psychology/cphd/index.php

1	2	3	4	5	6	7
Practice oriented		Equal emphasis				Research oriented

Percentage of faculty subscribing to each of the following orientations:

Psychodynamic/Psychoanalytic	10%
Applied behavioral analysis/Radical behavioral	0%
Family systems/Systems	0%
Existential/Phenomenological/Humanistic	60%
Cognitive/Cognitive-behavioral	30%

Courses required for incoming students prior to enrolling: None

Courses recommended but not mandatory:
None

GRE mean
Verbal 540   Quantitative 580
Analytical Writing not used for admission purposes

GPA mean
Overall GPA 3.6

Number of applications/admission offers/incoming students in 2008
40 applied/14 admission offers/6 incoming

% of students receiving:
Full tuition waiver only: 0%
Assistantship/fellowship only: 90%
Both full tuition waiver & assistantship/fellowship: 10%

Approximate percentage of incoming students with a B.A./B.S. only: 30%   Master's: 70%

Approximate percentage of students who are
Women: 85%   Ethnic Minority: 15%   International: 0%

Average years to complete the doctoral program (including internship): 5–6 years

Personal interview
In-person interview strongly preferred; telephone acceptable

Attrition rate in past 7 years: 15%

Percentage of students applying for internship last year accepted into APPIC or APA internships: 86%

Formal tracks/concentrations: none

Research areas	# Faculty	# Grants
career development	3	0
personality testing	1	0
Reversal theory	1	0
child/adolescent/developmental	1	0
adaptation to blindness	1	0
achievement motivation	1	0
relationships & gender roles	1	0
body image	1	0
psychological reactance theory	1	0
sleep quality/difficulty/habits	1	0

Clinical opportunities

university counseling center	medical center
community health centers	prison settings
VA medical centers	children's home
in-house clinic	developmental center

University of Louisville (Ph.D.)

Department of Educational and Counseling Psychology
Louisville, KY 40292
phone#: (502) 852-0588
e-mail: mmleaco1@louisville.edu
Web address: www.louisville.edu/education/degrees/med-cps-cp.html

1	2	3	4	5	6	7
Practice oriented		Equal emphasis				Research oriented

Percentage of faculty subscribing to each of the following orientations:

Psychodynamic/Psychoanalytic	43%
Family systems/Systems	43%
Existential/Phenomenological/Humanistic	43%
Cognitive/Cognitive-behavioral	86%

Courses required for incoming students to have completed prior to enrolling:
abnormal, development, statistics or methodology, social

Recommended but not mandatory courses:
Core psychology

GRE mean
Verbal 568   Quantitative 658
Analytical Writing 4.0

GPA mean
Overall undergraduate GPA 3.62
Overall master's GPA 3.9

Number of applications/admission offers/incoming students in 2009
72 applied/7 admission offers/6 incoming

% of incoming students receiving:
Full tuition waiver only: 0%
Assistantship/fellowship only: 0%
Both full tuition waiver & assistantship/fellowship: 100%

Approximate percentage of incoming students with a B.A./B.S. only: 100%   Master's: 0% (Note: We accept post-master's level also)

Approximate percentage of students who are
Women: 75% Ethnic Minority: 12.5% International: 12.5%

Average years to complete the doctoral program (including internship): 5.2 years entering with master's; 7 years entering with bachelors

Personal interview
No preference given

Attrition rate in past 7 years: 17%

Percentage of students applying for internship last year accepted into APPIC or APA internships: 100%

Formal tracks/concentrations: none

Research areas	# Faculty	# Grants
forgiveness	1	0
suicide	2	0
adolescent depression	1	3
depression & health	1	0
bullying	1	0
adolescent development	2	0
religion & spirituality	2	0
GBLT	1	0
school adjustment/diverse populations	3	1
cross cultural competency	2	0
microaggression	1	0
couples counseling	1	0
meta-analysis	1	2
vocational psychology	2	0
international psychology	1	0
prevention-school based	3	2

Clinical opportunities

college counseling center	group interventions
developmental disabilities	healthy lifestyle/positive
child treatment	psychology
school-based services	prison settings
sex offender treatment	psychological assessment/
hospital based services	neuropsychology
health psychology	vocational psychology
ADHD	prevention services

Loyola University of Chicago (Ph.D.)

School of Education
820 North Michigan Avenue
Chicago, IL 60611
phone#: (312) 915-6311
e-mail: sbrown@luc.edu
(Dr. Steven Brown, Graduate Program Director)
Web address: www.luc.edu/education/programs/cpsy-phd_main.shtml

1	2	3	**4**	5	6	7
Practice oriented		Equal emphasis				Research oriented

Percentage of faculty subscribing to each of the following orientations:

Psychodynamic/Psychoanalytic	0%
Applied behavioral analysis/Radical behavioral	0%
Family systems/Systems	25%
Existential/Phenomenological/Humanistic	25%
Cognitive/Cognitive-behavioral	50%

Courses required for incoming students to have completed prior to enrolling:
Master's degree in counseling, psychology, or related field

Recommended but not mandatory courses: None

GRE mean
Verbal 620   Quantitative 600
Psychology Subject Test 550
Analytical Writing not reported

GPA mean
Overall GPA 3.5   Psychology GPA 3.8
Junior/Senior GPA 3.8

Number of applications/admission offers/incoming students in 2009
60 applied/5 admission offers/4 incoming

% of students receiving:
Full tuition waiver only: 0%
Assistantship/fellowship only: 0%
Both full tuition waiver & assistantship/fellowship: 100%

Approximate percentage of incoming students with a B.A./B.S. only: 0%   **Master's:** 100%

Approximate percentage of students who are Women: 78%   **Ethnic Minority:** 37%   **International:** .03%

Average years to complete the doctoral program (including internship): 6 years

Personal interview
Required in person

Attrition rate in past 7 years: 7%

Percentage of students applying for internship last year accepted into APPIC or APA internships: 100%

Formal tracks/concentrations: none

Research areas	# Faculty	# Grants
adolescent risk behavior	2	1
child/adolescent development	2	0
counseling process	1	0
multicultural counseling	2	0
vocational psychology	1	0

Clinical opportunities
hospitals
universities (counseling centers)
clinics

Marquette University (Ph.D.)

Department of Counselor Education & Counseling Psychology
150 Schroeder Health Sciences & Education Complex
Milwaukee, WI 53201-1881
phone#: (414) 288-5790
E-mail: coreen.bukowski@marquette.edu
Web address: www.marquette.edu/education/grad/cecp_doctorate.shtml

1	2	3	4	**5**	6	7
Practice oriented		Equal emphasis				Research oriented

Percentage of faculty subscribing to each of the following orientations:

Psychodynamic/Psychoanalytic	28%
Applied behavioral analysis/Radical behavioral	14%

Family systems/Systems	14%
Existential/Phenomenological/Humanistic	57%
Cognitive/Cognitive-behavioral	57%

Courses required for incoming students to have completed prior to enrolling: None

Recommended but not mandatory courses:
Psychology or counseling majors are recommended. Masters degree in counseling or closely-related field enhances application.

GRE mean
Verbal 520   Quantitative 660
Psychology Subject Test not required
Analytical Writing 5.0

GPA mean
Overall GPA 3.8

Number of applications/admission offers/incoming students in 2009
87 applied/7 admission offers/4 incoming

% of students receiving:
Full tuition waiver only: 0%
Assistantship/fellowship only: 2%
Both full tuition waiver & assistantship/fellowship: 100%

Approximate percentage of incoming students with a B.A./B.S. only: 0%   **Master's:** 100%

Approximate percentage of students who are Women: 25%   **Ethnic Minority:** 25%   **International:** 0%

Average years to complete the doctoral program (including internship): 6 years

Personal interview
Preferred in person but telephone acceptable

Attrition rate in past 7 years: 8%

Percentage of students applying for internship last year accepted into APPIC or APA internships: 87.5%

Formal tracks/concentrations: addiction-mental health, child/adolescent, multicultural counseling

Research areas	# Faculty	# Grants
addictions	1	4
child maltreatment	2	0
multicultural	4	0
parenting	1	3
program evaluation in education	2	1
psychotherapy process	3	0
strengths, optimal functioning	3	0
clinical supervision	2	0

Clinical opportunities

Addiction	co-occurring disorders
Dept. clinics	clinical supervision
diverse populations	university counseling
homelessness	department of corrections
trauma	community mental health
parenting	medical centers
childhood disorders	schools
health/medical psychology	community clinics
neuropsychology	vocational rehabilitation

University of Maryland College Park (Ph.D.)
Department of Psychology and College of Education
College Park, MD 20742
phone#: (301) 405-5865
e-mail: cgorham@psyc.umd.edu, boblent@umd.edu
Web address: www.bsos.umd.edu/psyc/counseling/counsel2.html

1	2	3	4	5	6	7
Practice oriented			Equal emphasis			Research oriented

Percentage of faculty subscribing to each of the following orientations:

Psychodynamic/Psychoanalytic	57%
Applied behavioral analysis/Radical behavioral	0%
Family systems/Systems	0%
Existential/Phenomenological/Humanistic	28%
Cognitive/Cognitive-behavioral	14%
Interpersonal	42%
Feminist	0%

Courses required for incoming students to have completed prior to enrolling:
We require a minimum of 15 credits of coursework in psychology, including statistics, and 3 additional courses (in areas such as theories of personality, developmental psychology, social psychology, or cognitive-behavioral psychology)

Recommended but not mandatory courses:
Statistics, core psychology

GRE mean
Verbal 621   Quantitative 693
Analytical Writing not reported

GPA mean
Overall Undergraduate GPA 3.59
Overall master's GPA 3.9

Number of applications/admission offers/incoming students in 2009
165 applied/5 admission offers/4 incoming

% of students receiving:
Full tuition waiver only: 0%
Assistantship/fellowship only: 0%
Both full tuition waiver & assistantship/fellowship: 100%

Approximate percentage of incoming students with a B.A./B.S. only: 50%   **Master's:** 50%

Approximate percentage of students who are Women: 71%   **Ethnic Minority:** 49%   **International:** 23%

Average years to complete the doctoral program (including internship): 6 years

Personal interview
Telephone required

Attrition rate in past 7 years: 3%

Percentage of students applying for internship last year accepted into APPIC or APA internships: 100%

Formal tracks/concentrations: none

Research areas	# Faculty	# Grants
AIDS/HIV	1	0
career counseling	3	0
career/vocational psychology	3	0
counseling process	3	0
counseling relationship	3	0
countertransference	2	0
domestic violence	1	0
dreams (their use in therapy)	1	0
health/well-being	2	0
interpersonal relationships	1	0
multicultural	3	0
supervision/training	3	0

Clinical opportunities

multicultural	consultation
group	career
individual	supervision

McGill University (Ph.D.)

Department of Educational and Counseling Psychology
Faculty of Education
3700 McTavish Street
Montreal, Quebec H3A 1Y2, Canada
phone#: (514) 398-4245
e-mail: ada.sinacore@mcgill.ca (program director)
carole.grossman@mcgill.ca (program advisor)
Web address: www.mcgill.ca/edu-ecp/prospective/
graduate/counselling/phd/

1	2	3	**4**	5	6	7
Practice oriented		Equal emphasis				Research oriented

Percentage of faculty subscribing to each of the following orientations:

Psychodynamic/Psychoanalytic	40%
Applied behavioral analysis/Radical behavioral	0%
Family systems/Systems	20%
Existential/Phenomenological/Humanistic	60%
Cognitive/Cognitive-behavioral	60%
Feminist/multicultural	40%

Courses required for incoming students to have completed prior to enrolling:
Forty-two credits in the following core areas: biological, sociological and cognitive-affective domains, developmental psychology, history and systems of psychology, psychological measurement and assessment, research methods, statistics, personality and psychopathology

Recommended but not mandatory courses:
None

GRE mean
Not reported

GPA mean
Overall GPA 3.7

Number of applications/admission offers/incoming students in 2009
17 applied/7 admission offers/6 incoming
16 applied/4 admission offers/4 incoming

% of students receiving:
Full tuition waiver only: 0%
Assistantship/fellowship only: 100%
Both full tuition waiver & assistantship/fellowship: 0%

Approximate percentage of incoming students with a B.A./B.S. only: 0%   **Master's:** 100%

Approximate percentage of students who are Women: 75%   **Ethnic Minority:** this type of data is not collected in Canada **International:** not reported

Average years to complete the doctoral program (including internship): 7 years

Personal interview
Preferred in person but telephone acceptable

Attrition rate in past 7 years: 22%

Percentage of students applying for internship last year accepted into APPIC or APA internships: 40%

Formal tracks/concentrations: psychotherapy, multiculturalism, supervision, health psychology

Research areas	# Faculty	# Grants
development and training	1	0
feminism multicultural pedagogy	2	0
psychotherapy	2	2

Clinical opportunities

behavioral therapy clinic	psychiatry clinic
children's behavior clinic	psychotherapy clinic
eating disorders	

University of Memphis (Ph.D.)

Department of Counseling, Educational Psychology and Research
Ball Education Building, Room 100
Memphis, TN 38152
phone#: (901) 678-2841
e-mail: slease@memphis.edu
Web address: http://www.memphis.edu/cepr/counseling-psychology.htm

1	2	3	**4**	5	6	7
Practice oriented		Equal emphasis				Research oriented

Percentage of faculty subscribing to each of the following orientations:

Psychodynamic/Psychoanalytic	0%
Applied behavioral analysis/Radical behavioral	0%
Family systems/Systems	60%
Existential/Phenomenological/Humanistic	60%
Cognitive/Cognitive-behavioral	60%
Feminist	20%
Constructivist	40%

Courses required for incoming students to have completed prior to enrolling:
Master's degree in counseling, psychology, or related field. Must have theories of counseling, group counseling, career counseling, statistics/research, practicum.

Recommended but not mandatory courses:
Psychological assessment, psychopathology

GRE mean–incoming 2009 students
Verbal 523   Quantitative 626
Analytical Writing not used

GPA mean incoming students
Overall Graduate GPA 3.85   Undergraduate GPA 3.20

Number of applications/admission offers/incoming students in 2009
applied not reported/admission offers not reported/
45 applications/13 offers/8 incoming

% of students receiving:
Full tuition waiver only: 0%
Assistantship/fellowship only: 0%
Both full tuition waiver & assistantship/fellowship: 100%

Approximate percentage of incoming students with a B.A./B.S. only: 0%   **Master's:** 100%

Approximate percentage of students who are Women: 66%   **Ethnic Minority:** 14%   **International:** 8%

Average years to complete the doctoral program (including internship): 4.5 years

Personal interview
Preferred in person but telephone acceptable

Attrition rate in past 7 years: 3.7%

Percentage of students applying for internship last year accepted into APPIC or APA internships: 100%

Formal tracks/concentrations: diversity, international studies

Research areas	# Faculty	# Grants
AIDS/HIV counseling	1	0
at-risk families and children	1	1
consultation	1	0
gays, lesbians, and bisexuals	3	1
disabled persons	3	1
human sexuality	1	0
international psychology	2	1
masculinity	2	0
multicultural counseling	3	0
psychological resources	1	0
vocational psychology	2	1
health psychology	1	0

Clinical opportunities (all the following are clinical opportunities for our students)
children/adolescents
couples/families
university students
community mental health
inpatient
outpatient
neuropsychological assessment
vocational/learning disability assessment
Veterans Affairs Medical Center (substance abuse, PTSD, spinal cord injury)
domestic violence (perpetrators and survivors)
forensic psychology

University of Miami (Ph.D.)
Department of Educational and Psychological Studies
P.O. Box 248065
Coral Gables, FL 33124-2040
phone#: (305) 284-3711
e-mail: blewis@miami.edu
Web address: www.education.miami.edu/program/
Programs.asp?Program_ID=47

1	2	3	4	5	6	7
Practice oriented			Equal emphasis			Research oriented

Percentage of faculty subscribing to each of the following orientations:

Psychodynamic/Psychoanalytic	14%
Applied behavioral analysis/Radical behavioral	0%
Family systems/Systems	50%
Existential/Phenomenological/Humanistic	20%
Cognitive/Cognitive-behavioral	60%

Courses required for incoming students to have completed prior to enrolling:
Standard curriculum for master's in counseling

Recommended but not mandatory courses: None

GRE mean
Verbal 561   Quantitative 632
Analytical Writing not reported

GPA mean
Overall GPA 3.5   Psychology GPA N/A

Number of applications/admission offers/incoming students in 2008
114 applied/10 admission offers/7 incoming

% of students receiving:
Full tuition waiver only: 0%
Assistantship/fellowship only: 0%
Both full tuition waiver & assistantship/fellowship: 100%

Approximate percentage of incoming students with a B.A./B.S. only: 14%   **Master's:** 86%

Approximate percentage of students who are Women: 77%   **Ethnic Minority:** 43%
International: not reported

Average years to complete the doctoral program (including internship): 6 years

Personal interview
Preferred in person but telephone acceptable

Attrition rate in past 7 years: 14.5%

Percentage of students applying for internship last year accepted into APPIC or APA internships: 100%

Formal tracks/concentrations: multicultural counseling, health psychology, family therapy

Research areas	# Faculty	# Grants
couple violence	1	0
ethnic minorities	3	1
families	3	1
health psychology	3	1

Clinical opportunities
Tailored to students' interests

University of Minnesota–Department of Educational Psychology (Ph.D.)

Counseling and Student Personnel Psychology
250 Education Sciences Building
56 East River Road
Minneapolis, MN 55455
phone#: (612) 624-6827
e-mail: cspp@umn.edu
Web address: education.umn.edu/EdPsych/CSPP/

1	2	3	4	5	6	7
Practice oriented		Equal emphasis				Research oriented

Percentage of faculty subscribing to each of the following orientations:

Psychodynamic/Psychoanalytic	25%
Applied behavioral analysis/Radical behavioral	10%
Family systems/Systems	30%
Existential/Phenomenological/Humanistic	60%
Cognitive/Cognitive-behavioral	60%

Courses required for incoming students to have completed prior to enrolling: None

Recommended but not mandatory courses:
Foundational courses in undergraduate psychology

GRE mean
Verbal 558   Quantitative 686
Analytical Writing 5

GPA mean
Overall GPA 3.76

Number of applications/admission offers/incoming students in 2009
69 applied/10 admission offers/7 incoming

% of students receiving:
Full tuition waiver only: 0%
Assistantship/fellowship only: 0%
Both full tuition waiver & assistantship/fellowship: 100%

Approximate percentage of incoming students with a B.A./B.S. only: 10%   **Master's:** 90%

Approximate percentage of students who are Women: 68% **Ethnic Minority:** 25% **International:** 27%

Average years to complete the doctoral program (including internship): 6.5 years

Personal interview
Interview not required

Attrition rate in past 7 years: 14.5%

Percentage of students applying for internship last year accepted into APPIC or APA internships: 100%

Formal tracks/concentrations: none

Research areas	# Faculty	# Grants
burnout prevention	2	0
career development	2	4
genetic counseling	1	1
high-risk adolescents	2	1
international counseling	4	1
master therapist	2	1
multicultural counseling	4	4
multicultural integrative therapy	1	0
prevention	1	1
school counseling	3	2
supervision	2	1
therapist development	2	2
therapy outcome	1	0

Clinical opportunities
Multiple practicum sites in the Twin Cities

University of Minnesota–Department of Psychology (Ph.D.)

75 East River Road
Minneapolis, MN 55455
phone#: (612) 625-3873
e-mail: counpsy@umn.edu
Web address: www.psych.umn.edu/areas/counseling/index.htm

1	2	3	4	5	6	7
Practice oriented		Equal emphasis				Research oriented

Percentage of faculty subscribing to each of the following orientations:

Psychodynamic/Psychoanalytic	33%
Applied behavioral analysis/Radical behavioral	0%
Family systems/Systems	0%
Existential/Phenomenological/Humanistic	0%
Cognitive/Cognitive-behavioral	66%

Courses required for incoming students to have completed prior to enrolling:
Broad base of scientific training in psychology with a background in statistics

Recommended but not mandatory courses:
See above

GRE mean (for those offered admissions)
Verbal 574   Quantitative 734
Psychology Subject Test not required
Analytical Writing 4.9

GPA mean (for those offered admissions)
Overall GPA 3.75   Psychology GPA 3.93

Number of applications/admission offers/incoming students in 2008
80 applied/5 admission offers/2 incoming

% of students receiving:
Full tuition waiver only: 0%
Assistantship/fellowship only: 0%
Both full tuition waiver & assistantship/fellowship: 100%

Approximate percentage of incoming students with a B.A./B.S. only: 100%   **Master's:** 0%

Approximate percentage of students who are
Women: 81% **Ethnic Minority:** 27% **International:** 19%

Average years to complete the doctoral program
(including internship): 6 years

Personal interview
Interview not required

Attrition rate in past 7 years: 7%

Percentage of students applying for internship last year accepted into APPIC or APA internships: 100%

Formal tracks/concentrations: none

Research areas	# Faculty	# Grants
acculturation	1	1
career development and choice	1	1
coping with stressful life events	1	1
cultural socialization	1	1
ethnic and racial identity	1	2
interest measurement	1	1
international adoption	1	1
interpersonal relations	1	0
interventions with returning veterans	1	1
interventions with sexual assault survivors in the ER	1	1
multicultural counseling	1	0
occupational health psychology	1	0
stressful life events	1	0
perceived control over stressful life events	1	0
personality and adjustment	1	0
posttraumatic growth	1	0
Posttraumatic Stress Disorder	1	0
racism and discrimination	1	2
refugee mental health	1	1
reintegration issues among returning veterans	1	1
sexual assault recovery	1	1
values and work adjustment	1	0

Clinical opportunities
We use about 30 locations as practica and advanced practica locations. The sites are matched with students' interests.

University of Missouri–Columbia (Ph.D.)

Educational, School, and Counseling Psychology
Columbia, MO 65211-2130
phone#: (573) 882-7731
e-mail: HeppnerM@Missouri.edu
Web address: education.missouri.edu/ESCP/
program_areas/counseling_psychology/index.php

1	2	3	4	5	6	7
Practice oriented		Equal emphasis				Research oriented

Percentage of faculty subscribing to each of the following orientations:

Psychodynamic/Psychoanalytic	10%
Family systems/Systems	30%
Existential/Phenomenological/Humanistic	50%
Cognitive/Cognitive-behavioral	50%
Interpersonal	30%
Feminist	30%

Courses required for incoming students to have completed prior to enrolling:
If entering without a master's degree, 15 hours of prerequisite course work, including statistics, personality, social, and developmental

Recommended but not mandatory courses:
None

GRE mean
Verbal 515   Quantitative 660
Analytical Writing not reported
Psychology Subject Test not reported

GPA mean
Overall GPA 3.5

Number of applications/admission offers/incoming students in 2009
102 applied/7 admission offers/7 incoming

% of students receiving:
Full tuition waiver only: 0%
Assistantship/fellowship only: 0%
Both full tuition waiver & assistantship/fellowship: 100%

Approximate percentage of incoming students with a B.A./B.S. only: 10%–typical   **Master's:** 90%–typical, though most recent was 100%

Approximate percentage of students who are
Women: 100% **Ethnic Minority:** 28% **International:** 42%

Average years to complete the doctoral program
(including internship): 6 years

Personal interview
Students are phone interviewed and then invited to come to campus for a visitation where they can meet and interact with our faculty and other students.

Attrition rate in past 7 years: 7%

Percentage of students applying for internship last year accepted into APPIC or APA internships: 100%

Formal tracks/concentrations: multicultural minor; teaching minor; statistics minor, sports psychology, career development

Research areas	# Faculty	# Grants
addictions	2	0
African American adolescents	1	2
career development	5	2
counseling process	3	2
counseling supervision	2	1
counseling/therapy integration	1	0
disability	1	0
eating disorders	1	1
gender	2	0
group process	2	1
health psychology	2	1
identity development	1	0
multicultural counseling	5	2
perfectionism	1	0

problem solving	3	2
rape	1	1
scale construction	4	3

Clinical opportunities

cognitive-behavioral
family counseling center
learning disabilities clinic
rural community mental
  health centers
psychiatric clinic
psychology clinic
rehabilitation
state hospital

state prison
university/college
  counseling centers
university career center
university medical clinics
VA hospital
women's center
women's shelters

University of Missouri–Kansas City (Ph.D.)

Division of Counseling, Educational Psychology,
and Exercise Science
School of Education, Room 215
5100 Rockhill Road
Kansas City, MO 64110
phone#: (816) 235-2722
e-mail: umkccepsy@umkc.edu
Web address: http://education.umkc.edu/programs/view/18

1	2	3	4	5	6	7
Practice oriented		Equal emphasis				Research oriented

Percentage of faculty subscribing to each of the following orientations:

Psychodynamic/Psychoanalytic	10%
Applied behavioral analysis/Radical behavioral	5%
Family systems/Systems	20%
Existential/Phenomenological/Humanistic	25%
Cognitive/Cognitive-behavioral	40%

Courses required for incoming students to have completed prior to enrolling:

Undergraduate psychology major or master's degree in counseling or psychology

Recommended but not mandatory courses:
None

GRE mean
Verbal + Quantitative 1073

GPA mean
3.44

Number of applications/admission offers/incoming students in 2008
69 applied/7 admission offers/7 incoming

Percentage of students receiving:
Full tuition waiver only: 0%
Assistantship/fellowship only: 0%
Both full tuition waiver & assistantship/fellowship: 100%

Approximate percentage of incoming students with a B.A./B.S. only: 52%   Master's: 48% (Approximate for last five years only)

Approximate percentage of students who are
Women: 77.5%   **Ethnic Minority:** 32.5%
International: 2.5%

Average years to complete the doctoral program (including internship): 6 years

Personal interview
Preferred in person but telephone acceptable

Attrition rate in past 7 years: not reported

Percentage of students applying for internship last year accepted into APPIC or APA internships: 100%

Formal tracks/concentrations: none

Research areas	# Faculty	# Grants
cross-cultural counseling	5	1
family systems theory	2	0
interpersonal relations	3	0
professional issues	3	0
psychopathology prevention	3	0
psychotherapy process	3	0
sports psychology	1	0
stress and coping	1	0
supervision	2	0
vocational interests	3	0

Clinical opportunities
Not reported

University of Nebraska–Lincoln (Ph.D.)

Department of Educational Psychology
38 Teachers College Hall
Lincoln, NE 68588-0345
phone#: (402) 472-0573
e-mail: mscheel2@unl.edu
Web address: cehs.unl.edu/edpsych/graduate/copsych.shtml

1	2	3	4	5	6	7
Practice oriented		Equal emphasis				Research oriented

Percentage of faculty subscribing to each of the following orientations:

Psychodynamic/Psychoanalytic	20%
Applied behavioral analysis/Radical behavioral	0%
Family systems/Systems	20%
Existential/Phenomenological/Humanistic	20%
Cognitive/Cognitive-behavioral	40%

Courses required for incoming students to have completed prior to enrolling:
Bachelor's in a closely related area or master's in counseling or closely related field

Recommended but not mandatory courses:
None

GRE mean
Verbal 471   Quantitative 546

GPA mean
Overall GPA 3.5

Number of applications/admission offers/incoming students in 2009
75 applied/19 admission offers/15 incoming

% of students receiving:
Full tuition waiver only: 0%
Assistantship/fellowship only: 0%
Both full tuition waiver & assistantship/fellowship: 30%

Approximate percentage of incoming students with a B.A./B.S. only: 70%   **Master's:**30%

Approximate percentage of students who are Women: 77%   **Ethnic Minority:** 20%   **International:** 3%

Average years to complete the doctoral program (including internship): 5 years

Personal interview
Preferred in person but telephone acceptable

Attrition rate in past 7 years: not reported

Percentage of students applying for internship last year accepted into APPIC or APA internships: 100%

Formal tracks/concentrations: multicultural counseling; gender; couple and family counseling

Research areas	# Faculty	# Grants
family counseling	1	0
multicultural	3	0
gender	2	0
vocational	3	0
immigrant and refugees	1	0
psychotherapy process	1	0

Clinical opportunities
couple and family counseling
health psychology
multicultural counseling
psychological assessment
vocational counseling
immigrants and refugees
adolescence in schools

New Mexico State University (Ph.D.)
Department of Counseling and Educational Psychology
MSC 3CEP
P.O. Box 30001
Las Cruces, NM 88003-8001
phone#: (505) 646-2121
e-mail: eadams@nmsu.edu
Web address: education.nmsu.edu/cep/phd/index.html

1	2	3	4	5	6	7
Practice oriented			Equal emphasis			Research oriented

Percentage of faculty subscribing to each of the following orientations:
Psychodynamic/Psychoanalytic 22%
Applied behavioral analysis/Radical behavioral 0%
Family systems/Systems 11%
Existential/Phenomenological/Humanistic 33%
Cognitive/Cognitive-behavioral 22%

Courses required for incoming students to have completed prior to enrolling: None

Recommended but not mandatory courses:
Counseling practicum, human development, multicultural, counseling theory and techniques, family therapy, group work, career/life planning, counseling research, diagnosis, addictions

GRE mean
Verbal + Quantitative 1000
Analytical Writing 4.5

GPA mean
Master's GPA 3.76

Number of applications/admission offers/incoming students in 2009
65 applied/13 admission offers/6 incoming

% of students receiving:
Full tuition waiver only: 0%
Assistantship/fellowship only: 80%
Both full tuition waiver & assistantship/fellowship: 20%

Approximate percentage of incoming students with a B.A./B.S. only: 0%   **Master's:** 100%

Approximate percentage of students who are Women: 54%   **Ethnic Minority:** 46%   **International:** 4%

Average years to complete the doctoral program (including internship): 5 years

Personal interview
Preferred in person but telephone acceptable

Attrition rate in past 7 years: 8%

Percentage of students applying for internship last year accepted into APPIC or APA internships: 93%

Formal tracks/concentrations: multicultural counseling, supervision/training, health psychology

Research areas	# Faculty	# Grants
acculturation	3	0
career	2	0
family systems	1	0
gender	3	0
social identity	3	0
multicultural curriculum development	1	0
interpersonal relationship enhancement	1	1
health psychology	1	1
LGBT	3	1

Clinical opportunities
community organizations
departmental training center
families
groups
low income
medically underserved minorities
rural
substance abuse
university counseling center
vocational career development

New York University (Ph.D.)
Department of Applied Psychology
East Building, 4th Floor

239 Greene Street
New York, NY 10003
phone#: (212) 998-5559
e-mail: mm13@nyu.edu
Web address: steinhardt.nyu.edu/appsych/phd/
counseling_psychology

1	2	3	4	5	6	7
Practice oriented			Equal emphasis			Research oriented

Percentage of faculty subscribing to each of the following orientations:

Psychodynamic/Psychoanalytic	44%
Applied behavioral analysis/Radical behavioral	14%
Family systems/Systems	14%
Existential/Phenomenological/Humanistic	14%
Cognitive/Cognitive-behavioral	14%

Courses required for incoming students to have completed prior to enrolling:

18 credits of prerequisites in psychology at undergraduate or graduate level. Not necessary to complete prerequisites before enrollment.

Recommended but not mandatory courses:

Basic areas in psychology course work

GRE mean

Verbal + Quantitative 1348

GPA mean

Overall GPA 3.48

Number of applications/admission offers/incoming students in 2009

189 applied/6 admission offers/5 incoming

% of students receiving:

Full tuition waiver only: 0%
Assistantship/fellowship only: 0%
Both full tuition waiver & assistantship/fellowship: 100%

Approximate percentage of incoming students with a B.A./B.S. only: 40%   Master's: 60%

Approximate percentage of students who are Women: 20%   Ethnic Minority: 20%
International: not reported

Average years to complete the doctoral program (including internship): 7 years

Personal interview
Required

Attrition rate in past 7 years: 5%

Percentage of students applying for internship last year accepted into APPIC or APA internships: 50%

Formal tracks/concentrations: none

Research areas	# Faculty	# Grants
group process	1	0
multicultural counseling	2	0
psychoanalytic constructs	1	0
psychopathology and differential diagnosis	2	0
religion and spirituality	1	1

women's development/health	2	2
work as a developmental context	1	0
LGBT	1	1
positive psychology	1	1

Clinical opportunities

Wide range of specialized practica and externship sites are available in the New York metropolitan area

University of North Dakota (Ph.D.)

Department of Counseling Psychology and Community Services
290 Centennial Drive, Stop 8255
Grand Forks, ND 58202-8255
phone#: (701) 777-2729
fax#: (701) 777-3184
e-mail: cl.juntunen@und.edu
Web address: www.counseling.und.edu

1	2	3	4	5	6	7
Practice oriented			Equal emphasis			Research oriented

Percentage of faculty subscribing to each of the following orientations:

Psychodynamic/Psychoanalytic	30%
Applied behavioral analysis/Radical behavioral	0%
Family systems/Systems	20%
Existential/Phenomenological/Humanistic	40%
Cognitive/Cognitive-behavioral	50%
Feminist	50%

Courses required for incoming students to have completed prior to enrolling:

20 semester hours of undergraduate psychology including statistics, research methods, abnormal, developmental, personality (for both post-Master's and post-baccalaureate applicants)

Recommended but not mandatory courses:

Research methods, master's level practicum, 60 hours supervised practice (for post-master's applicants)

GRE mean

Verbal 545   Quantitative 590
Analytical Writing 4.8

GPA mean

Overall 3.7

Number of applications/admission offers/incoming students in 2009

38 applied/11 admission offers/8 incoming

% of students receiving:

Full tuition waiver only: 0%
Assistantship/fellowship only: 0%
Both full tuition waiver & assistantship/fellowship: 100%

Approximate percentage of incoming students with a B.A./B.S. only: 25%   Master's: 75%

Approximate percentage of students who are Women: 75%   Ethnic Minority: 20%   International: 8%

Average years to complete the doctoral program (including internship): 5 years

Personal interview
Preferred in person but telephone acceptable

Attrition rate in past 7 years: 7%

Percentage of students applying for internship last year accepted into APPIC or APA internships: 100%

Formal tracks/concentrations: none

Research areas	# Faculty	# Grants
body image	1	0
career development	1	0
deployment/military psychology	2	1
domestic violence	1	0
gay, lesbian, bisexual	2	1
geriatric psychology	1	1
group identity development	1	0
healthy relationships	1	1
HIV prevention	1	1
multicultural counseling	1	0
Native American career development	1	0
poverty	1	0
rural mental health	2	0
student self-efficacy	1	0
supervisor strategies	2	0
vocational interests testing	1	0
white privilege	1	0
women/career development	1	0

Clinical opportunities
variety of community and academic settings, including university counseling centers, hospitals, and community mental health agencies, with both psychotherapy and assessment services

University of North Texas (Ph.D.)
Department of Psychology
P.O. Box 311280
Denton, TX 76203-3587
phone#: (940) 565-2671
e-mail: amy.mayfield@unt.edu
Web address: www.psyc.unt.edu/gradcounseling.shtml

1	2	3	**4**	5	6	7
Practice oriented		Equal emphasis				Research oriented

Percentage of faculty subscribing to each of the following orientations:

Psychodynamic/Psychoanalytic	40%
Applied behavioral analysis/Radical behavioral	0%
Family systems/Systems	40%
Existential/Phenomenological/Humanistic	40%
Cognitive/Cognitive-behavioral	30%

Courses required for incoming students to have completed prior to enrolling:
Statistics and three of the following: experimental, cognition, learning, perception, motivation, physiological, psychological measurement, or research thesis

GRE mean
Verbal 521   Quantitative 615   Writing 4.5

GPA mean
Overall GPA 3.6

Number of applications/admission offers/incoming students in 2009
71 applied/12 admission offers/8 incoming

% of students receiving:
Full tuition waiver only: 0%
Assistantship/fellowship only: 88%
Both full tuition waiver & assistantship/fellowship: 12%

Approximate percentage of incoming students with a B.A./B.S. only: 75%   **Master's:** 25%

Approximate percentage of students who are Women: 75%   **Ethnic Minority:** 12%   **International:** 0%

Average years to complete the doctoral program (including internship): 6.5 years

Personal interview
Preferred in person but telephone may be acceptable in certain circumstances

Attrition rate in past 7 years: 9%

Percentage of students applying for internship last year accepted into APPIC or APA internships: 88%

Formal tracks/concentrations: marriage & family, aging, sport psychology

Research areas	# Faculty	# Grants
ADHD treatment	2	1
counseling and therapy	1	1
eating disorders	3	0
gerontology	1	0
marriage and family	3	2
minority and cross-cultural	2	0
professional issues	3	0
sports psychology	2	1
vocational development	3	0

Clinical opportunities
On-campus psychology clinic
University counseling and testing services
External agencies after completion of internal practicum requirements

University of Northern Colorado (Ph.D.)
School of Applied Psychology and Counselor Education
248 McKee Hall, Campus Box 131
Greeley, CO 80639
phone#: (970) 351-1631
e-mail: basilia.softas-nail@unco.edu
Web address: www.unco.edu/cebs/counspsych/

1	2	**3**	4	5	6	7
Practice oriented		Equal emphasis				Research oriented

Percentage of faculty subscribing to each of the following orientations:

Psychodynamic/Psychoanalytic	20%
Applied behavioral analysis/Radical behavioral	10%

Family systems/Systems	20%
Existential/Phenomenological/Humanistic	20%
Cognitive/Cognitive-behavioral	30%

Courses required for incoming students to have completed prior to enrolling:
Either a bachelor's or master's degree in psychology or a closely related field.

Recommended but not mandatory courses: none

GRE mean
Verbal 550   Quantitative 570
Recommended GRE total 1000
Analytical Writing 5.0

GPA mean
Overall GPA 3.65

Number of applications/admission offers/incoming students in 2009
86 applied/12admission offers/7 incoming

% of students receiving:
Full tuition waiver only: 15%
Assistantship/fellowship only: 70%
Both full tuition waiver & assistantship/fellowship: 15%

Approximate percentage of incoming students with a B.A./B.S. only: 25% **Master's:** 75%

Approximate percentage of students who are Women: 75% **Ethnic Minority:** 15% **International:** 10%

Average years to complete the doctoral program (including internship): 4–5 years

Personal interview
Preferred in person but video-taped responses to interview questions is acceptable.

Attrition rate in past 7 years: 12%

Percentage of students applying for internship last year accepted into APPIC or APA internships: 100%

Formal tracks/concentrations: none

Research areas	# Faculty	# Grants
child psychology	8	2
college student adjustment	2	0
counseling process	3	0
eating disorders	2	0
family dynamics	4	1
multicultural	6	0

Clinical opportunities

clinical hypnosis	group therapy
cognitive/academic assessment	play therapy (students can fulfill didactic requirements for RPT)
personality assessment	
neuropsychological assessment	clinical supervision (individual, group, CFT, and Play therapy)
individual therapy	
couples and family therapy	

University of Notre Dame (Ph.D.)
Department of Psychology

Notre Dame, IN 46556-5636
phone#: (574) 631-4501
fax#: (574) 631-8883
e-mail: Stewart47@nd.edu
Web address: psychology.nd.edu/graduate-studies/

1	2	3	4	5	6	7
Practice oriented			Equal emphasis			Research oriented

Percentage of faculty subscribing to each of the following orientations:

Psychodynamic/Psychoanalytic	0%
Applied behavioral analysis/Radical behavioral	10%
Family systems/Systems	20%
Existential/Phenomenological/Humanistic	10%
Cognitive/Cognitive-behavioral	60%

Courses required for incoming students to have completed prior to enrolling:
Undergraduate psychology major, statistics, research methods, and research experience

Recommended but not mandatory courses: Biology, Tests & Measurement, Abnormal Psychology, Psychology of Personality, Introduction to Clinical Psychology

GRE mean
Verbal + Quantitative 1250

GPA mean
Overall GPA 3.7   Psychology GPA 3.7

Number of applications/admission offers/incoming students in 2009
91 applied/5 admission offers/3 incoming

% of students receiving:
Full tuition waiver only: 0%
Assistantship/fellowship only: 0%
Both full tuition waiver & assistantship/fellowship: 100%

Approximate percentage of incoming students with a B.A./B.S. only: 100% **Master's:** 0%

Approximate percentage of students who are Women: 76% **Ethnic Minority:** 32% **International:** 12%

Average years to complete the doctoral program (including internship): 7 years

Personal interview
Preferred in person but telephone acceptable

Attrition rate in past 7 years: 19%

Percentage of students applying for internship last year accepted into APPIC or APA internships: 63%

Formal tracks/concentrations: none

Research areas	# Faculty	# Grants
behavioral medicine	1	1
health psychology	1	1
marital interaction	1	1
multicultural	2	1
narrative psychology	1	1
social/clinical interface	2	0
depression	3	1

Clinical opportunities

juvenile justice center	community outpatient hospital
community mental health center	university counseling center
legal aid clinic	

University of Oklahoma (Ph.D.)

Department of Educational Psychology
Norman, OK 73019-0260
phone#: (405) 325-5974
e-mail: dbeesley@ou.edu or gpoedpsych@ou.edu
Web address: www.ou.edu/content/education/
departments/edpy/programs/counseling-psychology.html

1	2	3	4	5	6	7
Practice oriented		Equal emphasis				Research oriented

Percentage of faculty subscribing to each of the following orientations:

Psychodynamic/Psychoanalytic	28%
Family systems/Systems	43%
Existential/Phenomenological/Humanistic	14%
Cognitive/Cognitive-behavioral	43%
Relational/Process Oriented	43%
Feminist	14%
Narrative	14%

Courses required for incoming students to have completed prior to enrolling:
Algebra, 2 semesters of English grammar and composition, 18 semester hours in psychology or related area

Recommended but not mandatory courses:
None

GRE mean
Verbal 591   Quantitative 637 Analytical 4.7

GPA mean
Overall 3.91

Number of applications/admission offers/incoming students in 2009
68 applied/7 admission offers/7 incoming

% of students receiving:
Full tuition waiver only: 0%
Assistantship/fellowship only: 0%
Both full tuition waiver & assistantship/fellowship: 100%

Approximate percentage of incoming students with a B.A./B.S. only: 14%   **Master's:** 86%

Approximate percentage of students who are Men: 57%   **Women:** 43%   **Ethnic Minority:** 29%
International: 0%

Average years to complete the doctoral program (including internship): 5 years

Personal interview
Preferred in person but telephone acceptable

Attrition rate in past 7 years: 5%

Percentage of students applying for internship last year accepted into APPIC or APA internships: 78%

Formal tracks/concentrations: marriage and family

Research areas	# Faculty	# Grants
American Indians	2	0
assessment	2	0
career	1	0
child treatment	4	0
clinical supervision	1	0
relational health	2	0
trauma/violence	2	0
at-risk youth/delinquency	2	0
counseling process and outcomes	2	0
ecopsychology	1	0
gender	3	0
ethics	1	0
health psychology	1	0
spirituality	2	0
marriage and family	1	0
multicultural counseling	5	0
narrative	1	0

Clinical opportunities

child abuse and neglect	Indian health service clinics
child study center	psychiatric hospitals
community mental health	rehabilitation clinics
correctional facilities	university counseling centers
health sciences center/ medical clinics	VA hospital
psychological and neuro-psychological assessment	schools

Oklahoma State University (Ph.D.)

School of Applied Health and Educational Psychology
434 Willard Hall
Stillwater, OK 74078
phone#: (405) 744-6040
e-mail: sue.c.jacobs@okstate.edu
Web address: education.okstate.edu/index.php/academic-units/school-of-applied-health-a-educational-psychology/counseling-psychology

1	2	3	4	5	6	7
Practice oriented		Equal emphasis				Research oriented

Percentage of faculty subscribing to each of the following orientations:

Psychodynamic/Psychoanalytic	10%
Applied behavioral analysis/Radical behavioral	0%
Family systems/Systems	20%
Existential/Phenomenological/Humanistic	40%
Cognitive/Cognitive-behavioral	30%

Courses required for incoming students to have completed prior to enrolling:
Bachelor's degree in psychology, sociology, or related fields, or master's degree in counseling, psychology, or related area; we have two tracks to our program: post-bachelor's and post-master's.

Recommended but not mandatory courses:
Statistics, research design

GRE mean
We recommend 500 for Verbal and 500 for Quantitative

315

Analytical Writing 4.5

GPA mean
Not reported

Number of applications/admission offers/incoming students in 2009
65 applied/12 admission offers/8 incoming (we usually accept 4 students in each track: post-bachelor's and post-master's)

% of students receiving:
Full tuition waiver only: 0%
Assistantship/fellowship only: 95%
Both full tuition waiver & assistantship/fellowship: 0%

Approximate percentage of incoming students with a B.A./B.S. only: 40%   **Master's:** 60%

Approximate percentage of students who are Women: 60%   **Ethnic Minority:** 30%   **International:** 5%

Average years to complete the doctoral program (including internship): 4.5 years (post-master's); 5.5 years post-bachelor's

Personal interview
Preferred in person

Attrition rate in past 7 years: 3%

Percentage of students applying for internship last year accepted into APPIC or APA internships: 100%

Formal tracks/concentrations: none

Research areas	# Faculty	# Grants
American Indian	3	0
at-risk youth	2	0
career	4	1
health psychology	2	0
LGBT	4	0
multicultural	6	0
professional	2	0
psychological assessment	1	0
rural mental health	1	0
sports psychology	1	0
supervision	3	0
women/gender issues	4	0

Clinical opportunities

correctional psychology unit	outpatient hospital
domestic violence center	rural mental health clinic
Indian health services	university counseling
inpatient hospital	centers
marriage and family clinic	youth and family services

University of Oregon (Ph.D.)
Counseling Psychology Program
5251 University of Oregon
Eugene, OR 97403-5251
phone#: (541) 346-2456
e-mail: cpsy@uoregon.edu
Web address: education.uoregon.edu/field.htm?id=46

1	2	3	4	**5**	6	7
Practice oriented			Equal emphasis			Research oriented

Percentage of faculty subscribing to each of the following orientations:

Psychodynamic/Psychoanalytic	0%
Applied behavioral analysis/Radical behavioral	0%
Family systems/Systems	50%
Existential/Phenomenological/Humanistic	25%
Cognitive/Cognitive-behavioral	100%

Courses required for incoming students to have completed prior to enrolling:
Some background in psychology

Recommended but not mandatory courses:
Research design, statistics, helping skills, human development, language (e.g. Spanish)

GRE mean
Verbal 550   Quantitative 620
Analytical Writing 4.63

GPA mean
Overall 3.52

Number of applications/admission offers/incoming students in 2009
164 applied/11 admission offers/8 incoming

% of students receiving:
Full tuition waiver only: 0%
Assistantship/fellowship only: 0%
Both full tuition waiver & assistantship/fellowship: 100%

Approximate percentage of incoming students with a B.A./B.S. only: 60%   **Master's:** 40%

Approximate percentage of students who are Women: 84%   **Ethnic Minority:** 58%   **International:** 7%

Average years to complete the doctoral program (including internship): 5.8 years

Personal interview
Preferred in person but telephone acceptable

Attrition rate in past 7 years: 12%

Percentage of students applying for internship last year accepted into APPIC or APA internships: 100%

Formal tracks/concentrations: none

Research areas	# Faculty	# Grants
child and family psychology	3	2
college student development	2	0
domestic violence	1	0
multicultural	4	1
prevention research	4	2
social support and interactions	3	0
treatment outcomes	4	2
vocational psychology	2	1

Clinical opportunities

child–family (English and Spanish)	community mental health inpatient settings
community prevention	VA hospital
university/college counseling centers	domestic violence agency (English and Spanish)

Our Lady of the Lake University (Psy.D.)

School of Professional Studies
Graduate Admissions Office
411 SW 24th Street
San Antonio, TX 78207-4689
phone#: (210) 431-3914
e-mail: clcastaneda@lake.ollusa.edu
Web address: www.ollusa.edu/s/1190/ollu.
aspx?sie=1190&gid=id=pgid=1748

1	2	3	4	5	6	7
Practice oriented		Equal emphasis				Research oriented

Percentage of faculty subscribing to each of the following orientations:

Psychodynamic/Psychoanalytic	0%
Applied behavioral analysis/Radical behavioral	0%
Family systems/Systems	90%
Existential/Phenomenological/Humanistic	10%
Cognitive/Cognitive-behavioral	0%

Courses required for incoming students to have completed prior to enrolling:
Master's or bachelor's degree in psychology or closely related area

Recommended but not mandatory courses: None

GRE mean
Verbal 490   Quantitative 548
Analytical Writing 4.5

GPA mean
3.1

Number of applications/admission offers/incoming students in 2009
24 applied/12 admission offers/7 incoming

% of students receiving:
Full tuition waiver only: 14%
Assistantship/fellowship only: 29%
Both full tuition waiver & assistantship/fellowship: 0%

Approximate percentage of incoming students with a B.A./B.S. only: 29%   Master's: 71%

Approximate percentage of students who are
Women: 71% Ethnic Minority: 43% International: 29%

Average years to complete the doctoral program (including internship): 5.5 years

Personal interview
Required in person

Attrition rate in past 7 years: 17.5%

Percentage of students applying for internship last year accepted into APPIC or APA internships: 80%

Formal tracks/concentrations: health psychology

Research areas	# Faculty	# Grants
brief therapy	3	2
ethics	1	0
reimbursement	1	0

Clinical opportunities
community counseling
health psychology
school-age population
Spanish-speaking
population

Pennsylvania State University (Ph.D.)

Department of Counselor Education, Counseling Psychology, and Rehabilitation Services
University Park, PA 16802
phone#: (814) 865-8304
e-mail: CnPsydoc@psu.edu
Web address: http://www.ed.psu.edu/educ/cecprs/counseling-psychology

1	2	3	4	5	6	7
Practice oriented		Equal emphasis				Research oriented

Percentage of faculty subscribing to each of the following orientations:

Psychodynamic/Psychoanalytic	70%
Applied behavioral analysis/Radical behavioral	0%
Family systems/Systems	30%
Existential/Phenomenological/Humanistic	0%
Cognitive/Cognitive-behavioral	0%

Courses required for incoming students to have completed prior to enrolling:
theories of counseling/psychotherapy, individual counseling practicum, assessment, statistics/research design, career counseling, multicultural counseling, group counseling, counselor skills training/pre-practicum

Recommended but not mandatory courses:
Development, core courses in psychology

GRE mean
Verbal 532   Quantitative 597   Analytical 597
Analytical Writing 4.5

GPA mean
Overall master's GPA 3.98

Number of applications/admission offers/incoming students in 2009
65 applied/8 admission offers/5 incoming

% of students receiving:
Full tuition waiver only: 0%
Assistantship/fellowship only: 0%
Both full tuition waiver & assistantship/fellowship: 100%

Approximate percentage of incoming students with a B.A./B.S. only: 0%   Master's: 100%

Approximate percentage of students who are
Women: 76% Ethnic Minority: 32% International: 10%

Average years to complete the doctoral program (including internship): 6 years

Personal interview
Preferred in person but telephone acceptable in certain circumstances.

Attrition rate in past 7 years: 10%

Percentage of students applying for internship last year accepted into APPIC or APA internships: 100%

Formal tracks/concentrations: none

Research areas	# Faculty	# Grants
family systems	2	1
lesbian/gay/bisexual	1	0
psychotherapy	1	0

Clinical opportunities
Not reported

Purdue University (Ph.D.)

Department of Educational Studies
BRNG Hall, 100 N. University St.,
West Lafayette, IN 47907-2098
phone#: (765) 494-9748 (Secretary: Ros Bol)
e-mail: servaty@purdue.edu
Web address: www.edst.purdue.edu/cd/psychology/index.html

1	2	3	4	5	6	7

Practice oriented   Equal emphasis   Research oriented

Percentage of faculty subscribing to each of the following orientations:

Psychodynamic/Psychoanalytic	0%
Applied behavioral analysis/Radical behavioral	0%
Family systems/Systems	20%
Existential/Phenomenological/Humanistic	65%
Cognitive/Cognitive-behavioral	15%

Courses required for incoming students to have completed prior to enrolling: None

Recommended but not mandatory courses:
Undergraduate psychology, statistics, research design

GRE mean
Verbal 568   Quantitative 672
Psychology Subject Test not used
Analytical Writing 4.4

GPA mean
Overall GPA 3.60

Number of applications/admission offers/incoming students in 2009
49 applied/11 admission offers/7 incoming

% of students receiving:
Full tuition waiver only: 0%
Assistantship/fellowship only: 0%
Both full tuition waiver & assistantship/fellowship: 60%

Approximate percentage of incoming students with a B.A./B.S. only: 50% **Master's:** 50%

Approximate percentage of students who are Women: 80% **Ethnic Minority:** 12% **International:** 25%

Average years to complete the doctoral program (including internship): 5 years

Personal interview
Preferred in person but telephone acceptable

Attrition rate in past 7 years: 2.6%

Percentage of students applying for internship last year accepted into APPIC or APA internships: 80%

Formal tracks/concentrations: none

Research areas	# Faculty	# Grants
adult attachment theory	1	1
career and talent development	1	0
grief and bereavement	1	1
adjustment of international students/immigration	1	1
therapeutic assessment	1	0
gambling	1	0

Clinical opportunities

university/department clinic	college counseling centers
hospitals	community mental health

Seton Hall University (Ph.D.)

Department of Professional Psychology and
Family Therapy
College of Education
400 South Orange Avenue
South Orange, NJ 07079
phone#: (973) 275-2740
e-mail: palmerla@shu.edu
Web address: www.shu.edu/academics/education/phd-counseling-psychology/index.cfm

1	2	3	4	5	6	7

Practice oriented   Equal emphasis   Research oriented

Percentage of faculty subscribing to each of the following orientations:

Psychodynamic/Psychoanalytic	25%
Applied behavioral analysis/Radical behavioral	0%
Family systems/Systems	0%
Existential/Phenomenological/Humanistic	25%
Cognitive/Cognitive-behavioral	50%

Courses required for incoming students to have completed prior to enrolling:
Group counseling, abnormal psychology, test and measurement, counseling skills, statistics and computer application I

Recommended, but not mandatory courses:
None

GRE mean
Verbal 567   Quantitative 620   Analytical Writing 4.6

GPA mean
Overall GPA 3.7

Number of applications/admission offers/incoming students in 2009
122 applied/7 admission offers/3 incoming

% of students receiving:
Full tuition waiver only: 0%

Assistantship/fellowship only: 100%
Both full tuition waiver & assistantship/fellowship: 0%

Approximate percentage of incoming students who entered with a B.A./B.S. only: 0% **Master's:** 100%

Approximate percentage of students who are Women: 67% **Ethnic Minority:** 33% **International:** 0%

Average years to complete the doctoral program (including internship): 5.8 years

Personal interview:
Preferred in person but telephone acceptable

Attrition rate in past 7 years: 14%

Percentage of students applying for internship last year was accepted into APPIC or APA internships? 67%

Formal tracks/concentrations: neuropsychology, multicultural, assessment, infant mental health, couples and families

Research areas	# Faculty	# Grants
career development	1	0
multicultural counseling	3	0
neuropsychology	1	0
psychological trauma	1	0
resiliency	1	0
student well-being	1	0
health and coping	1	0
spirituality	1	0
the advising relationship	1	0

Clinical opportunities
The university does not run any specialty clinics. The program has developed an extensive offering of diverse clinical training opportunities in the greater New York area.

Southern Illinois University (Ph.D.)

Department of Psychology
Carbondale, IL 62901
phone#: (618) 453-3564
e-mail: gradpsyc@siu.edu (graduate secretary)
chwalisz@siu.edu (program director)
Web address: www.psychology.siuc.edu/grad/counseling.html

1	2	3	4	5	6	7
Practice oriented		Equal emphasis				Research oriented

Percentage of faculty subscribing to each of the following orientations:
Psychodynamic/Psychoanalytic 0%
Applied behavioral analysis/Radical behavioral 0%
Family systems/Systems 0%
Existential/Phenomenological/Humanistic 67%
Cognitive/Cognitive-behavioral 33%

Courses required for incoming students to have completed prior to enrolling: None

Recommended but not mandatory courses:
At least 1 statistics course; if student was not an undergraduate psychology major, we look for coursework in core areas of psychology

GRE mean
Verbal 524 Quantitative 608
Analytical Writing 5.24

GPA mean
Overall GPA 3.51

Number of applications/admission offers/incoming students in 2008
84 applied/7admission offers/5 incoming

% of students receiving:
Full tuition waiver only: 0%
Assistantship/fellowship only: 0%
Both full tuition waiver & assistantship/fellowship: 100%

Approximate percentage of incoming students with a B.A./B.S. only: 90% **Master's:** 10%

Approximate percentage of students who are Women: 80% **Ethnic Minority:** 40% **International:** 18%

Average years to complete the doctoral program (including internship): 5.5 years

Personal interview
Preferred in person (open house) but telephone acceptable

Attrition rate in past 7 years: 8%

Percentage of students applying for internship last year accepted into APPIC or APA internships: 100%

Formal tracks/concentrations: none

Research areas	# Faculty	# Grants
academic self-concept, and achievement	1	0
adjustment to brain injury/disability	1	0
career assessment and counseling	2	1
career choice and development	2	1
caregiver burden	1	1
counseling supervision	1	0
expectations about counseling	1	0
gender/cultural influences	3	2
health psychology	1	0
occupational stress and health	1	0
psychological measurement	1	0
student development	1	0
qualitative research methodology	2	0
racial/ethnic identity	3	0
self-efficacy	1	0
spiritual/religious issues	2	0
stress and coping	2	0
women in management	1	0
workplace violence	1	0

Clinical opportunities
career development
marriage and family
rural mental health
partial hospitalization
university counseling center
community medical clinics
VA hospital

psychiatric (inpatient)
state correctional system
  (medium security facility)
student health service

vocational rehabilitation
substance abuse
stress management
sexuality counseling

University of Southern Mississippi (Ph.D.)

Department of Psychology
118 College Dr. #5025
Hattiesburg, MS 39406-0001
phone#: (601) 266-4602
e-mail: bonnie.nicholson@usm.edu
Web address: www.usm.edu/counselingpsy/dochome.html

1	2	3	4	5	6	7
Practice oriented			Equal emphasis			Research oriented

Percentage of faculty subscribing to each of the following orientations:

Psychodynamic/Psychoanalytic	0%
Applied behavioral analysis/Radical behavioral	0%
Family systems/Systems	0%
Existential/Phenomenological/Humanistic	17%
Cognitive/Cognitive-behavioral	83%

Courses required for incoming students to have completed prior to enrolling: None

Recommended but not mandatory courses:
Statistics, personality, testing and assessment

GRE mean
Verbal 522   Quantitative 574
Analytical Writing Data: not used in admission decisions

GPA mean
Overall GPA 3.82   Overall master's GPA n/a

Number of applications/admission offers/incoming students in 2009
70 applied/10 admission offers/6 incoming

% of students receiving:
Full tuition waiver only: 0%
Assistantship/fellowship only: 0%
Both full tuition waiver & assistantship/fellowship: 100%

Approximate percentage of incoming students with a B.A./B.S. only: 66% Master's: 33%

Approximate percentage of students who are Women: 83% Ethnic Minority: 17% International: 17%

Average years to complete the doctoral program (including internship): 6 post BA/BS; 5 post master's

Personal interview
Preferred in person but telephone acceptable

Attrition rate in past 7 years: 20%

Percentage of students applying for internship last year accepted into APPIC or APA internships: 100%

Formal tracks/concentrations: none

Research areas	# Faculty	# Grants
anger	1	1
diversity	1	5
empirically supported treatments	3	2
motivational interviewing	1	2
parenting	1	0
spirituality	1	1
vocational	1	0
criminal thinking	1	0
forensic psychology	2	0

Clinical opportunities

alcohol and drug treatment	outpatient
community mental health center	university counseling center
counseling assessment center	university medical center (Jackson, MS)
counseling training clinic	
inpatient	VA hospital (Biloxi, MS)

University of St. Thomas (Psy.D.)

Graduate School of Professional Psychology
TMH451, 1000 La Salle Avenue
Minneapolis, MN 55403-2005
phone#: (651) 962-4650
e-mail: GradPsych@St.Thomas.Edu
Web address: www.stthomas.edu/gradpsych/programs/psyd/default.html

1	2	3	4	5	6	7
Practice oriented			Equal emphasis			Research oriented

Percentage of faculty subscribing to each of the following orientations:

Psychodynamic/Psychoanalytic	10%
Applied behavioral analysis/Radical behavioral	0%
Family systems/Systems	20%
Existential/Phenomenological/Humanistic	40%
Cognitive/Cognitive-behavioral	30%

Courses required for incoming students to have completed prior to enrolling:
M.A. program in counseling psychology or equivalent

Recommended & mandatory courses:
Statistics, Psychobiology/psychophysiology, social/group dynamics, assessment, personality/counseling theory, development, psychopathology, counseling skills and counseling ethics, counseling practicum

GRE mean
Verbal 430   Quantitative 490
Analytical Writing 4.3

GPA mean
Overall GPA 3.9

Number of applications/admission offers/incoming students in 2009
34 applied/19 admission offers/15 incoming

% of students receiving:
Full tuition waiver only: 0%
Assistantship/fellowship only: 12%
Both full tuition waiver & assistantship/fellowship: 0%

Approximate percentage of incoming students with a B.A./B.S. only: 0%   **Master's:** 100%

Approximate percentage of 2009 students who are Women: 66%   **Ethnic Minority:** 40%   **International:** 0%

Average years to complete the doctoral program (including internship): 5.3 years

Personal interview
Preferred in person

Attrition rate in past 7 years: 6.7%

Percentage of students applying for internship last year (2008) accepted into APPIC or APA internships: 75%

Formal tracks/concentrations: none

Research areas	# Faculty	# Grants
counseling process	3	0
cultural sensitive therapy	4	0
interprofessional ethics	2	0
licensure and regulatory boards	1	0
master therapists	1	0
religion and psychotherapy	1	0

Clinical opportunities
Full range of diagnostic disorders in a variety of settings.

Teacher's College–Columbia University (Ph.D.)

Program in Counseling Psychology
Department of Counseling and Clinical Psychology
New York, NY 10027
phone#: (212)678-3397
e-mail: gug3@columbia.edu
Web address: www.tc.columbia.edu/CCP/CounPsych/index.asp?id=Doctor-of-Philosophy&Info=the+Ph%2ED%2E+Program+in+Counseling+Psychology#DoctorofPhilosophy

1	2	3	4	**5**	6	7
Practice oriented		Equal emphasis				Research oriented

Percentage of faculty subscribing to each of the following orientations:

Psychodynamic/Psychoanalytic	10%
Applied behavioral analysis/Radical behavioral	10%
Family systems/Systems	40%
Existential/Phenomenological/Humanistic	40%
Cognitive/Cognitive-behavioral	25%
Multicultural/Diversity	90%

Courses required for incoming students to have completed prior to enrolling:
Bachelor's, but master's degree preferred

Recommended but not mandatory courses: none

GRE mean
Verbal 570   Quantitative 570
Analytical Writing not reported

GPA mean
Overall GPA 3.75

Number of applications/admission offers/incoming students in 2009
180 applied/7 admission offers/7 incoming

% of incoming students receiving:
Full tuition waiver only: 100%
Assistantship/fellowship only: 25%
Both full tuition waiver & assistantship/fellowship: 75%

Approximate percentage of incoming students with a B.A./B.S. only: 15%   **Master's:** 85%

Approximate percentage of students who are Women: 100%   **Ethnic Minority:** 75%   **International:** 15%

Average years to complete the doctoral program (including internship): 6.5 years

Personal interview
Required in person

Attrition rate in past 7 years: 15%

Percentage of students applying for internship last year accepted into APPIC or APA internships: 85%

Formal tracks/concentrations: none

Research areas	# Faculty	# Grants
cognition and stereotypes	2	0
cultural competence	3	0
immigration		
multicultural counseling	7	0
prevention		
racism and racial identity	2	0
sexual harassment	1	0
women and leadership	1	0

Clinical opportunities:
Practicum in university clinic and off-site externships required

University of Tennessee–Knoxville (Ph.D.)

Department of Psychology
1404 Circle Dr., Rm. 312 Austin Peay
Knoxville, TN 37996-0900
phone#: (865) 974-3328
e-mail: bmallinc@utk.edu
Web address: psychology.utk.edu/gradstudy/counseling/index.shtml

1	2	3	**4**	5	6	7
Practice oriented		Equal emphasis				Research oriented

Percentage of faculty subscribing to each of the following orientations:

Psychodynamic/Psychoanalytic	0%
Applied behavioral analysis/Radical behavioral	0%
Family systems/Systems	0%
Existential/Phenomenological/Humanistic	17%
Cognitive/Cognitive-behavioral	50%

321

Feminist	17%
Interpersonal/experiential	17%

Courses required for incoming students to have completed prior to enrolling:
An undergraduate degree is required, but no particular courses.

Recommended but not mandatory courses:
experimental, personality, developmental, abnormal

GRE mean
Verbal 570   Quantitative 600
Analytical Writing not reported

GPA mean
Overall GPA 3.35 (Undergraduate); 3.78 (Graduate)

Number of applications/admission offers/incoming students in 2009
95 applied/8 admission offers/7 incoming

% of students receiving:
Full tuition waiver only: 0%
Assistantship/fellowship only: 0%
Both full tuition waiver & assistantship/fellowship: 100%

Approximate percentage of incoming students with a B.A./B.S. only: 40%   **Master's:** 60%

Approximate percentage of students who are:
Women: 77%   Ethnic Minority: 13%   International: 26%

Average years to complete the doctoral program (including internship): 5.5 years

Personal interview:
Interview not required

Attrition rate in past 7 years: 10%

Percentage of students applying for internship last year accepted into APPIC or APA internships: 86%

Formal tracks/concentrations: none

Research areas	# Faculty	# Grants
Trauma, military PTSD	1	none so far
LBGT identity development, heterosexism	1	0
Personality and optimum performance	1	0
Psychotherapy process and outcome	1	0
Multicultural psychology	3	0
Health psychology	1	1

Clinical opportunities
practicum at University Counseling Center
assistantships at Career Services, alcohol/drug treatment inpatient, domestic violence counseling, and community mental health centers

Tennessee State University (Ph.D.)
Department of Psychology
Nashville, TN 37209-1561
phone#: (615) 963-5141
e-mail: jcampbell21@tnstate.edu
Web address: www.tnstate.edu/psychology

1	2	3	4	5	6	7
Practice oriented		Equal emphasis				Research oriented

Percentage of faculty subscribing to each of the following orientations:

Psychodynamic/Psychoanalytic	60%
Applied behavioral analysis/Radical behavioral	0%
Family systems/Systems	20%
Existential/Phenomenological/Humanistic	17%
Cognitive/Cognitive-behavioral	20%

Courses required for incoming students to have completed prior to enrolling:
Learning or Cognitive Affective Bases of Behavior; statistics; research methodology; counseling; intellectual assessment; personality theory, developmental or psychometrics (2 out of 3); master's-level practicum; history & systems of psychology

Recommended but not mandatory courses: none

GRE mean
Verbal 500   Quantitative 500
Analytical Writing not reported

GPA mean
Overall GPA 3.25

Number of applications/admission offers/incoming students in 2009
35 applied/10 admission offers/7 incoming

% of students receiving:
Full tuition waiver only: 0%
Assistantship/fellowship only: 0%
Both full tuition waiver & assistantship/fellowship: 100%

Approximate percentage of incoming students with a B.A./B.S. only: 0%   **Master's:** 100%

Approximate percentage of students who are
Women: 72.2%   Ethnic Minority: 27.8%   International: 11%

Average years to complete the doctoral program (including internship): 5 years

Personal interview
Preferred in person but telephone acceptable

Attrition rate in past 7 years: 10.8%

Percentage of students applying for internship last year accepted into APPIC or APA internships: 100%

Formal tracks/concentrations: none

Research areas	# Faculty	# Grants
career/vocational	1	2
eating disorders	1	0
ethical issues	2	0
men's issues	3	1
multicultural concerns	2	1
resiliency/decision-making	2	0
religious/spirituality in counseling	1	0
teaching/training of psychology	1	0
marriage and family therapy	1	0

Clinical opportunities

adult, child, and adolescent psychiatry	university counseling center
behavioral health	community mental health

forensics
assessment clinics

VA hospital
correctional facilities

methods in psychological research	1	0
multicultural training	2	0
acculturation process	1	0
racial/ethnic minority groups	3	1
public health	2	1

Texas A&M University (Ph.D.)

Department of Educational Psychology
College Station, TX 77843
phone#: (979) 845-1833
e-mail: cpsy@tamu.edu
Web address: cpsy.tamu.edu

1	2	3	**4**	5	6	7

Practice oriented   Equal emphasis   Research oriented

Percentage of faculty subscribing to each of the following orientations:
Psychodynamic/Psychoanalytic   20%
Multicultural/Feminist   40%
Cognitive/Cognitive-behavioral   20%

Courses required for incoming students prior to enrolling: None

Courses recommended but not mandatory:
Courses in psychology, statistics, and research methods

GRE mean
Verbal 505   Quantitative 595
Analytical Writing not reported

GPA mean
Overall GPA 3.54   Psychology GPA N/A
Junior/Senior GPA 3.54

Number of applications/admission offers/incoming students in 2009
66 applied/11 admission offers/7 incoming

% of students receiving:
Full tuition waiver only: 0%
Assistantship/fellowship only: 50%
Both full tuition waiver & assistantship/fellowship: 50%

Approximate percentage of incoming students with a B.A./B.S. only: 73%   Master's: 27%

Approximate percentage of students who are:
Women: 74%   Ethnic Minority: 53%   International: 5%

Average years to complete the doctoral program (including internship): 6 years

Personal interview
Required in person

Attrition rate in past 7 years: 6%

Percentage of students applying for internship last year accepted into APPIC or APA internships: 91%

Formal tracks/concentrations: clinical geropsychology, multicultural counseling, public health, Mexican American health/mental health research

Research areas	# Faculty	# Grants
geropsychology	1	0
rehabilitation/caregivers	1	3

Clinical opportunities
university counseling centers
VA hospitals
community health clinics

University of Texas at Austin

Department of Educational Psychology
D 5800
Austin, TX 78712
phone#: (512) 471-4409
e-mail: aaren.rohlen@mail.utexas.edu
Web address: www.edb.utexas.edu/education/
departments/edp/admissions/programs/doctoral/
counseling/

1	2	3	4	**5**	6	7

Practice oriented   Equal emphasis   Research oriented

Percentage of faculty subscribing to each of the following orientations:
Psychodynamic/Psychoanalytic   25%
Applied behavioral analysis/Radical behavioral   0%
Existential/Phenomenological/Humanistic   12.5%
Interpersonal/Constructivist   12.5%
Cognitive/Cognitive-behavioral   25%
Multicultural   25%

Courses required for incoming students to have completed prior to enrolling:
Bachelor's degree

Recommended but not mandatory courses: None

GRE mean
Verbal + Quantitative 1212
Analytical Writing not reported 6

GPA mean
Overall GPA 3.77

Number of applications/admission offers/incoming students in 2008
153 Applied/14 admission offers/12 incoming

% of students receiving:
Full tuition waiver only: 0%
Assistantship/fellowship only: 67%
Both full tuition waiver & assistantship/fellowship: 33%

Approximate percentage of incoming students with a B.A./B.S. only: 59%   Master's: 41%

Approximate percentage of students who are
Women: 66%   Ethnic Minority: 41%   International: 0%

Average years to complete the doctoral program (including internship): 6 years

Personal interview
Preferred in person but telephone acceptable

Attrition rate in past 7 years: 10%

Percentage of students applying for internship last year accepted into APPIC or APA internships: 88%

Formal tracks/concentrations: n/a

Research areas	# Faculty	# Grants
depression	1	0
forensic psychology/assessment	1	0
psychology of men and masculinity	1	0
multicultural/cross-cultural	2	0
psychoanalysis	1	0
health psychology	1	0

Clinical opportunities
University counseling and career centers
Community agency counseling
Adolescent and adult inpatient units at state hospital
Outpatient practicum at VA
Community and hospital-based assessment
Neuropsychological assessment
Correctional facilities

Texas Tech University (Ph.D.)

Department of Psychology
Lubbock, TX 79409
phone#: (806) 742-3711, ext. 229
e-mail: sheila.garos@ttu.edu
Web address: www.depts.ttu.edu/psy/graduate/counseling/counseling.php

1	2	3	4	5	6	7
Practice oriented		Equal emphasis			Research oriented	

Percentage of faculty subscribing to each of the following orientations:

Psychodynamic/Psychoanalytic	14%
Applied behavioral analysis/Radical behavioral	14%
Family systems/Systems	14%
Existential/Phenomenological/Humanistic	14%
Cognitive/Cognitive-behavioral	28%
Interpersonal Therapy	14%

Courses required for incoming students to have completed prior to enrolling:
18 undergraduate hours in psychology and statistics

Recommended but not mandatory courses: None

GRE mean
Verbal 596   Quantitative 658
Analytical Writing 4.7

GPA mean
Overall GPA 3.70

Number of applications/admission offers/incoming students in 2009
82 applied/10 admission offers/5 incoming

% of students receiving:
Full tuition waiver only: 0%

Assistantship/fellowship only: 100%
Both full tuition waiver & assistantship/fellowship: 0%

Approximate percentage of incoming students with a B.A./B.S. only: 100%   **Master's:** 0%

Approximate percentage of students who are Women: 82%   **Ethnic Minority:** 18%   **International:** 0%

Average years to complete the doctoral program (including internship): 6 years

Personal interview
Required in person

Attrition rate in past 7 years: 14%

Percentage of students applying for internship last year accepted into APPIC or APA internships: 100%

Formal tracks/concentrations: none

Research areas	# Faculty	# Grants
Asian Americans	1	0
behavioral addictions	1	0
coping and stress	1	0
cultural differences in the self	1	0
depression	1	0
forensic/correctional	1	2+
gender and women	2	0
health psychology	1	0
multicultural counseling	2	0
positive psychology	1	0
relationships	1	0
religion	1	0
sexual behavior	1	0
vocational	2	0
women's sexual health	1	1

Clinical opportunities
inpatient psychiatric unit
community mental health (MHMR)
outpatient psychology clinic
health sciences center/cancer center
family practice
child advocacy
community neuropsychological assessment
personality assessment
psychiatric prison unit
university counseling center
adult probation center

Texas Woman's University (Ph.D.)

Department of Psychology and Philosophy
P.O. Box 425470
Denton, TX 76204
phone#: (940) 898-2303
e-mail: sstabb@mail.twu.edu
Web address: www.twu.edu/psychology-philosophy/counseling-psych-phd.asp

1	2	3	4	5	6	7
Practice oriented		Equal emphasis			Research oriented	

Percentage of faculty subscribing to each of the following orientations:
Psychodynamic/Psychoanalytic   33%

Applied behavioral analysis/Radical behavioral	—
Family systems/Systems	17%
Existential/Phenomenological/Humanistic	100%
Cognitive/Cognitive-behavioral	—
Integrative	33%
Feminist	67%

Courses required for incoming students to have completed prior to enrolling:
Development, statistics, learning, experimental, intro, 3 additional psychology credits

Recommended but not mandatory courses: None

GRE mean
Verbal 560   Quantitative 560
Analytical Writing not reported

GPA mean
Psychology GPA 3.7   Junior/Senior GPA 3.5

Number of applications/admission offers/incoming students in 2009
Approximately 70 applied/14 admission offers/9 incoming

% of students receiving:
Full tuition waiver only: 0%
Assistantship/fellowship only: 40%
Both full tuition waiver & assistantship/fellowship: 0%

Approximate percentage of incoming students with a B.A./B.S. only: 50%   **Master's:** 50%

Approximate percentage of students who are Women: 80% **Ethnic Minority:** 25% **International:** 10%

Average years to complete the doctoral program (including internship): 6 years

Personal interview
No

Attrition rate in past 7 years: 5 students have left in the last 7 years.

Percentage of students applying for internship last year accepted into APPIC or APA internships: 100%

Formal tracks/concentrations: Gender & Multicultural; family systems, sexuality

Research areas	# Faculty	# Grants
career development	1	0
ethics and regulation	2	1
gender	4	2
sexuality	3	1
prison populations	1	0
Integrative theory & Practice	1	0

Clinical opportunities

university counseling center	domestic violence agencies
community mental health	hospitals
prisons/corrections	youth & family agencies
HIV/AIDS agencies	chemical dependency treatment

University of Utah (Ph.D.)
Department of Educational Psychology

1705E Campus Center Drive, Room 327
Salt Lake City, UT 84112-9255
phone#: (801) 581-7148
e-mail: paul.gore@ed.utah.edu
Web address: cp.ed.utah.edu

1	2	3	4	5	6	7
Practice oriented		Equal emphasis				Research oriented

Percentage of faculty subscribing to each of the following orientations:

Psychodynamic/Psychoanalytic	13%
Applied behavioral analysis/Radical behavioral	0%
Family systems/Systems	0%
Existential/Phenomenological/Humanistic	2%
Cognitive/Cognitive-behavioral	35%
Feminist/Multicultural	25%
Interpersonal	25%

Courses required for incoming students to have completed prior to enrolling:
Undergraduate and/or graduate preparation in psychology is strongly encouraged but no specific courses are required.

Recommended but not mandatory courses:
Experimental, personality, developmental, physiological, abnormal, statistics, research methods, social, and learning

GRE mean
Verbal 540   Quantitative 600   Analytical not reported
Psychology Subject Test not required
Analytical Writing 4.7

GPA mean
Overall GPA 3.65

Number of applications/admission offers/incoming students in 2009
66 applied/9 admission offers/6 incoming

% of students receiving:
Full tuition waiver only: 0%
Assistantship/fellowship only: 0%
Both full tuition waiver & assistantship/fellowship: 100%

Approximate percentage of incoming students with a B.A./B.S. only: 52%   **Master's:** 48%

Approximate percentage of students who are Women: 66%   **Ethnic Minority:** 15% **International:** 0%

Average years to complete the doctoral program (including internship): 6.7 years for students entering with bachelors, 5.5 years for students entering with masters

Personal interview
In-person interview day scheduled for February, phone interview available.

Attrition rate in past 7 years: 5%

Percentage of students applying for internship last year accepted into APPIC or APA internships: 90%

Formal tracks/concentrations: none

Research areas	# Faculty	# Grants
applied gerontology	1	1
children and adolescents	3	2

gender and women's	2	0
human emotion	1	0
ethics	1	0
lesbian, gay, bisexual, transgender	2	0
multicultural counseling	2	0
professional education/training	1	0
psychotherapy process/outcome	1	0
substance abuse	1	1
career development	2	0

Clinical opportunities

community mental health	sexual abuse treatment
drug and alcohol treatment	university counseling center
ethnic student center	VA hospital
family medicine health center	pain clinic
gerontology services	women's resource center

Virginia Commonwealth University (Ph.D.)

Department of Psychology
Richmond, VA 23284-2018
phone#: (804) 828-2975
e-mail: mstern@vcu.edu, mccreary@vcu.edu
(Co-Directors)
Web address: www.psychology.vcu.edu/counseling/index.shtml

1	2	3	4	5	6	7
Practice oriented		Equal emphasis				Research oriented

Percentage of faculty subscribing to each of the following orientations:

Psychodynamic/Interpersonal	30%
Applied behavioral analysis/Radical behavioral	0%
Family systems/Systems	10%
Existential/Phenomenological/Humanistic	8%
Cognitive-behavioral/Feminist	28%
Developmental	8%

Courses required for incoming students to have completed prior to enrolling:
18 undergraduate credit hours in psychology, including courses in statistics, experimental and introductory psychology

Recommended but not mandatory courses: None

GRE mean
Verbal 585   Quantitative 626
Analytical Writing 4.6

GPA mean
Overall GPA 3.57

Number of applications/admission offers/incoming students in 2009
132 applied/6 admission offers/6 incoming

% of students receiving:
Full tuition waiver only: 0%
Assistantship/fellowship only: 0%
Both full tuition waiver & assistantship/fellowship: 73%

Approximate percentage of incoming students with a B.A./B.S. 100%

Approximate percentage of students who are
Women: 80.9% **Ethnic Minority:** 21.3% **International:** 2.1%

Average years to complete the doctoral program (including internship): 5.94 years

Personal interview
Preferred in person but telephone acceptable

Attrition rate in past 7 years: 10.9%

Percentage of students applying for internship last year accepted into APPIC or APA internships: 100%

Formal tracks/concentrations: health psychology

Research areas	# Faculty	# Grants
career intervention	1	1
minority mental health	3	0
forgiveness/religious values	2	3
health psychology	5	4
interventions	1	4
prevention	2	2
leadership and group dynamics	1	0
marital and family enrichment	2	0
teaching of life skills/community	1	0

Clinical opportunities

college mental health center	juvenile correctional system
university counseling center	state psychiatric hospital
child treatment center	substance abuse
federal correctional center	VA hospital
rehabilitation medicine unit	hospitals/medical centers
community mental health	church mental health

Washington State University (Ph.D.)

Department of Educational Leadership and Counseling Psychology
Pullman, WA 99164
phone#: (509) 335-7016 or 335-9195
e-mail: gradstudies@wsu.edu and mccubbin@wsu.edu
Web address: www.education.wsu.edu/graduate/specialization/index.html

1	2	3	4	5	6	7
Practice oriented		Equal emphasis				Research oriented

Percentage of faculty subscribing to each of the following orientations:

Psychodynamic/Psychoanalytic	0%
Applied behavioral analysis/Radical behavioral	0%
Family systems/Systems	10%
Existential/Phenomenological/Humanistic	40%
Cognitive/Cognitive-behavioral	50%

Courses required for incoming students to have completed prior to enrolling: None

Recommended but not mandatory courses: None

GRE mean
Verbal 520   Quantitative 490   Analytical not reported
Analytical Writing not reported
Psychology Subject Test not reported

GPA mean
Overall GPA 3.80
Overall master's GPA 3.89

Number of applications/admission offers/incoming students in 2009
94 applied/13 admission offers/5 incoming

% of students receiving:
Full tuition waiver only: 0%
Assistantship/fellowship only: 0%
Both full tuition waiver & assistantship/fellowship: 80%

Approximate percentage of incoming students with a B.A./B.S. only: 40%　**Master's:** 60%

Approximate percentage of students who are Women: 79.5%　**Ethnic Minority:** 66.7%
International: 7.7%

Average years to complete the doctoral program (including internship): 6 years

Personal interview
Interview not required

Attrition rate in past 7 years: 5%

Percentage of students applying for internship last year accepted into APPIC or APA internships: 83%

Formal tracks/concentrations: none

Research areas	# Faculty	# Grants
acculturation/ethnic identity	3	0
cross-cultural/multicultural	3	1
disabilities	0	1
eating disorders	1	0
hypnosis and attentional processes	2	1
measurement/assessment	3	1
personality	1	0
resiliency	1	0
social influence	1	0
supervision	1	0
vocational	2	0

Clinical opportunities
not reported

West Virginia University (Ph.D.)

Department of Counseling, Rehabilitation Counseling, and Counseling Psychology
P.O. Box 6122
Morgantown, WV 26506-6122
phone#: (304) 293-2227
e-mail: james.bartee@mail.wvu.edu
Web address: counseling.wvu.edu/counseling_psychology

1	2	3	4	5	6	7
Practice oriented		Equal emphasis				Research oriented

Percentage of faculty subscribing to each of the following orientations:
Psychodynamic/Psychoanalytic　20%
Applied behavioral analysis/Radical behavioral　0%
Family systems/Systems　20%

Existential/Phenomenological/Humanistic　40%
Cognitive/Cognitive-behavioral　20%

Courses required for incoming students to have completed prior to enrolling:
Master's degree in counseling psychology, clinical psychology, or related field

Recommended but not mandatory courses:
Supervised field experience, multivariate methods, psychopharmacology

GRE mean
Verbal 521　Quantitative 617
Analytical Writing 4.5

GPA mean
Overall GPA 3.25
Overall graduate GPA 3.7

Number of applications/admission offers/incoming students in 2009
41 applied/06 admission offers/6 incoming

% of students receiving:
Full tuition waiver only: 50%
Assistantship/fellowship only: 0%
Both full tuition waiver & assistantship/fellowship: 50%

Approximate percentage of incoming students with a B.A./B.S. only: 0%　**Master's:** 100%

Approximate percentage of students who are Women: 66%　**Ethnic Minority:** 16%
International: not reported 0%

Average years to complete the doctoral program (including internship): 5.5 years

Personal interview
Required in person

Attrition rate in past 7 years: 4%

Percentage of students applying for internship last year accepted into APPIC or APA internships: 86%

Formal tracks/concentrations: none

Research areas	# Faculty	# Grants
clinical supervision	2	0
consulting models	1	0
group counseling	1	0
injured athletes	1	0
personality assessment	2	0
psychiatric rehabilitation	1	0
psychology and mental health	3	0
psychology of disability	1	0
psychotherapeutic techniques	3	0
rehab counseling and psychology	2	0
self-efficacy and health	2	0
vocational counseling	2	0

Clinical opportunities
community agencies
correctional facilities
general hospitals out patient
  clinics/assessment centers
comprehensive mental
  health centers
crisis units
counseling centers
rehabilitation hospitals
psychiatric hospitals
VA hospital

Western Michigan University (Ph.D.)

Department of Counselor Education and
Counseling Psychology
3102 Sangren Hall
Kalamazoo, MI 49008-5226
phone#: (269) 387-5100 | (269) 387-5090 Fax
e-mail: carolyn.cardwell@wmich.edu
Web address: www.wmich.edu/coe/cecp/academics/
doctoral/phd-counselingpsychology.html

1	2	3	4	5	6	7
Practice oriented		Equal emphasis				Research oriented

Percentage of faculty subscribing to each of the following orientations:

Psychodynamic/Psychoanalytic	13%
Applied behavioral analysis/Radical behavioral	0%
Family systems/Systems	20%
Existential/Phenomenological/Humanistic	88%
Cognitive/Cognitive-behavioral	88%

Courses required for incoming students to have completed prior to enrolling:
Undergraduate degree required; master's degree preferred

Recommended but not mandatory courses:
Psychology or social science major

GRE mean
Verbal + Quantitative 1000
Analytical Writing not reported
Psychology Subject Test not reported

GPA mean
Overall graduate GPA 3.5
Overall undergraduate GPA 3.5

Number of applications/admission offers/incoming students in 2009
60 applied/13 admission offers/7 incoming

% of students receiving:
Full tuition waiver only: 0%
Assistantship/fellowship only: 33%
Both full tuition waiver & assistantship/fellowship: 67%

Approximate percentage of incoming students with a B.A./B.S. only: 10%   **Master's:** 90%

Approximate percentage of students who are Women: 70%   **Ethnic Minority:** 34%   **International:** 9%

Average years to complete the doctoral program (including internship): 5 years

Personal interview
Required in person

Attrition rate in past 7 years: 6%

Percentage of students applying for internship last year accepted into APPIC or APA internships: 84%

Formal tracks/concentrations: none

Research areas	# Faculty	# Grants
families	1	1
group work	1	1
multicultural concerns	4	0
psychological assessment	2	0
treatment	3	0

Clinical opportunities
In-house clinic and local hospitals, agencies, and schools

University of Wisconsin–Madison (Ph.D.)

Department of Counseling Psychology
321 Education Building, 1000 Bascom Mall
Madison, WI 53706
phone#: (608) 263-2746
e-mail: counpsych@education.wisc.edu
Web address: www.grad.wisc.edu/education/mas/237.html

1	2	3	4	5	6	7
Practice oriented		Equal emphasis				Research oriented

Percentage of faculty subscribing to each of the following orientations:

Psychodynamic/Psychoanalytic	30%
Applied behavioral analysis/Radical behavioral	0%
Family systems/Systems	10%
Existential/Phenomenological/Humanistic	40%
Cognitive/Cognitive-behavioral	30%
Multicultural	100%

Courses required for incoming students to have completed prior to enrolling:
Master's degree in counseling, including multicultural counseling and career psychology

Recommended but not mandatory courses: None

GRE mean
Verbal 535   Quantitative 580
Analytical Writing not reported

GPA mean
Junior/Senior GPA 3.6

Number of applications/admission offers/incoming students in 2009
83 applied/13 admission offers/8 incoming

% of students receiving:
Full tuition waiver only: 0%
Assistantship/fellowship only: 0%
Both full tuition waiver & assistantship/fellowship: 100%

Approximate percentage of incoming students with a B.A./B.S. only: 0%   **Master's:** 90%

Approximate percentage of students who are Women: 60%   **Ethnic Minority:** 50%
International: not reported

Average years to complete the doctoral program (including internship): 7 years

Personal interview
Telephone required

Attrition rate in past 7 years: 11%

Percentage of students applying for internship last year accepted into APPIC or APA internships: 67%

Formal tracks/concentrations: none

Research areas	# Faculty	# Grants
academic retention	2	0
career development	2	0
clinical supervision	1	1
ethnic identity	4	2
gender	4	0
group	1	0
multidisciplinary environments	2	1
multiethnic/cultural environments	5	3
process-outcome	3	0
school counseling	2	2

Clinical opportunities

not reported

University of Wisconsin–Milwaukee (Ph.D.)

Department of Educational Psychology
P.O. Box 413
Milwaukee, WI 53201
phone#: (414) 229-4939
e-mail: srwester@uwm.edu
Web address: www4.uwm.edu/soe/academics/ed_psych/
counseling_psych

1	2	3	4	5	6	7
Practice oriented		Equal emphasis			Research oriented	

Percentage of faculty subscribing to each of the following orientations:

Psychodynamic/Psychoanalytic	10%
Applied behavioral analysis/Radical behavioral	0%
Developmental Systems	20%
Interpersonal	10%
Existential/Phenomenological/Humanistic	0%
Cognitive/Cognitive-behavioral	60%

Courses required for incoming students to have completed prior to enrolling:

Group counseling, listening skills, statistics, multicultural counseling, theories of counseling, cognition, career development, personality

Recommended but not mandatory courses:

Cognition, personality

GRE mean

Verbal 525   Quantitative 550   Analytical 599

Analytical Writing 4.4
Psychology Subject Test not reported

GPA mean

Overall GPA 3.7

Number of applications/admission offers/incoming students in 2009

63 applied/10 admission offers/5 incoming

% of students receiving:

Full tuition waiver only: 0%
Assistantship/fellowship only: 0%
Both full tuition waiver & assistantship/fellowship: 70%

Approximate percentage of incoming students with a B.A./B.S. only: 10%   **Master's:** 90%

Approximate percentage of students who are Women: 80%   **Ethnic Minority:** 60%   **International:** 25%

Average years to complete the doctoral program (including internship): 5 years

Personal interview

Preferred in person but telephone acceptable

Attrition rate in past 7 years: 5%

Percentage of students applying for internship last year accepted into APPIC or APA internships: 88%

Formal tracks/concentrations: none

Research areas	# Faculty	# Grants
youth addictions	1	2
barriers for women in math/science	1	1
hypnosis and hypnotizability	1	0
international research	1	2
intervention programming	1	1
masculinity and male gender role	1	0
counseling training	1	1
multicultural counseling	2	2
pediatric behavioral health	1	0
vocational development	2	2

Clinical opportunities

children's hospital	medical college
community mental health	VA hospital
counseling center	day treatment for
family services	adolescents
inpatient psychiatric	eating disorders clinic

TIME LINE

Freshman and Sophomore Years

1. Take the core psychology courses—introduction, statistics, research methods, abnormal, cognitive, social.
2. Find out about faculty interests and research.
3. Make preliminary contact with faculty members whose research interests you.
4. Explore volunteer opportunities in clinical settings.
5. Investigate various career choices.
6. Join psychology student organizations and become an active member.
7. Attend departmental colloquia and social gatherings.
8. Enroll in courses helpful for graduate school, including biological sciences, mathematics, writing, and public speaking.
9. Learn to use library and electronic resources, such as scholarly journals and PsycLit.
10. Consider participating in your university's honors program, if you qualify.
11. Begin a career folder and place activities, honors, and other valuable reminders in it.
12. Discuss your career interests with faculty members and other mentors.

Junior Year

1. Take advanced psychology courses, for example, biopsychology, psychological testing.
2. Begin clinical work, both volunteer and practicum.
3. Volunteer for research with faculty and begin researching a potential honors thesis/independent project.
4. Continue contact with faculty and upperclassmen.
5. Enroll in professional organizations, for example, student affiliate of American Psychological Association or American Psychological Society.
6. Apply for membership in your local Psi Chi chapter.
7. Visit your career services office on campus and determine how the staff can assist you in applying to graduate school.
8. Draft a curriculum vitae to determine your strengths and weaknesses.
9. Attend a state or regional psychology convention.
10. Peruse graduate school bulletins online to acquaint yourself with typical requirements, offerings, and policies.
11. Surf the Web. Become comfortable with leading Web sites on graduate school admissions.
12. Access the GRE bulletin and information online. Begin preparation for the GRE by purchasing a study guide, attending a preparation course, and taking practice tests.
13. Update your folder by putting your curriculum vita/resume and reminders of your activities and accomplishments in it.
14. Try to focus your interests in particular research areas, theoretical orientations, and clinical populations.

15. Consider serving as an officer in one of the student organizations on campus.
16. Meet with your advisor or mentor before summer to review your plan for graduate applications.

Application Year

June–August

1. Continue to acquire research competencies and clinical experiences.
2. Surf the Web and begin to gather information from program Web sites.
3. Begin to narrow down potential schools to 20–40.
4. Prepare intensively for the GREs.
5. Consider taking the GRE General Test if you are prepared; this will afford ample time to retake them in the fall if necessary.
6. Investigate financial aid opportunities for graduate students.
7. Set aside money for the cost of the GREs and applications.

August–September

1. Download program information and applications from program Web sites and/or write to schools for applications.
2. Receive information packets and read through them.
3. Consult with advisors regarding graduate programs, application procedures, faculty of interest, etc.
4. Continue to study diligently for the GREs.
5. Update your curriculum vitae.
6. Investigate possible financial aid opportunities.
7. Begin a file in your institution's Office of Career Services.
8. Gather applications for salient fellowships and scholarships.

September–October

1. Take the GRE General Test (for first or second time).
2. Register for the GRE Psychology Subject Test administered in November and December.
3. Create a short list of schools using the worksheets.
4. Record the deadlines for submitting each application.

5. Choose the faculty at each school that most interest you.
6. Research your area of interest, focusing on the work of faculty with whom you would like to work.
7. Write to graduate faculty expressing interest in their work (if appropriate).
8. Request a copy of your own transcript and inspect it for any errors or omissions.
9. Begin first drafts of your personal statement and get feedback on it.
10. Update your CV or resume.
11. Calculate costs of applications and admission interviews and acquire the money for them.
12. Finalize the decision on whom you will ask for letters of recommendation.
13. Formulate your Plan B (i.e., what you will do if you are not accepted into a doctoral program).

October–November

1. Take the GRE Psychology Subject Test.
2. Take the MAT (only if necessary).
3. Prepare packets to distribute to your recommenders, including a complete vitae or resume.
4. Request letters of recommendation.
5. Arrange for the registrar to send your transcripts to schools.
6. Gather information on financial aid and loans available to graduate students.
7. Finalize your personal statements.

November–December

1. Complete applications.
2. Maintain a photocopy of each application for your records.
3. If the opportunity arises, visit professors with whom you have been in contact.
4. Submit applications.
5. Verify that the applications and all necessary materials have been received.
6. Request ETS forward your GRE scores to the appropriate institutions.

January–March

1. Wait patiently.
2. Insure that all of your letters of recommendation have been sent.
3. Complete the Free Application for Federal Student Aid at www.fafsa.ed.gov to determine what federal loans you can count on.

4. Be prepared for surprise telephone interviews.
5. Practice and prepare for admission interviews.
6. Travel to interviews as invited.
7. Develop contingency plans if not accepted into any programs.

April–May

1. If other programs make early offers, contact your top choices to determine the current status of your application.
2. Accept an offer of admission and promptly turn down less-preferred offers.
3. Finalize financial aid arrangements for next year.
4. Send official transcripts with Spring term grades to the program you plan to attend.
5. If not accepted to any schools, refer to Chapter 8.
6. Celebrate (if accepted) or regroup (if not accepted).
7. Inform people who wrote you letters of recommendation of the outcome.

WORKSHEET FOR CHOOSING PROGRAMS

Area of Interest	School	Research			Clinical			Self-Rating
		# Faculty	Funded	Rank	Orien-tation	Res/Clin	Rank	

Area of Interest	School	Research			Clinical			Self-Rating
		# Faculty	Funded	Rank	Orien-tation	Res/Clin	Rank	

A P P E N D I X   C

WORKSHEET
FOR ASSESSING
PROGRAM CRITERIA

School	Self-Rating	Courses	GRE-V	GRE-G	GRE-S	GPA	Research	Clinical	Compete	Total

A P P E N D I X D

WORKSHEET
FOR MAKING
FINAL CHOICES

School	School Criteria	Research	Clinical	Theoretical Orientation	Financial Aid	Program Outcomes	Quality of Life

A P P E N D I X   E
RESEARCH AREAS

	# Faculty	# Grants

Acceptance and Commitment Therapy

	# Faculty	# Grants
Georgia State University (Ph.D.) (Cl)	1	0
Illinois Institute of Technology (Ph.D.) (Cl)	1	0
University at Albany/State University of New York (Ph.D.) (Cl)	1	1
Utah State University (Ph.D.) (Cm)	1	1
Wichita State University (Ph.D.) (Cl)	1	0

Acculturation

	# Faculty	# Grants
New Mexico State University (Ph.D.) (Co)	3	0
Texas A&M University (Ph.D.) (Co)	1	0
University of Minnesota (Ph.D.) (Co)	1	1
Washington State University (Ph.D.) (Co)	3	0
Yeshiva University (Ph.D.) (Cl)	2	3

Acquired Immune Deficiency Syndrome/HIV

	# Faculty	# Grants
Argosy University, Phoenix (Psy.D.) (Cl)	1	0
Arizona State University (Ph.D.) (Co)	1	0
Carlos Albizu University–San Juan Campus (Ph.D.) (Cl)	1	0
DePaul University (Ph.D.) (Cl)	1	3
George Washington University (Ph.D.) (Cl)	1	2
Georgia State University (Ph.D.) (Cl)	2	4
Jackson State University (Ph.D.) (Cl)	3	3
Ponce School of Medicine (Psy.D.) (Cl)	3	2

	# Faculty	# Grants
San Diego State University/University of California, San Diego (Ph.D.) (Cl)	7	1
Southern Illinois University—Carbondale (Ph.D.) (Cl)	1	0
The University of Memphis (Ph.D.) (Co)	1	0
University of Illinois at Chicago (Ph.D.) (Cl)	2	2
University of Maryland—College Park (Ph.D.) (Co)	1	0
University of Miami (Ph.D.) (Cl)	6	2
University of Missouri—Kansas City (Ph.D.) (Cl)	2	3
University of North Dakota (Ph.D.) (Co)	1	1
University of North Texas (Ph.D.) (Cl)	2	0
University of North Texas and University of North Texas Health Sciences Center (Consortium) (Ph.D.) (Cl)	1	1
University of Wyoming (Ph.D.) (Cl)	1	1
Virginia Consortium Program in Clinical Psychology (Psy.D.) (Cl)	1	0
Western Michigan University (Ph.D.) (Cl)	1	0

Adjustment

	# Faculty	# Grants
Marquette University (Ph.D.) (Cl)	1	0
Purdue University (Ph.D.) (Co)	1	1
Southern Illinois University—Carbondale (Ph.D.) (Co)	1	0
St. Louis University (Ph.D.) (Cl)	2	0
University of Northern Colorado (Psy.D.) (Co)	2	0

Note. Cl, Clinical; Co, Counseling, Cm, combined psychology programs.

	# Faculty	# Grants
Virginia Consortium Program in Clinical Psychology (Psy.D.) (Cl)	2	0

Adolescent/At-Risk Adolescent

	# Faculty	# Grants
Argosy University, Chicago (Psy.D.) (Cl)	1	0
Boston College (Ph.D.) (Co)	3	2
Carlos Albizu University–San Juan Campus (Ph.D.) (Cl)	1	4
Catholic University of America (Ph.D.) (Cl)	4	2
Colorado State University (Ph.D.) (Co)	3	5
DePaul University (Ph.D.) (Cl)	2	2
Drexel University (Ph.D.) (Cl)	2	2
Duke University (Ph.D.) (Cl)	3	2
Emory University (Ph.D.) (Cl)	2	1
Fordham University (Ph.D.) (Cl)	1	0
George Washington University (Ph.D.) (Cl)	3	2
Howard University (Ph.D.) (Cl)	2	0
Indiana University—Bloomington (Ph.D.) (Co)	0	2
Kent State University (Ph.D.) (Cl)	1	1
Loyola University of Chicago (Ph.D.) (Cl)	6	5
Loyola University of Chicago (Ph.D.) (Co)	2	1
Northern Illinois University (Ph.D.) (Cl)	3	0
Northwestern University Medical School (Ph.D.) (Cl)	3	2
Oklahoma State University (Ph.D.) (Co)	2	0
Purdue University (Ph.D.) (Cl)	1	1
Rosalind Franklin University of Medicine and Science (Ph.D.) (Cl)	1	0
Rutgers, The State University of New Jersey (Psy.D.) (Cl)	3	1
Southern Illinois University—Carbondale (Ph.D.) (Cl)	2	0
Texas Tech University (Ph.D.) (Cl)	1	0
The University of Memphis (Ph.D.) (Co)	1	1
The Wright Institute (Psy.D.) (Cl)	2	0
University of Cincinnati (Ph.D.) (Cl)	4	4
University of Colorado at Colorado Springs (Ph.D.) (Cl)	1	0
University of Denver (Ph.D.) (Cl)	4	3
University of Georgia (Ph.D.) (Cl)	3	10
University of Georgia (Ph.D.) (Co)	2	0
University of Kentucky (Ph.D.) (Cl)	3	3
University of Louisville (Ph.D.) (Co)	3	3
University of Minnesota Ed (Ph.D.) (Co)	2	1
University of North Carolina at Chapel Hill (Ph.D.) (Cl)	3	3
University of Oklahoma (Ph.D.) (Co)	2	0
University of Pittsburgh (Ph.D.) (Cl)	8	28
University of Utah (Ph.D.) (Cl)	3	3
University of Vermont (Ph.D.) (Cl)	1	1
University of Virginia (Ph.D.) (Cl)	5	5
University of Wisconsin—Milwaukee (Ph.D.) (Co)	1	2
Virginia Commonwealth University (Ph.D.) (Cl)	5	4
Virginia Consortium Program in Clinical Psychology (Psy.D.) (Cl)	3	0
Yeshiva University (Psy.D.) (Cm)	2	0

Adoption/Foster Care

	# Faculty	# Grants
Rutgers, The State University of New Jersey (Psy.D.) (Cl)	1	1
University of Delaware (Ph.D.) (Cl)	1	2
University of Massachusetts—Amherst (Ph.D.) (Cl)	1	1

Affective Disorders/Depression/Mood Disorders

	# Faculty	# Grants
American University (Ph.D.) (Cl)	1	0
Baylor University (Psy.D.) (Cl)	3	0
Binghamton University/State University of New York (Ph.D.) (Cl)	1	1
Boston University (Ph.D.) (Cl)	2	1
Carlos Albizu University—Miami Campus (Psy.D.) (Cl)	3	0
Catholic University of America (Ph.D.) (Cl)	2	2
Clark University (Ph.D.) (Cl)	1	0
Drexel University (Ph.D.) (Cl)	2	1
Duke University (Ph.D.) (Cl)	3	2
Fuller Theological Seminary (Ph.D. & Psy.D.) (Cl)	1	0
George Washington University (Ph.D.) (Cl)	2	2
Georgia State University (Ph.D.) (Cl)	1	1
Harvard University (Ph.D.) (Cl)	4	5
Hofstra University (Ph.D.) (Cl)	1	0
Illinois Institute of Technology (Ph.D.) (Cl)	1	1
Indiana State University (Psy.D.) (Cl)	2	0
Jackson State University (Ph.D.) (Cl)	1	0
James Madison University (Psy.D.) (Cm)	1	0
Marquette University (Ph.D.) (Cl)	2	0
Marshall University (Psy.D.) (Cl)	1	0
McGill University (Ph.D.) (Cl)	2	2
Michigan State University (Ph.D.) (Cl)	1	0
Northern Illinois University (Ph.D.) (Cl)	2	0
Northwestern University (Ph.D.) (Cl)	3	0
Oklahoma State University (Ph.D.) (Cl)	1	0
Pacific Graduate School of Psychology/ Stanford University Medical School Consortium (Psy.D.) (Cl)	2	2
Pennsylvania State University (Ph.D.) (Cl)	2	0
San Diego State University/University of California, San Diego (Ph.D.) (Cl)	3	2

	# Faculty	# Grants
Simon Fraser University (Ph.D.) (Cl)	3	1
Southern Illinois University—Carbondale (Ph.D.) (Cl)	2	0
St. Louis University (Ph.D.) (Cl)	2	0
Stony Brook University/State University of New York (Ph.D.) (Cl)	1	2
Teachers College, Columbia University (Ph.D.) (Cl)	1	1
Texas Tech University (Ph.D.) (Co)	1	0
The Ohio State University (Ph.D.) (Cl)	3	1
Uniformed Services University of Health Sciences (Ph.D.) (Cl)	1	2
University at Buffalo/State University of New York (Ph.D.) (Cl)	1	0
University of Alabama at Tuscaloosa (Ph.D.) (Cl)	1	0
University of Arizona (Ph.D.) (Cl)	2	3
University of California, Berkeley (Ph.D.) (Cl)	3	3
University of California, Los Angeles (Ph.D.) (Cl)	4	5
University of Colorado at Boulder (Ph.D.) (Cl)	5	4
University of Connecticut (Ph.D.) (Cl)	4	2
University of Georgia (Ph.D.) (Cl)	2	2
University of Hawaii at Manoa (Ph.D.) (Cl)	2	0
University of Houston (Ph.D.) (Cl)	2	2
University of Illinois at Chicago (Ph.D.) (Cl)	2	0
University of Iowa (Ph.D.) (Cl)	2	1
University of Iowa (Ph.D.) (Co)	1	0
University of Kansas—Psychology (Ph.D.) (Cl)	3	1
University of Louisville (Ph.D.) (Co)	1	0
University of Maine (Ph.D.) (Cl)	1	0
University of Maryland—College Park (Ph.D.) (Cl)	1	0
University of Miami (Ph.D.) (Cl)	3	1
University of Michigan (Ph.D.) (Cl)	1	1
University of Minnesota (Ph.D.) (Cl)	—	—
University of Montana (Ph.D.) (Cl)	1	0
University of Nevada—Reno (Ph.D.) (Cl)	1	0
University of North Carolina at Greensboro (Ph.D.) (Cl)	1	0
University of North Texas (Ph.D.) (Cl)	1	0
University of Notre Dame (Ph.D.) (Co)	3	1
University of Oregon (Ph.D.) (Cl)	3	2
University of Pennsylvania (Ph.D.) (Cl)	3	4
University of Pittsburgh (Ph.D.) (Cl)	7	22
University of Rochester (Ph.D.) (Cl)	1	1
University of South Dakota (Ph.D.) (Cl)	2	0
University of South Florida (Ph.D.) (Cl)	2	2
University of Southern California (Ph.D.) (Cl)	5	0
University of Texas at Austin (Ph.D.) (Cl)	1	1
University of Texas at Austin (Ph.D.) (Co)	1	0
University of Texas Southwestern Medical Center (Ph.D.) (Cl)	3	3
University of Vermont (Ph.D.) (Cl)	2	2
University of Washington (Ph.D.) (Cl)	3	1
University of Waterloo (Ph.D.) (Cl)	2	2
University of Wisconsin—Madison (Ph.D.) (Cl)	6	6
University of Wisconsin—Milwaukee (Ph.D.) (Cl)	1	2
University of Wyoming (Ph.D.) (Cl)	3	2
Vanderbilt University (Ph.D.) (Cl)	8	5
Virginia Consortium Program in Clinical Psychology (Psy.D.) (Cl)	5	0
Virginia Polytechnic Institute and State University (Ph.D.) (Cl)	2	0
Western Michigan University (Ph.D.) (Cl)	3	1
Yale University (Ph.D.) (Cl)	3	1
Yeshiva University (Psy.D.) (Cl)	2	0
York University (Ph.D.) (Cl)	2	2

African American Studies

	# Faculty	# Grants
University of Georgia (Ph.D.) (Cl)	1	0
University of Georgia (Ph.D.) (Co)	1	1
University of Missouri—Columbia (Ph.D.) (Co)	1	2

Aggression/Anger Control

	# Faculty	# Grants
Colorado State University (Ph.D.) (Co)	1	0
Hofstra University (Ph.D.) (Cl)	2	0
Long Island University, C.W. Post Campus (Psy.D.) (Cl)	1	0
Marywood University (Psy.D.) (Cl)	1	0
McGill University (Ph.D.) (Cl)	1	1
Philadelphia College of Osteopathic Medicine (Psy.D.) (Cl)	1	0
Purdue University (Ph.D.) (Cl)	3	1
University of Arkansas (Ph.D.) (Cl)	3	1
University of Georgia (Ph.D.) (Cl)	4	0
University of Louisville (Ph.D.) (Co)	1	0
University of Southern Mississippi (Ph.D.) (Co)	1	1

Aging/Gerontology/Adult Development

	# Faculty	# Grants
Adler School of Professional Psychology (Psy.D.) (Cl)	1	0
Argosy University, Phoenix (Psy.D.) (Cl)	2	0
Boston University (Ph.D.) (Cl)	2	2
Carlos Albizu University—Miami Campus (Psy.D.) (Cl)	1	0
Carlos Albizu University–San Juan Campus (Ph.D.) (Cl)	2	1
Case Western Reserve University (Ph.D.) (Cl)	2	1

	# Faculty	# Grants
Colorado State University (Ph.D.) (Co)	3	1
Florida Institute of Technology (Psy.D.) (Cl)	1	2
Gallaudet University (Ph.D.) (Cl)	1	0
Immaculata University (Psy.D.) (Cl)	1	0
Long Island University, Brooklyn Campus (Ph.D) (Cl)	1	1
Loyola College in Maryland (Psy.D.) (Cl)	2	0
Marquette University (Ph.D.) (Cl)	1	0
Nova Southeastern University (Ph.D. & Psy.D.) (Cl)	1	0
Pacific Graduate School of Psychology (Ph.D.) (Cl)	1	0
San Diego State University/University of California, San Diego (Ph.D.) (Cl)	8	1
Teachers College, Columbia University (Ph.D.) (Cl)	1	0
Texas A&M University (Ph.D.) (Cl)	2	1
Texas A&M University (Ph.D.) (Co)	1	0
University of Alabama at Birmingham (Ph.D.) (Cl)	3	6
University of Alabama at Tuscaloosa (Ph.D.) (Cl)	6	5
University of Colorado at Colorado Springs (Ph.D.) (Cl)	6	1
University of Connecticut (Ph.D.) (Cl)	1	0
University of Georgia (Ph.D.) (Cl)	2	2
University of Indianapolis (Psy.D.) (Cl)	2	1
University of Kansas—Psychology (Ph.D.) (Cl)	1	1
University of Louisville (Ph.D.) (Cl)	3	1
University of Massachusetts—Amherst (Ph.D.) (Cl)	2	0
University of Missouri—St. Louis (Ph.D.) (Cl)	1	1
University of Nevada—Reno (Ph.D.) (Cl)	2	4
University of North Dakota (Ph.D.) (Co)	1	1
University of North Texas (Ph.D.) (Cl)	1	1
University of North Texas (Ph.D.) (Co)	1	0
University of Southern California (Ph.D.) (Cl)	4	5
University of Tulsa (Ph.D.) (Cl)	2	1
University of Utah (Ph.D.) (Co)	1	1
Washington University in St. Louis (Ph.D.) (Cl)	3	5
West Virginia University (Ph.D.) (Cl)	2	1
Wheaton College (Psy.D.) (Cl)	1	0
Wright State University (Psy.D.) (Cl)	1	0
Xavier University (Psy.D.) (Cl)	2	0
Yeshiva University (Psy.D.) (Cl)	1	1
Carlos Albizu University–San Juan Campus (Psy.D.) (Cl)	2	0
McGill University (Ph.D.) (Cl)	2	1
Rosalind Franklin University of Medicine and Science (Ph.D.) (Cl)	1	1
University of Victoria (Ph.D.) (Cl)	1	1

Alcohol (see also Substance Abuse/Addictive Behaviors)

	# Faculty	# Grants
Bowling Green State University (Ph.D.) (Cl)	1	0
Georgia State University (Ph.D.) (Cl)	1	1
Jackson State University (Ph.D.) (Cl)	2	0
Kent State University (Ph.D.) (Cl)	1	1
Nova Southeastern University (Ph.D. & Psy.D.) (Cl)	3	5
University of Central Florida (Ph.D.) (Cl)	1	—
University of Detroit Mercy (Ph.D.) (Cl)	1	1
University of Georgia (Ph.D.) (Cl)	1	1
University of Illinois at Chicago (Ph.D.) (Cl)	1	1
University of Southern California (Ph.D.) (Cl)	3	0
University of Wisconsin—Milwaukee (Ph.D.) (Cl)	1	0

Alzheimer's Disease

	# Faculty	# Grants
Marquette University (Ph.D.) (Cl)	1	0
San Diego State University/University of California, San Diego (Ph.D.) (Cl)	6	0
University of Texas Southwestern Medical Center (Ph.D.) (Cl)	1	1

Anxiety Disorders/Panic Disorders

	# Faculty	# Grants
American University (Ph.D.) (Cl)	1	0
Auburn University (Ph.D.) (Cl)	2	0
Binghamton University/State University of New York (Ph.D.) (Cl)	2	1
Boston University (Ph.D.) (Cl)	7	5
Brigham Young University (Ph.D.) (Cl)	1	1
Catholic University of America (Ph.D.) (Cl)	8	2
Central Michigan University (Ph.D.) (Cl)	1	1
Colorado State University (Ph.D.) (Co)	1	0
Concordia University (Ph.D.) (Cl)	2	3
Drexel University (Ph.D.) (Cl)	2	0
Eastern Michigan University (Ph.D.) (Cl)	2	0
Florida State University (Ph.D.) (Cl)	1	4
George Mason University (Ph.D.) (Cl)	1	0
George Washington University (Ph.D.) (Cl)	1	1
Georgia State University (Ph.D.) (Cl)	2	2
Harvard University (Ph.D.) (Cl)	3	0
Kent State University (Ph.D.) (Cl)	2	1
La Salle University (Psy.D.) (Cl)	3	0
Miami University (Ph.D.) (Cl)	3	1
Northern Illinois University (Ph.D.) (Cl)	3	1
Northwestern University (Ph.D.) (Cl)	2	1
Nova Southeastern University (Ph.D. & Psy.D.) (Cl)	1	0
Oklahoma State University (Ph.D.) (Cl)	1	0

	# Faculty	# Grants
Ontario Institute for Studies in Education/University of Toronto (Ph.D.) (Cm)	2	2
Pacific Graduate School of Psychology/Stanford University Medical School Consortium (Psy.D.) (Cl)	5	3
Pacific University (Psy.D.) (Cl)	1	0
Pennsylvania State University (Ph.D.) (Cl)	3	3
Philadelphia College of Osteopathic Medicine (Psy.D.) (Cl)	7	0
Purdue University (Ph.D.) (Cl)	1	0
Rosalind Franklin University of Medicine and Science (Ph.D.) (Cl)	1	1
Rutgers, The State University of New Jersey (Psy.D.) (Cl)	3	1
San Diego State University/University of California, San Diego (Ph.D.) (Cl)	4	1
Southern Illinois University—Carbondale (Ph.D.) (Cl)	3	0
St. Louis University (Ph.D.) (Cl)	2	0
Stony Brook University/State University of New York (Ph.D.) (Cl)	1	2
Texas A&M University (Ph.D.) (Cl)	3	1
The Ohio State University (Ph.D.) (Cl)	2	1
University at Albany/State University of New York (Ph.D.) (Cl)	1	1
University at Buffalo/State University of New York (Ph.D.) (Cl)	2	1
University of Arkansas (Ph.D.) (Cl)	4	2
University of British Columbia (Ph.D.) (Cl)	2	2
University of British Columbia (Ph.D.) (Co)	2	2
University of California, Los Angeles (Ph.D.) (Cl)	2	7
University of Connecticut (Ph.D.) (Cl)	2	1
University of Delaware (Ph.D.) (Cl)	3	1
University of Florida (Ph.D.) (Cl)	2	2
University of Georgia (Ph.D.) (Cl)	1	0
University of Hawaii at Manoa (Ph.D.) (Cl)	1	1
University of Houston (Ph.D.) (Cl)	3	3
University of Illinois at Chicago (Ph.D.) (Cl)	3	1
University of Kansas—Child (Ph.D.) (Cl)	1	—
University of Kansas—Psychology (Ph.D.) (Cl)	2	1
University of Louisville (Ph.D.) (Cl)	2	0
University of Maine (Ph.D.) (Cl)	2	1
University of Massachusetts—Boston (Ph.D.) (Cl)	1	1
University of Minnesota (Ph.D.) (Cl)	—	—
University of Missouri—Columbia (Ph.D.) (Cl)	2	1
University of Nebraska—Lincoln (Ph.D.) (Cl)	1	0
University of Nevada—Reno (Ph.D.) (Cl)	2	0

	# Faculty	# Grants
University of North Carolina at Chapel Hill (Ph.D.) (Cl)	1	0
University of North Dakota (Ph.D.) (Cl)	1	0
University of Oregon (Ph.D.) (Cl)	2	2
University of Pennsylvania (Ph.D.) (Cl)	2	5
University of Texas at Austin (Ph.D.) (Cl)	1	0
University of Toledo (Ph.D.) (Cl)	2	0
University of Vermont (Ph.D.) (Cl)	1	3
University of Virginia (Ph.D.) (Cl)	1	0
University of Washington (Ph.D.) (Cl)	3	1
University of Waterloo (Ph.D.) (Cl)	4	6
University of Wisconsin—Milwaukee (Ph.D.) (Cl)	4	7
University of Wyoming (Ph.D.) (Cl)	2	1
Vanderbilt University (Ph.D.) (Cl)	7	0
Virginia Commonwealth University (Ph.D.) (Cl)	2	1
Virginia Consortium Program in Clinical Psychology (Psy.D.) (Cl)	3	0
Virginia Polytechnic Institute and State University (Ph.D.) (Cl)	3	1
West Virginia University (Ph.D.) (Cl)	2	0
Western Michigan University (Ph.D.) (Cl)	1	1
Yale University (Ph.D.) (Cl)	2	1
Yeshiva University (Psy.D.) (Cl)	1	0

Applied Behavioral Analysis

	# Faculty	# Grants
Eastern Michigan University (Ph.D.) (Cl)	2	0
Rutgers, The State University of New Jersey (Ph.D.) (Cl)	2	1
Rutgers, The State University of New Jersey (Psy.D.) (Cl)	1	1
San Diego State University/University of California, San Diego (Ph.D.) (Cl)	4	0
University of Hartford (Psy.D.) (Cl)	1	0
University of North Dakota (Ph.D.) (Cl)	2	0

Asian Studies

	# Faculty	# Grants
Texas Tech University (Ph.D.) (Co)	1	0
University of British Columbia (Ph.D.) (Cl)	1	2
University of British Columbia (Ph.D.) (Co)	1	2

Assessment/Diagnosis

	# Faculty	# Grants
Alliant International University—Los Angeles (Psy.D.) (Cl)	3	—
Alliant International University—San Diego (Ph.D.) (Cl)	4	—
Alliant International University—San Diego (Psy.D.) (Cl)	2	—
Alliant International University—San Francisco Bay (Ph.D.) (Cl)	2	—
Alliant International University—San Francisco Bay (Psy.D.) (Cl)	1	—

	# Faculty	# Grants
Argosy University, Atlanta (Psy.D.) (Cl)	4	0
Azusa Pacific University (Psy.D.) (Cl)	2	0
Binghamton University/State University of New York (Ph.D.) (Cl)	4	0
Brigham Young University (Ph.D.) (Cl)	3	1
Catholic University of America (Ph.D.) (Cl)	1	1
Central Michigan University (Ph.D.) (Cl)	1	0
Clark University (Ph.D.) (Cl)	1	0
Colorado State University (Ph.D.) (Co)	3	1
Fairleigh Dickinson University (Ph.D.) (Cl)	5	1
Fordham University (Ph.D.) (Cl)	3	0
George Washington University (Psy.D.) (Cl)	3	0
Indiana State University (Psy.D.) (Cl)	2	0
Jackson State University (Ph.D.) (Cl)	6	0
McGill University (Ph.D.) (Cl)	2	0
Oklahoma State University (Ph.D.) (Co)	1	0
Pacific Graduate School of Psychology (Ph.D.) (Cl)	4	0
Pepperdine University (Psy.D.) (Cl)	6	0
Philadelphia College of Osteopathic Medicine (Psy.D.) (Cl)	3	0
Purdue University (Ph.D.) (Co)	1	0
Roosevelt University (Psy.D.) (Cl)	3	0
Rutgers, The State University of New Jersey (Psy.D.) (Cl)	2	0
Southern Illinois University—Carbondale (Ph.D.) (Cl)	8	0
St. Louis University (Ph.D.) (Cl)	2	0
Texas A&M University (Ph.D.) (Cl)	3	0
Texas Tech University (Ph.D.) (Cl)	1	0
The New School (Ph.D.) (Cl)	2	1
University at Buffalo/State University of New York (Ph.D.) (Cl)	1	1
University at Buffalo/State University of New York (Ph.D.) (Cm)	4	1
University of Alabama at Tuscaloosa (Ph.D.) (Cl)	2	0
University of British Columbia (Ph.D.) (Cl)	1	1
University of British Columbia (Ph.D.) (Co)	1	1
University of California, Santa Barbara (Ph.D.) (Cm)	—	—
University of Colorado at Boulder (Ph.D.) (Cl)	4	1
University of Detroit Mercy (Ph.D.) (Cl)	2	0
University of Georgia (Ph.D.) (Co)	1	1
University of Hartford (Psy.D.) (Cl)	1	0
University of Hawaii at Manoa (Ph.D.) (Cl)	7	2
University of Iowa (Ph.D.) (Cl)	3	1
University of Kentucky (Ph.D.) (Cl)	3	0
University of Massachusetts—Amherst (Ph.D.) (Cl)	1	1
University of Mississippi (Ph.D.) (Cl)	2	0

	# Faculty	# Grants
University of Montana (Ph.D.) (Cl)	4	1
University of Nevada—Reno (Ph.D.) (Cl)	3	0
University of North Carolina at Greensboro (Ph.D.) (Cl)	1	0
University of Oklahoma (Ph.D.) (Co)	2	0
University of Toledo (Ph.D.) (Cl)	2	1
Virginia Consortium Program in Clinical Psychology (Psy.D.) (Cl)	4	0
Western Michigan University (Ph.D.) (Co)	2	0
Widener University (Psy.D.) (Cl)	5	0
Yeshiva University (Psy.D.) (Cm)	3	0

Attachment

	# Faculty	# Grants
Argosy University, Twin Cities (Psy.D.) (Cl)	1	0
Catholic University of America (Ph.D.) (Cl)	1	1
Fordham University (Ph.D.) (Cl)	1	0
Iowa State University (Ph.D.) (Co)	1	0
James Madison University (Psy.D.) (Cm)	1	0
Long Island University, C.W. Post Campus (Psy.D.) (Cl)	1	1
Michigan State University (Ph.D.) (Cl)	2	0
Purdue University (Ph.D.) (Co)	1	1
Stony Brook University/State University of New York (Ph.D.) (Cl)	1	0
University of Delaware (Ph.D.) (Cl)	2	2
University of Houston (Ph.D.) (Co)	1	0
Yeshiva University (Psy.D.) (Cm)	3	0

Attention

	# Faculty	# Grants
Seattle Pacific University (Ph.D.) (Cl)	1	1
University of Missouri—Kansas City (Ph.D.) (Cl)	1	0

Attention Deficit/Hyperactivity Disorder

	# Faculty	# Grants
Argosy University, Schaumburg (Psy.D.) (Cl)	1	0
Carlos Albizu University–San Juan Campus (Ph.D.) (Cl)	2	1
Colorado State University (Ph.D.) (Co)	1	0
Emory University (Ph.D.) (Cl)	1	1
Illinois Institute of Technology (Ph.D.) (Cl)	1	0
Marquette University (Ph.D.) (Cl)	1	0
Marywood University (Psy.D.) (Cl)	1	0
McGill University (Ph.D.) (Cl)	1	1
Nova Southeastern University (Ph.D. & Psy.D.) (Cl)	2	1
Pepperdine University (Psy.D.) (Cl)	1	2
Regent University (Psy.D.) (Cl)	1	1

	# Faculty	# Grants
University at Buffalo/State University of New York (Ph.D.) (Cl)	2	10
University at Buffalo/State University of New York (Ph.D.) (Cm)	1	3
University of California, Berkeley (Ph.D.) (Cl)	1	2
University of California, Santa Barbara (Ph.D.) (Cm)	—	—
University of Central Florida (Ph.D.) (Cl)	1	—
University of Maine (Ph.D.) (Cl)	1	0
University of North Carolina at Greensboro (Ph.D.) (Cl)	1	2
University of North Texas (Ph.D.) (Co)	2	1
University of Pittsburgh (Ph.D.) (Cl)	1	2
University of Rochester (Ph.D.) (Cl)	1	0
University of Victoria (Ph.D.) (Cl)	1	1
University of Wyoming (Ph.D.) (Cl)	1	0
Utah State University (Ph.D.) (Cm)	1	0
Virginia Consortium Program in Clinical Psychology (Psy.D.) (Cl)	1	0
Virginia Polytechnic Institute and State University (Ph.D.) (Cl)	1	0
Yeshiva University (Psy.D.) (Cm)	2	0

Attitudes, Beliefs, and Values

Arizona State University (Ph.D.) (Co)	1	0
George Fox University (Psy.D.) (Cl)	1	0
University of La Verne (Psy.D.) (Cl)	2	0
University of Minnesota (Ph.D.) (Co)	1	0

Attributions

University of Georgia (Ph.D.) (Co)	2	0
Virginia Consortium Program in Clinical Psychology (Psy.D.) (Cl)	1	0

Autism/Asperger's Syndrome/ Developmental Disorders

Auburn University (Ph.D.) (Cl)	1	1
Binghamton University/State University of New York (Ph.D.) (Cl)	2	3
Brigham Young University (Ph.D.) (Cl)	2	2
Case Western Reserve University (Ph.D.) (Cl)	1	1
Georgia State University (Ph.D.) (Cl)	1	1
Long Island University, Brooklyn Campus (Ph.D) (Cl)	4	1
Long Island University, C.W. Post Campus (Psy.D.) (Cl)	1	0
Marquette University (Ph.D.) (Cl)	1	0
Michigan State University (Ph.D.) (Cl)	2	1
Pennsylvania State University (Ph.D.) (Cl)	3	1
Pepperdine University (Psy.D.) (Cl)	1	0

Rutgers, The State University of New Jersey (Ph.D.) (Cl)	1	1
Rutgers, The State University of New Jersey (Psy.D.) (Cl)	4	3
San Diego State University/University of California, San Diego (Ph.D.) (Cl)	2	0
Seattle Pacific University (Ph.D.) (Cl)	1	0
St. John's University (Ph.D.) (Cl)	1	1
Stony Brook University/State University of New York (Ph.D.) (Cl)	0	2
The Wright Institute (Psy.D.) (Cl)	2	0
University at Albany/State University of New York (Ph.D.) (Cl)	1	3
University of Alabama at Birmingham (Ph.D.) (Cl)	6	16
University of Alabama at Tuscaloosa (Ph.D.) (Cl)	1	2
University of California, Santa Barbara (Ph.D.) (Cm)	—	—
University of Connecticut (Ph.D.) (Cl)	4	3
University of Denver (Ph.D.) (Cl)	1	1
University of Michigan (Ph.D.) (Cl)	1	2
University of Missouri—Columbia (Ph.D.) (Cl)	1	0
University of Pittsburgh (Ph.D.) (Cl)	3	16
University of Rochester (Ph.D.) (Cl)	2	2
University of Texas at Austin (Ph.D.) (Cl)	1	0
University of Washington (Ph.D.) (Cl)	1	1
University of Wisconsin—Milwaukee (Ph.D.) (Cl)	1	1
Vanderbilt University (Ph.D.) (Cl)	2	1
Virginia Polytechnic Institute and State University (Ph.D.) (Cl)	2	0

Behavioral Analysis/Therapy

Hofstra University (Ph.D.) (Cl)	5	0
McGill University (Ph.D.) (Cl)	1	0
Nova Southeastern University (Ph.D. & Psy.D.) (Cl)	14	2
Pacific University (Psy.D.) (Cl)	7	0
University of Kentucky (Ph.D.) (Co)	2	1
University of Mississippi (Ph.D.) (Cl)	3	0
University of Nevada—Reno (Ph.D.) (Cl)	3	0
University of North Carolina at Greensboro (Ph.D.) (Cl)	1	0
Virginia Consortium Program in Clinical Psychology (Psy.D.) (Cl)	1	0
Western Michigan University (Ph.D.) (Cl)	4	0

Behavioral Medicine/Health Psychology

Adelphi University (Ph.D.) (Cl)	1	1
Alliant International University— Los Angeles (Ph.D.) (Cl)	5	—

	# Faculty	# Grants
Alliant International University—Los Angeles (Psy.D.) (Cl)	5	—
Alliant International University—San Diego (Ph.D.) (Cl)	4	—
Alliant International University—San Francisco Bay (Ph.D.) (Cl)	3	—
Alliant International University—San Francisco Bay (Psy.D.) (Cl)	4	—
Antioch University New England (Psy.D.)	1	1
Argosy University, Chicago (Psy.D.) (Cl)	4	3
Argosy University, Hawaii (Psy.D.) (Cl)	1	0
Argosy University, Phoenix (Psy.D.) (Cl)	2	0
Arizona State University (Ph.D.) (Cl)	8	5
Arizona State University (Ph.D.) (Co)	1	0
Ball State University (Ph.D.) (Co)	2	0
Baylor University (Psy.D.) (Cl)	1	0
Binghamton University/State University of New York (Ph.D.) (Cl)	1	1
Bowling Green State University (Ph.D.) (Cl)	2	1
Brigham Young University (Ph.D.) (Cl)	1	1
Carlos Albizu University—Miami Campus (Psy.D.) (Cl)	2	0
Case Western Reserve University (Ph.D.) (Cl)	1	1
Central Michigan University (Ph.D.) (Cl)	1	1
Colorado State University (Ph.D.) (Co)	8	4
Concordia University (Ph.D.) (Cl)	1	1
Concordia University (Ph.D.) (Cl)	1	0
Drexel University (Ph.D.) (Cl)	7	2
Duke University (Ph.D.) (Cl)	4	6
Eastern Michigan University (Ph.D.) (Cl)	1	0
Fairleigh Dickinson University (Ph.D.) (Cl)	3	0
Florida Institute of Technology (Psy.D.) (Cl)	3	0
Fordham University (Ph.D.) (Cl)	3	2
Fordham University (Ph.D.) (Co)	2	1
Fuller Theological Seminary (Ph.D. & Psy.D.) (Cl)	3	0
George Washington University (Ph.D.) (Cl)	2	0
Howard University (Ph.D.) (Cl)	3	2
Illinois Institute of Technology (Ph.D.) (Cl)	1	1
Indiana State University (Psy.D.) (Cl)	2	1
Indiana University of Pennsylvania (Psy.D.) (Cl)	2	0
Indiana University—Bloomington (Ph.D.) (Cl)	2	2
Indiana University—Purdue University Indianapolis (Ph.D.) (Cl)	6	1
Iowa State University (Ph.D.) (Co)	1	1
La Salle University (Psy.D.) (Cl)	3	1
Loma Linda University (Ph.D. & Psy.D.) (Cl)		6
Long Island University, Brooklyn Campus (Ph.D) (Cl)	1	1
Loyola College in Maryland (Psy.D.) (Cl)	3	0
McGill University (Ph.D.) (Cl)	4	4
New Mexico State University (Ph.D.) (Co)	1	1
Nova Southeastern University (Ph.D. & Psy.D.) (Cl)	6	2
Ohio University (Ph.D.) (Cl)	4	6
Oklahoma State University (Ph.D.) (Cl)	2	0
Oklahoma State University (Ph.D.) (Co)	2	0
Pacific Graduate School of Psychology (Ph.D.) (Cl)	4	1
Pacific Graduate School of Psychology/Stanford University Medical School Consortium (Psy.D.) (Cl)	2	1
Pacific University (Psy.D.) (Cl)	2	1
Pennsylvania State University (Ph.D.) (Cl)	2	0
Roosevelt University (Psy.D.) (Cl)	4	1
Rutgers, The State University of New Jersey (Ph.D.) (Cl)	5	1
Sam Houston State University (Ph.D.) (Cl)	2	0
San Diego State University/University of California, San Diego (Ph.D.) (Cl)	2	1
Seattle Pacific University (Ph.D.) (Cl)	3	0
Seton Hall University (Ph.D.) (Co)	1	0
Simon Fraser University (Ph.D.) (Cl)	1	1
Southern Illinois University—Carbondale (Ph.D.) (Cl)	2	0
Southern Illinois University—Carbondale (Ph.D.) (Co)	1	0
Southern Methodist University (Ph.D.) (Cl)	3	1
Spalding University (Psy.D.) (Cl)	1	0
St. John's University (Ph.D.) (Cl)	2	1
Texas A&M University (Ph.D.) (Cl)	2	1
Texas Tech University (Ph.D.) (Cl)	4	1
The University of Memphis (Ph.D.) (Cl)	4	3
The University of Memphis (Ph.D.) (Co)	1	0
Uniformed Services University of Health Sciences (Ph.D.) (Cl)	1	3
University at Albany/State University of New York (Ph.D.) (Cl)	2	0
University at Buffalo/State University of New York (Ph.D.) (Cl)	3	3
University at Buffalo/State University of New York (Ph.D.) (Cm)	4	3
University of Alabama at Birmingham (Ph.D.) (Cl)	2	2
University of Alabama at Tuscaloosa (Ph.D.) (Cl)	3	2
University of Arizona (Ph.D.) (Cl)	6	6
University of California, Los Angeles (Ph.D.) (Cl)	2	7
University of Cincinnati (Ph.D.) (Cl)	10	6
University of Connecticut (Ph.D.) (Cl)	1	1
University of Denver (Psy.D.) (Cl)	1	0
University of Florida (Ph.D.) (Cl)	3	3
University of Florida (Ph.D.) (Co)	1	2
University of Hawaii at Manoa (Ph.D.) (Cl)	1	0

345

	# Faculty	# Grants
University of Illinois at Chicago (Ph.D.) (Cl)	4	1
University of Iowa (Ph.D.) (Cl)	2	3
University of Kansas—Child (Ph.D.) (Cl)	2	1
University of Kansas—Psychology (Ph.D.) (Cl)	2	1
University of Kentucky (Ph.D.) (Cl)	2	1
University of Louisville (Ph.D.) (Cl)	3	1
University of Maine (Ph.D.) (Cl)	1	1
University of Maryland—Baltimore County (Ph.D.) (Cl)	3	3
University of Maryland—College Park (Ph.D.) (Co)	2	0
University of Massachusetts—Boston (Ph.D.) (Cl)	1	2
University of Miami (Ph.D.) (Cl)	14	2
University of Miami (Ph.D.) (Co)	3	1
University of Michigan (Ph.D.) (Cl)	1	—
University of Minnesota (Ph.D.) (Co)	1	0
University of Missouri—Columbia (Ph.D.) (Co)	2	1
University of Missouri—St. Louis (Ph.D.) (Cl)	2	1
University of Montana (Ph.D.) (Cl)	4	0
University of Nevada—Reno (Ph.D.) (Cl)	2	0
University of New Mexico (Ph.D.) (Cl)	2	2
University of North Carolina at Chapel Hill (Ph.D.) (Cl)	1	2
University of North Dakota (Ph.D.) (Cl)	2	0
University of North Texas and University of North Texas Health Sciences Center (Consortium) (Ph.D.) (Cl)	2	1
University of Notre Dame (Ph.D.) (Co)	2	2
University of Oklahoma (Ph.D.) (Co)	1	0
University of Pittsburgh (Ph.D.) (Cl)	14	38
University of Rhode Island (Ph.D.) (Cl)	4	7
University of South Florida (Ph.D.) (Cl)	5	8
University of Southern California (Ph.D.) (Cl)	3	3
University of Tennessee—Knoxville (Ph.D.) (Cl)	2	1
University of Tennessee—Knoxville (Ph.D.) (Co)	1	1
University of Texas at Austin (Ph.D.) (Cl)	1	1
University of Texas at Austin (Ph.D.) (Co)	1	0
University of Texas Southwestern Medical Center (Ph.D.) (Cl)	4	4
University of Utah (Ph.D.) (Cl)	1	1
University of Vermont (Ph.D.) (Cl)	1	1
University of Windsor (Ph.D.) (Cl)	3	5
University of Wisconsin—Madison (Ph.D.) (Cl)	3	3
University of Wisconsin—Milwaukee (Ph.D.) (Cl)	2	0
Utah State University (Ph.D.) (Cm)	3	2
Vanderbilt University (Ph.D.) (Cl)	7	5
Virginia Commonwealth University (Ph.D.) (Cl)	5	3
Virginia Commonwealth University (Ph.D.) (Co)	5	4
Virginia Consortium Program in Clinical Psychology (Psy.D.) (Cl)	6	0
Virginia Polytechnic Institute and State University (Ph.D.) (Cl)	3	2
Washington State University (Ph.D.) (Cl)	5	8
West Virginia University (Ph.D.) (Cl)	3	1
Western Michigan University (Ph.D.) (Cl)	1	1
Yale University (Ph.D.) (Cl)	3	4

Bereavement/Grief

	# Faculty	# Grants
Biola University (Ph.D. & Psy.D.) (Cl)	1	0
Loyola University of Chicago (Ph.D.) (Cl)	1	0
Pacific Graduate School of Psychology (Ph.D.) (Cl)	1	0
Purdue University (Ph.D.) (Co)	1	1
San Diego State University/University of California, San Diego (Ph.D.) (Cl)	2	0

Biofeedback/Relaxation

	# Faculty	# Grants
Fuller Theological Seminary (Ph.D. & Psy.D.) (Cl)	1	0
George Washington University (Ph.D.) (Cl)	1	0
Hofstra University (Ph.D.) (Cl)	1	0
James Madison University (Psy.D.) (Cm)	1	0
Nova Southeastern University (Ph.D. & Psy.D.) (Cl)	1	1
Pennsylvania State University (Ph.D.) (Cl)	2	1
San Diego State University/University of California, San Diego (Ph.D.) (Cl)	1	0
Seattle Pacific University (Ph.D.) (Cl)	1	1
University of North Dakota (Ph.D.) (Cl)	1	0
Virginia Consortium Program in Clinical Psychology (Psy.D.) (Cl)	2	0
Brigham Young University (Ph.D.) (Cl)	1	1
Georgia State University (Ph.D.) (Cl)	4	1
University of Montana (Ph.D.) (Cl)	1	0
University of Victoria (Ph.D.) (Cl)	2	2

Brain Injury/Head Injury

	# Faculty	# Grants
Brigham Young University (Ph.D.) (Cl)	1	1
Georgia State University (Ph.D.) (Cl)	4	1
University of Montana (Ph.D.) (Cl)	1	0
University of Victoria (Ph.D.) (Cl)	2	2

	# Faculty	# Grants

Bullying

	# Faculty	# Grants
Miami University (Ph.D.) (Cl)	3	2
Michigan State University (Ph.D.) (Cl)	1	0
University of Louisville (Ph.D.) (Co)	1	0

Cardiovascular Health/Function

Brigham Young University (Ph.D.) (Cl)	1	1
Kent State University (Ph.D.) (Cl)	1	1
San Diego State University/University of California, San Diego (Ph.D.) (Cl)	4	1
The Ohio State University (Ph.D.) (Cl)	3	4
Uniformed Services University of Health Sciences (Ph.D.) (Cl)	2	4
University of Georgia (Ph.D.) (Cl)	1	1
University of Maryland—Baltimore County (Ph.D.) (Cl)	1	1
University of Miami (Ph.D.) (Cl)	4	2
University of North Texas and University of North Texas Health Sciences Center (Consortium) (Ph.D.) (Cl)	2	1
University of Pittsburgh (Ph.D.) (Cl)	4	13
Virginia Consortium Program in Clinical Psychology (Psy.D.) (Cl)	1	1
West Virginia University (Ph.D.) (Cl)	1	0
Yeshiva University (Ph.D.) (Cl)	1	0

Child Abuse/Neglect/Sexual Abuse

Carlos Albizu University–San Juan Campus (Ph.D.) (Cl)	1	0
Clark University (Ph.D.) (Cl)	1	1
DePaul University (Ph.D.) (Cl)	1	1
Marquette University (Ph.D.) (Co)	2	0
Northern Illinois University (Ph.D.) (Cl)	3	1
Ontario Institute for Studies in Education/University of Toronto (Ph.D.) (Cm)	2	1
Southern Illinois University—Carbondale (Ph.D.) (Cl)	1	0
St. John's University (Ph.D.) (Cl)	1	2
Texas Tech University (Ph.D.) (Cl)	1	0
University of California, Santa Barbara (Ph.D.) (Cm)	—	—
University of Michigan (Ph.D.) (Cl)	1	—
University of Nebraska—Lincoln (Ph.D.) (Cl)	2	2
University of Rochester (Ph.D.) (Cl)	1	6
University of Victoria (Ph.D.) (Cl)	1	1
Virginia Consortium Program in Clinical Psychology (Psy.D.) (Cl)	2	0

Child and Family

Antioch University New England (Psy.D.)	2	0
Argosy University, Hawaii (Psy.D.) (Cl)	3	0

Argosy University, Washington, DC (Psy.D.) (Cl)	4	—
Carlos Albizu University—Miami Campus (Psy.D.) (Cl)	3	2
Central Michigan University (Ph.D.) (Cl)	1	2
Eastern Michigan University (Ph.D.) (Cl)	3	1
Fordham University (Ph.D.) (Cl)	2	1
Indiana University—Bloomington (Ph.D.) (Cl)	1	2
Jackson State University (Ph.D.) (Cl)	1	0
Kent State University (Ph.D.) (Cl)	2	1
Miami University (Ph.D.) (Cl)	1	1
Oklahoma State University (Ph.D.) (Cl)	1	0
Pacific Graduate School of Psychology (Ph.D.) (Cl)	4	0
Philadelphia College of Osteopathic Medicine (Psy.D.) (Cl)	2	1
Roosevelt University (Psy.D.) (Cl)	4	1
San Diego State University/University of California, San Diego (Ph.D.) (Cl)	7	0
The Ohio State University (Ph.D.) (Cl)	2	4
University at Albany/State University of New York (Ph.D.) (Cl)	4	2
University at Buffalo/State University of New York (Ph.D.) (Cl)	3	1
University of Arkansas (Ph.D.) (Cl)	2	0
University of Central Florida (Ph.D.) (Cl)	1	—
University of Hawaii at Manoa (Ph.D.) (Cl)	3	4
University of Houston (Ph.D.) (Co)	1	1
University of Indianapolis (Psy.D.) (Cl)	2	1
University of Kansas—Child (Ph.D.) (Cl)	2	1
University of Massachusetts—Amherst (Ph.D.) (Cl)	7	1
University of Michigan (Ph.D.) (Cl)	4	3
University of New Mexico (Ph.D.) (Cl)	1	0
University of North Carolina at Greensboro (Ph.D.) (Cl)	3	2
University of North Texas (Ph.D.) (Cl)	1	1
University of Oregon (Ph.D.) (Co)	3	2
University of Ottawa (Ph.D.) (Cl)	6	3
University of Pittsburgh (Ph.D.) (Cl)	14	45
University of South Carolina (Ph.D.) (Cl)	4	14
University of Southern California (Ph.D.) (Cl)	4	1
University of Toledo (Ph.D.) (Cl)	1	0
University of Utah (Ph.D.) (Co)	3	2
Utah State University (Ph.D.) (Cm)	2	0
Widener University (Psy.D.) (Cl)	3	1
Yeshiva University (Psy.D.) (Cl)	1	0
Yeshiva University (Psy.D.) (Cm)	2	0

Child/Child Clinical/Pediatric

Adelphi University (Ph.D.) (Cl)	2	2
Adler School of Professional Psychology (Psy.D.) (Cl)	2	0
American University (Ph.D.) (Cl)	1	0

347

	# Faculty	# Grants
Argosy University, Atlanta (Psy.D.) (Cl)	2	0
Argosy University, Schaumburg (Psy.D.) (Cl)	1	1
Arizona State University (Ph.D.) (Cl)	7	8
Auburn University (Ph.D.) (Cl)	5	1
Azusa Pacific University (Psy.D.) (Cl)	2	1
Ball State University (Ph.D.) (Co)	2	0
Binghamton University/State University of New York (Ph.D.) (Cl)	3	3
Bowling Green State University (Ph.D.) (Cl)	2	1
Brigham Young University (Ph.D.) (Cl)	3	2
Carlos Albizu University–San Juan Campus (Ph.D.) (Cl)	3	0
Catholic University of America (Ph.D.) (Cl)	7	5
Chicago School of Professional Psychology (Psy.D.) (Cl)	1	0
Clark University (Ph.D.) (Cl)	2	1
Colorado State University (Ph.D.) (Co)	5	1
Concordia University (Ph.D.) (Cl)	8	10
Duke University (Ph.D.) (Cl)	1	1
Emory University (Ph.D.) (Cl)	1	1
Fairleigh Dickinson University (Ph.D.) (Cl)	2	0
Fuller Theological Seminary (Ph.D. & Psy.D.) (Cl)	3	1
George Washington University (Ph.D.) (Cl)	2	1
George Washington University (Psy.D.) (Cl)	5	4
Georgia State University (Ph.D.) (Cl)	1	2
Harvard University (Ph.D.) (Cl)	1	4
Hofstra University (Ph.D.) (Cl)	1	0
Illinois Institute of Technology (Ph.D.) (Cl)	4	2
Immaculata University (Psy.D.) (Cl)	16	0
Indiana State University (Psy.D.) (Cl)	1	0
Kent State University (Ph.D.) (Cl)	1	1
La Salle University (Psy.D.) (Cl)	1	0
Loma Linda University (Ph.D. & Psy.D.) (Cl)	1	2
Louisiana Tech University (Ph.D.) (Co)	1	0
Loyola University of Chicago (Ph.D.) (Cl)	1	2
Loyola University of Chicago (Ph.D.) (Co)	2	0
Marquette University (Ph.D.) (Cl)	4	1
McGill University (Ph.D.) (Cl)	1	1
McGill University (Ph.D.) (Cl)	1	1
McGill University (Ph.D.) (Co)	1	0
Northern Illinois University (Ph.D.) (Cl)	2	0
Nova Southeastern University (Ph.D. & Psy.D.) (Cl)	20	2
Oklahoma State University (Ph.D.) (Cl)	2	1
Pace University (Psy.D.) (Cm)	3	0
Pennsylvania State University (Ph.D.) (Cl)	5	3
Philadelphia College of Osteopathic Medicine (Psy.D.) (Cl)	1	0
Seattle Pacific University (Ph.D.) (Cl)	4	2
Simon Fraser University (Ph.D.) (Cl)	10	16
Southern Illinois University—Carbondale (Ph.D.) (Cl)	4	0
Spalding University (Psy.D.) (Cl)	1	0
St. Louis University (Ph.D.) (Cl)	2	1
Texas A&M University (Ph.D.) (Cl)	4	3
Texas Tech University (Ph.D.) (Cl)	1	0
The New School (Ph.D.) (Cl)	2	1
The Ohio State University (Ph.D.) (Cl)	2	3
The University of Memphis (Ph.D.) (Cl)	3	5
The Wright Institute (Psy.D.) (Cl)	2	0
University of Alabama at Tuscaloosa (Ph.D.) (Cl)	3	4
University of Cincinnati (Ph.D.) (Cl)	5	4
University of Colorado at Boulder (Ph.D.) (Cl)	8	5
University of Colorado at Colorado Springs (Ph.D.) (Cl)	1	0
University of Delaware (Ph.D.) (Cl)	9	6
University of Florida (Ph.D.) (Cl)	5	5
University of Georgia (Ph.D.) (Cl)	4	6
University of Hartford (Psy.D.) (Cl)	2	2
University of Houston (Ph.D.) (Cl)	3	2
University of Iowa (Ph.D.) (Co)	1	1
University of Kentucky (Ph.D.) (Cl)	2	1
University of Miami (Ph.D.) (Cl)	9	4
University of Michigan (Ph.D.) (Cl)	2	—
University of Nebraska—Lincoln (Ph.D.) (Cl)	3	2
University of Nevada—Las Vegas (Ph.D.) (Cl)	2	1
University of New Mexico (Ph.D.) (Cl)	1	0
University of North Carolina at Chapel Hill (Ph.D.) (Cl)	1	2
University of Northern Colorado (Psy.D.) (Co)	8	2
University of Oklahoma (Ph.D.) (Co)	4	0
University of Oregon (Ph.D.) (Cl)	2	1
University of Rhode Island (Ph.D.) (Cl)	1	0
University of South Dakota (Ph.D.) (Cl)	7	2
University of Southern Mississippi (Ph.D.) (Cl)	3	2
University of Texas Southwestern Medical Center (Ph.D.) (Cl)	6	4
University of Toledo (Ph.D.) (Cl)	3	0
University of Vermont (Ph.D.) (Cl)	4	2
University of Virginia (Ph.D.) (Cl)	8	4
University of Washington (Ph.D.) (Cl)	3	3
University of Windsor (Ph.D.) (Cl)	4	3
University of Wisconsin—Milwaukee (Ph.D.) (Cl)	3	1
University of Wisconsin—Milwaukee (Ph.D.) (Co)	1	0
Utah State University (Ph.D.) (Cm)	4	2
Virginia Commonwealth University (Ph.D.) (Cl)	5	4
Virginia Consortium Program in Clinical Psychology (Psy.D.) (Cl)	4	0

	# Faculty	# Grants
Virginia Polytechnic Institute and State University (Ph.D.) (Cl)	7	5
Washington State University (Ph.D.) (Cl)	4	4
West Virginia University (Ph.D.) (Cl)	1	0
Western Michigan University (Ph.D.) (Cl)	3	0
Wheaton College (Psy.D.) (Cl)	3	1
Wright State University (Psy.D.) (Cl)	2	0

Chronic Disease/Illness

DePaul University (Ph.D.) (Cl)	1	3
Jackson State University (Ph.D.) (Cl)	3	1
San Diego State University/University of California, San Diego (Ph.D.) (Cl)	4	1
The Wright Institute (Psy.D.) (Cl)	1	0
University of Michigan (Ph.D.) (Cl)	1	—
University of Pittsburgh (Ph.D.) (Cl)	2	6
Wright State University (Psy.D.) (Cl)	1	0

Chronic/Severe Mental Illness

Case Western Reserve University (Ph.D.) (Cl)	1	0
Nova Southeastern University (Ph.D. & Psy.D.) (Cl)	2	0
University of Houston (Ph.D.) (Cl)	3	1
University of Louisville (Ph.D.) (Cl)	2	0

Clinical Judgment

Ball State University (Ph.D.) (Co)	1	0
Indiana State University (Psy.D.) (Cl)	1	0
Indiana University of Pennsylvania (Psy.D.) (Cl)	1	0
Southern Illinois University—Carbondale (Ph.D.) (Cl)	1	0

Cognition/Social Cognition

Argosy University, Washington, DC (Psy.D.) (Cl)	1	0
Arizona State University (Ph.D.) (Co)	1	0
Baylor University (Psy.D.) (Cl)	2	0
Catholic University of America (Ph.D.) (Cl)	3	1
Clark University (Ph.D.) (Cl)	1	0
Concordia University (Ph.D.) (Cl)	4	5
Drexel University (Ph.D.) (Cl)	2	2
Duke University (Ph.D.) (Cl)	3	2
Fuller Theological Seminary (Ph.D. & Psy.D.) (Cl)	1	0
George Mason University (Ph.D.) (Cl)	4	0
Marywood University (Psy.D.) (Cl)	1	0
McGill University (Ph.D.) (Cl)	1	0
Northwestern University (Ph.D.) (Cl)	2	1

Pennsylvania State University (Ph.D.) (Cl)	2	0
Philadelphia College of Osteopathic Medicine (Psy.D.) (Cl)	2	0
Roosevelt University (Psy.D.) (Cl)	1	0
San Diego State University/University of California, San Diego (Ph.D.) (Cl)	13	0
Seattle Pacific University (Ph.D.) (Cl)	1	1
Simon Fraser University (Ph.D.) (Cl)	4	4
Southern Methodist University (Ph.D.) (Cl)	1	0
Teachers College, Columbia University (Ph.D.) (Co)	2	0
University of Colorado at Colorado Springs (Ph.D.) (Cl)	2	1
University of Denver (Psy.D.) (Cl)	1	0
University of Pittsburgh (Ph.D.) (Cl)	4	10
University of Waterloo (Ph.D.) (Cl)	1	1
Yale University (Ph.D.) (Cl)	3	0
York University (Ph.D.) (Cl)	1	1

Cognitive Therapy/Cognitive-Behavioral Therapy

Argosy University, Washington, DC (Psy.D.) (Cl)	3	—
Arizona State University (Ph.D.) (Co)	1	1
Baylor University (Psy.D.) (Cl)	3	0
Brigham Young University (Ph.D.) (Cl)	1	0
Drexel University (Ph.D.) (Cl)	5	1
Gallaudet University (Ph.D.) (Cl)	1	0
Philadelphia College of Osteopathic Medicine (Psy.D.) (Cl)	11	0
San Diego State University/University of California, San Diego (Ph.D.) (Cl)	2	0
Texas Tech University (Ph.D.) (Cl)	3	0
University of Southern California (Ph.D.) (Cl)	2	0
University of Toledo (Ph.D.) (Cl)	2	0
University of Washington (Ph.D.) (Cl)	4	2
Virginia Consortium Program in Clinical Psychology (Psy.D.) (Cl)	2	0
Xavier University (Psy.D.) (Cl)	5	1

Communication—Verbal/Nonverbal

Drexel University (Ph.D.) (Cl)	1	0
Hofstra University (Ph.D.) (Cl)	2	0
Loyola College in Maryland (Psy.D.) (Cl)	1	0
University of Nevada—Reno (Ph.D.) (Cl)	4	0
Vanderbilt University (Ph.D.) (Cl)	1	0

Community Psychology

Adler School of Professional Psychology (Psy.D.) (Cl)	1	1
Alliant International University—Los Angeles (Ph.D.) (Cl)	1	—

349

	# Faculty	# Grants
Alliant International University—San Francisco Bay (Ph.D.) (Cl)	4	—
Alliant International University—San Francisco Bay (Psy.D.) (Cl)	4	—
Antioch University New England (Psy.D.)	2	2
Arizona State University (Ph.D.) (Cl)	7	5
Boston University (Ph.D.) (Cl)	1	0
Bowling Green State University (Ph.D.) (Cl)	1	1
Catholic University of America (Ph.D.) (Cl)	2	2
Fairleigh Dickinson University (Ph.D.) (Cl)	2	0
George Washington University (Ph.D.) (Cl)	6	1
George Washington University (Psy.D.) (Cl)	3	1
John F. Kennedy University (Psy.D.) (Cl)	2	0
Loyola University of Chicago (Ph.D.) (Cl)	3	0
Nova Southeastern University (Ph.D. & Psy.D.) (Cl)	4	0
Pace University (Psy.D.) (Cm)	1	0
Pepperdine University (Psy.D.) (Cl)	1	0
Rutgers, The State University of New Jersey (Psy.D.) (Cl)	2	1
San Diego State University/University of California, San Diego (Ph.D.) (Cl)	1	0
Southern Illinois University— Carbondale (Ph.D.) (Cl)	1	0
St. Louis University (Ph.D.) (Cl)	1	0
Texas Tech University (Ph.D.) (Cl)	1	0
University of Denver (Ph.D.) (Cl)	2	1
University of Hartford (Psy.D.) (Cl)	2	0
University of Illinois at Chicago (Ph.D.) (Cl)	1	1
University of Illinois at Urbana–Champaign (Ph.D.) (Cl)	5	4
University of La Verne (Psy.D.) (Cl)	12	0
University of Maryland—Baltimore County (Ph.D.) (Cl)	4	2
University of Mississippi (Ph.D.) (Cl)	2	0
University of Missouri—Kansas City (Ph.D.) (Cl)	1	1
University of North Dakota (Ph.D.) (Cl)	2	0
University of Ottawa (Ph.D.) (Cl)	4	3
University of Rhode Island (Ph.D.) (Cl)	1	1
University of South Carolina (Ph.D.) (Cl)	2	3
University of Southern California (Ph.D.) (Cl)	1	2
University of Texas Southwestern Medical Center (Ph.D.) (Cl)	1	0
University of Virginia (Ph.D.) (Cl)	3	3
University of Windsor (Ph.D.) (Cl)	2	2
Virginia Commonwealth University (Ph.D.) (Cl)	5	3
Virginia Consortium Program in Clinical Psychology (Psy.D.) (Cl)	1	0

Compliance

University of Mississippi (Ph.D.) (Cl)	1	0
Virginia Consortium Program in Clinical Psychology (Psy.D.) (Cl)	1	0

Conduct Disorder

Duke University (Ph.D.) (Cl)	2	3
Florida State University (Ph.D.) (Cl)	1	1
Seattle Pacific University (Ph.D.) (Cl)	1	1
University of Alabama at Tuscaloosa (Ph.D.) (Cl)	2	1
University of Vermont (Ph.D.) (Cl)	1	1

Consultation

Arizona State University (Ph.D.) (Co)	2	0
Georgia State University (Ph.D.) (Co)	1	1
Miami University (Ph.D.) (Cl)	3	2
Regent University (Psy.D.) (Cl)	4	3
The University of Memphis (Ph.D.) (Co)	1	0
Virginia Consortium Program in Clinical Psychology (Psy.D.) (Cl)	1	0
West Virginia University (Ph.D.) (Co)	1	0

Counseling/Process and Outcomes

Arizona State University (Ph.D.) (Co)	4	0
Arizona State University (Ph.D.) (Co)	7	2
Azusa Pacific University (Psy.D.) (Cl)	2	1
Florida State University (Ph.D.) (Cm)	4	1
Loyola University of Chicago (Ph.D.) (Co)	1	0
Northeastern University (Ph.D.) (Cm)	1	1
Seattle Pacific University (Ph.D.) (Cl)	1	0
University of British Columbia (Ph.D.) (Cl)	1	0
University of British Columbia (Ph.D.) (Co)	1	0
University of Maryland—College Park (Ph.D.) (Co)	6	0
University of Missouri—Columbia (Ph.D.) (Co)	4	2
University of North Texas (Ph.D.) (Co)	1	1
University of Northern Colorado (Psy.D.) (Co)	3	0
University of Oklahoma (Ph.D.) (Co)	2	0
University of St. Thomas (Psy.D.) (Co)	3	0
University of Wisconsin—Milwaukee (Ph.D.) (Co)	1	1

Crisis/Critical Incident

Brigham Young University (Ph.D.) (Co)	1	1
Philadelphia College of Osteopathic Medicine (Psy.D.) (Cl)	2	0

	# Faculty	# Grants
University of Detroit Mercy (Ph.D.) (Cl)	2	0

Deafness/Hard of Hearing

Gallaudet University (Ph.D.) (Cl)	10	3

Diabetes

Rosalind Franklin University of Medicine and Science (Ph.D.) (Cl)	1	0
University of Miami (Ph.D.) (Cl)	3	2
Yeshiva University (Ph.D.) (Cl)	1	1

Disabilities/Disabled Persons

DePaul University (Ph.D.) (Cl)	2	2
John F. Kennedy University (Psy.D.) (Cl)	1	0
Loyola University of Chicago (Ph.D.) (Cl)	1	2
Rutgers, The State University of New Jersey (Psy.D.) (Cl)	1	1
The University of Memphis (Ph.D.) (Co)	3	1
University of Missouri—Columbia (Ph.D.) (Co)	1	0
Washington State University (Ph.D.) (Co)	0	1
West Virginia University (Ph.D.) (Co)	1	0

Disaster/Trauma

Adelphi University (Ph.D.) (Cl)	2	1
Alliant International University—Los Angeles (Ph.D.) (Cl)	2	—
Alliant International University—Los Angeles (Psy.D.) (Cl)	3	—
Alliant International University—San Diego (Ph.D.) (Cl)	2	—
Alliant International University—San Diego (Psy.D.) (Cl)	2	—
Alliant International University—San Francisco Bay (Ph.D.) (Cl)	3	—
Alliant International University—San Francisco Bay (Psy.D.) (Cl)	2	—
Argosy University, Chicago (Psy.D.) (Cl)	1	0
Argosy University, Washington, DC (Psy.D.) (Cl)	1	0
Chicago School of Professional Psychology (Psy.D.) (Cl)	1	0
City University of New York at City College (Ph.D.) (Cl)	3	2
Georgia State University (Ph.D.) (Co)	1	0
Idaho State University (Ph.D.) (Cl)	2	1
Long Island University, Brooklyn Campus (Ph.D) (Cl)	1	1
Long Island University, C.W. Post Campus (Psy.D.) (Cl)	1	1
Miami University (Ph.D.) (Cl)	4	1

	# Faculty	# Grants
Northern Illinois University (Ph.D.) (Cl)	3	1
Nova Southeastern University (Ph.D. & Psy.D.) (Cl)	8	0
Pacific Graduate School of Psychology/ Stanford University Medical School Consortium (Psy.D.) (Cl)	2	0
Sam Houston State University (Ph.D.) (Cl)	1	0
Seattle Pacific University (Ph.D.) (Cl)	1	0
Seton Hall University (Ph.D.) (Co)	1	0
Spalding University (Psy.D.) (Cl)	1	0
Teachers College, Columbia University (Ph.D.) (Cl)	2	1
Texas Tech University (Ph.D.) (Cl)	2	0
University of British Columbia (Ph.D.) (Cl)	3	3
University of British Columbia (Ph.D.) (Co)	3	3
University of California, Santa Barbara (Ph.D.) (Cm)	—	—
University of Colorado at Colorado Springs (Ph.D.) (Cl)	1	2
University of Connecticut (Ph.D.) (Cl)	4	3
University of Denver (Ph.D.) (Cl)	1	1
University of Georgia (Ph.D.) (Co)	1	1
University of Kansas—Child (Ph.D.) (Cl)	2	1
University of Massachusetts—Boston (Ph.D.) (Cl)	2	1
University of Miami (Ph.D.) (Cl)	4	2
University of Missouri—St. Louis (Ph.D.) (Cl)	2	2
University of Nebraska—Lincoln (Ph.D.) (Cl)	2	1
University of New Mexico (Ph.D.) (Cl)	1	0
University of North Texas (Ph.D.) (Cl)	2	0
University of Oklahoma (Ph.D.) (Co)	2	0
University of South Dakota (Ph.D.) (Cl)	4	1
University of Southern California (Ph.D.) (Cl)	1	1
University of Tennessee—Knoxville (Ph.D.) (Co)	1	—
University of Wyoming (Ph.D.) (Cl)	1	2
Virginia Consortium Program in Clinical Psychology (Psy.D.) (Cl)	1	0
Yeshiva University (Psy.D.) (Cl)	2	0

Dreams

Miami University (Ph.D.) (Cl)	1	0
University of Maryland—College Park (Ph.D.) (Co)	1	0

Early Intervention

Florida State University (Ph.D.) (Cl)	2	1
Northeastern University (Ph.D.) (Cm)	1	1

Eating Disorders/Body Image

	# Faculty	# Grants
Alliant International University—Fresno (Ph.D.) (Cl)	1	—
American University (Ph.D.) (Cl)	1	0
Argosy University, Chicago (Psy.D.) (Cl)	1	0
Argosy University, Schaumburg (Psy.D.) (Cl)	1	1
Argosy University, Washington, DC (Psy.D.) (Cl)	2	—
Boston University (Ph.D.) (Cl)	1	1
Brigham Young University (Ph.D.) (Cl)	1	1
Colorado State University (Ph.D.) (Co)	1	0
Drexel University (Ph.D.) (Cl)	1	1
Duke University (Ph.D.) (Cl)	3	3
Emory University (Ph.D.) (Cl)	1	0
Fairleigh Dickinson University (Ph.D.) (Cl)	1	1
Florida Institute of Technology (Psy.D.) (Cl)	2	0
Florida State University (Ph.D.) (Cl)	3	3
Hofstra University (Ph.D.) (Cl)	2	0
Indiana State University (Psy.D.) (Cl)	1	1
Indiana University—Bloomington (Ph.D.) (Cl)	1	0
Kent State University (Ph.D.) (Cl)	1	0
Louisiana Tech University (Ph.D.) (Co)	1	0
Marquette University (Ph.D.) (Cl)	1	0
McGill University (Ph.D.) (Cl)	1	1
Miami University (Ph.D.) (Cl)	1	0
Michigan State University (Ph.D.) (Cl)	1	2
Northeastern University (Ph.D.) (Cm)	3	1
Pacific Graduate School of Psychology/ Stanford University Medical School Consortium (Psy.D.) (Cl)	2	1
Philadelphia College of Osteopathic Medicine (Psy.D.) (Cl)	1	0
Rutgers, The State University of New Jersey (Ph.D.) (Cl)	1	0
Rutgers, The State University of New Jersey (Psy.D.) (Cl)	1	1
St. Louis University (Ph.D.) (Cl)	1	1
Tennessee State University (Ph.D.) (Co)	1	0
Texas Tech University (Ph.D.) (Cl)	1	0
Uniformed Services University of Health Sciences (Ph.D.) (Cl)	1	1
University at Albany/State University of New York (Ph.D.) (Cl)	1	1
University of Alabama at Birmingham (Ph.D.) (Cl)	1	1
University of Central Florida (Ph.D.) (Cl)	2	—
University of Denver (Ph.D.) (Cl)	1	0
University of Georgia (Ph.D.) (Cl)	1	1
University of Hawaii at Manoa (Ph.D.) (Cl)	2	1
University of Illinois at Chicago (Ph.D.) (Cl)	1	0
University of Illinois at Urbana–Champaign (Ph.D.) (Co)	1	0
University of Kentucky (Ph.D.) (Cl)	1	1
University of Minnesota (Ph.D.) (Cl)	—	—
University of Missouri—Columbia (Ph.D.) (Co)	1	1
University of Missouri—Kansas City (Ph.D.) (Cl)	2	0
University of Nevada—Las Vegas (Ph.D.) (Cl)	1	0
University of New Mexico (Ph.D.) (Cl)	2	0
University of North Carolina at Chapel Hill (Ph.D.) (Cl)	1	0
University of North Dakota (Ph.D.) (Co)	1	0
University of North Texas (Ph.D.) (Co)	3	0
University of Northern Colorado (Psy.D.) (Co)	2	0
University of Pittsburgh (Ph.D.) (Cl)	1	4
University of South Florida (Ph.D.) (Cl)	2	1
University of Windsor (Ph.D.) (Cl)	2	1
Vanderbilt University (Ph.D.) (Cl)	2	2
Virginia Consortium Program in Clinical Psychology (Psy.D.) (Cl)	2	1
Washington State University (Ph.D.) (Co)	1	0
Yale University (Ph.D.) (Cl)	2	0
York University (Ph.D.) (Cl)	1	1

Emotion

	# Faculty	# Grants
Boston University (Ph.D.) (Cl)	3	0
Catholic University of America (Ph.D.) (Cl)	2	1
Colorado State University (Ph.D.) (Co)	1	0
Georgia State University (Ph.D.) (Cl)	3	0
McGill University (Ph.D.) (Cl)	1	1
Northern Illinois University (Ph.D.) (Cl)	4	0
Pennsylvania State University (Ph.D.) (Cl)	5	1
Sam Houston State University (Ph.D.) (Cl)	1	0
The New School (Ph.D.) (Cl)	1	0
University at Albany/State University of New York (Ph.D.) (Cl)	7	5
University of California, Berkeley (Ph.D.) (Cl)	4	5
University of Delaware (Ph.D.) (Cl)	2	1
University of Georgia (Ph.D.) (Cl)	1	0
University of Illinois at Urbana–Champaign (Ph.D.) (Cl)	5	10
University of Mississippi (Ph.D.) (Cl)	2	1
University of Missouri—Kansas City (Ph.D.) (Cl)	2	1
University of Pittsburgh (Ph.D.) (Cl)	5	19
University of South Florida (Ph.D.) (Cl)	2	2
University of Utah (Ph.D.) (Co)	1	0
University of Waterloo (Ph.D.) (Cl)	1	5
University of Wisconsin—Milwaukee (Ph.D.) (Cl)	2	1

	# Faculty	# Grants
Vanderbilt University (Ph.D.) (Cl)	9	2
Virginia Consortium Program in Clinical Psychology (Psy.D.) (Cl)	1	0

Empirically Supported Treatment Research

Rutgers, The State University of New Jersey (Psy.D.) (Cl)	2	1
University of Southern Mississippi (Ph.D.) (Co)	3	2

Epidemiology

Florida State University (Ph.D.) (Cl)	1	1
University of Virginia (Ph.D.) (Cl)	2	1
Yale University (Ph.D.) (Cl)	1	0

Ethical Issues

Catholic University of America (Ph.D.) (Cl)	1	0
Colorado State University (Ph.D.) (Co)	1	0
Fairleigh Dickinson University (Ph.D.) (Cl)	2	0
Immaculata University (Psy.D.) (Cl)	2	0
Indiana University of Pennsylvania (Psy.D.) (Cl)	2	0
Iowa State University (Ph.D.) (Co)	1	0
Loyola College in Maryland (Psy.D.) (Cl)	2	0
Loyola University of Chicago (Ph.D.) (Cl)	1	0
Our Lady of the Lake University (Psy.D.) (Co)	1	0
Philadelphia College of Osteopathic Medicine (Psy.D.) (Cl)	1	0
Rutgers, The State University of New Jersey (Psy.D.) (Cl)	1	0
St. Louis University (Ph.D.) (Cl)	2	0
Tennessee State University (Ph.D.) (Co)	2	0
Texas Tech University (Ph.D.) (Cl)	1	0
Texas Woman's University (Ph.D.) (Co)	2	1
University of British Columbia (Ph.D.) (Cl)	1	0
University of British Columbia (Ph.D.) (Co)	1	0
University of Denver (Ph.D.) (Co)	1	0
University of Iowa (Ph.D.) (Co)	2	1
University of Oklahoma (Ph.D.) (Co)	1	0
University of South Dakota (Ph.D.) (Cl)	1	0
University of Utah (Ph.D.) (Co)	1	0
Utah State University (Ph.D.) (Cm)	2	1
Vanderbilt University (Ph.D.) (Cl)	1	0
Virginia Consortium Program in Clinical Psychology (Psy.D.) (Cl)	1	0

Evolutionary Psychology

The Wright Institute (Psy.D.) (Cl)	1	1
University of Colorado at Colorado Springs (Ph.D.) (Cl)	1	1

Family/Family Therapy/Family Systems

Alliant International University—Fresno (Ph.D.) (Cl)	3	—
Alliant International University—Los Angeles (Psy.D.) (Cl)	2	—
Alliant International University—San Diego (Ph.D.) (Cl)	4	—
Alliant International University—San Diego (Psy.D.) (Cl)	7	—
Alliant International University—San Francisco Bay (Ph.D.) (Cl)	2	—
Alliant International University—San Francisco Bay (Psy.D.) (Cl)	10	—
Argosy University, Schaumburg (Psy.D.) (Cl)	1	0
Arizona State University (Ph.D.) (Cl)	5	3
Arizona State University (Ph.D.) (Co)	1	0
Azusa Pacific University (Psy.D.) (Cl)	2	0
Boston University (Ph.D.) (Cl)	2	1
Bowling Green State University (Ph.D.) (Cl)	2	0
Catholic University of America (Ph.D.) (Cl)	4	2
Chestnut Hill College (Psy.D.) (Cl)	1	1
Clark University (Ph.D.) (Cl)	3	2
Florida Institute of Technology (Psy.D.) (Cl)	2	0
Fordham University (Ph.D.) (Cl)	1	0
Fuller Theological Seminary (Ph.D. & Psy.D.) (Cl)	2	1
George Washington University (Ph.D.) (Cl)	2	1
Georgia State University (Ph.D.) (Cl)	1	1
Hofstra University (Ph.D.) (Cl)	1	0
Howard University (Ph.D.) (Cl)	2	0
Illinois Institute of Technology (Ph.D.) (Cl)	1	0
Immaculata University (Psy.D.) (Cl)	2	0
Indiana University of Pennsylvania (Psy.D.) (Cl)	1	0
Iowa State University (Ph.D.) (Co)	2	1
James Madison University (Psy.D.) (Cm)	2	0
Lehigh University (Ph.D.) (Co)	2	—
Marquette University (Ph.D.) (Cl)	2	1
McGill University (Ph.D.) (Cl)	2	1
Miami University (Ph.D.) (Cl)	3	1
Michigan State University (Ph.D.) (Cl)	3	1
New Mexico State University (Ph.D.) (Co)	1	0
Ohio University (Ph.D.) (Cl)	2	2
Pennsylvania State University (Ph.D.) (Cl)	2	1

	# Faculty	# Grants
Pennsylvania State University (Ph.D.) (Co)	2	1
Pepperdine University (Psy.D.) (Cl)	1	0
Purdue University (Ph.D.) (Cl)	2	2
Rutgers, The State University of New Jersey (Psy.D.) (Cl)	3	1
Sam Houston State University (Ph.D.) (Cl)	1	0
Seattle Pacific University (Ph.D.) (Cl)	2	0
Simon Fraser University (Ph.D.) (Cl)	3	3
Southern Illinois University—Carbondale (Ph.D.) (Cl)	1	0
Southern Methodist University (Ph.D.) (Cl)	5	2
St. Louis University (Ph.D.) (Cl)	3	0
The Wright Institute (Psy.D.) (Cl)	1	0
University at Albany/State University of New York (Ph.D.) (Co)	2	1
University at Buffalo/State University of New York (Ph.D.) (Cm)	1	0
University of Arizona (Ph.D.) (Cl)	2	4
University of Arkansas (Ph.D.) (Cl)	3	0
University of California, Los Angeles (Ph.D.) (Cl)	5	5
University of Colorado at Boulder (Ph.D.) (Cl)	4	4
University of Denver (Ph.D.) (Cl)	1	1
University of Georgia (Ph.D.) (Cl)	2	0
University of Houston (Ph.D.) (Cl)	3	2
University of Kentucky (Ph.D.) (Co)	2	0
University of Massachusetts—Boston (Ph.D.) (Cl)	1	1
University of Miami (Ph.D.) (Cl)	2	1
University of Miami (Ph.D.) (Co)	3	1
University of Michigan (Ph.D.) (Cl)	5	3
University of Missouri—Kansas City (Ph.D.) (Co)	2	0
University of Nebraska—Lincoln (Ph.D.) (Co)	1	0
University of North Carolina at Chapel Hill (Ph.D.) (Cl)	1	1
University of Northern Colorado (Psy.D.) (Co)	4	1
University of Pennsylvania (Ph.D.) (Cl)	1	0
University of Rhode Island (Ph.D.) (Cl)	2	0
University of South Dakota (Ph.D.) (Cl)	2	0
University of South Florida (Ph.D.) (Cl)	1	0
University of Tennessee—Knoxville (Ph.D.) (Cl)	7	5
University of Utah (Ph.D.) (Cl)	1	1
University of Victoria (Ph.D.) (Cl)	2	2
University of Virginia (Ph.D.) (Cl)	3	2
Virginia Consortium Program in Clinical Psychology (Psy.D.) (Cl)	5	0
Western Michigan University (Ph.D.) (Co)	1	1
Yeshiva University (Psy.D.) (Cl)	1	0
Yeshiva University (Psy.D.) (Cm)	2	0

Fetal Alcohol Syndrome

Miami University (Ph.D.) (Cl)	1	0
University of Victoria (Ph.D.) (Cl)	1	1

Forensic/Psychology and Law

Alliant International University—San Francisco Bay (Psy.D.) (Cl)	3	—
Argosy University, Washington, DC (Psy.D.) (Cl)	3	—
Azusa Pacific University (Psy.D.) (Cl)	3	1
Carlos Albizu University—Miami Campus (Psy.D.) (Cl)	1	0
Carlos Albizu University–San Juan Campus (Psy.D.) (Cl)	3	0
Chicago School of Professional Psychology (Psy.D.) (Cl)	2	0
Drexel University (Ph.D.) (Cl)	6	4
Fairleigh Dickinson University (Ph.D.) (Cl)	2	1
Florida State University (Ph.D.) (Cl)	1	0
Fordham University (Ph.D.) (Co)	1	1
George Fox University (Psy.D.) (Cl)	1	0
George Mason University (Ph.D.) (Cl)	1	1
Georgia State University (Ph.D.) (Cl)	2	1
Georgia State University (Ph.D.) (Co)	1	0
Iowa State University (Ph.D.) (Co)	1	0
Loma Linda University (Ph.D. & Psy.D.) (Cl)	2	0
Long Island University, Brooklyn Campus (Ph.D) (Cl)	2	0
Northwestern University Medical School (Ph.D.) (Cl)	2	2
Nova Southeastern University (Ph.D. & Psy.D.) (Cl)	3	2
Pacific Graduate School of Psychology (Ph.D.) (Cl)	5	0
Pacific University (Psy.D.) (Cl)	2	0
Pepperdine University (Psy.D.) (Cl)	1	0
Philadelphia College of Osteopathic Medicine (Psy.D.) (Cl)	1	0
Rutgers, The State University of New Jersey (Psy.D.) (Cl)	1	0
Sam Houston State University (Ph.D.) (Cl)	8	1
Simon Fraser University (Ph.D.) (Cl)	4	9
Southern Illinois University—Carbondale (Ph.D.) (Cl)	1	1
Spalding University (Psy.D.) (Cl)	1	0
Texas Tech University (Ph.D.) (Co)	1	2+
Texas Woman's University (Ph.D.) (Co)	1	0
The Wright Institute (Psy.D.) (Cl)	2	0
University of Alabama at Tuscaloosa (Ph.D.) (Cl)	4	0
University of Colorado at Colorado Springs (Ph.D.) (Cl)	1	0
University of Denver (Psy.D.) (Cl)	2	0
University of Florida (Ph.D.) (Co)	1	0
University of Georgia (Ph.D.) (Co)	2	2

	# Faculty	# Grants
University of Houston (Ph.D.) (Cl)	2	1
University of Indianapolis (Psy.D.) (Cl)	1	0
University of La Verne (Psy.D.) (Cl)	2	0
University of Louisville (Ph.D.) (Cl)	1	0
University of Maine (Ph.D.) (Cl)	2	1
University of Nebraska—Lincoln (Ph.D.) (Cl)	2	4
University of North Texas (Ph.D.) (Cl)	3	1
University of Rhode Island (Ph.D.) (Cl)	2	3
University of Southern Mississippi (Ph.D.) (Co)	3	0
University of Texas at Austin (Ph.D.) (Co)	1	0
University of Utah (Ph.D.) (Cl)	1	0
University of Virginia (Ph.D.) (Cl)	4	1
University of Wyoming (Ph.D.) (Cl)	2	1
Virginia Commonwealth University (Ph.D.) (Cl)	1	1
West Virginia University (Ph.D.) (Cl)	2	1
West Virginia University (Ph.D.) (Co)	3	0
Wright State University (Psy.D.) (Cl)	1	0
Yeshiva University (Psy.D.) (Cl)	1	0

Forgiveness

Iowa State University (Ph.D.) (Co)	1	1
University of Louisville (Ph.D.) (Co)	1	0
Virginia Commonwealth University (Ph.D.) (Co)	2	3

Gambling

Loyola College in Maryland (Psy.D.) (Cl)	1	0
Purdue University (Ph.D.) (Co)	1	0
University of Windsor (Ph.D.) (Cl)	1	3

Gay/Lesbian/Bisexuality

Alliant International University— Los Angeles (Psy.D.) (Cl)	2	—
Alliant International University— San Diego (Psy.D.) (Cl)	1	—
Alliant International University— San Francisco Bay (Ph.D.) (Cl)	2	—
Argosy University, Chicago (Psy.D.) (Cl)	2	0
Argosy University, Hawaii (Psy.D.) (Cl)	2	0
Argosy University, Washington, DC (Psy.D.) (Cl)	2	—
George Mason University (Ph.D.) (Cl)	1	0
John F. Kennedy University (Psy.D.) (Cl)	3	0
Loyola College in Maryland (Psy.D.) (Cl)	1	0
Marquette University (Ph.D.) (Cl)	1	0
Marshall University (Psy.D.) (Cl)	1	0
New Mexico State University (Ph.D.) (Co)	3	1
New York University (Ph.D.) (Co)	1	1
Oklahoma State University (Ph.D.) (Co)	4	0

Pacific Graduate School of Psychology (Ph.D.) (Cl)	1	1
Pennsylvania State University (Ph.D.) (Co)	1	0
The University of Memphis (Ph.D.) (Co)	3	1
University of California, Santa Barbara (Ph.D.) (Cm)	—	—
University of Louisville (Ph.D.) (Co)	1	0
University of Montana (Ph.D.) (Cl)	2	0
University of North Dakota (Ph.D.) (Co)	2	1
University of Tennessee—Knoxville (Ph.D.) (Co)	1	0
University of Utah (Ph.D.) (Co)	2	0
University of Vermont (Ph.D.) (Cl)	1	0
Virginia Consortium Program in Clinical Psychology (Psy.D.) (Cl)	1	0

Gender Roles/Sex Differences

Alliant International University— Los Angeles (Ph.D.) (Cl)	2	—
Alliant International University— San Diego (Ph.D.) (Cl)	2	—
Alliant International University— San Diego (Psy.D.) (Cl)	3	—
Alliant International University— San Francisco Bay (Ph.D.) (Cl)	4	—
Alliant International University— San Francisco Bay (Psy.D.) (Cl)	2	—
Arizona State University (Ph.D.) (Co)	2	0
Biola University (Psy.D.) (Cl)	2	1
Boston College (Ph.D.) (Co)	2	1
Boston University (Ph.D.) (Cl)	1	0
Clark University (Ph.D.) (Cl)	1	1
Concordia University (Ph.D.) (Cl)	2	1
Georgia State University (Ph.D.) (Cl)	1	1
Georgia State University (Ph.D.) (Co)	2	0
Indiana State University (Psy.D.) (Cl)	2	0
Indiana University of Pennsylvania (Psy.D.) (Cl)	1	0
Iowa State University (Ph.D.) (Co)	1	0
McGill University (Ph.D.) (Cl)	1	1
New Mexico State University (Ph.D.) (Co)	3	0
Pace University (Psy.D.) (Cm)	2	0
San Diego State University/University of California, San Diego (Ph.D.) (Cl)	4	0
Seattle Pacific University (Ph.D.) (Cl)	5	1
Southern Illinois University— Carbondale (Ph.D.) (Cl)	1	0
Southern Illinois University— Carbondale (Ph.D.) (Co)	3	2
St. John's University (Ph.D.) (Cl)	2	0
Texas Tech University (Ph.D.) (Co)	2	0
Texas Woman's University (Ph.D.) (Co)	4	2
The Wright Institute (Psy.D.) (Cl)	3	0
University of Florida (Ph.D.) (Co)	1	1
University of Georgia (Ph.D.) (Cl)	1	0
University of Houston (Ph.D.) (Co)	1	0

	# Faculty	# Grants
University of Kentucky (Ph.D.) (Co)	3	1
University of La Verne (Psy.D.) (Cl)	2	0
University of Missouri—Columbia (Ph.D.) (Co)	2	0
University of Montana (Ph.D.) (Cl)	2	1
University of Nebraska—Lincoln (Ph.D.) (Co)	2	0
University of North Dakota (Ph.D.) (Cl)	2	0
University of Oklahoma (Ph.D.) (Co)	3	0
University of Utah (Ph.D.) (Co)	2	0
University of Wisconsin—Madison (Ph.D.) (Co)	4	0
Vanderbilt University (Ph.D.) (Cl)	2	0
Virginia Consortium Program in Clinical Psychology (Psy.D.) (Cl)	2	0
Wheaton College (Psy.D.) (Cl)	3	1
Wright State University (Psy.D.) (Cl)	3	0

Genetics/Behavioral Genetics

Boston University (Ph.D.) (Cl)	1	1
Duke University (Ph.D.) (Cl)	2	2
Emory University (Ph.D.) (Cl)	2	1
Indiana University—Bloomington (Ph.D.) (Cl)	3	4
McGill University (Ph.D.) (Cl)	1	1
Michigan State University (Ph.D.) (Cl)	3	4
Northwestern University (Ph.D.) (Cl)	1	0
Southern Illinois University—Carbondale (Ph.D.) (Cl)	1	0
University of Colorado at Boulder (Ph.D.) (Cl)	3	3
University of Denver (Ph.D.) (Cl)	2	2
University of Illinois at Urbana–Champaign (Ph.D.) (Cl)	2	2
University of Minnesota (Ph.D.) (Cl)	—	—
University of Minnesota (Ph.D.) (Cl)	—	—
University of Minnesota Ed (Ph.D.) (Co)	1	1
University of Pittsburgh (Ph.D.) (Cl)	4	11
University of Southern California (Ph.D.) (Cl)	4	1
University of Texas at Austin (Ph.D.) (Cl)	1	0
University of Virginia (Ph.D.) (Cl)	2	1
Yale University (Ph.D.) (Cl)	1	0

Group Process and Therapy

Antioch University New England (Psy.D.)	1	0
Arizona State University (Ph.D.) (Co)	1	0
Baylor University (Psy.D.) (Cl)	1	0
Brigham Young University (Ph.D.) (Cl)	3	0
Fuller Theological Seminary (Ph.D. & Psy.D.) (Cl)	1	0
George Washington University (Psy.D.) (Cl)	3	0

Indiana University—Bloomington (Ph.D.) (Co)	2	0
Iowa State University (Ph.D.) (Co)	1	0
Marquette University (Ph.D.) (Cl)	1	0
New York University (Ph.D.) (Co)	1	0
Roosevelt University (Psy.D.) (Cl)	1	0
University of Denver (Ph.D.) (Co)	1	0
University of Houston (Ph.D.) (Co)	1	1
University of Missouri—Columbia (Ph.D.) (Co)	2	1
University of North Dakota (Ph.D.) (Co)	1	0
University of Wisconsin—Madison (Ph.D.) (Co)	1	0
West Virginia University (Ph.D.) (Co)	1	0
Western Michigan University (Ph.D.) (Co)	1	1

Health Care/Primary Care

Jackson State University (Ph.D.) (Cl)	3	0
Philadelphia College of Osteopathic Medicine (Psy.D.) (Cl)	3	2
University of Alabama at Tuscaloosa (Ph.D.) (Cl)	3	3
University of Hawaii at Manoa (Ph.D.) (Cl)	2	0
University of Montana (Ph.D.) (Cl)	2	0
University of Nevada—Reno (Ph.D.) (Cl)	1	1
University of Wyoming (Ph.D.) (Cl)	2	1

Help-Seeking

Iowa State University (Ph.D.) (Co)	1	0
Marquette University (Ph.D.) (Cl)	2	1

Hispanic Studies

Arizona State University (Ph.D.) (Cl)	3	1
Chicago School of Professional Psychology (Psy.D.) (Cl)	1	0
Marquette University (Ph.D.) (Cl)	1	0
Texas Tech University (Ph.D.) (Cl)	1	1
University of Georgia (Ph.D.) (Co)	1	0
University of Illinois at Urbana–Champaign (Ph.D.) (Co)	1	1

Humor

San Diego State University/University of California, San Diego (Ph.D.) (Cl)	1	0
Virginia Consortium Program in Clinical Psychology (Psy.D.) (Cl)	1	0

Hypnosis

Binghamton University/State University of New York (Ph.D.) (Cl)	1	1

	# Faculty	# Grants
Pennsylvania State University (Ph.D.) (Cl)	1	0
Seattle Pacific University (Ph.D.) (Cl)	2	0
University of Wisconsin—Milwaukee (Ph.D.) (Co)	1	0
Washington State University (Ph.D.) (Co)	2	1

Identity Development

University of Detroit Mercy (Ph.D.) (Cl)	2	0
University of Missouri—Columbia (Ph.D.) (Co)	1	0

Immigration

John F. Kennedy University (Psy.D.) (Cl)	1	0
Miami University (Ph.D.) (Cl)	2	0
Teachers College, Columbia University (Ph.D.) (Co)	—	—
University of California, Santa Barbara (Ph.D.) (Cm)	—	—
University of Nebraska—Lincoln (Ph.D.) (Co)	1	0

Indigenous/Native American

Brigham Young University (Ph.D.) (Co)	1	1
Oklahoma State University (Ph.D.) (Co)	3	0
Seattle Pacific University (Ph.D.) (Cl)	1	0
University of British Columbia (Ph.D.) (Cl)	3	7
University of British Columbia (Ph.D.) (Co)	3	7
University of Illinois at Urbana–Champaign (Ph.D.) (Cl)	2	2
University of Montana (Ph.D.) (Cl)	2	1
University of North Dakota (Ph.D.) (Co)	1	0
University of Oklahoma (Ph.D.) (Co)	2	0
University of Wyoming (Ph.D.) (Cl)	2	1
Utah State University (Ph.D.) (Cm)	1	0

Interpersonal Relationships/Friendships

Adelphi University (Ph.D.) (Cl)	1	1
Arizona State University (Ph.D.) (Co)	3	0
Catholic University of America (Ph.D.) (Cl)	2	1
Colorado State University (Ph.D.) (Co)	1	0
Indiana State University (Psy.D.) (Cl)	1	0
Marquette University (Ph.D.) (Cl)	2	0
McGill University (Ph.D.) (Cl)	2	2
New Mexico State University (Ph.D.) (Co)	1	1
San Diego State University/University of California, San Diego (Ph.D.) (Cl)	1	0
University of Denver (Ph.D.) (Cl)	2	5
University of Georgia (Ph.D.) (Cl)	1	0

University of Maryland—Baltimore County (Ph.D.) (Cl)	1	0
University of Maryland—College Park (Ph.D.) (Co)	1	0
University of Minnesota (Ph.D.) (Co)	1	0
University of Missouri—Kansas City (Ph.D.) (Co)	3	0
University of North Dakota (Ph.D.) (Cl)	2	0
University of North Dakota (Ph.D.) (Co)	1	1
University of Oklahoma (Ph.D.) (Co)	2	0
University of St. Thomas (Psy.D.) (Co)	2	0
University of Waterloo (Ph.D.) (Cl)	1	5
Virginia Consortium Program in Clinical Psychology (Psy.D.) (Cl)	2	0
Wichita State University (Ph.D.) (Cl)	1	0

Intervention

Alliant International University—Los Angeles (Psy.D.) (Cl)	10	—
Alliant International University—San Diego (Psy.D.) (Cl)	10	—
Chicago School of Professional Psychology (Psy.D.) (Cl)	1	0
Seattle Pacific University (Ph.D.) (Cl)	1	0
St. John's University (Ph.D.) (Cl)	1	1
University of Illinois at Urbana–Champaign (Ph.D.) (Cl)	2	2
University of Minnesota (Ph.D.) (Co)	2	2
University of Wisconsin—Milwaukee (Ph.D.) (Co)	1	1
Vanderbilt University (Ph.D.) (Cl)	4	3
Virginia Commonwealth University (Ph.D.) (Co)	1	4
Virginia Consortium Program in Clinical Psychology (Psy.D.) (Cl)	1	0
Yeshiva University (Psy.D.) (Cm)	3	0
Northeastern University (Ph.D.) (Cm)	3	1
Seattle Pacific University (Ph.D.) (Cl)	1	0
Virginia Commonwealth University (Ph.D.) (Co)	1	0

Leadership

Northeastern University (Ph.D.) (Cm)	3	1
Seattle Pacific University (Ph.D.) (Cl)	1	0
Virginia Commonwealth University (Ph.D.) (Co)	1	0

Learning Disabilities

Argosy University, Phoenix (Psy.D.) (Cl)	4	0
Binghamton University/State University of New York (Ph.D.) (Cl)	1	1
Case Western Reserve University (Ph.D.) (Cl)	1	1
Colorado State University (Ph.D.) (Co)	1	0
Marshall University (Psy.D.) (Cl)	1	0

	# Faculty	# Grants
Pace University (Psy.D.) (Cm)	1	0
Roosevelt University (Psy.D.) (Cl)	1	0
Southern Illinois University—Carbondale (Ph.D.) (Cl)	2	1
University of California, Santa Barbara (Ph.D.) (Cm)	—	—
University of Texas Southwestern Medical Center (Ph.D.) (Cl)	1	0
University of Virginia (Ph.D.) (Cl)	2	0
University of Wisconsin—Milwaukee (Ph.D.) (Cl)	1	0
Virginia Consortium Program in Clinical Psychology (Psy.D.) (Cl)	1	0
Widener University (Psy.D.) (Cl)	3	0
Yeshiva University (Psy.D.) (Cm)	3	0

Malingering

Marywood University (Psy.D.) (Cl)	1	0
University of Montana (Ph.D.) (Cl)	1	0
University of North Texas (Ph.D.) (Cl)	2	0

Marital/Intimate Partner Violence

Argosy University, Schaumburg (Psy.D.) (Cl)	2	0
George Mason University (Ph.D.) (Cl)	1	0
Indiana University—Bloomington (Ph.D.) (Cl)	1	1
Long Island University, C.W. Post Campus (Psy.D.) (Cl)	2	0
Loyola College in Maryland (Psy.D.) (Cl)	1	0
Michigan State University (Ph.D.) (Cl)	2	2
Northern Illinois University (Ph.D.) (Cl)	4	0
Nova Southeastern University (Ph.D. & Psy.D.) (Cl)	3	1
Purdue University (Ph.D.) (Cl)	2	0
Stony Brook University/State University of New York (Ph.D.) (Cl)	2	5
University of Connecticut (Ph.D.) (Cl)	1	1
University of Hartford (Psy.D.) (Cl)	1	1
University of Iowa (Ph.D.) (Cl)	2	1
University of Kansas—Child (Ph.D.) (Cl)	1	1
University of Maryland—Baltimore County (Ph.D.) (Cl)	1	0
University of Maryland—College Park (Ph.D.) (Co)	1	0
University of Montana (Ph.D.) (Cl)	2	1
University of North Dakota (Ph.D.) (Co)	1	0
University of Oregon (Ph.D.) (Co)	1	0
University of Washington (Ph.D.) (Cl)	2	1
Western Michigan University (Ph.D.) (Cl)	1	0
Miami University (Ph.D.) (Cl)	4	2
University of Miami (Ph.D.) (Co)	1	0

Marriage/Couples

Adelphi University (Ph.D.) (Cl)	2	1
Argosy University, Chicago (Psy.D.) (Cl)	1	0
Argosy University, Schaumburg (Psy.D.) (Cl)	1	1
Auburn University (Ph.D.) (Cl)	1	1
Binghamton University/State University of New York (Ph.D.) (Cl)	1	1
Catholic University of America (Ph.D.) (Cl)	1	1
Fairleigh Dickinson University (Ph.D.) (Cl)	4	0
Forest Institute of Professional Psychology (Psy.D.) (Cl)	1	1
Fuller Theological Seminary (Ph.D. & Psy.D.) (Cl)	4	0
George Fox University (Psy.D.) (Cl)	1	1
Georgia State University (Ph.D.) (Cl)	1	0
Hofstra University (Ph.D.) (Cl)	1	0
Illinois Institute of Technology (Ph.D.) (Cl)	1	1
Indiana University—Bloomington (Ph.D.) (Co)	2	3
Louisiana Tech University (Ph.D.) (Co)	1	0
Northern Illinois University (Ph.D.) (Cl)	3	0
Pepperdine University (Psy.D.) (Cl)	1	0
Regent University (Psy.D.) (Cl)	2	1
Rutgers, The State University of New Jersey (Ph.D.) (Cl)	2	1
Sam Houston State University (Ph.D.) (Cl)	1	0
Seattle Pacific University (Ph.D.) (Cl)	1	0
Southern Illinois University—Carbondale (Ph.D.) (Cl)	1	0
Southern Illinois University—Carbondale (Ph.D.) (Cl)	2	0
Tennessee State University (Ph.D.) (Co)	1	0
Texas A&M University (Ph.D.) (Cl)	5	3
Texas Tech University (Ph.D.) (Co)	1	0
The Wright Institute (Psy.D.) (Cl)	3	0
University of California, Los Angeles (Ph.D.) (Cl)	2	5
University of Delaware (Ph.D.) (Cl)	1	1
University of Denver (Ph.D.) (Cl)	1	4
University of Denver (Psy.D.) (Cl)	2	0
University of Detroit Mercy (Ph.D.) (Cl)	2	0
University of Georgia (Ph.D.) (Cl)	1	3
University of Houston (Ph.D.) (Cl)	2	1
University of Iowa (Ph.D.) (Cl)	1	0
University of Kansas—Psychology (Ph.D.) (Cl)	1	0
University of Louisville (Ph.D.) (Co)	1	0
University of Nevada—Reno (Ph.D.) (Cl)	2	0
University of North Carolina at Chapel Hill (Ph.D.) (Cl)	1	2
University of North Texas (Ph.D.) (Co)	3	2
University of Notre Dame (Ph.D.) (Co)	1	1
University of Oklahoma (Ph.D.) (Co)	1	0
University of Rochester (Ph.D.) (Cl)	1	1
University of South Carolina (Ph.D.) (Cl)	1	0

	# Faculty	# Grants
University of Southern California (Ph.D.) (Cl)	2	0
University of Victoria (Ph.D.) (Cl)	1	1
University of Waterloo (Ph.D.) (Cl)	3	2
Virginia Commonwealth University (Ph.D.) (Co)	2	0
Virginia Consortium Program in Clinical Psychology (Psy.D.) (Cl)	6	0
Virginia Polytechnic Institute and State University (Ph.D.) (Cl)	1	0
Wheaton College (Psy.D.) (Cl)	4	0
York University (Ph.D.) (Cl)	1	1

Media

Marywood University (Psy.D.) (Cl)	2	0
Pepperdine University (Psy.D.) (Cl)	1	0
University of Massachusetts—Boston (Ph.D.) (Cl)	1	0
University of Toledo (Ph.D.) (Cl)	2	1

Memory

Binghamton University/State University of New York (Ph.D.) (Cl)	2	0
Case Western Reserve University (Ph.D.) (Cl)	2	0
Drexel University (Ph.D.) (Cl)	1	0
George Fox University (Psy.D.) (Cl)	2	1
Idaho State University (Ph.D.) (Cl)	1	0
Marquette University (Ph.D.) (Cl)	1	2
McGill University (Ph.D.) (Cl)	2	1
Philadelphia College of Osteopathic Medicine (Psy.D.) (Cl)	1	0
The New School (Ph.D.) (Cl)	2	1
University of Montana (Ph.D.) (Cl)	1	0
York University (Ph.D.) (Cl)	2	2

Men's Issues

Argosy University, Schaumburg (Psy.D.) (Cl)	1	0
Colorado State University (Ph.D.) (Co)	1	0
Tennessee State University (Ph.D.) (Co)	3	1
The University of Memphis (Ph.D.) (Co)	2	0
University of Iowa (Ph.D.) (Co)	3	0
University of Texas at Austin (Ph.D.) (Co)	1	0
University of Wisconsin—Milwaukee (Ph.D.) (Co)	1	0

Mental Health Services/Policy

Northwestern University Medical School (Ph.D.) (Cl)	2	1
Philadelphia College of Osteopathic Medicine (Psy.D.) (Cl)	1	0

Rutgers, The State University of New Jersey (Psy.D.) (Cl)	2	1
University of Arizona (Ph.D.) (Cl)	1	1
University of California, Santa Barbara (Ph.D.) (Cm)	—	—
University of Hawaii at Manoa (Ph.D.) (Cl)	5	6
University of Houston (Ph.D.) (Co)	1	0

Meta-Analysis

Marshall University (Psy.D.) (Cl)	1	0
University of Louisville (Ph.D.) (Co)	1	2
Wheaton College (Psy.D.) (Cl)	1	0

Methodology

Arizona State University (Ph.D.) (Co)	2	0
Hofstra University (Ph.D.) (Cl)	2	0
Sam Houston State University (Ph.D.) (Cl)	1	0
Southern Illinois University—Carbondale (Ph.D.) (Co)	2	0
Texas A&M University (Ph.D.) (Co)	1	0
University at Albany/State University of New York (Ph.D.) (Co)	1	0

Mindfulness

Catholic University of America (Ph.D.) (Cl)	2	0
Drexel University (Ph.D.) (Cl)	2	1
La Salle University (Psy.D.) (Cl)	2	1
University at Albany/State University of New York (Ph.D.) (Cl)	3	2
University of Montana (Ph.D.) (Cl)	1	0

Minority/Cross-Cultural/Diversity

Adelphi University (Ph.D.) (Cl)	6	3
Alliant International University—Fresno (Ph.D.) (Cl)	2	—
Alliant International University—Los Angeles (Ph.D.) (Cl)	3	—
Alliant International University—Los Angeles (Psy.D.) (Cl)	3	—
Alliant International University—San Diego (Ph.D.) (Cl)	2	—
Alliant International University—San Diego (Psy.D.) (Cl)	5	—
Alliant International University—San Francisco Bay (Ph.D.) (Cl)	4	—
Alliant International University—San Francisco Bay (Psy.D.) (Cl)	11	—
Antioch University New England (Psy.D.)	1	0
Argosy University, Atlanta (Psy.D.) (Cl)	3	0

	# Faculty	# Grants
Argosy University, Chicago (Psy.D.) (Cl)	4	1
Argosy University, Hawaii (Psy.D.) (Cl)	9	0
Argosy University, Phoenix (Psy.D.) (Cl)	5	0
Argosy University, Schaumburg (Psy.D.) (Cl)	1	0
Argosy University, Schaumburg (Psy.D.) (Cl)	2	1
Argosy University, Twin Cities (Psy.D.) (Cl)	2	0
Argosy University, Washington, DC (Psy.D.) (Cl)	4	—
Arizona State University (Ph.D.) (Cl)	5	1
Arizona State University (Ph.D.) (Co)	5	1
Azusa Pacific University (Psy.D.) (Cl)	2	0
Ball State University (Ph.D.) (Co)	4	1
Biola University (Ph.D. & Psy.D.) (Cl)	4	0
Boston College (Ph.D.) (Co)	1	1
Boston University (Ph.D.) (Cl)	1	0
Brigham Young University (Ph.D.) (Co)	2	2
Carlos Albizu University—Miami Campus (Psy.D.) (Cl)	6	0
Central Michigan University (Ph.D.) (Cl)	1	0
Chicago School of Professional Psychology (Psy.D.) (Cl)	9	1
Colorado State University (Ph.D.) (Co)	6	3
DePaul University (Ph.D.) (Cl)	4	1
Eastern Michigan University (Ph.D.) (Cl)	2	0
Fairleigh Dickinson University (Ph.D.) (Cl)	2	0
Fordham University (Ph.D.) (Co)	5	0
Forest Institute of Professional Psychology (Psy.D.) (Cl)	1	1
Fuller Theological Seminary (Ph.D. & Psy.D.) (Cl)	2	0
George Washington University (Ph.D.) (Cl)	4	3
Georgia State University (Ph.D.) (Cl)	6	1
Harvard University (Ph.D.) (Cl)	1	0
Hofstra University (Ph.D.) (Cl)	2	0
Howard University (Ph.D.) (Cl)	9	5
Immaculata University (Psy.D.) (Cl)	4	0
Indiana University of Pennsylvania (Psy.D.) (Cl)	3	0
Indiana University—Bloomington (Ph.D.) (Co)	3	1
Iowa State University (Ph.D.) (Co)	3	0
James Madison University (Psy.D.) (Cm)	4	1
John F. Kennedy University (Psy.D.) (Cl)	10	0
Lehigh University (Ph.D.) (Co)	4	1
Long Island University, Brooklyn Campus (Ph.D) (Cl)	4	1
Loyola College in Maryland (Psy.D.) (Cl)	3	0
Loyola University of Chicago (Ph.D.) (Cl)	3	3
Loyola University of Chicago (Ph.D.) (Co)	2	0
Marquette University (Ph.D.) (Cl)	5	0
Marquette University (Ph.D.) (Co)	4	0
Marshall University (Psy.D.) (Cl)	1	0
Marywood University (Psy.D.) (Cl)	2	0
Michigan State University (Ph.D.) (Cl)	3	0
New Mexico State University (Ph.D.) (Co)	1	0
New York University (Ph.D.) (Co)	2	0
Northern Illinois University (Ph.D.) (Cl)	4	0
Nova Southeastern University (Ph.D. & Psy.D.) (Cl)	4	0
Oklahoma State University (Ph.D.) (Co)	6	0
Pace University (Psy.D.) (Cm)	2	0
Pacific Graduate School of Psychology (Ph.D.) (Cl)	7	0
Pacific Graduate School of Psychology/ Stanford University Medical School Consortium (Psy.D.) (Cl)	2	1
Pennsylvania State University (Ph.D.) (Cl)	1	1
Pepperdine University (Psy.D.) (Cl)	5	2
Philadelphia College of Osteopathic Medicine (Psy.D.) (Cl)	4	0
Purdue University (Ph.D.) (Cl)	2	0
Rutgers, The State University of New Jersey (Psy.D.) (Cl)	2	0
Sam Houston State University (Ph.D.) (Cl)	2	0
San Diego State University/University of California, San Diego (Ph.D.) (Cl)	12	0
Seattle Pacific University (Ph.D.) (Cl)	3	0
Seton Hall University (Ph.D.) (Co)	3	0
Southern Illinois University— Carbondale (Ph.D.) (Co)	3	0
St. John's University (Ph.D.) (Cl)	5	1
St. Louis University (Ph.D.) (Cl)	1	0
Teachers College, Columbia University (Ph.D.) (Co)	12	0
Tennessee State University (Ph.D.) (Co)	2	1
Texas A&M University (Ph.D.) (Co)	5	0
Texas Tech University (Ph.D.) (Cl)	1	2
Texas Tech University (Ph.D.) (Co)	3	0
The University of Akron (Ph.D.) (Co)	2	0
The University of Memphis (Ph.D.) (Co)	5	1
The Wright Institute (Psy.D.) (Cl)	3	0
University at Albany/State University of New York (Ph.D.) (Co)	3	2
University at Buffalo/State University of New York (Ph.D.) (Cm)	1	0
University of Alabama at Tuscaloosa (Ph.D.) (Cl)	5	5
University of Arkansas (Ph.D.) (Cl)	2	1
University of California, Berkeley (Ph.D.) (Cl)	1	1
University of California, Los Angeles (Ph.D.) (Cl)	3	5
University of California, Santa Barbara (Ph.D.) (Cm)	—	—
University of Central Florida (Ph.D.) (Cl)	1	—
University of Connecticut (Ph.D.) (Cl)	2	1

	# Faculty	# Grants
University of Denver (Ph.D.) (Co)	1	1
University of Denver (Psy.D.) (Cl)	1	0
University of Florida (Ph.D.) (Co)	1	0
University of Georgia (Ph.D.) (Co)	4	3
University of Hawaii at Manoa (Ph.D.) (Cl)	4	3
University of Houston (Ph.D.) (Cl)	3	2
University of Houston (Ph.D.) (Co)	3	1
University of Illinois at Urbana–Champaign (Ph.D.) (Cl)	7	7
University of Illinois at Urbana–Champaign (Ph.D.) (Co)	6	3
University of Indianapolis (Psy.D.) (Cl)	2	1
University of Iowa (Ph.D.) (Co)	2	1
University of Kansas—Child (Ph.D.) (Cl)	4	0
University of Kentucky (Ph.D.) (Co)	4	0
University of La Verne (Psy.D.) (Cl)	7	2
University of Louisville (Ph.D.) (Co)	3	0
University of Maryland—College Park (Ph.D.) (Co)	3	0
University of Massachusetts—Boston (Ph.D.) (Cl)	3	2
University of Miami (Ph.D.) (Co)	3	1
University of Michigan (Ph.D.) (Cl)	2	—
University of Minnesota (Ph.D.) (Cl)	—	—
University of Minnesota (Ph.D.) (Co)	5	6
University of Minnesota Ed (Ph.D.) (Co)	9	5
University of Mississippi (Ph.D.) (Cl)	1	0
University of Missouri—Columbia (Ph.D.) (Co)	5	2
University of Missouri—Kansas City (Ph.D.) (Co)	5	1
University of Missouri—St. Louis (Ph.D.) (Cl)	1	1
University of Nebraska—Lincoln (Ph.D.) (Co)	3	0
University of Nevada—Reno (Ph.D.) (Cl)	1	0
University of New Mexico (Ph.D.) (Cl)	2	1
University of North Carolina at Chapel Hill (Ph.D.) (Cl)	2	0
University of North Dakota (Ph.D.) (Cl)	4	1
University of North Dakota (Ph.D.) (Co)	1	0
University of North Texas (Ph.D.) (Cl)	1	0
University of North Texas (Ph.D.) (Co)	2	0
University of Northern Colorado (Psy.D.) (Co)	6	0
University of Notre Dame (Ph.D.) (Co)	2	1
University of Oklahoma (Ph.D.) (Co)	5	0
University of Oregon (Ph.D.) (Cl)	1	1
University of Oregon (Ph.D.) (Co)	4	1
University of Rhode Island (Ph.D.) (Cl)	1	0
University of South Dakota (Ph.D.) (Cl)	7	0
University of Southern California (Ph.D.) (Cl)	8	4
University of Southern Mississippi (Ph.D.) (Co)	1	5
University of St. Thomas (Psy.D.) (Co)	4	0
University of Tennessee—Knoxville (Ph.D.) (Co)	3	0
University of Texas at Austin (Ph.D.) (Cl)	1	0
University of Texas at Austin (Ph.D.) (Co)	2	0
University of Texas Southwestern Medical Center (Ph.D.) (Cl)	2	0
University of Toledo (Ph.D.) (Cl)	2	0
University of Utah (Ph.D.) (Cl)	1	1
University of Utah (Ph.D.) (Co)	2	0
University of Victoria (Ph.D.) (Cl)	1	1
University of Virginia (Ph.D.) (Cl)	4	2
University of Washington (Ph.D.) (Cl)	5	4
University of Waterloo (Ph.D.) (Cl)	1	0
University of Wisconsin—Madison (Ph.D.) (Co)	9	5
University of Wisconsin—Milwaukee (Ph.D.) (Cl)	1	0
University of Wisconsin—Milwaukee (Ph.D.) (Co)	3	4
Virginia Commonwealth University (Ph.D.) (Cl)	2	1
Virginia Commonwealth University (Ph.D.) (Co)	3	0
Virginia Consortium Program in Clinical Psychology (Psy.D.) (Cl)	7	0
Virginia Polytechnic Institute and State University (Ph.D.) (Cl)	1	1
Washington State University (Ph.D.) (Co)	3	1
West Virginia University (Ph.D.) (Cl)	1	0
Western Michigan University (Ph.D.) (Co)	4	0
Wright State University (Psy.D.) (Cl)	3	0
Yeshiva University (Psy.D.) (Cl)	2	0
Yeshiva University (Psy.D.) (Cm)	3	1

MMPI

	# Faculty	# Grants
Fordham University (Ph.D.) (Cl)	3	0
Kent State University (Ph.D.) (Cl)	1	1
Nova Southeastern University (Ph.D. & Psy.D.) (Cl)	1	0
Texas Tech University (Ph.D.) (Cl)	1	0
Virginia Consortium Program in Clinical Psychology (Psy.D.) (Cl)	1	2
Wichita State University (Ph.D.) (Cl)	1	0

Moral Development

	# Faculty	# Grants
Azusa Pacific University (Psy.D.) (Cl)	2	1
St. John's University (Ph.D.) (Cl)	3	0
The New School (Ph.D.) (Cl)	1	0
Virginia Consortium Program in Clinical Psychology (Psy.D.) (Cl)	1	0

	# Faculty	# Grants

Motivation

	# Faculty	# Grants
Adelphi University (Ph.D.) (Cl)	1	1
Clark University (Ph.D.) (Cl)	1	1
Idaho State University (Ph.D.) (Cl)	1	1
Louisiana Tech University (Ph.D.) (Co)	1	0
University of Rochester (Ph.D.) (Cl)	1	5
University of Waterloo (Ph.D.) (Cl)	1	5
York University (Ph.D.) (Cl)	1	1

Multiple Sclerosis

	# Faculty	# Grants
University of Kansas—Psychology (Ph.D.) (Cl)	1	1
Yeshiva University (Ph.D.) (Cl)	1	3

Multisystemic Interventions/Therapy

	# Faculty	# Grants
Seattle Pacific University (Ph.D.) (Cl)	1	0
University of Missouri—Columbia (Ph.D.) (Cl)	1	1

Narrative Psychology

	# Faculty	# Grants
Miami University (Ph.D.) (Cl)	2	0
The New School (Ph.D.) (Cl)	2	0
The Wright Institute (Psy.D.) (Cl)	4	0
University of Notre Dame (Ph.D.) (Co)	1	1
University of Oklahoma (Ph.D.) (Co)	1	0
University of Saskatchewan (Ph.D.) (Cl)	1	1
York University (Ph.D.) (Cl)	1	1

Neuroimaging/Functional Neuroimaging

	# Faculty	# Grants
Brigham Young University (Ph.D.) (Cl)	1	1
Drexel University (Ph.D.) (Cl)	3	0
Georgia State University (Ph.D.) (Cl)	3	1
Michigan State University (Ph.D.) (Cl)	1	1
University of Florida (Ph.D.) (Cl)	2	3
University of Illinois at Urbana–Champaign (Ph.D.) (Cl)	3	8
University of New Mexico (Ph.D.) (Cl)	3	3
University of Pittsburgh (Ph.D.) (Cl)	7	27
Vanderbilt University (Ph.D.) (Cl)	6	5

Neuropsychology

	# Faculty	# Grants
Adler School of Professional Psychology (Psy.D.) (Cl)	4	1
Alliant International University—Fresno (Psy.D.) (Cl)	1	—
Alliant International University—Los Angeles (Psy.D.) (Cl)	2	—
Alliant International University—San Diego (Ph.D.) (Cl)	2	—
Alliant International University—San Francisco Bay (Psy.D.) (Cl)	1	—
Argosy University, Atlanta (Psy.D.) (Cl)	3	0
Argosy University, Hawaii (Psy.D.) (Cl)	2	0
Argosy University, Phoenix (Psy.D.) (Cl)	2	0
Azusa Pacific University (Psy.D.) (Cl)	1	0
Biola University (Ph.D. & Psy.D.) (Cl)	2	1
Boston University (Ph.D.) (Cl)	2	2
Brigham Young University (Ph.D.) (Cl)	3	3
Carlos Albizu University—Miami Campus (Psy.D.) (Cl)	2	0
Central Michigan University (Ph.D.) (Cl)	1	1
Concordia University (Ph.D.) (Cl)	2	5
Drexel University (Ph.D.) (Cl)	7	2
Duke University (Ph.D.) (Cl)	1	1
Eastern Michigan University (Ph.D.) (Cl)	2	1
Emory University (Ph.D.) (Cl)	1	0
Fielding Graduate University (Ph.D.) (Cl)	—	—
Florida Institute of Technology (Psy.D.) (Cl)	2	1
Fordham University (Ph.D.) (Cl)	1	2
Fuller Theological Seminary (Ph.D. & Psy.D.) (Cl)	2	0
Georgia State University (Ph.D.) (Cl)	3	2
Howard University (Ph.D.) (Cl)	2	1
Immaculata University (Psy.D.) (Cl)	3	0
John F. Kennedy University (Psy.D.) (Cl)	1	0
Kent State University (Ph.D.) (Cl)	1	2
Loma Linda University (Ph.D. & Psy.D.) (Cl)	2	0
Long Island University, Brooklyn Campus (Ph.D) (Cl)	1	1
Loyola College in Maryland (Psy.D.) (Cl)	2	0
Marquette University (Ph.D.) (Cl)	3	0
McGill University (Ph.D.) (Cl)	1	1
Northeastern University (Ph.D.) (Cm)	1	0
Northwestern University Medical School (Ph.D.) (Cl)	3	1
Nova Southeastern University (Ph.D. & Psy.D.) (Cl)	4	2
Ohio University (Ph.D.) (Cl)	1	1
Pacific Graduate School of Psychology (Ph.D.) (Cl)	5	1
Pacific University (Psy.D.) (Cl)	2	0
Pennsylvania State University (Ph.D.) (Cl)	2	1
Pepperdine University (Psy.D.) (Cl)	3	1
Roosevelt University (Psy.D.) (Cl)	3	0
Rosalind Franklin University of Medicine and Science (Ph.D.) (Cl)	1	2
Sam Houston State University (Ph.D.) (Cl)	1	0
San Diego State University/University of California, San Diego (Ph.D.) (Cl)	9	1
Seton Hall University (Ph.D.) (Co)	1	0
Simon Fraser University (Ph.D.) (Cl)	2	3
St. Louis University (Ph.D.) (Cl)	1	0
Texas Tech University (Ph.D.) (Cl)	1	0

	# Faculty	# Grants
Uniformed Services University of Health Sciences (Ph.D.) (Cl)	1	1
University at Albany/State University of New York (Ph.D.) (Cl)	1	1
University of Alabama at Birmingham (Ph.D.) (Cl)	3	2
University of Arizona (Ph.D.) (Cl)	3	3
University of California, Santa Barbara (Ph.D.) (Cm)	—	—
University of Cincinnati (Ph.D.) (Cl)	6	5
University of Connecticut (Ph.D.) (Cl)	3	2
University of Denver (Ph.D.) (Cl)	1	1
University of Florida (Ph.D.) (Cl)	6	4
University of Georgia (Ph.D.) (Cl)	1	1
University of Hawaii at Manoa (Ph.D.) (Cl)	1	0
University of Houston (Ph.D.) (Cl)	4	4
University of Illinois at Chicago (Ph.D.) (Cl)	1	4
University of Illinois at Urbana–Champaign (Ph.D.) (Cl)	2	4
University of Indianapolis (Psy.D.) (Cl)	3	1
University of Kentucky (Ph.D.) (Cl)	2	1
University of Massachusetts—Boston (Ph.D.) (Cl)	2	3
University of Michigan (Ph.D.) (Cl)	2	2
University of Missouri—Columbia (Ph.D.) (Cl)	2	1
University of Missouri—Kansas City (Ph.D.) (Cl)	2	2
University of Montana (Ph.D.) (Cl)	1	0
University of Nevada—Las Vegas (Ph.D.) (Cl)	1	1
University of New Mexico (Ph.D.) (Cl)	2	0
University of North Texas (Ph.D.) (Cl)	1	0
University of Oregon (Ph.D.) (Cl)	2	2
University of Pittsburgh (Ph.D.) (Cl)	7	27
University of South Carolina (Ph.D.) (Cl)	2	2
University of South Florida (Ph.D.) (Cl)	2	0
University of Texas at Austin (Ph.D.) (Cl)	4	3
University of Texas Southwestern Medical Center (Ph.D.) (Cl)	4	4
University of Tulsa (Ph.D.) (Cl)	1	1
University of Utah (Ph.D.) (Cl)	1	0
University of Victoria (Ph.D.) (Cl)	1	1
University of Virginia (Ph.D.) (Cl)	1	1
University of Windsor (Ph.D.) (Cl)	4	4
University of Wisconsin—Milwaukee (Ph.D.) (Cl)	2	1
Vanderbilt University (Ph.D.) (Cl)	4	3
Virginia Consortium Program in Clinical Psychology (Psy.D.) (Cl)	2	0
Virginia Polytechnic Institute and State University (Ph.D.) (Cl)	2	1
Washington State University (Ph.D.) (Cl)	1	1
Washington University in St. Louis (Ph.D.) (Cl)	4	7
Yeshiva University (Ph.D.) (Cl)	2	2
York University (Ph.D.) (Cl)	1	1

Nicotine/Tobacco/Smoking (see also Substance Abuse/Addictive Behaviors)

	# Faculty	# Grants
DePaul University (Ph.D.) (Cl)	1	1
San Diego State University/University of California, San Diego (Ph.D.) (Cl)	7	1
Southern Illinois University—Carbondale (Ph.D.) (Cl)	1	—
St. John's University (Ph.D.) (Cl)	1	0
Texas Tech University (Ph.D.) (Cl)	1	1
University of Illinois at Chicago (Ph.D.) (Cl)	3	5
University of Mississippi (Ph.D.) (Cl)	1	1
University of Missouri—Kansas City (Ph.D.) (Cl)	3	2
University of North Texas and University of North Texas Health Sciences Center (Consortium) (Ph.D.) (Cl)	1	0

Oncology/Cancer Care

	# Faculty	# Grants
Rosalind Franklin University of Medicine and Science (Ph.D.) (Cl)	1	0
San Diego State University/University of California, San Diego (Ph.D.) (Cl)	6	2
The Ohio State University (Ph.D.) (Cl)	3	6
Uniformed Services University of Health Sciences (Ph.D.) (Cl)	1	0
University of Illinois at Urbana–Champaign (Ph.D.) (Co)	2	2
University of Iowa (Ph.D.) (Co)	2	1
University of Miami (Ph.D.) (Cl)	4	1
University of Pittsburgh (Ph.D.) (Cl)	1	3
University of South Florida (Ph.D.) (Cl)	2	8
Yeshiva University (Ph.D.) (Cl)	1	2
York University (Ph.D.) (Cl)	1	1

Organizational

	# Faculty	# Grants
Ball State University (Ph.D.) (Co)	1	0
Marquette University (Ph.D.) (Cl)	1	0
Pacific University (Psy.D.) (Cl)	5	0
Rutgers, The State University of New Jersey (Psy.D.) (Cl)	1	0

Pain Management

	# Faculty	# Grants
Binghamton University/State University of New York (Ph.D.) (Cl)	1	1
George Fox University (Psy.D.) (Cl)	1	1
Philadelphia College of Osteopathic Medicine (Psy.D.) (Cl)	1	0
Rosalind Franklin University of Medicine and Science (Ph.D.) (Cl)	1	1

	# Faculty	# Grants
San Diego State University/University of California, San Diego (Ph.D.) (Cl)	2	0
University of Alabama at Tuscaloosa (Ph.D.) (Cl)	2	3
University of Florida (Ph.D.) (Cl)	2	3
University of Georgia (Ph.D.) (Cl)	1	1
University of Kentucky (Ph.D.) (Cl)	1	1
University of North Dakota (Ph.D.) (Cl)	1	0
University of Texas Southwestern Medical Center (Ph.D.) (Cl)	1	1
University of Tulsa (Ph.D.) (Cl)	1	2
Virginia Consortium Program in Clinical Psychology (Psy.D.) (Cl)	1	0
Virginia Polytechnic Institute and State University (Ph.D.) (Cl)	2	0
West Virginia University (Ph.D.) (Cl)	1	0
York University (Ph.D.) (Cl)	1	1

Parent–Child Interactions/Parenting

Argosy University, Chicago (Psy.D.) (Cl)	1	0
Biola University (Ph.D. & Psy.D.) (Cl)	3	0
Case Western Reserve University (Ph.D.) (Cl)	2	0
Catholic University of America (Ph.D.) (Cl)	5	2
Clark University (Ph.D.) (Cl)	2	1
Colorado State University (Ph.D.) (Co)	1	0
DePaul University (Ph.D.) (Cl)	1	1
Fordham University (Ph.D.) (Cl)	2	0
Georgia State University (Ph.D.) (Cl)	1	1
Idaho State University (Ph.D.) (Cl)	1	0
Indiana University of Pennsylvania (Psy.D.) (Cl)	4	1
James Madison University (Psy.D.) (Cm)	2	0
Long Island University, C.W. Post Campus (Psy.D.) (Cl)	1	1
Marquette University (Ph.D.) (Cl)	3	1
Marquette University (Ph.D.) (Co)	1	3
Miami University (Ph.D.) (Cl)	4	3
Northern Illinois University (Ph.D.) (Cl)	4	0
Pennsylvania State University (Ph.D.) (Cl)	3	2
Stony Brook University/State University of New York (Ph.D.) (Cl)	1	1
Texas Tech University (Ph.D.) (Cl)	1	0
University of Georgia (Ph.D.) (Cl)	2	5
University of Houston (Ph.D.) (Cl)	2	1
University of Indianapolis (Psy.D.) (Cl)	1	1
University of Montana (Ph.D.) (Cl)	1	0
University of Southern Mississippi (Ph.D.) (Co)	1	0
University of Virginia (Ph.D.) (Cl)	2	0
Virginia Consortium Program in Clinical Psychology (Psy.D.) (Cl)	3	1
Virginia Polytechnic Institute and State University (Ph.D.) (Cl)	2	2
Wheaton College (Psy.D.) (Cl)	1	0
Wright State University (Psy.D.) (Cl)	3	0

Yeshiva University (Psy.D.) (Cl)	1	0
Yeshiva University (Psy.D.) (Cm)	2	0

Person Perception

Idaho State University (Ph.D.) (Cl)	1	1
Sam Houston State University (Ph.D.) (Cl)	1	0

Personality Assessment

Arizona State University (Ph.D.) (Cl)	1	0
Auburn University (Ph.D.) (Cl)	1	0
Baylor University (Psy.D.) (Cl)	3	0
Florida Institute of Technology (Psy.D.) (Cl)	3	0
George Washington University (Psy.D.) (Cl)	3	0
Immaculata University (Psy.D.) (Cl)	4	0
Pennsylvania State University (Ph.D.) (Cl)	5	1
Philadelphia College of Osteopathic Medicine (Psy.D.) (Cl)	3	0
Purdue University (Ph.D.) (Cl)	1	0
The New School (Ph.D.) (Cl)	1	0
The University of Akron (Ph.D.) (Co)	2	0
University of Illinois at Urbana–Champaign (Ph.D.) (Co)	1	1
University of Kentucky (Ph.D.) (Cl)	3	1
University of Minnesota (Ph.D.) (Cl)	—	—
University of North Dakota (Ph.D.) (Cl)	2	0
University of South Florida (Ph.D.) (Cl)	1	0
University of Utah (Ph.D.) (Cl)	1	0
Virginia Consortium Program in Clinical Psychology (Psy.D.) (Cl)	3	0
West Virginia University (Ph.D.) (Co)	2	0

Personality Disorders

Alliant International University—Los Angeles (Psy.D.) (Cl)	2	—
Argosy University, Chicago (Psy.D.) (Cl)	1	0
Binghamton University/State University of New York (Ph.D.) (Cl)	1	1
Boston University (Ph.D.) (Cl)	1	0
Case Western Reserve University (Ph.D.) (Cl)	1	6
Eastern Michigan University (Ph.D.) (Cl)	1	1
Fordham University (Ph.D.) (Cl)	2	1
Harvard University (Ph.D.) (Cl)	1	0
Indiana State University (Psy.D.) (Cl)	1	0
Indiana University—Bloomington (Ph.D.) (Cl)	3	2
Miami University (Ph.D.) (Cl)	3	0
Michigan State University (Ph.D.) (Cl)	1	2
Michigan State University (Ph.D.) (Cl)	1	1
Northern Illinois University (Ph.D.) (Cl)	2	0
Pennsylvania State University (Ph.D.) (Cl)	2	0

	# Faculty	# Grants
Philadelphia College of Osteopathic Medicine (Psy.D.) (Cl)	1	0
Rutgers, The State University of New Jersey (Psy.D.) (Cl)	2	0
St. Louis University (Ph.D.) (Cl)	2	0
University of Colorado at Boulder (Ph.D.) (Cl)	1	1
University of Iowa (Ph.D.) (Cl)	1	1
University of Kentucky (Ph.D.) (Cl)	2	0
University of Michigan (Ph.D.) (Cl)	1	—
University of Minnesota (Ph.D.) (Cl)	—	—
University of Missouri—Columbia (Ph.D.) (Cl)	1	2
University of Montana (Ph.D.) (Cl)	1	1
University of North Carolina at Greensboro (Ph.D.) (Cl)	1	0
University of North Dakota (Ph.D.) (Cl)	3	0
University of Tulsa (Ph.D.) (Cl)	2	0
University of Virginia (Ph.D.) (Cl)	1	1
University of Wisconsin—Madison (Ph.D.) (Cl)	1	1
Wichita State University (Ph.D.) (Cl)	2	2

Personality/Temperament

	# Faculty	# Grants
Adelphi University (Ph.D.) (Cl)	3	1
Alliant International University— Los Angeles (Ph.D.) (Cl)	1	—
Alliant International University— San Diego (Ph.D.) (Cl)	8	—
Alliant International University— San Francisco Bay (Ph.D.) (Cl)	3	—
Alliant International University— San Francisco Bay (Psy.D.) (Cl)	4	—
Case Western Reserve University (Ph.D.) (Cl)	1	1
Emory University (Ph.D.) (Cl)	2	2
George Mason University (Ph.D.) (Cl)	1	1
Hofstra University (Ph.D.) (Cl)	2	0
Iowa State University (Ph.D.) (Co)	1	0
Louisiana Tech University (Ph.D.) (Co)	1	0
McGill University (Ph.D.) (Cl)	1	1
Northern Illinois University (Ph.D.) (Cl)	1	0
Northwestern University (Ph.D.) (Cl)	4	2
Purdue University (Ph.D.) (Cl)	3	1
Regent University (Psy.D.) (Cl)	1	1
Sam Houston State University (Ph.D.) (Cl)	1	1
Southern Illinois University— Carbondale (Ph.D.) (Cl)	3	0
The Ohio State University (Ph.D.) (Cl)	1	0
University of California, Berkeley (Ph.D.) (Cl)	1	1
University of Florida (Ph.D.) (Co)	1	0
University of Georgia (Ph.D.) (Cl)	1	0
University of Maryland—College Park (Ph.D.) (Cl)	1	0
University of Minnesota (Ph.D.) (Co)	1	0
University of Tennessee—Knoxville (Ph.D.) (Co)	1	0

	# Faculty	# Grants
Vanderbilt University (Ph.D.) (Cl)	1	1
Washington State University (Ph.D.) (Co)	1	0

Positive Psychology/Resilience

	# Faculty	# Grants
Alliant International University— Los Angeles (Psy.D.) (Cl)	1	—
Carlos Albizu University—Miami Campus (Psy.D.) (Cl)	1	0
George Mason University (Ph.D.) (Cl)	3	1
Immaculata University (Psy.D.) (Cl)	3	0
Marywood University (Psy.D.) (Cl)	1	0
New York University (Ph.D.) (Co)	1	1
Pepperdine University (Psy.D.) (Cl)	3	0
Seton Hall University (Ph.D.) (Co)	1	0
Tennessee State University (Ph.D.) (Co)	2	0
Texas Tech University (Ph.D.) (Co)	1	0
University of Indianapolis (Psy.D.) (Cl)	1	0
University of Kansas (Ph.D.) (Co)	3	1
University of Montana (Ph.D.) (Cl)	1	0
University of Texas at Austin (Ph.D.) (Cl)	1	0
Washington State University (Ph.D.) (Co)	1	0

Posttraumatic Stress Disorder

	# Faculty	# Grants
Binghamton University/State University of New York (Ph.D.) (Cl)	2	0
Florida Institute of Technology (Psy.D.) (Cl)	1	0
Fuller Theological Seminary (Ph.D. & Psy.D.) (Cl)	2	0
Jackson State University (Ph.D.) (Cl)	1	0
La Salle University (Psy.D.) (Cl)	1	1
Loyola College in Maryland (Psy.D.) (Cl)	4	0
Miami University (Ph.D.) (Cl)	1	1
Nova Southeastern University (Ph.D. & Psy.D.) (Cl)	8	0
Pace University (Psy.D.) (Cm)	1	0
Pacific University (Psy.D.) (Cl)	1	0
Pepperdine University (Psy.D.) (Cl)	6	3
San Diego State University/University of California, San Diego (Ph.D.) (Cl)	1	0
University of Denver (Ph.D.) (Co)	1	1
University of Detroit Mercy (Ph.D.) (Cl)	2	0
University of Indianapolis (Psy.D.) (Cl)	1	0
University of Minnesota (Ph.D.) (Co)	1	0
University of Mississippi (Ph.D.) (Cl)	1	0
University of Montana (Ph.D.) (Cl)	3	2
University of North Texas (Ph.D.) (Cl)	2	0
University of Tulsa (Ph.D.) (Cl)	3	2
West Virginia University (Ph.D.) (Cl)	1	0

Poverty

	# Faculty	# Grants
Marshall University (Psy.D.) (Cl)	1	0
University of Denver (Ph.D.) (Cl)	2	1
University of North Dakota (Ph.D.) (Co)	1	0

	# Faculty	# Grants

Prevention

Arizona State University (Ph.D.) (Cl)	6	4
Binghamton University/State University of New York (Ph.D.) (Cl)	3	1
Clark University (Ph.D.) (Cl)	4	2
Duke University (Ph.D.) (Cl)	3	3
Fordham University (Ph.D.) (Cl)	1	0
George Mason University (Ph.D.) (Cl)	3	2
Hofstra University (Ph.D.) (Cl)	2	0
Indiana University of Pennsylvania (Psy.D.) (Cl)	1	0
Loyola University of Chicago (Ph.D.) (Cl)	3	2
Northern Illinois University (Ph.D.) (Cl)	1	0
Rutgers, The State University of New Jersey (Ph.D.) (Cl)	2	1
Teachers College, Columbia University (Ph.D.) (Co)	—	—
The New School (Ph.D.) (Cl)	2	1
University at Albany/State University of New York (Ph.D.) (Co)	1	0
University of Central Florida (Ph.D.) (Cl)	1	—
University of Colorado at Boulder (Ph.D.) (Cl)	3	2
University of Denver (Ph.D.) (Cl)	2	1
University of Georgia (Ph.D.) (Cl)	1	5
University of Georgia (Ph.D.) (Co)	2	3
University of Louisville (Ph.D.) (Co)	3	2
University of Minnesota Ed (Ph.D.) (Co)	1	1
University of Missouri—Kansas City (Ph.D.) (Co)	3	0
University of Nevada—Reno (Ph.D.) (Cl)	4	2
University of Oregon (Ph.D.) (Co)	4	2
University of Pittsburgh (Ph.D.) (Cl)	3	9
University of South Carolina (Ph.D.) (Cl)	3	4
University of Southern California (Ph.D.) (Cl)	2	0
University of Vermont (Ph.D.) (Cl)	3	3
University of Virginia (Ph.D.) (Cl)	2	2
Vanderbilt University (Ph.D.) (Cl)	3	2
Virginia Commonwealth University (Ph.D.) (Co)	2	2
Virginia Consortium Program in Clinical Psychology (Psy.D.) (Cl)	2	1
Virginia Polytechnic Institute and State University (Ph.D.) (Cl)	4	3

Problem Solving

Drexel University (Ph.D.) (Cl)	2	1
San Diego State University/University of California, San Diego (Ph.D.) (Cl)	1	0
University of Missouri—Columbia (Ph.D.) (Co)	3	2
Widener University (Psy.D.) (Cl)	4	1

Professional Issues/Training

Alliant International University— Los Angeles (Psy.D.) (Cl)	3	—
ternational University—San Diego (Ph.D.) (Cl)	2	—
Alliant International University— San Diego (Psy.D.) (Cl)	2	—
Alliant International University— San Francisco Bay (Ph.D.) (Cl)	2	—
Alliant International University— San Francisco Bay (Psy.D.) (Cl)	3	—
Auburn University (Ph.D.) (Co)	1	0
Indiana State University (Psy.D.) (Cl)	1	0
Indiana University of Pennsylvania (Psy.D.) (Cl)	5	1
Long Island University, C.W. Post Campus (Psy.D.) (Cl)	1	0
Oklahoma State University (Ph.D.) (Co)	2	0
Pepperdine University (Psy.D.) (Cl)	1	0
Philadelphia College of Osteopathic Medicine (Psy.D.) (Cl)	1	0
St. Louis University (Ph.D.) (Cl)	2	0
University of Alabama at Tuscaloosa (Ph.D.) (Cl)	2	0
University of Missouri—Kansas City (Ph.D.) (Co)	3	0
University of North Texas (Ph.D.) (Co)	3	0
University of Utah (Ph.D.) (Co)	1	0
Virginia Consortium Program in Clinical Psychology (Psy.D.) (Cl)	2	0
Yeshiva University (Psy.D.) (Cm)	3	0

Program Evaluation

American University (Ph.D.) (Cl)	1	0
DePaul University (Ph.D.) (Cl)	4	1
George Mason University (Ph.D.) (Cl)	3	2
Marquette University (Ph.D.) (Co)	2	1
Miami University (Ph.D.) (Cl)	2	2
Pepperdine University (Psy.D.) (Cl)	4	0
Rutgers, The State University of New Jersey (Psy.D.) (Cl)	1	0
Seattle Pacific University (Ph.D.) (Cl)	2	1
Spalding University (Psy.D.) (Cl)	2	2
University of Colorado at Colorado Springs (Ph.D.) (Cl)	2	2
University of Illinois at Urbana– Champaign (Ph.D.) (Cl)	4	3
University of Pittsburgh (Ph.D.) (Cl)	2	3
University of Toledo (Ph.D.) (Cl)	2	1
Virginia Consortium Program in Clinical Psychology (Psy.D.) (Cl)	2	0

Psychoanalysis/Psychodynamics

Adelphi University (Ph.D.) (Cl)	8	3
Biola University (Ph.D. & Psy.D.) (Cl)	4	0

	# Faculty	# Grants
California Institute of Integral Studies (Psy.D.) (Cl)	2	0
Loma Linda University (Ph.D. & Psy.D.) (Cl)	2	2
New York University (Ph.D.) (Co)	1	0
Nova Southeastern University (Ph.D. & Psy.D.) (Cl)	2	0
Pennsylvania State University (Ph.D.) (Cl)	2	0
Rutgers, The State University of New Jersey (Psy.D.) (Cl)	4	1
Seattle Pacific University (Ph.D.) (Cl)	1	0
The New School (Ph.D.) (Cl)	2	0
University of Pennsylvania (Ph.D.) (Cl)	1	1
University of Texas at Austin (Ph.D.) (Co)	1	0
Virginia Consortium Program in Clinical Psychology (Psy.D.) (Cl)	2	0
Xavier University (Psy.D.) (Cl)	4	0
Yeshiva University (Psy.D.) (Cl)	5	0

Psychometrics/Measurement

	# Faculty	# Grants
Argosy University, Twin Cities (Psy.D.) (Cl)	2	0
Auburn University (Ph.D.) (Co)	1	0
Brigham Young University (Ph.D.) (Cl)	1	1
Carlos Albizu University–San Juan Campus (Ph.D.) (Cl)	2	0
Hofstra University (Ph.D.) (Cl)	1	0
Northern Illinois University (Ph.D.) (Cl)	3	0
Pace University (Psy.D.) (Cm)	3	0
Ponce School of Medicine (Psy.D.) (Cl)	4	1
San Diego State University/University of California, San Diego (Ph.D.) (Cl)	4	0
Southern Illinois University—Carbondale (Ph.D.) (Co)	1	0
University of Minnesota (Ph.D.) (Co)	1	1
University of Missouri—Columbia (Ph.D.) (Co)	4	3
Washington State University (Ph.D.) (Co)	3	1

Psychoneuroimmunology

	# Faculty	# Grants
The Ohio State University (Ph.D.) (Cl)	2	5
University of Kentucky (Ph.D.) (Cl)	1	1
University of Miami (Ph.D.) (Cl)	6	2
University of North Texas and University of North Texas Health Sciences Center (Consortium) (Ph.D.) (Cl)	1	0
University of Pittsburgh (Ph.D.) (Cl)	3	9

Psychopathology/Adult Psychopathology

	# Faculty	# Grants
Binghamton University/State University of New York (Ph.D.) (Cl)	8	2
Brigham Young University (Ph.D.) (Cl)	1	0
Catholic University of America (Ph.D.) (Cl)	3	1
Clark University (Ph.D.) (Cl)	2	0
Colorado State University (Ph.D.) (Co)	3	0
Drexel University (Ph.D.) (Cl)	1	0
George Washington University (Psy.D.) (Cl)	4	0
Indiana State University (Psy.D.) (Cl)	2	0
Indiana University of Pennsylvania (Psy.D.) (Cl)	3	0
Loyola University of Chicago (Ph.D.) (Cl)	1	0
McGill University (Ph.D.) (Cl)	2	2
New York University (Ph.D.) (Co)	2	0
Northern Illinois University (Ph.D.) (Cl)	4	0
Ohio University (Ph.D.) (Cl)	2	0
Pacific Graduate School of Psychology (Ph.D.) (Cl)	1	1
Pennsylvania State University (Ph.D.) (Cl)	5	1
Rutgers, The State University of New Jersey (Ph.D.) (Cl)	1	1
San Diego State University/University of California, San Diego (Ph.D.) (Cl)	3	0
Simon Fraser University (Ph.D.) (Cl)	8	7
Southern Methodist University (Ph.D.) (Cl)	3	2
Texas A&M University (Ph.D.) (Cl)	2	1
The New School (Ph.D.) (Cl)	2	0
University at Albany/State University of New York (Ph.D.) (Cl)	1	0
University of Alabama at Tuscaloosa (Ph.D.) (Cl)	3	2
University of Colorado at Boulder (Ph.D.) (Cl)	5	3
University of Connecticut (Ph.D.) (Cl)	5	4
University of Georgia (Ph.D.) (Cl)	4	2
University of Houston (Ph.D.) (Cl)	6	3
University of Kansas—Psychology (Ph.D.) (Cl)	1	0
University of Kentucky (Ph.D.) (Cl)	4	1
University of Manitoba (Ph.D.) (Cl)	3	—
University of Miami (Ph.D.) (Cl)	6	2
University of Nebraska—Lincoln (Ph.D.) (Cl)	3	2
University of North Dakota (Ph.D.) (Cl)	6	0
University of Pittsburgh (Ph.D.) (Cl)	8	19
University of Southern California (Ph.D.) (Cl)	5	0
University of Tennessee—Knoxville (Ph.D.) (Cl)	—	1
University of Utah (Ph.D.) (Cl)	1	0
University of Virginia (Ph.D.) (Cl)	3	3
Vanderbilt University (Ph.D.) (Cl)	12	5
Vanderbilt University (Ph.D.) (Cl)	1	0
Virginia Commonwealth University (Ph.D.) (Cl)	1	1
Virginia Consortium Program in Clinical Psychology (Psy.D.) (Cl)	3	0
Washington State University (Ph.D.) (Cl)	5	6
Washington University in St. Louis (Ph.D.) (Cl)	4	0

	# Faculty	# Grants
Yale University (Ph.D.) (Cl)	5	0
York University (Ph.D.) (Cl)	2	2

Psychopathology—Child/Developmental

Baylor University (Psy.D.) (Cl)	2	0
Catholic University of America (Ph.D.) (Cl)	4	3
Concordia University (Ph.D.) (Cl)	2	1
Duke University (Ph.D.) (Cl)	3	3
Florida State University (Ph.D.) (Cl)	3	3
Harvard University (Ph.D.) (Cl)	3	4
Idaho State University (Ph.D.) (Cl)	1	1
Indiana University of Pennsylvania (Psy.D.) (Cl)	1	0
Indiana University—Bloomington (Ph.D.) (Cl)	4	4
Long Island University, Brooklyn Campus (Ph.D) (Cl)	2	0
Loyola College in Maryland (Psy.D.) (Cl)	5	0
Loyola University of Chicago (Ph.D.) (Cl)	11	7
McGill University (Ph.D.) (Cl)	1	1
Miami University (Ph.D.) (Cl)	6	4
Northern Illinois University (Ph.D.) (Cl)	4	0
Pacific University (Psy.D.) (Cl)	5	0
San Diego State University/University of California, San Diego (Ph.D.) (Cl)	3	0
Seattle Pacific University (Ph.D.) (Cl)	3	3
Simon Fraser University (Ph.D.) (Cl)	4	6
The Ohio State University (Ph.D.) (Cl)	3	4
University of Alabama at Tuscaloosa (Ph.D.) (Cl)	1	0
University of Central Florida (Ph.D.) (Cl)	1	—
University of Connecticut (Ph.D.) (Cl)	14	8
University of Denver (Ph.D.) (Cl)	2	2
University of Georgia (Ph.D.) (Cl)	3	3
University of Kentucky (Ph.D.) (Cl)	1	1
University of Massachusetts—Amherst (Ph.D.) (Cl)	1	0
University of Massachusetts—Boston (Ph.D.) (Cl)	2	1
University of Miami (Ph.D.) (Cl)	5	2
University of Minnesota (Ph.D.) (Cl)	—	—
University of Montana (Ph.D.) (Cl)	3	1
University of Oregon (Ph.D.) (Cl)	4	1
University of Southern California (Ph.D.) (Cl)	5	0
University of Tennessee—Knoxville (Ph.D.) (Cl)	3	1
University of Virginia (Ph.D.) (Cl)	3	2
University of Wisconsin—Madison (Ph.D.) (Cl)	3	3
Virginia Consortium Program in Clinical Psychology (Psy.D.) (Cl)	1	0
West Virginia University (Ph.D.) (Cl)	1	0
Yale University (Ph.D.) (Cl)	2	0

Psychopharmacology

Argosy University, Phoenix (Psy.D.) (Cl)	1	0
Idaho State University (Ph.D.) (Cl)	1	1
McGill University (Ph.D.) (Cl)	2	1
San Diego State University/University of California, San Diego (Ph.D.) (Cl)	6	2
University of Minnesota (Ph.D.) (Cl)	—	—
University of Pennsylvania (Ph.D.) (Cl)	3	3
University of Pittsburgh (Ph.D.) (Cl)	3	8
Vanderbilt University (Ph.D.) (Cl)	2	2

Psychophysiology

Binghamton University/State University of New York (Ph.D.) (Cl)	2	0
Howard University (Ph.D.) (Cl)	1	1
McGill University (Ph.D.) (Cl)	2	1
Pennsylvania State University (Ph.D.) (Cl)	7	0
Rutgers, The State University of New Jersey (Psy.D.) (Cl)	1	0
San Diego State University/University of California, San Diego (Ph.D.) (Cl)	5	0
Seattle Pacific University (Ph.D.) (Cl)	1	0
Syracuse University (Ph.D.) (Cl)	3	2
University of Alabama at Birmingham (Ph.D.) (Cl)	1	1
University of Delaware (Ph.D.) (Cl)	3	1
University of Illinois at Urbana–Champaign (Ph.D.) (Cl)	3	8
University of Kentucky (Ph.D.) (Cl)	2	1
University of Michigan (Ph.D.) (Cl)	1	—
University of Minnesota (Ph.D.) (Cl)	—	—
University of North Dakota (Ph.D.) (Cl)	1	0
University of Pittsburgh (Ph.D.) (Cl)	5	16
Vanderbilt University (Ph.D.) (Cl)	6	2
Virginia Commonwealth University (Ph.D.) (Cl)	2	0
Virginia Consortium Program in Clinical Psychology (Psy.D.) (Cl)	1	0

Psychotherapy/Process and Outcome/Integrative Approaches

Adelphi University (Ph.D.) (Cl)	4	3
Alliant International University—Fresno (Ph.D.) (Cl)	2	—
Alliant International University—Los Angeles (Ph.D.) (Cl)	5	—
Alliant International University—San Diego (Ph.D.) (Cl)	5	—
Alliant International University—San Francisco Bay (Ph.D.) (Cl)	5	—
Alliant International University—San Francisco Bay (Psy.D.) (Cl)	14	—
Antioch University New England (Psy.D.)	2	0
Argosy University, Chicago (Psy.D.) (Cl)	1	0

	# Faculty	# Grants
Argosy University, Schaumburg (Psy.D.) (Cl)	2	1
Argosy University, Tampa (Psy.D.) (Cl)	2	0
Argosy University, Twin Cities (Psy.D.) (Cl)	2	0
Argosy University, Washington, DC (Psy.D.) (Cl)	2	—
Brigham Young University (Ph.D.) (Cl)	3	3
Brigham Young University (Ph.D.) (Co)	3	3
California Institute of Integral Studies (Psy.D.) (Cl)	2	0
Carlos Albizu University—Miami Campus (Psy.D.) (Cl)	6	0
Catholic University of America (Ph.D.) (Cl)	10	0
Clark University (Ph.D.) (Cl)	1	1
Colorado State University (Ph.D.) (Co)	1	0
Drexel University (Ph.D.) (Cl)	4	1
George Mason University (Ph.D.) (Cl)	1	0
Hofstra University (Ph.D.) (Cl)	1	2
Immaculata University (Psy.D.) (Cl)	5	0
James Madison University (Psy.D.) (Cm)	4	0
Loma Linda University (Ph.D. & Psy.D.) (Cl)	1	0
Long Island University, Brooklyn Campus (Ph.D) (Cl)	3	1
Loyola College in Maryland (Psy.D.) (Cl)	1	0
Loyola University of Chicago (Ph.D.) (Cl)	4	1
Marquette University (Ph.D.) (Cl)	6	0
Marquette University (Ph.D.) (Co)	3	0
Marshall University (Psy.D.) (Cl)	1	0
Marywood University (Psy.D.) (Cl)	1	0
McGill University (Ph.D.) (Cl)	1	1
McGill University (Ph.D.) (Co)	2	2
Miami University (Ph.D.) (Cl)	3	0
Northwestern University (Ph.D.) (Cl)	1	0
Pacific Graduate School of Psychology (Ph.D.) (Cl)	5	1
Pacific University (Psy.D.) (Cl)	7	0
Pennsylvania State University (Ph.D.) (Cl)	4	3
Pennsylvania State University (Ph.D.) (Co)	1	0
Pepperdine University (Psy.D.) (Cl)	12	2
Philadelphia College of Osteopathic Medicine (Psy.D.) (Cl)	2	0
Rutgers, The State University of New Jersey (Ph.D.) (Cl)	5	1
Rutgers, The State University of New Jersey (Psy.D.) (Cl)	3	1
Sam Houston State University (Ph.D.) (Cl)	1	1
San Diego State University/University of California, San Diego (Ph.D.) (Cl)	4	0
Stony Brook University/State University of New York (Ph.D.) (Cl)	1	1
Teachers College, Columbia University (Ph.D.) (Cl)	3	1
Texas A&M University (Ph.D.) (Cl)	7	2
Texas Woman's University (Ph.D.) (Co)	1	0
The New School (Ph.D.) (Cl)	3	1
The University of Memphis (Ph.D.) (Cl)	5	4
The Wright Institute (Psy.D.) (Cl)	2	0
University at Albany/State University of New York (Ph.D.) (Co)	1	0
University of Alabama at Tuscaloosa (Ph.D.) (Cl)	3	0
University of Arizona (Ph.D.) (Cl)	3	4
University of California, Santa Barbara (Ph.D.) (Cm)	—	—
University of Colorado at Boulder (Ph.D.) (Cl)	4	4
University of Delaware (Ph.D.) (Cl)	2	0
University of Denver (Ph.D.) (Cl)	2	1
University of Detroit Mercy (Ph.D.) (Cl)	4	0
University of Hawaii at Manoa (Ph.D.) (Cl)	4	4
University of Illinois at Urbana–Champaign (Ph.D.) (Cl)	1	1
University of Kansas (Ph.D.) (Co)	1	0
University of Kansas—Psychology (Ph.D.) (Cl)	1	0
University of La Verne (Psy.D.) (Cl)	3	0
University of Maine (Ph.D.) (Cl)	3	0
University of Maryland—College Park (Ph.D.) (Cl)	2	2
University of Massachusetts—Amherst (Ph.D.) (Cl)	5	0
University of Minnesota Ed (Ph.D.) (Co)	3	1
University of Missouri—Kansas City (Ph.D.) (Co)	3	0
University of Montana (Ph.D.) (Cl)	3	0
niversity of Nebraska—Lincoln (Ph.D.) (Co)	1	0
University of Nevada—Reno (Ph.D.) (Cl)	3	1
University of Oregon (Ph.D.) (Co)	4	2
University of St. Thomas (Psy.D.) (Co)	1	0
University of Tennessee—Knoxville (Ph.D.) (Cl)	5	2
University of Tennessee—Knoxville (Ph.D.) (Co)	1	0
University of Toledo (Ph.D.) (Cl)	3	1
University of Utah (Ph.D.) (Co)	1	0
University of Washington (Ph.D.) (Cl)	1	1
University of Windsor (Ph.D.) (Cl)	3	2
University of Wisconsin—Madison (Ph.D.) (Co)	3	0
University of Wisconsin—Milwaukee (Ph.D.) (Cl)	3	9
Virginia Commonwealth University (Ph.D.) (Cl)	3	3
Virginia Consortium Program in Clinical Psychology (Psy.D.) (Cl)	6	0
Virginia Polytechnic Institute and State University (Ph.D.) (Cl)	2	2
West Virginia University (Ph.D.) (Co)	3	0
Western Michigan University (Ph.D.) (Cl)	4	0
Yeshiva University (Psy.D.) (Cl)	3	0
York University (Ph.D.) (Cl)	3	3

	# Faculty	# Grants

Public Health

	# Faculty	# Grants
Texas A&M University (Ph.D.) (Co)	2	1
University of Iowa (Ph.D.) (Co)	2	0
University of Toledo (Ph.D.) (Cl)	2	1
Yale University (Ph.D.) (Cl)	1	1

Quantitative/Mathematical Models of Psychopathology

	# Faculty	# Grants
Indiana University—Bloomington (Ph.D.) (Cl)	2	1
University of Iowa (Ph.D.) (Cl)	2	0

Reading/Literacy

	# Faculty	# Grants
Georgia State University (Ph.D.) (Cl)	1	4
Ontario Institute for Studies in Education/University of Toronto (Ph.D.) (Cm)	5	7
University of Waterloo (Ph.D.) (Cl)	1	0

Rehabilitation

	# Faculty	# Grants
Ball State University (Ph.D.) (Co)	2	1
Florida State University (Ph.D.) (Cm)	2	1
Georgia State University (Ph.D.) (Co)	1	0
Illinois Institute of Technology (Ph.D.) (Cl)	2	1
Philadelphia College of Osteopathic Medicine (Psy.D.) (Cl)	1	0
Texas A&M University (Ph.D.) (Co)	1	3
University at Buffalo/State University of New York (Ph.D.) (Cm)	2	0
University of Texas Southwestern Medical Center (Ph.D.) (Cl)	1	1
Virginia Consortium Program in Clinical Psychology (Psy.D.) (Cl)	1	0
West Virginia University (Ph.D.) (Co)	3	0

Religion/Spirituality

	# Faculty	# Grants
Argosy University, Schaumburg (Psy.D.) (Cl)	1	1
Azusa Pacific University (Psy.D.) (Cl)	4	1
Biola University (Ph.D. & Psy.D.) (Cl)	4	2
Bowling Green State University (Ph.D.) (Cl)	2	1
Brigham Young University (Ph.D.) (Co)	6	3
California Institute of Integral Studies (Psy.D.) (Cl)	4	1
Fuller Theological Seminary (Ph.D. & Psy.D.) (Cl)	7	0
George Fox University (Psy.D.) (Cl)	1	1
Howard University (Ph.D.) (Co)	2	0
Loyola College in Maryland (Psy.D.) (Cl)	2	0

	# Faculty	# Grants
New York University (Ph.D.) (Co)	1	1
Pepperdine University (Psy.D.) (Cl)	5	3
Regent University (Psy.D.) (Cl)	1	1
Seattle Pacific University (Ph.D.) (Cl)	4	1
Seton Hall University (Ph.D.) (Co)	1	0
Southern Illinois University—Carbondale (Ph.D.) (Cl)	1	0
Southern Illinois University—Carbondale (Ph.D.) (Co)	2	0
Spalding University (Psy.D.) (Cl)	1	0
Teachers College, Columbia University (Ph.D.) (Cl)	1	1
Tennessee State University (Ph.D.) (Co)	1	0
Texas Tech University (Ph.D.) (Co)	1	0
University at Albany/State University of New York (Ph.D.) (Co)	1	0
University of Detroit Mercy (Ph.D.) (Cl)	3	0
University of Iowa (Ph.D.) (Co)	2	0
University of Louisville (Ph.D.) (Co)	2	0
University of Maryland—Baltimore County (Ph.D.) (Cl)	1	0
University of Missouri—St. Louis (Ph.D.) (Cl)	1	0
University of Oklahoma (Ph.D.) (Co)	2	0
University of Southern Mississippi (Ph.D.) (Co)	1	1
University of St. Thomas (Psy.D.) (Co)	1	0
Virginia Consortium Program in Clinical Psychology (Psy.D.) (Cl)	1	0
Wheaton College (Psy.D.) (Cl)	4	1

Rural Mental Health

	# Faculty	# Grants
Marshall University (Psy.D.) (Cl)	2	1
Oklahoma State University (Ph.D.) (Co)	1	0
Pennsylvania State University (Ph.D.) (Cl)	1	1
University of Alabama at Tuscaloosa (Ph.D.) (Cl)	4	2
University of Florida (Ph.D.) (Cl)	1	1
University of Mississippi (Ph.D.) (Cl)	2	0
University of North Dakota (Ph.D.) (Cl)	2	2
University of North Dakota (Ph.D.) (Co)	2	0
University of South Dakota (Ph.D.) (Cl)	6	0
Utah State University (Ph.D.) (Cm)	2	1
Wheaton College (Psy.D.) (Cl)	2	0

Schizophrenia

	# Faculty	# Grants
Boston University (Ph.D.) (Cl)	1	0
Emory University (Ph.D.) (Cl)	1	1
Harvard University (Ph.D.) (Cl)	1	1
Hofstra University (Ph.D.) (Cl)	2	1
Indiana University—Bloomington (Ph.D.) (Cl)	2	4
Kent State University (Ph.D.) (Cl)	1	1
Long Island University, C.W. Post Campus (Psy.D.) (Cl)	1	0
Rosalind Franklin University of Medicine and Science (Ph.D.) (Cl)	1	0

	# Faculty	# Grants
San Diego State University/University of California, San Diego (Ph.D.) (Cl)	7	2
St. John's University (Ph.D.) (Cl)	1	0
University of California, Los Angeles (Ph.D.) (Cl)	2	6
University of Central Florida (Ph.D.) (Cl)	1	—
University of Georgia (Ph.D.) (Cl)	1	0
University of Hawaii at Manoa (Ph.D.) (Cl)	5	1
University of Houston (Ph.D.) (Cl)	2	1
University of Illinois at Chicago (Ph.D.) (Cl)	1	4
University of Illinois at Urbana–Champaign (Ph.D.) (Cl)	2	5
University of Indianapolis (Psy.D.) (Cl)	2	1
University of Michigan (Ph.D.) (Cl)	1	—
University of Minnesota (Ph.D.) (Cl)	—	—
University of Missouri—Columbia (Ph.D.) (Cl)	1	1
University of Montana (Ph.D.) (Cl)	1	0
University of North Carolina at Chapel Hill (Ph.D.) (Cl)	1	2
University of North Carolina at Greensboro (Ph.D.) (Cl)	1	1
University of North Texas (Ph.D.) (Cl)	2	0
University of Pittsburgh (Ph.D.) (Cl)	1	1
University of Wisconsin—Madison (Ph.D.) (Cl)	1	0
University of Wyoming (Ph.D.) (Cl)	1	0
Vanderbilt University (Ph.D.) (Cl)	2	2
Virginia Consortium Program in Clinical Psychology (Psy.D.) (Cl)	1	0
York University (Ph.D.) (Cl)	2	2

School/Educational

	# Faculty	# Grants
Azusa Pacific University (Psy.D.) (Cl)	2	1
Boston College (Ph.D.) (Co)	6	3
Brigham Young University (Ph.D.) (Co)	3	2
Colorado State University (Ph.D.) (Co)	1	1
Florida State University (Ph.D.) (Cm)	3	1
George Fox University (Psy.D.) (Cl)	1	1
Immaculata University (Psy.D.) (Cl)	2	0
Indiana University—Bloomington (Ph.D.) (Co)	0	1
Miami University (Ph.D.) (Cl)	8	6
Northern Illinois University (Ph.D.) (Cl)	1	0
Seton Hall University (Ph.D.) (Co)	1	0
Southern Illinois University—Carbondale (Ph.D.) (Co)	2	0
University of California, Los Angeles (Ph.D.) (Cl)	2	3
University of California, Santa Barbara (Ph.D.) (Cm)	—	—
University of Georgia (Ph.D.) (Co)	4	1
University of Kansas—Child (Ph.D.) (Cl)	2	1
University of Louisville (Ph.D.) (Co)	3	1

	# Faculty	# Grants
University of Minnesota Ed (Ph.D.) (Co)	3	2
University of North Dakota (Ph.D.) (Co)	1	0
University of Southern California (Ph.D.) (Cl)	2	0
University of Virginia (Ph.D.) (Cl)	4	2
University of Wisconsin—Madison (Ph.D.) (Co)	4	2
Utah State University (Ph.D.) (Cm)	1	0
Virginia Consortium Program in Clinical Psychology (Psy.D.) (Cl)	1	0

Self-Esteem/Self-Efficacy/Self-Psychology

	# Faculty	# Grants
Case Western Reserve University (Ph.D.) (Cl)	1	0
Catholic University of America (Ph.D.) (Cl)	2	0
George Mason University (Ph.D.) (Cl)	1	0
John F. Kennedy University (Psy.D.) (Cl)	1	0
Seattle Pacific University (Ph.D.) (Cl)	1	0
Southern Illinois University—Carbondale (Ph.D.) (Co)	1	0
University of Detroit Mercy (Ph.D.) (Cl)	2	0
University of North Dakota (Ph.D.) (Cl)	1	1
University of South Carolina (Ph.D.) (Cl)	2	2
Virginia Consortium Program in Clinical Psychology (Psy.D.) (Cl)	1	0
West Virginia University (Ph.D.) (Co)	2	0
Wichita State University (Ph.D.) (Cl)	1	5

Severe Mental Illness

	# Faculty	# Grants
Central Michigan University (Ph.D.) (Cl)	1	1
Concordia University (Ph.D.) (Cl)	2	1
Illinois Institute of Technology (Ph.D.) (Cl)	2	1
Indiana University—Purdue University Indianapolis (Ph.D.) (Cl)	2	3
Philadelphia College of Osteopathic Medicine (Psy.D.) (Cl)	1	0
Rosalind Franklin University of Medicine and Science (Ph.D.) (Cl)	1	0
Rutgers, The State University of New Jersey (Psy.D.) (Cl)	2	1
Seattle Pacific University (Ph.D.) (Cl)	1	1
University of Cincinnati (Ph.D.) (Cl)	2	1
University of Maryland—College Park (Ph.D.) (Cl)	2	2
University of Massachusetts—Boston (Ph.D.) (Cl)	1	1
University of Missouri—Kansas City (Ph.D.) (Cl)	1	1
University of Nebraska—Lincoln (Ph.D.) (Cl)	1	1
University of South Dakota (Ph.D.) (Cl)	2	0

	# Faculty	# Grants

Sexuality/Sexual Dysfunction

	# Faculty	# Grants
Alliant International University—San Diego (Psy.D.) (Cl)	1	—
Auburn University (Ph.D.) (Cl)	1	1
Carlos Albizu University–San Juan Campus (Psy.D.) (Cl)	2	0
Eastern Michigan University (Ph.D.) (Cl)	1	0
Hofstra University (Ph.D.) (Cl)	1	0
Idaho State University (Ph.D.) (Cl)	2	2
Indiana University—Bloomington (Ph.D.) (Cl)	1	3
Loyola College in Maryland (Psy.D.) (Cl)	2	0
McGill University (Ph.D.) (Cl)	1	1
Ohio University (Ph.D.) (Cl)	1	1
Regent University (Psy.D.) (Cl)	1	3
San Diego State University/University of California, San Diego (Ph.D.) (Cl)	1	0
Simon Fraser University (Ph.D.) (Cl)	2	2
Syracuse University (Ph.D.) (Cl)	2	4
Teachers College, Columbia University (Ph.D.) (Co)	1	0
Texas Tech University (Ph.D.) (Co)	1	0
Texas Woman's University (Ph.D.) (Co)	3	1
The University of Memphis (Ph.D.) (Co)	1	0
Uniformed Services University of Health Sciences (Ph.D.) (Cl)	1	0
University of Florida (Ph.D.) (Co)	1	0
University of Minnesota (Ph.D.) (Co)	1	1
University of Montana (Ph.D.) (Cl)	1	0
University of Nevada—Reno (Ph.D.) (Cl)	1	1
University of Texas at Austin (Ph.D.) (Cl)	1	1
University of Utah (Ph.D.) (Cl)	2	1
University of Vermont (Ph.D.) (Cl)	3	0
University of Waterloo (Ph.D.) (Cl)	1	0
Western Michigan University (Ph.D.) (Cl)	1	1

Sleep Disorders

	# Faculty	# Grants
Argosy University, Schaumburg (Psy.D.) (Cl)	1	1
Drexel University (Ph.D.) (Cl)	1	0
Louisiana Tech University (Ph.D.) (Co)	1	0
San Diego State University/University of California, San Diego (Ph.D.) (Cl)	4	0
Southern Illinois University—Carbondale (Ph.D.) (Cl)	1	0
University of Alabama at Tuscaloosa (Ph.D.) (Cl)	1	1
University of Arizona (Ph.D.) (Cl)	1	2
University of California, Berkeley (Ph.D.) (Cl)	1	2
University of Michigan (Ph.D.) (Cl)	1	—
University of North Texas and University of North Texas Health Sciences Center (Consortium) (Ph.D.) (Cl)	1	1

	# Faculty	# Grants
University of Texas Southwestern Medical Center (Ph.D.) (Cl)	1	1
Virginia Consortium Program in Clinical Psychology (Psy.D.) (Cl)	3	1
Yeshiva University (Psy.D.) (Cl)	1	0

Social Justice Issues

	# Faculty	# Grants
Pepperdine University (Psy.D.) (Cl)	2	0
University at Albany/State University of New York (Ph.D.) (Co)	3	1
University of California, Santa Barbara (Ph.D.) (Cm)	—	—

Social Skills/Competence

	# Faculty	# Grants
Binghamton University/State University of New York (Ph.D.) (Cl)	1	0
Carlos Albizu University–San Juan Campus (Ph.D.) (Cl)	2	1
Concordia University (Ph.D.) (Cl)	1	1
Florida State University (Ph.D.) (Cl)	1	1
James Madison University (Psy.D.) (Cm)	4	0
Long Island University, Brooklyn Campus (Ph.D) (Cl)	1	0
Purdue University (Ph.D.) (Cl)	2	0
San Diego State University/University of California, San Diego (Ph.D.) (Cl)	1	0
University of Alabama at Tuscaloosa (Ph.D.) (Cl)	2	1
University of Houston (Ph.D.) (Cl)	4	3
University of Maine (Ph.D.) (Cl)	2	2
University of Michigan (Ph.D.) (Cl)	3	3
University of Mississippi (Ph.D.) (Cl)	2	0
University of Nevada—Las Vegas (Ph.D.) (Cl)	1	0
University of Nevada—Reno (Ph.D.) (Cl)	3	0
Virginia Polytechnic Institute and State University (Ph.D.) (Cl)	3	0
Yeshiva University (Psy.D.) (Cm)	3	1

Social Support

	# Faculty	# Grants
DePaul University (Ph.D.) (Cl)	2	1
Fordham University (Ph.D.) (Cl)	2	0
Illinois Institute of Technology (Ph.D.) (Cl)	1	0
Iowa State University (Ph.D.) (Co)	1	0
San Diego State University/University of California, San Diego (Ph.D.) (Cl)	2	0
University of Denver (Ph.D.) (Co)	1	1
University of Oregon (Ph.D.) (Co)	3	0
University of Pittsburgh (Ph.D.) (Cl)	1	4

	# Faculty	# Grants

Social–Psychological Approaches

Argosy University, Washington, DC (Psy.D.) (Cl)	1	—
Arizona State University (Ph.D.) (Co)	2	0
Ball State University (Ph.D.) (Co)	3	0
George Mason University (Ph.D.) (Cl)	4	0
Indiana University—Bloomington (Ph.D.) (Cl)	3	1
James Madison University (Psy.D.) (Cm)	1	0
La Salle University (Psy.D.) (Cl)	1	0
Loyola College in Maryland (Psy.D.) (Cl)	1	0
Rutgers, The State University of New Jersey (Psy.D.) (Cl)	1	1
Sam Houston State University (Ph.D.) (Cl)	1	0
University of Colorado at Colorado Springs (Ph.D.) (Cl)	1	1
University of Notre Dame (Ph.D.) (Co)	2	0
Washington State University (Ph.D.) (Co)	1	0
Xavier University (Psy.D.) (Cl)	1	0

Somatization Disorders

Philadelphia College of Osteopathic Medicine (Psy.D.) (Cl)	1	0
Rutgers, The State University of New Jersey (Ph.D.) (Cl)	1	0

Sports Psychology

American University (Ph.D.) (Cl)	2	0
Carlos Albizu University–San Juan Campus (Ph.D.) (Cl)	1	0
Carlos Albizu University–San Juan Campus (Psy.D.) (Cl)	2	0
Catholic University of America (Ph.D.) (Cl)	1	0
Oklahoma State University (Ph.D.) (Co)	1	0
Rosalind Franklin University of Medicine and Science (Ph.D.) (Cl)	1	0
Spalding University (Psy.D.) (Cl)	1	0
St. Louis University (Ph.D.) (Cl)	1	0
University of Missouri—Kansas City (Ph.D.) (Co)	1	0
University of North Texas (Ph.D.) (Co)	2	1
West Virginia University (Ph.D.) (Co)	1	0

Statistics

Fairleigh Dickinson University (Ph.D.) (Cl)	2	0
Loma Linda University (Ph.D. & Psy.D.) (Cl)	3	0
San Diego State University/University of California, San Diego (Ph.D.) (Cl)	4	0

University of Nevada—Las Vegas (Ph.D.) (Cl)	1	0
University of Pittsburgh (Ph.D.) (Cl)	2	2
Vanderbilt University (Ph.D.) (Cl)	2	1
Xavier University (Psy.D.) (Cl)	2	0

Stigma

Iowa State University (Ph.D.) (Co)	1	0
Jackson State University (Ph.D.) (Cl)	2	0
Marquette University (Ph.D.) (Cl)	1	1
Marquette University (Ph.D.) (Cl)	2	0
Pepperdine University (Psy.D.) (Cl)	1	0
Sam Houston State University (Ph.D.) (Cl)	1	1
University of California, Berkeley (Ph.D.) (Cl)	1	1
University of Hartford (Psy.D.) (Cl)	1	1

Stress and Coping

American University (Ph.D.) (Cl)	1	0
Catholic University of America (Ph.D.) (Cl)	5	2
Colorado State University (Ph.D.) (Co)	2	0
Drexel University (Ph.D.) (Cl)	1	0
Duke University (Ph.D.) (Cl)	4	4
Fairleigh Dickinson University (Ph.D.) (Cl)	1	0
Fordham University (Ph.D.) (Cl)	2	1
Fuller Theological Seminary (Ph.D. & Psy.D.) (Cl)	1	0
George Fox University (Psy.D.) (Cl)	1	1
George Mason University (Ph.D.) (Cl)	2	0
George Washington University (Ph.D.) (Cl)	3	1
Georgia State University (Ph.D.) (Co)	2	1
Indiana State University (Psy.D.) (Cl)	2	0
Indiana University—Bloomington (Ph.D.) (Cl)	1	1
Kent State University (Ph.D.) (Cl)	1	1
Marywood University (Psy.D.) (Cl)	3	0
McGill University (Ph.D.) (Cl)	1	1
Philadelphia College of Osteopathic Medicine (Psy.D.) (Cl)	2	1
San Diego State University/University of California, San Diego (Ph.D.) (Cl)	13	0
Simon Fraser University (Ph.D.) (Cl)	1	1
Southern Illinois University—Carbondale (Ph.D.) (Cl)	1	0
Southern Illinois University—Carbondale (Ph.D.) (Co)	3	0
St. John's University (Ph.D.) (Cl)	1	1
St. Louis University (Ph.D.) (Cl)	2	0
Texas Tech University (Ph.D.) (Co)	1	0
The Wright Institute (Psy.D.) (Cl)	1	0
Uniformed Services University of Health Sciences (Ph.D.) (Cl)	1	3

	# Faculty	# Grants
University of British Columbia (Ph.D.) (Cl)	1	2
University of British Columbia (Ph.D.) (Co)	1	2
University of Georgia (Ph.D.) (Cl)	2	0
University of Kansas—Child (Ph.D.) (Cl)	2	1
University of Kansas—Psychology (Ph.D.) (Cl)	1	0
University of Louisville (Ph.D.) (Cl)	2	0
University of Massachusetts—Amherst (Ph.D.) (Cl)	1	1
University of Miami (Ph.D.) (Cl)	9	2
University of Michigan (Ph.D.) (Cl)	1	—
University of Minnesota (Ph.D.) (Cl)	—	—
University of Minnesota (Ph.D.) (Co)	3	1
University of Missouri—Kansas City (Ph.D.) (Co)	1	0
University of North Dakota (Ph.D.) (Cl)	6	0
University of North Texas (Ph.D.) (Cl)	2	1
University of Oregon (Ph.D.) (Cl)	2	1
University of Pittsburgh (Ph.D.) (Cl)	4	15
University of Texas at Austin (Ph.D.) (Cl)	1	1
University of Tulsa (Ph.D.) (Cl)	4	2
Virginia Commonwealth University (Ph.D.) (Cl)	2	0
Virginia Consortium Program in Clinical Psychology (Psy.D.) (Cl)	3	0
Virginia Polytechnic Institute and State University (Ph.D.) (Cl)	1	1
Widener University (Psy.D.) (Cl)	5	2
Wright State University (Psy.D.) (Cl)	1	0
Yeshiva University (Psy.D.) (Cl)	4	1

Substance Abuse/Addictive Behaviors (see also Alcohol and Nicotine/Tobacco/Smoking)

	# Faculty	# Grants
Alliant International University—Los Angeles (Ph.D.) (Cl)	2	—
Alliant International University—San Diego (Psy.D.) (Cl)	2	—
Alliant International University—San Francisco Bay (Ph.D.) (Cl)	3	—
Alliant International University—San Francisco Bay (Psy.D.) (Cl)	4	—
American University (Ph.D.) (Cl)	2	2
Argosy University, Chicago (Psy.D.) (Cl)	1	0
Argosy University, Phoenix (Psy.D.) (Cl)	1	0
Argosy University, Schaumburg (Psy.D.) (Cl)	1	1
Arizona State University (Ph.D.) (Cl)	3	2
Auburn University (Ph.D.) (Co)	0	1
Binghamton University/State University of New York (Ph.D.) (Cl)	1	1
Boston University (Ph.D.) (Cl)	3	2

	# Faculty	# Grants
City University of New York at City College (Ph.D.) (Cl)	2	1
Colorado State University (Ph.D.) (Co)	4	3
Eastern Michigan University (Ph.D.) (Cl)	1	0
Florida State University (Ph.D.) (Cl)	2	1
Fordham University (Ph.D.) (Cl)	2	1
Fuller Theological Seminary (Ph.D. & Psy.D.) (Cl)	1	0
Harvard University (Ph.D.) (Cl)	1	0
Hofstra University (Ph.D.) (Cl)	3	1
Idaho State University (Ph.D.) (Cl)	3	1
Indiana State University (Psy.D.) (Cl)	1	1
Indiana University—Bloomington (Ph.D.) (Cl)	4	4
Indiana University—Bloomington (Ph.D.) (Co)	1	1
Marquette University (Ph.D.) (Co)	1	4
McGill University (Ph.D.) (Cl)	1	1
Oklahoma State University (Ph.D.) (Cl)	2	0
Pacific Graduate School of Psychology (Ph.D.) (Cl)	2	0
Pacific Graduate School of Psychology/ Stanford University Medical School Consortium (Psy.D.) (Cl)	2	0
Rutgers, The State University of New Jersey (Ph.D.) (Cl)	3	1
Rutgers, The State University of New Jersey (Psy.D.) (Cl)	4	2
Sam Houston State University (Ph.D.) (Cl)	1	1
San Diego State University/University OF California, San Diego (Ph.D.) (Cl)	12	5
Seattle Pacific University (Ph.D.) (Cl)	1	1
Spalding University (Psy.D.) (Cl)	1	0
Syracuse University (Ph.D.) (Cl)	3	6
Texas A&M University (Ph.D.) (Cl)	1	1
Texas Tech University (Ph.D.) (Cl)	1	1
The Wright Institute (Psy.D.) (Cl)	2	0
Uniformed Services University of Health Sciences (Ph.D.) (Cl)	1	3
University at Albany/State University of New York (Ph.D.) (Cl)	2	2
University at Buffalo/State University of New York (Ph.D.) (Cl)	4	8
University of Alabama at Birmingham (Ph.D.) (Cl)	3	5
University of Arkansas (Ph.D.) (Cl)	3	2
University of California, Los Angeles (Ph.D.) (Cl)	1	3
University of California, Santa Barbara (Ph.D.) (Cm)	—	—
University of Cincinnati (Ph.D.) (Cl)	4	5
University of Colorado at Boulder (Ph.D.) (Cl)	2	2
University of Florida (Ph.D.) (Co)	1	0
University of Georgia (Ph.D.) (Cl)	3	11
University of Georgia (Ph.D.) (Co)	1	1
University of Hartford (Psy.D.) (Cl)	1	0
University of Hawaii at Manoa (Ph.D.) (Cl)	1	3

	# Faculty	# Grants
University of Kentucky (Ph.D.) (Cl)	4	3
University of Maryland—Baltimore County (Ph.D.) (Cl)	2	3
University of Maryland—College Park (Ph.D.) (Cl)	3	4
University of Massachusetts—Amherst (Ph.D.) (Cl)	1	0
University of Minnesota (Ph.D.) (Cl)	—	—
University of Missouri—Columbia (Ph.D.) (Cl)	5	10
University of Missouri—Columbia (Ph.D.) (Co)	2	0
University of Montana (Ph.D.) (Cl)	2	1
University of Nevada—Reno (Ph.D.) (Cl)	2	1
University of New Mexico (Ph.D.) (Cl)	6	4
University of North Dakota (Ph.D.) (Cl)	1	0
University of Pennsylvania (Ph.D.) (Cl)	1	1
University of Pittsburgh (Ph.D.) (Cl)	8	21
University of South Dakota (Ph.D.) (Cl)	2	2
University of South Florida (Ph.D.) (Cl)	3	5
University of Texas at Austin (Ph.D.) (Cl)	1	1
University of Utah (Ph.D.) (Co)	1	1
University of Victoria (Ph.D.) (Cl)	1	1
University of Washington (Ph.D.) (Cl)	3	3
University of Windsor (Ph.D.) (Cl)	2	1
University of Wisconsin—Madison (Ph.D.) (Cl)	1	1
University of Wyoming (Ph.D.) (Cl)	1	1
Utah State University (Ph.D.) (Cm)	1	0
Vanderbilt University (Ph.D.) (Cl)	3	0
Virginia Commonwealth University (Ph.D.) (Cl)	1	1
Virginia Polytechnic Institute and State University (Ph.D.) (Cl)	1	2

Suicide

Alliant International University—San Diego (Psy.D.) (Cl)	2	—
Catholic University of America (Ph.D.) (Cl)	2	1
Florida State University (Ph.D.) (Cl)	1	0
Harvard University (Ph.D.) (Cl)	2	4
Howard University (Ph.D.) (Cl)	1	0
La Salle University (Psy.D.) (Cl)	1	0
Texas Tech University (Ph.D.) (Cl)	4	2
The University of Akron (Ph.D.) (Co)	2	0
University of Georgia (Ph.D.) (Cl)	1	0
University of Illinois at Urbana–Champaign (Ph.D.) (Cl)	1	1
University of Iowa (Ph.D.) (Co)	1	0
University of Louisville (Ph.D.) (Co)	2	0
University of Maryland—Baltimore County (Ph.D.) (Cl)	1	0
University of Nevada—Reno (Ph.D.) (Cl)	1	0
University of North Dakota (Ph.D.) (Cl)	1	1
University of South Florida (Ph.D.) (Cl)	1	2

| University of Washington (Ph.D.) (Cl) | 1 | 1 |
| West Virginia University (Ph.D.) (Cl) | 1 | 1 |

Supervision/Mentoring/Training

Antioch University New England (Psy.D.)	2	0
Argosy University, Chicago (Psy.D.) (Cl)	2	1
Arizona State University (Ph.D.) (Co)	4	0
Colorado State University (Ph.D.) (Co)	2	0
Florida Institute of Technology (Psy.D.) (Cl)	1	0
Fordham University (Ph.D.) (Co)	3	2
George Fox University (Psy.D.) (Cl)	1	0
Howard University (Ph.D.) (Cl)	4	2
Iowa State University (Ph.D.) (Co)	1	0
James Madison University (Psy.D.) (Cm)	4	0
Lehigh University (Ph.D.) (Co)	2	1
Marquette University (Ph.D.) (Co)	2	0
Marywood University (Psy.D.) (Cl)	4	0
Miami University (Ph.D.) (Cl)	2	1
Oklahoma State University (Ph.D.) (Co)	3	0
Pacific University (Psy.D.) (Cl)	3	1
Pepperdine University (Psy.D.) (Cl)	5	0
Philadelphia College of Osteopathic Medicine (Psy.D.) (Cl)	1	0
Seattle Pacific University (Ph.D.) (Cl)	1	0
Southern Illinois University—Carbondale (Ph.D.) (Co)	1	0
University at Albany/State University of New York (Ph.D.) (Co)	2	0
University of Hartford (Psy.D.) (Cl)	1	0
University of Indianapolis (Psy.D.) (Cl)	1	0
University of Maryland—College Park (Ph.D.) (Co)	3	0
University of Minnesota Ed (Ph.D.) (Co)	4	3
University of Missouri—Columbia (Ph.D.) (Co)	2	1
University of Missouri—Kansas City (Ph.D.) (Co)	2	0
University of North Dakota (Ph.D.) (Co)	2	0
University of Oklahoma (Ph.D.) (Co)	1	0
University of Wisconsin—Madison (Ph.D.) (Co)	1	1
Virginia Consortium Program in Clinical Psychology (Psy.D.) (Cl)	2	0
Washington State University (Ph.D.) (Co)	1	0
West Virginia University (Ph.D.) (Co)	2	0

Teaching

Colorado State University (Ph.D.) (Co)	1	0
Roosevelt University (Psy.D.) (Cl)	1	0
Spalding University (Psy.D.) (Cl)	1	0
Tennessee State University (Ph.D.) (Co)	1	0
Texas Tech University (Ph.D.) (Cl)	2	0
Virginia Commonwealth University (Ph.D.) (Co)	1	0
Wichita State University (Ph.D.) (Cl)	1	1

	# Faculty	# Grants

Teenage Pregnancy/Sexuality

	# Faculty	# Grants
Argosy University, Atlanta (Psy.D.) (Cl)	2	0
DePaul University (Ph.D.) (Cl)	2	1
Wichita State University (Ph.D.) (Cl)	1	2

Tic Disorders

Loyola College in Maryland (Psy.D.) (Cl)	1	0
Western Michigan University (Ph.D.) (Cl)	1	0

Veteran/Military Issues

Catholic University of America (Ph.D.) (Cl)	3	1
University of Minnesota (Ph.D.) (Co)	1	1
University of North Dakota (Ph.D.) (Co)	2	1

Violence/Abuse/Sexual Abuse/Rape

Alliant International University—San Francisco Bay (Ph.D.) (Cl)	3	—
Boston University (Ph.D.) (Cl)	1	0
Catholic University of America (Ph.D.) (Cl)	1	1
Central Michigan University (Ph.D.) (Cl)	1	0
Colorado State University (Ph.D.) (Co)	2	0
DePaul University (Ph.D.) (Cl)	3	3
Fairleigh Dickinson University (Ph.D.) (Cl)	3	0
Florida Institute of Technology (Psy.D.) (Cl)	1	1
Indiana University of Pennsylvania (Psy.D.) (Cl)	1	0
Northern Illinois University (Ph.D.) (Cl)	6	0
Nova Southeastern University (Ph.D. & Psy.D.) (Cl)	2	0
Pennsylvania State University (Ph.D.) (Cl)	3	0
Sam Houston State University (Ph.D.) (Cl)	2	0
Simon Fraser University (Ph.D.) (Cl)	6	7
Southern Illinois University—Carbondale (Ph.D.) (Cl)	1	0
Southern Illinois University—Carbondale (Ph.D.) (Co)	1	0
St. Louis University (Ph.D.) (Cl)	2	1
University of Alabama at Tuscaloosa (Ph.D.) (Cl)	2	2
University of Colorado at Boulder (Ph.D.) (Cl)	1	0
University of Denver (Ph.D.) (Cl)	2	2
University of Georgia (Ph.D.) (Cl)	5	0
University of Kansas—Child (Ph.D.) (Cl)	2	1
University of Kentucky (Ph.D.) (Cl)	1	2
University of Mississippi (Ph.D.) (Cl)	2	0
University of Missouri—Columbia (Ph.D.) (Co)	1	1
University of North Texas (Ph.D.) (Cl)	2	0
University of South Carolina (Ph.D.) (Cl)	2	0
University of Virginia (Ph.D.) (Cl)	2	2

Vocational Interests/Career Development

Arizona State University (Ph.D.) (Co)	3	1
Ball State University (Ph.D.) (Co)	4	0
Boston College (Ph.D.) (Co)	1	1
Colorado State University (Ph.D.) (Co)	2	0
Florida State University (Ph.D.) (Cm)	3	1
Fordham University (Ph.D.) (Co)	3	1
Georgia State University (Ph.D.) (Co)	1	0
Iowa State University (Ph.D.) (Co)	2	0
Lehigh University (Ph.D.) (Co)	1	1
Louisiana Tech University (Ph.D.) (Co)	3	0
Loyola University of Chicago (Ph.D.) (Co)	1	0
New Mexico State University (Ph.D.) (Co)	2	0
Oklahoma State University (Ph.D.) (Co)	4	1
Purdue University (Ph.D.) (Co)	1	0
Seattle Pacific University (Ph.D.) (Cl)	3	0
Seton Hall University (Ph.D.) (Co)	1	0
Southern Illinois University—Carbondale (Ph.D.) (Co)	4	2
Tennessee State University (Ph.D.) (Co)	1	2
Texas Tech University (Ph.D.) (Co)	2	0
Texas Woman's University (Ph.D.) (Co)	1	0
The University of Akron (Ph.D.) (Co)	2	0
The University of Memphis (Ph.D.) (Co)	2	1
University at Albany/State University of New York (Ph.D.) (Co)	1	1
University at Buffalo/State University of New York (Ph.D.) (Cm)	2	0
University of British Columbia (Ph.D.) (Cl)	4	4
University of British Columbia (Ph.D.) (Co)	4	4
University of California, Santa Barbara (Ph.D.) (Cm)	—	—
University of Florida (Ph.D.) (Co)	1	0
University of Houston (Ph.D.) (Co)	2	0
University of Illinois at Urbana–Champaign (Ph.D.) (Co)	2	1
University of Iowa (Ph.D.) (Co)	1	1
University of Kansas (Ph.D.) (Co)	1	0
University of Louisville (Ph.D.) (Co)	2	0
University of Maryland—College Park (Ph.D.) (Co)	6	0
University of Minnesota (Ph.D.) (Co)	1	1
University of Minnesota Ed (Ph.D.) (Co)	2	4
University of Missouri—Columbia (Ph.D.) (Co)	5	2
University of Missouri—Kansas City (Ph.D.) (Co)	3	0

	# Faculty	# Grants
University of Nebraska—Lincoln (Ph.D.) (Co)	3	0
University of North Dakota (Ph.D.) (Co)	2	0
University of North Texas (Ph.D.) (Co)	3	0
University of Oklahoma (Ph.D.) (Co)	1	0
University of Oregon (Ph.D.) (Co)	2	1
University of Southern Mississippi (Ph.D.) (Co)	1	0
University of Utah (Ph.D.) (Co)	2	0
University of Wisconsin—Madison (Ph.D.) (Co)	2	0
University of Wisconsin—Milwaukee (Ph.D.) (Co)	2	2
Virginia Commonwealth University (Ph.D.) (Co)	1	1
Washington State University (Ph.D.) (Co)	2	0
West Virginia University (Ph.D.) (Co)	2	0

Weight Management

	# Faculty	# Grants
Drexel University (Ph.D.) (Cl)	2	2
University of Florida (Ph.D.) (Cl)	2	2
University of Pittsburgh (Ph.D.) (Cl)	1	4
Yeshiva University (Ph.D.) (Cl)	1	0

Women's Studies/Feminism

	# Faculty	# Grants
Antioch University New England (Psy.D.)	2	0
Argosy University, Chicago (Psy.D.) (Cl)	1	0
Arizona State University (Ph.D.) (Co)	2	0
Ball State University (Ph.D.) (Co)	2	0
Boston University (Ph.D.) (Cl)	1	1
Brigham Young University (Ph.D.) (Co)	2	1
Colorado State University (Ph.D.) (Co)	3	1
Drexel University (Ph.D.) (Cl)	3	0
Fairleigh Dickinson University (Ph.D.) (Cl)	2	0
Indiana State University (Psy.D.) (Cl)	2	0
Indiana University of Pennsylvania (Psy.D.) (Cl)	2	0
Indiana University—Bloomington (Ph.D.) (Co)	1	0
Iowa State University (Ph.D.) (Co)	1	1
Loyola College in Maryland (Psy.D.) (Cl)	2	0
Marshall University (Psy.D.) (Cl)	1	0
McGill University (Ph.D.) (Co)	2	0
New York University (Ph.D.) (Co)	2	2
Oklahoma State University (Ph.D.) (Co)	4	0
Pacific University (Psy.D.) (Cl)	1	0
Rutgers, The State University of New Jersey (Psy.D.) (Cl)	1	0
San Diego State University/University of California, San Diego (Ph.D.) (Cl)	3	0
Seattle Pacific University (Ph.D.) (Cl)	2	2

	# Faculty	# Grants
Southern Illinois University—Carbondale (Ph.D.) (Co)	1	0
Teachers College, Columbia University (Ph.D.) (Co)	1	0
Texas Tech University (Ph.D.) (Co)	1	1
The University of Akron (Ph.D.) (Co)	3	0
University at Albany/State University of New York (Ph.D.) (Co)	1	0
University of British Columbia (Ph.D.) (Cl)	2	1
University of British Columbia (Ph.D.) (Co)	2	1
University of Florida (Ph.D.) (Co)	1	0
University of Illinois at Urbana–Champaign (Ph.D.) (Cl)	3	2
University of Indianapolis (Psy.D.) (Cl)	2	0
University of Kansas (Ph.D.) (Co)	3	1
University of Kansas—Psychology (Ph.D.) (Cl)	1	0
University of Maine (Ph.D.) (Cl)	1	0
University of Missouri—St. Louis (Ph.D.) (Cl)	1	2
University of Nevada—Las Vegas (Ph.D.) (Cl)	1	0
University of North Dakota (Ph.D.) (Cl)	2	0
University of North Dakota (Ph.D.) (Co)	1	0
University of Wisconsin—Milwaukee (Ph.D.) (Co)	1	1
Virginia Consortium Program in Clinical Psychology (Psy.D.) (Cl)	5	0

Workplace Issues

	# Faculty	# Grants
Hofstra University (Ph.D.) (Cl)	1	0
New York University (Ph.D.) (Co)	1	0
Uniformed Services University of Health Sciences (Ph.D.) (Cl)	—	—
University of Denver (Ph.D.) (Co)	1	1

Miscellaneous

	# Faculty	# Grants
abortion issues—Southern Illinois University—Carbondale (Ph.D.) (Cl)	1	0
action research—Miami University (Ph.D.) (Cl)	2	1
adaptation to blindness—Louisiana Tech University (Ph.D.) (Co)	1	0
adult clinical—University of Southern Mississippi (Ph.D.) (Cl)	5	3
adult—University of Ottawa (Ph.D.) (Cl)	9	4
advocacy/social policy/activism—Alliant International University—Los Angeles (Ph.D.) (Cl)	2	—
altruism—Teachers College, Columbia University (Ph.D.) (Cl)	1	0
animal behavior—Marshall University (Psy.D.) (Cl)	1	0
asthma—Yeshiva University (Ph.D.) (Cl)	1	1

	# Faculty	# Grants
attitudes and attitude change—Hofstra University (Ph.D.) (Cl)	1	0
battering—University of Georgia (Ph.D.) (Cl)	1	0
behavioral addictions—Texas Tech University (Ph.D.) (Co)	1	0
behavioral dentistry—West Virginia University (Ph.D.) (Cl)	1	1
behavioral undercontrol—University of Maryland—College Park (Ph.D.) (Cl)	2	1
beliefs and values—James Madison University (Psy.D.) (Cm)	3	1
bias—Spalding University (Psy.D.) (Cl)	1	0
bilingualism—St. John's University (Ph.D.) (Cl)	2	0
biopsychosocial—Fuller Theological Seminary (Ph.D. & Psy.D.) (Cl)	3	2
blame & responsibility attribution—Sam Houston State University (Ph.D.) (Cl)	1	1
brief therapy—Our Lady of the Lake University (Psy.D.) (Co)	3	2
burnout prevention—University of Minnesota Ed (Ph.D.) (Co)	2	0
caregiver burden—Southern Illinois University—Carbondale (Ph.D.) (Co)	1	1
caregiving—University of Alabama at Tuscaloosa (Ph.D.) (Cl)	1	2
citizen participation—University of South Carolina (Ph.D.) (Cl)	1	1
clinic-based research—Pepperdine University (Psy.D.) (Cl)	4	1
college student development—University of Oregon (Ph.D.) (Co)	2	0
competency issues—Virginia Consortium Program in Clinical Psychology (Psy.D.) (Cl)	1	0
computer-based research—University of Mississippi (Ph.D.) (Cl)	1	1
constructivist psychology—University of Florida (Ph.D.) (Co)	1	0
countertransference—University of Maryland—College Park (Ph.D.) (Co)	2	0
creativity—University of Kansas (Ph.D.) (Co)	1	1
data-based case management—University of Hawaii at Manoa (Ph.D.) (Cl)	2	0
death and dying—Indiana University of Pennsylvania (Psy.D.) (Cl)	1	0
decision making—San Diego State University/University of California, San Diego (Ph.D.) (Cl)	1	0
descriptive experience sampling—University of Nevada—Las Vegas (Ph.D.) (Cl)	2	0
developmental psychobiology—Idaho State University (Ph.D.) (Cl)	1	2
dialectic behavior therapy in inpatient hospital settings—Philadelphia College of Osteopathic Medicine (Psy.D.) (Cl)	1	0
discrimination—Iowa State University (Ph.D.) (Co)	1	0
disruptive behavior disorders—Yale University (Ph.D.) (Cl)	1	0
dissociative disorders—Rutgers, The State University of New Jersey (Psy.D.) (Cl)	1	0
divorce—Virginia Commonwealth University (Ph.D.) (Cl)	1	0
drug policy—Drexel University (Ph.D.) (Cl)	1	1
dynamic psychotherapy—Pacific University (Psy.D.) (Cl)	2	0
ecopsychology—University of Oklahoma (Ph.D.) (Co)	1	0
emerging adulthood—Loyola University of Chicago (Ph.D.) (Cl)	1	0
emotional freedom technique—Argosy University, Schaumburg (Psy.D.) (Cl)	1	1
empowerment—Georgia State University (Ph.D.) (Cl)	1	0
evidence based practices—Philadelphia College of Osteopathic Medicine (Psy.D.) (Cl)	12	0
existential-humanistic—Immaculata University (Psy.D.) (Cl)	2	0
expectations about counseling—Southern Illinois University—Carbondale (Ph.D.) (Co)	1	0
experiential therapy—Argosy University, Schaumburg (Psy.D.) (Cl)	3	1
experimental psychopathology—University of Arkansas (Ph.D.) (Cl)	5	2
extracurricular activities—Loyola University of Chicago (Ph.D.) (Cl)	1	1
fear conditioning and extinction—Ponce School of Medicine (Psy.D.) (Cl)	1	1
fear conditioning—Marquette University (Ph.D.) (Cl)	1	0
geopolitical conflict—Argosy University, Washington, DC (Psy.D.) (Cl)	1	—
gestalt therapy—Pacific University (Psy.D.) (Cl)	1	0
gifted/talent development—Florida State University (Ph.D.) (Cm)	1	1
helping behavior—University of Detroit Mercy (Ph.D.) (Cl)	1	0
homelessness/HIV—Azusa Pacific University (Psy.D.) (Cl)	1	0
hope in counseling—Howard University (Ph.D.) (Co)	1	0
human error—Hofstra University (Ph.D.) (Cl)	1	0
human-computer interaction—Drexel University (Ph.D.) (Cl)	1	0
hypertension—University of Miami (Ph.D.) (Cl)	3	1

	# Faculty	# Grants
impact of managed care on clinical training—Northeastern University (Ph.D.) (Cm)	1	0
incest survivors—University of Nevada—Reno (Ph.D.) (Cl)	2	0
infertility—University of British Columbia (Ph.D.) (Cl & Co)	1	0
informant discrepancies/rater biases in child assessment—Texas Tech University (Ph.D.) (Cl)	1	0
information processing—San Diego State University/University of California, San Diego (Ph.D.) (Cl)	4	0
instructional psychology—Pace University (Psy.D.) (Cm)	1	1
internalizing disorders—Indiana University—Bloomington (Ph.D.) (Cl)	2	1
language development—Catholic University of America (Ph.D.) (Cl)	1	1
learning—Pace University (Psy.D.) (Cm)	1	0
licensure and regulatory boards—University of St. Thomas (Psy.D.) (Co)	1	0
mental imagery—Marquette University (Ph.D.) (Cl)	1	0
mental retardation—University of Wyoming (Ph.D.) (Cl)	2	1
migraines—Yeshiva University (Ph.D.) (Cl)	1	3
mind/body/health—Rutgers, The State University of New Jersey (Psy.D.) (Cl)	1	1
motivational interviewing—University of Southern Mississippi (Ph.D.) (Co)	1	2
multidisciplinary environments—University of Wisconsin—Madison (Ph.D.) (Co)	2	1
multigenerational health—Chicago School of Professional Psychology (Psy.D.) (Cl)	1	0
multimedia-based treatment—Western Michigan University (Ph.D.) (Cl)	2	2
neuroscience/psychobiology—Concordia University (Ph.D.) (Cl)	9	12
nonlinear dynamic systems—University of Montana (Ph.D.) (Cl)	1	0
nutrition—San Diego State University/ University of California, San Diego (Ph.D.) (Cl)	3	0
olfaction—McGill University (Ph.D.) (Cl)	1	1
patient non-adherence to medical advice—Philadelphia College of Osteopathic Medicine (Psy.D.) (Cl)	1	0
peace psychology—Alliant International University—Los Angeles (Ph.D.) (Cl)	1	—
perception and eye movement—University of Detroit Mercy (Ph.D.) (Cl)	1	1
perfectionism—University of Missouri—Columbia (Ph.D.) (Co)	1	0
personal meaning-making processes—Texas Tech University (Ph.D.) (Cl)	1	0
person-centered interventions—Argosy University, Chicago (Psy.D.) (Cl)	2	0
philosophical issues—Rutgers, The State University of New Jersey (Ph.D.) (Cl)	1	0
philosophy and psychology—Rutgers, The State University of New Jersey (Psy.D.) (Cl)	2	0
play therapy—Argosy University, Chicago (Psy.D.) (Cl)	1	0
population psychology—Alliant International University—Los Angeles (Ph.D.) (Cl)	1	—
pregnancy issues—Virginia Commonwealth University (Ph.D.) (Cl)	1	1
prejudice and intergroup relations—Seattle Pacific University (Ph.D.) (Cl)	1	0
program and policy development—Seattle Pacific University (Ph.D.) (Cl)	2	1
projective techniques—Long Island University, Brooklyn Campus (Ph.D) (Cl)	2	0
pseudoscience in clinical psychology—University of Arkansas (Ph.D.) (Cl)	1	0
psychological games—John F. Kennedy University (Psy.D.) (Cl)	1	0
psychological reactance theory—Louisiana Tech University (Ph.D.) (Co)	1	0
psychological resources—The University of Memphis (Ph.D.) (Co)	1	0
psychological treatment—Washington University in St. Louis (Ph.D.) (Cl)	3	5
psychologies of peace and war—Seattle Pacific University (Ph.D.) (Cl)	1	0
psychosocial aspects of medical illness—Marquette University (Ph.D.) (Cl)	1	0
refugee mental health—University of Minnesota (Ph.D.) (Co)	1	1
reimbursement—Our Lady of the Lake University (Psy.D.) (Co)	1	0
retention—Arizona State University (Ph.D.) (Co)	4	1
reversal theory—Louisiana Tech University (Ph.D.) (Co)	1	0
risk and resilience—Teachers College, Columbia University (Ph.D.) (Cl)	2	1
shame—George Fox University (Psy.D.) (Cl)	1	0
short-term, dynamic therapy—Argosy University, Atlanta (Psy.D.) (Cl)	2	0
shyness—Virginia Polytechnic Institute and State University (Ph.D.) (Cl)	1	0
single case research—Pacific University (Psy.D.) (Cl)	2	0
single subject design, time series regression, dynamic factor analysis—Texas Tech University (Ph.D.) (Cl)	2	0

	# Faculty	# Grants
social development—University of Maine (Ph.D.) (Cl)	1	1
social identity—New Mexico State University (Ph.D.) (Co)	3	0
spatial ability and cognitive transfer—Northeastern University (Ph.D.) (Cm)	2	0
strengths, optimal functioning—Marquette University (Ph.D.) (Co)	3	0
stroop effect—George Fox University (Psy.D.) (Cl)	1	1
symbolic play—Yeshiva University (Psy.D.) (Cm)	1	0
technology and education—Marywood University (Psy.D.) (Cl)	3	0
terrorism—Pacific Graduate School of Psychology/Stanford University Medical School Consortium (Psy.D.) (Cl)	2	2
the advising relationship—Seton Hall University (Ph.D.) (Co)	1	0
theoretical scholarship—Pepperdine University (Psy.D.) (Cl)	2	0
theoretical unification—James Madison University (Psy.D.) (Cm)	1	0
therapeutic relationship—Adelphi University (Ph.D.) (Cl)	2	1
treatment dissemination—University of Missouri—Columbia (Ph.D.) (Cl)	2	1
treatment utilization—Marquette University (Ph.D.) (Cl)	2	0
treatment—Western Michigan University (Ph.D.) (Co)	3	0
videotapes in training—Howard University (Ph.D.) (Co)	1	1
white privilege—University of North Dakota (Ph.D.) (Co)	1	0
worldview, racial identity, and self-efficacy—Howard University (Ph.D.) (Co)	1	1

APPENDIX F
SPECIALTY CLINICS AND PRACTICA SITES

Acceptance/Acceptance & Commitment Therapy

Hofstra University (Ph.D.) (Cl)
The Wright Institute (Psy.D.) (Cl)
University at Albany/State University of New York (Ph.D.) (Cl)
University of Wisconsin—Milwaukee (Ph.D.) (Cl)

Acquired Immune Deficiency Syndrome/HIV

Argosy University, Phoenix (Psy.D.) (Cl)
Azusa Pacific University (Psy.D.) (Cl)
George Washington University (Ph.D.) (Cl)
Georgia State University (Ph.D.) (Cl)
Loyola University of Chicago (Ph.D.) (Cl)
Pacific Graduate School of Psychology (Ph.D.) (Cl)
Pacific Graduate School of Psychology/Stanford University Medical School Consortium (Psy.D.) (Cl)
Pepperdine University (Psy.D.) (Cl)
Texas Woman's University (Ph.D.) (Co)
The Wright Institute (Psy.D.) (Cl)
University of Illinois at Chicago (Ph.D.) (Cl)
University of La Verne (Psy.D.) (Cl)
University of Miami (Ph.D.) (Cl)
University of Nevada—Reno (Ph.D.) (Cl)
University of Vermont (Ph.D.) (Cl)
Wright State University (Psy.D.) (Cl)

Adjustment

Georgia State University (Ph.D.) (Cl)
University of Illinois at Chicago (Ph.D.) (Cl)

Adolescent Psychotherapy/At-Risk Adolescents/Delinquency

Binghamton University/State University of New York (Ph.D.) (Cl)
Boston University (Ph.D.) (Cl)
Brigham Young University (Ph.D.) (Cl)
Colorado State University (Ph.D.) (Co)
Florida State University (Ph.D.) (Cl)
George Fox University (Psy.D.) (Cl)
George Washington University (Ph.D.) (Cl)
Harvard University (Ph.D.) (Cl)
Loyola College in Maryland (Psy.D.) (Cl)
Marshall University (Psy.D.) (Cl)
Miami University (Ph.D.) (Cl)
Pacific Graduate School of Psychology/Stanford University Medical School Consortium (Psy.D.) (Cl)
Pepperdine University (Psy.D.) (Cl)
Rutgers, The State University of New Jersey (Ph.D. & Psy.D.) (Cl)
Seattle Pacific University (Ph.D.) (Cl)
Southern Illinois University—Carbondale (Ph.D.) (Cl)
University at Albany/State University of New York (Ph.D.) (Cl & Co)
University of Alabama at Tuscaloosa (Ph.D.) (Cl)
University of Georgia (Ph.D.) (Co)
University of Houston (Ph.D.) (Cl)
University of Maine (Ph.D.) (Cl)
University of Montana (Ph.D.) (Cl)
University of Nebraska—Lincoln (Ph.D.) (Co)
University of Notre Dame (Ph.D.) (Co)
University of Pittsburgh (Ph.D.) (Cl)

Note. Cl, Clinical; Co, Counseling, Cm, combined psychology programs.

University of Saskatchewan (Ph.D.) (Cl)
University of Texas at Austin (Ph.D.) (Co)
University of Utah (Ph.D.) (Cl)
University of Vermont (Ph.D.) (Cl)
University of Victoria (Ph.D.) (Cl)
Virginia Commonwealth University (Ph.D.) (Co)
Virginia Consortium Program in Clinical Psychology
    (Psy.D.) (Cl)
Yale University (Ph.D.) (Cl)

Adoption

Pepperdine University (Psy.D.) (Cl)
University of California, Los Angeles (Ph.D.) (Cl)

Affective Disorders/Depression/

Mood Disorders
Baylor University (Psy.D.) (Cl)
Binghamton University/State University of New York
    (Ph.D.) (Cl)
Boston University (Ph.D.) (Cl)
Case Western Reserve University (Ph.D.) (Cl)
Duke University (Ph.D.) (Cl)
Eastern Michigan University (Ph.D.) (Cl)
George Washington University (Ph.D.) (Cl)
Harvard University (Ph.D.) (Cl)
Hofstra University (Ph.D.) (Cl)
Illinois Institute of Technology (Ph.D.) (Cl)
Indiana University—Bloomington (Ph.D.) (Cl)
La Salle University (Psy.D.) (Cl)
Long Island University, C.W. Post Campus (Psy.D.)
    (Cl)
Miami University (Ph.D.) (Cl)
Michigan State University (Ph.D.) (Cl)
Northwestern University (Ph.D.) (Cl)
Nova Southeastern University (Ph.D. & Psy.D.) (Cl)
Pacific Graduate School of Psychology/Stanford Uni-
    versity Medical School Consortium (Psy.D.) (Cl)
Purdue University (Ph.D.) (Cl)
Rutgers, The State University of New Jersey (Ph.D. &
    Psy.D.) (Cl)
The Ohio State University (Ph.D.) (Cl)
The University of Memphis (Ph.D.) (Cl)
The Wright Institute (Psy.D.) (Cl)
University at Buffalo/State University of New York
    (Ph.D.) (Cl)
University of Arizona (Ph.D.) (Cl)
University of California, Los Angeles (Ph.D.) (Cl)
University of Connecticut (Ph.D.) (Cl)
University of Delaware (Ph.D.) (Cl)
University of Georgia (Ph.D.) (Cl)
University of Hartford (Psy.D.) (Cl)

University of Illinois at Urbana–Champaign (Ph.D.)
    (Cl)
University of Iowa (Ph.D.) (Cl)
University of Louisville (Ph.D.) (Cl)
University of Minnesota (Ph.D.) (Cl)
University of Montana (Ph.D.) (Cl)
University of Nevada—Reno (Ph.D.) (Cl)
University of North Dakota (Ph.D.) (Cl)
University of North Texas (Ph.D.) (Cl)
University of Oregon (Ph.D.) (Cl)
University of Ottawa (Ph.D.) (Cl)
University of Pittsburgh (Ph.D.) (Cl)
University of South Florida (Ph.D.) (Cl)
University of Texas at Austin (Ph.D.) (Cl)
University of Texas Southwestern Medical Center
    (Ph.D.) (Cl)
University of Utah (Ph.D.) (Cl)
University of Vermont (Ph.D.) (Cl)
University of Virginia (Ph.D.) (Cl)
University of Wisconsin—Madison (Ph.D.) (Cl)
University of Wyoming (Ph.D.) (Cl)
Vanderbilt University (Ph.D.) (Cl)
Virginia Commonwealth University (Ph.D.) (Cl)
Virginia Polytechnic Institute and State University
    (Ph.D.) (Cl)
Wichita State University (Ph.D.) (Cl)
Wright State University (Psy.D.) (Cl)
Yeshiva University (Psy.D.) (Cl)
York University (Ph.D.) (Cl)

Aggression/Anger Control/Impulse Control

Baylor University (Psy.D.) (Cl)
George Washington University (Ph.D.) (Cl)
Hofstra University (Ph.D.) (Cl)
La Salle University (Psy.D.) (Cl)
Long Island University, C.W. Post Campus (Psy.D.)
    (Cl)
Rutgers, The State University of New Jersey (Psy.D.)
    (Cl)
Vanderbilt University (Ph.D.) (Cl)

Aging/Gerontology

Argosy University, Chicago (Psy.D.) (Cl)
Argosy University, Washington, DC (Psy.D.) (Cl)
Arizona State University (Ph.D.) (Cl)
Azusa Pacific University (Psy.D.) (Cl)
Baylor University (Psy.D.) (Cl)
Boston University (Ph.D.) (Cl)
Case Western Reserve University (Ph.D.) (Cl)
Fairleigh Dickinson University (Ph.D.) (Cl)
Fuller Theological Seminary (Ph.D. & Psy.D.) (Cl)

George Fox University (Psy.D.) (Cl)
Harvard University (Ph.D.) (Cl)
Michigan State University (Ph.D.) (Cl)
Oklahoma State University (Ph.D.) (Cl)
Pacific Graduate School of Psychology (Ph.D.) (Cl)
Pacific Graduate School of Psychology/Stanford University Medical School Consortium (Psy.D.) (Cl)
Pepperdine University (Psy.D.) (Cl)
Philadelphia College of Osteopathic Medicine (Psy.D.) (Cl)
The Ohio State University (Ph.D.) (Cl)
University of Alabama at Tuscaloosa (Ph.D.) (Cl)
University of Alabama at Tuscaloosa (Ph.D.) (Cl)
University of Arizona (Ph.D.) (Cl)
University of Colorado at Colorado Springs (Ph.D.) (Cl)
University of Houston (Ph.D.) (Cl)
University of Houston (Ph.D.) (Co)
University of Louisville (Ph.D.) (Cl)
University of Massachusetts—Amherst (Ph.D.) (Cl)
University of Missouri—St. Louis (Ph.D.) (Cl)
University of Nevada—Reno (Ph.D.) (Cl)
University of Ottawa (Ph.D.) (Cl)
University of Southern California (Ph.D.) (Cl)
University of Utah (Ph.D.) (Co)
Virginia Polytechnic Institute and State University (Ph.D.) (Cl)
Wayne State University (Ph.D.) (Cl)
West Virginia University (Ph.D.) (Cl)
Wright State University (Psy.D.) (Cl)
Yeshiva University (Ph.D. & Psy.D.) (Cl)
York University (Ph.D.) (Cl)

Anxiety Disorders/Panic Disorders

Argosy University, Tampa (Psy.D.) (Cl)
Argosy University, Washington, DC (Psy.D.) (Cl)
Auburn University (Ph.D.) (Cl)
Baylor University (Psy.D.) (Cl)
Binghamton University/State University of New York (Ph.D.) (Cl)
Boston University (Ph.D.) (Cl)
Case Western Reserve University (Ph.D.) (Cl)
Eastern Michigan University (Ph.D.) (Cl)
Fairleigh Dickinson University (Ph.D.) (Cl)
Florida State University (Ph.D.) (Cl)
George Washington University (Ph.D.) (Cl)
Georgia State University (Ph.D.) (Cl)
Harvard University (Ph.D.) (Cl)
Hofstra University (Ph.D.) (Cl)
Hofstra University (Ph.D.) (Cl)
Indiana University—Bloomington (Ph.D.) (Cl)
Kent State University (Ph.D.) (Cl)

La Salle University (Psy.D.) (Cl)
Long Island University, C.W. Post Campus (Psy.D.) (Cl)
Miami University (Ph.D.) (Cl)
Northern Illinois University (Ph.D.) (Cl)
Northwestern University (Ph.D.) (Cl)
Nova Southeastern University (Ph.D. & Psy.D.) (Cl)
Oklahoma State University (Ph.D.) (Cl)
Purdue University (Ph.D.) (Cl)
Roosevelt University (Psy.D.) (Cl)
Rosalind Franklin University of Medicine and Science (Ph.D.) (Cl)
Rutgers, The State University of New Jersey (Ph.D. & Psy.D.) (Cl)
San Diego State University/University of California, San Diego (Ph.D.) (Cl)
Southern Methodist University (Ph.D.) (Cl)
St. Louis University (Ph.D.) (Cl)
Syracuse University (Ph.D.) (Cl)
Temple University (Ph.D.) (Cl)
Temple University (Ph.D.) (Cl)
The Ohio State University (Ph.D.) (Cl)
The University of Memphis (Ph.D.) (Cl)
University at Albany/State University of New York (Ph.D.) (Cl)
University at Buffalo/State University of New York (Ph.D.) (Cl)
University of Alabama at Tuscaloosa (Ph.D.) (Cl)
University of California, Los Angeles (Ph.D.) (Cl)
University of Connecticut (Ph.D.) (Cl)
University of Delaware (Ph.D.) (Cl)
University of Florida (Ph.D.) (Co)
University of Georgia (Ph.D.) (Cl)
University of Hartford (Psy.D.) (Cl)
University of Houston (Ph.D.) (Cl)
University of Illinois at Chicago (Ph.D.) (Cl)
University of Illinois at Urbana–Champaign (Ph.D.) (Cl)
University of Kansas—Psychology (Ph.D.) (Cl)
University of Louisville (Ph.D.) (Cl)
University of Maine (Ph.D.) (Cl)
University of Minnesota (Ph.D.) (Cl)
University of Missouri—Kansas City (Ph.D.) (Cl)
University of Montana (Ph.D.) (Cl)
University of Nebraska—Lincoln (Ph.D.) (Cl)
University of Nevada—Las Vegas (Ph.D.) (Cl)
University of Nevada—Reno (Ph.D.) (Cl)
University of New Mexico (Ph.D.) (Cl)
University of North Carolina at Chapel Hill (Ph.D.) (Cl)
University of North Dakota (Ph.D.) (Cl)
University of North Texas (Ph.D.) (Cl)
University of Oregon (Ph.D.) (Cl)

University of Ottawa (Ph.D.) (Cl)
University of Pittsburgh (Ph.D.) (Cl)
University of South Florida (Ph.D.) (Cl)
University of South Florida (Ph.D.) (Cl)
University of Texas at Austin (Ph.D.) (Cl)
University of Toledo (Ph.D.) (Cl)
University of Utah (Ph.D.) (Cl)
University of Vermont (Ph.D.) (Cl)
University of Virginia (Ph.D.) (Cl)
University of Washington (Ph.D.) (Cl)
University of Wisconsin—Madison (Ph.D.) (Cl)
University of Wyoming (Ph.D.) (Cl)
Vanderbilt University (Ph.D.) (Cl)
Virginia Commonwealth University (Ph.D.) (Cl)
Virginia Polytechnic Institute and State University
  (Ph.D.) (Cl)
West Virginia University (Ph.D.) (Cl)
Wichita State University (Ph.D.) (Cl)
Yale University (Ph.D.) (Cl)
Yeshiva University (Psy.D.) (Cl)
York University (Ph.D.) (Cl)

Assessment

American University (Ph.D.) (Cl)
Antioch University New England (Psy.D.)
Argosy University, Atlanta (Psy.D.) (Cl)
Argosy University, Phoenix (Psy.D.) (Cl)
Arizona State University (Ph.D.) (Cl)
Catholic University of America (Ph.D.) (Cl)
Central Michigan University (Ph.D.) (Cl)
DePaul University (Ph.D.) (Cl)
Emory University (Ph.D.) (Cl)
Fairleigh Dickinson University (Ph.D.) (Cl)
Fuller Theological Seminary (Ph.D. & Psy.D.) (Cl)
Gallaudet University (Ph.D.) (Cl)
George Fox University (Psy.D.) (Cl)
George Mason University (Ph.D.) (Cl)
George Washington University (Ph.D. & Psy.D.) (Cl)
Georgia State University (Ph.D.) (Cl)
Indiana University of Pennsylvania (Psy.D.) (Cl)
Indiana University—Bloomington (Ph.D.) (Cl)
Kent State University (Ph.D.) (Cl)
La Salle University (Psy.D.) (Cl)
Long Island University, C.W. Post Campus (Psy.D.)
  (Cl)
Loyola University of Chicago (Ph.D.) (Cl)
Miami University (Ph.D.) (Cl)
Michigan State University (Ph.D.) (Cl)
Northern Illinois University (Ph.D.) (Cl)
Nova Southeastern University (Ph.D. & Psy.D.) (Cl)
Pacific Graduate School of Psychology (Ph.D.) (Cl)
Pepperdine University (Psy.D.) (Cl)

Purdue University (Ph.D.) (Cl)
Rutgers, The State University of New Jersey (Ph.D. &
  Psy.D.) (Cl)
Sam Houston State University (Ph.D.) (Cl)
Southern Methodist University (Ph.D.) (Cl)
St. Louis University (Ph.D.) (Cl)
Tennessee State University (Ph.D.) (Co)
Texas Tech University (Ph.D.) (Co)
The Wright Institute (Psy.D.) (Cl)
University of Colorado at Boulder (Ph.D.) (Cl)
University of Denver (Ph.D.) (Co)
University of Denver (Psy.D.) (Cl)
University of Georgia (Ph.D.) (Cl)
University of Hawaii at Manoa (Ph.D.) (Cl)
University of Houston (Ph.D.) (Cl)
University of Indianapolis (Psy.D.) (Cl)
University of Kentucky (Ph.D.) (Cl)
University of Louisville (Ph.D.) (Co)
University of Massachusetts—Amherst (Ph.D.) (Cl)
University of Mississippi (Ph.D.) (Cl)
University of Missouri—St. Louis (Ph.D.) (Cl)
University of Montana (Ph.D.) (Cl)
University of Nebraska—Lincoln (Ph.D.) (Co)
University of New Mexico (Ph.D.) (Cl)
University of North Carolina at Chapel Hill (Ph.D.)
  (Cl)
University of North Dakota (Ph.D.) (Cl)
University of Northern Colorado (Psy.D.) (Co)
University of Oklahoma (Ph.D.) (Co)
University of Oregon (Ph.D.) (Cl)
University of Pennsylvania (Ph.D.) (Cl)
University of Pittsburgh (Ph.D.) (Cl)
University of South Florida (Ph.D.) (Cl)
University of Southern California (Ph.D.) (Cl)
University of Texas at Austin (Ph.D.) (Cl)
University of Toledo (Ph.D.) (Cl)
University of Virginia (Ph.D.) (Cl)
University of Wisconsin—Madison (Ph.D.) (Cl)
Virginia Commonwealth University (Ph.D.) (Cl)
Widener University (Psy.D.) (Cl)
Wright State University (Psy.D.) (Cl)
Yeshiva University (Psy.D.) (Cl)
York University (Ph.D.) (Cl)

Attention Deficit/Hyperactivity Disorder

Auburn University (Ph.D.) (Cl)
Case Western Reserve University (Ph.D.) (Cl)
George Washington University (Ph.D.) (Cl)
Indiana State University (Psy.D.) (Cl)
Iowa State University (Ph.D.) (Co)
Long Island University, C.W. Post Campus (Psy.D.)
  (Cl)

Marquette University (Ph.D.) (Cl)
Miami University (Ph.D.) (Cl)
Miami University (Ph.D.) (Cl)
Northern Illinois University (Ph.D.) (Cl)
Pepperdine University (Psy.D.) (Cl)
Purdue University (Ph.D.) (Cl)
Rutgers, The State University of New Jersey (Psy.D.) (Cl)
St. Louis University (Ph.D.) (Cl)
University at Buffalo/State University of New York (Ph.D.) (Cl)
University of Alabama at Tuscaloosa (Ph.D.) (Cl)
University of Florida (Ph.D.) (Cl)
University of Louisville (Ph.D.) (Co)
University of Maine (Ph.D.) (Cl)
University of Minnesota (Ph.D.) (Cl)
University of Pittsburgh (Ph.D.) (Cl)
University of Rochester (Ph.D.) (Cl)
University of South Florida (Ph.D.) (Cl)
University of Texas at Austin (Ph.D.) (Cl)
Virginia Polytechnic Institute and State University (Ph.D.) (Cl)

Behavioral Medicine/Health Psychology

Antioch University New England (Psy.D.)
Argosy University, Atlanta (Psy.D.) (Cl)
Argosy University, Chicago (Psy.D.) (Cl)
Arizona State University (Ph.D.) (Cl)
Azusa Pacific University (Psy.D.) (Cl)
Baylor University (Psy.D.) (Cl)
Baylor University (Psy.D.) (Cl)
Binghamton University/State University of New York (Ph.D.) (Cl)
Boston University (Ph.D.) (Cl)
Bowling Green State University (Ph.D.) (Cl)
California Institute of Integral Studies (Psy.D.) (Cl)
Chicago School of Professional Psychology (Psy.D.) (Cl)
Drexel University (Ph.D.) (Cl)
Duke University (Ph.D.) (Cl)
Eastern Michigan University (Ph.D.) (Cl)
Fairleigh Dickinson University (Ph.D.) (Cl)
Florida Institute of Technology (Psy.D.) (Cl)
Florida State University (Ph.D.) (Cl)
George Fox University (Psy.D.) (Cl)
George Washington University (Ph.D.) (Cl)
Georgia State University (Ph.D.) (Cl & Co)
Harvard University (Ph.D.) (Cl)
Howard University (Ph.D.) (Cl)
Illinois Institute of Technology (Ph.D.) (Cl)
Indiana State University (Psy.D.) (Cl)
Indiana University of Pennsylvania (Psy.D.) (Cl)

Indiana University—Bloomington (Ph.D.) (Cl)
Indiana University—Purdue University Indianapolis (Ph.D.) (Cl)
Jackson State University (Ph.D.) (Cl)
Kent State University (Ph.D.) (Cl)
La Salle University (Psy.D.) (Cl)
Loma Linda University (Ph.D. & Psy.D.) (Cl)
Loyola College in Maryland (Psy.D.) (Cl)
Loyola University of Chicago (Ph.D.) (Cl)
Marquette University (Ph.D.) (Co)
Massachusetts School of Professional Psychology, Inc. (Psy.D.) (Cl)
Oklahoma State University (Ph.D.) (Cl)
Our Lady of the Lake University (Psy.D.) (Co)
Pacific Graduate School of Psychology (Ph.D.) (Cl)
Pacific Graduate School of Psychology/Stanford University Medical School Consortium (Psy.D.) (Cl)
Pepperdine University (Psy.D.) (Cl)
Regent University (Psy.D.) (Cl)
Roosevelt University (Psy.D.) (Cl)
Rosalind Franklin University of Medicine and Science (Ph.D.) (Cl)
Rutgers, The State University of New Jersey (Ph.D. & Psy.D.) (Cl)
San Diego State University/University of California, San Diego (Ph.D.) (Cl)
Seattle Pacific University (Ph.D.) (Cl)
Spalding University (Psy.D.) (Cl)
St. Louis University (Ph.D.) (Cl)
Syracuse University (Ph.D.) (Cl)
Tennessee State University (Ph.D.) (Co)
Texas Tech University (Ph.D.) (Co)
The Ohio State University (Ph.D.) (Cl)
The University of Memphis (Ph.D.) (Cl)
University at Albany/State University of New York (Ph.D.) (Cl)
University of Alabama at Birmingham (Ph.D.) (Cl)
University of Alabama at Tuscaloosa (Ph.D.) (Cl)
University of Arizona (Ph.D.) (Cl)
University of Cincinnati (Ph.D.) (Cl)
University of Colorado at Colorado Springs (Ph.D.) (Cl)
University of Connecticut (Ph.D.) (Cl)
University of Denver (Psy.D.) (Cl)
University of Hawaii at Manoa (Ph.D.) (Cl)
University of Houston (Ph.D.) (Cl & Co)
University of Illinois at Chicago (Ph.D.) (Cl)
University of Illinois at Urbana–Champaign (Ph.D.) (Co)
University of Indianapolis (Psy.D.) (Cl)
University of Iowa (Ph.D.) (Cl)
University of Kansas—Psychology (Ph.D.) (Cl)
University of Kentucky (Ph.D.) (Cl)

University of Louisville (Ph.D.) (Cl & Co)
University of Maine (Ph.D.) (Cl)
University of Miami (Ph.D.) (Cl)
University of Mississippi (Ph.D.) (Cl)
University of Missouri—Columbia (Ph.D.) (Cl)
University of Missouri—St. Louis (Ph.D.) (Cl)
University of Nebraska—Lincoln (Ph.D.) (Co)
University of Nevada—Reno (Ph.D.) (Cl)
University of New Mexico (Ph.D.) (Cl)
University of North Carolina at Chapel Hill (Ph.D.) (Cl)
University of North Dakota (Ph.D.) (Cl)
University of Oklahoma (Ph.D.) (Co)
University of Pittsburgh (Ph.D.) (Cl)
University of Rhode Island (Ph.D.) (Cl)
University of South Carolina (Ph.D.) (Cl)
University of South Florida (Ph.D.) (Cl)
University of Texas at Austin (Ph.D.) (Cl)
University of Texas Southwestern Medical Center (Ph.D.) (Cl)
University of Utah (Ph.D.) (Cl)
University of Vermont (Ph.D.) (Cl)
University of Virginia (Ph.D.) (Cl)
University of Wisconsin—Milwaukee (Ph.D.) (Cl)
Utah State University (Ph.D.) (Cm)
Vanderbilt University (Ph.D.) (Cl)
Virginia Polytechnic Institute and State University (Ph.D.) (Cl)
Washington State University (Ph.D.) (Cl)
Wayne State University (Ph.D.) (Cl)
West Virginia University (Ph.D.) (Cl)
Widener University (Psy.D.) (Cl)
Yale University (Ph.D.) (Cl)
Yeshiva University (Ph.D.) (Cl)
York University (Ph.D.) (Cl)

Behavioral Therapy/Analysis

Arizona State University (Ph.D.) (Cl)
Central Michigan University (Ph.D.) (Cl)
Emory University (Ph.D.) (Cl)
Long Island University, Brooklyn Campus (Ph.D) (Cl)
Long Island University, C.W. Post Campus (Psy.D.) (Cl)
McGill University (Ph.D.) (Co)
Northern Illinois University (Ph.D.) (Cl)
Nova Southeastern University (Ph.D. & Psy.D.) (Cl)
Pepperdine University (Psy.D.) (Cl)
University of Colorado at Boulder (Ph.D.) (Cl)
University of Georgia (Ph.D.) (Cl)
University of Maryland—Baltimore County (Ph.D.) (Cl)

University of Minnesota (Ph.D.) (Cl)
University of Pennsylvania (Ph.D.) (Cl)
University of Texas Southwestern Medical Center (Ph.D.) (Cl)
University of Wisconsin—Milwaukee (Ph.D.) (Cl)

Biofeedback

Nova Southeastern University (Ph.D. & Psy.D.) (Cl)
Widener University (Psy.D.) (Cl)

Career Counseling/Development

Florida State University (Ph.D.) (Cm)
Southern Illinois University—Carbondale (Ph.D.) (Co)
University of California, Santa Barbara (Ph.D.) (Cm)
University of Florida (Ph.D.) (Co)
University of Maryland—College Park (Ph.D.) (Co)
University of Tennessee—Knoxville (Ph.D.) (Co)

Child Abuse/Neglect

Argosy University, Washington, DC (Psy.D.) (Cl)
Duke University (Ph.D.) (Cl)
Georgia State University (Ph.D.) (Cl)
University of California, Santa Barbara (Ph.D.) (Cm)
University of Delaware (Ph.D.) (Cl)
University of Kansas—Child (Ph.D.) (Cl)
University of Nebraska—Lincoln (Ph.D.) (Cl)
University of Oklahoma (Ph.D.) (Co)

Child/Pediatric

Adelphi University (Ph.D.) (Cl)
Adler School of Professional Psychology (Psy.D.) (Cl)
Alliant International University—San Francisco Bay (Ph.D. & Psy.D.) (Cl)
Antioch University New England (Psy.D.)
Argosy University, Atlanta (Psy.D.) (Cl)
Argosy University, Chicago (Psy.D.) (Cl)
Argosy University, Hawaii (Psy.D.) (Cl)
Argosy University, Schaumburg (Psy.D.) (Cl)
Argosy University, Washington, DC (Psy.D.) (Cl)
Arizona State University (Ph.D.) (Cl)
Arizona State University (Ph.D.) (Cl)
Auburn University (Ph.D.) (Cl)
Azusa Pacific University (Psy.D.) (Cl)
Ball State University (Ph.D.) (Co)
Baylor University (Psy.D.) (Cl)
Binghamton University/State University of New York (Ph.D.) (Cl)
Biola University (Ph.D. & Psy.D.) (Cl)

Bowling Green State University (Ph.D.) (Cl)
California Institute of Integral Studies (Psy.D.) (Cl)
Carlos Albizu University—Miami Campus (Psy.D.)
 (Cl)
Case Western Reserve University (Ph.D.) (Cl)
Central Michigan University (Ph.D.) (Cl)
Chicago School of Professional Psychology (Psy.D.)
 (Cl)
City University of New York at City College (Ph.D.)
 (Cl)
Clark University (Ph.D.) (Cl)
Concordia University (Ph.D.) (Cl)
DePaul University (Ph.D.) (Cl)
Drexel University (Ph.D.) (Cl)
Duke University (Ph.D.) (Cl)
Florida State University (Ph.D.) (Cl)
Forest Institute of Professional Psychology (Psy.D.)
 (Cl)
Fuller Theological Seminary (Ph.D. & Psy.D.) (Cl)
George Fox University (Psy.D.) (Cl)
George Washington University (Ph.D. & Psy.D.) (Cl)
Georgia State University (Ph.D.) (Cl)
Harvard University (Ph.D.) (Cl)
Howard University (Ph.D.) (Cl)
Illinois Institute of Technology (Ph.D.) (Cl)
Indiana University of Pennsylvania (Psy.D.) (Cl)
Indiana University—Bloomington (Ph.D.) (Cl)
Indiana University—Purdue University Indianapolis
 (Ph.D.) (Cl)
James Madison University (Psy.D.) (Cm)
Kent State University (Ph.D.) (Cl)
La Salle University (Psy.D.) (Cl)
Loma Linda University (Ph.D. & Psy.D.) (Cl)
Long Island University, Brooklyn Campus (Ph.D)
 (Cl)
Long Island University, C.W. Post Campus (Psy.D.)
 (Cl)
Louisiana Tech University (Ph.D.) (Co)
Loyola College in Maryland (Psy.D.) (Cl)
Marquette University (Ph.D.) (Cl & Co)
McGill University (Ph.D.) (Co)
Miami University (Ph.D.) (Cl)
Michigan State University (Ph.D.) (Cl)
Northeastern University (Ph.D.) (Cm)
Northern Illinois University (Ph.D.) (Cl)
Northwestern University Medical School (Ph.D.) (Cl)
Nova Southeastern University (Ph.D. & Psy.D.) (Cl)
Ohio University (Ph.D.) (Cl)
Oklahoma State University (Ph.D.) (Cl & Co)
Pace University (Psy.D.) (Cm)
Pacific Graduate School of Psychology (Ph.D.) (Cl)
Pacific Graduate School of Psychology/Stanford Uni-
 versity Medical School Consortium (Psy.D.) (Cl)

Pepperdine University (Psy.D.) (Cl)
Purdue University (Ph.D.) (Cl)
Regent University (Psy.D.) (Cl)
Roosevelt University (Psy.D.) (Cl)
Rutgers, The State University of New Jersey (Psy.D.)
 (Cl)
San Diego State University/University of California,
 San Diego (Ph.D.) (Cl)
Seattle Pacific University (Ph.D.) (Cl)
St. John's University (Ph.D.) (Cl)
Suffolk University (Ph.D.) (Cl)
Teachers College, Columbia University (Ph.D.) (Cl)
Tennessee State University (Ph.D.) (Co)
Texas Tech University (Ph.D.) (Co)
Texas Woman's University (Ph.D.) (Co)
The Ohio State University (Ph.D.) (Cl)
The University of Akron (Ph.D.) (Co)
The University of Memphis (Ph.D.) (Cl & Co)
The Wright Institute (Psy.D.) (Cl)
Uniformed Services University of Health Sciences
 (Ph.D.) (Cl)
University at Albany/State University of New York
 (Ph.D.) (Cl)
University at Buffalo/State University of New York
 (Ph.D.) (Cl)
University of Arkansas (Ph.D.) (Cl)
University of California, Los Angeles (Ph.D.) (Cl)
University of Cincinnati (Ph.D.) (Cl)
University of Connecticut (Ph.D.) (Cl)
University of Delaware (Ph.D.) (Cl)
University of Denver (Ph.D.) (Cl)
University of Florida (Ph.D.) (Cl & Co)
University of Georgia (Ph.D.) (Cl)
University of Hartford (Psy.D.) (Cl)
University of Hawaii at Manoa (Ph.D.) (Cl)
University of Houston (Ph.D.) (Cl & Co)
University of Illinois at Urbana–Champaign (Ph.D.)
 (Cl & Co)
University of Indianapolis (Psy.D.) (Cl)
University of Iowa (Ph.D.) (Cl)
University of Kansas—Child (Ph.D.) (Cl)
University of Kansas—Psychology (Ph.D.) (Cl)
University of Kentucky (Ph.D.) (Cl)
University of La Verne (Psy.D.) (Cl)
University of Louisville (Ph.D.) (Cl & Co)
University of Maine (Ph.D.) (Cl)
University of Maryland—Baltimore County (Ph.D.)
 (Cl)
University of Massachusetts—Amherst (Ph.D.) (Cl)
University of Miami (Ph.D.) (Cl)
University of Michigan (Ph.D.) (Cl)
University of Minnesota (Ph.D.) (Cl)
University of Mississippi (Ph.D.) (Cl)

University of Missouri—Columbia (Ph.D.) (Cl)
University of Missouri—St. Louis (Ph.D.) (Cl)
University of Nebraska—Lincoln (Ph.D.) (Cl)
University of Nevada—Las Vegas (Ph.D.) (Cl)
University of New Mexico (Ph.D.) (Cl)
University of North Carolina at Chapel Hill (Ph.D.) (Cl)
University of North Texas (Ph.D.) (Cl)
University of Northern Colorado (Psy.D.) (Co)
University of Oklahoma (Ph.D.) (Co)
University of Oregon (Ph.D.) (Cl & Co)
University of Pittsburgh (Ph.D.) (Cl)
University of Rhode Island (Ph.D.) (Cl)
University of Rochester (Ph.D.) (Cl)
University of Rochester (Ph.D.) (Cl)
University of South Carolina (Ph.D.) (Cl)
University of South Florida (Ph.D.) (Cl)
University of Southern California (Ph.D.) (Cl)
University of Southern Mississippi (Ph.D.) (Cl)
University of Texas at Austin (Ph.D.) (Cl)
University of Texas Southwestern Medical Center (Ph.D.) (Cl)
University of Toledo (Ph.D.) (Cl)
University of Utah (Ph.D.) (Cl)
University of Vermont (Ph.D.) (Cl)
University of Virginia (Ph.D.) (Cl)
University of Washington (Ph.D.) (Cl)
University of Waterloo (Ph.D.) (Cl)
University of Wisconsin—Madison (Ph.D.) (Cl)
University of Wisconsin—Milwaukee (Ph.D.) (Cl & Co)
Utah State University (Ph.D.) (Cm)
Vanderbilt University (Ph.D.) (Cl)
Vanderbilt University (Ph.D.) (Cl)
Virginia Commonwealth University (Ph.D.) (Cl & Co)
Virginia Consortium Program in Clinical Psychology (Psy.D.) (Cl)
Virginia Polytechnic Institute and State University (Ph.D.) (Cl)
Wright State University (Psy.D.) (Cl)
Yale University (Ph.D.) (Cl)
Yeshiva University (Psy.D.) (Cm)

Christian Counseling

Regent University (Psy.D.) (Cl)
Seattle Pacific University (Ph.D.) (Cl)

Chronic/Severe Mental Illness

Argosy University, Chicago (Psy.D.) (Cl)
Azusa Pacific University (Psy.D.) (Cl)
California Institute of Integral Studies (Psy.D.) (Cl)

Fuller Theological Seminary (Ph.D. & Psy.D.) (Cl)
Georgia State University (Ph.D.) (Cl)
Northeastern University (Ph.D.) (Cm)
Northwestern University Medical School (Ph.D.) (Cl)
Pepperdine University (Psy.D.) (Cl)
Roosevelt University (Psy.D.) (Cl)
University of Alabama at Tuscaloosa (Ph.D.) (Cl)
University of Connecticut (Ph.D.) (Cl)
University of Hartford (Psy.D.) (Cl)
University of Houston (Ph.D.) (Co)
University of Kentucky (Ph.D.) (Cl)
University of Miami (Ph.D.) (Cl)
University of Minnesota (Ph.D.) (Cl)
University of Mississippi (Ph.D.) (Cl)
University of Missouri—Kansas City (Ph.D.) (Cl)
University of Pittsburgh (Ph.D.) (Cl)
University of Toledo (Ph.D.) (Cl)
University of Vermont (Ph.D.) (Cl)
Utah State University (Ph.D.) (Cm)
Virginia Commonwealth University (Ph.D.) (Cl)

Cognitive/Cognitive-Behavioral Therapy

American University (Ph.D.) (Cl)
Antioch University New England (Psy.D.)
Argosy University, Chicago (Psy.D.) (Cl)
Boston University (Ph.D.) (Cl)
Central Michigan University (Ph.D.) (Cl)
Concordia University (Ph.D.) (Cl)
Drexel University (Ph.D.) (Cl)
Duke University (Ph.D.) (Cl)
Emory University (Ph.D.) (Cl)
George Mason University (Ph.D.) (Cl)
Harvard University (Ph.D.) (Cl)
Idaho State University (Ph.D.) (Cl)
Northern Illinois University (Ph.D.) (Cl)
Pepperdine University (Psy.D.) (Cl)
San Diego State University/University of California, San Diego (Ph.D.) (Cl)
St. John's University (Ph.D.) (Cl)
University of Colorado at Boulder (Ph.D.) (Cl)
University of Colorado at Colorado Springs (Ph.D.) (Cl)
University of Denver (Psy.D.) (Cl)
University of Florida (Ph.D.) (Cl)
University of Houston (Ph.D.) (Cl)
University of Iowa (Ph.D.) (Cl)
University of Kansas—Psychology (Ph.D.) (Cl)
University of Kentucky (Ph.D.) (Cl)
University of Massachusetts—Amherst (Ph.D.) (Cl)
University of Minnesota (Ph.D.) (Cl)
University of Missouri—Columbia (Ph.D.) (Co)
University of Northern Colorado (Psy.D.) (Co)

University of Oregon (Ph.D.) (Cl)
University of Pennsylvania (Ph.D.) (Cl)
University of Pittsburgh (Ph.D.) (Cl)
University of Southern California (Ph.D.) (Cl)
University of Toledo (Ph.D.) (Cl)
University of Utah (Ph.D.) (Cl)
University of Wisconsin—Madison (Ph.D.) (Cl)
Widener University (Psy.D.) (Cl)
Yeshiva University (Psy.D.) (Cl)

Community Psychology

Adler School of Professional Psychology (Psy.D.) (Cl)
Alliant International University—San Francisco Bay
    (Ph.D. & Psy.D.) (Cl)
Antioch University New England (Psy.D.)
Argosy University, Chicago (Psy.D.) (Cl)
Argosy University, Hawaii (Psy.D.) (Cl)
Argosy University, Schaumburg (Psy.D.) (Cl)
Argosy University, Washington, DC (Psy.D.) (Cl)
Azusa Pacific University (Psy.D.) (Cl)
Baylor University (Psy.D.) (Cl)
Boston College (Ph.D.) (Co)
Boston University (Ph.D.) (Cl)
Bowling Green State University (Ph.D.) (Cl)
Bowling Green State University (Ph.D.) (Cl)
Brigham Young University (Ph.D.) (Cl)
California Institute of Integral Studies (Psy.D.) (Cl)
Chicago School of Professional Psychology (Psy.D.)
    (Cl)
Colorado State University (Ph.D.) (Co)
DePaul University (Ph.D.) (Cl)
Fairleigh Dickinson University (Ph.D.) (Cl)
Fordham University (Ph.D.) (Co)
George Fox University (Psy.D.) (Cl)
George Mason University (Ph.D.) (Cl)
Georgia State University (Ph.D.) (Cl)
Howard University (Ph.D.) (Cl)
Iowa State University (Ph.D.) (Co)
John F. Kennedy University (Psy.D.) (Cl)
Loma Linda University (Ph.D. & Psy.D.) (Cl)
Long Island University, Brooklyn Campus (Ph.D)
    (Cl)
Louisiana Tech University (Ph.D.) (Co)
Marquette University (Ph.D.) (Co)
Marshall University (Psy.D.) (Cl)
Marywood University (Psy.D.) (Cl)
McGill University (Ph.D.) (Co)
Miami University (Ph.D.) (Cl)
New Mexico State University (Ph.D.) (Co)
Nova Southeastern University (Ph.D. & Psy.D.) (Cl)
Our Lady of the Lake University (Psy.D.) (Co)

Pacific Graduate School of Psychology/Stanford Uni-
    versity Medical School Consortium (Psy.D.) (Cl)
Pepperdine University (Psy.D.) (Cl)
Purdue University (Ph.D.) (Co)
Rutgers, The State University of New Jersey (Ph.D. &
    Psy.D.) (Cl)
Seattle Pacific University (Ph.D.) (Cl)
Southern Illinois University—Carbondale (Ph.D.)
    (Co)
Suffolk University (Ph.D.) (Cl)
Syracuse University (Ph.D.) (Cl)
Tennessee State University (Ph.D.) (Co)
Texas A&M University (Ph.D.) (Cl & Co)
Texas Tech University (Ph.D.) (Co)
Texas Woman's University (Ph.D.) (Co)
The University of Akron (Ph.D.) (Co)
University at Albany/State University of New York
    (Ph.D.) (Co)
University at Buffalo/State University of New York
    (Ph.D.) (Cm)
University of Arizona (Ph.D.) (Cl)
University of Arkansas (Ph.D.) (Cl)
University of California, Los Angeles (Ph.D.) (Cl)
University of California, Santa Barbara (Ph.D.) (Cm)
University of Cincinnati (Ph.D.) (Cl)
University of Florida (Ph.D.) (Co)
University of Hartford (Psy.D.) (Cl)
University of Illinois at Urbana–Champaign (Ph.D.)
    (Cl & Co)
University of Indianapolis (Psy.D.) (Cl)
University of Iowa (Ph.D.) (Co)
University of Kansas—Child (Ph.D.) (Cl)
University of Kentucky (Ph.D.) (Cl & Co)
University of Maine (Ph.D.) (Cl)
University of Minnesota (Ph.D.) (Cl)
University of Mississippi (Ph.D.) (Cl)
University of Montana (Ph.D.) (Cl)
University of North Dakota (Ph.D.) (Cl & Co)
University of Notre Dame (Ph.D.) (Co)
University of Oklahoma (Ph.D.) (Co)
University of Oregon (Ph.D.) (Co)
University of Ottawa (Ph.D.) (Cl)
University of Rhode Island (Ph.D.) (Cl)
University of Southern Mississippi (Ph.D.) (Co)
University of Tennessee—Knoxville (Ph.D.) (Co)
University of Texas at Austin (Ph.D.) (Cl & Co)
University of Texas Southwestern Medical Center
    (Ph.D.) (Cl)
University of Utah (Ph.D.) (Co)
University of Virginia (Ph.D.) (Cl)
University of Washington (Ph.D.) (Cl)
University of Wisconsin—Milwaukee (Ph.D.) (Co)
Utah State University (Ph.D.) (Cm)

Virginia Commonwealth University (Ph.D.) (Cl & Co)
Wayne State University (Ph.D.) (Cl)
West Virginia University (Ph.D.) (Co)

Conduct Disorder

Antioch University New England (Psy.D.)
Binghamton University/State University of New York
(Ph.D.) (Cl)
George Washington University (Ph.D.) (Cl)
Miami University (Ph.D.) (Cl)
Purdue University (Ph.D.) (Cl)
Rutgers, The State University of New Jersey (Psy.D.)
(Cl)
University of Alabama at Tuscaloosa (Ph.D.) (Cl)
University of Delaware (Ph.D.) (Cl)
University of Houston (Ph.D.) (Cl)
University of Miami (Ph.D.) (Cl)
University of Minnesota (Ph.D.) (Cl)
University of Pittsburgh (Ph.D.) (Cl)
University of Tennessee—Knoxville (Ph.D.) (Cl)
Virginia Polytechnic Institute and State University
(Ph.D.) (Cl)
Yale University (Ph.D.) (Cl)

Consultation

Miami University (Ph.D.) (Cl)
Northern Illinois University (Ph.D.) (Cl)
Nova Southeastern University (Ph.D. & Psy.D.) (Cl)
Purdue University (Ph.D.) (Cl)
University of Denver (Ph.D.) (Co)
University of Hawaii at Manoa (Ph.D.) (Cl)
University of Maryland—College Park (Ph.D.) (Co)
University of Mississippi (Ph.D.) (Cl)
University of Ottawa (Ph.D.) (Cl)
University of Virginia (Ph.D.) (Cl)
Virginia Polytechnic Institute and State University
(Ph.D.) (Cl)

Correctional Psychology/Prisons

Adler School of Professional Psychology (Psy.D.) (Cl)
Argosy University, Schaumburg (Psy.D.) (Cl)
Brigham Young University (Ph.D.) (Cl)
Forest Institute of Professional Psychology (Psy.D.)
(Cl)
George Fox University (Psy.D.) (Cl)
Iowa State University (Ph.D.) (Co)
Louisiana Tech University (Ph.D.) (Co)
Loyola College in Maryland (Psy.D.) (Cl)
Marquette University (Ph.D.) (Co)
Marshall University (Psy.D.) (Cl)

Oklahoma State University (Ph.D.) (Co)
Roosevelt University (Psy.D.) (Cl)
Sam Houston State University (Ph.D.) (Cl)
Seattle Pacific University (Ph.D.) (Cl)
Southern Illinois University—Carbondale (Ph.D.)
(Co)
Tennessee State University (Ph.D.) (Co)
University of Indianapolis (Psy.D.) (Cl)
University of Missouri—Columbia (Ph.D.) (Co)
University of Oklahoma (Ph.D.) (Co)
University of Southern California (Ph.D.) (Cl)
University of Texas at Austin (Ph.D.) (Co)
Virginia Commonwealth University (Ph.D.) (Cl & Co)
West Virginia University (Ph.D.) (Co)

Crisis Intervention

Argosy University, Atlanta (Psy.D.) (Cl)
Baylor University (Psy.D.) (Cl)
Howard University (Ph.D.) (Cl)
Indiana University—Purdue University Indianapolis
(Ph.D.) (Cl)
Northwestern University (Ph.D.) (Cl)
Nova Southeastern University (Ph.D. & Psy.D.) (Cl)
Syracuse University (Ph.D.) (Cl)
The Ohio State University (Ph.D.) (Cl)
The Wright Institute (Psy.D.) (Cl)
University of Florida (Ph.D.) (Co)
University of Houston (Ph.D.) (Co)
University of Maine (Ph.D.) (Cl)
University of Minnesota (Ph.D.) (Cl)
University of South Dakota (Ph.D.) (Cl)
University of Texas at Austin (Ph.D.) (Cl)
University of Virginia (Ph.D.) (Cl)
West Virginia University (Ph.D.) (Co)
Wright State University (Psy.D.) (Cl)

Day Treatment

Alliant International University—Los Angeles (Ph.D.
& Psy.D.) (Cl)
Argosy University, Hawaii (Psy.D.) (Cl)
Roosevelt University (Psy.D.) (Cl)
University at Albany/State University of New York
(Ph.D.) (Co)
University of Wisconsin—Milwaukee (Ph.D.) (Co)

Developmental Disabilities/

Autism/Assessment
Argosy University, Hawaii (Psy.D.) (Cl)
Auburn University (Ph.D.) (Cl)

Binghamton University/State University of New York (Ph.D.) (Cl)
Bowling Green State University (Ph.D.) (Cl)
George Washington University (Ph.D. & Psy.D.) (Cl)
Georgia State University (Ph.D.) (Cl)
Long Island University, C.W. Post Campus (Psy.D.) (Cl)
Miami University (Ph.D.) (Cl)
Northern Illinois University (Ph.D.) (Cl)
Pepperdine University (Psy.D.) (Cl)
Rutgers, The State University of New Jersey (Ph.D. & Psy.D.) (Cl)
Seattle Pacific University (Ph.D.) (Cl)
The University of Memphis (Ph.D.) (Cl)
The Wright Institute (Psy.D.) (Cl)
University at Albany/State University of New York (Ph.D.) (Cl)
University of Alabama at Tuscaloosa (Ph.D.) (Cl)
University of Arkansas (Ph.D.) (Cl)
University of California, Los Angeles (Ph.D.) (Cl)
University of California, Santa Barbara (Ph.D.) (Cm)
University of Cincinnati (Ph.D.) (Cl)
University of Colorado at Colorado Springs (Ph.D.) (Cl)
University of Connecticut (Ph.D.) (Cl)
University of Delaware (Ph.D.) (Cl)
University of Denver (Ph.D.) (Cl)
University of Georgia (Ph.D.) (Co)
University of Hawaii at Manoa (Ph.D.) (Cl)
University of Louisville (Ph.D.) (Cl & Co)
University of Miami (Ph.D.) (Cl)
University of North Carolina at Chapel Hill (Ph.D.) (Cl)
University of Pittsburgh (Ph.D.) (Cl)
University of Rochester (Ph.D.) (Cl)
University of Texas Southwestern Medical Center (Ph.D.) (Cl)
University of Washington (Ph.D.) (Cl)
University of Wisconsin—Milwaukee (Ph.D.) (Cl)
University of Wyoming (Ph.D.) (Cl)
Vanderbilt University (Ph.D.) (Cl)

Dialectical Behavior Therapy/Analysis

Duke University (Ph.D.) (Cl)
Harvard University (Ph.D.) (Cl)
Pepperdine University (Psy.D.) (Cl)
The Wright Institute (Psy.D.) (Cl)
University of Kansas—Psychology (Ph.D.) (Cl)
University of Kentucky (Ph.D.) (Cl)

Disabilities

Argosy University, Phoenix (Psy.D.) (Cl)
Utah State University (Ph.D.) (Cm)

Disaster/Trauma

Argosy University, Tampa (Psy.D.) (Cl)
Hofstra University (Ph.D.) (Cl)
Marquette University (Ph.D.) (Cl & Co)
Oklahoma State University (Ph.D.) (Cl)
University of Denver (Ph.D. & Psy.D.) (Cl)
University of Montana (Ph.D.) (Cl)
University of South Florida (Ph.D.) (Cl)
University of Texas at Austin (Ph.D.) (Cl)
Virginia Commonwealth University (Ph.D.) (Cl)

Dissociative Disorder

George Washington University (Ph.D.) (Cl)
Rutgers, The State University of New Jersey (Psy.D.) (Cl)

Divorce/Child Custody

University of Houston (Ph.D.) (Cl)
University of Iowa (Ph.D.) (Cl)
Virginia Commonwealth University (Ph.D.) (Cl)

Early Intervention

University of Kansas—Child (Ph.D.) (Cl)
Utah State University (Ph.D.) (Cm)
Wayne State University (Ph.D.) (Cl)

Eating Disorders/Body Image

Argosy University, Chicago (Psy.D.) (Cl)
Baylor University (Psy.D.) (Cl)
Boston University (Ph.D.) (Cl)
Duke University (Ph.D.) (Cl)
George Washington University (Ph.D.) (Cl)
Harvard University (Ph.D.) (Cl)
Kent State University (Ph.D.) (Cl)
Long Island University, C.W. Post Campus (Psy.D.) (Cl)
Loyola College in Maryland (Psy.D.) (Cl)
Loyola University of Chicago (Ph.D.) (Cl)
McGill University (Ph.D.) (Co)
Michigan State University (Ph.D.) (Cl)
Pepperdine University (Psy.D.) (Cl)
Roosevelt University (Psy.D.) (Cl)

Rutgers, The State University of New Jersey (Ph.D. & Psy.D.) (Cl)
St. Louis University (Ph.D.) (Cl)
The Ohio State University (Ph.D.) (Cl)
The University of Memphis (Ph.D.) (Cl)
University at Albany/State University of New York (Ph.D.) (Cl)
University of Central Florida (Ph.D.) (Cl)
University of Georgia (Ph.D.) (Cl)
University of Hawaii at Manoa (Ph.D.) (Cl)
University of Iowa (Ph.D.) (Cl)
University of Manitoba (Ph.D.) (Cl)
University of Miami (Ph.D.) (Cl)
University of Minnesota (Ph.D.) (Cl)
University of Mississippi (Ph.D.) (Cl)
University of North Carolina at Chapel Hill (Ph.D.) (Cl)
University of Pittsburgh (Ph.D.) (Cl)
University of South Florida (Ph.D.) (Cl)
University of Vermont (Ph.D.) (Cl)
University of Wisconsin—Milwaukee (Ph.D.) (Co)
Utah State University (Ph.D.) (Cm)
Yale University (Ph.D.) (Cl)
York University (Ph.D.) (Cl)

Emergency Services

Argosy University, Chicago (Psy.D.) (Cl)
Boston College (Ph.D.) (Co)
George Fox University (Psy.D.) (Cl)
University of Hartford (Psy.D.) (Cl)
University of Maryland—Baltimore County (Ph.D.) (Cl)
University of Pittsburgh (Ph.D.) (Cl)
University of Texas Southwestern Medical Center (Ph.D.) (Cl)

Empirically Supported Treatments/Interventions

DePaul University (Ph.D.) (Cl)
The Wright Institute (Psy.D.) (Cl)
University of Arizona (Ph.D.) (Cl)
University of Wisconsin—Milwaukee (Ph.D.) (Cl)
University of Wyoming (Ph.D.) (Cl)
Wright State University (Psy.D.) (Cl)

Family/Family Therapy/Family Systems

Alliant International University—San Francisco Bay (Ph.D.) (Cl)
Antioch University New England (Psy.D.)
Argosy University, Chicago (Psy.D.) (Cl)

Argosy University, Phoenix (Psy.D.) (Cl)
Argosy University, Schaumburg (Psy.D.) (Cl)
Argosy University, Tampa (Psy.D.) (Cl)
Arizona State University (Ph.D.) (Cl)
Baylor University (Psy.D.) (Cl)
Binghamton University/State University of New York (Ph.D.) (Cl)
Boston University (Ph.D.) (Cl)
Bowling Green State University (Ph.D.) (Cl)
Carlos Albizu University–San Juan Campus (Psy.D.) (Cl)
Catholic University of America (Ph.D.) (Cl)
City University of New York at City College (Ph.D.) (Cl)
Colorado State University (Ph.D.) (Co)
Concordia University (Ph.D.) (Cl)
DePaul University (Ph.D.) (Cl)
Duke University (Ph.D.) (Cl)
Fairleigh Dickinson University (Ph.D.) (Cl)
Florida Institute of Technology (Psy.D.) (Cl)
Fuller Theological Seminary (Ph.D. & Psy.D.) (Cl)
George Washington University (Ph.D. & Psy.D.) (Cl)
Georgia State University (Ph.D.) (Cl)
Howard University (Ph.D.) (Cl)
Idaho State University (Ph.D.) (Cl)
Illinois Institute of Technology (Ph.D.) (Cl)
Long Island University, Brooklyn Campus (Ph.D) (Cl)
Long Island University, C.W. Post Campus (Psy.D.) (Cl)
Loyola University of Chicago (Ph.D.) (Cl)
Marquette University (Ph.D.) (Cl)
Miami University (Ph.D.) (Cl)
Michigan State University (Ph.D.) (Cl)
New Mexico State University (Ph.D.) (Co)
Northeastern University (Ph.D.) (Cm)
Northern Illinois University (Ph.D.) (Cl)
Northwestern University (Ph.D.) (Cl)
Nova Southeastern University (Ph.D. & Psy.D.) (Cl)
Oklahoma State University (Ph.D.) (Cl)
Pacific Graduate School of Psychology (Ph.D.) (Cl)
Pacific Graduate School of Psychology/Stanford University Medical School Consortium (Psy.D.) (Cl)
Philadelphia College of Osteopathic Medicine (Psy.D.) (Cl)
Rutgers, The State University of New Jersey (Ph.D. & Psy.D.) (Cl)
Seattle Pacific University (Ph.D.) (Cl)
Southern Illinois University—Carbondale (Ph.D.) (Cl)
Spalding University (Psy.D.) (Cl)
St. Louis University (Ph.D.) (Cl)
Syracuse University (Ph.D.) (Cl)

Texas A&M University (Ph.D.) (Cl)
Texas Tech University (Ph.D.) (Co)
The Ohio State University (Ph.D.) (Cl)
The University of Memphis (Ph.D.) (Cl)
The Wright Institute (Psy.D.) (Cl)
University of Alabama at Tuscaloosa (Ph.D.) (Cl)
University of California, Santa Barbara (Ph.D.) (Cm)
University of Central Florida (Ph.D.) (Cl)
University of Colorado at Boulder (Ph.D.) (Cl)
University of Delaware (Ph.D.) (Cl)
University of Denver (Ph.D.) (Cl)
University of Florida (Ph.D.) (Co)
University of Houston (Ph.D.) (Cl & Co)
University of Illinois at Urbana–Champaign (Ph.D.)
    (Cl)
University of La Verne (Psy.D.) (Cl)
University of Maryland—Baltimore County (Ph.D.)
    (Cl)
University of Miami (Ph.D.) (Cl)
University of Minnesota (Ph.D.) (Cl)
University of Mississippi (Ph.D.) (Cl)
University of Missouri—Columbia (Ph.D.) (Co)
University of Nevada—Las Vegas (Ph.D.) (Cl)
University of Pittsburgh (Ph.D.) (Cl)
University of Rhode Island (Ph.D.) (Cl)
University of South Florida (Ph.D.) (Cl)
University of Southern California (Ph.D.) (Cl)
University of Texas Southwestern Medical Center
    (Ph.D.) (Cl)
University of Toledo (Ph.D.) (Cl)
University of Utah (Ph.D.) (Cl & Co)
University of Vermont (Ph.D.) (Cl)
University of Virginia (Ph.D.) (Cl)
University of Washington (Ph.D.) (Cl)
University of Wisconsin—Madison (Ph.D.) (Cl)
University of Wisconsin—Milwaukee (Ph.D.) (Cl &
    Co)
Widener University (Psy.D.) (Cl)
Wright State University (Psy.D.) (Cl)
Yeshiva University (Psy.D.) (Cl)

Forensic

Alliant International University—Fresno (Ph.D.) (Cl)
Alliant International University—San Francisco Bay
    (Ph.D. & Psy.D.) (Cl)
Antioch University New England (Psy.D.)
Argosy University, Atlanta (Psy.D.) (Cl)
Argosy University, Chicago (Psy.D.) (Cl)
Argosy University, Hawaii (Psy.D.) (Cl)
Argosy University, Phoenix (Psy.D.) (Cl)
Argosy University, Schaumburg (Psy.D.) (Cl)
Argosy University, Tampa (Psy.D.) (Cl)

Argosy University, Washington, DC (Psy.D.) (Cl)
Azusa Pacific University (Psy.D.) (Cl)
Binghamton University/State University of New York
    (Ph.D.) (Cl)
Carlos Albizu University–San Juan Campus (Psy.D.)
    (Cl)
Central Michigan University (Ph.D.) (Cl)
Chicago School of Professional Psychology (Psy.D.)
    (Cl)
Drexel University (Ph.D.) (Cl)
Florida Institute of Technology (Psy.D.) (Cl)
Fuller Theological Seminary (Ph.D. & Psy.D.) (Cl)
George Washington University (Ph.D.) (Cl)
Georgia State University (Ph.D.) (Co)
Indiana State University (Psy.D.) (Cl)
Jackson State University (Ph.D.) (Cl)
James Madison University (Psy.D.) (Cm)
Kent State University (Ph.D.) (Cl)
Loma Linda University (Ph.D. & Psy.D.) (Cl)
Long Island University, Brooklyn Campus (Ph.D)
    (Cl)
Massachusetts School of Professional Psychology,
    Inc. (Psy.D.) (Cl)
McGill University (Ph.D.) (Co)
Northern Illinois University (Ph.D.) (Cl)
Nova Southeastern University (Ph.D. & Psy.D.) (Cl)
Pacific Graduate School of Psychology (Ph.D.) (Cl)
Pepperdine University (Psy.D.) (Cl)
Regent University (Psy.D.) (Cl)
Rutgers, The State University of New Jersey (Psy.D.)
    (Cl)
Sam Houston State University (Ph.D.) (Cl)
Southern Illinois University—Carbondale (Ph.D.)
    (Cl)
Suffolk University (Ph.D.) (Cl)
Tennessee State University (Ph.D.) (Co)
Texas A&M University (Ph.D.) (Cl)
Texas Tech University (Ph.D.) (Co)
Texas Woman's University (Ph.D.) (Co)
The Wright Institute (Psy.D.) (Cl)
University of Alabama at Tuscaloosa (Ph.D.) (Cl)
University of Florida (Ph.D.) (Cl & Co)
University of Hartford (Psy.D.) (Cl)
University of Houston (Ph.D.) (Cl & Co)
University of Illinois at Urbana–Champaign (Ph.D.)
    (Cl)
University of Iowa (Ph.D.) (Co)
University of Kansas—Psychology (Ph.D.) (Cl)
University of Kentucky (Ph.D.) (Co)
University of La Verne (Psy.D.) (Cl)
University of Louisville (Ph.D.) (Co)
University of Maryland—Baltimore County (Ph.D.)
    (Cl)

University of Minnesota (Ph.D.) (Cl)
University of Montana (Ph.D.) (Cl)
University of Nebraska—Lincoln (Ph.D.) (Cl)
University of New Mexico (Ph.D.) (Cl)
University of North Texas (Ph.D.) (Cl)
University of Saskatchewan (Ph.D.) (Cl)
University of South Dakota (Ph.D.) (Cl)
University of Texas Southwestern Medical Center
    (Ph.D.) (Cl)
University of Victoria (Ph.D.) (Cl)
University of Virginia (Ph.D.) (Cl)
University of Wisconsin—Madison (Ph.D.) (Cl)
West Virginia University (Ph.D.) (Cl)
Widener University (Psy.D.) (Cl)
Wright State University (Psy.D.) (Cl)
York University (Ph.D.) (Cl)

Functional Analytic Therapy

University of Montana (Ph.D.) (Cl)
University of Wisconsin—Milwaukee (Ph.D.) (Cl)

Gay/Lesbian/Bisexual/Transgender

Antioch University New England (Psy.D.)
Argosy University, Chicago (Psy.D.) (Cl)
California Institute of Integral Studies (Psy.D.) (Cl)
Pacific Graduate School of Psychology (Ph.D.) (Cl)
Pacific Graduate School of Psychology/Stanford Uni-
    versity Medical School Consortium (Psy.D.) (Cl)
The Wright Institute (Psy.D.) (Cl)
University of California, Santa Barbara (Ph.D.) (Cm)
University of Montana (Ph.D.) (Cl)
University of Pittsburgh (Ph.D.) (Cl)
Wright State University (Psy.D.) (Cl)

Group Therapy

Antioch University New England (Psy.D.)
Argosy University, Chicago (Psy.D.) (Cl)
Baylor University (Psy.D.) (Cl)
DePaul University (Ph.D.) (Cl)
Fuller Theological Seminary (Ph.D. & Psy.D.) (Cl)
George Mason University (Ph.D.) (Cl)
George Washington University (Ph.D.) (Cl)
Long Island University, C.W. Post Campus (Psy.D.)
    (Cl)
Marquette University (Ph.D.) (Cl)
Miami University (Ph.D.) (Cl)
New Mexico State University (Ph.D.) (Co)
Nova Southeastern University (Ph.D. & Psy.D.) (Cl)
Pepperdine University (Psy.D.) (Cl)

Rutgers, The State University of New Jersey (Psy.D.)
    (Cl)
The Wright Institute (Psy.D.) (Cl)
University of Colorado at Boulder (Ph.D.) (Cl)
University of Denver (Psy.D.) (Cl)
University of Illinois at Urbana–Champaign (Ph.D.)
    (Cl)
University of Louisville (Ph.D.) (Co)
University of Maryland—College Park (Ph.D.) (Co)
University of Miami (Ph.D.) (Cl)
University of Northern Colorado (Psy.D.) (Co)
University of Pennsylvania (Ph.D.) (Cl)
University of Pittsburgh (Ph.D.) (Cl)
University of Rhode Island (Ph.D.) (Cl)
Widener University (Psy.D.) (Cl)
Wright State University (Psy.D.) (Cl)

Homelessness

Long Island University, Brooklyn Campus (Ph.D) (Cl)
Marquette University (Ph.D.) (Co)
Pacific Graduate School of Psychology/Stanford Uni-
    versity Medical School Consortium (Psy.D.) (Cl)
Pepperdine University (Psy.D.) (Cl)
University of Georgia (Ph.D.) (Co)
University of Iowa (Ph.D.) (Co)
University of Utah (Ph.D.) (Cl)

Hospice

University of Alabama at Tuscaloosa (Ph.D.) (Cl)
University of Florida (Ph.D.) (Co)

Hypnosis

Rutgers, The State University of New Jersey (Psy.D.)
    (Cl)
University of Denver (Psy.D.) (Cl)
University of Northern Colorado (Psy.D.) (Co)
University of Tennessee—Knoxville (Ph.D.) (Cl)
University of Waterloo (Ph.D.) (Cl)

Interpersonal Therapy

Emory University (Ph.D.) (Cl)
Fuller Theological Seminary (Ph.D. & Psy.D.) (Cl)
Rutgers, The State University of New Jersey (Psy.D.)
    (Cl)
University of Colorado at Boulder (Ph.D.) (Cl)
University of Houston (Ph.D.) (Cl)
University of Louisville (Ph.D.) (Cl)
University of North Dakota (Ph.D.) (Cl)

University of Utah (Ph.D.) (Cl)
Yeshiva University (Psy.D.) (Cl)

Learning Disabilities

Binghamton University/State University of New York (Ph.D.) (Cl)
George Washington University (Psy.D.) (Cl)
James Madison University (Psy.D.) (Cm)
St. Louis University (Ph.D.) (Cl)
University of Florida (Ph.D.) (Cl)
University of Georgia (Ph.D.) (Co)
University of Houston (Ph.D.) (Cl)
University of Iowa (Ph.D.) (Cl)
University of Missouri—Columbia (Ph.D.) (Co)
University of South Florida (Ph.D.) (Cl)
University of Wisconsin—Milwaukee (Ph.D.) (Cl)

Marriage/Couples

Adelphi University (Ph.D.) (Cl)
Argosy University, Chicago (Psy.D.) (Cl)
Arizona State University (Ph.D.) (Cl)
Auburn University (Ph.D.) (Cl)
Binghamton University/State University of New York (Ph.D.) (Cl)
Carlos Albizu University–San Juan Campus (Psy.D.) (Cl)
Catholic University of America (Ph.D.) (Cl)
Clark University (Ph.D.) (Cl)
Concordia University (Ph.D.) (Cl)
Forest Institute of Professional Psychology (Psy.D.) (Cl)
Fuller Theological Seminary (Ph.D. & Psy.D.) (Cl)
George Washington University (Ph.D.) (Cl)
Idaho State University (Ph.D.) (Cl)
Illinois Institute of Technology (Ph.D.) (Cl)
Indiana University—Bloomington (Ph.D.) (Cl)
Kent State University (Ph.D.) (Cl)
Long Island University, C.W. Post Campus (Psy.D.) (Cl)
McGill University (Ph.D.) (Co)
Michigan State University (Ph.D.) (Cl)
Northwestern University (Ph.D.) (Cl)
Oklahoma State University (Ph.D.) (Cl & Co)
Pepperdine University (Psy.D.) (Cl)
Rutgers, The State University of New Jersey (Psy.D.) (Cl)
Southern Illinois University—Carbondale (Ph.D.) (Co)
Southern Methodist University (Ph.D.) (Cl)
St. Louis University (Ph.D.) (Cl)
Stony Brook University/State University of New York (Ph.D.) (Cl)

Syracuse University (Ph.D.) (Cl)
The Wright Institute (Psy.D.) (Cl)
University of California, Los Angeles (Ph.D.) (Cl)
University of Colorado at Boulder (Ph.D.) (Cl)
University of Delaware (Ph.D.) (Cl)
University of Denver (Ph.D.) (Cl)
University of Houston (Ph.D.) (Cl)
University of Iowa (Ph.D.) (Cl)
University of Miami (Ph.D.) (Cl)
University of Missouri—St. Louis (Ph.D.) (Cl)
University of Montana (Ph.D.) (Cl)
University of Nebraska—Lincoln (Ph.D.) (Co)
University of Nevada—Las Vegas (Ph.D.) (Cl)
University of Nevada—Reno (Ph.D.) (Cl)
University of North Carolina at Chapel Hill (Ph.D.) (Cl)
University of North Dakota (Ph.D.) (Cl)
University of Northern Colorado (Psy.D.) (Co)
University of Oregon (Ph.D.) (Cl)
University of Ottawa (Ph.D.) (Cl)
University of Rhode Island (Ph.D.) (Cl)
University of Southern California (Ph.D.) (Cl)
University of Tennessee—Knoxville (Ph.D.) (Cl)
University of Texas at Austin (Ph.D.) (Cl)
University of Virginia (Ph.D.) (Cl)
University of Washington (Ph.D.) (Cl)
University of Waterloo (Ph.D.) (Cl)
Virginia Polytechnic Institute and State University (Ph.D.) (Cl)
Widener University (Psy.D.) (Cl)
Wright State University (Psy.D.) (Cl)
Yeshiva University (Psy.D.) (Cl)

Medical Center/Hospital-Based Services

Alliant International University—Fresno (Ph.D.) (Cl)
Alliant International University—Los Angeles (Ph.D.) (Cl)/18
Alliant International University—San Francisco Bay (Ph.D. & Psy.D.) (Cl)
Argosy University, Hawaii (Psy.D.) (Cl)
Argosy University, Tampa (Psy.D.) (Cl)
Boston College (Ph.D.) (Co)
Brigham Young University (Ph.D.) (Cl)
Florida State University (Ph.D.) (Cl)
John F. Kennedy University (Psy.D.) (Cl)
Lehigh University (Ph.D.) (Co)
Loma Linda University (Ph.D. & Psy.D.) (Cl)
Long Island University, Brooklyn Campus (Ph.D) (Cl)
Louisiana Tech University (Ph.D.) (Co)
Loyola University of Chicago (Ph.D.) (Co)
Marquette University (Ph.D.) (Co)

Marshall University (Psy.D.) (Cl)
Purdue University (Ph.D.) (Co)
Sam Houston State University (Ph.D.) (Cl)
Southern Illinois University—Carbondale (Ph.D.)
    (Co)
St. John's University (Ph.D.) (Cl)
Texas Woman's University (Ph.D.) (Co)
University at Albany/State University of New York
    (Ph.D.) (Co)
University at Buffalo/State University of New York
    (Ph.D.) (Cm)
University of Alabama at Tuscaloosa (Ph.D.) (Cl)
University of Denver (Ph.D.) (Co)
University of Florida (Ph.D.) (Cl)
University of Hartford (Psy.D.) (Cl)
University of Houston (Ph.D.) (Co)
University of Illinois at Urbana–Champaign (Ph.D.)
    (Co)
University of Indianapolis (Psy.D.) (Cl)
University of Iowa (Ph.D.) (Co)
University of Louisville (Ph.D.) (Co)
University of Maryland—Baltimore County (Ph.D.)
    (Cl)
University of Missouri—Columbia (Ph.D.) (Cl & Co)
University of North Dakota (Ph.D.) (Co)
University of Virginia (Ph.D.) (Cl)
University of Wisconsin—Milwaukee (Ph.D.) (Co)
Virginia Commonwealth University (Ph.D.) (Co)
West Virginia University (Ph.D.) (Co)
Western Michigan University (Ph.D.) (Co)

Men's Issues

The Wright Institute (Psy.D.) (Cl)
Wright State University (Psy.D.) (Cl)

Mental Retardation

University of Mississippi (Ph.D.) (Cl)
University of Vermont (Ph.D.) (Cl)

Mindfulness

Pepperdine University (Psy.D.) (Cl)
University of Colorado at Boulder (Ph.D.) (Cl)
University of Montana (Ph.D.) (Cl)

Minority/Cross-Cultural/Multicultural

Argosy University, Chicago (Psy.D.) (Cl)
Argosy University, Phoenix (Psy.D.) (Cl)
Biola University (Ph.D. & Psy.D.) (Cl)
Carlos Albizu University—Miami Campus (Psy.D.) (Cl)

Catholic University of America (Ph.D.) (Cl)
Chicago School of Professional Psychology (Psy.D.)
    (Cl)
DePaul University (Ph.D.) (Cl)
Fairleigh Dickinson University (Ph.D.) (Cl)
Florida State University (Ph.D.) (Cl)
Forest Institute of Professional Psychology (Psy.D.)
    (Cl)
George Washington University (Ph.D.) (Cl)
Georgia State University (Ph.D.) (Cl & Co)
Howard University (Ph.D.) (Cl)
Illinois Institute of Technology (Ph.D.) (Cl)
Marquette University (Ph.D.) (Co)
Miami University (Ph.D.) (Cl)
Michigan State University (Ph.D.) (Cl)
New Mexico State University (Ph.D.) (Co)
Nova Southeastern University (Ph.D. & Psy.D.) (Cl)
Pacific Graduate School of Psychology (Ph.D.) (Cl)
Pacific Graduate School of Psychology/Stanford University Medical School Consortium (Psy.D.) (Cl)
Pepperdine University (Psy.D.) (Cl)
Philadelphia College of Osteopathic Medicine
    (Psy.D.) (Cl)
Rutgers, The State University of New Jersey (Ph.D. &
    Psy.D.) (Cl)
Seattle Pacific University (Ph.D.) (Cl)
St. Louis University (Ph.D.) (Cl)
The University of Memphis (Ph.D.) (Cl)
The Wright Institute (Psy.D.) (Cl)
University at Albany/State University of New York
    (Ph.D.) (Cl)
University of Arkansas (Ph.D.) (Cl)
University of California, Los Angeles (Ph.D.) (Cl)
University of Connecticut (Ph.D.) (Cl)
University of Denver (Ph.D.) (Cl & Co)
University of Hawaii at Manoa (Ph.D.) (Cl)
University of Houston (Ph.D.) (Cl)
University of Illinois at Urbana–Champaign (Ph.D.) (Cl)
University of Maryland—College Park (Ph.D.) (Co)
University of Massachusetts—Amherst (Ph.D.) (Cl)
University of Miami (Ph.D.) (Cl)
University of Nebraska—Lincoln (Ph.D.) (Cl & Co)
University of New Mexico (Ph.D.) (Cl)
University of North Dakota (Ph.D.) (Cl)
University of Pittsburgh (Ph.D.) (Cl)
University of Rhode Island (Ph.D.) (Cl)
University of South Dakota (Ph.D.) (Cl)
University of Southern California (Ph.D.) (Cl)
University of Texas at Austin (Ph.D.) (Cl)
University of Utah (Ph.D.) (Cl & Co)
University of Vermont (Ph.D.) (Cl)
University of Washington (Ph.D.) (Cl)
Utah State University (Ph.D.) (Cm)

Wayne State University (Ph.D.) (Cl)
Widener University (Psy.D.) (Cl)
Wright State University (Psy.D.) (Cl)
Yeshiva University (Psy.D.) (Cm)

Motivational Interviewing

Boston University (Ph.D.) (Cl)
University of Montana (Ph.D.) (Cl)

Native American Health Services

George Fox University (Psy.D.) (Cl)
Oklahoma State University (Ph.D.) (Co)
University of Oklahoma (Ph.D.) (Co)

Neuroimaging

University of Connecticut (Ph.D.) (Cl)
University of New Mexico (Ph.D.) (Cl)

Neuropsychology

Adelphi University (Ph.D.) (Cl)
Alliant International University—San Francisco Bay (Ph.D.) (Cl)
American University (Ph.D.) (Cl)
Antioch University New England (Psy.D.)
Argosy University, Atlanta (Psy.D.) (Cl)
Argosy University, Chicago (Psy.D.) (Cl)
Argosy University, Phoenix (Psy.D.) (Cl)
Argosy University, Tampa (Psy.D.) (Cl)
Argosy University, Washington, DC (Psy.D.) (Cl)
Baylor University (Psy.D.) (Cl)
Binghamton University/State University of New York (Ph.D.) (Cl)
Boston University (Ph.D.) (Cl)
Brigham Young University (Ph.D.) (Cl)
California Institute of Integral Studies (Psy.D.) (Cl)
Catholic University of America (Ph.D.) (Cl)
Central Michigan University (Ph.D.) (Cl)
Colorado State University (Ph.D.) (Co)
Drexel University (Ph.D.) (Cl)
Eastern Michigan University (Ph.D.) (Cl)
Emory University (Ph.D.) (Cl)
Fairleigh Dickinson University (Ph.D.) (Cl)
Florida Institute of Technology (Psy.D.) (Cl)
Forest Institute of Professional Psychology (Psy.D.) (Cl)
Fuller Theological Seminary (Ph.D. & Psy.D.) (Cl)
George Fox University (Psy.D.) (Cl)
George Washington University (Ph.D.) (Cl)
Georgia State University (Ph.D.) (Cl)

Harvard University (Ph.D.) (Cl)
Howard University (Ph.D.) (Cl)
Idaho State University (Ph.D.) (Cl)
Illinois Institute of Technology (Ph.D.) (Cl)
Indiana University—Bloomington (Ph.D.) (Cl)
Jackson State University (Ph.D.) (Cl)
James Madison University (Psy.D.) (Cm)
Kent State University (Ph.D.) (Cl)
Loma Linda University (Ph.D. & Psy.D.) (Cl)
Long Island University, Brooklyn Campus (Ph.D) (Cl)
Loyola University of Chicago (Ph.D.) (Cl)
Marquette University (Ph.D.) (Cl & Co)
McGill University (Ph.D.) (Co)
Northwestern University (Ph.D.) (Cl)
Northwestern University Medical School (Ph.D.) (Cl)
Nova Southeastern University (Ph.D. & Psy.D.) (Cl)
Ohio University (Ph.D.) (Cl)
Pace University (Psy.D.) (Cm)
Pacific Graduate School of Psychology (Ph.D.) (Cl)
Pacific Graduate School of Psychology/Stanford University Medical School Consortium (Psy.D.) (Cl)
Pepperdine University (Psy.D.) (Cl)
Purdue University (Ph.D.) (Cl)
Regent University (Psy.D.) (Cl)
Roosevelt University (Psy.D.) (Cl)
Rosalind Franklin University of Medicine and Science (Ph.D.) (Cl)
Rutgers, The State University of New Jersey (Psy.D.) (Cl)
Sam Houston State University (Ph.D.) (Cl)
San Diego State University/University of California, San Diego (Ph.D.) (Cl)
Seattle Pacific University (Ph.D.) (Cl)
Southern Illinois University—Carbondale (Ph.D.) (Cl)
St. John's University (Ph.D.) (Cl)
St. Louis University (Ph.D.) (Cl)
Suffolk University (Ph.D.) (Cl)
Syracuse University (Ph.D.) (Cl)
Temple University (Ph.D.) (Cl)
Texas A&M University (Ph.D.) (Cl)
The Ohio State University (Ph.D.) (Cl)
The Wright Institute (Psy.D.) (Cl)
University at Albany/State University of New York (Ph.D.) (Cl & Co)
University of Alabama at Birmingham (Ph.D.) (Cl)
University of Alabama at Tuscaloosa (Ph.D.) (Cl)
University of Arizona (Ph.D.) (Cl)
University of Arkansas (Ph.D.) (Cl)
University of California, Santa Barbara (Ph.D.) (Cm)
University of Central Florida (Ph.D.) (Cl)
University of Cincinnati (Ph.D.) (Cl)

University of Colorado at Colorado Springs (Ph.D.) (Cl)
University of Connecticut (Ph.D.) (Cl)
University of Denver (Ph.D.) (Cl)
University of Florida (Ph.D.) (Cl)
University of Georgia (Ph.D.) (Cl)
University of Hawaii at Manoa (Ph.D.) (Cl)
University of Houston (Ph.D.) (Cl)
University of Illinois at Urbana–Champaign (Ph.D.) (Cl)
University of Indianapolis (Psy.D.) (Cl)
University of Iowa (Ph.D.) (Cl)
University of Kentucky (Ph.D.) (Cl)
University of Maryland—Baltimore County (Ph.D.) (Cl)
University of Miami (Ph.D.) (Cl)
University of Minnesota (Ph.D.) (Cl)
University of Montana (Ph.D.) (Cl)
University of Nebraska—Lincoln (Ph.D.) (Cl)
University of New Mexico (Ph.D.) (Cl)
University of Northern Colorado (Psy.D.) (Co)
University of Oregon (Ph.D.) (Cl)
University of Pittsburgh (Ph.D.) (Cl)
University of South Florida (Ph.D.) (Cl)
University of Southern California (Ph.D.) (Cl)
University of Texas at Austin (Ph.D.) (Cl & Co)
University of Texas Southwestern Medical Center (Ph.D.) (Cl)
University of Utah (Ph.D.) (Cl)
University of Victoria (Ph.D.) (Cl)
University of Virginia (Ph.D.) (Cl)
University of Washington (Ph.D.) (Cl)
University of Waterloo (Ph.D.) (Cl)
University of Wisconsin—Madison (Ph.D.) (Cl)
University of Wisconsin—Milwaukee (Ph.D.) (Cl)
Utah State University (Ph.D.) (Cm)
Vanderbilt University (Ph.D.) (Cl)
Virginia Commonwealth University (Ph.D.) (Cl)
Virginia Polytechnic Institute and State University (Ph.D.) (Cl)
Wayne State University (Ph.D.) (Cl)
Widener University (Psy.D.) (Cl)
Wright State University (Psy.D.) (Cl)
Yeshiva University (Ph.D.) (Cl)
York University (Ph.D.) (Cl)

Oncology/Cancer Care

Ball State University (Ph.D.) (Co)
Howard University (Ph.D.) (Co)
Indiana University—Purdue University Indianapolis (Ph.D.) (Cl)
Northeastern University (Ph.D.) (Cm)

Seattle Pacific University (Ph.D.) (Cl)
The Ohio State University (Ph.D.) (Cl)
The University of Memphis (Ph.D.) (Cl)
University of Delaware (Ph.D.) (Cl)
University of Kansas—Psychology (Ph.D.) (Cl)
University of South Florida (Ph.D.) (Cl)
University of Tennessee—Knoxville (Ph.D.) (Cl)

Organizational

Chicago School of Professional Psychology (Psy.D.) (Cl)
Rutgers, The State University of New Jersey (Psy.D.) (Cl)
Widener University (Psy.D.) (Cl)

Pain Management

Argosy University, Phoenix (Psy.D.) (Cl)
Binghamton University/State University of New York (Ph.D.) (Cl)
Forest Institute of Professional Psychology (Psy.D.) (Cl)
George Fox University (Psy.D.) (Cl)
Illinois Institute of Technology (Ph.D.) (Cl)
Marquette University (Ph.D.) (Cl)
Nova Southeastern University (Ph.D.) (Cl)
Nova Southeastern University (Psy.D.) (Cl)
Ohio University (Ph.D.) (Cl)
Pacific Graduate School of Psychology/Stanford University Medical School Consortium (Psy.D.) (Cl)
University of Alabama at Tuscaloosa (Ph.D.) (Cl)
University of Florida (Ph.D.) (Cl)
University of Kentucky (Ph.D.) (Cl)
University of Montana (Ph.D.) (Cl)
University of Ottawa (Ph.D.) (Cl)
University of Pittsburgh (Ph.D.) (Cl)
University of Utah (Ph.D.) (Co)
Virginia Commonwealth University (Ph.D.) (Cl)

Parent–Child Interaction/Parent Training

Arizona State University (Ph.D.) (Cl)
Central Michigan University (Ph.D.) (Cl)
Hofstra University (Ph.D.) (Cl)
Idaho State University (Ph.D.) (Cl)
Long Island University, C.W. Post Campus (Psy.D.) (Cl)
Marquette University (Ph.D.) (Co)
Miami University (Ph.D.) (Cl)
Northern Illinois University (Ph.D.) (Cl)
Nova Southeastern University (Ph.D. & Psy.D.) (Cl)
Nova Southeastern University (Psy.D.) (Cl)

St. Louis University (Ph.D.) (Cl)
University at Buffalo/State University of New York (Ph.D.) (Cl)
University of Alabama at Tuscaloosa (Ph.D.) (Cl)
University of Florida (Ph.D.) (Cl)
University of Ottawa (Ph.D.) (Cl)
University of Pittsburgh (Ph.D.) (Cl)
University of Southern California (Ph.D.) (Cl)
University of Virginia (Ph.D.) (Cl)
West Virginia University (Ph.D.) (Cl)
Yeshiva University (Psy.D.) (Cl & Cm)

Personality Disorders

Antioch University New England (Psy.D.)
Argosy University, Chicago (Psy.D.) (Cl)
Baylor University (Psy.D.) (Cl)
Case Western Reserve University (Ph.D.) (Cl)
Eastern Michigan University (Ph.D.) (Cl)
George Washington University (Ph.D.) (Cl)
Georgia State University (Ph.D.) (Cl)
Loyola University of Chicago (Ph.D.) (Cl)
Northwestern University (Ph.D.) (Cl)
Pacific Graduate School of Psychology/Stanford University Medical School Consortium (Psy.D.) (Cl)
Purdue University (Ph.D.) (Cl)
Rutgers, The State University of New Jersey (Ph.D. & Psy.D.) (Cl)
St. Louis University (Ph.D.) (Cl)
The Wright Institute (Psy.D.) (Cl)
University at Buffalo/State University of New York (Ph.D.) (Cl)
University of Georgia (Ph.D.) (Cl)
University of Minnesota (Ph.D.) (Cl)
University of Montana (Ph.D.) (Cl)
University of Nevada—Reno (Ph.D.) (Cl)
University of New Mexico (Ph.D.) (Cl)
University of North Dakota (Ph.D.) (Cl)
University of Pittsburgh (Ph.D.) (Cl)
University of Southern California (Ph.D.) (Cl)
University of Tennessee—Knoxville (Ph.D.) (Cl)
University of Texas at Austin (Ph.D.) (Cl)
University of Texas Southwestern Medical Center (Ph.D.) (Cl)
University of Utah (Ph.D.) (Cl)
University of Washington (Ph.D.) (Cl)
Vanderbilt University (Ph.D.) (Cl)
Wright State University (Psy.D.) (Cl)

Posttraumatic Stress Disorder/Trauma

Argosy University, Washington, DC (Psy.D.) (Cl)
Auburn University (Ph.D.) (Cl)

Boston University (Ph.D.) (Cl)
Florida Institute of Technology (Psy.D.) (Cl)
Miami University (Ph.D.) (Cl)
Michigan State University (Ph.D.) (Cl)
Pacific Graduate School of Psychology/Stanford University Medical School Consortium (Psy.D.) (Cl)
Pepperdine University (Psy.D.) (Cl)
University of Alabama at Tuscaloosa (Ph.D.) (Cl)
University of Connecticut (Ph.D.) (Cl)
University of Houston (Ph.D.) (Cl & Co)
University of Maine (Ph.D.) (Cl)
University of Minnesota (Ph.D.) (Cl)
University of Mississippi (Ph.D.) (Cl)
University of Missouri—St. Louis (Ph.D.) (Cl)
University of Nevada—Reno (Ph.D.) (Cl)
University of North Texas (Ph.D.) (Cl)
University of Ottawa (Ph.D.) (Cl)
University of Wisconsin—Milwaukee (Ph.D.) (Cl)
University of Wyoming (Ph.D.) (Cl)

Prevention

Argosy University, Chicago (Psy.D.) (Cl)
Arizona State University (Ph.D.) (Cl)
Clark University (Ph.D.) (Cl)
Harvard University (Ph.D.) (Cl)
Miami University (Ph.D.) (Cl)
University of Illinois at Chicago (Ph.D.) (Cl)
University of Louisville (Ph.D.) (Co)
University of Maryland—Baltimore County (Ph.D.) (Cl)
University of Vermont (Ph.D.) (Cl)
Virginia Polytechnic Institute and State University (Ph.D.) (Cl)

Primary Care

Auburn University (Ph.D.) (Cl)
Colorado State University (Ph.D.) (Co)
Forest Institute of Professional Psychology (Psy.D.) (Cl)
George Fox University (Psy.D.) (Cl)
Loma Linda University (Ph.D. & Psy.D.) (Cl)
Ohio University (Ph.D.) (Cl)
The Wright Institute (Psy.D.) (Cl)
University of Colorado at Colorado Springs (Ph.D.) (Cl)
University of Missouri—Kansas City (Ph.D.) (Cl)
University of Texas Southwestern Medical Center (Ph.D.) (Cl)
University of Wyoming (Ph.D.) (Cl)
West Virginia University (Ph.D.) (Cl)

Private Practice

Brigham Young University (Ph.D.) (Cl)
Chicago School of Professional Psychology (Psy.D.) (Cl)
Iowa State University (Ph.D.) (Co)
University at Albany/State University of New York
    (Ph.D.) (Co)

Program Evaluation

George Mason University (Ph.D.) (Cl)
The Wright Institute (Psy.D.) (Cl)
Wright State University (Psy.D.) (Cl)

Psychiatry Clinic

McGill University (Ph.D.) (Co)
University of Missouri—Columbia (Ph.D.) (Co)
University of Missouri—Kansas City (Ph.D.) (Cl)

Psychoanalytic/Psychodynamic Therapy

Adelphi University (Ph.D.) (Cl)
American University (Ph.D.) (Cl)
Antioch University New England (Psy.D.)
Argosy University, Chicago (Psy.D.) (Cl)
Central Michigan University (Ph.D.) (Cl)
Concordia University (Ph.D.) (Cl)
Emory University (Ph.D.) (Cl)
George Washington University (Ph.D.) (Cl)
Nova Southeastern University (Ph.D. & Psy.D.) (Cl)
Pepperdine University (Psy.D.) (Cl)
Rutgers, The State University of New Jersey (Psy.D.)
    (Cl)
St. John's University (Ph.D.) (Cl)
St. Louis University (Ph.D.) (Cl)
Teachers College, Columbia University (Ph.D.) (Cl)
The Wright Institute (Psy.D.) (Cl)
University of Colorado at Boulder (Ph.D.) (Cl)
University of Denver (Psy.D.) (Cl)
University of Massachusetts—Amherst (Ph.D.) (Cl)
University of Pennsylvania (Ph.D.) (Cl)
University of Rochester (Ph.D.) (Cl)
University of Toledo (Ph.D.) (Cl)
Widener University (Psy.D.) (Cl)
Wright State University (Psy.D.) (Cl)
Yeshiva University (Psy.D.) (Cl)

Rehabilitation

Alliant International University—Fresno (Ph.D.) (Cl)
Alliant International University—Los Angeles (Ph.D.
    & Psy.D.) (Cl)

Argosy University, Atlanta (Psy.D.) (Cl)
Argosy University, Chicago (Psy.D.) (Cl)
Auburn University (Ph.D.) (Co)
Georgia State University (Ph.D.) (Cl)
Pacific Graduate School of Psychology/Stanford
    University Medical School Consortium (Psy.D.)
    (Cl)
Pepperdine University (Psy.D.) (Cl)
Seattle Pacific University (Ph.D.) (Cl)
The Wright Institute (Psy.D.) (Cl)
University of Hawaii at Manoa (Ph.D.) (Cl)
University of Houston (Ph.D.) (Cl)
University of Illinois at Urbana–Champaign (Ph.D.)
    (Co)
University of Maryland—Baltimore County (Ph.D.)
    (Cl)
University of Missouri—Columbia (Ph.D.) (Cl &
    Co)
University of Oklahoma (Ph.D.) (Co)
University of Texas Southwestern Medical Center
    (Ph.D.) (Cl)
University of Victoria (Ph.D.) (Cl)
University of Washington (Ph.D.) (Cl)
Utah State University (Ph.D.) (Cm)
Virginia Commonwealth University (Ph.D.) (Co)
Wayne State University (Ph.D.) (Cl)
West Virginia University (Ph.D.) (Co)
Wright State University (Psy.D.) (Cl)

Religion/Spirituality

Argosy University, Chicago (Psy.D.) (Cl)
Biola University (Ph.D. & Psy.D.) (Cl)
George Fox University (Psy.D.) (Cl)
Pepperdine University (Psy.D.) (Cl)
Virginia Commonwealth University (Ph.D.) (Co)

Rural Mental Health/Psychology

Antioch University New England (Psy.D.)
Baylor University (Psy.D.) (Cl)
George Fox University (Psy.D.) (Cl)
Indiana State University (Psy.D.) (Cl)
Marshall University (Psy.D.) (Cl)
Miami University (Ph.D.) (Cl)
New Mexico State University (Ph.D.) (Co)
Oklahoma State University (Ph.D.) (Co)
Southern Illinois University—Carbondale (Ph.D.)
    (Co)
Texas A&M University (Ph.D.) (Cl)
University of Florida (Ph.D.) (Cl & Co)
University of Georgia (Ph.D.) (Co)
University of Kentucky (Ph.D.) (Co)

University of Missouri—Columbia (Ph.D.) (Co)
University of Montana (Ph.D.) (Cl)
University of New Mexico (Ph.D.) (Cl)
University of North Dakota (Ph.D.) (Cl)
University of South Dakota (Ph.D.) (Cl)
University of Wyoming (Ph.D.) (Cl)

Schizophrenia/Psychosis/

Serious Mental Illness
Argosy University, Phoenix (Psy.D.) (Cl)
Baylor University (Psy.D.) (Cl)
Binghamton University/State University of New York
    (Ph.D.) (Cl)
Case Western Reserve University (Ph.D.) (Cl)
George Washington University (Ph.D. & Psy.D.)
    (Cl)
Howard University (Ph.D.) (Cl)
Illinois Institute of Technology (Ph.D.) (Cl)
Indiana University—Bloomington (Ph.D.) (Cl)
Indiana University—Purdue University Indianapolis
    (Ph.D.) (Cl)
Kent State University (Ph.D.) (Cl)
Nova Southeastern University (Ph.D. & Psy.D.) (Cl)
Pacific Graduate School of Psychology/Stanford Uni-
    versity Medical School Consortium (Psy.D.) (Cl)
Pepperdine University (Psy.D.) (Cl)
Rutgers, The State University of New Jersey (Psy.D.)
    (Cl)
Seattle Pacific University (Ph.D.) (Cl)
Southern Illinois University—Carbondale (Ph.D.)
    (Cl)
The Wright Institute (Psy.D.) (Cl)
University of California, Los Angeles (Ph.D.) (Cl)
University of Cincinnati (Ph.D.) (Cl)
University of Hawaii at Manoa (Ph.D.) (Cl)
University of Houston (Ph.D.) (Cl)
University of Louisville (Ph.D.) (Cl)
University of Maryland—Baltimore County (Ph.D.)
    (Cl)
University of Minnesota (Ph.D.) (Cl)
University of Montana (Ph.D.) (Cl)
University of Nebraska—Lincoln (Ph.D.) (Cl)
University of North Texas (Ph.D.) (Cl)
University of Pennsylvania (Ph.D.) (Cl)
University of Pittsburgh (Ph.D.) (Cl)
University of South Dakota (Ph.D.) (Cl)
University of Southern California (Ph.D.) (Cl)
University of Virginia (Ph.D.) (Cl)
University of Wisconsin—Madison (Ph.D.) (Cl)
Vanderbilt University (Ph.D.) (Cl)
Wright State University (Psy.D.) (Cl)
York University (Ph.D.) (Cl)

School/Educational

Adler School of Professional Psychology (Psy.D.) (Cl)
Alliant International University—Fresno (Ph.D.) (Cl)
Alliant International University—San Francisco Bay
    (Ph.D. & Psy.D.) (Cl)
Antioch University New England (Psy.D.)
Argosy University, Atlanta (Psy.D.) (Cl)
Argosy University, Chicago (Psy.D.) (Cl)
Argosy University, Hawaii (Psy.D.) (Cl)
Argosy University, Phoenix (Psy.D.) (Cl)
Argosy University, Tampa (Psy.D.) (Cl)
Argosy University, Washington, DC (Psy.D.) (Cl)
Azusa Pacific University (Psy.D.) (Cl)
Baylor University (Psy.D.) (Cl)
Binghamton University/State University of New York
    (Ph.D.) (Cl)
Boston College (Ph.D.) (Co)
Bowling Green State University (Ph.D.) (Cl)
Brigham Young University (Ph.D.) (Cl)
Central Michigan University (Ph.D.) (Cl)
Chicago School of Professional Psychology (Psy.D.)
    (Cl)
Clark University (Ph.D.) (Cl)
George Fox University (Psy.D.) (Cl)
Indiana University—Bloomington (Ph.D.) (Cl)
Indiana University—Purdue University Indianapolis
    (Ph.D.) (Cl)
James Madison University (Psy.D.) (Cm)
Long Island University, C.W. Post Campus (Psy.D.)
    (Cl)
Marquette University (Ph.D.) (Co)
Marshall University (Psy.D.) (Cl)
Miami University (Ph.D.) (Cl)
Northern Illinois University (Ph.D.) (Cl)
Our Lady of the Lake University (Psy.D.) (Co)
Pepperdine University (Psy.D.) (Cl)
Rutgers, The State University of New Jersey (Psy.D.)
    (Cl)
San Diego State University/University of California,
    San Diego (Ph.D.) (Cl)
Suffolk University (Ph.D.) (Cl)
Syracuse University (Ph.D.) (Cl)
The University of Memphis (Ph.D.) (Cl)
University at Buffalo/State University of New York
    (Ph.D.) (Cm)
University of Arkansas (Ph.D.) (Cl)
University of California, Los Angeles (Ph.D.) (Cl)
University of California, Santa Barbara (Ph.D.) (Cm)
University of Georgia (Ph.D.) (Co)
University of Houston (Ph.D.) (Co)
University of Illinois at Urbana–Champaign (Ph.D.)
    (Cl)

University of Indianapolis (Psy.D.) (Cl)
University of Iowa (Ph.D.) (Co)
University of Louisville (Ph.D.) (Co)
University of Maryland—Baltimore County (Ph.D.)
(Cl)
University of North Carolina at Greensboro (Ph.D.)
(Cl)
University of Oklahoma (Ph.D.) (Co)
University of Virginia (Ph.D.) (Cl)
University of Waterloo (Ph.D.) (Cl)
Virginia Commonwealth University (Ph.D.) (Cl)
West Virginia University (Ph.D.) (Cl)
Western Michigan University (Ph.D.) (Co)
Widener University (Psy.D.) (Cl)
Yeshiva University (Psy.D.) (Cm)

Sexuality/Sex Therapy/Sexual Offenders

Adler School of Professional Psychology (Psy.D.) (Cl)
Argosy University, Phoenix (Psy.D.) (Cl)
Argosy University, Washington, DC (Psy.D.) (Cl)
Baylor University (Psy.D.) (Cl)
Carlos Albizu University–San Juan Campus (Psy.D.)
(Cl)
Chicago School of Professional Psychology (Psy.D.)
(Cl)
Idaho State University (Ph.D.) (Cl)
La Salle University (Psy.D.) (Cl)
Southern Illinois University—Carbondale (Ph.D.)
(Co)
The Ohio State University (Ph.D.) (Cl)
University of Florida (Ph.D.) (Co)
University of Louisville (Ph.D.) (Co)
University of Mississippi (Ph.D.) (Cl)
University of Ottawa (Ph.D.) (Cl)
University of Utah (Ph.D.) (Cl)
Widener University (Psy.D.) (Cl)

Sleep Disorders

University of Alabama at Tuscaloosa (Ph.D.) (Cl)
University of Arizona (Ph.D.) (Cl)
University of Texas at Austin (Ph.D.) (Cl)
University of Texas Southwestern Medical Center
(Ph.D.) (Cl)

Spanish-Speaking Clients

Brigham Young University (Ph.D.) (Co)
California Institute of Integral Studies (Psy.D.) (Cl)
Our Lady of the Lake University (Psy.D.) (Co)

Stress

Georgia State University (Ph.D.) (Co)
Indiana University of Pennsylvania (Psy.D.) (Cl)
Long Island University, C.W. Post Campus (Psy.D.)
(Cl)
Loyola College in Maryland (Psy.D.) (Cl)
Nova Southeastern University (Ph.D. & Psy.D.) (Cl)
Nova Southeastern University (Psy.D.) (Cl)
Southern Illinois University—Carbondale (Ph.D.)
(Co)
University of Georgia (Ph.D.) (Cl)

Substance Abuse/Addiction

Adelphi University (Ph.D.) (Cl)
Alliant International University—Los Angeles
(Psy.D.) (Cl)
Alliant International University—San Francisco Bay
(Ph.D.) (Cl)
Argosy University, Atlanta (Psy.D.) (Cl)
Argosy University, Chicago (Psy.D.) (Cl)
Argosy University, Hawaii (Psy.D.) (Cl)
Argosy University, Phoenix (Psy.D.) (Cl)
Argosy University, Tampa (Psy.D.) (Cl)
Argosy University, Washington, DC (Psy.D.) (Cl)
Auburn University (Ph.D.) (Cl & Co)
Azusa Pacific University (Psy.D.) (Cl)
Baylor University (Psy.D.) (Cl)
Binghamton University/State University of New York
(Ph.D.) (Cl)
Boston University (Ph.D.) (Cl)
California Institute of Integral Studies (Psy.D.) (Cl)
Fairleigh Dickinson University (Ph.D.) (Cl)
George Fox University (Psy.D.) (Cl)
George Washington University (Ph.D.) (Cl)
Howard University (Ph.D.) (Cl)
Idaho State University (Ph.D.) (Cl)
Indiana University—Bloomington (Ph.D.) (Cl)
Loyola University of Chicago (Ph.D.) (Cl)
Marquette University (Ph.D.) (Co)
New Mexico State University (Ph.D.) (Co)
Nova Southeastern University (Ph.D. & Psy.D.) (Cl)
Ohio University (Ph.D.) (Cl)
Oklahoma State University (Ph.D.) (Cl)
Pacific Graduate School of Psychology/Stanford Uni-
versity Medical School Consortium (Psy.D.) (Cl)
Pepperdine University (Psy.D.) (Cl)
Rutgers, The State University of New Jersey (Ph.D. &
Psy.D.) (Cl)
Southern Illinois University—Carbondale (Ph.D.) (Cl
& Co)
Syracuse University (Ph.D.) (Cl)

Texas A&M University (Ph.D.) (Cl)
Texas Woman's University (Ph.D.) (Co)
The University of Memphis (Ph.D.) (Cl)
The Wright Institute (Psy.D.) (Cl)
Uniformed Services University of Health Sciences
    (Ph.D.) (Cl)
University at Albany/State University of New York
    (Ph.D.) (Cl & Co)
University at Buffalo/State University of New York
    (Ph.D.) (Cl)
University of Arizona (Ph.D.) (Cl)
University of Arkansas (Ph.D.) (Cl)
University of Central Florida (Ph.D.) (Cl)
University of Cincinnati (Ph.D.) (Cl)
University of Connecticut (Ph.D.) (Cl)
University of Florida (Ph.D.) (Co)
University of Hawaii at Manoa (Ph.D.) (Cl)
University of Houston (Ph.D.) (Co)
University of Illinois at Chicago (Ph.D.) (Cl)
University of Kansas—Psychology (Ph.D.) (Cl)
University of La Verne (Psy.D.) (Cl)
University of Maryland—Baltimore County (Ph.D.)
    (Cl)
University of Miami (Ph.D.) (Cl)
University of Minnesota (Ph.D.) (Cl)
University of Mississippi (Ph.D.) (Cl)
University of Missouri—Kansas City (Ph.D.) (Cl)
University of Montana (Ph.D.) (Cl)
University of Nebraska—Lincoln (Ph.D.) (Cl)
University of Nevada—Reno (Ph.D.) (Cl)
University of New Mexico (Ph.D.) (Cl)
University of North Dakota (Ph.D.) (Cl)
University of Pittsburgh (Ph.D.) (Cl)
University of Rochester (Ph.D.) (Cl)
University of South Florida (Ph.D.) (Cl)
University of Southern California (Ph.D.) (Cl)
University of Southern Mississippi (Ph.D.) (Co)
University of Tennessee—Knoxville (Ph.D.) (Cl &
    Co)
University of Texas at Austin (Ph.D.) (Cl)
University of Utah (Ph.D.) (Cl & Co)
University of Vermont (Ph.D.) (Cl)
University of Washington (Ph.D.) (Cl)
University of Wisconsin—Madison (Ph.D.) (Cl)
Vanderbilt University (Ph.D.) (Cl)
Virginia Commonwealth University (Ph.D.) (Cl &
    Co)
Virginia Polytechnic Institute and State University
    (Ph.D.) (Cl)
Wayne State University (Ph.D.) (Cl)
Wright State University (Psy.D.) (Cl)
Yale University (Ph.D.) (Cl)

Suicide/Prevention

Baylor University (Psy.D.) (Cl)
University of Pittsburgh (Ph.D.) (Cl)

Supervision

Binghamton University/State University of New York
    (Ph.D.) (Cl)
Fuller Theological Seminary (Ph.D. & Psy.D.) (Cl)
Georgia State University (Ph.D.) (Cl)
James Madison University (Psy.D.) (Cm)
Marquette University (Ph.D.) (Co)
University of California, Los Angeles (Ph.D.) (Cl)
University of Denver (Psy.D.) (Cl)
University of Georgia (Ph.D.) (Co)
University of Maryland—College Park (Ph.D.) (Co)
University of Massachusetts—Amherst (Ph.D.) (Cl)
University of Northern Colorado (Psy.D.) (Co)

Tourette Syndrome

Rutgers, The State University of New Jersey (Ph.D.) (Cl)
University of Wisconsin—Milwaukee (Ph.D.) (Cl)

Traumatic Brain Injury

Eastern Michigan University (Ph.D.) (Cl)
University of Connecticut (Ph.D.) (Cl)
University of Houston (Ph.D.) (Cl)

Veterans Hospital/Medical Center

Argosy University, Hawaii (Psy.D.) (Cl)
Auburn University (Ph.D.) (Cl)
Boston College (Ph.D.) (Co)
Chicago School of Professional Psychology (Psy.D.)
    (Cl)
Eastern Michigan University (Ph.D.) (Cl)
Iowa State University (Ph.D.) (Co)
Louisiana Tech University (Ph.D.) (Co)
McGill University (Ph.D.) (Co)
Ohio University (Ph.D.) (Cl)
Pacific Graduate School of Psychology (Ph.D.) (Cl)
Pacific Graduate School of Psychology/Stanford Uni-
    versity Medical School Consortium (Psy.D.) (Cl)
Pepperdine University (Psy.D.) (Cl)
Regent University (Psy.D.) (Cl)
Roosevelt University (Psy.D.) (Cl)
Southern Illinois University—Carbondale (Ph.D.)
    (Co)
Tennessee State University (Ph.D.) (Co)
Texas A&M University (Ph.D.) (Co)

Uniformed Services University of Health Sciences
    (Ph.D.) (Cl)
University of Alabama at Tuscaloosa (Ph.D.) (Cl)
University of Denver (Ph.D.) (Co)
University of Houston (Ph.D.) (Co)
University of Illinois at Urbana–Champaign (Ph.D.)
    (Co)
University of Iowa (Ph.D.) (Co)
University of Kentucky (Ph.D.) (Co)
University of Missouri—Columbia (Ph.D.) (Cl & Co)
University of Missouri—Kansas City (Ph.D.) (Cl)
University of New Mexico (Ph.D.) (Cl)
University of Oklahoma (Ph.D.) (Co)
University of Oregon (Ph.D.) (Co)
University of Pittsburgh (Ph.D.) (Cl)
University of Southern Mississippi (Ph.D.) (Co)
University of Texas at Austin (Ph.D.) (Cl)
University of Utah (Ph.D.) (Co)
University of Wisconsin—Milwaukee (Ph.D.) (Co)
Virginia Commonwealth University (Ph.D.) (Co)
West Virginia University (Ph.D.) (Co)

Victim/Violence/Sexual Abuse

Antioch University New England (Psy.D.)
Argosy University, Chicago (Psy.D.) (Cl)
Baylor University (Psy.D.) (Cl)
Boston College (Ph.D.) (Co)
Carlos Albizu University–San Juan Campus (Psy.D.)
    (Cl)
Florida Institute of Technology (Psy.D.) (Cl)
Fuller Theological Seminary (Ph.D. & Psy.D.) (Cl)
George Washington University (Ph.D.) (Cl)
Georgia State University (Ph.D.) (Cl)
Howard University (Ph.D.) (Cl)
Long Island University, C.W. Post Campus (Psy.D.)
    (Cl)
Loyola University of Chicago (Ph.D.) (Cl)
McGill University (Ph.D.) (Co)
Michigan State University (Ph.D.) (Cl)
Northern Illinois University (Ph.D.) (Cl)
Nova Southeastern University (Ph.D. & Psy.D.) (Cl)
Oklahoma State University (Ph.D.) (Co)
Pacific Graduate School of Psychology/Stanford Uni-
    versity Medical School Consortium (Psy.D.) (Cl)
Rutgers, The State University of New Jersey (Psy.D.)
    (Cl)
Southern Illinois University—Carbondale (Ph.D.)
    (Cl)
St. Louis University (Ph.D.) (Cl)
Texas Woman's University (Ph.D.) (Co)
University of Florida (Ph.D.) (Co)
University of Georgia (Ph.D.) (Cl)

University of Houston (Ph.D.) (Cl)
University of Manitoba (Ph.D.) (Cl)
University of Maryland—Baltimore County (Ph.D.)
    (Cl)
University of Miami (Ph.D.) (Cl)
University of Montana (Ph.D.) (Cl)
University of Nevada—Reno (Ph.D.) (Cl)
University of North Dakota (Ph.D.) (Cl)
University of Oregon (Ph.D.) (Co)
University of Pittsburgh (Ph.D.) (Cl)
University of Tennessee—Knoxville (Ph.D.) (Cl & Co)
University of Utah (Ph.D.) (Co)
University of Virginia (Ph.D.) (Cl)

Vocational/Career Development

Florida State University (Ph.D.) (Cm)
Marquette University (Ph.D.) (Co)
New Mexico State University (Ph.D.) (Co)
Southern Illinois University—Carbondale (Ph.D.)
    (Co)
University of Louisville (Ph.D.) (Co)
University of Nebraska—Lincoln (Ph.D.) (Co)
University of Texas Southwestern Medical Center
    (Ph.D.) (Cl)

Weight Management

Loma Linda University (Ph.D.) (Cl)/Loma Linda Uni-
    versity (Psy.D.) (Cl)
University of Florida (Ph.D.) (Cl)
University of Illinois at Chicago (Ph.D.) (Cl)
University of Kansas—Psychology (Ph.D.) (Cl)
University of Pittsburgh (Ph.D.) (Cl)
University of South Florida (Ph.D.) (Cl)
Yeshiva University (Ph.D.) (Cl)

Women's Issues

Indiana University—Purdue University Indianapolis
    (Ph.D.) (Cl)
The Wright Institute (Psy.D.) (Cl)
University of Iowa (Ph.D.) (Co)
University of Missouri—Columbia (Ph.D.) (Co)
University of Utah (Ph.D.) (Co)
Wright State University (Psy.D.) (Cl)

Miscellaneous

achievement and intelligence testing—Long Island
    University, C.W. Post Campus (Psy.D.) (Cl)
advanced traineeships (supervision, leadership)—
    University of Indianapolis (Psy.D.) (Cl)

agencies—Western Michigan University (Ph.D.) (Co)

altruism—The Wright Institute (Psy.D.) (Cl)

Asian clinic—Harvard University (Ph.D.) (Cl)

assertiveness training—Long Island University, C.W. Post Campus (Psy.D.) (Cl)

assisted living placements—University of Colorado at Colorado Springs (Ph.D.) (Cl)

asthma and anxiety—Yeshiva University (Ph.D.) (Cl)

attachment disorders—Miami University (Ph.D.) (Cl) University of Montana (Ph.D.) (Cl)

behavioral cardiology—Duke University (Ph.D.) (Cl)

behavioral dentistry—West Virginia University (Ph.D.) (Cl)

behavioral genetics—University of Oregon (Ph.D.) (Cl)

body dysmorphic disorder clinic—University of Maine (Ph.D.) (Cl)

cardiovascular psychology—Yeshiva University (Ph.D.) (Cl)

center on sickle cell anemia—Howard University (Ph.D.) (Co)

child and adult mental health—University of Victoria (Ph.D.) (Cl)

clinical outcome studies—George Washington University (Psy.D.) (Cl)

co-occurring disorders—Marquette University (Ph.D.) (Co)

couples, family, and group treatment—University of Victoria (Ph.D.) (Cl)

creative and expressive arts—Chicago School of Professional Psychology (Psy.D.) (Cl)

data management systems—Virginia Polytechnic Institute and State University (Ph.D.) (Cl)

diabetes—University of Miami (Ph.D.) (Cl)

diagnostic interviewing—Northwestern University (Ph.D.) (Cl)

disruptive behavior problems (child)—Purdue University (Ph.D.) (Cl)

domestic violence—Carlos Albizu University–San Juan Campus (Ph.D. & Psy.D.) (Cl)

dual diagnoses—University of Hawaii at Manoa (Ph.D.) (Cl)

existential-humanistic psychotherapy—Pepperdine University (Psy.D.) (Cl)

factitious disorder—University of Alabama at Tuscaloosa (Ph.D.) (Cl)

family-school collaboration—Yeshiva University (Psy.D.) (Cm)

foster care—Seattle Pacific University (Ph.D.) (Cl)

gambling—The University of Memphis (Ph.D.) (Cl)

general population—Azusa Pacific University (Psy.D.) (Cl)

genome center—Howard University (Ph.D.) (Co)

hoarding—University of Texas at Austin (Ph.D.) (Cl)

human services center—Florida State University (Ph.D.) (Cm)

human/health care systems change assessment—University of Illinois at Urbana–Champaign (Ph.D.) (Cl)

inner city and rural populations—Chicago School of Professional Psychology (Psy.D.) (Cl)

intake interviews—Indiana University of Pennsylvania (Psy.D.) (Cl)

intensive services for serious emotional disorders—University of Kansas—Child (Ph.D.) (Cl)

internal medicine—Philadelphia College of Osteopathic Medicine (Psy.D.) (Cl)

legal aid clinic—University of Notre Dame (Ph.D.) (Co)

low income—New Mexico State University (Ph.D.) (Co)

military teaching hospitals—Uniformed Services University of Health Sciences (Ph.D.) (Cl)

multidisciplinary assessment—James Madison University (Psy.D.) (Cm)

neuropsychiatric—Rosalind Franklin University of Medicine and Science (Ph.D.) (Cl)

outpatient/inpatient—Biola University (Ph.D.) (Cl)/ Biola University (Psy.D.) (Cl)

palliative care—Kent State University (Ph.D.) (Cl)

person-centered and experiential psychotherapy—Argosy University, Chicago (Psy.D.) (Cl)

person-centered therapy—American University (Ph.D.) (Cl)

pre-/postpartum psychopathology—University of Iowa (Ph.D.) (Cl)

pre-surgery evaluation—University of Missouri—Kansas City (Ph.D.) (Cl)

psycho-education evaluations—The Ohio State University (Ph.D.) (Cl)

psychoeducational (coping skills) training—University of Washington (Ph.D.) (Cl)

psychological center—Stony Brook University/State University of New York (Ph.D.) (Cl)

psychology clinic—University of Missouri—Columbia (Ph.D.) (Co)

public and private community Mental Health Centers agencies—Alliant International University—Los Angeles (Ph.D. & Psy.D.) (Cl)

public policy/advocacy—The Wright Institute (Psy.D.) (Cl) Wright State University (Psy.D.) (Cl)

rational-emotive therapy—University of Utah (Ph.D.) (Cl)

research institutes—St. John's University (Ph.D.) (Cl)

research protocol assessment and prevention—University of Missouri—Columbia (Ph.D.) (Cl)

selective mutism—University of South Florida (Ph.D.) (Cl)

shelters—University of Indianapolis (Psy.D.) (Cl)

shyness program—Pacific Graduate School of Psychology (Ph.D.) (Cl)

social justice—The Wright Institute (Psy.D.) (Cl)

socialization difficulties—Long Island University, C.W. Post Campus (Psy.D.) (Cl)

somatization disorders—Rutgers, The State University of New Jersey (Ph.D.) (Cl)

special education—University of Virginia (Ph.D.) (Cl)

sports psychology—Argosy University, Chicago (Psy.D.) (Cl)

Carlos Albizu University–San Juan Campus (Psy.D.) (Cl)

stroke—University of Houston (Ph.D.) (Cl)

surgical centers—Argosy University, Phoenix (Psy.D.) (Cl)

systems management—Virginia Polytechnic Institute and State University (Ph.D.) (Cl)

telemedicine—University of Kansas—Psychology (Ph.D.) (Cl)

torture survivors—Roosevelt University (Psy.D.) (Cl)

unique military settings—Uniformed Services University of Health Sciences (Ph.D.) (Cl)

women's shelters—University of Missouri—Columbia (Ph.D.) (Co)

A P P E N D I X   G
PROGRAM CONCENTRATIONS AND TRACKS

Adult/Adult Clinical

Alliant International University—San Francisco Bay (Psy.D.) (Cl)
Antioch University New England (Psy.D.)
Argosy University, Atlanta (Psy.D.) (Cl)
Boston University (Ph.D.) (Cl)
Case Western Reserve University (Ph.D.) (Cl)
Catholic University of America (Ph.D.) (Cl)
Duke University (Ph.D.) (Cl)
George Washington University (Psy.D.) (Cl)
Howard University (Ph.D.) (Cl)
Kent State University (Ph.D.) (Cl)
Marquette University (Ph.D.) (Cl)
Miami University (Ph.D.) (Cl)
Northwestern University Medical School (Ph.D.) (Cl)
Pennsylvania State University (Ph.D.) (Cl)
Southern Illinois University—Carbondale (Ph.D.) (Cl)
Spalding University (Psy.D.) (Cl)
Texas A&M University (Ph.D.) (Co)
The Ohio State University (Ph.D.) (Cl)
University of California, Los Angeles (Ph.D.) (Cl)
University of Central Florida (Ph.D.) (Cl)
University of Houston (Ph.D.) (Cl)
University of Indianapolis (Psy.D.) (Cl)
University of Iowa (Ph.D.) (Cl)
University of Massachusetts—Amherst (Ph.D.) (Cl)
University of Miami (Ph.D.) (Cl)
University of Minnesota (Ph.D.) (Cl)
University of Missouri—Columbia (Ph.D.) (Cl)
University of Nebraska—Lincoln (Ph.D.) (Cl)
University of North Carolina at Chapel Hill (Ph.D.) (Cl)

University of Pittsburgh (Ph.D.) (Cl)
University of Southern Mississippi (Ph.D.) (Cl)
University of Utah (Ph.D.) (Cl)
University of Washington (Ph.D.) (Cl)
University of Windsor (Ph.D.) (Cl)
Vanderbilt University (Ph.D.) (Cl)
Wisconsin School of Professional Psychology (Psy.D.) (Cl)
York University (Ph.D.) (Cl)

Aging/Geropsychology/Adult Developmental

Argosy University, Tampa (Psy.D.) (Cl)
Concordia University (Ph.D.) (Cl)
University of Alabama at Birmingham (Ph.D.) (Cl)
University of Alabama at Tuscaloosa (Ph.D.) (Cl)
University of Colorado at Colorado Springs (Ph.D.) (Cl)
University of Delaware (Ph.D.) (Cl)
University of La Verne (Psy.D.) (Cl)
University of North Texas (Ph.D.) (Co)
University of Southern California (Ph.D.) (Cl)
University of Victoria (Ph.D.) (Cl)
West Virginia University (Ph.D.) (Cl)
Xavier University (Psy.D.) (Cl)
Yeshiva University (Psy.D.) (Cl)

Applied Behavioral Analysis

Alliant International University—San Diego (Ph.D. & Psy.D.) (Cl)
Eastern Michigan University (Ph.D.) (Cl)

Assessment

Chestnut Hill College (Psy.D.) (Cl)
George Washington University (Psy.D.) (Cl)
Kent State University (Ph.D.) (Cl)
Seton Hall University (Ph.D.) (Co)
University of Georgia (Ph.D.) (Co)

Child & Family

Catholic University of America (Ph.D.) (Cl)
La Salle University (Psy.D.) (Cl)
Nova Southeastern University (Ph.D. & Psy.D.) (Cl)
Spalding University (Psy.D.) (Cl)
University of Rhode Island (Ph.D.) (Cl)
University of South Carolina (Ph.D.) (Cl)
Vanderbilt University (Ph.D.) (Cl)
Xavier University (Psy.D.) (Cl)

Child/Pediatric

Adler School of Professional Psychology (Psy.D.) (Cl)
Antioch University New England (Psy.D.)
Argosy University, Chicago (Psy.D.) (Cl)
Argosy University, Tampa (Psy.D.) (Cl)
Argosy University, Twin Cities (Psy.D.) (Cl)
Arizona State University (Ph.D.) (Cl)
Auburn University (Ph.D.) (Cl)
Boston University (Ph.D.) (Cl)
Bowling Green State University (Ph.D.) (Cl)
Brigham Young University (Ph.D.) (Cl)
Carlos Albizu University—Miami Campus (Psy.D.)
    (Cl)
Case Western Reserve University (Ph.D.) (Cl)
Chicago School of Professional Psychology (Psy.D.)
    (Cl)
DePaul University (Ph.D.) (Cl)
Duke University (Ph.D.) (Cl)
Forest Institute of Professional Psychology (Psy.D.)
    (Cl)
George Washington University (Psy.D.) (Cl)
Howard University (Ph.D.) (Cl)
Indiana University of Pennsylvania (Psy.D.) (Cl)
Loma Linda University (Ph.D.) (Cl)
Loma Linda University (Psy.D.) (Cl)
Long Island University, C.W. Post Campus (Psy.D.)
    (Cl)
Loyola University of Chicago (Ph.D.) (Cl)
Marquette University (Ph.D.) (Co)
Massachusetts School of Professional Psychology,
    Inc. (Psy.D.) (Cl)
Miami University (Ph.D.) (Cl)
Northwestern University Medical School (Ph.D.) (Cl)

Ohio University (Ph.D.) (Cl)
Oklahoma State University (Ph.D.) (Cl)
Pacific Graduate School of Psychology/Stanford University Medical School Consortium (Psy.D.) (Cl)
Pacific University (Psy.D.) (Cl)
Pennsylvania State University (Ph.D.) (Cl)
Regent University (Psy.D.) (Cl)
Seton Hall University (Ph.D.) (Co)
Simon Fraser University (Ph.D.) (Cl)
Southern Illinois University—Carbondale (Ph.D.)
    (Cl)
St. John's University (Ph.D.) (Cl)
Suffolk University (Ph.D.) (Cl)
Teachers College, Columbia University (Ph.D.) (Cl)
The Ohio State University (Ph.D.) (Cl)
The University of Memphis (Ph.D.) (Cl)
University of Alabama at Birmingham (Ph.D.) (Cl)
University of Alabama at Tuscaloosa (Ph.D.) (Cl)
University of California, Los Angeles (Ph.D.) (Cl)
University of Central Florida (Ph.D.) (Cl)
University of Connecticut (Ph.D.) (Cl)
University of Denver (Ph.D.) (Cl)
University of Denver (Psy.D.) (Cl)
University of Florida (Ph.D.) (Cl)
University of Georgia (Ph.D.) (Cl)
University of Hartford (Psy.D.) (Cl)
University of Indianapolis (Psy.D.) (Cl)
University of Kansas—Child (Ph.D.) (Cl)
University of Kansas—Child (Ph.D.) (Cl)
University of Maine (Ph.D.) (Cl)
University of Maryland—Baltimore County (Ph.D.)
    (Cl)
University of Miami (Ph.D.) (Cl)
University of Miami (Ph.D.) (Cl)
University of Minnesota (Ph.D.) (Cl)
University of Missouri—Columbia (Ph.D.) (Cl)
University of North Carolina at Chapel Hill (Ph.D.)
    (Cl)
University of North Carolina at Chapel Hill (Ph.D.)
    (Cl)
University of North Carolina at Greensboro (Ph.D.)
    (Cl)
University of Pittsburgh (Ph.D.) (Cl)
University of Rochester (Ph.D.) (Cl)
University of South Florida (Ph.D.) (Cl)
University of Southern Mississippi (Ph.D.) (Cl)
University of Texas Southwestern Medical Center
    (Ph.D.) (Cl)
University of Toledo (Ph.D.) (Cl)
University of Utah (Ph.D.) (Cl)
University of Virginia (Ph.D.) (Cl)
University of Washington (Ph.D.) (Cl)
University of Windsor (Ph.D.) (Cl)

Utah State University (Ph.D.) (Cm)
Virginia Commonwealth University (Ph.D.) (Cl)
Wayne State University (Ph.D.) (Cl)
West Virginia University (Ph.D.) (Cl)
Wisconsin School of Professional Psychology (Psy.D.) (Cl)
Yeshiva University (Psy.D.) (Cm)

Cognitive/Cognitive-Behavioral

Concordia University (Ph.D.) (Cl)
Pepperdine University (Psy.D.) (Cl)
University of Toledo (Ph.D.) (Cl)
Yeshiva University (Psy.D.) (Cl)

Community

Arizona State University (Ph.D.) (Cl)
Bowling Green State University (Ph.D.) (Cl)
DePaul University (Ph.D.) (Cl)
Georgia State University (Ph.D.) (Cl)
Pacific Graduate School of Psychology (Ph.D.) (Cl)
Rutgers, The State University of New Jersey (Psy.D.) (Cl)
University of Maryland—Baltimore County (Ph.D.) (Cl)
Wayne State University (Ph.D.) (Cl)

Family/Marriage & Family

Adler School of Professional Psychology (Psy.D.) (Cl)
Alliant International University—Los Angeles (Ph.D. & Psy.D.) (Cl)
Alliant International University—San Diego (Ph.D. & Psy.D.) (Cl)
Alliant International University—San Francisco Bay (Ph.D. & Psy.D.) (Cl)
Argosy University, Atlanta (Psy.D.) (Cl)
Argosy University, Chicago (Psy.D.) (Cl)
Argosy University, Hawaii (Psy.D.) (Cl)
Argosy University, Schaumburg (Psy.D.) (Cl)
Argosy University, Tampa (Psy.D.) (Cl)
Argosy University, Washington, DC (Psy.D.) (Cl)
Azusa Pacific University (Psy.D.) (Cl)
Ball State University (Ph.D.) (Co)
Chestnut Hill College (Psy.D.) (Cl)
Florida Institute of Technology (Psy.D.) (Cl)
Fordham University (Ph.D.) (Cl)
Forest Institute of Professional Psychology (Psy.D.) (Cl)
Fuller Theological Seminary (Ph.D. & Psy.D.) (Cl)
Kent State University (Ph.D.) (Cl)
Loma Linda University (Psy.D.) (Cl)

Long Island University, C.W. Post Campus (Psy.D.) (Cl)
Marquette University (Ph.D.) (Cl)
Massachusetts School of Professional Psychology, Inc. (Psy.D.) (Cl)
Miami University (Ph.D.) (Cl)
Pacific Graduate School of Psychology (Ph.D.) (Cl)
Pepperdine University (Psy.D.) (Cl)
Regent University (Psy.D.) (Cl)
Seton Hall University (Ph.D.) (Co)
Texas Woman's University (Ph.D.) (Co)
University of Alabama at Birmingham (Ph.D.) (Cl)
University of California, Los Angeles (Ph.D.) (Cl)
University of Georgia (Ph.D.) (Co)
University of Houston (Ph.D.) (Cl)
University of Massachusetts—Amherst (Ph.D.) (Cl)
University of Miami (Ph.D.) (Co)
University of Montana (Ph.D.) (Cl)
University of Nebraska—Lincoln (Ph.D.) (Cl)
University of Nebraska—Lincoln (Ph.D.) (Co)
University of North Texas (Ph.D.) (Co)
University of Oklahoma (Ph.D.) (Co)
University of Southern California (Ph.D.) (Cl)
University of Toledo (Ph.D.) (Cl)
University of Virginia (Ph.D.) (Cl)

Forensic/Psychology & Law

Alliant International University—Fresno (Ph.D. & Psy.D.) (Cl)
Alliant International University—San Diego (Ph.D. & Psy.D.) (Cl)
Alliant International University—San Francisco Bay (Psy.D.) (Cl)
Argosy University, Chicago (Psy.D.) (Cl)
Argosy University, Schaumburg (Psy.D.) (Cl)
Argosy University, Twin Cities (Psy.D.) (Cl)
Argosy University, Washington, DC (Psy.D.) (Cl)
Azusa Pacific University (Psy.D.) (Cl)
Carlos Albizu University—Miami Campus (Psy.D.) (Cl)
Chicago School of Professional Psychology (Psy.D.) (Cl)
City University of New York at City College (Ph.D.) (Cl)
Drexel University (Ph.D.) (Cl)
Florida Institute of Technology (Psy.D.) (Cl)
Fordham University (Ph.D.) (Cl)
Forest Institute of Professional Psychology (Psy.D.) (Cl)
Loma Linda University (Psy.D.) (Cl)
Massachusetts School of Professional Psychology, Inc. (Psy.D.) (Cl)
Nova Southeastern University (Ph.D. & Psy.D.) (Cl)

Pacific Graduate School of Psychology (Ph.D.) (Cl)
Pacific Graduate School of Psychology (Ph.D.) (Cl)
Pacific University (Psy.D.) (Cl)
Pepperdine University (Psy.D.) (Cl)
Sam Houston State University (Ph.D.) (Cl)
Simon Fraser University (Ph.D.) (Cl)
Spalding University (Psy.D.) (Cl)
University of Alabama at Tuscaloosa (Ph.D.) (Cl)
University of Denver (Psy.D.) (Cl)
University of La Verne (Psy.D.) (Cl)
University of Nebraska—Lincoln (Ph.D.) (Cl)
University of Virginia (Ph.D.) (Cl)

Gender Studies

Alliant International University—San Francisco Bay
    (Ph.D. & Psy.D.) (Cl)
City University of New York at City College (Ph.D.)
    (Cl)
Texas Woman's University (Ph.D.) (Co)
University of Missouri—St. Louis (Ph.D.) (Cl)
University of Nebraska—Lincoln (Ph.D.) (Co)

Generalist

Carlos Albizu University—Miami Campus (Psy.D.)
    (Cl)
Indiana State University (Psy.D.) (Cl)
Kent State University (Ph.D.) (Cl)
La Salle University (Psy.D.) (Cl)
Suffolk University (Ph.D.) (Cl)
University of Kansas—Psychology (Ph.D.) (Cl)
University of Maine (Ph.D.) (Cl)

Health/Behavioral Medicine

Alliant International University—Fresno (Ph.D. &
    Psy.D.) (Cl)
Alliant International University—Los Angeles (Ph.D.
    & Psy.D.) (Cl)
Alliant International University—San Diego (Ph.D. &
    Psy.D.) (Cl)
Alliant International University—San Francisco Bay
    (Ph.D. & Psy.D.) (Cl)
Antioch University New England (Psy.D.)
Argosy University, Atlanta (Psy.D.) (Cl)
Argosy University, Chicago (Psy.D.) (Cl)
Argosy University, Hawaii (Psy.D.) (Cl)
Argosy University, Schaumburg (Psy.D.) (Cl)
Argosy University, Twin Cities (Psy.D.) (Cl)
Argosy University, Washington, DC (Psy.D.) (Cl)
Arizona State University (Ph.D.) (Cl)

Ball State University (Ph.D.) (Co)
Bowling Green State University (Ph.D.) (Cl)
Chicago School of Professional Psychology (Psy.D.)
    (Cl)
City University of New York at City College (Ph.D.)
    (Cl)
Concordia University (Ph.D.) (Cl)
Drexel University (Ph.D.) (Cl)
Duke University (Ph.D.) (Cl)
Florida Institute of Technology (Psy.D.) (Cl)
Fordham University (Ph.D.) (Cl)
Kent State University (Ph.D.) (Cl)
La Salle University (Psy.D.) (Cl)
Loma Linda University (Ph.D. & Psy.D.) (Cl)
Massachusetts School of Professional Psychology,
    Inc. (Psy.D.) (Cl)
McGill University (Ph.D.) (Co)
New Mexico State University (Ph.D.) (Co)
Nova Southeastern University (Ph.D. & Psy.D.) (Cl)
Ohio University (Ph.D.) (Cl)
Oklahoma State University (Ph.D.) (Cl)
Our Lady of the Lake University (Psy.D.) (Co)
Pacific Graduate School of Psychology (Ph.D.) (Cl)
Pacific University (Psy.D.) (Cl)
Ponce School of Medicine (Psy.D.) (Cl)
Regent University (Psy.D.) (Cl)
Rosalind Franklin University of Medicine and Sci-
    ence (Ph.D.) (Cl)
San Diego State University/University of California,
    San Diego (Ph.D.) (Cl)
Spalding University (Psy.D.) (Cl)
Syracuse University (Ph.D.) (Cl)
Texas A&M University (Ph.D.) (Co)
The Ohio State University (Ph.D.) (Cl)
The University of Memphis (Ph.D.) (Cl)
Uniformed Services University of Health Sciences
    (Ph.D.) (Cl)
University of Alabama at Tuscaloosa (Ph.D.) (Cl)
University of California, Los Angeles (Ph.D.) (Cl)
University of Cincinnati (Ph.D.) (Cl)
University of Connecticut (Ph.D.) (Cl)
University of Florida (Ph.D.) (Cl)
University of Indianapolis (Psy.D.) (Cl)
University of Iowa (Ph.D.) (Cl)
University of Kansas—Psychology (Ph.D.) (Cl)
University of Kentucky (Ph.D.) (Cl)
University of Maryland—Baltimore County (Ph.D.)
    (Cl)
University of Miami (Ph.D.) (Cl)
University of Miami (Ph.D.) (Co)
University of Missouri—Kansas City (Ph.D.) (Cl)
University of Missouri—St. Louis (Ph.D.) (Cl)

University of North Texas and University of North
    Texas Health Sciences Center (Consortium)
    (Ph.D.) (Cl)
University of Pittsburgh (Ph.D.) (Cl)
University of Rhode Island (Ph.D.) (Cl)
University of South Florida (Ph.D.) (Cl)
University of Texas Southwestern Medical Center
    (Ph.D.) (Cl)
University of Utah (Ph.D.) (Cl)
Utah State University (Ph.D.) (Cm)
Virginia Commonwealth University (Ph.D.) (Cl)
Virginia Commonwealth University (Ph.D.) (Co)
Wayne State University (Ph.D.) (Cl)
West Virginia University (Ph.D.) (Cl)
York University (Ph.D.) (Cl)

Multicultural/Cross-Cultural/Diversity

Alliant International University—Los Angeles (Ph.D.
    & Psy.D.) (Cl)
Alliant International University—San Diego (Ph.D. &
    Psy.D.) (Cl)
Alliant International University—San Francisco Bay
    (Ph.D. & Psy.D.) (Cl)
Argosy University, Chicago (Psy.D.) (Cl)
Argosy University, Hawaii (Psy.D.) (Cl)
Argosy University, Schaumburg (Psy.D.) (Cl)
Argosy University, Washington, DC (Psy.D.) (Cl)
Ball State University (Ph.D.) (Co)
Chicago School of Professional Psychology (Psy.D.)
    (Cl)
Immaculata University (Psy.D.) (Cl)
Loma Linda University (Ph.D.) (Cl)
Loma Linda University (Psy.D.) (Cl)
Marquette University (Ph.D.) (Co)
McGill University (Ph.D.) (Co)
New Mexico State University (Ph.D.) (Co)
Nova Southeastern University (Ph.D. & Psy.D.) (Cl)
Pacific University (Psy.D.) (Cl)
Pepperdine University (Psy.D.) (Cl)
Seton Hall University (Ph.D.) (Co)
Texas A&M University (Ph.D.) (Co)
Texas A&M University (Ph.D.) (Co)
The University of Memphis (Ph.D.) (Co)
The University of Memphis (Ph.D.) (Co)
University of California, Los Angeles (Ph.D.) (Cl)
University of La Verne (Psy.D.) (Cl)
University of Miami (Ph.D.) (Co)
University of Missouri—Columbia (Ph.D.) (Co)
University of Nebraska—Lincoln (Ph.D.) (Co)
University of Rhode Island (Ph.D.) (Cl)
Utah State University (Ph.D.) (Cm)

Neuropsychology

Adler School of Professional Psychology (Psy.D.) (Cl)
Argosy University, Atlanta (Psy.D.) (Cl)
Argosy University, Chicago (Psy.D.) (Cl)
Argosy University, Schaumburg (Psy.D.) (Cl)
Argosy University, Tampa (Psy.D.) (Cl)
Boston University (Ph.D.) (Cl)
Brigham Young University (Ph.D.) (Cl)
Carlos Albizu University—Miami Campus (Psy.D.)
    (Cl)
Concordia University (Ph.D.) (Cl)
Drexel University (Ph.D.) (Cl)
Florida Institute of Technology (Psy.D.) (Cl)
Forest Institute of Professional Psychology (Psy.D.)
    (Cl)
Georgia State University (Ph.D.) (Cl)
Immaculata University (Psy.D.) (Cl)
Loma Linda University (Ph.D. & Psy.D.) (Cl)
Loyola University of Chicago (Ph.D.) (Cl)
Northwestern University Medical School (Ph.D.) (Cl)
Nova Southeastern University (Ph.D. & Psy.D.) (Cl)
Pacific Graduate School of Psychology (Ph.D.) (Cl)
Pacific University (Psy.D.) (Cl)
Ponce School of Medicine (Psy.D.) (Cl)
Rosalind Franklin University of Medicine and Sci-
    ence (Ph.D.) (Cl)
San Diego State University/University of California,
    San Diego (Ph.D.) (Cl)
Seton Hall University (Ph.D.) (Co)
Simon Fraser University (Ph.D.) (Cl)
Suffolk University (Ph.D.) (Cl)
University of Alabama at Birmingham (Ph.D.) (Cl)
University of Cincinnati (Ph.D.) (Cl)
University of Colorado at Boulder (Ph.D.) (Cl)
University of Connecticut (Ph.D.) (Cl)
University of Florida (Ph.D.) (Cl)
University of Florida (Ph.D.) (Cl)
University of Florida (Ph.D.) (Cl)
University of Georgia (Ph.D.) (Cl)
University of Houston (Ph.D.) (Cl)
University of Iowa (Ph.D.) (Cl)
University of Kentucky (Ph.D.) (Cl)
University of Montana (Ph.D.) (Cl)
University of Ottawa (Ph.D.) (Cl)
University of Rhode Island (Ph.D.) (Cl)
University of South Florida (Ph.D.) (Cl)
University of Texas Southwestern Medical Center
    (Ph.D.) (Cl)
University of Utah (Ph.D.) (Cl)
University of Victoria (Ph.D.) (Cl)
University of Windsor (Ph.D.) (Cl)

Virginia Consortium Program in Clinical Psychology (Psy.D.) (Cl)
Wayne State University (Ph.D.) (Cl)
Widener University (Psy.D.) (Cl)
York University (Ph.D.) (Cl)

Organizational/Consulting

Argosy University, Chicago (Psy.D.) (Cl)
Chicago School of Professional Psychology (Psy.D.) (Cl)
Pacific University (Psy.D.) (Cl)

Psychoanalytic/Psychodynamic Therapy

Alliant International University—San Diego (Ph.D. & Psy.D.) (Cl)
Argosy University, Chicago (Psy.D.) (Cl)
Immaculata University (Psy.D.) (Cl)
McGill University (Ph.D.) (Co)
Nova Southeastern University (Ph.D.) (Cl)
Nova Southeastern University (Psy.D.) (Cl)
Pepperdine University (Psy.D.) (Cl)
The University of Memphis (Ph.D.) (Cl)
University of Toledo (Ph.D.) (Cl)
Yeshiva University (Psy.D.) (Cl)

School/Educational

Florida State University (Ph.D.) (Cm)
Miami University (Ph.D.) (Cl)
Northeastern University (Ph.D.) (Cm)
University of California, Santa Barbara (Ph.D.) (Cm)
University of Virginia (Ph.D.) (Cl)
Widener University (Psy.D.) (Cl)

Sports Psychology

La Salle University (Psy.D.) (Cl)
Rutgers, The State University of New Jersey (Psy.D.) (Cl)
University of Denver (Psy.D.) (Cl)
University of Missouri—Columbia (Ph.D.) (Co)
University of North Texas (Ph.D.) (Co)

Substance Abuse/Addiction

Adler School of Professional Psychology (Psy.D.) (Cl)
Immaculata University (Psy.D.) (Cl)
Marquette University (Ph.D.) (Co)
Syracuse University (Ph.D.) (Cl)
University of South Florida (Ph.D.) (Cl)

Supervision/Clinical Supervision

McGill University (Ph.D.) (Co)
New Mexico State University (Ph.D.) (Co)
University of Georgia (Ph.D.) (Co)

Trauma/Disaster

Argosy University, Twin Cities (Psy.D.) (Cl)
Miami University (Ph.D.) (Cl)
Nova Southeastern University (Ph.D. & Psy.D.) (Cl)
University of Denver (Psy.D.) (Cl)
University of Missouri—St. Louis (Ph.D.) (Cl)
University of South Dakota (Ph.D.) (Cl)

Miscellaneous

ADHD specialization—University of North Carolina at Greensboro (Ph.D.) (Cl)
Adlerian psychotherapy—Adler School of Professional Psychology (Psy.D.) (Cl)
applied methodology—University of Rhode Island (Ph.D.) (Cl)
behavior analysis—West Virginia University (Ph.D.) (Cl)
behavioral genetics—University of Colorado at Boulder (Ph.D.) (Cl)
biofeedback—Widener University (Psy.D.) (Cl)
career development—University of Missouri—Columbia (Ph.D.) (Co)
client-centered/experiential psychotherapies—Argosy University, Chicago (Psy.D.) (Cl)
close relationships—Stony Brook University/State University of New York (Ph.D.) (Cl)
combined rehab/clinical—Illinois Institute of Technology (Ph.D.) (Cl)
consulting psychology—Regent University (Psy.D.) (Cl)
ecosystemic clinical child psychology—Alliant International University—Fresno (Ph.D.) (Cl)
experimental psychopathology—San Diego State University/
University of California, San Diego (Ph.D.) (Cl)
group psychotherapy—Adler School of Professional Psychology (Psy.D.) (Cl)
HIV/AIDS—Syracuse University (Ph.D.) (Cl)
human factors—University of Cincinnati (Ph.D.) (Cl)
individuals with severe mental illness—Xavier University (Psy.D.) (Cl)
integrated behavioral health focus—University of Wyoming (Ph.D.) (Cl)
integrative therapy—Immaculata University (Psy.D.) (Cl)

leadership psychology—Fuller Theological Seminary (Psy.D.) (Cl)

mental health counseling—Yeshiva University (Psy.D.) (Cl)

mental health research—Texas A&M University (Ph.D.) (Co)

military clinical psychology—Uniformed Services University of Health Sciences (Ph.D.) (Cl)

personality psychology—University of Iowa (Ph.D.) (Cl)

personality/psychopathology—University of South Florida (Ph.D.) (Cl)

preparing future faculty—University of Georgia (Ph.D.) (Co)

primary care psychology—Adler School of Professional Psychology (Psy.D.) (Cl)

psychological testing—Immaculata University (Psy.D.) (Cl)

psychology & spirituality—Argosy University, Chicago (Psy.D.) (Cl)

psychopathology—Rosalind Franklin University of Medicine and Science (Ph.D.) (Cl)

religion—Regent University (Psy.D.) (Cl)

scientifically validated psychosocial interventions—University of Wisconsin—Milwaukee (Ph.D.) (Cl)

scientist-practitioner training model—The New School (Ph.D.) (Cl)

serious and persistent mental disorders—Long Island University, C.W. Post Campus (Psy.D.) (Cl)

sexuality—Texas Woman's University (Ph.D.) (Co)

social justice—Ball State University (Ph.D.) (Co)

spirituality—Fordham University (Ph.D.) (Cl)

statistics minor—University of Missouri—Columbia (Ph.D.) (Co)

teaching minor—University of Missouri—Columbia (Ph.D.) (Co)

vocational psychology—Ball State University (Ph.D.) (Co)

REFERENCES

Accredited doctoral programs in professional psychology: 2010. (2010). *American Psychologist, 65,* 894–908.

Actkinson, T. R. (2000, Winter). Master's and myth. *Eye on Psi Chi, 4,* 19–25.

American Psychological Association. (1986). *Careers in psychology.* Washington, DC: Author.

American Psychological Association. (2002). Ethical principles of psychologists and code of conduct. *American Psychologist, 57,* 1060–1073.

American Psychological Association Research Office. (2003). *2001 doctorate employment survey.* Washington, DC: Author.

American Psychological Association. (2006). *The APAGS resource guide for LGBT students in psychology.* Washington, DC: Author.

American Psychological Association. (2011). *2011 graduate study in psychology.* Washington, DC: Author.

American Psychological Association Center for Workforce Studies. (2009). *2007 Doctorate employment survey.* Washington, DC: Author.

Anderson, N. B. (2009). Rebalancing the internship imbalance. *Monitor on Psychology, 40*(6), 9.

Anderson, N., & Shackleton, V. (1990). Decision making in the graduate selection interview: A field study. *Journal of Occupational Psychology, 63,* 63–76.

APA Practice Directorate. (2005). *Summary of psychology licensing or certification laws.* Washington, DC: Author.

Appleby, D. C., & Appleby, K. M. (2003, August). *The "kisses of death" in the graduate school application process.* Poster presented at the annual convention of the American Psychological Association, Toronto.

Appleby, D., Keenan, J., & Mauer, B. (1999, Spring).

Applicant characteristics valued by graduate programs in psychology. *Eye on Psi Chi, 3,* 39.

Asher, D. (2008). *Graduate admissions essays: How to write your way into the graduate program of your choice* (3rd ed.). Berkeley, CA: Ten Speed Press.

Association of American Medical Colleges Staff. (2009). *Medical school admission requirements (MSAR) 2009-20010: The most authoritative guide to U.S. and Canadian medical schools* (59th ed.). Association of American Medical Colleges.

Association of State and Provincial Psychology Boards and National Register of Health Service Providers in Psychology. (2005). *Doctoral psychology programs meeting designation criteria.* Washington, DC: National Register.

Astin, A. W., Green, K. C., & Korn, W. S. (1987). *The American freshman: Twenty-year trends 1966–85.* University of California, Cooperative Institutional Research Program, American Council on Education.

Ault, R. L. (1993). To waive or not to waive? Students' misconceptions about the confidentiality choice for letters of recommendation. *Teaching of Psychology, 20,* 44–45.

Baker, T. B., McFall, R. M., & Shoham, V. (2008). Current status and future prospects of clinical psychology: Toward a scientifically principled approach to mental and behavioral health care. *Perspectives on Psychological Science in the Public Interest, 9*(2), 67–103.

Barron, J. (1986). Search for survival and identity—and power. *The Clinical Psychologist, 39,* 61–63.

Bartsch, R. A., Warren, T. D., Sharp, A. D., & Green, M. A. (2003). Assessment of psychology graduate program information on the Web. *Teaching of Psychology, 30,* 167–170.

Bechtoldt, H., Norcross, J. C., Wyckoff, L. A., Pokrywa, M. L., & Campbell, L. F. (2001). Theoretical orientations and employment settings of clinical and counseling psychologists: A comparative study. *The Clinical Psychologist, 54*(1), 3–6.

Bendersky, K., Isaac, W. L., Stover, J. H., & Zook, J. M. (2008). Psychology students and online graduate programs: A need to reexamine undergraduate advisement. *Teaching of Psychology, 35*, 38–41.

Bernal, M. E., Sirolli, A. A., Weisser, S. K., Ruiz, J. A., Chamberlain, V. J., & Knight, G. P. (1999). Relevance of multicultural training to students' applications to clinical psychology programs. *Cultural Diversity and Ethnic Minority Psychology, 5*, 43–55.

Bernstein, B. L., & Kerr, B. (1993). Counseling psychology and the scientist–practitioner model: Implementation and implications. *The Counseling Psychologist, 21*, 136–151.

Bersoff, D. N., Goodman-Delahunty, J., Grisso, J. T., Hans, V. P., Poythress, N. G., & Roesch, R. G. (1997). Training in law and psychology: Models from the Villanova Conference. *American Psychologist, 52*, 1301–1310.

Beutler, L. E., & Fisher, D. (1994). Combined specialty training in counseling, clinical, and school psychology: An idea whose time has returned. *Professional Psychology: Research and Practice, 25*, 62–69.

Biaggio, M., Orchard, S., Larson, J., Petrino, K., & Mihara, R. (2003). Guidelines for gay/lesbian/bisexual-affirmative educational practices in graduate psychology programs. *Professional Psychology: Research & Practice, 34*, 548–554.

Boitano, J. J. (1999, August). *Graduate training in neuroscience.* Paper presented at the 107th annual convention of the American Psychological Association, Boston, MA.

Bolles, R. N. (2006). *What color is your parachute? A practical manual for job-hunters and career-changes.* Berkeley, CA: Ten Speed Press.

Bonifzi, D. Z., Crespy, S. D., & Reiker, P. (1997). Value of a master's degree for gaining admission to doctoral programs in psychology. *Teaching of Psychology, 24*, 176–182.

Bottoms, B. L., & Nysse, K. L. (1999, Fall). Applying to graduate school: Writing a compelling personal statement. *Eye on Psi Chi, 4*, 20–22.

Boudreau, R. A., Killip, S. M., MacInnis, S. H., Milloy, D. G., & Rogers, T. B. (1983). An evaluation of Graduate Record Examinations as predictors of graduate success in a Canadian context. *Canadian Psychology, 24*, 191–199.

Brems, C., & Johnson, M. E. (1997). Comparison of recent graduates of clinical versus counseling psychology programs. *Journal of Psychology, 131*, 91–99.

Briihl, D. S., & Wasieleski, D. T. (2004). A survey of master's-level psychology programs: Admissions criteria and program policies. *Teaching of Psychology, 31*, 252–256.

Briihl, D. S., & Wasieleski, D. T. (2007). The GRE Analytical Writing Test: Description and utilization. *Teaching of Psychology, 34*, 191–193.

Bullock, M. (1997, July/August). Federal funding is available for psychology graduate students. *Psychological Science Agenda*, p. 4.

Burgess, D., Keeley, J., & Blashfield, R. (2008). Full disclosure data on clinical psychology doctorate programs. *Training and Education in Professional Psychology, 2*, 117–122.

Burke, K. L., Sachs, M. L., Fry, S. J., & Schweighardt, S. L. (2008). *Directory of graduate programs in applied sport psychology* (9th ed.). Morgantown, WV: Fitness Information Technology.

Buskist, W., & Mixon, A. (1998). *Master's programs in psychology and counseling psychology.* Needham Heights, MA: Allyn & Bacon.

Callahan, J. L., Collins, Jr., F. L., & Klonoff, E. A. (2010). An examination of applicant characteristics of successfully matched interns: Is the glass half empty or half full or leaking miserably? *Journal of Clinical Psychology, 66*, 1–16.

Cashin, J. R., & Landrum, R. E. (1991). Undergraduate students' perceptions of graduate admissions in psychology. *Psychological Reports, 69*, 1107–1110.

Castle, P. H., & Norcross, J. C. (2002, August). *Empirical data and integrative perspectives on combined doctoral programs.* Paper presented at the 110th annual convention of the American Psychological Association, Chicago, IL.

Ceci, S. J., & Peters, D. (1984). Letters of reference: A naturalistic study of the effects of confidentiality. *American Psychologist, 39*, 29–31.

Chapman, C. P., & Lane, H. C. (1997). Perceptions about the use of letters of recommendation. *The Advisor, 17*, 31–36.

Chernyshenko, O. S., & Ones, D. S. (1999). How selective are psychology graduate programs? The effect of the selection ratio on GRE score validity. *Educational and Psychological Measurement, 59*, 951–961.

CIRP (Cooperative Institutional Research Program). (2005). *The American freshman: National norms for Fall 2005.* Los Angeles, CA: Higher Education Research Institute.

Cobb, H. C., Reeve, R. E., Shealy, C. N., Norcross, J. C., et al. (2004). Overlap among clinical, counseling, and school psychology: Implications for the profession and combined-integrated training. *Journal of Clinical Psychology, 60*, 939–956.

Collins, L. H. (2001, Winter). Does research experience make a significant difference in graduate admissions? *Eye on Psi Chi, 5*, 26–28.

Conway, J. B. (1988). Differences among clinical psychologists: Scientists, practitioners, and scientist–

415

practitioners. *Professional Psychology: Research and Practice, 19*, 642–655.

Coyle, S. L., & Bae, Y. (1987). *Summary report 1986: Doctorate recipients from United States universities*. Washington, DC: National Academy Press.

Crowe, M. B., Grogan, J. M., Jacobs, R. R., Lindsay, C. A., & Mack, M. M. (1985). Delineation of the roles of clinical psychology: A survey of practice in psychology. *Professional Psychology: Research and Practice, 16*, 124–137.

Dattilio, F. (1992). Doctoral studies for master's level licensed psychologists. *The Pennsylvania Psychologist Quarterly, 52*(2), 7, 11.

Dollinger, S. J. (1989). Predictive validity of the Graduate Record Examination in a clinical psychology program. *Professional Psychology: Research and Practice, 20*, 56–58.

Drummond, F., Rodolfa, E., & Smith, D. (1981). A survey of APA- and non-APA-approved internship programs. *American Psychologist, 36*, 411–414.

Eddy, B., Lloyd, P. J., & Lubin, B. (1987). Enhancing the application to doctoral professional programs: Suggestions from a national survey. *Teaching of Psychology, 14*, 160–163.

Educational Testing Service (ETS). (1984). *Analysis of score change patterns of examinees repeating the GRE General Test*. Princeton, NJ: Educational Testing Service.

Educational Testing Service (ETS). (1995). *Practicing to take the GRE Psychology Test* (3rd ed.). Princeton, NJ: Educational Testing Service.

Educational Testing Service (ETS). (2007, August). *The GRE(R) Analytical Writing measure: An asset in admissions*. http://www.ets.org/Media/Tests/GRE/pdf/gre_aw_an_asset.pdf

Elam, C. L., et al. (1998). Letters of recommendation: Medical school admission committee members' recommendations. *The Advisor, 18*, 4–6.

Farry, J., Norcross, J. C., Mayne, T. J., & Sayette, M. A. (1995, August). *Acceptance rates and financial aid in clinical psychology: An update*. Poster presented at the 103rd annual convention of the American Psychological Association, New York, NY.

Fauber, R. L. (2006). Graduate admissions in clinical psychology: Observations on the present and thoughts on the future. *Clinical Psychology: Science and Practice, 13*, 227–234.

Fennell, K., & Kohout, J. (2002). *Characteristics of graduate departments of psychology: 1999–2000*. Washington, DC: American Psychological Association.

Ferrari, J. R., & Hemovich, V. B. (2004). Student-based psychology journals: Perceptions by graduate program directors. *Teaching of Psychology, 31*, 272–275.

Fitzgerald, L. F., & Osipow, S. H. (1986). An occupational analysis of counseling psychology. How special is the specialty? *American Psychologist, 41*, 535–544.

Fretz, B. R. (1976, Spring). Finding careers with a bachelor's degree in psychology. *Psi Chi Newsletter, 2*, 5–13.

Fretz, B. R., & Stang, D. J. (1980). *Preparing for graduate study in psychology: Not for seniors only!* Washington, DC: American Psychological Association.

Gaddy, C. D., Charlot-Swilley, D., Nelson, P. D., & Reich, J. N. (1995). Selected outcomes of accredited programs. *Professional Psychology: Research and Practice, 26*, 507–513.

Gartner, J. D. (1986). Antireligious prejudice in admissions to doctoral programs in clinical psychology. *Professional Psychology: Research and Practice, 17*, 473–475.

Gehlman, S., Wicherski, M., & Kohout, J. (1995). *Characteristics of graduate departments of psychology: 1993–1994*. Washington, DC: American Psychological Association Research Office.

Goldberg, E. L., & Alliger, G. M. (1992). Assessing the validity of the GRE for students in psychology: A validity generalization approach. *Educational and Psychological Measurement, 52*, 1019–1027.

Golding, J. M., Lang, K., Eymard, L. A., & Shadish, W. R. (1988). The buck stops here: A survey of the financial status of Ph.D. graduate students in psychology, 1966–1987. *American Psychologist, 43*, 1089–1091.

Goliszek, A. (2000). *The complete medical school preparation and admissions guide*. New York: Healthnet Press.

Goodyear, R. K., Murdock, N., Lichtenberg, J. W., McPherson, R., Koetting, K., & Petren, S. (2008). Stability and change in counseling psychologists' identities, roles, functions, and career satisfactions across 15 years. *The Counseling Psychologist, 36*, 220–249.

Gordon, R. A. (1990). Research productivity in master's-level psychology programs. *Professional Psychology: Research and Practice, 21*, 33–36.

Graduate Record Examinations. (2007). *2007–2008 GRE information and registration bulletin*. Princeton, NJ: Educational Testing Service.

Graham, J. M., & Kim, Y. (2011). Predictors of doctoral success in professional psychology: Characteristics of students, programs, and universities. *Journal of Clinical Psychology, 67*, 350–354.

Grote, C. L., Robiner, W. N., & Haut, A. (2001). Disclosure of negative information in letters of recommendation: Writers' intentions and readers' experiences. *Professional Psychology: Research and Practice, 32*, 655–661.

Halgin, R. P. (1986). Advising undergraduates who wish to become clinicians. *Teaching of Psychology, 13*, 7–12.

Hall, J. E., Wexelbaum, S. F., & Boucher, A. P. (2007). Looking ahead: Planning for a successful career as a psychologist. *Eye on Psi Chi, 12*(2), 10–12.

Hasan, N. T., Fouad, N. A., & Williams-Nickelson, C. (Eds.). (2008). *Studying psychology in the United*

States: Expert guidance for international students. Washington, DC: American Psychological Association.

Hayes, S. C., & Hayes, L. J. (1989). Writing your vitae. *APS Observor, 2*(3), 15–17.

Heppner, P. P., & Downing, N. E. (1982). Job interviewing for new psychologists: Riding the emotional rollercoaster. *Professional Psychology, 13,* 334–341.

Hersh, J. B., & Poey, K. (1984). A proposed interviewing guide for intern applicants. *Professional Psychology, 15,* 3–5.

Hershey, J. M., Kopplin, D. A., & Cornell, J. E. (1991). Doctors of psychology: Their career experiences and attitudes toward degree and training. *Professional Psychology: Research and Practice, 22,* 351–356.

Hines, D. (1985). Admissions criteria for ranking master's-level applicants to clinical doctoral programs. *Teaching of Psychology, 13,* 64–66.

Holmes, C. B., & Beishline, M. J. (1996, August). *Doctoral admission rates for students with GRE scores below 1000.* Poster presented at the 104th annual meeting of the American Psychological Association, Toronto.

Huss, M. T., Randall, B. A., Patry, M., Davis, S. F., & Hansen, D. J. (2002). Factors influencing self-rated preparedness for graduate school: A survey of graduate schools. *Teaching of Psychology, 29,* 275–281.

Ilardi, S. S., Rodriguez-Hanley, A., Roberts, M. G., & Seigel, J. (2000). On the origins of clinical psychology faculty: Who is training the trainers? *Clinical Psychology: Science and Practice, 7,* 346–354.

Ingram, R. E. (1983). The GRE in the graduate admissions process: Is how it is used justified by the evidence of its validity? *Professional Psychology: Research and Practice, 14,* 711–714.

Jacob, M. C. (1987). Managing the internship application experience: Advice from an exhausted but content survivor. *The Counseling Psychologist, 15,* 146–155.

Jensen, A. R. (1998). *The g factor: The science of mental ability.* Westport, CT: Praeger.

Kaiser, J. C., Kaiser, A. J., Richardson, N. J., & Fox, E. J. (2007). Undergraduate research experiences: "Are all research experiences rated equally?" *Eye on Psi Chi, 12(2),* 22–24.

Kalat, J. W., & Matlin, M. W. (2000). The GRE Psychology Test: A useful but poorly understood test. *Teaching of Psychology, 27,* 24–27.

Keith-Spiegel, P. (1991). *The complete guide to graduate school admission.* Hillsdale, NJ: Lawrence Erlbaum.

Keith-Spiegel, P., Tabachnick, B. G., & Spiegel, G. B. (1994). When demand exceeds supply: Second-order criteria used by graduate school selection committees. *Teaching of Psychology, 21,* 79–81.

Keith-Spiegel, P., & Wiederman, M. W. (2000). *The complete guide to graduate school admission* (2nd ed.). Mahwah, NJ: Lawrence Erlbaum.

Keller, J. W., Beam, K. J., Maier, K. A., & Pietrowski, C. (1995, April). *Research or clinical experience: What doctoral applicants need to know.* Paper presented at the annual meeting of the Southeastern Psychological Association, Savannah, GA.

Kellogg, R. T. (2003). *GRE Psychology with CD-ROM – The best test prep for the GRE.* Piscataway, NJ: Research & Education Association.

Khubchandani, A. (2002). To disclose or not to disclose: That is the question. *The APAGS Newsletter, 14*(4), 24–26.

King, D. W., Beehr, T. A., & King, L. A. (1986). Doctoral student selection in one professional psychology program. *Journal of Clinical Psychology, 42,* 399–407.

Kluger, J. (2002, June 10). Pumping up your past. *Time,* p. 45.

Kohout, J. L., & Wicherski, M. M. (1992). *1991 salaries in psychology.* Washington, DC: American Psychological Association.

Kohout, J., & Wicherski, M. (1993). *1991–1992 characteristics of graduate departments of psychology.* Washington, DC: American Psychological Association.

Kohout, J. & Wicherski, M. (1999). *1997 doctorate employment survey.* Washington, DC: American Psychological Association Research Office.

Kopala, M., Keitel, M. A., Suzuki, L. A., Alexander, C. M., Ponterotto, J. G., Reynolds, A. L., & Hennessy, J. J. (1995). Doctoral admissions in counseling psychology at Fordham University. *Teaching of Psychology, 22,* 133–135.

Korn, J. H. (1984). New odds on acceptance into Ph.D. programs in psychology. *American Psychologist, 39,* 179–180.

Kuncel, N. R., Hezlett, S. A., & Ones, D. S. (2001). A comprehensive meta-analysis of the predictive validity of the graduate record examinations: Implications for graduate student selection and performance. *Psychological Bulletin, 127,* 162–181.

Kupfersmid, J., & Fiola, M. (1991). Comparison of EPPP scores among graduates of varying psychology programs. *American Psychologist, 46,* 534–535.

Kyle, T. M. (2000, July/August). Investigating and choosing: The decision-making process among first-year graduate students. *APA Monitor,* p. 19.

Landrum, R. E. (2003). Graduate admissions in psychology: Transcripts and the effect of withdrawals. *Teaching of Psychology, 30,* 323–325.

Landi, G. (2010). International students seeking graduate study in the U.S. *Eye on Psi Chi, 15*(3), 7.

Landrum, R. E., & Nelson, L. R. (2002). The undergraduate research assistantship: An analysis of benefits. *Teaching of Psychology, 29,* 15–19.

Lark, J. S., & Croteau, J. M. (1998). Lesbian, gay, and bisexual doctoral students' mentoring relationships with faculty in counseling psychology: A qualitative study. *The Counseling Psychologist, 26*, 754–776.

Lipson, C. (2008). *Succeeding as an international student in the United States and Canada*. Chicago; University of Chicago Press.

Lovitts, B. E., & Nelson, C. (2000, November–December). Attrition from Ph.D. programs. *Academe*, pp. 44–50.

Lubin, B. (1993, Winter). Message of the president. *Psi Chi Newsletter, 19*, 1.

Maher, B. A. (1999). Changing trends in doctoral training programs in psychology: A comparative analysis of research-oriented versus professional-applied programs. *Psychological Sciences, 10*, 475–481.

Mayne, T. J., Norcross, J. C., & Sayette, M. A. (1994). Admission requirements, acceptance rates, and financial assistance in clinical psychology programs: Diversity across the practice–research continuum. *American Psychologist, 49*, 605–611.

McFall, R. M. (2002). Training for prescriptions vs. prescriptions for training: Where are we now? Where should we be? How do we get there? *Journal of Clinical Psychology, 58*, 659–676.

McWade, P. (1996). *Financing graduate school*. Princeton, NJ: Peterson's Guides.

Megargee, E. I. (1990). *A guide to obtaining a psychology internship*. Muncie, IN: Accelerated Development.

Megargee, E. I. (2001). *Megargee's guide to obtaining a psychology internship* (4th ed.). New York: Taylor & Francis.

Minke, K. M., & Brown, D. T. (1996). Preparing psychologists to work with children: A comparison of curricula in child-clinical and school psychology programs. *Professional Psychology: Research and Practice, 27*, 631–634.

Mitchell, S. L. (1996). Getting a foot in the door: The written internship application. *Professional Psychology: Research and Practice, 27*, 90–92.

Morgan, R. D., & Cohen, L. M. (2003, August). *Counseling and clinical psychology: Are we training students differently?* Poster presented at the annual convention of the American Psychological Association, Toronto.

Morrison, T., & Morrison, M. (1995). A meta-analytic assessment of the predictive validity of the quantitative and verbal components of the Graduate Record Examination with graduate grade point average representing the criterion of graduate success. *Educational and Psychological Measurement, 55*, 309–316.

Mulvey, T. A., Wicherski, M., & Kohout, J. L. (2010). *Availability and levels of financial support for U.S. master's and doctoral students in graduate departments of psychology: 2009–2010*. Washington, DC: APA Center for Workforce Studies.

Munoz-Dunbar, R., & Stanton, A. L. (1999). Ethnic diversity in clinical psychology: Recruitment and admis-

sion practices among doctoral programs. *Teaching of Psychology, 26*, 259–263.

Murphy, M. J., Levant, R. F., Hall, J. E., & Glueckauf, R. L. (2007). Distance education in professional training in psychology. *Professional Psychology: Research and Practice, 38*, 97–103.

Murray, B. (1996). Psychology remains top college major. *APA Monitor, 27*, 1, 42.

Murray, T. M., & Williams, S. (1999). *Analyses of data from graduate study in psychology: 1997–98*. Washington, DC: American Psychological Association Research Office.

National Association of Colleges and Employers. (2007). *Career Services Benchmark Survey*. Retrieved July 26, 2007 from www.naceweb.org/press/current.asp.

National Center for Education Statistics. (2009). *IPEDS completion survey*. Washington, DC: U.S. Department of Education.

Nauta, M. M. (2000). Assessing the accuracy of psychology undergraduates' perceptions of graduate admissions criteria. *Teaching of Psychology, 27*, 277–280.

Neimeyer, G. J., Saferstein, J., & Rice, K. G. (2005). Does the model matter? The relationship between science-practice emphasis and outcomes in academic training programs in counseling psychology. *The Counseling Psychologist, 33(5)*, 635–654.

Nevid, J. S., & Gildea, T. J. (1984). The admissions process in clinical training: The role of the personal interview. *Professional Psychology: Research and Practice, 15*, 18–25.

Norcross, J. C., & Cannon, J. T. (2008, Fall). You're writing your own letter of recommendation. *Eye on Psi Chi, 12(4)*, 24–28.

Norcross, J. C., Castle, P. H., Sayette, M. A. & Mayne, T. J. (2004). The Psy.D.: Heterogeneity in practitioner training. *Professional Psychology: Research and Practice, 35*, 412–419.

Norcross, J. C., Ellis, J. L., & Sayette, M. A. (2010). Getting in and getting money: A comparative analysis of admission standards, acceptance rates, and financial assistance across the research-practice continuum in clinical psychology programs. *Training and Education in Professional Psychology, 4*, 99–104.

Norcross, J. C., Evans, K. L., & Ellis, J. L. (2010). The model does matter II: Admissions and training in APA-accredited counseling psychology programs. *The Counseling Psychologist, 38*, 257–268.

Norcross, J. C., Gallagher, K. M., & Prochaska, J. O. (1989). The Boulder and/or the Vail model: Training preferences of clinical psychologists. *Journal of Clinical Psychology, 45*, 822–828.

Norcross, J. C., & Goldfried, M. R. (Eds.). (2005). *Handbook of psychotherapy integration*. New York: Oxford University Press.

Norcross, J. C., Hanych, J. M., & Terranova, R. D. (1996).

Graduate study in psychology: 1992–1993. *American Psychologist, 51*, 631–643.

Norcross, J. C., Hedges, M., & Prochaska, J. O. (2002). The face of 2010: A Delphi poll on the future of psychotherapy. *Professional Psychology: Research and Practice, 33*, 316–322.

Norcross, J. C., & Kaplan, K. J. (1995). Training in psychotherapy integration. Integrative/eclectic programs. *Journal of Psychotherapy Integration, 5*(3).

Norcross, J. C., Karg, R. S., & Prochaska, J. O. (1997). Clinical psychologists in the 1990s: Part II. *The Clinical Psychologist, 50*(3), 4–11.

Norcross, J. C., Karpiak, C. P., & Santoro, S. O. (2005). Clinical psychologists across the years: The Division of Clinical Psychology from 1960 to 2003. *Journal of Clinical Psychology, 61*, 1467–1483.

Norcross, J. C., Kohout, J. L., & Wicherski, M. (2005). Graduate study in psychology, 1971–2004. *American Psychologist, 60*, 840–850.

Norcross, J. C., & Oliver, J. M. (2005, March). *An update on PsyD programs: Acceptance rates, financial assistance, and selected outcomes by program setting.* Poster presented at the 76th annual meeting of the Eastern Psychological Association, Boston, MA.

Norcross, J. C., Sayette, M. A., Mayne, T. J., Karg, R. S., & Turkson, M. A. (1998). Selecting a doctoral program in professional psychology: Some comparisons among Ph.D. counseling, Ph.D. clinical, and Psy.D. clinical psychology programs. *Professional Psychology: Research and Practice, 29*, 609–614.

O'Donohue, W., Plaud, J. J., Mowatt, A. M., & Fearon, J. R. (1989). Current status of curricula of doctoral training programs in clinical psychology. *Professional Psychology: Research and Practice, 20*, 196–197.

Oliver, J. M., Norcross, J. C., Sayette, M. A., Griffin, K., & Mayne, T. J. (2005, March). *Doctoral study in clinical, counseling, and combined psychology: Admission requirements and student characteristics.* Poster presented at the 76th annual meeting of the Eastern Psychological Association, Boston, MA.

O'Neill, J. V. (2001, September). Image seen as key to social work's future. *NASW News*, p. 3.

Osborne, R. E. (1996, Fall). The "personal" side of graduate school personal statements. *Eye on Psi Chi, 1*, 14–15.

Otto, R. K., & Heilbrun, K. (2002). The practice of forensic psychology: A look toward the future in light of the past. *American Psychologist, 57*, 5–18.

Parent, M. C., & Williamson, J. B. (2010). Program disparities in unmatched internship applicants. *Training and Education in Professional Psychology, 4*, 116–120.

Pate, W. E. II. (2001). *Analyses of data from Graduate Study in Psychology: 1999–2000.* Washington, DC: American Psychological Association Research Office.

Pate, W. E. II, & Finno, A. A. (2009, August). *Graduate school debt and starting salaries in psychology.* Presented at the annual convention of the American Psychological Association, Toronto, Canada.

Peterson, D. R. (1976). Need for the doctor of psychology degree in professional psychology. *American Psychologist, 31*, 792–798.

Peterson, D. R. (1982). Origins and development of the Doctor of Psychology concept. In G. R. Caddy, D. C. Rimm, H. Watson, & J. H. Johnson (Eds.), *Educating professional psychologists* (pp. 19–38). New Brunswick, NJ: Transaction Books.

Peterson, D. R., Eaton, M. M., Levine, A. R., & Snepp, F. P. (1982). Career experiences of doctors of psychology. *Professional Psychology, 13*, 268–277.

Peterson's grants for graduate and postdoctoral study (5th ed.). (1998). Princeton, NJ: Peterson's.

Piotrowski, C., & Keller, J. W. (1996). Research or clinical experience: What doctoral applicants need to know. *Journal of Instructional Psychology, 23*, 126–127.

Prevoznak, M. A., & Bubka, A. (1999, April). *Word-a-day method in preparation for the GRE.* Poster presented at the annual meeting of the Eastern Psychological Association, Providence, RI.

Princeton Review. (2005). *Paying for graduate school without going broke* (2005 edition). Princeton: Author.

Princeton Review. (2005). *Cracking the GRE Psychology.* Princeton: Author.

Psychological Corporation. (1994). *Miller Analogies Test: Technical manual.* San Antonio, TX: Author.

Purdy, J. E., Reinehr, R. C., & Swartz, J. D. (1989). Graduate admissions criteria of leading psychology departments. *American Psychologist, 44*, 960–961.

Rader, J. (2000). Disclosing a lesbian, gay, or bisexual identity in graduate psychology programs: Risk and rewards. *APAGS, 12*(2).

Raphael, S., & Halpert, L. H. (1999). *Graduate Record Examination—Psychology* (3rd ed.). New York: Prentice Hall.

Rem, R., Oren, E. M., & Childrey, G. (1987). Selection of graduate students in clinical psychology: Use of cutoff scores and interviews. *Professional Psychology: Research and Practice, 18*, 485–488.

Resnick, J. H. (1991). Finally, a definition of clinical psychology: A message from the President, Division 12. *The Clinical Psychologist, 44*(1), 3–4.

Rheingold, H. L. (1994). *The psychologist's guide to an academic career.* Washington, DC: American Psychological Association.

Robyak, J. E., & Goodyear, R. K. (1984). Graduate school origins of diplomates and fellows in professional psychology. *Professional Psychology: Research and Practice, 15*, 379–387.

Rogers, M. R., & Molina, L. E. (2006). Exemplary efforts in psychology to recruit and retain graduate students of color. *American Psychologist, 61*, 143–156.

REFERENCES

Salzinger, K. (Chair). (1998, August). *Combined professional–scientific psychology: Greater than the sum of its parts?* Symposium presented at the 106th annual convention of the American Psychological Association, San Francisco, CA.

Sayette, M. A., & Mayne, T. J. (1990). Survey of current clinical and research trends in clinical psychology. *American Psychologist, 45*, 1263–1267.

Sayette, M. A., Mayne, T. J., Norcross, J. C., & Giuffre, D. E. (1999, June). *Letting a hundred flowers bloom? Ph.D. clinical psychology training in the 1990s*. Paper presented at the annual meeting of the Academy of Psychological Clinical Science, Denver, CO.

Sayette, M. A., Norcross, J. C., & Dimoff, J. D. (2011). The heterogeneity of clinical psychology Ph.D. programs and the distinctiveness of APCS programs. *Clinical Psychology: Science & Practice, 18*, 4–11.

Schaefer, S. E. (1995). Stigmatization of psychology doctoral program applicants who have a history of psychological counseling. *Dissertation Abstracts, 57*(02B), 1427.

Scott, W. C., & Silka, L. D. (1974). Applying to graduate school in psychology: A perspective and guide. *Journal Supplement Abstract Service*, MS. 597.

Shaffer, D. R., & Tomarelli, M. (1981). Bias in the ivory tower: An unintended consequence of the Buckley Amendment for graduate admissions. *Journal of Applied Psychology, 66*, 7–11.

Shealy, C. N. (Ed.). (2004). Special issues: The Consensus Conference and combined-integrated model of doctoral training in professional psychology. *Journal of Clinical Psychology, 60*, issues 9 and 10.

Smith, R. A. (1985). Advising beginning psychology majors for graduate school. *Teaching of Psychology, 12*, 194–198.

Snepp, F. P., & Peterson, D. R. (1988). Evaluative comparison of Psy.D. and Ph.D. students by clinical internship supervisors. *Professional Psychology: Research and Practice, 19*, 180–183.

Society for Industrial and Organizational Psychology. (2009). *Graduate training in industrial/organizational psychology and related fields*. Bowling Green, OH: Author.

Stapp, J., Tucker, A. M., & VandenBos, G. R. (1985). Census of psychological personnel: 1983. *American Psychologist, 40*, 1317–1351.

Steinpreis, R., Queen, L., & Tennen, H. (1992). The education of clinical psychologists: A survey of training directors. *The Clinical Psychologist, 45*, 87–94.

Sternberg, R. J. (Ed.). (2006). *Career paths in psychology: Where your degree can take you* (2nd ed.). Washington, DC: American Psychological Association.

Sternberg, R. J., & Williams, W. M. (1997). Does the graduate record examination predict meaningful success in the graduate training of psychologists? *American Psychologist, 52*, 630–641.

Stewart, A. E., & Stewart, E. A. (1996). A decision-making technique for choosing a psychology internship. *Professional Psychology: Research and Practice, 27*, 521–526.

Stewart, D. W., & Spille, H. A. (1988). *Diploma mills: Degrees of fraud*. New York: Macmillan.

Strickland, B. R. (1985). Over the Boulder(s) and through the Vail. *The Clinical Psychologist, 38*, 52–56.

Stewart, P. K., Roberts, M. C., & Roy, K. M. (2007). Scholarly productivity in clinical psychology PhD programs: A normative assessment of publication rates. *Clinical Psychology: Science and Practice, 14*, 157–171.

Stoloff, M., McCarthy, M., Keller, L., Varfolomeeva, V., Lynch, J., Makara, K., et al. (2010). The undergraduate psychology major: An examination of structure and sequence. *Teaching of Psychology, 37*, 4–15.

Templer, D. I., Stroup, K., Mancuso, L. J., & Tangen, K. (2008). Comparative decline of professional school graduates' performance on the Examination for Professional Practice in Psychology. *Psychological Reports, 102*, 551–560.

Terry, R. L. (1996, December). Characteristics of psychology departments at primarily undergraduate institutions. *Council on Undergraduate Research Quarterly*, pp. 86–90.

Tibbits-Kleber, A. L., & Howell, R. J. (1987). Doctoral training in clinical psychology: A students' perspective. *Professional Psychology: Research and Practice, 18*, 634–639.

Tipton, R. M. (1983). Clinical and counseling psychology: A study of roles and functions. *Professional Psychology: Research and Practice, 14*, 837–846.

Titus, J. B., & Buxman, N. J. (1999, Spring). Is Psi Chi meeting its mission statement? *Eye on Psi Chi, 3*, 16–18.

Todd, D. M., & Farinato, D. (1992). A local resource for advising applicants to clinical psychology graduate programs. *Teaching of Psychology, 19*, 52–54.

Toia, A., Herron, W. G., Primavera, L. H., & Javier, R. A. (1997). Ethnic diversification in clinical psychology training. *Cultural Diversity and Mental Health, 3*, 193–206.

Toma, J. D., & Cross, M. E. (1998). Intercollegiate athletics and student college choice: Exploring the impact of championship seasons on undergraduate applications. *Research in Higher Education, 39*, 633–661.

Tryon, G. S. (1985). What can our students learn from regional psychology conventions? *Teaching of Psychology, 12*, 227–228.

Tryon, G. S. (2000). Doctoral training issues in school and clinical child psychology. *Professional Psychology: Research and Practice, 31*, 85–87.

Turkington, C. (1986). Practitioner training. *APA Monitor, 17*(1), 14, 17.

Turkson, M. A., & Norcross, J. C. (1996, March). *Doctoral training in counseling psychology: Admission statistics, student characteristics, and financial assistance*. Paper presented at the annual conference of the Eastern Psychological Association, Philadelphia, PA.

VandeCreek, L., & Fleisher, M. (1984). The role of practicum in the undergraduate psychology curriculum. *Teaching of Psychology, 11*, 9–14.

VandenBos, G. E., Stapp, J., & Kilburg, R. R. (1981). Health service providers in psychology. *American Psychologist, 36*, 1395–1418.

Walfish, S. (2004). An eye-opening experience: Taking an online practice Graduate Record Examination. *Eye on Psi Chi, Winter 2004*, 18, 19, 69.

Walfish, S., Stenmark, D. E., Shealy, J. S., & Shealy, S. E. (1989). Reasons why applicants select clinical psychology graduate programs. *Professional Psychology: Research and Practice, 20*, 350–354.

Walfish, S., & Sumprer, G. F. (1984). Employment opportunities for graduates of APA-approved and non-APA-approved training programs. *American Psychologist, 39*, 1199–1200.

Wang, A. Y. (2010). Be Telemachus, find Mentor. *Eye on Psi Chi, 15*(2), 4.

Waters, J., Drew, B., & Ayers, J. (1988). Integrating conflicting needs in curriculum planning: Advice to faculty. In P. J. Woods (Ed.), *Is psychology for them?*

Washington, DC: American Psychological Association.

Watkins, C. E., Lopez, F. G., Campbell, V. L., & Himmell, C. D. (1986a). Contemporary counseling psychology: Results of a national survey. *Journal of Counseling Psychology, 33*, 301–309.

Watkins, C. E., Lopez, F. G., Campbell, V. L., & Himmell, C. D. (1986b). Counseling psychology and clinical psychology: Some preliminary comparative data. *American Psychologist, 41*, 581–582.

Whitbourne, S. K. (1999, April). *A guide to personal statements*. Paper presented at the 70th annual meeting of the Eastern Psychological Association, Boston, MA.

Wicherski, M., & Kohout, J. (2005). *2003 Doctorate Employment Survey*. Retrieved on July 27, 2007 from research.apa.org/des03.html#salaries.

Wittenberg, R. (2003). *Opportunities in social work careers*. Lincolnwood, IL: McGraw-Hill.

Young, K. S., & VandeCreek, L. (1996, March). *Ethnic minority selection procedures in clinical training graduate admissions*. Paper presented at the 67th annual meeting of the Eastern Psychological Association, Philadelphia, PA.